# English Grammar and Composition

## Complete Course

**John E. Warriner**

FRANKLIN EDITION

**Harcourt Brace Jovanovich, Publishers**
New York Chicago San Francisco Atlanta Dallas *and* London

**THE SERIES:**

**English Grammar and Composition: First Course**
**English Grammar and Composition: Second Course**
**English Grammar and Composition: Third Course**
**English Grammar and Composition: Fourth Course**
**English Grammar and Composition: Fifth Course**
**English Grammar and Composition: Complete Course**

**Test booklet and teacher's manual for each above title.**

**CORRELATED SERIES:**

**English Workshop: First Course**
**English Workshop: Second Course**
**English Workshop: Third Course**
**English Workshop: Fourth Course**
**English Workshop: Fifth Course**
**English Workshop: Review Course**

**Composition: Models and Exercises, First Course**
**Composition: Models and Exercises, Second Course**
**Composition: Models and Exercises, Third Course**
**Composition: Models and Exercises, Fourth Course**
**Composition: Models and Exercises, Fifth Course**
**Advanced Composition: A Book of Models for Writing, Complete Course**

**Vocabulary Workshop: First Course**
**Vocabulary Workshop: Second Course**
**Vocabulary Workshop: Third Course**
**Vocabulary Workshop: Fourth Course**
**Vocabulary Workshop: Fifth Course**
**Vocabulary Workshop: Complete Course**

**John E. Warriner** taught English for thirty-two years in junior and senior high schools and in college. He is chief author of the *English Grammar and Composition* series, coauthor of the *English Workshop* series, general editor of the *Composition: Models and Exercises* series, and editor of *Short Stories: Characters in Conflict*. His co-authors have been active in English education.



Printed in the United States of America

ISBN 0-15-311885-7

# To the Student

Now you are probably thinking, "Here we go again—another English class, another textbook." You are, of course, quite right. Since almost everything you do involves the use of language, schools make the study of English a required subject in every year, and in any English class, a textbook is an essential tool.

This textbook is designed to help you master the skills required for the effective use of standard English. Although the book will help you to *speak* better, its primary purpose is to help you to *write* better.

You have been learning to write almost as long as you have been going to school, which, at this point, may seem to you to be a very long time. To be sure, you have already studied many composition skills. This book reviews those skills while it carries you further into the study of more advanced skills which lead to better writing.

As your experience increases, your ideas become more sophisticated and consequently more difficult to express. Additional skills are needed. This textbook provides instruction in these skills and the opportunity to practice their use. Practice is important because you learn to write by writing. No one ever learned to write in any other way.

Your textbook is also designed as a useful reference book: it offers the solution to almost any writing problem you are likely to encounter. By familiarizing yourself with the contents and organization of the book, and by using the index freely, you can easily find out what you need to know, whether it is a question about punctuation or usage or sentence structure, or a suggestion about the form of an outline, of a bibliography, or of a business letter. Keep this book nearby whenever you write. Develop the habit of looking up the answers to questions that arise concerning the use of standard English.

J.W.

# Contents

# PART TWO: Usage

# PART SEVEN: College Entrance and Other Examinations



# PART EIGHT: Speaking and Listening

# English Grammar and Composition

FRANKLIN EDITION

COMPLETE COURSE

# Grammar

## PART ONE

Chapter 1

# The Parts of Speech

## Their Identification and Function

By this time in your educational career, you understand the importance of being able to speak and write effectively. A principal goal of instruction in English is to increase your competence in speaking and writing. Every year your English courses take you further toward mastering language skills.

Since English is a cumulative subject, some things that you encounter each year are bound to be familiar. Among these is grammar, which you have probably been studying since elementary school. There is a good chance that by now you already know enough English grammar to meet your needs. You may, however, find your knowledge of grammar somewhat tarnished and in need of polishing.

Grammar is important. By giving names to the kinds of words and the parts of a sentence, it provides the terminology you need in your study of language. By making you aware of the basic patterns of English sentences, it helps you to develop a varied and interesting style. You should, therefore, find out early in the school year whether your knowledge of grammar is adequate. The way to do this is to test yourself and then review what you still need to learn.

Chapter 1 deals with the most fundamental grammatical knowledge—the parts of speech, or the names of words according to their function in the sentence.

## Diagnostic Test

Number your paper 1–33. Copy the numbered words in the following passage and write what part of speech each of the words is, using abbreviations: *n.*, noun; *pron.*, pronoun; *adj.*, adjective; *v.*, verb; *adv.*, adverb; *conj.*, conjunction; *prep.*, preposition; *inter.*, interjection.

There are (1) *various* ways (2) *we* can look at the grammar (3) *of* a language. One analogy (4) *might be* the (5) *rules* of such a game as chess. The basic rules of chess are (6) *quite* simple. There are only (7) *six* kinds of pieces, (8) *each* of which (9) *has* the privilege of moving in a particular way. (10) *When* certain combinations occur, certain moves are obligatory. (11) *Otherwise* the players have (12) *many* options each time it is their turn to move. (13) *As* they (14) *move* in turn, the two players construct a (15) *series* of patterns (16) *on* the board (17) *which* is not like any series either of them (18) *has seen* before. In the same way the words of a language are classified as belonging (19) *to* certain classes, (20) *traditionally* called (21) *parts* of speech. The functions of (22) *these* are (23) *different,* just as the moves of the chess pieces are. Nouns can be subjects (24) *and* objects, (25) *adjectives* are modifiers, pronouns substitute for nouns, and so on. The rules are (26) *more* complicated than (27) *those* of chess, but not so complicated that (28) *they* cannot be learned by a five-year-old child. Just as the chess players (29) *create* a (30) *new* game, unlike any other played (31) *in* the past, so speakers are (32) *constantly* making up new sentences, (33) *many*—perhaps most—of which are unlike any they ever heard or spoke in the past.



## THE NOUN

**1a. A *noun* is a word used to name a person, place, thing, or idea.**

Nouns may be classified in three ways: *proper* or *common; abstract* or *concrete;* and *collective.*

A *proper noun* names a particular person, place, or thing and is capitalized: *Kay, Miami, White House.*

A *common noun* is a noun that does not name a particular person, place, or thing. Common nouns are not capitalized: *woman, city, building.*

An *abstract noun* names a quality, a characteristic, an idea: *beauty, strength, love, courage.*

A *concrete noun* names an object that can be perceived by the senses: *hat, desk, book, box.*

A *collective noun* names a group: *crowd, team, class.*

► NOTE A *compound noun* is a noun of more than one word: *First National Bank, Ringling Brothers Circus, high school.*

## THE PRONOUN

**1b. A pronoun is a word used in place of a noun or of more than one noun.**

EXAMPLES Anglers complained about the weather forecast. **They** said **it** had not warned **them** of the storm. [The pronouns *they* and *them* take the place of the noun *anglers.* The pronoun *it* takes the place of the noun *forecast.*]

An umbrella and a book were left in the cafeteria. **They** have not been claimed. [The pronoun *they* takes the place of two nouns, *umbrella* and *book.*]

Sometimes a pronoun takes the place of another pronoun.

EXAMPLE **One** of the film projectors is broken. **It** has been sent out for repair. [The pronoun *it* takes the place of the pronoun *one.*]

The word to which a pronoun refers (whose place it takes) is the *antecedent* of the pronoun. In the preceding example *one* is the antecedent of *it.*

Pronouns are classified as: *personal, reflexive, intensive, relative, interrogative, demonstrative,* and *indefinite.*

### *Personal Pronouns*

| | | | |
|---|---|---|---|
| I, me | he, him | it | they, them |
| you | she, her | we, us | |

### *Possessive Forms*

| | | | |
|---|---|---|---|
| my, mine | his | its | their, theirs |
| your, yours | her, hers | our, ours | |

Some of the possessive forms—*my, your, his, her, its, our, their*—are used before a noun in the same way adjectives are used to limit the meaning of a noun: *my* parents, *your* home, *her* coat, etc. They are possessive pronouns functioning as adjectives. In this book these words are called pronouns. Your teacher may, however, prefer to have you call them possessive adjectives. Follow your teacher's instructions in labeling these words.

### *Reflexive and Intensive Pronouns*

| | |
|---|---|
| myself | ourselves |
| yourself | yourselves |
| himself, herself, itself | themselves |

Personal pronouns combined with *–self, –selves* may be used in two ways:

1. They may be used *reflexively.*

   Carmen hurt **herself.**

2. They may be used *intensively* for emphasis.

   Carmen **herself** was not hurt.

### *Relative Pronouns*

| | | |
|---|---|---|
| who | which | whose |
| whom | that | |

*Relative pronouns* are used to introduce subordinate clauses (see page 56).

EXAMPLES The people **who** live there are on vacation.
The copy **that** I read was from the library.
Do you know the woman **whose** car was stolen?

### *Interrogative Pronouns*

| | | |
|---|---|---|
| who | which | whose |
| whom | what | |

*Interrogative pronouns* are used in questions.

EXAMPLES **Who** borrowed my pen?
**What** was the name of the book?

### *Demonstrative Pronouns*

this these that those

*Demonstrative pronouns* are used to point out persons or things.

EXAMPLES **That** is an excellent question.
**This** seems to be my lucky day.

### *Most Commonly Used Indefinite Pronouns*

| | | | |
|---|---|---|---|
| all | each | most | other |
| another | either | neither | several |
| any | everybody | nobody | some |
| anybody | everyone | none | somebody |
| anyone | few | no one | someone |
| both | many | one | such |

Pronouns that do not fall into the classifications above are called *indefinite pronouns*. Most indefinite pronouns express the idea of quantity: *all, few, none*.

EXAMPLES **All** of us are here.
**Few** of the cars were new.

**EXERCISE 1.** Number your paper 1–10. After the number of each sentence, write in order the pronouns in the sentence.

1. Last year our school gave two photography courses, neither of which had been offered before.
2. The course that I took dealt with the ways in which people perceive their environment.
3. Most of us block out our everyday surroundings, ignoring details which we have learned to take for granted.
4. You can prove to yourselves how blind all of us become to our surroundings.

5. Which of you, upon returning home from a trip, suddenly notices how different all of the rooms look to you?
6. Some of your possessions may look unfamiliar to you, and a few of them may seem totally alien.
7. Eventually, the impression of newness wears off, and your house takes on its familiar appearance.
8. Each of us can regain the ability to see freshly if we make full use of our sense of sight.
9. We must see the shapes of the objects themselves instead of thinking about their function.
10. According to Claude Monet, a French impressionist painter whose works are world-famous, in order to see as an artist, we must forget the names of the things that we are looking at.

## THE ADJECTIVE

**1c. An *adjective* is a word used to modify a noun or a pronoun.**

*To modify* means "to limit," or to make more definite the meaning of a word. Adjectives may modify nouns or pronouns in any one of three different ways.

1. By telling *what kind:*

   **blue** eyes, **large** city, **capable** student

2. By pointing out *which one:*

   **this** woman, **that** suggestion

3. By telling *how many:*

   **several** reasons, **ten** players

As the preceding examples show, the normal position of an adjective is directly before the word it modifies. Occasionally, for stylistic reasons, a writer may use adjectives after the word they modify.

EXAMPLE The night, **cold** and **foggy**, drove us indoors.

A *predicate adjective* (see page 32) is separated from the word it modifies by a verb.

EXAMPLES Deborah is **practical.**
He looks **thoughtful.**
The stew tasted **delicious.**
Her hand felt **cold.**

## The Same Word as Adjective and Pronoun

A word may be used as more than one part of speech. This rule is especially true of the words in the list below, which may be used both as pronouns and as adjectives.

| | | | |
|---|---|---|---|
| all | either | one | these |
| another | few | other | this |
| any | many | several | those |
| both | more | some | what |
| each | neither | that | which |

ADJECTIVE **Which** pen do you want? [*Which* modifies the noun *pen.*]

PRONOUN **Which** do you want? [*Which* takes the place of a noun previously mentioned.]

ADJECTIVE I like **this** picture. [*This* modifies the noun *picture.*]

PRONOUN I like **this.** [*This* takes the place of a noun previously mentioned.]

## Nouns Used as Adjectives

Nouns are sometimes used as adjectives.

| | |
|---|---|
| **sofa** cushion | **hotel** lobby |
| **bread** pudding | **glass** beads |

When you are identifying parts of speech and you encounter a noun used as an adjective, label it an adjective.

**EXERCISE 2.** Some of the nouns, pronouns, and adjectives in the following sentences are italicized. For each sentence, list these words in order in a column, numbering as in the example. After each word, tell what part of speech it is. If a word is an adjective, write after it the word the adjective modifies.

EXAMPLE 1. A *hobby* is something *you* like to do in your *spare* time.

*1. hobby n.*
*you pron.*
*spare adj. (time)*

1. *Some* people take up a hobby because *it* is fun; *others* seek in hobbies relief from their *tensions.*
2. In *this* complex culture of *ours, everyday* living imposes stresses and strains *which* affect many people adversely.
3. A hobby offers *them* a release from strain and a chance to share *enjoyment* and relaxation with *other* hobbyists.
4. In *their* hobbies Franklin Delano Roosevelt and Dwight D. Eisenhower found relaxation from the *exhausting* responsibilities of the *Presidency.*
5. President Roosevelt's hobbies were stamps and *ship* models; President Eisenhower took up painting after *he* met Sir Winston Churchill, *who* was also a painter, during the Second World War.
6. *All* hobbies provide fun and relaxation, but *some* are also *educational.*
7. One of President John F. Kennedy's favorite *leisure* pursuits was a *word* game in which players suggested *unlikely* answers, *such* as "income taxes."
8. *Other* players had to invent questions to *which* the phrase was an answer, like, "What happens in *your* country every year when the government budget comes out?"
9. *Crossword* puzzles are an educational hobby for *millions* all over the world, and provide *vocabulary* exercise as well as enjoyable relaxation.
10. The nature and *type* of hobbies and leisure pursuits are limited only by *one's* imagination and skills.

## THE VERB

**1d. A *verb* is a word that expresses action or otherwise helps to make a statement.**

All verbs help to make a statement. Some help to make a statement by expressing action. The action expressed may be physical, as in such verbs as *hit, play, move,* and *run,* or it may be mental, as in *think, know, imagine, believe.*

## Transitive and Intransitive Verbs

Action verbs may or may not take an *object*—a noun or pronoun that completes the action by showing *who* or *what* is affected by the action. Verbs that have an object are called *transitive.* The verbs in the following examples are transitive:

The catcher **dropped** the ball. [*Ball* is the object of *dropped.*]
The people **believed** the politician. [*Politician* is the object.]
The waiter **ignored** the customers. [*Customers* is the object.]

Verbs that express action without objects are called *intransitive.*

The catcher **shrugged.**
The people **chuckled.**
The waiter **quit.**

Although some verbs are transitive only (*ignore, complete*) and some intransitive only (*arrive, sleep*), most verbs in English can be either.

EXAMPLES The judges **explained** the contest rules. [transitive]
Patiently, the judges **explained.** [intransitive]
The contestants still **misunderstood** them. [transitive]
The contestants still **misunderstood.** [intransitive]

► NOTE Most dictionaries group the meanings of verbs according to whether they are transitive (*v.t.* in most dictionaries) or intransitive (*v.i.*). Remembering the difference will help you to find readily the meaning you want.

## Linking Verbs

Some intransitive verbs help to make a statement not by expressing action, but by expressing a state or condition.

These verbs link to the subject a noun, pronoun, or adjective that describes or identifies it. They are called *linking verbs*. The word that is linked to the subject is called a *subject complement*.

EXAMPLES The author **is** our guest. [The subject complement *guest* refers to the subject *author*.]

This **is** she. [*She* refers to the subject *this*.]

She **looks** serious. [*Serious* refers to the subject *she*.

The subject complement always refers to the subject of the linking verb. It may identify the subject, as in the first two examples, or describe the subject, as in the third one.

The most common linking verb is the verb *be*,[1] which has the following forms: *am, is, are, was, were, be, being, been* (and all verb phrases ending in *be, being,* or *been,* such as *can be, is being,* and *could have been*). Other common linking verbs are listed below.

### *Common Linking Verbs*

| | | | |
|---|---|---|---|
| appear | grow | seem | stay |
| become | look | smell | taste |
| feel | remain | sound | |

Many of the verbs in the preceding list can also be used as action verbs—that is, without a subject complement.

LINKING The detectives **looked** puzzled.

ACTION The detective **looked** for clues.

In general, a verb is a linking verb if you can substitute for it some form of the verb *seem*.

EXAMPLES Hank Aaron **looked** [seemed] pleased.

Everyone in the stadium **felt** [seemed] happy.

All of the passengers **remained** [seemed] calm.

[1] The verb *be* can also be followed by certain adverbs and adverb phrases: We were *there;* the men were *at work.* In this situation, *be* is not considered a linking verb.

## The Helping Verb and the Verb Phrase

A *verb phrase* is made up of a main verb and one or more *helping verbs* (sometimes called *auxiliary verbs*). Helping verbs are so called because they *help* the main verb to express action or make a statement. The helping verbs in the following phrases are printed in bold-faced type:

| | |
|---|---|
| **has** played | **will be** coming |
| **should have** paid | **must have been** injured |

In other words, a verb phrase is a verb of more than one word.

### *Common Helping Verbs*

| | | |
|---|---|---|
| am | has | can (may) have |
| are | had | could (would, should) be |
| is | can | could (would, should) have |
| was | may | will (shall) have been |
| were | will (shall) be | might have |
| do | will (shall) have | might have been |
| did | has (had) been | must |
| have | can (may) be | must have |
| | | must have been |

The parts of a verb phrase may be separated from one another by other words; i.e., the helping verb may be separated from the main verb.

EXAMPLES **Did** you **see** Lorraine Hansberry's play?

**I am** not **going** with you.

We **had** finally **completed** our work.

**EXERCISE 3.** List in order the verbs and verb phrases in the following sentences, placing before each the number of the sentence in which it appears. After each verb, tell whether it is transitive, intransitive, or (intransitive) linking. You may use abbreviations: *v.t.*, *v.i.*, or *l.v.* (linking verb). Be sure to list all words in a verb phrase.

1. The modern shopping center is a response to the migration to the suburbs that began after World War II and is continuing.
2. We have tens of thousands of shopping centers in this country, and many more are on the architects' drawing boards.
3. With art galleries, theaters, concerts, and festivals, the big shopping centers are also cultural centers.
4. A typical center contains acres of parking space and scores of stores where one can buy almost anything.
5. A whole town may rapidly develop around a new shopping center, and the center then becomes the downtown area of the community.
6. Because most shoppers are busy people, architects design the centers for efficiency.
7. Parking spaces are ample, and people can move quickly from store to store.
8. The variety of stores interests shoppers who enjoy bargain hunting, but because most stores in a shopping center cater to people of the same income level, prices actually do not vary greatly.
9. Although the primary aim of shopping centers is convenience, they also provide recreation and entertainment.

## THE ADVERB

### 1e. An *adverb* is a word used to modify a verb, an adjective, or another adverb.

The adverb is used most commonly as the modifier of a verb. It may tell *how, when, where,* or *to what extent* (how often or how much) the action of the verb is done.

EXAMPLES She drives **carefully.** [*Carefully* tells *how* she drives.]

She drives **early** and **late.** [*Early* and *late* tell *when* she drives.]

She drives **everywhere.** [*Everywhere* tells *where* she drives.]

She can **almost** drive. [*Almost* tells *to what extent* she can drive.]

She drives **daily.** [*Daily* tells *how often* she drives.]

Some adverbs, such as *really, actually, truly, indeed,* are used mostly for emphasis. Classify these as adverbs of extent.

EXAMPLES Ramona can **really** cook. [*Really* emphasizes the high quality of Ramona's cooking.]

He can **actually** drive. [*Actually* emphasizes the fact that he is able to drive, which apparently is surprising to the speaker.]

She is **indeed** a fine player. [*Indeed* emphasizes the fact that she is a fine player.]

An adverb may modify an adjective.

EXAMPLE She is a **really** good driver. [*Really* modifies the adjective *good,* telling how good or to what extent she is good at driving.]

An adverb may modify another adverb.

He behaved **very** well. [The adverb *very* modifies the adverb *well,* telling how well.]

► NOTE The word *not* is classified as an adverb. Because it occurs so frequently, especially in contractions, you may ignore it in doing the exercises on parts of speech.

## Nouns Used as Adverbs

Some nouns may be used adverbially.

I called her **yesterday.**

She is leaving **tomorrow.**

We expect them **Monday.**

In identifying parts of speech, label nouns used in this way as adverbs.

**EXERCISE 4.** On your paper, list in order the adverbs in the following sentences, placing before each the number of the sentence in which it appears. After each adverb, write the word or words it modifies, and state whether the adverb tells how, when, where, or to what extent.

1. Dr. Cora Russell spoke interestingly here today.
2. Although she is a physicist, her topic was really astronomy.
3. She recalled that discoveries have often been made accidentally, despite the precision with which scientists always try to work.
4. In 1973, she recalled, radiation from the Gum Nebula unexpectedly affected the trip of Mariner 10.
5. Mariner 10 was headed for Mercury, there to inspect its atmosphere at close range.
6. Intense radiations from the Gum Nebula were detected by the spacecraft in the unusually clear conditions that prevail everywhere in interplanetary space.
7. The radiations were in the low ultraviolet wavelengths, lengths almost as short as X-rays, with uniquely high temperatures.
8. When they became known, scientists who were working here and abroad quickly realized that they were observing something never recorded before, which might soon alter their ideas of galactic evolution.
9. The Gum Nebula is the galaxy closest to what we popularly call the Milky Way—that is, to our own galaxy.
10. If the temperatures of the Gum Nebula are now to be our guide, every galaxy—a word long associated with milk because of the ancient Greek word it comes from—was once very hot milk, hotter than we ever suspected.

**EXERCISE 5.** Copy the numbered, italicized words. After each word, tell what part of speech it is; then after each adjective or adverb, tell what word or word it modifies.

Lizards may be sleek, slender, and (1) *graceful;* or they may be (2) *fantastically* ugly, with grotesque (3) *horns,* spines, and frilly collars. (4) *They* have startling habits. They may snap off (5) *their* tails when they are seized. (6) *Some* may rear up and run (7) *away* on their hind legs. (8) *Certainly* there is nothing (9) *commonplace* about lizards.

(10) *Warmer* portions of the earth (11) *have* the (12) *greatest* number and variety of lizards, but (13) *they* are (14) *also* found in temperate latitudes. There are about 125 (15) *different* kinds in the United States. (16) *One* of the most familiar is the little chameleon, also called anolis. (17) *It* (18) *belongs* to the iguana family, and is (19) *quite* different from the (20) *true* chameleon

family of Africa. (21) *Both* families are interesting for their (22) *ability* to change color. The chameleons' (23) *large*, powerful relatives, the iguanas, (24) *dwell* in the jungles of Mexico, Central, and South America, the (25) *West Indies*, and the Galápagos Islands.[1]

## THE PREPOSITION

**1f. A *preposition* is a word used to show the relation of a noun or pronoun to some other word in the sentence.**

In the following sentences the prepositions are shown in bold-faced type. The words between which the prepositions show relationship are underscored.

> The Oriental rug **in** the hall is a Sarouk.
> Moss will not grow **under** these trees.
> Both **of** us bought the same gift **for** you.

### Object of a Preposition

A preposition always appears in a phrase, usually at the beginning (see page 37). The noun or pronoun at the end of a prepositional phrase is the *object* of the preposition that begins the phrase.

EXAMPLES before **lunch** at the **game**

***Commonly Used Prepositions***

| | | |
|---|---|---|
| about | at | but (meaning "except") |
| above | before | by |
| across | behind | concerning |
| after | below | down |
| against | beneath | during |
| along | beside | except |
| amid | besides | for |
| among | between | from |
| around | beyond | in |

[1] From "The Scaly Dragons of Modern Times" in *Compton's Pictured Encyclopedia and Fact-Index*, Volume 8, 1956 Edition. Copyright © 1956 by F. E. Compton Company, a division of Encyclopaedia Britannica, Inc. Reprinted by permission of the publisher.

### *Commonly Used Prepositions* (*cont.*)

| | | |
|---|---|---|
| into | since | until |
| like | through | unto |
| of | throughout | up |
| off | to | upon |
| on | toward | with |
| over | under | within |
| past | underneath | without |

A group of words may act as a preposition: *on account of, in spite of.*

**EXERCISE 6.** Write ten sentences, each containing a different one of the following prepositions. Draw a line under the phrase which each preposition introduces, and draw a circle around the object of each preposition.

| | | | | |
|---|---|---|---|---|
| 1. above | 3. below | 5. during | 7. into | 9. until |
| 2. against | 4. by | 6. for | 8. of | 10. up |

## THE CONJUNCTION

**1g. A *conjunction* is a word that joins words or groups of words.**

In the following sentences the conjunctions are printed in bold-faced type; the words or groups of words that the conjunctions join are underscored.

> Bring your lunch **and** one dollar.
> You must pass every subject **and** maintain a good average.
> We placed an ad, **but** no one responded.
> I can use the truck **or** the jeep.
> You can **either** stay here **or** come with us.
> She invited both Martin **and** me.
> I will let you know **when** I hear from him.
> She succeeds **because** she works hard.

There are three kinds of conjunctions: *coordinating* conjunctions, *correlative* conjunctions, and *subordinating* conjunctions.

### *Coordinating Conjunctions*

| | | | | |
|---|---|---|---|---|
| and | but | or | nor | for |

Correlative conjunctions are always used in pairs.

EXAMPLES The work is **not only** profitable **but also** pleasant.
Do you know **whether** Sara is coming alone **or** with her parents?

### *Correlative Conjunctions*

| | |
|---|---|
| either . . . or | not only . . . but (also) |
| neither . . . nor | whether . . . or |
| both . . . and | |

Subordinating conjunctions are used to begin subordinate clauses (see page 63), usually adverb clauses.

In the following sentences the subordinate clauses are printed in bold-faced type, and the subordinating conjunctions that introduce them are underscored.

There is no use arguing, **<u>since</u> you have already made your decision.**

We stayed indoors **<u>until</u> the storm abated.**

You may stay **<u>where</u> you are.**

A subordinating conjunction need not come between the sentence parts that it joins. It may come at the beginning of the sentence.

**<u>Although</u> speed is important,** accuracy is more important.

**<u>When</u> I take an examination,** I become frightened.

### *Commonly Used Subordinating Conjunctions*[1]

| | | | |
|---|---|---|---|
| after | before | provided | unless |
| although | how | since | until |
| as | if | than | when |
| as much as | in order that | that | where |
| because | inasmuch as | though | while |

[1] Some of these words may be used as prepositions: *after, before, since, until;* others may be used as adverbs: *how, when, where. That* is often used as a relative pronoun.

## THE INTERJECTION

**1h. An *interjection* is a word that expresses emotion and has no grammatical relation to other words in the sentence.**

EXAMPLES Oh! My goodness! Hurry! Ah! Ouch! Alas!

## THE SAME WORD AS DIFFERENT PARTS OF SPEECH

You have already learned that there are many words in English which can be used as more than one part of speech. For example, *these* may be an adjective (these books) or a pronoun (I want these); *blue* may be an adjective (the blue car) or a noun (Blue is my favorite color); *Tuesday* can be a noun (Tuesday is my birthday) or an adverb (Come Tuesday). There are thousands of words like these which can be classified by part of speech only when you see them in sentences.

EXAMPLES The **plant** was growing in a terrarium. [*Plant* names a living thing; it is a noun.]

We usually **plant** tomatoes in the spring. [*Plant* expresses action; it is a verb.]

Bacteria cause many **plant** diseases. [*Plant* modifies *diseases;* it is an adjective.]

**EXERCISE 7.** This is an exercise in identifying the same word when used as different parts of speech. Copy on your paper the italicized words in the following sentences. After each word, write what part of speech it is. Be prepared to explain your answers.

1. The manager likes to hear the *ring* of the cash registers as the salespeople *ring* up their sales.
2. According to the *daily* schedule, the boat makes three trips *daily*.
3. She chose an especially large *book* at the *book* sale.
4. Be sure to turn *right* at the *right* corner; our house is the first one on the *right*.
5. *That* shows you didn't read *that* explanation carefully.

## SUMMARY OF PARTS OF SPEECH

| Rule | Part of Speech | Use | Examples |
|---|---|---|---|
| 1a | noun | names | man, Iowa, corn, wealth, team |
| 1b | pronoun | takes the place of a noun | you, we, herself, them, this, who |
| 1c | adjective | modifies a noun or pronoun | red, large, two |
| 1d | verb | shows action or helps to make a statement | is, does, have wanted, seems |
| 1e | adverb | modifies a verb, an adjective, or another adverb | rapidly, well, somewhat, too |
| 1f | preposition | relates a noun or a pronoun to another word | into, below, from, of |
| 1g | conjunction | joins words or groups of words | and, but, or, for, after, as, until |
| 1h | interjection | shows strong feeling | ow! |

**REVIEW EXERCISE.** In a column on your paper, copy in order the italicized words in the following paragraphs. Carefully consider the use of each word, and write after it what part of speech it is.

(1) *Our* new neighbors, the Whartons, moved (2) *into* (3) *that* vacant house (4) *across* the street (5) *today.* I (6) *enjoyed* watching and helping (7) *whenever* I could. The (8) *enormous* moving van arrived (9) *about* eleven o'clock, followed (10) *closely* by Mr. and Mrs. Wharton, (11) *their* four children, (12) *and* their dog in a station wagon loaded above the windows.

(13) *Moving* is (14) *like* an exhibition exposing (15) *all* of your secrets to the public, for neighbors (16) *like* to gather (17) *around* and inspect each bed, table, chair, and lamp as the movers

carry (18) *it* into the house. (19) *Other* delivery trucks arrived. (20) *Soon* movers, drivers, Mr. and Mrs. Wharton, the (21) *four* children, the dog, and (22) *others* were getting in one another's way as (23) *they* rushed into and out of the house. I (24) *offered* to help unload the (25) *wagon.* I wanted to do (26) *this* (27) *not only* (28) *because* I was feeling friendly (29) *but also* because I wanted to see what the Whartons were bringing with (30) *them.*

The Whartons became more and more (31) *distraught* as they directed the placing (32) *of* furniture and rugs, (33) *cautioned* the movers about marring the (34) *freshly* (35) *painted* walls, and tried (36) *vainly* to keep the children out of the way. The children (37) *barely* missed destruction a (38) *dozen* times. (39) *At* seven o'clock, as the evening was growing dark and the van was finally pulling away, I heard the youngest Wharton saying to his parents, (40) "*Hey,* why can't we go home now?"

Chapter 2

# The Parts of a Sentence

## The Functions of Subjects, Predicates, and Complements

In order to achieve an understanding of English sentences, you need terms to use in referring to the basic parts of the sentence. With only two terms—*subject* and *predicate*—you could begin to describe most sentences. After you had started, however, you would find out that you need to know the name and function of some other important sentence elements: *object, predicate nominative,* and *predicate adjective,* to name only the most important. You have encountered all of these terms in previous English classes. To find out how well you remember them, take the following diagnostic test to see which terms, if any, you need to review.

### Diagnostic Test

From each of the following sentences, copy the subject, verb, and complement, if there is one. After each complement, tell what kind it is: indirect object (*i.o.*), direct object (*d.o.*), predicate nominative (*p.n.*), predicate adjective (*p.a.*).

EXAMPLE 1. Her employers gave my mother a bonus.
1. *employers, gave, mother* (*i.o.*), *bonus* (*d.o.*)

1. Some of your classmates will attend.
2. This experience taught me a valuable lesson.

3. Out of the darkness came a huge, lumbering creature.
4. To everyone's surprise, Jane and I were not late.
5. The water in the bay seemed very cold.
6. The only people in the water were the children.
7. This morning the mail carrier left this letter for you.
8. He gave me this one, too.
9. Lee Trevino is an excellent golfer.
10. Mechanics had just assembled and checked all parts of the motor.

**2a. A *sentence* is a group of words expressing a complete thought.**

SENTENCE The importance of the minority party in American politics must be understood.

NOT A SENTENCE The importance of the minority party in American politics

SENTENCE This third political party will appeal to the dissatisfied in both of the established parties.

NOT A SENTENCE This third political party, appealing to the dissatisfied in both of the established parties

## SUBJECT AND PREDICATE

**2b. A sentence consists of two parts: the *subject* and the *predicate*. The *subject* of the sentence is that part about which something is being said. The *predicate* is that part which says something about the subject.**

| SUBJECT | PREDICATE |
|---|---|
| Faculty and students | planned a new class schedule. |

| PREDICATE | SUBJECT |
|---|---|
| At the end of the day comes | our activity period. |

These two main parts of sentences may consist of a single word or many words. The whole subject is called the *complete subject;* the whole predicate, the *complete predicate.* However long a subject or predicate may be, it always has a core – an essential part.

### The Simple Subject

**2c. The *simple subject* is the principal word or group of words in the subject.**

EXAMPLES A duplicating machine in constant use requires servicing every day. [subject: *A duplicating machine in constant use;* simple subject: *machine*]

The University of North Carolina at Chapel Hill has many computers. [subject: *The University of North Carolina at Chapel Hill;* simple subject: *University of North Carolina*]

► NOTE Throughout this book the term *subject,* when used in connection with the sentence, refers to the simple subject; the term *verb* refers to the simple predicate.

### The Simple Predicate, or Verb

**2d. The principal word or group of words in the predicate is called the *simple predicate,* or the *verb.***

EXAMPLE Faculty and students planned a new class schedule. [predicate: *planned a new class schedule;* simple predicate, or verb: *planned*]

### Compound Subjects and Verbs

**2e. A *compound subject* consists of two or more subjects that are joined by a conjunction and have the same verb. The usual connecting words are *and* and *or.***

EXAMPLE The **White House** and the **Pentagon** called a new press conference. [compound subject: *White House . . . Pentagon*]

**2f. A *compound verb* consists of two or more verbs that are joined by a conjunction and have the same subject.**

EXAMPLE Mary McLeod Bethune **established** schools and **worked** on government committees. [compound verb: *established . . . worked*]

## How to Find the Subject of a Sentence

To find the subject of a sentence, first find the verb (the simple predicate); then ask yourself the question "Who or what . . .?" For instance, in the sentence "Outside the wall walked an armed guard," the verb is *walked.* Ask the question, "Who or what walked?" You find the answer to be *guard walked. Guard* is the subject of the sentence.

In addition to this simple formula for locating the subject, here are some other facts you should keep in mind:

1. In sentences expressing a command or a request, the subject is always *you,* even though the word *you* may not appear in the sentence.

(You) Stamp the envelopes before mailing them.

(You) Please run some errands for me.

2. The subject of a sentence is never in a prepositional phrase.

Neither of the rivals survived the duel. [verb: *survived.* Who survived? *Neither. Neither* is the subject. *Rivals* is not the subject. It is in the phrase *of the rivals.*]

Knowledge of grammar is an aid to good writing. [verb: *is.* What is? *Knowledge. Knowledge* is the subject. *Grammar* is not the subject. It is in the phrase *of grammar.*]

3. To find the subject in a question, turn the question into statement form.

QUESTION What drawer did you put the box of pencils in?

STATEMENT You did put the box of pencils in what drawer. [subject: *you;* verb: *did put*]

4. *There* and *here* are not usually the subjects of a verb.

Except in a statement like rule 4, *there* and *here* are either adverbs or expletives.

**Here** is the book. [verb: *is;* subject: *book.* In this sentence the word *here* is an adverb telling where.]

**There** are arguments on both sides. [verb: *are;* subject: *arguments.* In this use *there* is called an *expletive,* a word used to get the sentence started. The word *it* may also be used as an expletive: *It* is useless to argue.]

**EXERCISE 1.** Number your paper 1–20. Write after the proper number the subject and the verb in each sentence. Underline subjects once and verbs twice. Be careful to include all parts of compound subjects and verbs, as well as all words in a verb phrase.

1. Your weight, according to the doctor, is 55 kilograms.
2. Should you drop sundaes from your diet or add them to it?
3. Your ability to decide depends upon your working knowledge of the metric system.
4. In 1821 John Quincy Adams proposed adoption of the metric system in the United States.
5. Most countries already employ this system of weights and measures.
6. Adoption of this system in the United States has been debated in Congress.
7. The United States Metric Board guides the proper implementation of the system.
8. The changeover will probably take many years.
9. The necessary changes and adjustments will also cost a good deal.
10. The cost of replacing all speed limit signs in the United States will, by itself, be enormous.
11. Under this system, the basic unit for measuring distance is the *meter,* equal to about $3\frac{1}{3}$ feet.
12. Weight will be calculated under the metric system in *grams* or *kilograms* instead of ounces or pounds.
13. To imagine the weight of a gram, lift a paper clip.
14. A shopper buys milk by the *liter,* roughly equivalent to a quart.
15. Prefixes for these units, such as *kilo-, milli-,* and *centi-,* indicate an increase or decrease in size.
16. A kilogram, or 1000 grams, equals 2.2 pounds.
17. We would substitute the Celsius for the Fahrenheit scale in measuring temperature.
18. On the Celsius scale, zero represents the freezing point of water.
19. There will be, undoubtedly, many changes in everyday speech.
20. No longer could you be offered an inch and take a mile.

## COMPLEMENTS

Some sentences express a complete thought by means of a subject and verb only.

| | |
|---|---|
| S V<br>He thinks. | S V<br>Everybody left. |

Most sentences, however, have in the predicate one or more words that complete the meaning of the subject and verb. These completing words are called complements.

| | |
|---|---|
| Frank caught | a large **tuna.** |
| She handed | **me** a **note.** |
| Maria is | the class **president.** |
| The best ones are | **these.** |
| She seems | **happy.** |
| He called | **me lazy.** |
| Who appointed | **him leader?** |

► NOTE An adverb modifying the verb is not a complement. Only nouns, pronouns, and adjectives act as complements.

Mrs. Clark is **here.** [The adverb *here* modifies the verb *is*. It is not a complement.]

Mrs. Clark is a **teacher.** [The noun *teacher* is a complement.]

Mrs. Clark is **young.** [The adjective *young* is a complement.]

### Direct and Indirect Objects

Complements that receive or are affected by the action of the verb are called *objects.* They are of two kinds: the *direct object* and the *indirect object.*

**2g. The *direct object* of the verb receives the action of the verb or shows the result of the action. It answers the question "What?" or "Whom?" after an action verb.**

I took **Lena** with me. [I took *whom?*]

Jean has written her **composition.** [Jean has written *what?*]

Except when it ends in *-self* (*myself, himself*), the object of a verb never refers to the same person or thing as the subject.

▶ **NOTE** The diagrams are included as an aid to those students who have already studied diagraming. No attempt is made in this book to teach diagraming or to give practice in diagraming. However, a review explanation may be appropriate. Sentence diagrams are "pictures" of the structure of a sentence—that is, ways of placing the words of a sentence into a pattern, so that their functions can be more easily seen. On the main line the subject comes first, then a vertical line crossing the main line, then the verb. Between the verb and the direct object is a vertical line which does not cross the main line. Between the verb and a predicate adjective or a predicate nominative (see pages 32–33) is a similar line slanted to the left. The indirect object occupies a lower horizontal line joined to the verb by a slanted line. Single-word modifiers slant downward from the words they modify.

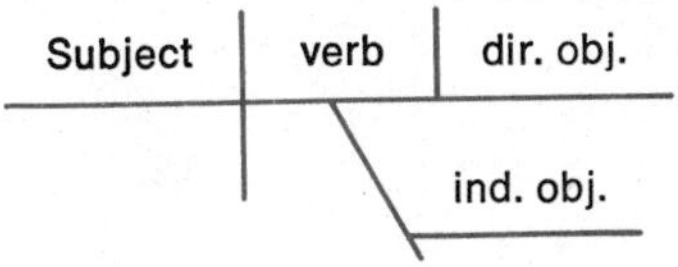


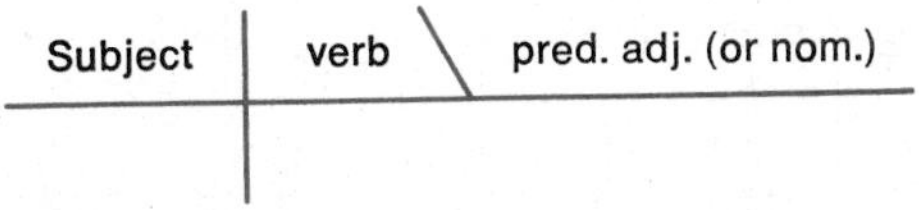


**2h. The *indirect object* of the verb precedes the direct object and usually tells to whom or for whom the action of the verb is done.**

If the word *to* or *for* is used, the noun or pronoun following it is part of a prepositional phrase; it is not an indirect object. Like subjects, objects of verbs are never part of a prepositional phrase.

> Father promised **me** the car. [*Me* is an indirect object.]
> Father promised the car **to me.** [*Me* is part of phrase *to me.*]

EXAMPLES He gave **us** his permission. [gave *to* us]

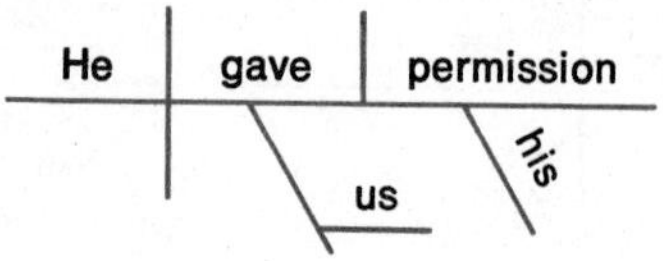


Bob made his **mother** a writing desk. [made *for* his mother]

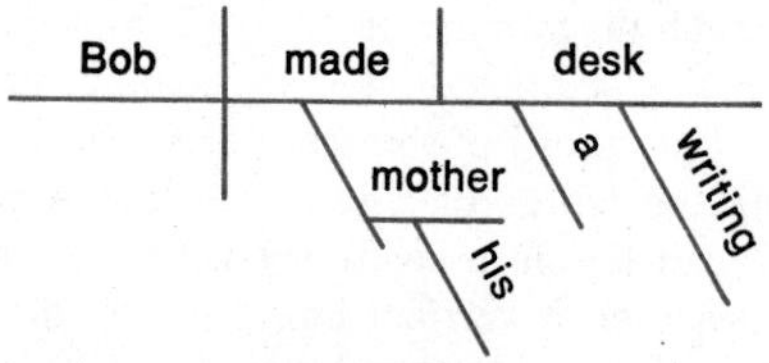


Objects of the verb may be compound.

Mrs. Spiers praised the stage **crew** and the **cast**.

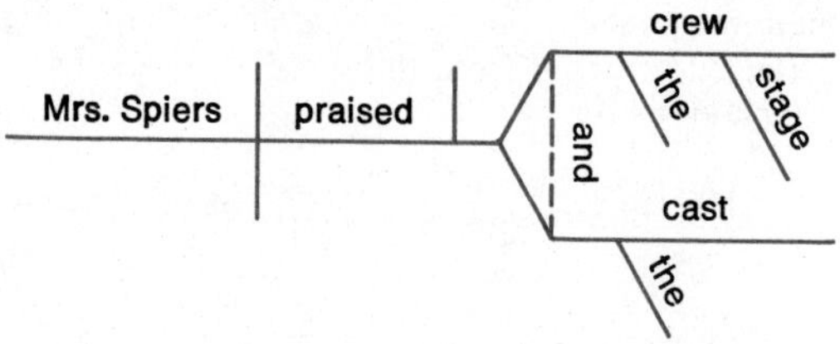


She gave **George** and **me** several suggestions.

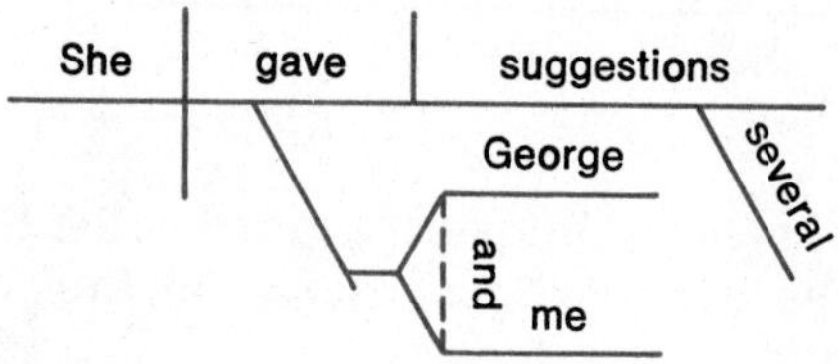


## The Objective Complement

To complete their meaning, some action verbs require an additional complement following their objects. This additional complement is called an *objective complement* because it refers to the object; it may be a noun or an adjective.

They elected Mary **chairwoman.** [The noun *chairwoman* refers to the direct object *Mary* and helps to complete the meaning of the verb *elected.* It is an objective complement.]

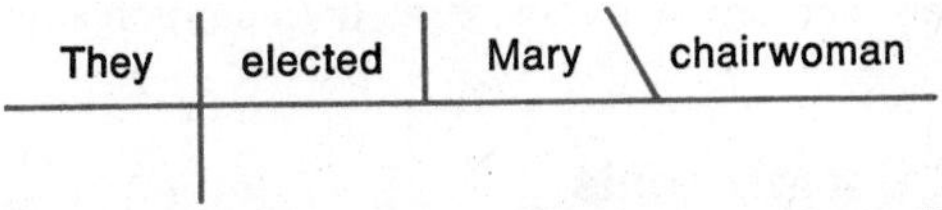


You made her **angry.** [The adjective *angry* modifies the direct object *her* and helps to complete the meaning of the verb *made.* It is an objective complement.]

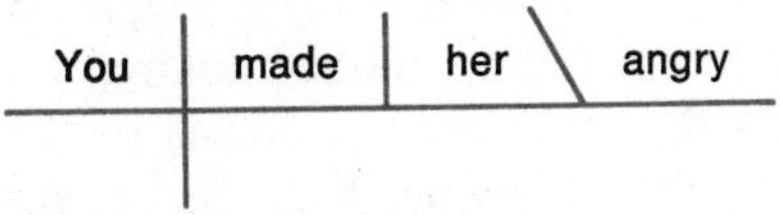


Only a few verbs meaning "make" or "consider" take an objective complement: *elect, appoint, name, choose, render, make, consider,* etc.

The dog licked the dish **clean.** [*made* the dish clean]
The barber cut my hair **short.** [*made* my hair short]
We thought the clown **funny.** [*considered* the clown funny]

**EXERCISE 2.** Number your paper 1–10. Copy after the proper number the objects of the verb or verbs in each sentence. After each object, write *i.o.* for indirect object, or *d.o.* for direct object. If a sentence has no object, write *0* after the number on your paper.

1. Modern medicine leaves some patients in a unique condition.
2. The science pages of the newspapers tell us strange stories.
3. Modern medicine is so advanced that even doctors have difficulty keeping up with their own profession.
4. There is so much for them to do, and so little time, that they work under great pressures.
5. A doctor had told a cancer patient the sad news that the amputation of her leg would be necessary.
6. His patient had protested the operation with great force.
7. She told the doctor stories she had heard about new leg bones made of metal alloys.
8. The doctor knew some of the developments in the field, but not all.

9. He gave his patient the benefit of the doubt, and offered her a new operation instead of the amputation.
10. Years later, the healthy patient still laughed aloud and proudly tapped her leg, with its new titanium-polyethylene thighbone.

## Subject Complements

Complements that refer to (describe, explain, or identify) the subject are *subject complements*. There are two kinds: the *predicate nominative* and the *predicate adjective*.

Subject complements follow linking verbs only. The common linking verbs are the forms of the verb *be* (see page 12), and the following: *become, seem, grow, appear, look, feel, smell, taste, remain, sound, stay.*

**2i. A *predicate nominative* is a noun or pronoun complement that refers to the same person or thing as the subject of the verb. It follows a linking verb.**

New York is our largest **city.** [*City* refers to the subject *New York.*]

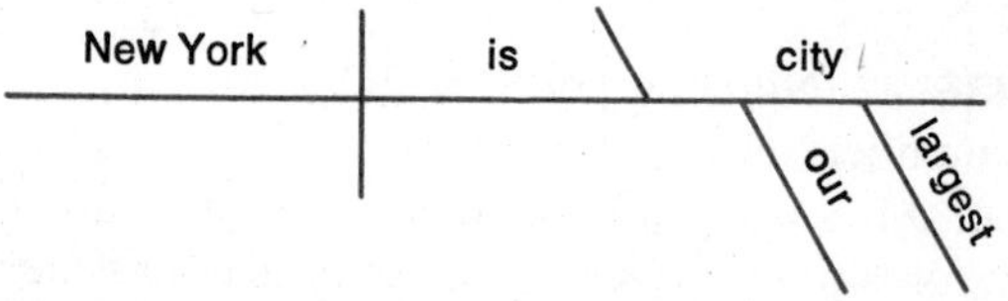


My best friends were **Agnes** and **she.** [Compound predicate nominative; *Agnes* and *she* refer to the same persons as the subject *friends.*]

**2j. A *predicate adjective* is an adjective complement that modifies the subject of the verb. It follows a linking verb.**

This book is **dull.** [The predicate adjective *dull* modifies the subject *book.*]

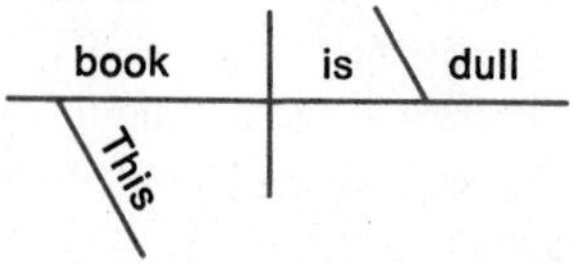


His speech seemed **repetitious** and **tiresome.** [compound predicate adjective modifying the subject *speech*]

In the normal order of an English sentence, complements follow the verb. However, a complement may precede the verb.

This **song** he wrote in 1980. [*Song* is the direct object of the verb *wrote*.]

**Fortunate** are those who can learn from their mistakes. [*Fortunate* is a predicate adjective modifying the subject *those*.]

**EXERCISE 3.** Number your paper 1–20. After the proper number, write the predicate nominatives or predicate adjectives in each of the following sentences; identify each with the abbreviation *p.n.* or *p.a.* Some sentences contain more than one complement.

1. Pablo Casals was a famous cellist.
2. Her speech before the committee seemed effective.
3. About noon the sky became dark and ominous.
4. The loss of his fortune was a fatal blow.
5. Before a match I always feel extremely nervous.
6. Consuelo has been an excellent captain.
7. Deep are the roots of this family.
8. Some of the new regulations seem quite unfair.
9. Long and perilous was Ulysses' voyage home.
10. It was Helen who appeared happy at the news.
11. The outcome of the election was uncertain for a long time, and both candidates eventually became tired and irritable.
12. Although the teacher was absent, the class remained orderly.
13. You can be sure that your anonymous benefactor is either he or Mrs. Graham.
14. If you had been ready, no one would have been late.
15. After her vacation, Aunt Jo looked better and felt better.
16. In spite of many corrupting influences, he remained honest.
17. The ocean mist smelled fishy and tasted salty.
18. The older boys grew tall, but the youngest stayed short.
19. If you were president, you would not be so dictatorial.
20. Shortly after graduating, she became a pilot in the United States Air Force.

## SUMMARY OF SENTENCE PATTERNS

You have learned that every sentence has two basic parts—subject and predicate. Within the subject there is a simple subject, commonly called just the subject; within the predicate there is a simple predicate, commonly called the verb. The pattern of some sentences consists of subject and verb only.

| S | V |
|---|---|
| Children | play. |

Modifiers may be added to the subject and verb without changing the basic pattern of such a sentence.

Many children (S) from this neighborhood play (V) in the park every day.

You have learned also that certain additions to the predicate create other sentence patterns. These additions are complements, which complete the meaning begun by the subject and verb. The different kinds of complements produce the different sentence patterns. The seven common sentence patterns are as follows:

| | | | |
|---|---|---|---|
| S<br>Children | V<br>play. | | |
| S<br>Children | V<br>play | D.O.<br>games. | |
| S<br>He | V<br>gave | I.O.<br>the children | D.O.<br>toys. |
| S<br>This | V<br>made | D.O.<br>the children | OBJ. COMP. (ADJ.)<br>happy. |
| S<br>They | V<br>made | D.O.<br>her | OBJ. COMP. (NOUN)<br>director. |
| S<br>She | V<br>is | P.N.<br>director. | |
| S<br>She | V<br>seems | P.A.<br>competent. | |

**REVIEW EXERCISE.** Number your paper 1–15. Write after the proper number the subject, the verb, and the complements in each sentence. After the complement, tell what kind it is, using abbreviations as follows: direct object, *d.o.;* indirect object, *i.o.;* predicate nominative, *p.n.;* predicate adjective, *p.a.*

1. O. Henry is the pseudonym of the American writer William Sydney Porter.
2. Although born in Greensboro, North Carolina, O. Henry is most famous for his stories about New York City.
3. As a result of his frequent, long walks through the city streets, he knew all aspects of the rapidly growing metropolis.
4. Through his writing, he gave us a clear, if romantic, picture of the city in the early 1900's.
5. The *New York World* paid O. Henry one hundred dollars for each of his weekly stories.
6. Many of his characters were people in poor or modest circumstances.
7. In O. Henry's time, the population of New York City was four million.
8. O. Henry describes the troubles, hardships, and joys of the "four million" in his short stories.
9. The vivid descriptions in his stories give the reader a sympathetic understanding of the characters.
10. The typical O. Henry story is sentimental and full of stereotyped characters.
11. His best-known story is "The Gift of the Magi."
12. In "The Gift of the Magi," a young husband sells his prized watch, and his wife sells her beautiful long hair.
13. With the proceeds he buys her a set of combs for Christmas, and she buys him a fob for his watch.
14. The stories usually have a surprise ending.
15. In spite of their faults, the stories are interesting, and they re-create for us the New York of generations ago.

Chapter 3

# The Phrase

## Kinds of Phrases and Their Functions

Words in a sentence act not only individually but also in groups. The grouped words act together as a unit which may function as a modifier, a subject, a verb, an object, or a predicate nominative. The most common group of related words is the phrase. In Chapter 1 you learned about the verb phrase, which is a verb of more than one word (*is coming, might have been*). This chapter provides a review of the makeup and function in the sentence of other kinds of phrases.

### Diagnostic Test

To determine which parts of this chapter you need to study in your review of phrases, take the following two-part test.

A. Number your paper 1–10. Copy in order the ten prepositional phrases in the following sentences. After each phrase, tell whether it is an adjective or an adverb phrase.

1. Alicia and I are in the same math class, but her assignment is different from mine.
2. When traffic in town is heavy, walking downtown is faster than driving the car.
3. When you confer with your guidance counselor, you will receive information about several colleges which are suitable for you.
4. Accepting my counselor's suggestions, I wrote immediately to several colleges in the Middle West.

5. The President, facing a difficult decision, called a meeting of the Security Council.
6. To raise your grades during the last quarter is more difficult than to maintain them all year.

**B.** Copy on your paper two participial phrases, two gerund phrases, and two infinitive phrases from the test sentences in Part **A.** Label each phrase and give before it the number of the sentence in which it appears.

**3a. A *phrase* is a group of words not containing a verb and its subject. A phrase is used as a single part of speech.**

Five kinds of phrases are explained on the following pages: *prepositional phrases, participial phrases, gerund phrases, infinitive phrases,* and *appositive phrases.*

## THE PREPOSITIONAL PHRASE

**3b. A *prepositional phrase* is a group of words beginning with a preposition and usually ending with a noun or pronoun.**

| | |
|---|---|
| **for** Peg and you | **in** the classroom |
| **after** the exam | **to** bed |

The noun or pronoun that concludes the prepositional phrase is the object of the preposition that begins the phrase.

| | |
|---|---|
| on the **steps** | from **Hazel** and **me** |
| with a **grin** | for **Josie** or **Mary** |

Prepositional phrases are usually used as modifiers—as adjectives or adverbs. Occasionally, a prepositional phrase is used as a noun:

**After dinner** will be too late. [The prepositional phrase is the subject of the sentence; it is used as a noun.]

## The Adjective Phrase

**3c. An *adjective phrase* is a prepositional phrase that modifies a noun or a pronoun.**

Tucson has been the locale **of many Westerns.**

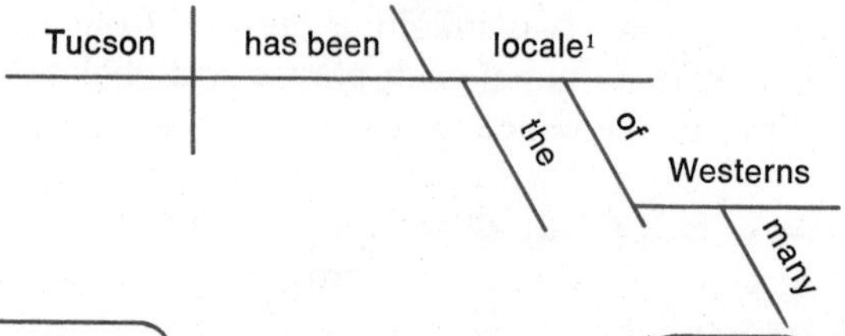


Tourists **from the East** visit the old frontier towns **in the West.**

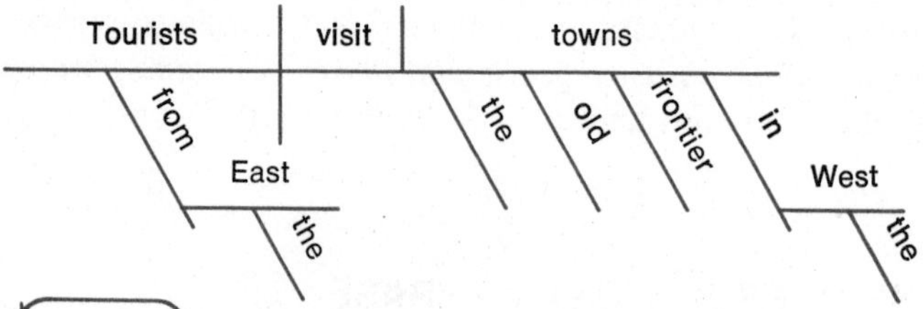


Many **of the tourists** like historical places.

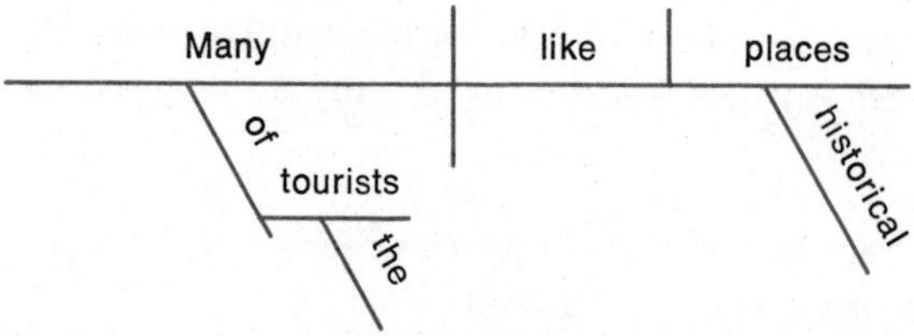


**EXERCISE 1.** Copy in a column the adjective phrases in the following sentences. Before each phrase, place the number of the sentence in which it appears. After each phrase, write the noun the phrase modifies.

1. Once inhabited primarily by American Indians and dreaded by pioneers, the deserts of the Southwest are now popular areas for business and recreation.

[1] In a diagram the preposition which begins the phrase is placed on a line slanting downward from the word the phrase modifies. The object of the preposition is placed on a horizontal line extending to the right from the line with the preposition. Single-word modifiers are diagramed in the usual way.

2. Caves beneath the rims of the desert canyons were once the homes of small bands of Pueblos.
3. These lofty homes provided protection from enemies, but life in cliff dwellings was hard and tedious.
4. The flatlands below the abandoned ruins were once irrigated by a system of canals.
5. A visit to the desert intrigues tourists from states without deserts.

## The Adverb Phrase

**3d. An *adverb phrase* is a prepositional phrase that modifies a verb, an adjective, or another adverb.**

The following sentences show the ways in which an adverb phrase can modify a verb.

> She practices **with diligence.** [*how* she practices]
> She practices **before a concert tour.** [*when* she practices]
> She practices **in her studio.** [*where* she practices]
> She practices **for weeks.** [*to what extent* she practices]
> She practices **for her own good.** [*why* she practices]

See the following diagram.

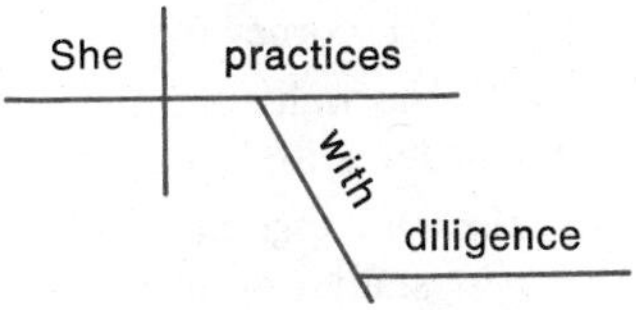


In the sentence below, the adverb phrase modifies an adjective.

> He was true **to his word.**

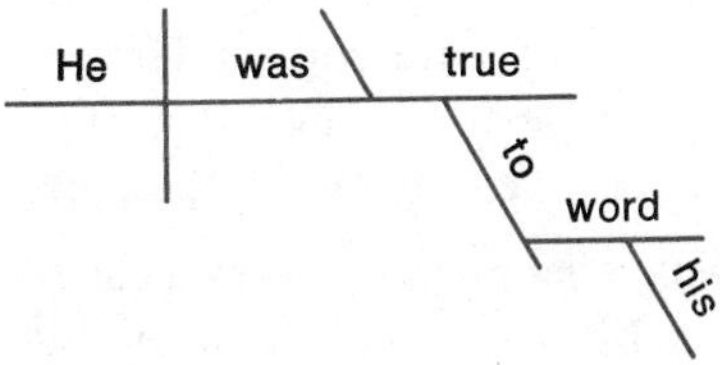

The following sentence illustrates an adverb phrase modifying an adverb.

He threw the ball far **to the left.**

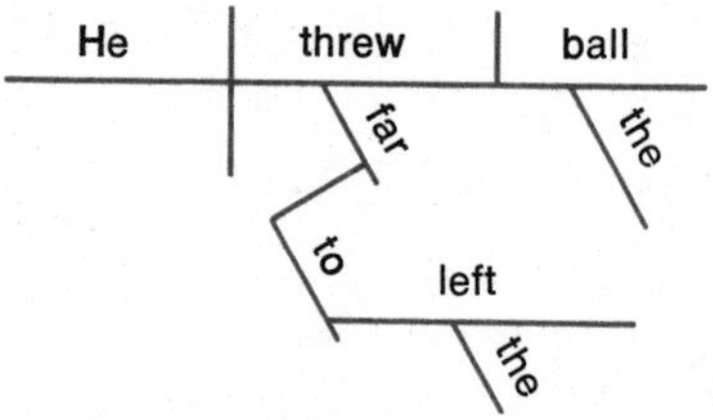


**EXERCISE 2.** Number your paper 1–10. After the proper number, list the adverb phrases in each of the following sentences. After each phrase, write the word(s) the phrase modifies.

1. After the concert, everyone praised Gail for her performance.
2. She had practiced at her home for hours.
3. When she was playing at her best, she became unaware of her surroundings.
4. Although she played at home with complete abandon, she was modest about her coming performance.
5. She practiced far beyond the necessary hours, knowing she would not be content with a merely mechanical rendition.
6. Bill, however, practiced for only a short time and, after practicing, always went to the corner for a pizza.
7. If he succeeded with the right notes, he thought, his music teacher would be satisfied with him.
8. After their first rehearsal together, Gail's cool reaction to his interpretation was shattering to his self-respect.
9. Bill, the best pianist among the boys, practiced in terror for the remaining three days.
10. When he spoke with us after the recital, he raved about Gail's playing and groaned over his own mistakes.

**EXERCISE 3.** Demonstrate your understanding of the way a prepositional phrase functions as an adjective or adverb by writing complete sentences as indicated.

EXAMPLE 1. with quiet pride [Use as an adverb phrase.]

1. *Sandra spoke about her work with quiet pride.*

1. in great haste [Use as an adverb phrase.]
2. of surprising value [Use as an adjective phrase.]
3. for her own good [Use as an adverb phrase.]
4. without really trying [Use as an adverb phrase.]
5. with a generous nature [Use as an adjective phrase.]
6. of unexpected courage [Use as an adjective phrase.]
7. to success [Use as an adjective phrase.]
8. by fair means or foul [Use as an adverb phrase.]
9. of the joke [Use as an adjective phrase.]
10. after another disappointment [Use as an adverb phrase.]

## PHRASES CONTAINING VERBALS

Less common than the prepositional phrase but still very useful to a writer are the verbal phrases: the *participial phrase,* the *gerund phrase,* and the *infinitive phrase.* They are called verbal phrases because the most important word in them is a verbal. Verbals are so called because they are formed from verbs. In some respects they act like verbs. They may express action; they may have modifiers; and they may be followed by complements. In one important respect, however, they are not like verbs; verbals are not used as verbs in a sentence. They are used as other parts of speech—as nouns, as adjectives, or as adverbs.

Before you can understand verbal phrases, you must understand the verbals on which the phrases are based. On the following pages you will find an explanation of each kind of verbal, followed by a discussion of the verbal as it is most commonly used—in a phrase.

### The Participle and the Participial Phrase

**3e. A *participle* is a verb form that is used as an adjective.**

The rapidly **developing** storm kept small boats in port.
**Developing** rapidly, the storm kept small boats in port.
The storm, **developing** rapidly, kept small boats in port.

In these sentences, *developing,* which is formed from the verb *develop,* is used as an adjective, modifying the noun *storm.*

In the following sentence the participle *crying,* which is formed from the verb *cry,* is used as an adjective, modifying the pronoun *him.*

I found him **crying.**

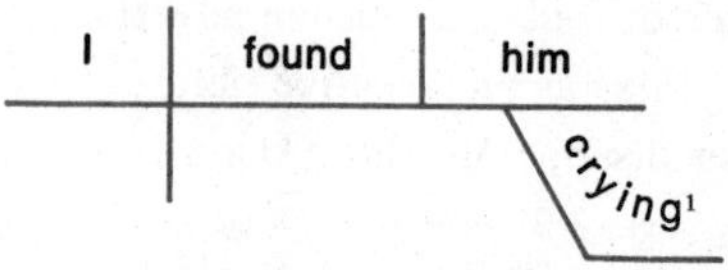


There are two kinds of participles: *present participles* and *past participles.* A present participle, like those in the preceding examples, ends in *–ing.* A past participle may end in *–ed, –d, –t, –en,* or *–n:* ask*ed,* save*d,* deal*t,* eat*en,* see*n.*

PRESENT PARTICIPLE They saw their children **sleeping.**

PAST PARTICIPLE The children, **awakened,** began to stir.

Although participles are formed from verbs, they are not used alone as verbs. A participle may, however, be used with a helping verb to form a verb phrase.

PARTICIPLE The **moving** car gathered speed rapidly. [*Moving* modifies *car.*]

VERB PHRASE The car **was moving** rapidly. [The verb phrase *was moving* consists of the helping verb *was* plus the present participle *moving.*]

When participles are used in verb phrases, they are considered part of the verb and are not considered adjectives.

**3f. A *participial phrase* is a phrase containing a participle and any complements or modifiers it may have.**[2]

[1] In a diagram the participle is written on a bent line drawn downward from the word the participle modifies.

[2] For work on the participial phrase as a sentence fragment, see page 198. For exercises on the dangling participle, see pages 233–36.

**Removing his coat,** Jack rushed to the river bank. [The participial phrase is made up of the participle *removing* and the complement *coat,* which is the direct object of *removing.* Like verbs, participles may take an object.]

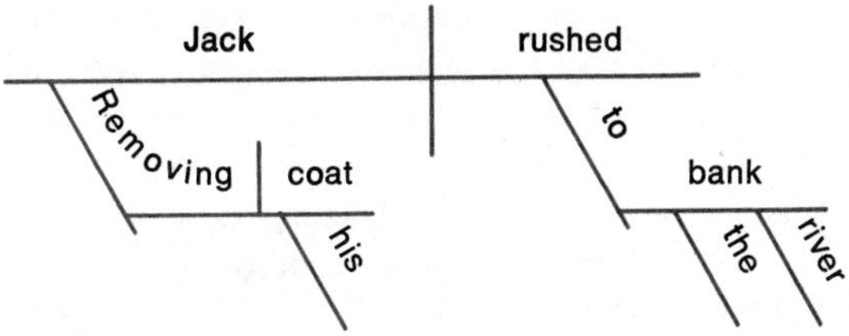


**Hesitating there for a moment,** he quickly grasped the situation. [The participial phrase is made up of the participle *hesitating* plus its modifiers—the adverb *there* and the adverb phrase *for a moment.*]

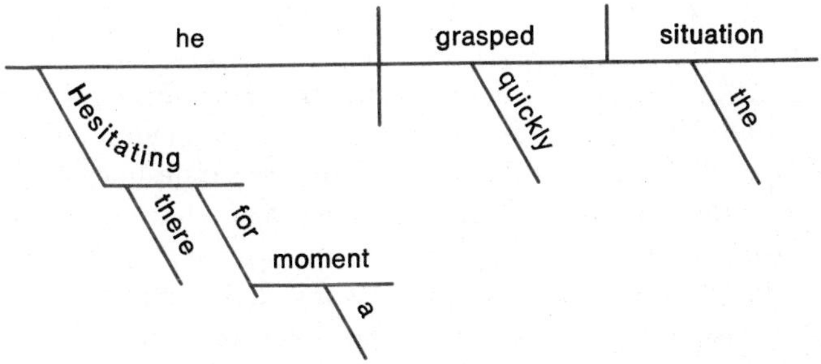


The participle usually introduces the phrase, and the entire phrase acts as an adjective to modify a noun or pronoun.

Arthur Ashe, **playing with skill,** won the tournament.

**Getting up at five,** we got an early start.

**Destroyed by fire,** the church was never rebuilt.

**EXERCISE 4.** List on your paper the participial phrases in the following sentences. Be sure to include all complements and modifiers. Before each phrase, write the number of the sentence in which it appears. After each phrase, write the word the phrase modifies.

1. High school graduates replying to a questionnaire about their college courses often mention freshman English as the course giving them the most trouble.
2. Facing college standards, the graduates realize that they did not work hard enough on the themes assigned in high school.
3. Statistics reported by the National Education Association revealed that the vast majority of American colleges offer remedial English classes emphasizing composition.
4. Handicapped by their writing deficiencies, graduates seeking employment or advancement in their occupations are often denied desirable opportunities.
5. Recognizing the importance of practice, teachers of composition, imitating the athletic coach, conduct regular practice sessions.

**EXERCISE 5.** For each of the following sentences, copy the numbered and italicized phrases in order on your paper. Place each phrase and its number on a separate line. After each phrase, write the word it modifies, and tell whether it is a *participial* phrase, an *adjective* prepositional phrase, or an *adverb* prepositional phrase. Do not list separately the prepositional phrase within a larger italicized phrase.

EXAMPLE (1) *Living far from the city,* I developed an interest (2) *in nature* (3) *at an early age.*

1. *Living far from the city, I,* **participial**
2. *in nature, interest,* **adjective**
3. *at an early age, developed,* **adverb**

a. (1) *Having studied hard,* Karen walked rapidly (2) *to school,* confident that she would do well on her test (3) *in chemistry.*

b. (4) *By next week* all of the students (5) *trying out for the soccer team* will have heard (6) *from the coach or his assistant.*

c. Those (7) *going on the field trip in the morning* will meet (8) *at either Debbie's house at eight-thirty or the school at nine o'clock.*

d. Today's newspaper, (9) *printed last night,* made no mention (10) *of this morning's traffic tie-up.*

e. Many (11) *of the articles* (12) *written for a newspaper* are based (13) *on news-wire reports.*

f. (14) *Annoyed by the mosquitoes,* Mr. Sims, (15) *slapping at his neck and face,* went (16) *into his house* (17) *for a while.*

g. (18) *Rinsed with hot water,* the dishes were stacked in the sink, (19) *waiting to be washed.*

h. The gift (20) *given to our principal, Mrs. Scott,* was a necklace (21) *made of silver and turquoise.*

i. (22) *Addressing her audience,* the principal spoke words (23) *of encouragement.*

j. At the end of the speech we heard some people (24) *clapping politely in the front rows* and others (25) *cheering hoarsely from the balcony.*

## The Gerund and the Gerund Phrase

**3g. A *gerund* is a verb form ending in *–ing* that is used as a noun.**

**Traveling** is fun. [*Traveling* is formed from the verb *travel* and, as the subject of the sentence, is used as a noun.]

A gerund is a verbal noun. It may be used in any way that a noun may be used.

Good **writing** comes from much practice. [gerund used as subject]

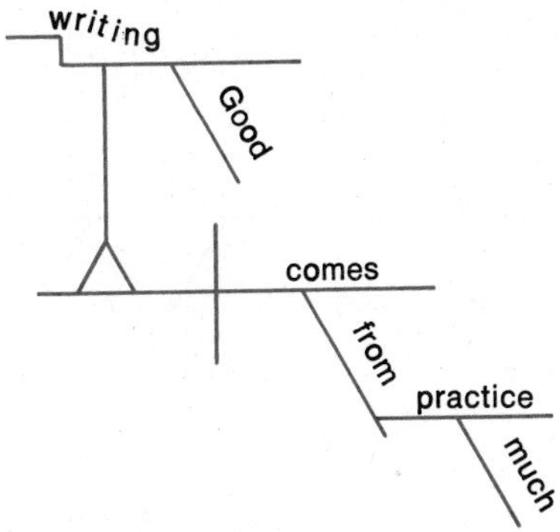

They do not appreciate my **singing.** [gerund used as object of verb]

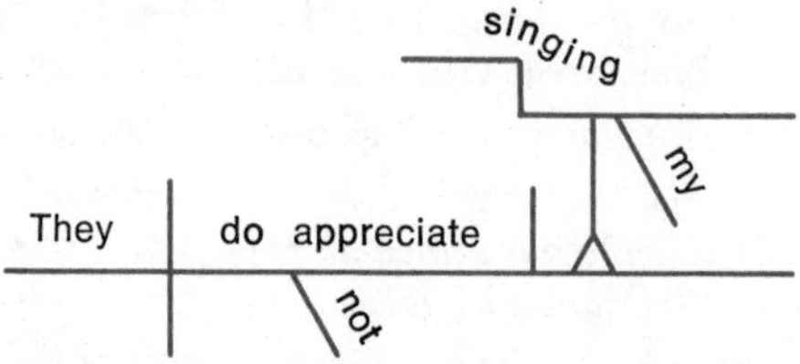


By **studying,** you can pass the course. [gerund used as object of a preposition]

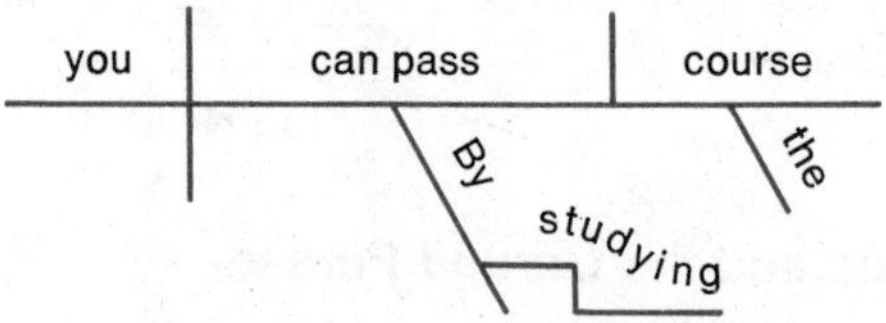


**3h. A *gerund phrase* is a phrase consisting of a gerund and any complements or modifiers it may have.**

**Carrying coals to Newcastle** is a traditional example of the unnecessary. [The gerund *Carrying* has *coals* as its direct object and is modified by the adverb phrase *to Newcastle.*]

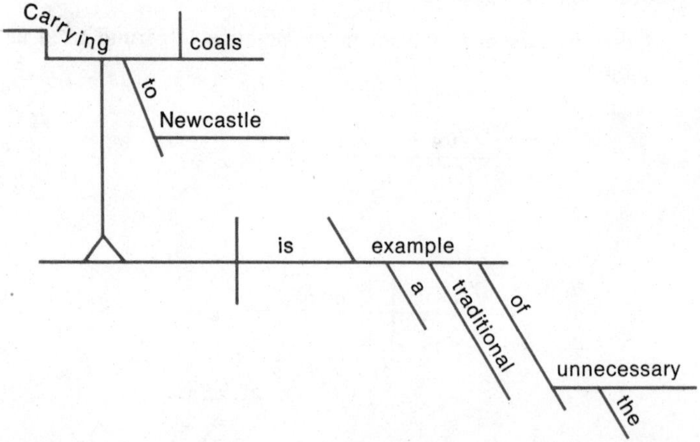


Like the gerund alone, the gerund phrase may be used in any place that a noun would fit:

**Telling your sister** was a mistake. [gerund phrase as subject]

The college advises **sending applications early.** [gerund phrase as object]

He won the game by **kicking a field goal.** [gerund phrase as object of preposition]

Her most important achievement was **winning the national championship.** [gerund phrase as predicate nominative]

## The Infinitive and the Infinitive Phrase

**3i. An *infinitive* is a verb form, usually preceded by *to,* that is used as a noun or a modifier.**

to go     to speak     to believe     to be

An infinitive is generally used as a noun, but it may also be used as an adjective or an adverb.

The infinitive used as a noun:

**To wait** for the bus is tiresome. [infinitive as subject]

Everyone wanted **to go.** [infinitive as object of the verb]

Her ambition is **to fly.** [infinitive as predicate nominative]

The infinitive used as an adjective:

We lacked the strength **to resist.** [infinitive modifies *strength*]

The infinitive used as an adverb:

We study **to learn.** [infinitive modifies the verb *study*]

► NOTE Do not confuse the infinitive, a verbal of which *to* is a part, with a prepositional phrase beginning with *to,* which consists of *to* plus a noun or pronoun.

| INFINITIVES | PREPOSITIONAL PHRASES |
|---|---|
| to fly | to her |
| to draw | to school |

The word *to,* called the sign of the infinitive, is sometimes omitted.

She made me [to] **leave.**
Help me [to] **do** my homework.

**3j. An *infinitive phrase* consists of an infinitive and any complements or modifiers it may have.**[1]

We intend **to leave early.** [*Early* is an adverb modifying the infinitive *to leave.*]

I have a paper **to write before class.** [*Before class* modifies *to write.*]

No one wants **to help us.** [*Us* is the object of *to help.*]

Like infinitives alone, infinitive phrases can be used as nouns or as modifiers:

We tried **to reason with her.** [The infinitive phrase *to reason with her* is the object of the verb *tried.*]

**To save money** became her obsession. [*To save money* is the subject of the sentence.]

There must be a way **to solve this problem.** [The infinitive phrase modifies the noun *way.*]

I am too busy **to go to the movies tonight.** [The infinitive phrase modifies the adjective *busy.*]

His plan is **to go to college for two years.** [The infinitive phrase is a predicate nominative, referring back to *plan.*]

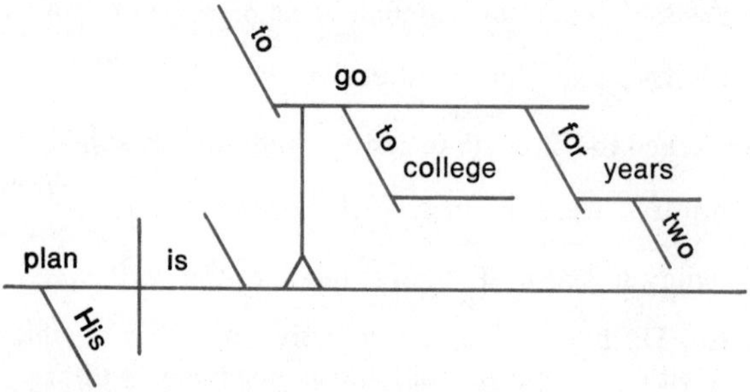


## The Infinitive Clause

Unlike other verbals, an infinitive may have a subject as well as complements and modifiers.

I expected **Gloria to vote for me.** [*Gloria* is the subject of the infinitive *to vote.*]

[1] For exercises on the use of the infinitive phrase to reduce wordiness, see pages 257–61.

I asked **her to help me.** [*Her* is the subject of the infinitive *to help.*]

I believe **it to be John.** [*It* is the subject of the infinitive *to be,* and *John* is a predicate nominative referring back to *it.*]

I believe **it to be good.** [*It* is the subject of the infinitive *to be,* and the adjective *good* is a predicate adjective referring back to *it.*]

When an infinitive has a subject, as in the preceding examples, the construction is called an *infinitive clause.* Notice that the subject of an infinitive is in the objective case.[1]

**REVIEW EXERCISE A.** Number your paper 1–20. In the following sentences most prepositional, participial, gerund, and infinitive phrases are numbered and italicized. Study the entire phrase, and after the corresponding number on your paper, tell what kind of phrase it is. If it is a prepositional phrase, tell whether it is an adjective phrase or an adverb phrase.

a. (1) *Reading the newspapers,* I was struck (2) *by the difference* (3) *between fact and fiction.*

b. (4) *Writing fiction* does not require the same kind of talent as (5) *writing nonfiction.*

c. (6) *Realizing they are likely* (7) *to be sued* for what they write, writers of nonfiction are very careful about (8) *qualifying what they say* (9) *with frequent attributions.*

d. (10) *Rarely claiming any direct certainty,* they credit others with saying what they report (11) *in their stories* (12) *through phrases* like "unofficial sources report," "it is said," and the like.

e. Fiction never claims (13) *to be fact,* and the writer of fiction seems to aim at (14) *distorting facts deliberately.*

f. This writing, though written (15) *by real people* and (16) *shaped by real experiences,* aims at the creation (17) *of unreal characters and events* and depends upon the reader's imagination (18) *to make them real.*

g. The difference (19) *between fact and fiction* in writing comes from (20) *aiming at two very different uses* of the printed word.

[1] For rules concerning the use of the objective case, see pages 108–11.

## THE APPOSITIVE[1]

**3k. An *appositive* is a noun or pronoun—often with modifiers—set beside another noun or pronoun to explain or identify it.**

Your friend **Tina** is in town.

The *Daily News,* a **tabloid,** has the largest circulation in the city.

An *appositive phrase* is a phrase consisting of an appositive and its modifiers.

My brother's car, **a sporty red hatchback with bucket seats,** is the envy of my friends.

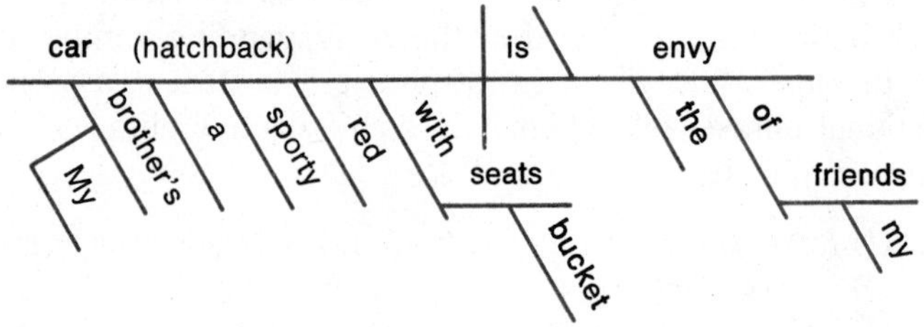


An appositive phrase usually follows the word it explains or identifies, but it may precede it.

**A beautiful collie,** Skip was my favorite dog.

**REVIEW EXERCISE B.** Number your paper 1–25. In the following sentences most of the phrases have been numbered and italicized. Write after its number on your paper the name of each phrase: prepositional, participial, gerund, infinitive, or appositive. In the case of a prepositional phrase, tell only whether it is an adjective phrase or an adverb phrase.

a. As its population increases (1) *by leaps and bounds,* the world faces a shortage (2) *of fresh water.*

[1] For rules on the punctuation of appositives, see pages 546–47. For the use of the appositive in subordination of ideas, see page 217.

b. An obvious way (3) *to increase the fresh water supply* is (4) *to convert sea water.*

c. (5) *Converting sea water* is, therefore, one (6) *of our greatest scientific problems.*

d. Scientists are experimenting (7) *with two methods,* (8) *the well-known distillation process and the freeze-separation process,* which separates fresh water by freezing it (9) *into removable crystals.*

e. (10) *Using one billion gallons a day,* a city (11) *of four million people* spends, (12) *under present circumstances,* approximately one dollar a thousand gallons; but converted water (13) *produced by existing methods* often costs five times as much.

f. (14) *Faced by this economic problem,* scientists are exploring the possibilities (15) *of a large nuclear reactor,* (16) *a controversial source of energy.*

g. It is possible (17) *to build a nuclear reactor* which will produce enough heat (18) *to distill one billion gallons a day* (19) *for a relatively small expense.*

h. Such a reactor, (20) *being built with all the necessary safeguards,* would represent a scientific achievement (21) *of the first magnitude.*

i. (22) *Solving the water problem in this way* would be a result (23) *of the determination* (24) *to provide fresh water* (25) *for every citizen.*

# Chapter 4

# The Clause

## The Function of Clauses

As you have been reminded in Chapter 3, most sentences are made up not only of single words functioning as parts of speech but also of word groups functioning as single parts of speech. The phrase is one such word group; the clause is another. Knowledge of the subordinate clause, which you will review in this chapter, is essential for all those wishing to improve their writing.

### Diagnostic Test

Give yourself the following diagnostic test. There are ten subordinate clauses in the following sentences. Copy them in order on your paper. After each clause, tell whether it is an adjective, adverb, or noun clause.

1. It is only human nature to like people who seem to like you.
2. No one can resist the flatterer who raises one's self-esteem.
3. When negotiations began, hopes were high for a quick agreement between company and union.
4. What actually happened to the ill-fated expedition will probably never be known.
5. Ms. Jordan refused to comment until she had studied the ambassador's report.
6. Since economic necessity is the thing that makes people work hard, firms won't hire anyone who offers to work for nothing.
7. If students are on the honor roll, they may spend any free period in the library reading whatever they wish.

**4a. A *clause* is a group of words containing a subject and predicate and used as part of a sentence.**

Clauses are classified according to grammatical completeness. Those that can stand alone if removed from their sentences are called *independent clauses.* Those that do not express a complete thought and cannot stand alone are called *subordinate clauses.*

## INDEPENDENT CLAUSES

When removed from its sentence, an independent clause[1] makes complete sense. Written with a capital at the beginning and a period at the end, it becomes a simple sentence. It is an independent *clause* only when combined in a larger sentence with one or more additional clauses, independent or subordinate.

When two or more independent clauses are joined together into a single sentence, the usual connecting words are *and, but, or, nor,* and *for.*

EXAMPLES It was after midnight, **and** the last bus home had already left. [The conjunction *and* joins two independent clauses.]

The soup was delicious, **but** the main course tasted bland. [The independent clauses are joined by *but.*]

## SUBORDINATE CLAUSES

Subordinate clauses,[2] which cannot stand alone as sentences, are used as nouns or modifiers in the same way as single words and phrases. A subordinate clause is always combined in some way with an independent clause. The following are examples of subordinate clauses.

[1] Independent clauses are sometimes called *main* clauses.
[2] Subordinate clauses are sometimes called *dependent* clauses.

whoever knows the song
which everyone in the family likes
as she had thought

Combined with an independent clause, each of these subordinate clauses plays its part in a sentence:

**Whoever knows the song** may join in.
We ordered spaghetti, **which everyone in the family likes.**
**As she had thought,** the right front tire had blown out.

**EXERCISE 1.** In each of the following sentences, a clause is printed in italics. If the italicized clause is an independent clause, place *I* after the proper number. If it is a subordinate clause, place *S* after the proper number.

1. Egyptology is the branch of learning *which is concerned with the language and culture of ancient Egypt.*
2. *Until the Rosetta Stone was discovered in 1799,* the ancient Egyptian language was an enigma to scholars.
3. Boussard, *who was a captain in the engineers under Napoleon,* found the stone in the trenches near Rosetta, a city near the mouth of the Nile.
4. Before the French had a chance to analyze its inscriptions, *the stone was captured by the British.*
5. Because the stone contained the same message in two kinds of Egyptian writing and in Greek script, *it provided the needed key for deciphering the Egyptian language.*
6. *When the Rosetta Stone was found,* part of the hieroglyphic portion was missing.
7. Scholars could easily read the Greek inscription, *which was nearly complete.*
8. *In 1818 Thomas Young succeeded in isolating a number of hieroglyphics* that he took to represent names.
9. *The message* that was written on the stone *was not very exciting in itself.*
10. Since the priests of Egypt were grateful for benefits from the king, *they were formally thanking the king for his generosity.*

## The Adjective Clause

Like a phrase, a subordinate clause acts as a single part of speech—as an adjective, adverb, or noun.

**4b. An *adjective clause* is a subordinate clause that, like an adjective, modifies a noun or a pronoun.**

EXAMPLES The house **where he was born** has been made a national shrine.

She is one **who earned her honors.**

This composition, **which I wrote last year,** received a grade of *C*.

Since a subordinate clause, like a sentence, has a verb and a subject and may contain complements and modifiers, it is diagramed very much like a sentence. Adjective and adverb clauses are placed on a horizontal line below the main line. An adjective clause begun by a relative pronoun is joined to the word it modifies by a slanting broken line drawn neatly from the modified word to the relative pronoun.

EXAMPLES Students **whose work represents their second-best** are not real students. [The subordinate clause *whose work represents their second-best* modifies the noun *students.*]

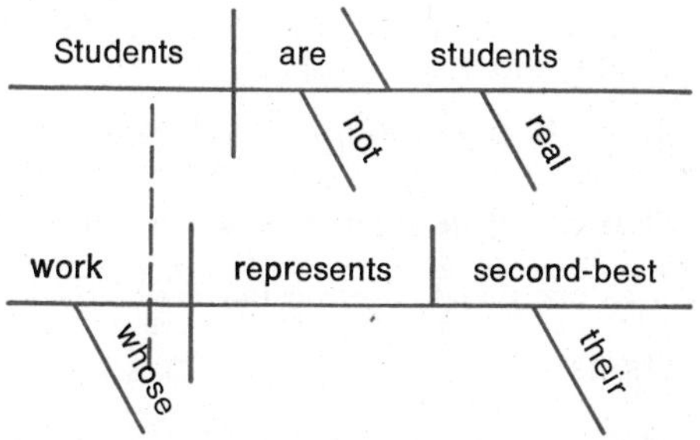

Bob spent on an old car all the money **that he had earned during the summer.** [The subordinate clause *that he had earned during the summer* modifies the noun *money.*]

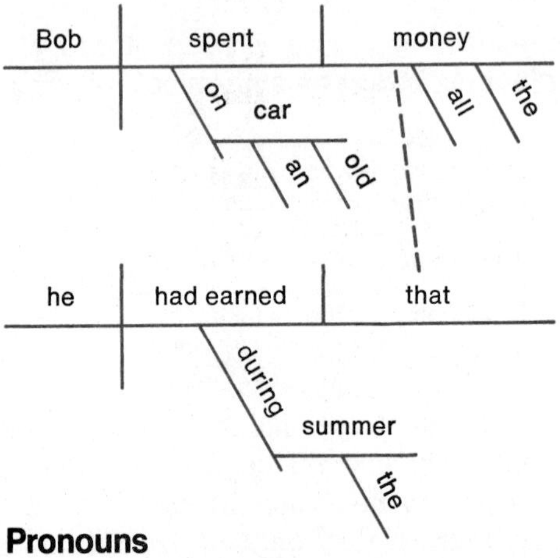


## Relative Pronouns

Adjective clauses often begin with the pronouns *who, whom, which,* or *that.* These pronouns refer to, or are *related* to, a noun or pronoun that has come before.

**4c. A *relative pronoun* is a pronoun that begins a subordinate adjective clause and is related to a noun or a pronoun already mentioned or understood. The word to which the relative pronoun is related is its *antecedent.***

A relative pronoun does three things.

1. It refers to a preceding noun or pronoun:

   Ms. Garcia is a woman **whom we can trust.**

   The joke was one **that I had heard before.**

2. It connects its clause with the rest of the sentence:

   I don't admire anyone **who acts like that.** [The subordinate clause is joined to the independent clause by the relative pronoun *who.*]

You need a watch **that keeps time.** [The subordinate clause is joined to the independent clause by the relative pronoun *that.*]

**3.** It performs a function within its own clause by serving as the subject, object, etc., of the subordinate clause:

The principal appointed George, **who is a reliable student.** [*Who* is the subject of the verb *is* in the adjective clause *who is a reliable student.*]

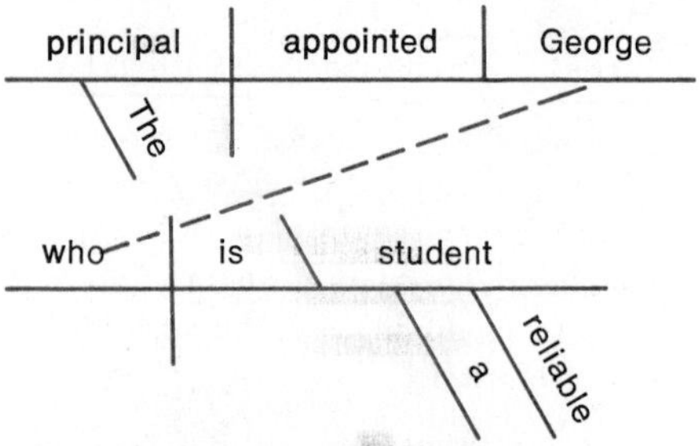


These are the assignments **for which you are responsible.** [*Which* is the object of the preposition *for.*][1]

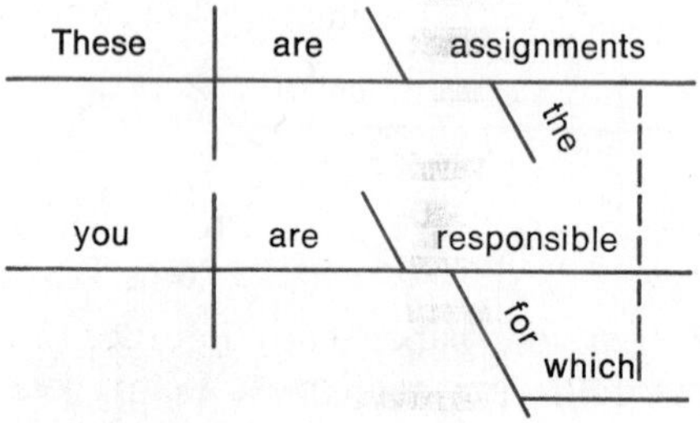


Show me the book **that you read.** [*That* is the object of the verb *read* (read *what?*).]

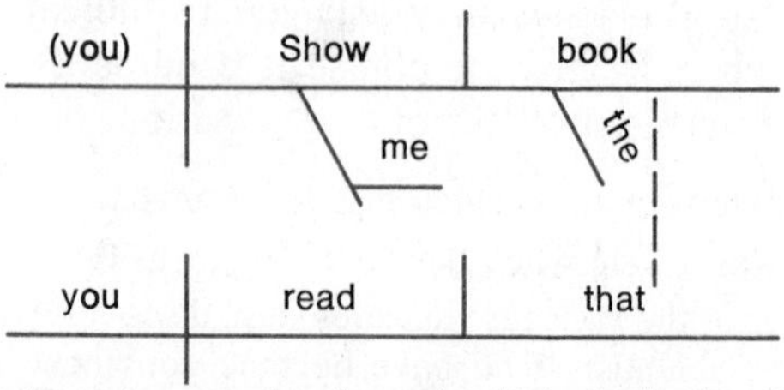


[1] In this sentence two words—*for* and *which*—begin the clause. Other two-word combinations of a preposition and a relative pronoun to begin a clause are *in which, by whom, for whom, from whom,* etc.

An adjective clause may also begin with the relative adjective *whose* or with the relative adverb *where* or *when.*

He is a coach **whose record has been amazing.** [*Whose,* the possessive form of the relative pronoun *who,* functions as an adjective modifying *record.*]

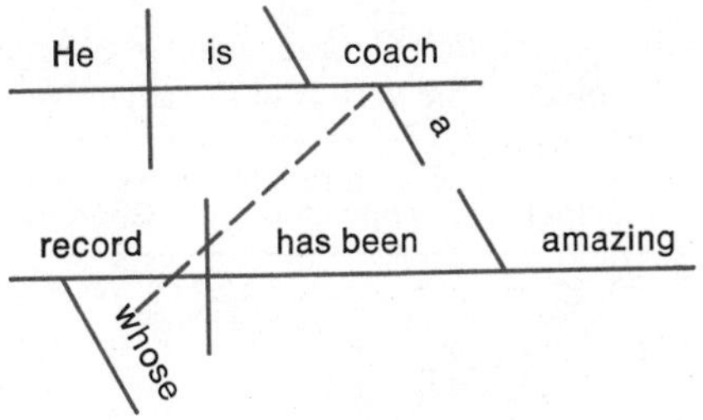


Do you remember the restaurant **where we ate lunch?** [*Where* acts as an adverb modifying *ate,* the verb in the clause. The antecedent is *restaurant.*]

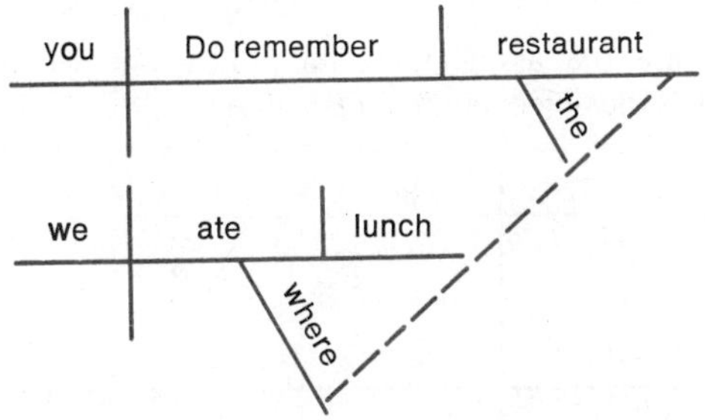


**EXERCISE 2.** On your paper, copy in order the adjective clauses in the following sentences. Before each clause, write the number of the sentence in which it appears. After each clause, write the noun or pronoun that the clause modifies. Your teacher may ask you to indicate whether the word which begins the clause is used as a subject, an object of a verb, an object of a preposition, or a modifier.

1. Black holes are stars which puzzle scientists.
2. There was a time when their existence was only a theory.
3. But during the past few decades new discoveries have been made by scientists who have become convinced of the real existence of black holes.
4. A black hole is a star which behaves very mysteriously.

5. It has collapsed to a size which is astonishingly small.
6. Therefore it possesses a density that is astonishingly great.
7. These properties give it powers which are quite peculiar.
8. There are stars which spaceships can pass by easily, and others near which special maneuvering might be required.
9. But the gravity of a black hole would probably capture anyone who entered its field, which is nearly inescapable.
10. Colliding with a black hole would be an accident that could hardly be enjoyable, and that would probably be unforgettable.
11. Our own galaxy contains black holes, according to scientists who attempt to explain various unsolved mysteries by the fact.
12. They are studying reports of meteors which seem to have suddenly vanished from sight.
13. A black hole, which is smaller and denser than anything known, can absorb or capture in orbit whatever material is attracted to it.
14. A scientist who became attracted in this way to a black hole would be a scientist who could not be questioned afterward.
15. The riddle of the existence of black holes, which remains unanswered, is a mystery that may never be fully solved.

## The Noun Clause

**4d. A *noun clause* is a subordinate clause used as a noun.**

In diagraming, a noun clause is pictured as a unit by being placed at the top of a vertical line rising from the part of the diagram (subject, object, predicate nominative) to which the clause belongs.

EXAMPLE **Whoever wins the election** will have many problems.

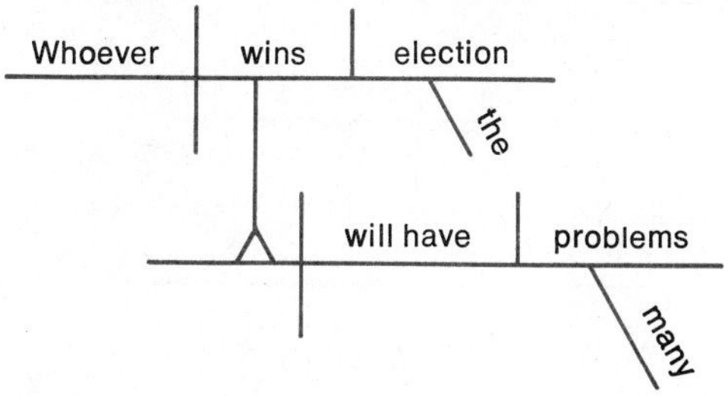

The entire noun clause *whoever wins the election* is the subject of the verb *will have.* Study the following pairs of sentences to see how a noun clause functioning in the same way that a noun functions may be a predicate nominative, an object of a verb, or an object of a preposition.

This is her **job.** [*Job* is a noun used as a predicate nominative after the linking verb *is.*]
This is **what she does.** [*What she does* is a noun clause used as a predicate nominative.]

Do you know the **score?** [*Score* is a noun used as the object of the verb *do know.*]
Do you know **what the score is?** [*What the score is* is a noun clause used as an object of a verb.]

Here is a copy of my **speech.** [*Speech* is a noun used as the object of the preposition *of.*]
Here is a copy of **what I said.** [*What I said* is a noun clause used as an object of a preposition.]

A noun clause may begin with an indefinite relative pronoun – *that, what, whatever, who, which, whoever, whichever.* Unlike a (definite) relative pronoun, an indefinite relative pronoun does not have an antecedent in its sentence.

EXAMPLE He told me **what he wanted.**

A noun clause may also begin with an indefinite relative adjective – *whose, which, whatever* – or an indefinite relative adverb – *where, when, how,* etc.

I know **whose car this is.**

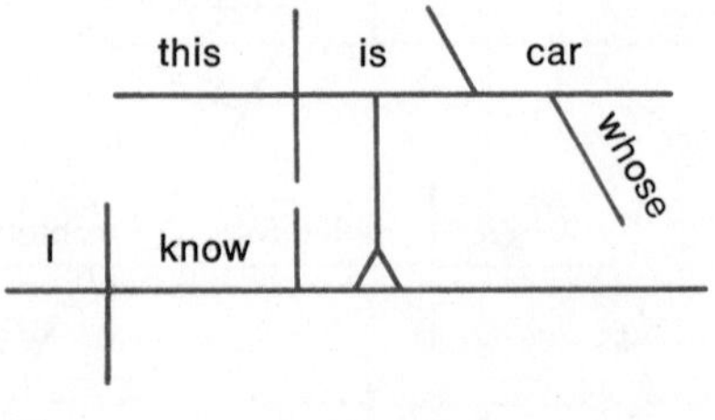

I know <u>**where**</u> **she went.**

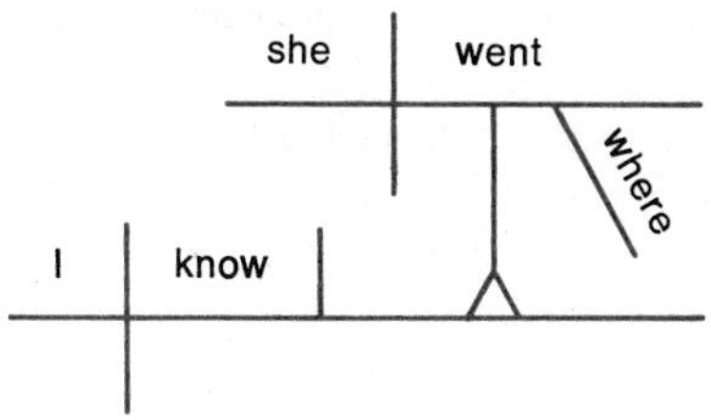


► **NOTE** Adjective and noun clauses are sometimes used without an introductory word. Note that the introductory word is omitted in the second sentence in each of the following pairs.

James Earl Jones is an actor **whom I admire.**

James Earl Jones is an actor **I admire.**

She says **that I. M. Pei designed the building.**

She says **I. M. Pei designed the building.**

**EXERCISE 3.** List in order on your paper the subordinate clauses in the following sentences. Before each clause, place the number of the sentence in which it appears. After each clause, tell what kind it is—adjective or noun. Be prepared to tell what word each adjective clause modifies and how each noun clause is used in the sentence—as a subject, an object of a verb or of a preposition, or a predicate nominative.

1. The processes which go on in a clock are interesting to study.
2. Ask someone who knows clocks what makes them tick.
3. Whatever a clockmaker says will be filled with the jargon of the trade of keeping time.
4. On the left is a timepiece that is really a clock, and on the right is what someone wrongly called a clock.
5. Whatever can properly be called a clock always strikes the hours on a bell.
6. What does not strike the hours on a bell should not be called a clock.
7. The history of the words we use is what determines their correct meaning.

8. Whoever knows the history of the word *clock* will know how its meaning has changed.
9. *Cloche* and *Glocke* are what the French and the Germans say when they mean "bell."
10. Anyone who wants to can call any timepiece a clock, but technically speaking, only whichever ones ring out the time actually deserve the name.

## The Adverb Clause

**4e. An *adverb clause* is a subordinate clause that, like an adverb, modifies a verb, an adjective, or an adverb.**

In the following examples each adverb clause illustrates one of the typical adverbial functions of telling *how, when, where, why, to what extent,* or *under what conditions.*

She plays golf **as though she were in a hurry.** [*how* she plays]
She plays golf **whenever she can.** [*when* she plays]
She plays golf **wherever she travels.** [*where* she plays]
She plays golf **because she enjoys it.** [*why* she plays]
She plays golf more **than I do.** [*how much* more]
She plays golf **if the weather permits.** [*under what conditions* she plays]

In diagraming, an adverb clause is written on a horizontal line below the main line of the diagram. The subordinating conjunction beginning the clause is written on a slanting broken line which links the verb of the clause to the word the clause modifies.

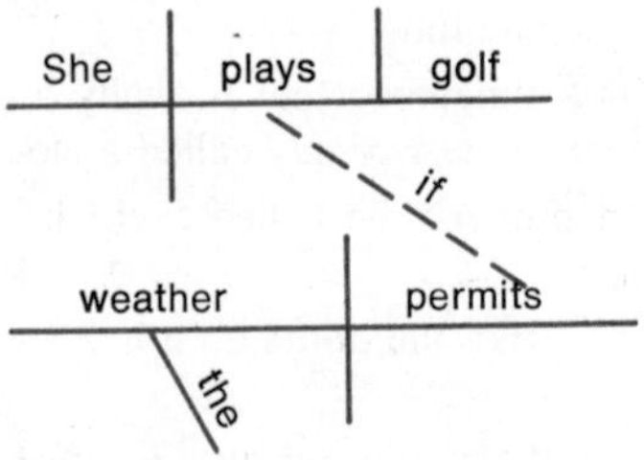

Adverb clauses may also modify adjectives and other adverbs.

She is confident **that she will win.** [The adverb clause *that she will win* modifies the adjective *confident.*]

He played better **than I did.** [The adverb clause *than I did* modifies the adverb *better.*]

## The Subordinating Conjunction

Adverb clauses often begin with a word like *after, because,* or *when* that expresses the relation between the clause and the rest of the sentence.

**4f. A conjunction that begins an adverb clause is called a subordinating conjunction. It joins the clause to the rest of the sentence.**

The following words are subordinating conjunctions. (Many may also be used as other parts of speech.)

***Common Subordinating Conjunctions***

| | | | |
|---|---|---|---|
| after | because | so that | whenever |
| although | before | than | where |
| as | if | though | wherever |
| as if | in order that | unless | whether |
| as long as | provided that | until | while |
| as though | since | when | |

## The Elliptical (Incomplete) Clause

Sometimes in our writing and speaking, we do not complete the adverb clauses we use.

EXAMPLES I am stronger than you [are].

While [I was] waiting for the dentist, I read a magazine.

In these adverb clauses the part of the clause given in brackets has been omitted. The missing part, however, could be readily supplied. Such incomplete clauses are said to be "elliptical."[1]

**EXERCISE 4.** Copy on your paper the adverb clauses in the following sentences. Before each clause, write the number of the sentence in which it appears. Draw a line under the subordinating conjunction that introduces the clause. After each clause, write what the clause tells: *how, when, where, why, to what extent, under what conditions.*

1. Because company was coming for dinner, Lola Gomez and her father prepared a special treat of Cuban black beans.
2. After Lola had soaked a pound of black beans overnight, she drained them and covered them with fresh water.
3. Before she lit the stove, she added chopped onion and green pepper, a bay leaf, coriander leaves, oregano, and salt pork to the beans.
4. While the mixture was simmering, Mr. Gomez prepared the sofrito.
5. Whenever a recipe calls for sofrito, you finely chop some onion, green pepper, and garlic.
6. Then you fry these vegetables in a little oil until they are tender.
7. As soon as the sofrito was ready, Mr. Gomez added it to the bean mixture.
8. He then crushed some of the beans against the side of the pot so that the bean mixture would become thicker.
9. When the mixture was thick, Lola put in some vinegar and sugar.
10. Although this dish is usually served with rice, Lola and her father prepared a green salad instead.

**REVIEW EXERCISE.** Each of the following sentences contains one or more subordinate clauses. Copy the clauses

[1] The definition of *ellipsis,* as applied to grammar, is an omission of one or more words, obviously understood, but necessary to make the expression grammatically complete. For the correct usage of pronouns in elliptical clauses, see page 117.

in order on your paper. Before each, write the number of the sentence in which it appears. After each, write what kind it is—adjective, noun, adverb.

1. When you drive a car, you must carry insurance, which pays for any damage or injury that you may inflict on others.
2. Insurance in some places is cheaper than it is in others.
3. How much insurance costs depends on how congested traffic is in the area.
4. An unmarried male who is under twenty-five pays the highest premium because statistics show that he is the worst risk.
5. Drivers who have a record of accidents must also pay a high premium since they have cost their insurance companies a great deal of money.
6. Insurance companies divide accidents into two categories: those that happen because of unforeseeable events and those that are made to happen.
7. When a tire blows out while you are driving in heavy traffic, the resulting accident is classed as unforeseeable.
8. If a driver passes another car on a turn, the resulting accident is one that was made to happen.
9. What is most alarming about our accidents is that four fifths of them are made to happen.
10. Insurance is costly for all of us because so many drivers make accidents happen.

## SENTENCES CLASSIFIED BY STRUCTURE

**4g. Classified according to their structure, there are four kinds of sentences: *simple, compound, complex,* and *compound-complex.***

**(1) A *simple sentence* is a sentence with one independent clause and no subordinate clauses.**

Great literature stirs the imagination.

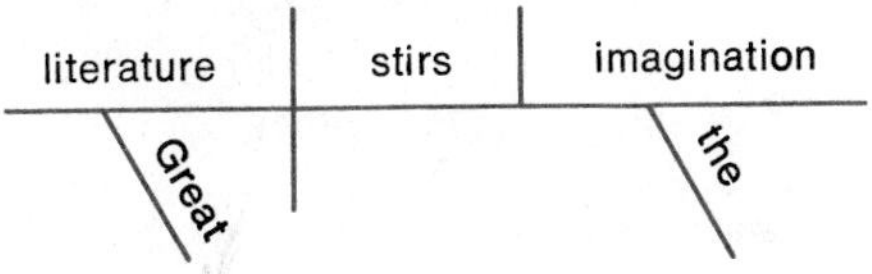

**(2) A *compound sentence* is a sentence composed of two or more independent clauses but no subordinate clauses.**[1]

Great literature stirs the imagination, and it challenges the intellect.
Great literature stirs the imagination; moreover, it challenges the intellect.

► **NOTE** Do not confuse the compound predicate of simple sentences with the two subjects and verbs of compound sentences.

Study the following diagrams.

Great literature **stirs** the imagination and **challenges** the intellect. [simple sentence with compound predicate]

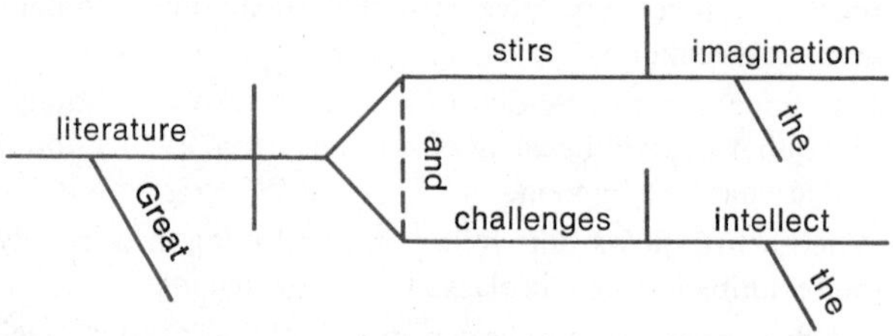


Great **literature stirs** the imagination, and **it challenges** the intellect. [compound sentence with two subjects and two verbs]

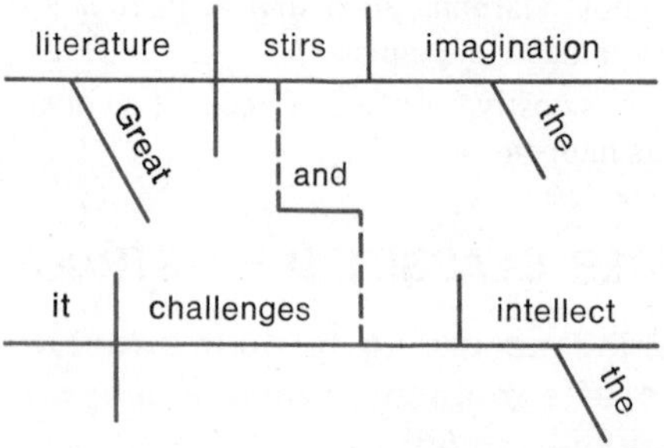


Independent clauses are joined by coordinating conjunctions:

and but nor or for yet

or by conjunctive adverbs:

| | | | |
|---|---|---|---|
| also | furthermore | nevertheless | therefore |
| besides | however | otherwise | thus |
| consequently | moreover | then | still |

[1] For rules concerning the punctuation of compound sentences, see pages 539 and 554–55.

**(3) A *complex sentence* is a sentence that contains one independent clause and at least one subordinate clause.**

Great literature, which stirs the imagination, also challenges the intellect.

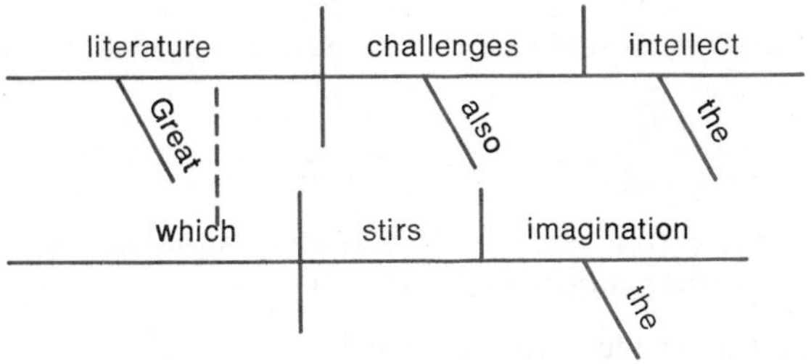


**(4) A *compound-complex sentence* is a sentence that contains two or more independent clauses and at least one subordinate clause.**

Great literature, which challenges the intellect, is sometimes difficult, but it is also rewarding. [The independent clauses are *Great literature is sometimes difficult* and *it is also rewarding.* The subordinate clause is *which challenges the intellect.*]

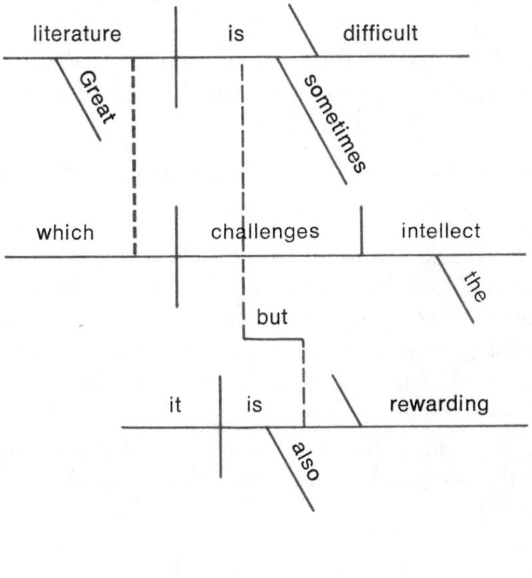

## SENTENCES CLASSIFIED BY PURPOSE

**4h. Classified according to their purpose, there are four kinds of sentences: *declarative, imperative, interrogative,* and *exclamatory.***

**(1) A *declarative sentence* is a sentence that makes a statement.**

In 1945 the United Nations had fifty-one members.

**(2) An *imperative sentence* is a sentence that gives a command or makes a request.**

Stop talking and open your books.
Please write to me.

**(3) An *interrogative sentence* is a sentence that asks a question.**

Which book did you like most?

**(4) An *exclamatory sentence* is a sentence that expresses strong feeling.**

How beautiful it is!

**EXERCISE 5.** After the proper number, classify each of the following sentences in two ways: (1) according to its structure and (2) according to its purpose.

EXAMPLE 1. Let me have your order tomorrow if you can.
1. *complex* *imperative*

1. According to the dictionary, the word *speliology* is formed from a Greek word meaning "cave" and the suffix *-logy,* meaning "study of" or "science of."
2. Speliology, which, then, is the scientific study of caves, is the pursuit of the National Speliological Society, which sponsors exploration of caves.
3. If a scientific explorer of caves is a speliologist, what do we call the many amateurs for whom cave exploration is just an exciting hobby?

4. These people, whose primary interest is adventure, are called *spelunkers,* and this word is derived from *spelunca,* the Latin word for cave.
5. Read a book on spelunking and enjoy vicariously some of the excitement of underground exploration.
6. Did you know that the techniques and equipment used by spelunkers are similar to those used by mountain climbers?
7. In limestone ice caves, where water seeps through ceilings and walls, surfaces are glazed and very slippery.
8. How perilous an adventure such a cave offers!
9. In the eight hundred feet of explored passages in Wyoming's Fossil Mountain Ice Cave, the temperature is −1° C.
10. Dripping water is transformed into sparkling icicles and columns of ice, and where water drops have splashed and frozen, the floor glitters as if it were covered with diamonds.

# Usage

# PART TWO

Chapter 5

# Levels of Usage

Because we are all part of one society, there are a number of matters we do not have to decide independently for ourselves. Instead, we more or less unconsciously comply with social conventions—the customary ways in in which groups of people behave together. The styles of clothing we wear derive from such conventions; so do our styles of etiquette. This chapter is about the conventions that govern our uses of language. But before considering conventional language, consider the more obvious and familiar conventions that affect the way we dress.

Although everyone knows the expression "clothes make the man," few really believe it. We like to think that we can recognize the admirable qualities in people whether they are wearing bathing suits or business suits. Yet we cannot truthfully say that people's clothes make no impression on us at all. We pay no particular attention to what people wear so long as their clothes are more or less what we would expect under the circumstances. We expect to see bathing suits at the beach and business suits at the office. We would notice a business suit at the beach or a bathing suit at the office. In other words, it is only when clothing is obviously singular or inappropriate that we are drawn to notice it emphatically and forced to consider the motives of its wearer.

## Appropriate Language

It is much the same with the language a person uses. As long as it is appropriate—"fits in" with what others use—we do not pay special attention to the way in which people form their sentences, or to the vocabulary they use. However, when a person's use of language strikes us as clearly unsuitable to the situation, we become distracted from *what* is being said and begin to think mainly about *how* it is being said. Language that deliberately calls attention to itself gets in the way of communication instead of making communication easier.

Language conveys more than mere ideas. It also conveys the speaker's own personality. If you speak stiffly you may give the impression of being standoffish, whether you mean to or not. If you speak as casually with a prospective employer as you do in conversation with close friends, the impression you create of yourself may lose you the job. In conversational use of the language you would probably say, "No one knew who the President had chosen." In a formal written report, however, you would write, "No one knew *whom* the President had chosen."

# THE VARIETIES OF ENGLISH

We can distinguish several different kinds of English, all by the differing situations in which each is used. In general, we can distinguish two broad categories of English: *standard* and *nonstandard.*

## Standard English

Standard English is the kind of English usage most widely recognized as acceptable. It is the language of most educational, legal, governmental, and professional documents. Although standard English differs, as we shall see, in different situations, it has certain conventions regularly observed by all who use it. And because the people who use standard English include educators, government leaders, journalists, authors, and business people, their language conventions are respected. That is why this variety of English is called *standard*—a term that denotes an example or model which others may follow.

As a model of English which others may follow, standard English is taught in schools and in textbooks such as this one because, for one reason, many occasions, such as a job interview or the writing of a business letter, require standard English. Learning the conventions of standard English, therefore, is an important task for every student.

## Nonstandard English

Standard and nonstandard English are not, of course, different languages. While there are some words that appear only in one or the other, most English words can appear in either. The main differences appear in the use of pronouns and certain verb forms. A user of standard English would use *brought* where a user of nonstandard English might use *brung*. Similarly:

| ***Standard*** | ***Nonstandard*** |
|---|---|
| He did it **himself.** | He did it **hisself.** |
| You and **she** fight all the time. | You and **her** fight all the time. |
| He **doesn't** trust me. | He **don't** trust me. |
| She **ran** right into me. | She **run** right into me. |

Sentences like those in the right-hand column above are spoken by thousands of native speakers of English. It has always been a major technique of literature to create characterization through the device of having characters use recognizably nonstandard speech. Eudora Welty and William Faulkner are among the great artists admired for their ability to capture the special lilt of certain dialects of nonstandard English. Occasionally it happens that a speaker of nonstandard English makes a style of usage a popular trademark. Dizzy Dean, a famous pitcher for the St. Louis Cardinals and later a radio and television announcer, made his own nonstandard speech a great asset, as did Casey Stengel, when he was manager of the New York Yankees and, later, the New York Mets. The following excerpt from an interview in the *New York Times* gives an idea of what nonstandard English in the Dizzy Dean style is like (as well as offering Mr. Dean's personal opinions about usage):

> And I reckon that's why that now I come up with an *ain't* once in a while, and have the Missouri teachers all stirred up. They don't like it because I say that Marty Marion or Vern Stephens *slud* into second base. What do they want me to say—*slidded?*
>
> Me and Paul [Dizzy's brother, also a pitcher for the Cards] didn't have to worry about that sort of stuff when we were winning games for the old Gas House Gang. And I don't know why I should get a sweat up now.
>
> Paul, he'd win one game and I'd win the next.
>
> Didn't nobody come around after the game and ask whether we'd throwed or threw the ball in there to make a play.
>
> We won 'em, no questions asked.[1]

There are so many varieties of nonstandard English—as there are nonstandard varieties of all living languages—that it seems best to describe it simply as the observance of conventions that are recognizably different from those of the standard language.

Language may vary according to audience and occasion. Standard English is the medium of communication certain to reach the broadest audience of speakers of English and find a hearing. Nonstandard English is by definition, as its name suggests, a form of usage proper to a smaller group than the whole of the English-speaking world. The more general the audience one is trying to reach, the more one tends to use the standard language. The more personal and informal the occasion, the less one needs to be conscious of the conventions and rules applying to standard usage.

[1] From "Dizzy Dean." The *New York Times*, July 26, 1946. © 1946 by The New York Times Company. Reprinted by permission.

# TWO KINDS OF STANDARD ENGLISH

Standard English is used in so many different situations—ranging from casual telephone conversations to formal speeches—that it would be impossible to name a particular kind appropriate for each situation. But we can distinguish two varieties of standard English: *formal* and *informal.*

## Formal English

Formal English, like formal dress and formal manners, is language for special occasions. Sometimes referred to as "literary" English, it is the language of all serious writing. It should be used in formal essays, essay answers to examination questions, formal reports, research papers, literary criticism, scholarly writings, and addresses on serious or solemn occasions.

As you might expect, formal English is likely to include words that rarely come up in ordinary conversation. The sentences are likely to be more elaborately constructed and longer than those of ordinary writing. Contractions are rarely used. Formal English pays close attention to refinements in usage, and seldom admits any slang. It is language in formal dress.

In the following example of formal English, note the long and carefully constructed sentences. Notice also the extremely formal vocabulary: *colossus, infidel, grandeur, promontory.*

Formidable and grand on a hilltop in Picardy, the five-towered castle of Coucy dominated the approach to Paris from the north, but whether as guardian or as challenger of the monarchy in the capital was an open question. Thrusting up from the castle's center, a gigantic cylinder rose to twice the height of the four corner towers. This was the *donjon* or central citadel, the largest in Europe, the mightiest of its kind ever built in the Middle Ages or thereafter. Ninety feet in diameter, 180 feet high, capable of housing a thousand men in a siege, it dwarfed and protected the castle at its base, the clustered roofs of the town, the bell tower of the church, and the thirty turrets of the massive wall enclosing the whole complex on the hill. Travelers coming from any direction could see this colossus of baronial power from miles away and, on approaching it, feel the awe of the traveler in infidel lands at first sight of the pyramids.

Seized by grandeur, the builders had carried out the scale of the *donjon* in interior features of more than mortal size: risers of steps were fifteen to sixteen inches, window seats three and a half feet from the ground, as if for use by a race of titans. Stone lintels measuring two cubic yards were no less heroic. For more than four hundred years the dynasty reflected by these arrangements had exhibited the same quality of excess. Ambitious, dangerous, not infrequently ferocious, the Coucys had planted themselves on a promontory of land which was formed by nature for command.[1]

## Informal English

Informal English is the language most English-speaking people use most of the time. It is the language of magazines, newspapers, and most books, and of business letters and talks intended for general audiences.

The conventions of informal English are less rigid than those of formal English. Sentences may be long or short and they are likely to sound more like conversation than the stately rhythms of formal English. Contractions often appear in informal English and sometimes a slang expression is admitted. Here is an example of written informal English:

One day General Littlefield picked our company out of the whole regiment and tried to get it mixed up by putting it through one movement after another as fast as we could execute them: squads right, squads left, squads on right into line, squads right about, squads left front into line, etc. In about three minutes one hundred and nine men were marching in one direction and I was marching away from them at an angle of forty-five degrees, all alone. "Company; halt!" shouted General Littlefield. "That man is the only man who has it right!" I was made a corporal for my achievement.

[1] From *A Distant Mirror: The Calamitous 14th Century* by Barbara W. Tuchman. Copyright © 1978 by Barbara W. Tuchman. Reprinted by permission of Alfred A. Knopf, Inc.

The next day General Littlefield summoned me to his office. He was swatting flies when I went in. I was silent and he was silent too, for a long time. I don't think he remembered me or why he had sent for me, but he didn't want to admit it. He swatted some more flies, keeping his eyes on them narrowly before he let go with the swatter. "Button up your coat" he snapped. Looking back on it now I can see that he meant me, although he was looking at a fly, but I just stood there. Another fly came to rest on a paper in front of the general and began rubbing its hind legs together. The general lifted the swatter cautiously. I moved restlessly and the fly flew away. "You startled him!" barked General Littlefield, looking at me severely. I said I was sorry. "That won't help the situation!" snapped the general, with cold military logic. I didn't see what I could do except offer to chase some more flies toward his desk, but I didn't say anything. He stared out the window at the faraway figures of co-eds crossing the campus toward the library. Finally, he told me I could go. So I went. He either didn't know which cadet I was or else he forgot what he wanted to see me about. It may have been that he wished to apologize for having called me the main trouble with the university; or maybe he had decided to compliment me on my brilliant drilling of the day before and then at the last minute decided not to. I don't know. I don't think about it much any more.[1]

**EXERCISE 1.** Read each of the following passages carefully and identify the type of English to which it belongs—formal, informal, or nonstandard. Note the particular words and constructions that cause you to label the passage as you do.

1

In a few weeks, you will each receive a copy of the treasurer's report. Anyone who wants to gripe about the way we're spending the club's money will get a chance at next Saturday's business meeting.

2

If I'd of known they was goin' to let you feed the elephants I'd of went with you.

[1] From "University Days" from *My Life and Hard Times,* copyright 1933, © 1961 by James Thurber. Published by Harper & Row. Originally printed in *The New Yorker.* (Published in Great Britain as *Vintage Thurber,* copyright © 1963 by Hamish Hamilton, London.) Reprinted by permission of Hamish Hamilton Ltd. and Helen Thurber.

3

Those actions of his former subordinates that the General was now powerless to oppose, he elected to support. In his eagerness to anticipate any new mischief that might occur to the junta, he promulgated a series of new laws, each more harshly repressive than the last, which even the most rabid of the young officers would not have dared to propose.

4

One thing is, she don't take long walks like she used to. Every morning we used to see her out there, takin' those brisk steps. Just as fast! You'd of thought there was something after her. And if you was to meet her, she'd never stop to say nothing to you. Just bob her head at you and go right on. Now that she ain't comin' by anymore, we sort of miss it. When you get used to something, you kind of want it to keep on.

5

I passed all the other courses that I took at my university, but I could never pass botany. This was because all botany students had to spend several hours a week in a laboratory looking through a microscope at plant cells, and I could never see through a microscope. I never once saw a cell through a microscope. This used to enrage my instructor. He would wander around the laboratory pleased with the progress all the students were making in drawing the involved and, so I am told, interesting structure of flower cells, until he came to me. I would just be standing there. "I can't see anything," I would say. He would begin patiently enough, explaining how anybody can see through a microscope, but he would always end up in a fury, claiming that I could *too* see through a microscope but just pretended that I couldn't. . . .[1]

**EXERCISE 2.** Each of the following brief passages is written, as indicated, in a kind of English typical of certain circumstances. Rewrite each of the passages in English suited to the circumstances specified.

[1] From "University Days" from *My Life and Hard Times,* copyright 1933, © 1961 by James Thurber. Published by Harper & Row. Originally printed in *The New Yorker*. (Published in Great Britain as *Vintage Thurber,* copyright © 1963 by Hamish Hamilton, London.) Reprinted by permission of Hamish Hamilton Ltd. and Helen Thurber.

1. *Nonstandard English used in an oral summary of an article. Rewrite in standard informal English.*

   The President finally got his dander up and told them Russians to get their stuff out of Cuba fast or else! He said the Navy would search ships headed for Cuba and if they didn't stop they'd be sorry.

2. *A student reports to her friends in the lunchroom a conversation she has had with the school principal. Rewrite in language she would use if reporting the same conversation to her class.*

   Yeah, old Sherlock Holmes told me that any kids caught sneaking out of assembly would get kicked out of school.

3. *Nonstandard English used in relating an incident. Rewrite in standard informal English.*

   When Mom and me come home, we seen right away they'd been somebody messing around with the car.

4. *The mayor talking informally to the City Commission. Rewrite in the kind of English the mayor would use in making the same explanation to an audience of citizens.*

   In a couple of weeks you'll all receive the report recommending a new high school. You can bet that there'll be plenty of moaning from those people up on the Hill.

## IMPROVING YOUR USAGE

While we can speak generally about three kinds of English —formal standard, informal standard, and nonstandard— the lines between them are not always easy to draw. One kind of usage shades into another; an expression we think of as being informal may turn up in a formal address; a slang word that originates in nonstandard English may become an acceptable part of the informal vocabulary; many words and constructions that we think of as belonging to standard speech may come into use among speakers of nonstandard English. The great majority of our words and our ways of putting them together are common to all three.

### Sources of Usage Information

If your usage habits conform to the conventions of standard English, your main concern will be in suiting your language to the occasion in which you speak or write. If you are in a conversation, the usage of those you are talking with will give you valuable clues. If you are writing, keeping your audience in mind should help.

There will be times, however, when you cannot be sure whether a particular word or expression is suitable for a particular situation. Or there may be a few nonstandard forms that you habitually use in your writing and speaking. You can deal with these questions by studying a textbook like this one, by referring to a dictionary, or by consulting a special book on usage like those listed on page 83. And most important of all, you can develop habits of noticing the usage preferences of careful users of English.

You will find the rules of grammar a useful but not invariably reliable guide to usage. Grammar describes the system of a language; usage is concerned with appropriate forms of expression. The two are not always the same, for language is a living and growing thing, and life and growth are not always logical. Changes are brought about by the people who use a language, and grammar rules, which can only be stated when the changes have occurred, necessarily come afterward. The rules of grammar describe the way the language works. When the system changes, the rules change.

## The Importance of Good English

Using English according to the conventions established by educated users of the language and adapting it to the circumstances in which we use it will not, of course, make us effective speakers and writers. Conventional usage is only one of the qualities of good speech and good writing. Perhaps it is not even the most important. It is not so important, for example, as clarity, or forcefulness of expression. It is not so important as honesty or originality or freshness. Yet good usage is important, nevertheless. We like to be noticed for things that are worthwhile and admirable, not just for things that are different. The person who is out of step in a parade attracts more attention than all the rest of those marching, but we do not usually seek that kind of notice.

People will judge you by your usage. If you deviate from the conventions of standard English, they will think more about how you are expressing yourself than they will about what you are saying.

**EXERCISE 3.** The words and expressions listed below present usage problems that trouble some people. Look them up in this and whatever other textbooks are available to you—most of these problems will be listed in the index. Consult also the usage books listed below.

1. *It's me.* [pronoun usage]
2. *shall* or *will*
3. *imply* or *infer*
4. double negatives
5. *between* or *among*
6. (*the*) *reason* is *because* . . .
7. split infinitive
8. *due to*

## Guides to Usage

The following books contain accurate information about usage problems. You will find additional information on usage in your dictionary (see page 617). Neither the books listed below nor your dictionary can tell you exactly what to say or write in a particular situation. What they can do is help you to make up your own mind.

*American Heritage Dictionary of the English Language: New College Edition,* Boston, Houghton Mifflin Company, 1978.

Bernstein, Theodore M., *The Careful Writer: A Modern Guide to English Usage,* New York, Atheneum, 1979.

Bryant, Margaret M., *Current American Usage,* New York, Funk & Wagnalls, 1962.

Evans, Bergen and Cornelia, *A Dictionary of Contemporary American Usage,* New York, Random House, 1957.

Fowler, Henry W., *A Dictionary of Modern English Usage: Second Edition,* Ernest Gowers, ed., New York, Oxford University Press, 1965.

Morris, William and Mary, *Harper Dictionary of Contemporary Usage,* New York, Harper & Row, 1975.

## SUMMARY: STANDARD AND NONSTANDARD ENGLISH

| ***Standard English*** | ***Typical Uses*** | ***Typical Features*** |
|---|---|---|
| Formal | research papers, serious speeches, books and articles for special audiences | words little used in ordinary speech; longer sentences; few contractions; no slang |
| Informal | conversations of educated people; most writing in books, newspapers, and magazines; business letters, lectures to general audiences, political speeches, most textbooks | wide variety of sentence length; less difficult vocabulary than formal; sentences that sound like good conversation, even when written; contractions; some slang |

| ***Nonstandard English*** | ***Typical Uses*** | ***Typical Features*** |
|---|---|---|
| | conversations in recognizably nonstandard words and phrases, dialogue intended to represent local dialects in movies, books, comic strips, radio, and television | verb and pronoun forms not appearing in standard English (you was, he don't, hisself, etc.); adverbs without the –ly ending (She sings bad); regular use of slang words and localisms |

Chapter 6

# Agreement

## Subject and Verb, Pronoun and Antecedent

Some words in English have matching forms to show grammatical relationships. Forms that match in this way are said to *agree*. For example, a subject and verb agree if both are singular or both plural. Pronouns also agree with their antecedents—the words pronouns stand for.

## AGREEMENT OF SUBJECT AND VERB

**6a. A word that refers to one person or thing is *singular* in number. A word that refers to more than one is *plural* in number.**

| SINGULAR | PLURAL |
|---|---|
| book | books |
| child | children |
| this | these |
| either | both |
| he, she, it | they |

**6b. A verb agrees with its subject in number.**

**(1) Singular subjects take singular verbs.**

A young **woman lives** next door.

This **exhibit was prepared** by the art department.

**(2) Plural subjects take plural verbs.**

Young **women live** next door.

These **exhibits were prepared** by the art department.

You will find it helpful to remember that *is, was, has,* and most verbs ending in a single *s* are singular: he *thinks,* she *works,* it *counts,* etc. *Are, were, have,* and most verbs not ending in a single *s* are plural: they *think,* they *work,* they *count.* The exceptions, which should cause you little difficulty, are verbs used with *I* and singular *you:* I *think,* you *work,* etc.

Notice that all the verbs given as examples in the preceding paragraph are in the present tense. All past tense verbs have the same form in the singular and plural except for the verb *be,* which has a special form *was* that is used with *I, he, she,* and *it,* and all singular nouns.

| SINGULAR | PLURAL |
| --- | --- |
| I went | they went |
| he carried | we carried |
| I was | we were |
| it was | they were |

If English is your native language, you probably have little trouble in making verbs agree with their subjects when they directly follow the subjects as in the examples above. You will encounter sentences, however, in which it is not so easy to identify the subject correctly or determine whether it is singular or plural. These constructions, which create most agreement problems, are taken up separately below.

## Intervening Phrase

**6c. The number of the subject is not changed by a phrase following the subject.**

A phrase that comes between a singular subject and its verb can easily mislead you if it contains a plural word. Remember that the verb agrees with its subject, not with any modifiers the subject may have.

EXAMPLES The **performance was** very funny.

The **performance** of the first three clowns **was** very funny. [*Performance,* not *clowns,* is the subject of the sentence.]

**A solution has been found.**

A **solution** to these problems **has been found.** [*solution has,* not *problems have*]

In formal writing, singular subjects followed by phrases beginning with *together with, as well as, in addition to,* and *accompanied by* take singular verbs.

EXAMPLE The captain, as well as the coaches, **was** disappointed in the team.

**EXERCISE 1.** Number your paper 1–10. Write after the proper number the subject of each sentence. After the subject, write the one of the two verbs in parentheses that agrees in number with the subject. Check your answers.

1. The cause of heartbeats (has, have) been a subject of continuous inquiry in the scientific and medical community.
2. The heartbeat, as well as other factors, (cause, causes) blood to flow throughout the body.
3. H. Allen and others (has, have) shown that the control of the nervous system is not linked to the beating of the heart.
4. The power of rhythmic contractions (belong, belongs) to the cardiac muscle itself, unassisted by other impulses.
5. All strips of muscle in the heart (is, are) capable of rhythmic action.
6. The power to trigger contractions (differ, differs) from part to part of the heart, however.
7. The greatest centralization of energies, as in many other organs and organisms, (is, are) located at the top.
8. The lesser energies of the heart (is, are) centered toward the bottom.
9. The number of beats of the heart per minute usually (decline, declines) with age, from as much as 140 at birth to 50 in an adult male.
10. The sequence of events in a single heartbeat (is, are) complex and well worth studying.

## Indefinite Pronouns as Subjects

Pronouns like *everybody, someone, everything, all,* and *none,* all of which are more or less indefinite in meaning, present some special usage problems. Some of them are always singular, some are always plural, and some others may be singular or plural, depending on the meaning of the sentence. In addition, such pronouns are often followed by a phrase. Therefore, you must first determine the number of the pronoun and then remember the rule about phrases that come between subjects and verbs.

**6d. The following common words are singular:** ***each, either, neither, one, no one, every one, anyone, someone, everyone, anybody, somebody, everybody.***

EXAMPLES **Each does** his own cooking.

**Each** of the boys **does** [not *do*] his own cooking.

**Everyone wants** more money.

**Every one** of the workers **wants** [not *want*] more money.

**6e. The following common words are plural:** ***several, few, both, many.***

EXAMPLES **Several** of the regular members **were** absent.

**Few** of my family really **understand** me.

**Both** of your excuses **sound** plausible.

**Many were** surprised at the final score.

**6f. The words** ***some, any, none, all,*** **and** ***most*** **may be singular or plural, depending on the meaning of the sentence.**

Usually, when the words *some, any, none, all,* and *most* refer to a singular word, they are singular; when they refer to a plural word, they are plural.[1] Compare the following examples:

[1] Since the word referred to appears in a phrase following the subject, this rule is an exception to rule 6c.

**Some** of the money **was** missing. [*Some* is singular because it refers to *money,* which is singular.]

**Some** of the dimes **were** missing. [*Some* is plural because it refers to *dimes,* which is plural.]

**All** of the fruit **looks** ripe.

**All** of the cherries **look** ripe.

**Most** of the book **was** interesting. [an indefinite part of a book]

**Most** of the books **were** interesting. [a number of separate books]

**Has any** of this evidence been presented?

**Have any** of my friends called me?

**None** of the evidence **points** to his guilt.

**None** of our students **were** involved.

► **USAGE NOTE** *Was* could have been used in the last example, but modern English usage prefers a plural verb in this situation. If you want the subject to be singular in such a sentence, use *no one* or *not one* instead of *none.*

**EXERCISE 2.** Number your paper 1–10. Write after the proper number on your paper the subject in each sentence. After it, write the one of the two verbs in parentheses which agrees in number with the subject.

1. Each of the pictures (was, were) in a silver frame.
2. One of my friends (play, plays) the tuba.
3. All of our belongings (is, are) still unpacked.
4. Some of these rare books (has, have) leather covers.
5. None of the people in the theater audience (was, were) pleased with the film.
6. Every one of these jeans (is, are) too small.
7. A few in my class (was, were) asked to help out.
8. The lack of funds (present, presents) a problem.
9. Everybody living in Lewis Heights (go, goes) to George Washington Carver High School.
10. A band with two trumpet players and thirty-five clarinetists (sound, sounds) terrible.

**EXERCISE 3.** Rewrite these ten sentences, following the instructions that appear in brackets after each of them. Sometimes the addition will affect agreement. Be sure to make the subject and verb of the new sentence agree. Underline each subject once and each verb twice.

EXAMPLE 1. Every one of the new buildings was damaged in the earthquake. [Change *every one* to *all.*]

1. *All of the new buildings were damaged in the earthquake.*

1. This group sings better than any of the others. [Add *Two members of* before "This group."]
2. A porpoise swims near the surface. [Add *like whales and sharks* after "porpoise." Put a comma before and after the added phrase.]
3. Apples were shipped from New York state to Chicago. [Add *One carload of* before "Apples."]
4. Several were unfairly treated. [Add *of our group* after "Several."]
5. Every one of the offices has been equipped with electric typewriters. [Change *Every one* to *All but three.*]
6. Each of the other witnesses agrees with my account of the accident. [Change *Each* to *All.*]
7. All of the money has been used up. [Change *money* to *tickets.*]
8. Her struggle to overcome illness was finally successful. [Add *and financial reverses* after "illness."]
9. The sky looks promising. [Add *as well as the wind and the water* after "sky." Set off the addition with commas.]
10. Morgan, one of our regular pinch hitters, usually strikes out. [Change *one* to *like the rest.*]

**EXERCISE 4.** Number your paper 1–20. Read each of the following sentences aloud. If the verb in a sentence agrees with its subject, write a + after the proper number on your paper; if the verb does not agree, write the correct form of the verb on your paper.

1. Each of the students are responsible for one lesson.
2. The goal of their efforts were to raise one million dollars.

3. Neither of the stories were good enough to publish.
4. Every one of the stations was out of gasoline.
5. Some of the crops have been ruined by frost.
6. The height of the office buildings are unusually great.
7. One of the club members has not yet voted.
8. The Russian ambassador, together with the Polish and Hungarian ambassadors, has called a press conference.
9. All of the mines has been closed.
10. The principal, as well as the school board and the faculty, was enthusiastic.
11. The desire for property and great riches ruin many lives.
12. Some of the criminal's motives were apparent.
13. The result of so many attempts was disappointing.
14. Each of the sales people have a definite territory to cover.
15. The ocean, as well as the gulf and the bay, provides good fishing.
16. Neither of her paternal grandparents are living.
17. Several of our best news sources have been cut off.
18. Few members of the party approve the committee's appointments.
19. A sophomore, as well as a freshman, is allowed to take public speaking.
20. The vessel, with its entire crew and cargo, were lost.

## Compound Subjects

As you will recall from Chapter 2, two words or groups of words may be connected to form the subject of a verb. These words, usually joined by *and* or *or,* are called a *compound subject.* Compound subjects may take singular or plural verbs, depending on whether the words joined are singular or plural and what the connecting word is.

### 6g. Subjects joined by *and* take a plural verb.

EXAMPLES A **horse and** an **elephant are** mammals.

**Julia and** her twin **sister** naturally **look** a lot alike.

The **walls and** the **ceiling were** beautifully decorated.

EXCEPTION When the parts of a compound subject are considered as a unit or when they refer to the same thing, a singular verb is used.

> **Macaroni and cheese is** the cafeteria special again today.
>
> **The Stars and Stripes is** our national emblem.
>
> His **friend and** fellow **author was** cool to the idea of collaborating on a new cookbook.

**6h. Singular subjects joined by *or* or *nor* take a singular verb.**

EXAMPLES My **brother or** my **sister is** likely to be at home.
Neither the **president** of the company **nor** the **sales manager is** a college graduate.
Either **Trina or Maria is** sure to know the answer.

**6i. When a singular and a plural subject are joined by *or* or *nor*, the verb agrees with the nearer subject.**

ACCEPTABLE Either the judge or the lawyers **are** wrong.

It is usually possible to avoid this awkward construction altogether:

BETTER Either the judge is wrong or the lawyers are.

Another reason for avoiding this construction is that the subjects may be different in person. If this is so, the verb must agree with the nearer subject in person as well as number. In the following example, the verb must not only be singular to agree with *I*, but it must also have the form (am) that matches *I* as a subject:

ACCEPTABLE Neither my sisters nor I am going to summer camp.

BETTER My sisters are not going to summer camp, and neither am I.

► **USAGE NOTE** The rules in this chapter are consistently followed in standard formal English but are often departed from in informal speaking and writing. Formal usage is likely to call for a singular verb after a singular subject in a strictly logical way.

Informal usage, on the other hand, often permits the use of a plural verb, whatever the logical number of the subject, if the meaning is clearly plural. Compare the following examples of formal and informal practices:

FORMAL Neither Lucy nor Carol has any money left.

INFORMAL Neither Lucy nor Carol have any money left. [Although joined by *nor,* which strictly calls for a singular verb, the meaning of the sentence is essentially plural: both Lucy and Carol have spent all of their money.]

FORMAL Every one of the campers was hungry.

INFORMAL Every one of the campers were hungry. [Strictly speaking, the subject *one* is singular and takes a singular verb. However, the meaning is essentially the same as that expressed by "All the campers were hungry." Informal usage permits a plural verb in such circumstances.]

FORMAL My aunt, along with my uncle and three of my cousins, is coming to our house this weekend.

INFORMAL My aunt, along with my uncle and three of my cousins, are coming to our house this weekend. [Although the construction logically calls for a singular verb, the meaning is clearly plural—all of them are coming, not just the aunt. It is usually wise to avoid constructions that set up a conflict between logic and meaning. The example would be better if it were written as "My aunt, my uncle, and three of my cousins *are* . . ."]

In some of the exercise sentences in this chapter, you will encounter such differences between formal and informal usage. For the purposes of these exercises, follow the rules of formal usage.

**EXERCISE 5.** Number your paper 1–25. Read each of the following sentences aloud. If the verb in a sentence agrees with its subject, write a + after the proper number. If the verb does not agree, write the correct form of the verb on your paper. Follow the practices of formal usage.

1. One of the oldest foods in the world is cheese.
2. Neither the Greeks nor the Romans were ignorant of its strength-giving properties in ancient times.
3. The extent of its uses have yet to be exhausted.
4. Neither shepherd nor astronaut has failed to appreciate it.
5. Cheeses of every kind has nourished both.
6. The art of making various cheeses are older than recorded history.
7. The appearance and the nutritional value of different kinds of cheese varies widely.
8. Each of the many different varieties have a unique history.
9. In fact, every cheese found on our dining tables has a rather involved history.
10. Not one of the familiar cheeses occur naturally without human intervention.
11. Special equipment, as well as careful planning, is necessary to make any kind of cheese.
12. Few of the familiar cookbooks shows how to make even the simplest cheese.
13. Curds of whole milk without the whey is the essence of cheese.
14. The processing of the curds by various methods are the latest development in the manufacture of cheese.
15. Several of the most healthful kinds of cheese have always been inexpensive.
16. Cottage cheese and cream cheese ranks high among these kinds.
17. One of the more striking types is Roquefort cheese.
18. Moldy bread crumbs in the curd brings about the distinctive ripening of Roquefort cheese.
19. The development of small cultures of penicillium fungi give the Roquefort curd its blue, marbled appearance.
20. The cheese called American cheese and known by many other names is cheddar cheese.
21. Differences in the cooking of the curd, or the method of curing, or the packaging, explains the great variety of flavors and textures of cheese.
22. The milk of goats, sheep, reindeer, zebras, and yaks, as well as the milk of cows, are used in cheese making.

23. The milk of sheep are used for Roquefort cheese.
24. Cheese with crackers or cheese with a few slices of good bread make a nourishing meal.
25. Neither milk nor cream, it appears, satisfies the human imagination, to judge by the astonishing phenomenon of cheese.

## Other Problems in Subject-Verb Agreement

**6j. When the subject follows the verb, as in questions and in sentences beginning with *here* and *there*, be careful to determine the subject and make sure that the verb agrees with it.**

NONSTANDARD There's three routes you can take.
STANDARD There **are** three **routes** you can take.

NONSTANDARD Where's your mother and father?
STANDARD Where **are** your **mother and father**?

**6k. Collective nouns may be either singular or plural.**

A collective noun names a group: *crowd, committee, jury, class.* A collective noun takes a plural verb when the speaker is thinking of the individual members of the group; it takes a singular verb when the speaker is thinking of the group as a unit.

The **crowd were fighting** for their lives. [The speaker is thinking of the individuals in the crowd.]

The **crowd was** an orderly one. [The speaker is thinking of the crowd as a single thing, a unit.]

The **team were** talking over some new plays.

The **team was** ranked first in the nation.

The **family have** agreed among themselves to share one car.

The **family is** the basic unit of our society.

SOME COMMON COLLECTIVE WORDS

| | | |
|---|---|---|
| army | crowd | orchestra |
| audience | flock | public |
| class | group | swarm |
| club | herd | team |
| committee | jury | troop |

**6l. Expressions stating amount (time, money, measurement, weight, volume, fractions) are usually singular when the amount is considered as a unit.**

EXAMPLES **Three years** in a strange land **seems** like a long time.

**Ten dollars is** not enough.

**Three fourths** of the money **has** been recovered.

However, when the amount is considered as a number of separate units, a plural verb is used.

EXAMPLES These last **three years have** been full of surprises.

There **are two silver dollars** in each of the stockings.

**6m. The title of a book or the name of an organization or country, even when plural in form, usually takes a singular verb.**

EXAMPLES ***The Adventures of Huckleberry Finn*** **was** published in 1884.

The **Knights of Columbus is** sponsoring a carnival.

The **United States remains** the leader of the Western bloc.

EXCEPTION Some names of organizations (Veterans of Foreign Wars, New York Yankees, Chicago Bears, etc.) customarily take a plural verb when you are thinking of the members and a singular verb when you mean the organization:

The **Veterans of Foreign Wars attend** this meeting.

The **Veterans of Foreign Wars is** a large organization.

**6n. A few nouns, such as *mumps, measles, civics, economics, mathematics, physics,* although plural in form, take a singular verb.**

EXAMPLES **Measles is** a disease to take seriously.

World **economics bears** directly on world peace.

The following similar words are more often plural than singular: *athletics, acoustics, gymnastics, tactics.* The word *politics* may be either singular or plural, and *scissors* and *trousers* are always plural.

For more information on the use of words ending in *–ics,* look up *–ics* in your dictionary.

**6o. When the subject and the predicate nominative are different in number, the verb agrees with the subject, not with the predicate nominative.**

ACCEPTABLE The most appreciated **gift was** the clothes that you sent us.

ACCEPTABLE The **clothes** that you sent us **were** the most appreciated gift.

BETTER Most of all we appreciated the clothes that you sent us.

Although the first two examples are acceptable, the third is clearly better. Avoid writing sentences in which the subject and predicate nominative are different in number.

**6p. *Every* or *many a* before a word or series of words is followed by a singular verb.**

EXAMPLES **Every man, woman,** and **child was** asked to contribute.

**Many a** college **student wishes** to return to the easy days of high school.

**Many a person** in these circumstances **has** hoped for a lucky break.

**6q. *Don't* and *doesn't* must agree with their subjects.**

With the subjects *I* and *you,* use *don't* (*do not*). With other subjects, use *doesn't* (*does not*) when the subject is singular and *don't* (*do not*) when the subject is plural.

EXAMPLES **I don't** like her painting.

**You don't** look happy.

**It [He, She, This] doesn't** run fast enough.

**They don't** swim.

By using *doesn't* after *it, he,* and *she,* you can eliminate most of the common errors in the use of *don't.*

**6r. In formal English, verbs in clauses that follow *one of those* are always plural.**

Even though informal usage often permits a singular verb in the clause following *one of those,* the plural verb is always correct. Therefore, if you always use a plural verb in such constructions you cannot go wrong.

EXAMPLES That is **one of those** remarks that **are** intended to start arguments.

Joan is **one of those** people who **go** out of their way to be helpful.

**6s. The word *number* is singular when preceded by *the;* it is plural when preceded by *a.***

EXAMPLES **The number** of volunteers **is** surprising.

**A number** of volunteers **are** signing up right now.

**EXERCISE 6.** Number your paper 1–25. After the proper number, write the correct one of the two verbs in parentheses in each sentence.

1. The cost of his research (was, were) paid by the UN.
2. Neither the President nor the FBI (was, were) willing to release any information.
3. Every one of her daughters (has, have) been successful.
4. *The Case of the Missing Butler* is one of those books that (is, are) easy to put down.
5. The question of taxes (doesn't, don't) pertain here.
6. Neither our car nor the cars of the others (was, were) able to plow through the drifts.
7. Fifteen minutes (is, are) enough time for this exercise.
8. There (seems, seem) to be many arguments on both sides.
9. Every planet, including the earth, (revolves, revolve) around the sun.
10. *The Magnificent Ambersons* (is, are) worth reading.

11. Many of Abigail Adams' letters (has, have) been collected and published.
12. The mayor of the city and the governor of the state (has, have) been in conference.
13. It (doesn't, don't) matter to me where you go.
14. Neither his secular music nor his religious compositions (appeals, appeal) to the popular taste.
15. Some of the oranges (doesn't, don't) ripen until April.
16. The fruit on the outdoor stands (looks, look) tempting.
17. Neither the doctor nor the nurse (was, were) in the patient's room when the crisis came.
18. College life and high school life (is, are) vastly different.
19. (There's, There are) not many selfish people in the world.
20. Two weeks (is, are) enough for a trip of that length.
21. She is one of those people who (is, are) never late.
22. The acoustics in this room (has, have) always been bad.
23. Each of the cheeses (was, were) sampled by the inspector.
24. Few members of the scientific world (is, are) able to explain Professor Von Faber's new theory.
25. Measles (is, are) not exclusively a children's disease.

## AGREEMENT OF PRONOUN AND ANTECEDENT

### 6t. A pronoun agrees with its antecedent in number and gender.[1]

All that you have learned about agreement of subject and verb will be useful to you in making pronouns agree with their antecedents. The antecedent of a pronoun is the word to which the pronoun refers. Study the following examples, in which the antecedents and the pronouns referring

[1] Pronouns also agree with their antecedents in *person* (see page 105):

> **I** should have thought of it **myself.**
> **You** will be late for **your** appointment.
> **George** is devoted to **his** aged mother.

Agreement in person rarely presents usage problems.

to them are printed in bold-faced type. Notice that as a rule the pronoun is singular when the antecedent is singular, and plural when the antecedent is plural. Notice, too, that the pronoun is masculine (*he, him, his*) when the antecedent is masculine; feminine (*she, her, hers*) when the antecedent is feminine; neuter (*it, its*) when the antecedent is neither masculine nor feminine. This kind of agreement is agreement in *gender*.

**Ms. Jameson** did **her** best.

**One** of the boys injured **his** ankle.

**Neither** of the girls achieved **her** purpose.

The **women** in the League expressed **their** opinions forcefully.

The **city** is proud of **its** parks.

I recognized **one** of the girls, but I didn't speak to **her**.

**(1) The words *each, either, neither, one, everyone, everybody, no one, nobody, anyone, anybody, someone, somebody* are referred to by a singular pronoun—*he, him, his, she, her, hers, it, its.***

The use of a phrase after the antecedent does not change the number of the antecedent.

EXAMPLES **Each** of the women had removed **her** shoes.

**Nobody** in a position of authority had given **his** approval of the bill.

If **anyone** calls, tell **him** I'll be back later.

► **USAGE NOTE** When the antecedent may be either masculine or feminine, use the masculine pronoun, which is acceptable standard usage. Avoid the awkward use of two pronouns: "If anyone calls, tell him or her I'll call back." The traditional usage is most frequent: ". . . tell **him** I'll call back." In informal spoken English, the plural is an acceptable way of avoiding the determination of gender: "If **someone** calls, tell **them** I'll call back."

Strict adherence to the general rule of agreement between pronoun and antecedent may lead to a construction so absurd that no one would use it:

ABSURD Did *everybody* leave the dance early because *he* wasn't enjoying *himself*?

In instances of this kind, use the plural pronoun or recast the sentence to avoid the problem:

BETTER Did **everybody** leave the dance early because **they** weren't enjoying **themselves**?

*or*

Did the **guests** leave the dance early because **they** weren't enjoying **themselves**?

**(2) Two or more singular antecedents joined by *or* or *nor* should be referred to by a singular pronoun.**

**Neither** Lynn **nor** Bess had **her** keys with **her.**

**(3) Two or more antecedents joined by *and* should be referred to by a plural pronoun.**

Lynn **and** Bess sat with **their** coats on.

► **USAGE NOTE** Like some of the rules for agreement of subject and verb, the rules for agreement of pronoun and antecedent show variations between formal and informal usage. Standard informal usage follows meaning rather than strict grammatical agreement. The sentences below marked "informal" are acceptable in informal writing and speaking. In exercises, however, follow the practices of formal English.

FORMAL **Neither** of the girls had brought **her** skis with **her.**

INFORMAL Neither of the girls had brought their skis with them.

FORMAL **Every one** of the campers had been advised to put **his** name on everything belonging to **him.**

INFORMAL Every one of the campers had been advised to put their names on everything belonging to them.

**REVIEW EXERCISE A.** This exercise covers errors in agreement of verb and subject and of pronoun and antecedent. Number your paper 1–25. If a sentence is correct, write a + after the proper number; if it is incorrect, write a 0. One error makes a sentence incorrect. Be prepared to revise all incorrect sentences.

1. One out of every twenty students are dropped from the course each term.
2. At this point the law of diminishing returns begins to operate.
3. The effect of the comics on young people are not so drastic as some believe.
4. Neither of the proposed bills were accepted in their entirety.
5. Each of the papers read in class were good.
6. Two thirds of the estate was left to the children.
7. Has either of the orders been sent?
8. When an employer is interviewing you, one of the first things they ask about is experience.
9. After a person retires, they usually prefer to live in the city.
10. A certain degree of privacy and security seem desirable.
11. Neither the Department of Agriculture nor the farmers were sure of their position.
12. He was one of those advisers who were with the Big Three at Yalta.
13. Each of these suggestions must be taken only for what they are worth.
14. Every member of the crew was decorated for his part in the rescue.
15. Everyone needs a few spare moments to themselves to do as they wish.
16. This is one of those pens that writes under water.
17. People who enter politics know that they will have to take criticism.
18. The frequency of fatal traffic accidents are rising.
19. In the past, close cooperation among nations have brought many improvements to the world.
20. Is there any old magazines in the cellar?
21. Assault and battery is a criminal offense.
22. Are you one of the boys who were tardy?
23. Anyone who does not get their parents' permission will not be permitted to make the trip.
24. Only one of his objections were sensible.
25. After the government has chosen somebody for an important position, they should consider carefully before turning it down.

**REVIEW EXERCISE B.** Rewrite the following sentences according to the directions given for each. Be sure to make changes or additions in verb forms, pronouns, etc., if necessary.

1. Some famous sports stars have made television commercials. [Change *Some famous sports stars* to *Many a famous sports star*.]
2. Where's my book? [Add *and my pen* after *book*.]
3. Both of the candidates have promised to reduce taxes. [Change *Both* to *Neither*.]
4. She writes neatly. [Add *is one of those students who* after *She*.]
5. Our basketball team has won the championship. [Add *Neither our football team nor* at the beginning of the sentence.]
6. People need friends to confide in. [Change *People* to *A person*.]
7. An application blank is required by the state university. [After *blank* add *together with a recent photograph and an autobiographical essay*. Put a comma before *together* and after *essay*.]
8. The tigers are growling ferociously. [At the beginning of the sentence, add *Either the lion or*.]
9. The movie screen is hard to see. [At the beginning of the sentence, add *The captions on*.]
10. A day in the library is all the time I need to finish my research. [Change *A day* to *Two days*.]

Chapter 7

# Correct Use of Pronouns

## Nominative and Objective Case; Special Problems with Pronouns

The function of a pronoun in a sentence is shown by the case form of the pronoun. Different functions demand different forms. For instance, a pronoun that acts as a subject is in the *nominative case;* a pronoun that acts as an object is in the *objective case;* and a pronoun that shows possession is in the *possessive case*. The following examples illustrate these three functions of pronouns.

| | |
|---|---|
| PRONOUN AS SUBJECT | **I** paid the manager. |
| PRONOUN AS OBJECT | The manager paid **me**. |
| POSSESSIVE PRONOUN | This is **my** money. |

Observe that the pronoun has a different form (*I, me, my*) in each case.

► **NOTE** Since they are used in the same ways that pronouns are used, nouns may also be said to have case. The nouns in the following sentence illustrate the three cases of nouns:

The *people's vote* will decide the *issue*.

| | |
|---|---|
| *people's* | noun in the possessive case |
| *vote* | noun in the nominative case—subject |
| *issue* | noun in the objective case—direct object |

However, since nouns have identical forms for the nominative and objective cases and form the possessive in a regular way, case presents no problems as far as nouns are concerned.

## 7a. Learn the case forms of pronouns and the uses of each form.

Personal pronouns are those pronouns which change form in the different persons. There are three persons—first, second, and third—which are distinguished as follows.

> First person is the person speaking: *I* (*We*) go.
>
> Second person is the person spoken to: *You* are going.
>
> Third person is a person or thing other than the speaker or the one spoken to: *He* (*She, It, They*) will go.

### *Personal Pronouns*

| *Singular* | NOMINATIVE CASE | OBJECTIVE CASE | POSSESSIVE CASE |
|---|---|---|---|
| FIRST PERSON | I | me | my, mine |
| SECOND PERSON | you | you | your, yours |
| THIRD PERSON | he, she, it | him, her, it | his, her, hers, its |

| *Plural* | NOMINATIVE CASE | OBJECTIVE CASE | POSSESSIVE CASE |
|---|---|---|---|
| FIRST PERSON | we | us | our, ours |
| SECOND PERSON | you | you | your, yours |
| THIRD PERSON | they | them | their, theirs |

Since *you* and *it* do not change their forms, ignore them. Memorize the following lists of nominative and objective forms.

| NOMINATIVE CASE | OBJECTIVE CASE |
|---|---|
| I | me |
| he | him |
| she | her |
| we | us |
| they | them |

## USES OF NOMINATIVE FORMS

**7b. The subject of a verb is in the nominative case.**

This rule means that whenever you use a pronoun as a subject, you should use one of the pronouns from the left-hand column on page 105. Ordinarily, you do this without thinking about it. When the subject is compound, however, many persons do make mistakes in their selection of pronouns. Whereas they would never say "Me am seventeen years old," they will say "Myra and me are seventeen years old." Since the pronoun is used as a subject in both sentences, it should be in the nominative case in both: "*Myra and I* are seventeen years old."

**(1) To determine the correct pronoun in a compound subject, try each subject separately with the verb, adapting the form as necessary. Your ear will tell you which form is correct.**

NONSTANDARD Her and me are good friends. [*Her* is a good friend? *Me* am a good friend?]

STANDARD **She** and **I** are good friends. [*She* is a good friend. *I* am a good friend.]

NONSTANDARD Neither Bill nor him was in school today. [*Him* was in school today?]

STANDARD Neither **Bill** nor **he** was in school today. [*He* was in school today.]

**(2) When the pronoun is used with a noun (*we girls, we seniors,* etc.), determine the correct form by reading the sentence without the noun.**

EXAMPLE **We girls** will do the job. [*We* (not *Us*) will do the job.]

**7c. A predicate nominative is in the nominative case.**

A predicate nominative is a noun or pronoun in the predicate that refers to the same thing as the subject of the sentence. For the present purpose, think of a predicate nominative as any pronoun that follows a form of the verb *be*.

| COMMON FORMS OF BE | | PREDICATE NOMINATIVE |
|---|---|---|
| am<br>is, are<br>was, were<br>may be, can be, will be, etc.<br>may have been, etc.<br>must be, might be | are followed by | I<br>he<br>she<br>we<br>you<br>they |

EXAMPLES Are you sure it was **they?**
It might have been **she.**
This may be **he** coming up the walk.

► **USAGE NOTE** It is now perfectly acceptable to use *me* as a predicate nominative in informal usage: *It's me*. (The construction rarely comes up in formal situations.) The plural form (*It's us*) is also generally accepted. However, using the objective case for the third person form of the pronoun (*It's him, It's them*) is still often frowned on in standard English. When you encounter any of these expressions in the exercises in this book or in the various tests you take, you will be wise to take a conservative attitude and use the nominative forms in all instances.

**EXERCISE 1.** Number your paper 1–15. After the proper number, write the personal pronoun that can be substituted for each italicized expression. In those sentences calling for [1st person pron.], use the appropriate one of the following pronouns: *I, we, me, us.*

EXAMPLES 1. George and *Sally* are late again.
1. *she*
2. Only Jean and [1st person pron.] know our secret.
2. *I*

1. Pedro and *his brother* are going out for basketball.
2. He and *Betty* are related in some way.
3. [1st person pron.] students will support the team.
4. That might have been *the Browns*.

5. Did you think that Sally and *Helen* were close friends?
6. Can you or *Mr. Graham* do these problems?
7. Are [1st person pron.] boys invited too?
8. I wish that I were *that girl.*
9. Neither Sandra nor *Agnes* was chosen.
10. Stan and [1st person pron.] won our matches.
11. You and *the boys* are wrong.
12. Either *your teacher* or the guidance counselor will advise you.
13. First she thought she had seen the lost children; then she said she wasn't sure it was *the lost children.*
14. Mildred and *Jane* borrowed my homework paper.
15. If *John* or Bill is absent, I'll get the assignment.

## USES OF OBJECTIVE FORMS

### 7d. The object of a verb is in the objective case.

The object of a verb answers the question "What?" or "Whom?" after an action verb.

EXAMPLE I saw **her.** [Saw whom? Answer: *her,* which is the object.]

As their name suggests, the objective forms (*me, him, her, us, them*) are used as objects.

EXAMPLES I saw **him** in the library.
She greeted **me** cordially.
**Him** I remember very well.

Since both direct and indirect objects are in the objective case, there is no point in distinguishing between them in applying this rule.

EXAMPLES I stopped **her.** [direct object]
I told **her** the story. [indirect object]

Like the nominative forms of pronouns, the objective forms are troublesome principally when they are used in compounds. Although you would hardly make the mistake of saying, "I saw *he* in the library," you might say, "I saw *Jim and he* in the library." Trying each object separately with the verb will help you to choose the correct pronoun for compound objects: "I saw *him* in the library."

Remember that when a pronoun is used with a noun (*we girls, us girls*), we determine the correct form by omitting the noun.

They blame **us** pedestrians. [They blame *us,* not *we.*]

**EXERCISE 2.** Referring to the list of objective forms, supply the correct pronouns for the italicized words in the following sentences. In sentences calling for [1st person pron.], use the appropriate one of the following: *I, we, me, us.*

1. Did you tell the superintendent or *Ms. Marshal?*
2. Carla and *Dave* I would never doubt.
3. Leave [1st person pron.] girls alone for a while.
4. Michelle will be inviting both you and [1st person pron.]
5. Did you see Lois or *Andy* today?
6. I sent a letter to the admissions director and *her assistant.*
7. The coach chose Joan and *Carmen and me.*
8. The principal should have notified *Sven* and Gail.
9. Ron just passed Tina and [1st person pron.] in the hall.
10. [1st person pron.] athletes have to go to team practice.

**EXERCISE 3.** This exercise covers the use of personal pronouns as subjects of verbs, predicate nominatives, and objects of verbs. Number your paper 1–20. After the proper number write the correct one of the two forms in parentheses in each sentence.

1. Who told Sue and (she, her)?
2. Have you and (she, her) had an argument?
3. That was probably Steve and (they, them).
4. Mr. Thompson said that (we, us) girls were late.
5. Tell the principal and (he, him) what you did.

6. Are you expecting Jean and (she, her)?
7. I don't believe it was (he, him).
8. Did you know that Bill and (she, her) are engaged?
9. Please tell (we, us) girls where you were.
10. Do not annoy (I, me) or the driver.
11. Certainly you must remember Edna and (I, me).
12. You misunderstood the teacher and (I, me).
13. Who will drive Peggy and (she, her) to the airport?
14. That must be (he, him).
15. I'll send you and (he, him) by different routes.
16. The doctor offered to treat her husband and (she, her).
17. We didn't want to leave Anne and (she, her) behind.
18. Our callers were probably (they, them).
19. Ray and (I, me) don't need advice.
20. We know it was (she, her).

**EXERCISE 4.** Write three sentences of your own, each containing a pronoun as part of a compound subject; three sentences, each containing a pronoun as part of a compound predicate nominative; and four sentences, each containing a pronoun as part of a compound object.

### 7e. The object of a preposition is in the objective case.

Prepositions, as well as verbs, take objects. The noun or pronoun at the end of a prepositional phrase is the object of the preposition that begins the phrase. In the following prepositional phrases the objects are printed in boldfaced type:

| | | |
|---|---|---|
| at **home** | in the **morning** | from **him** |
| to **Chicago** | under the **house** | for **George** and **them** |

Errors in the use of the pronoun as the object of a preposition, like those made when it is the object of a verb, usually occur when the object is compound. Since you would not say "I had a letter from *she*," you should not say "I had a letter from *Geraldine* and *she*." By omitting the first of the two objects in a compound object, you can usually tell what the correct pronoun is.

NONSTANDARD Give the message to either Belle or she.
STANDARD Give the message **to** either Belle or **her.** [to *her*]

NONSTANDARD I begged a ride with Frank and he.
STANDARD I begged a ride **with** Frank and **him.** [with *him*]

NONSTANDARD Dad bought the typewriter for my brother and I.
STANDARD Dad bought the typewriter **for** my brother and **me.** [for *me*]

**EXERCISE 5.** Number your paper 1–10. Select the preposition from each sentence, and write it after the proper number on your paper. After the preposition, write the correct one of the two pronouns in parentheses. Remember to choose the objective form.

1. The chess team sent a challenge to Don and (he, him).
2. The slide show was presented by my sister and (I, me).
3. We are planning to leave with (they, them) and Alice.
4. I dedicated my poem to both Marcia and (she, her).
5. Frank arrived right after Juanita and (I, me).
6. The responsibility has fallen upon (we, us) students.
7. Were you sitting near Tony and (she, her)?
8. The matter is strictly between Ms. James and (they, them).
9. Consuelo has been asking about you and (she, her).
10. Would you draw a cartoon for the girls and (we, us)?

**EXERCISE 6.** This exercise covers four uses of the personal pronouns: a. subject of a verb; b. predicate nominative (after a form of *be*); c. object of a verb (direct or indirect); d. object of a preposition. Number your paper 1–25. Select the correct one of the pronouns in parentheses in each sentence and write it after the proper number on your paper. After each pronoun, write the letter of its use as listed above.

EXAMPLE 1. Please ask Tommy and (she, her) for supper to-night.

1. *her, c*

1. I will ask Carter and (he, him).
2. Have you heard from the Whites or (they, them)?
3. Paula and (I, me) did our homework in school.
4. They thought it was (she, her).
5. Tell Mr. Clark and (he, him) what you want.
6. It might have been (they, them).
7. (He, Him) and (I, me) are on our way to the movies.
8. The book was written by Ms. Hall and (she, her).
9. You can count on (we, us) students.
10. (She, Her) and (I, me) volunteered to help.
11. It was (he, him) who invented the electric light.
12. If (we, us) seniors support the production, others will, too.
13. Have you ever worked for either Ms. Berger or (she, her)?
14. Did you leave the baby and (she, her) together?
15. Do I look like my mother or (she, her)?
16. Don't go without (we, us) girls.
17. When Jean and (I, me) saw what was coming, we ran.
18. How do you know it was (he, him)?
19. When do you expect your family and (they, them)?
20. Bring Isabel and (she, her) with you.
21. Neither you nor (I, me) was right.
22. The trouble with Bob and (I, me) is that we are lazy.
23. The Browns and (they, them) are arriving later.
24. She thought it was (they, them) who owned the house.
25. I talked to Rick and (he, him) for twenty minutes.

## USES OF *WHO* AND *WHOM*

Like the personal pronouns, the pronouns *who* and *who-ever* have three different case forms:

| NOMINATIVE | OBJECTIVE | POSSESSIVE |
|---|---|---|
| who | whom | whose |
| whoever | whomever | whosever |

## *Who* and *Whom* as Interrogative Pronouns

*Who* and *whom* are interrogative pronouns when they are used to ask a question. The four rules on pages 106–10 governing the case forms of the personal pronouns apply also to *who* and *whom*.

EXAMPLES **Who** left his books here? [The nominative form is required because *who* is the subject of *left.*]

**Whom** did Mary call? [The objective form is required because *whom* is the object of *did call.*]

You may find it helpful, at first, to substitute *he, she—him, her* for *who—whom,* respectively. If *he* or *she,* nominative, fits the sentence, then *who,* also nominative, will be correct. If *him* or *her* fits, then *whom* will be correct.

EXAMPLES (*Who, Whom*) left his books here? [***He*** left his books here. Hence, ***Who*** left his books here?]

(*Who, Whom*) did Mary call? [Mary did call **him.** Hence, Mary did call *whom.* ***Whom*** did Mary call?]

Interrogative pronouns appear in both direct and indirect questions. A direct question uses the exact words of the speaker and is followed by a question mark. An indirect question does not use the exact words of the speaker and is not followed by a question mark.

DIRECT QUESTION **Who** is the captain?
INDIRECT QUESTION She asked **who** the captain was.

DIRECT QUESTION **Whom** did she meet?
INDIRECT QUESTION They asked **whom** she had met.

When the interrogative pronoun is used immediately after a preposition, *whom* is always the correct form.

EXAMPLES **To whom** were you speaking?

**With whom** did you go?

► **USAGE NOTE** In informal usage, *whom* is not usually used as an interrogative pronoun. *Who* is used regardless of the case.

INFORMAL **Who** do you know in Toledo?

**Who** does the manager want?

In formal usage, the distinction between *who* and *whom* is still recognized:

FORMAL **Whom** do you know in Toledo? [*Whom* is the object of the verb *do know.*]

**Whom** does the manager want? [*Whom* is the object of the verb *does want.*]

## *Who* and *Whom* as Relative Pronouns

When *who* and *whom* (*whoever* and *whomever*) are used to begin a subordinate clause, they are relative pronouns. Their case is governed by the same rules that govern the case of a personal pronoun. Although *whom* is becoming increasingly uncommon in spoken English, the distinction between *who* and *whom* in subordinate clauses is usually observed in writing. Study the following explanations and refer to them whenever you need help with relative pronouns in your own writing.

**7f. The case of the pronoun beginning a subordinate clause is determined by its use in the clause that it begins. The case is not affected by any word outside the clause.**

In order to analyze a *who–whom* problem, follow these steps:

1. Pick out the subordinate clause.
2. Determine how the pronoun is used in the clause—subject, predicate nominative, object of verb, object of preposition—and decide its case according to the rules.
3. Select the correct form of the pronoun.

PROBLEM The new teacher, (who, whom) has taken Mr. Green's position, came from the South.

*Step 1* The subordinate clause is (*who, whom*) *has taken Mr. Green's position.*

*Step 2* In this clause the pronoun is used as the subject of the verb *has taken;* as a subject it should be, according to rule, in the nominative case.

*Step 3* The nominative form is *who.*

SOLUTION The new teacher, **who** has taken Mr. Green's position, came from the South.

PROBLEM The new teacher, (who, whom) I met today, came from the South.

*Step 1* The subordinate clause is (*who, whom*) *I met today.*

*Step 2* In the clause the subject is *I;* the verb is *met;* and the pronoun is the object of the verb *met* (*I met whom*). As an object it is in the objective case according to rule.

*Step 3* The objective form is *whom.*

SOLUTION The new teacher, **whom** I met today, came from the South.

PROBLEM Does anyone know (who, whom) the new teacher is?

*Step 1* The subordinate clause is (*who, whom*) *the new teacher is.*

*Step 2* In the clause, *teacher* is the subject, *is* is the verb; the pronoun is a predicate nominative (*the new teacher is who*). As a predicate nominative it is in the nominative case according to rule.

*Step 3* The nominative form is *who.*

SOLUTION Does anyone know **who** the new teacher is?

In writing the preceding sentence, one might tend to use *whom,* thinking it the object of the verb *know,* but *know* is outside the clause and cannot affect the case of a word in the clause. The object of the verb *know* is the entire clause *who the new teacher is.*

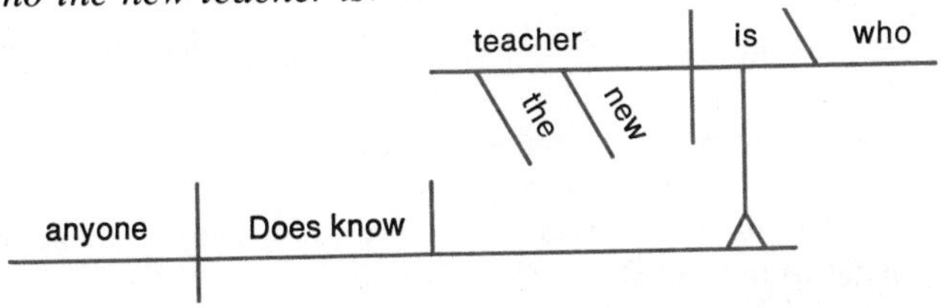


PROBLEM I do not remember (who, whom) I lent the book to. [Following the three steps, you will find that the pronoun here is used as the object of the preposition *to;* it should be in the objective case, hence *whom.*]

SOLUTION I do not remember **whom** I lent the book to.

SOLUTION I do not remember **to whom** I lent the book.

► **USAGE NOTE** In determining whether to use *who* or *whom,* do not be misled by a parenthetical expression like *I think, he said,* etc.

EXAMPLES They are the people **who,** I think, are the foundation of society. [*who* are the foundation of society]

She is the woman **who** Mr. Bryan thinks should be rewarded. [*who* should be rewarded]

**EXERCISE 7.** Number your paper 1–20. Using the three steps described on page 114 for determining the case of a relative pronoun, determine the pronoun's correct form for each of the following sentences and write it on your paper after the proper number. Take plenty of time. Don't guess.

1. In *Hamlet* the two characters (who, whom) I remember best are Hamlet and Ophelia.
2. If I had known (who, whom) she was, I would have been more cordial.
3. Next month's leader will be (whoever, whomever) the delegates elect.
4. Since I did not know (who, whom) the caller wanted, I instructed her to call again later.
5. Everybody (who, whom) received an invitation sent a reply.
6. The club members (who, whom) have paid their dues are qualified to vote.
7. She was one of those (who, whom) the politicians could not influence.
8. No one has figured out to (who, whom) the teacher was referring.
9. The church is looking for someone (who, whom) it can assign to lead the young people's group.
10. Harriet Tubman was a woman (who, whom), I think, we ought to remember.
11. The poets (who, whom) the reading public takes to its heart are not always great poets.
12. Everyone in the courtroom wondered (who, whom) the mysterious witness would be.
13. Many women (who, whom) are on strike would prefer to be working.

14. She is one of those students (who, whom), I believe, would make the most of an opportunity to study abroad.
15. The two men (who, whom) the police arrested for a parking violation were wanted for robbery in three states.
16. She couldn't plan her strategy until she knew (who, whom) her opponents would be.
17. You may tell anyone (who, whom) you think is interested that our fight has just begun.
18. The reporters must rely for information on certain persons (who, whom) they know well.
19. The coach's reply to the grandstand strategists (who, whom) were criticizing him was an undefeated season.
20. Ralph Bunche was a man (who, whom) many people respected.

## PRONOUNS IN INCOMPLETE CONSTRUCTIONS

An "incomplete construction" occurs most commonly after the words *than* and *as*. To avoid repetition, we say "The captain played better than he." (*Played* is omitted.) "Are you as tall as she?" (as she *is*). The interpretation of the sentence may depend upon the form of the pronoun used.

EXAMPLES I like Rosa better than **she**. [than she likes Rosa]
I like Rosa better than **her**. [than I like her]

**7g. After *than* and *as* introducing an incomplete construction, use the form of the pronoun you would use if the construction were completed.**

**EXERCISE 8.** Number your paper 1–10. Write after the proper number the part of each sentence beginning with *than* or *as,* using the correct pronoun and completing the sentence to show that the pronoun is correct. In several sentences either pronoun may be correct, depending on how the sentence is completed.

EXAMPLE 1. Nolan has worked longer than (he, him).
1. *than he has worked*

1. Have you lived in this city as long as (they, them)?
2. I don't know Brenda as well as (she, her).

3. Eva is shorter than (I, me).
4. The senior class scored higher than (they, them).
5. Mr. Cranley was more generous than (he, him).
6. Is she really prettier than (I, me)?
7. The results show that I do better on multiple-choice tests than (he, him).
8. Can they hit safely as often as (we, us)?
9. I understand him better than (she, her).
10. Can Ms. Edwards tutor Paula as well as (I, me)?

## MINOR PROBLEMS IN THE USE OF PRONOUNS

**7h. In standard formal English the pronouns ending in *–self, –selves* are usually used only to refer to another word in the sentence or to emphasize another word.**

EXAMPLES **I** hurt **myself.** [*Myself* refers to *I*.]

**She** told me the whole story **herself.** [*Herself* emphasizes *she*.]

The **boys themselves** made the suggestion. [*Themselves* emphasizes *boys*.]

Avoid the use of pronouns ending in *–self, –selves* in place of other personal pronouns used as subjects.

EXAMPLES Dinah and **I** [not *myself*] are seventeen years old.
Did anyone take longer than **you** [not *yourself*]?

**7i. An appositive is in the same case as the word with which it is in apposition.**

NONSTANDARD Two seniors, Abe and her, made the best speeches.

STANDARD Two seniors, **Abe and she,** made the best speeches.

*Abe* and *she* are in apposition with *seniors,* the subject of the sentence. Since the subject of a verb is nominative, the appositive is also nominative; hence, *she* is correct.

STANDARD For the leads in the play, the director chose two people, **Abe and her.**

In apposition with *people,* which is the object of *chose, Abe* and *her* are also in the objective case; hence, *her* is correct.

**7j. Use the possessive case of a noun or a pronoun before a gerund.**

This use of the possessive case will appear reasonable if you understand that a gerund is a noun form.

EXAMPLES I was surprised by the **child's question.**

I was surprised by the **child's asking** such a question.

Do you object to **my presence?**

Do you object to **my being** present?

Sometimes a participle ending in *-ing* may be confused with a gerund. The following use of the objective case before a participle is correct.

EXAMPLE I watched **him running** down the street.

The use of the possessive *his* in this sentence would change the meaning to a far less likely idea: *I watched his running down the street.*

Whether or not you should use the possessive form of a word preceding a word ending in *-ing* often depends on which word you wish to emphasize. If you wish to emphasize the action in the *-ing* word, you use the possessive. If you wish to emphasize the preceding word, you do not use the possessive.

What do you think of Helen's singing? [In this sentence the emphasis is on the kind of singing Helen does.]

Can you imagine Helen singing? [In this sentence the emphasis is on Helen, who apparently is not likely to be a singer.]

**EXERCISE 9.** Number your paper 1–10. Write a + after the proper number for each correct sentence; write a 0 for each incorrect sentence. After each 0, write the correct form.

1. The school's being open on a holiday surprised us.
2. Jean and myself did not have dates.

3. I do not enjoy her playing.
4. No one could understand Bob failing a math course.
5. The best players, Maria and her, were too ill to play.
6. After him warning us, we decided to study for the test.
7. Somebody, either Claudia or he, answered the question.
8. I had not been notified of their coming.
9. His friend and himself were offered the job.
10. The class's taking the test without preparing for it was a mistake.

**REVIEW EXERCISE A.** Number your paper 1–33. Select the correct one of the pronouns in parentheses in each sentence and write it after the proper number on your paper. Be prepared to explain your answers.

1. Helen and (I, me) stayed after school.
2. Have you seen Sally and (she, her)?
3. No one could be sure that it was (they, them).
4. Today I had letters from both Nancy and (she, her).
5. The Senator (who, whom) I talked with objected to the bill.
6. He is a boy (who, whom), I think, has always had his own way.
7. You should have seen Denise and (I, me).
8. I do not know (who, whom) she had in mind.
9. He said that you and (I, me) are his best friends.
10. How can anyone be sure (who, whom) it was?
11. He could not sing as well as (she, her).
12. These are the students (who, whom), I think, Mr. Langley meant.
13. The disagreement between Jenny and (he, him) was easily settled.
14. My sister and (I, me) did most of the cooking.
15. I do not know (who, whom) it was.
16. She knows that it might have been (she, her).
17. His sister is handsomer than (he, him).
18. Please call on either Miss Nash or (I, me) if you need help.
19. (He, Him) and (I, me) have been in the same homeroom for three years.

20. The flowers came from Helen and (I, me).
21. You go ahead and (we, us) girls will follow later.
22. Why do you dislike Tom and (he, him)?
23. That was the girl (who, whom) Betty wanted her to meet.
24. Bob and (he, him) have their driver's licenses.
25. She refused to let (we, us) boys drive her car.
26. Ask the co-editors, Roy and (she, her), when the yearbook will be published.
27. It was (his, him) whistling that annoyed us.
28. Two teachers, Mr. Bryce and (she, her), are sponsoring the Ski Club.
29. Did you hear about (him, his) breaking his leg?
30. Sue and (I, me, myself) did the homework together.
31. I do not approve of (their, them) habitually talking in class.
32. Aretha and (I, me) took turns at the wheel.
33. An investigation uncovered the story of (their, them) refusing a bribe.

**REVIEW EXERCISE B.** Some of the following sentences contain errors in the use of pronouns. Others are correct. Number your paper 1–20. If a sentence is correct, write a + after the proper number. If it is incorrect, write the correct form of the pronoun.

1. Melissa was older than her.
2. No one knew who the winner was.
3. I can't tell her sister and her apart.
4. Please wait for Andrea and I.
5. Are him and Maggie going to the movies?
6. Consult Mrs. Torres, who, I think, will advise you wisely.
7. Is the captain him or Tom?
8. You can never depend on him being anywhere on time.
9. Sally, Sue, and me are giving a party.
10. He is a man who has been highly recommended.
11. Sue and me had lunch downtown with our mothers.
12. We have some members whom I have never met.
13. I will talk with whoever gets the assignment.

14. Two teachers, Mrs. Dalton and he, are in charge.
15. Get Terri and she to finish the job.
16. Whom did she say is the best-qualified candidate?
17. I want to know who you elected.
18. I was glad to hear about you winning an award.
19. It's easy to mislead gullible people like you and he.
20. There is a man whom prosperity ruined.

Chapter 8

# Correct Form and Use of Verbs

## Principal Parts; Tense, Voice, and Mood

A verb is a word that expresses action or otherwise helps to make a statement.

### KINDS OF VERBS

All verbs help to make statements about their subjects. Those that do so by expressing action performed by the subject are called *action verbs*.

ACTION VERBS Bob **dived** into the icy water.

Anne **tapped** the egg firmly against the rim of the bowl.

She **thought** at length about the problem.

Some verbs help to make statements by linking the subject and a word in the predicate that explains, describes, or in some other way makes the subject more definite. Such verbs are called *linking verbs*.

LINKING VERBS Our chances **looked** good. [*Good,* an adjective, modifies the subject *chances*.]

Martina **is** my sister. [*Sister,* a noun, identifies Martina.]

George **became** an electrician. [*Electrician* identifies George.]

Some verbs can be either action verbs or linking verbs:

ACTION VERB We **looked** everywhere for the missing puppy. [*Looked* expresses action.]

LINKING VERB The test **looked** hard. [This time, *looked* links the subject, *test,* with a word that describes it, *hard.*]

There are many fewer linking verbs than action verbs. (You will find a list of the most common linking verbs on page 12.) The verb used most often as a linking verb is *be,* whose forms are *am, is, are, was, were,* and all verb phrases ending in *be, being,* or *been: may be, was being, has been,* etc.

In addition to functioning as a linking verb, *be* can also be followed by an adverb or adverb phrase:

She was **there.**
The house is **in the country.**

Although it resembles an action verb in this use, *be* is not generally classified as one. Just remember that *be* is always a linking verb except when followed by an adverb.

## THE PRINCIPAL PARTS OF A VERB

Every verb has four basic forms called principal parts: the *infinitive, present participle, past,* and *past participle.* All other forms are derived from these principal parts.

| INFINITIVE | PRESENT PARTICIPLE | PAST | PAST PARTICIPLE |
|---|---|---|---|
| work | (is) working | worked | (have) worked |

The words *is* and *have* are given with the present participle and past participle forms to remind you that these forms are used with a helping verb: *am, is, are, was, were, has been, will be, have, has, had,* etc.

### Regular Verbs

A regular verb is one that forms its past and past participle by adding *–d* or *–ed* to the infinitive form.

| INFINITIVE | PAST | PAST PARTICIPLE |
|---|---|---|
| live | lived | (have) lived |
| play | played | (have) played |

## Irregular Verbs

An irregular verb is one that forms its past and past participle in some other way than a regular verb.

This "other way" may involve changing the spelling of the verb or making no change at all.

| INFINITIVE | PAST | PAST PARTICIPLE |
|---|---|---|
| swim | swam | (have) swum |
| write | wrote | (have) written |
| hit | hit | (have) hit |

The major problem in the correct use of verbs is the choice of the correct past and past participle forms of irregular verbs. Since irregular past tenses and past participles are formed in a variety of ways, you must know the principal parts of each irregular verb.

Three principal parts of common irregular verbs are given in the following alphabetical list. Use this list for reference. For the principal parts of other irregular verbs, consult a dictionary. Drill exercises on irregular verbs frequently misused are given following the list.

### *Principal Parts of Irregular Verbs*

| INFINITIVE | PAST | PAST PARTICIPLE |
|---|---|---|
| bear | bore | (have) borne |
| beat | beat | (have) beaten *or* beat |
| begin | began | (have) begun |
| bite | bit | (have) bitten |
| blow | blew | (have) blown |
| break | broke | (have) broken |
| bring | brought | (have) brought |
| burst | burst | (have) burst |
| catch | caught | (have) caught |
| choose | chose | (have) chosen |
| come | came | (have) come |

| INFINITIVE | PAST | PAST PARTICIPLE |
|---|---|---|
| creep | crept | (have) crept |
| dive | dived[1] | (have) dived |
| do | did | (have) done |
| draw | drew | (have) drawn |
| drink | drank | (have) drunk |
| drive | drove | (have) driven |
| eat | ate | (have) eaten |
| fall | fell | (have) fallen |
| fling | flung | (have) flung |
| fly | flew | (have) flown |
| freeze | froze | (have) frozen |
| get | got | (have) got *or* gotten |
| give | gave | (have) given |
| go | went | (have) gone |
| grow | grew | (have) grown |
| know | knew | (have) known |
| lay | laid | (have) laid |
| lead | led | (have) led |
| lend | lent | (have) lent |
| lie | lay | (have) lain |
| lose | lost | (have) lost |
| ride | rode | (have) ridden |
| ring | rang | (have) rung |
| rise | rose | (have) risen |
| run | ran | (have) run |
| say | said | (have) said |
| see | saw | (have) seen |
| set | set | (have) set |
| shake | shook | (have) shaken |
| shine | shone *or* shined | (have) shone *or* shined |
| sing | sang *or* sung | (have) sung |
| sink | sank *or* sunk | (have) sunk |
| sit | sat | (have) sat |
| speak | spoke | (have) spoken |
| steal | stole | (have) stolen |
| sting | stung | (have) stung |
| swear | swore | (have) sworn |
| swim | swam | (have) swum |
| swing | swung | (have) swung |

[1] Informal, *dove*.

| INFINITIVE | PAST | PAST PARTICIPLE |
|---|---|---|
| take | took | (have) taken |
| tear | tore | (have) torn |
| throw | threw | (have) thrown |
| wear | wore | (have) worn |
| write | wrote | (have) written |

**8a. Learn the principal parts of common irregular verbs.**

To help you learn the correct use of irregular verbs, those which are commonly misused are presented on the following pages in four groups. Memorize the principal parts of the verbs in each group and do the exercises. In doing the exercises, remember that the past participle is used with helping, or auxiliary, verbs: *is, are, was, were, have, has, had, have been,* etc. As you say the principal parts, place *have* before the past participle: *begin, began, have begun.*

## *Group I*

| INFINITIVE | PAST | PAST PARTICIPLE |
|---|---|---|
| beat | beat | (have) beaten *or* beat |
| begin | began | (have) begun |
| blow | blew | (have) blown |
| break | broke | (have) broken |
| burst | burst | (have) burst |
| choose | chose | (have) chosen |
| come | came | (have) come |
| do | did | (have) done |

**EXERCISE 1.** Number your paper 1–20. After the proper number, write either the past or the past participle of the verb given at the beginning of each sentence, whichever will fill correctly the blank in the sentence.

1. *begin* I had already —— to work.
2. *blow* The wind has —— hard all day.
3. *come* He —— in last night at ten o'clock.
4. *choose* Has everyone —— a partner?
5. *beat* We —— them three times last season.

| | | |
|---|---|---|
| 6. | *do* | Marta —— the best she could. |
| 7. | *break* | Was his arm ——? |
| 8. | *burst* | Thousands died when the Johnstown dam ——. |
| 9. | *do* | We —— what was expected of us. |
| 10. | *begin* | You should have —— earlier. |
| 11. | *blow* | His boat had been —— out to sea. |
| 12. | *choose* | They —— Dr. Burns as the keynote speaker. |
| 13. | *burst* | They thought the water pipes had ——. |
| 14. | *come* | We watched as the band —— slowly up the street. |
| 15. | *choose* | I wished we had —— the other route. |
| 16. | *break* | She has —— her promise. |
| 17. | *come* | I —— along right after the accident happened. |
| 18. | *do* | The actors —— well in last night's performance. |
| 19. | *begin* | When the news came, I —— to regret my choice. |
| 20. | *come* | She has —— to get your advice. |

## *Group II*

| INFINITIVE | PAST | PAST PARTICIPLE |
|---|---|---|
| draw | drew | (have) drawn |
| drink | drank | (have) drunk |
| drive | drove | (have) driven |
| fall | fell | (have) fallen |
| fly | flew | (have) flown |
| freeze | froze | (have) frozen |
| give | gave | (have) given |
| go | went | (have) gone |

**EXERCISE 2.** Number your paper 1–20. After the proper number, write either the past or the past participle of the verb, whichever will fill correctly the blank in the sentence.

| | | |
|---|---|---|
| 1. | *drink* | Have you —— all the milk? |
| 2. | *fall* | If I hadn't ——, I'd have caught him. |
| 3. | *freeze* | The water hasn't —— yet. |
| 4. | *go* | He has —— to Chicago. |
| 5. | *give* | She —— me a makeup test yesterday. |
| 6. | *fly* | Have you —— in a helicopter? |

| | | |
|---|---|---|
| 7. | *drive* | Loretta has —— since she was sixteen. |
| 8. | *draw* | Marilyn —— the cartoons for the yearbook last year. |
| 9. | *go* | Marsha has —— to the library. |
| 10. | *give* | I —— him the money last week. |
| 11. | *freeze* | All of us were nearly ——. |
| 12. | *fly* | You could have —— up here in two hours. |
| 13. | *draw* | No child could have —— that picture. |
| 14. | *drink* | Although I had worked hard, he —— more water than I did. |
| 15. | *drive* | We have —— more than 500 kilometers today. |
| 16. | *fall* | I thought she had —— from the tree. |
| 17. | *give* | He —— me only a dollar. |
| 18. | *drive* | If you had —— a little farther, you would have found us. |
| 19. | *go* | He had —— home already. |
| 20. | *give* | She should have —— me more time for the test. |

**EXERCISE 3.** ***Group I*** and ***Group II.*** Number your paper 1–33. After the proper number, write a + for each sentence in which the italicized verb is correct; for each sentence in which the verb is incorrect, write the correct form of the verb.

1. Janet *drew* the picture for us.
2. I *begun* to think you had forgotten me.
3. No one *drunk* very much.
4. The boys *have broke* the window.
5. She has *drove* this road hundreds of times.
6. You *should have chosen* Jimmy.
7. She *had* not *fell* very far.
8. The older boys *done* the heavy work.
9. I *had flown* as far as St. Louis.
10. She *come* home an hour ago.
11. The food *must be frozen* immediately.
12. During the cold weather the water pipe *had bursted.*
13. He *give* me what I wanted.

14. Strong winds *blowed* us off our course.
15. We *could* not *have gone* any farther.
16. Rice Lake *was froze* to a depth of two feet.
17. His plow *was drawed* by a team of mules.
18. *Have* you ever *drunk* papaya juice?
19. She *had chose* him for her partner.
20. You *could have flew* to Newark.
21. As I reached the car, the bag of groceries suddenly *burst* open.
22. You *should have went* earlier.
23. Since then he *has* never *been beaten.*
24. Who *give* you the pearls?
25. Lola *come* in third in the first race.
26. You *might have fallen* on your head.
27. The axle *must be broke.*
28. The game *begun* about two o'clock.
29. She *had drunk* too much soda.
30. We *had driven* for miles in the fog.
31. Who *done* it?
32. The river *had frozen* solid.
33. The bus driver *come* after us about noon.

## *Group III*

| INFINITIVE | PAST | PAST PARTICIPLE |
|---|---|---|
| grow | grew | (have) grown |
| know | knew | (have) known |
| ride | rode | (have) ridden |
| ring | rang | (have) rung |
| run | ran | (have) run |
| see | saw | (have) seen |
| sing | sang *or* sung | (have) sung |
| speak | spoke | (have) spoken |

**EXERCISE 4.** Number your paper 1–20. After the proper number, write either the past or past participle of the verb given at the beginning of each sentence, whichever will correctly fill the blank in the sentence.

1. *ring* The fire alarm has ——.
2. *run* The shortstop —— toward third base.
3. *sing* Have you ever —— a round before?
4. *speak* We had —— to the plumber about the leak.
5. *see* The science club —— a filmstrip yesterday.
6. *ride* Have you ever —— on a burro?
7. *know* No one could have —— the outcome.
8. *grow* Our baby hamster has —— rapidly.
9. *see* We —— the parade on television.
10. *know* No one —— the formula for baking soda.
11. *ride* A few of us had —— on the roller coaster.
12. *grow* My dog Finn has —— old.
13. *speak* Have you —— to them about it?
14. *sing* We had never —— this song before.
15. *run* When I washed my new shirt, the dye ——.
16. *ring* Has the bell —— yet?
17. *speak* She hasn't —— to anyone about the party.
18. *see* I —— a flash of lightning just now.
19. *ring* If my alarm clock hadn't ——, I would still be sleeping.
20. *run* She —— all the way to the bus stop.

## *Group IV*

| INFINITIVE | PAST | PAST PARTICIPLE |
|---|---|---|
| spring | sprang *or* sprung | (have) sprung |
| steal | stole | (have) stolen |
| swim | swam | (have) swum |
| swing | swung | (have) swung |
| take | took | (have) taken |
| tear | tore | (have) torn |
| throw | threw | (have) thrown |
| write | wrote | (have) written |

**EXERCISE 5.** Number your paper 1–20. After the proper number, write either the past or past participle of the verb given at the beginning of each sentence, whichever will correctly fill the blank in the sentence.

1. *spring* The lock had been —— by force.
2. *swim* I could not have —— another stroke.
3. *tear* Have you —— your coat?
4. *write* Has she —— to you?
5. *throw* Dee —— him out at first base.
6. *take* She should have —— the children with her.
7. *swing* Last year they —— in the playground swings nearly every day.
8. *steal* They thought their car had been ——.
9. *throw* The first pitch Mary —— was a wide curve.
10. *write* My uncle has —— several books.
11. *tear* You have —— my homework paper.
12. *swim* Yesterday she —— alone to the raft.
13. *spring* In a moment he had —— onto his horse and galloped away.
14. *take* I should have —— a course in typing.
15. *swing* All morning the balloon —— back and forth on its cable.
16. *steal* I'm sure no one has —— your wallet.
17. *write* If you had —— to me, I'd have helped you.
18. *swim* Where were you when we —— the channel?
19. *throw* A sudden lurch of the boat —— everyone overboard.
20. *write* When you have —— your essay, show it to me.

**EXERCISE 6.** ***Group III*** and ***Group IV***. Number your paper 1–33. After the proper number, write a + for each sentence in which the italicized verb is correct; for each sentence in which the verb is incorrect, write the correct form of the verb.

1. You *have growed* much taller this year.
2. Who *had rang* the bell?
3. He *has ran* his last race.
4. We *have sung* that number in every concert.
5. He *has spoke* at our school several times.
6. They *swam* until they were tired.
7. I *had tore* my shirt.

8. You *have* never *wrote* a better story.
9. *Had* I *known* your number, I'd have called you.
10. I *had* not *rode* horseback for years.
11. She thinks I *seen* her there.
12. Who *throwed* you out?
13. We *should have taken* more money with us.
14. Several pages *have been torn* from this book.
15. The acrobat *swung* himself over the swinging bar.
16. Someone *must have stolen* my watch.
17. On both plays they *threw* us for a loss.
18. Mrs. Maxwell *seen* at once what the trouble was.
19. Dad thought we *had ridden* far enough.
20. She *would have knowed* what to do.
21. *Have* you *wrote* your composition yet?
22. The gale *had tore* both sails.
23. No one *could have swum* that far.
24. I *have* not *spoken* to Everett.
25. She *has sung* her way to stardom.
26. When Mr. Stoltz appeared, the boys *run* away.
27. I did not know the bell *had rang.*
28. This town *has grown* rapidly.
29. You *should have knowed* better.
30. Nothing *had been stolen.*
31. She *had tore* her new gloves.
32. You *could have took* Jane to the dance.
33. I *shall have written* my letter by that time.

**EXERCISE 7.** ***Groups I–IV.*** Number your paper 1–50. After the proper number, write either the past or past participle of the verb at the beginning of each sentence, whichever will fill correctly the blank in the sentence.

1. *burst* In the bus station my suitcase suddenly —— open.
2. *freeze* The doctor said I had —— both feet.
3. *break* Were any bones ——?
4. *fly* We'd be home now if we had ——.
5. *blow* The storm had —— down a telephone pole.

| | | |
|---|---|---|
| 6. | *fall* | She could not have —— more than two meters. |
| 7. | *begin* | We —— the job yesterday morning. |
| 8. | *know* | You should have —— what to do. |
| 9. | *beat* | We —— them twice last season. |
| 10. | *ring* | Someone had —— the bell. |
| 11. | *drive* | How far have you —— today? |
| 12. | *ride* | Grover had never —— in the back seat before. |
| 13. | *drink* | During the recent flood, we —— bottled water. |
| 14. | *run* | When I saw her pass the house, I —— after her. |
| 15. | *do* | She —— her homework before school was out. |
| 16. | *swim* | When I called for help, Helen —— out to me. |
| 17. | *come* | He —— in about an hour ago. |
| 18. | *steal* | Lydia thought someone had —— her bicycle. |
| 19. | *choose* | The council could have —— a better representative. |
| 20. | *sing* | You should have —— louder. |
| 21. | *grow* | The school has —— beyond capacity. |
| 22. | *speak* | How many times have I —— to you about that? |
| 23. | *go* | Alice had —— to the movies. |
| 24. | *see* | I'm sure Raymond —— me as I left the room. |
| 25. | *give* | What —— you the black eye? |
| 26. | *take* | I wish she had —— me with her. |
| 27. | *tear* | The trainer said I had —— a ligament. |
| 28. | *throw* | We lost the game when Bob —— the ball over Ben's head. |
| 29. | *tear* | Someone had —— the draperies. |
| 30. | *write* | Have you —— your paper on Maggie Lena Walker, the banker? |
| 31. | *throw* | Who —— away this fountain pen? |
| 32. | *go* | We could not have —— any earlier. |
| 33. | *see* | How do you know they —— you last night? |
| 34. | *freeze* | The milk has —— solid. |
| 35. | *run* | The truck —— into us as we parked at the curb. |
| 36. | *come* | Last night, Lupe —— over to hear some records. |
| 37. | *write* | You should have —— more. |
| 38. | *drink* | Who —— the milk I left here? |
| 39. | *know* | I had —— June when she was a little girl. |

| | |
|---|---|
| 40. *break* | Two convicts had —— away from the work gang. |
| 41. *begin* | A little later I —— to see what she meant. |
| 42. *swim* | During last week's cold wave we —— in the pool. |
| 43. *fall* | We thought he must have —— through the ice. |
| 44. *beat* | The defendant claimed his jailers —— him. |
| 45. *see* | I —— him at the dance last night. |
| 46. *throw* | That horse has never —— a rider. |
| 47. *run* | Mrs. Smith —— for mayor last year. |
| 48. *speak* | I wish she had —— about her travels. |
| 49. *come* | I couldn't find the family when I —— home. |
| 50. *write* | Both women have —— an autobiography. |

## THREE TROUBLESOME PAIRS OF VERBS

Three pairs of verbs require special study and drill because they are more difficult to use correctly than any other verbs. These special verbs are *lie* and *lay, sit* and *set, rise* and *raise*. The most difficult to use correctly are the verbs *lie* and *lay*.

### *Lie* and *Lay*

The verb *lie* means "to assume a lying position" or "to be in a lying position." Its principal parts are *lie,* (*is*) *lying, lay,* (*have*) *lain.*

The verb *lay* means "to put" or "to place something." Its principal parts are *lay,* (*is*) *laying, laid,* (*have*) *laid.*

The verb *lie* is intransitive (see page 11); that is, it never has an object. You never "lie" anything down.

The verb *lay* is transitive; that is, it may have an object, or be in the passive voice. (See page 11.)

| | |
|---|---|
| INTRANSITIVE | The metal **lies** in a mold until thoroughly cooled. [no object] |
| TRANSITIVE | Workers **lay** the molds in a cooling chamber. [object: *molds*] |
| TRANSITIVE | The molds **are laid** in a cooling chamber. [passive voice] |

Memorize the principal parts of these verbs:

| INFINITIVE | PRESENT PARTICIPLE | PAST | PAST PARTICIPLE |
|---|---|---|---|
| lie (to recline) | (is) lying | lay | (have) lain |
| lay (to put) | (is) laying | laid | (have) laid |

If you do not habitually use these verbs correctly, you must begin your work on them slowly and thoughtfully. Only by taking time to think through each form you use can you eventually establish the habit of using the verbs correctly. When faced with a *lie–lay* problem, ask yourself two questions:

1. What is the meaning I intend? Is it "to be in a lying position," or is it "to put something down"?[1]

2. What is the time expressed by the verb and which principal part is required to express this time?

| | |
|---|---|
| PROBLEM | After the alarm had awakened me, I (lay, laid) in bed too long. |
| *Question 1* | Meaning? The meaning here is "to remain in a lying position." The verb which means "to remain in a lying position" is *lie.* |
| *Question 2* | Principal part? The time is past and requires the past form, which is *lay.* [lie, *lay,* lain] |
| SOLUTION | After the alarm had awakened me, I **lay** in bed too long. |
| PROBLEM | Linda (lay, laid) her coat on the table. |
| *Question 1* | Meaning? The meaning here is "to put." The verb which means "to put" is *lay.* |
| *Question 2* | Principal part? The time is past and therefore requires the past form, which is *laid.* [lay, *laid,* laid] |
| SOLUTION | Linda **laid** her coat on the table. |
| PROBLEM | How long had it (lain, laid) there? |

[1] You should be warned against two fairly common misconceptions about *lie* and *lay.* The first is that only people and animals *lie.* A moment's thought, however, will make clear that inanimate objects may also be in a lying position. The second misconception is that because an inanimate object in a lying position must have been put there, one should use *lay,* the verb meaning "to put," to say that the object is at rest. Regardless of its having once *been put down,* the object *lies* (not *lays*) there.

*Question 1* Meaning? The meaning here is "to be in a lying position." The verb which means "to be in a lying position" is *lie*.

*Question 2* Principal part? The time requires the past participle with *had*. The past participle of *lie* is *lain*. [lie, lay, *lain*]

SOLUTION How long **had** it **lain** there?

PROBLEM The dog is (lying, laying) on the doormat.

*Question 1* Meaning? The meaning here is "to be in a lying position." The verb which means "to be in a lying position" is *lie*.

*Question 2* Principal part? The time here requires the present participle, which is *lying*.

SOLUTION The dog is **lying** on the doormat.

It will pay you to use this two-question formula each time you are in doubt about a problem in the use of *lie* and *lay*. Although slow at first, the process will speed up after a few trials, and you will be able to select the correct verb quickly. Of course, you must memorize the principal parts of the verbs before you can use the formula.

Two facts about the use of *lie* and *lay* may be of additional help.

1. Most errors in the use of these verbs are made when the speaker means "to assume or to be in a lying position." When this is the meaning you intend, be especially cautious.

2. When you wish to express the idea of "putting or placing something" in the past tense, always use *laid*.

**EXERCISE 8.** Number your paper 1–10. After the proper number, write the correct one of the two words in parentheses. Use the two-question formula.

1. If you are sick, you should be (lying, laying) down.
2. They (lay, laid) the heavy crate on the handcart.
3. She had (lain, laid) a great deal of emphasis on usage.
4. Amy (lay, laid) down for a while.
5. I left my gloves (lying, laying) on the counter.
6. She had just (lain, laid) down when the doorbell rang.

7. They (lay, laid) their plans before the committee.
8. The calf (lay, laid) on a pile of straw.
9. She (lay, laid) her pen down and closed her notebook.
10. Don't leave your shoes (lying, laying) in the middle of the floor.

**EXERCISE 9.** Choose the correct form of *lie* or *lay* to fill the blank in each sentence. Use the two-question formula.

1. The book —— open to page 231.
2. —— on your back and stretch yourself.
3. An hour ago I —— down for a nap.
4. The tiger was —— asleep near the tree.
5. Have they —— the flooring yet?
6. I think she is —— in the hammock.
7. He —— the boxes on the porch yesterday.
8. She had —— there only a short time.
9. The dog was —— in the shade.
10. She —— the dress pattern on the material.

**EXERCISE 10.** Number your paper 1–20. After the proper number, write the correct one of the two verbs in parentheses. Use the two-question formula.

1. The wreck (lay, laid) in twenty feet of water.
2. The cat loves to (lie, lay) on the window sill.
3. The missing book was (lying, laying) on the top shelf.
4. Do you remember where you (lay, laid) my pen?
5. You shouldn't have (lain, laid) there so long.
6. Cheryl was (lying, laying) on the deck.
7. Here the coal (lies, lays) near the surface.
8. We gathered driftwood while Doris (lay, laid) a fire.
9. I planned to (lie, lay) down for only ten minutes.
10. Gently she (lay, laid) down the injured child.
11. Sandy usually (lies, lays) near the fire.
12. I could not persuade him to (lie, lay) down.
13. Yesterday Dad and I (lay, laid) the new carpet.
14. The cat never (lies, lays) in the bed we made for her.

15. Someone had (lain, laid) a paintbrush on the chair.
16. His clothes were (lying, laying) about the room.
17. Flora had (lain, laid) her camera on the railing.
18. The fossils had (lain, laid) there for a million years.
19. Beneath his rough exterior (lies, lays) a kind heart.
20. I keep forgetting where I have (lain, laid) the hammer.

## *Sit* and *Set*

*Sit* usually means "to assume or to be in an upright, sitting position."[1] The principal parts of *sit* are *sit, (is) sitting, sat, (have) sat. Sit* is almost always an intransitive verb; it rarely takes an object.

*Set* usually means "to put, to place something." The principal parts of *set* are *set, (is) setting, set, (have) set.* Like *lay, set* is a transitive verb; it may take an object.

Since all forms of *set* are made without changing the vowel, the problem of using these two verbs is rather simple. You need only keep in mind the fact that when you mean "to put something down," you use *set* or *setting.* For all other meanings use *sit* or *sat* or *sitting.*[2]

Memorize the principal parts of these verbs:

| INFINITIVE | PRESENT PARTICIPLE | PAST | PAST PARTICIPLE |
|---|---|---|---|
| sit (to rest) | (is) sitting | sat | (have) sat |
| set (to put) | (is) setting | set | (have) set |

**EXERCISE 11.** Number your paper 1–10. After the proper number, write the correct one of the two verbs in parentheses in each sentence.

1. He has been (sitting, setting) by the telephone all evening.
2. Nancy just (sat, set) still and said nothing.
3. In what row were you (sitting, setting)?
4. Extra chairs were (sat, set) in the aisles by the ushers.

[1] Such expressions as "Sit the baby in the high chair" or "Sit him up" really mean "to put" or "to place," and these expressions, which are acceptable, are exceptions to the general rule.
[2] The expressions "The sun sets," "the setting hen," and "Wait for the cement to set" are exceptions to the rule.

5. Had you (sat, set) there longer, you would have caught a fish.
6. We decided to (sit, set) quietly and await results.
7. Passengers (sitting, setting) in the rear seats were not injured.
8. If you (sit, set) on the damp ground, you may catch a cold.
9. He plans to (sit, set) the new cabin on the beach.
10. Someone had (sat, set) in the fresh paint.

## *Rise* and *Raise*

The verb *rise* means "to go up." Its principal parts are *rise, (is) rising, rose, (have) risen.* In other words, when the subject of the verb is itself moving upward, use *rise.* Like *lie, rise* is intransitive; it never takes an object.

The verb *raise* means "to force something to move upward." Its principal parts are *raise, (is) raising, raised, (have) raised.* When the subject of the verb is acting on something, forcing it upward, use *raise.* Like *lay* and *set, raise* is transitive; it may take an object.

Memorize the principal parts of these verbs:

| INFINITIVE | PRESENT PARTICIPLE | PAST | PAST PARTICIPLE |
|---|---|---|---|
| rise (to go up) | (is) rising | rose | (have) risen |
| raise (to force up or be forced up) | (is) raising | raised | (have) raised |

**EXERCISE 12.** Number your paper 1–10. After the proper number, write the correct one of the two verbs in parentheses in each sentence.

1. Air bubbles have been (rising, raising) to the surface.
2. Increasing the duty on imports will (rise, raise) retail prices.
3. The speaker (rose, raised) from her chair and approached the microphone.
4. This month, the star has been (rising, raising) in the east.
5. The rooster (rises, raises) early.
6. During the Revolutionary War, many American colonists decided to (rise, raise) up against King George III.

7. Balloons can (rise, raise) because they contain heated air, which is less dense than the surrounding air.
8. The Wilsons (rose, raised) six adopted children.
9. Mist was (rising, raising) from the ground.
10. The dough has been (rising, raising) for the past hour.

**EXERCISE 13.** For each of the following verbs, write a brief sentence in which the verb is correctly used.

1. lie
2. raising
3. laying
4. set
5. lying
6. raised
7. rises
8. have lain
9. lay (past tense)
10. has laid
11. rising
12. rose
13. setting
14. risen
15. sat

**EXERCISE 14.** Number your paper 1–25. After the proper number, write the correct one of the two words in parentheses in each sentence. Work slowly. Try for 100 percent.

1. A film of oil (lay, laid) on the water.
2. Can't you (sit, set) a while longer?
3. If her temperature (rises, raises), call the doctor.
4. The dog had been (lying, laying) on the sofa.
5. We hardly (sat, set) down at all during the final quarter of the game.
6. Your letter was (lying, laying) at the bottom of the pile.
7. The waves (rose, raised) to mountainous heights.
8. I had (lain, laid) the flashlight on the car seat.
9. From where we were (sitting, setting), the stage was barely visible.
10. She forgot where she had (lain, laid) her gloves.
11. Piles of books and papers were (lying, laying) on the desk.
12. Clouds of black smoke were (rising, raising) from the hills behind us.
13. If we (sit, set) here much longer, we'll be late.
14. (Lie, Lay) down, Butch!
15. Boulders and jagged rocks (lay, laid) across the highway.
16. Since the election, stocks have been (rising, raising) steadily.
17. The dog must have been (lying, laying) under the car.

18. We spent the afternoon just (sitting, setting) and talking.
19. Where do you want to (sit, set)?
20. The child refused to (lie, lay) under the beach umbrella.
21. Beyond this point the road (rises, raises) sharply.
22. Who (lay, laid) out this tennis court?
23. No one expected the tide to (rise, raise) so high.
24. We were (sitting, setting) before the fireplace.
25. The ties on which the track (lies, lays) must be firm and level.

## TENSE

Verbs change in form to show the time of their action or of the idea they express. The time expressed by a verb (present, past, future) is its tense. There are six tenses. As the following conjugations of the verbs *go* and *be* will show you, the six tenses are made from the principal parts of the verb. Study these conjugations and use them for reference in your work on tense.

**8b. Learn the names of the six tenses and how the tenses are formed.**

### *Conjugation of the Verb* Go

Present infinitive: *to go* Perfect infinitive: *to have gone*

*Principal Parts*

| INFINITIVE | PRESENT PARTICIPLE | PAST | PAST PARTICIPLE |
|---|---|---|---|
| go | going | went | gone |

***Present Tense***

| *Singular* | *Plural* |
|---|---|
| I go | we go |
| you go | you go |
| he, she, it goes | they go |

Present progressive: *I am going,* etc.

### *Past Tense*

| *Singular* | *Plural* |
|---|---|
| I went | we went |
| you went | you went |
| he, she, it went | they went |

Past progressive: *I was going,* etc.

### *Future Tense*

(*will* or *shall* + the infinitive[1])

| *Singular* | *Plural* |
|---|---|
| I will (shall) go | we will (shall) go |
| you will go | you will go |
| he, she, it will go | they will go |

Future progressive: *I will (shall) be going,* etc.

### *Present Perfect Tense*

(*have* or *has* + the past participle)

| *Singular* | *Plural* |
|---|---|
| I have gone | we have gone |
| you have gone | you have gone |
| he, she, it has gone | they have gone |

Present perfect progressive: *I have been going,* etc.

### *Past Perfect Tense*

(*had* + the past participle)

| *Singular* | *Plural* |
|---|---|
| I had gone | we had gone |
| you had gone | you had gone |
| he, she, it had gone | they had gone |

Past perfect progressive: *I had been going,* etc.

### *Future Perfect Tense*

(*will have* or *shall have* + the past participle)

| *Singular* | *Plural* |
|---|---|
| I will (shall) have gone | we will (shall) have gone |
| you will have gone | you will have gone |
| he, she, it will have gone | they will have gone |

Future perfect progressive: *I will have (shall have) been going,* etc.

[1] For a discussion of the use of *shall* and *will,* see page 188.

## *Conjugation of the Verb* Be

Present infinitive: *to be*  Perfect infinitive: *to have been*

### *Principal Parts*

| INFINITIVE | PRESENT PARTICIPLE | PAST | PAST PARTICIPLE |
|---|---|---|---|
| be | being | was, were | been |

### ***Present Tense***

| *Singular* | *Plural* |
|---|---|
| I am | we are |
| you are | you are |
| he, she, it is | they are |

Present progressive: *I am being,* etc.

### ***Past Tense***

| *Singular* | *Plural* |
|---|---|
| I was | we were |
| you were | you were |
| he, she, it was | they were |

Past progressive: *I was being,* etc.

### ***Future Tense***

(*will* or *shall* + the infinitive)

| *Singular* | *Plural* |
|---|---|
| I will (shall) be | we will (shall) be |
| you will be | you will be |
| he, she, it will be | they will be |

### ***Present Perfect Tense***

(*have* or *has* + the past participle)

| *Singular* | *Plural* |
|---|---|
| I have been | we have been |
| you have been | you have been |
| he, she, it has been | they have been |

### *Past Perfect Tense*

(*had* + the past participle)

| *Singular* | *Plural* |
|---|---|
| I had been | we had been |
| you had been | you had been |
| he, she, it had been | they had been |

### *Future Perfect Tense*

(*will have* or *shall have* + the past participle)

| *Singular* | *Plural* |
|---|---|
| I will (shall) have been | we will (shall) have been |
| you will have been | you will have been |
| he, she, it will have been | they will have been |

## 8c. Learn the uses of each of the six tenses.

Each of the six tenses has its own particular uses, some of which require explanation. Study the following explanations of these uses; learn rules for the uses of the tenses; do the exercises. Use these pages for reference when you are confronted by a problem in tense in your own writing.

**(1) The *present tense* is used to express action (or to help make a statement about something) occurring now, at the present time.**

EXAMPLES I **work** here.

I **am working** now. [progressive form]

I **do work.** [The verb with *do* or *did* is called the emphatic form.]

► NOTE In all tenses, as in the second example, continuing action may be shown by the use of the progressive form, which ends in *–ing*. The third example illustrates the emphatic form, consisting of a form of *do* plus the first principal part of a verb. The normal way of making a sentence emphatic is to pronounce the helping verb with unusual stress. When there is no helping verb, *do* or *did* is added to carry this stress. These emphatic forms can be used in the present and past tense only.

The present tense is also used to indicate habitual action.

EXAMPLE She **works** every day.

The present tense is often used to express a general truth, something which is true at all times.

EXAMPLES She apparently thought that seeing **is** [instead of *was*] believing.

I did not know that Salem **is** [instead of *was*] the capital of Oregon.

The present tense is also used occasionally to achieve vividness in writing about past events. This use of the present tense is known as the *historical present.*

EXAMPLE Florence Nightingale promptly **senses** the needs of the patients and **comes** to their aid.

**(2) The *past tense* is used to express action (or to help make a statement about something) that occurred in the past but did not continue into the present. The past tense is formed regularly by adding *-d* or *-ed* to the verb.**

EXAMPLES I **worked** there during the holidays.

I **was working** there during the holidays.

► NOTE Past action may be shown in other ways.

EXAMPLES I **used to work** there.

I **did work** there. [emphatic form]

**(3) The *future tense* is used to express action (or to help make a statement about something) occurring at some time in the future. The future tense is formed with *will* or *shall.***

EXAMPLES I **will work** in the library after school.

I **will be working** in the library after school.

► NOTE The future may also be indicated in other ways.

EXAMPLES I **am going to work** there.

I **am about to work.**

I **work** there **tomorrow.** [present with another word indicating future time]

**(4) The *present perfect tense* is used to express action (or to help make a statement about something) occurring at no definite time in the past. It is formed with *have* or *has*.**

EXAMPLE He **has worked** for us many times.

The present perfect tense is also used to express action (or to help make a statement about something) occurring in the past and continuing into the present.

EXAMPLES I **have worked** here for six weeks. [I am still working here.]

I **have been working** here for six weeks. [I am still working here.]

**(5) The *past perfect tense* is used to express action (or to help make a statement about something) completed in the past before some other past action or event. It is formed with *had*.**

EXAMPLES When I **had worked** for a week, I **asked** for my pay. [The working preceded the asking.]

When I **had been working** for a week, I **asked** for my pay.

**(6) The *future perfect tense* is used to express action (or to help make a statement about something) which will be completed in the future before some other future action or event. It is formed with *will have* or *shall have*.**

EXAMPLES By the time school **opens, I will have worked** here eight weeks. [The working precedes the opening of school.]

By the time school **opens, I will have been working** here eight weeks.

**EXERCISE 15.** Explain the difference in meaning between the sentences in the following pairs. The sentences are correct. Name the tense used in each sentence.

1. Katherine went to high school for two years.
   Katherine has gone to high school for two years.
2. How long has she been here?

How long was she here?

3. What has been going on here?
   What went on here?
4. Have the ballots been counted?
   Had the ballots been counted?
5. We learned that he had been there for three hours.
   We learned that he has been there for three hours.
6. I suppose Mary will have finished college when they return from abroad.
   I suppose Mary will finish college when they return from abroad.
7. Was she sleeping?
   Had she been sleeping?
8. After July 1, I will have been studying here a year.
   After July 1, I will be studying here for a year.
9. We'll have given them more pay.
   We'll give them more pay.
10. What had she done?
    What has she done?

## SPECIAL PROBLEMS OF TENSE USAGE

### The Past Perfect Tense

The past perfect tense requires special consideration because young writers frequently fail to employ it in expressing two actions which happened at different times in the past. The function of the past perfect tense is to make clear which of the actions preceded the other.

**8d. Use the past perfect tense for the earlier of two past actions.**

NONSTANDARD Suddenly she remembered (past) that she promised (past) to meet her at eight. [The same tense has been incorrectly used for two actions which did not happen at the same time. Since the promising preceded the remembering, the past perfect form of promise should be used.]

STANDARD Suddenly she **remembered** (past) that she **had promised** (past perfect) to meet her at eight.

NONSTANDARD Everything he told (past) me I heard (past) before. [The hearing preceded the telling.]

STANDARD Everything he **told** (past) me I **had heard** (past perfect) before.

NONSTANDARD There was (past) a beautiful park where the city dump was (past). [Since the two verbs in this sentence are in the same tense, the sentence suggests that the park and the dump were there together.]

STANDARD There **was** (past) a beautiful park where the city dump **had been** (past perfect). [The past perfect *had been* makes it clear that the dump was there before the park.]

STANDARD There **had been** (past perfect) a beautiful park where the city dump **was** (past). [Making the other verb past perfect reverses the time order; the park preceded the dump.]

**8e. Avoid the use of *would have* in "if clauses" expressing the earlier of two past actions. Use the past perfect.**

NONSTANDARD If he would have worked harder, he'd have made the honor roll.

STANDARD If he **had worked** harder, he'd have made the honor roll.

NONSTANDARD If I would have thought of it, I'd have called for you.

STANDARD If I **had thought** of it, I'd have called for you.

**EXERCISE 16.** Correct the following sentences, which contain errors in the use of tenses. Refer, if necessary, to the rules on pages 145–48 for the uses of the various tenses.

1. The class officers canceled the party after I made all the arrangements for it.

2. Debbie based her decision on the old proverb that honesty was the best policy.
3. By the time I graduate, my sister will be practicing law for five years.
4. Even though his innocence was previously proved, he was not released.
5. If you would have been here earlier, you'd have met Maria.
6. When I finally got to the dentist, my tooth already stopped hurting.
7. The company hired Ms. Littmann because she lived for many years in Japan.
8. We thought that Bill went already.
9. We especially enjoyed a speech given by a woman who was in the People's Republic of China.
10. When I introduced them, they acted as if they never met before.
11. He already lost confidence in himself a long time before he was fired.
12. By that time we will make new arrangements for our trip.
13. If she would have asked me, I could have helped her.
14. The police said they thought we probably imagined the whole incident.
15. If we had matches, we could have built a fire.
16. When I was doing my homework last night, I was sure I took down the assignment correctly in class.
17. By the end of the summer, I will be working here two years.
18. When we totaled the scores, we found that we won by twenty points.
19. If we would have stayed at home, we'd have missed a good show.
20. The receptionist thought that Dr. Berg has been out of town until this morning.
21. I was surprised to learn that the world's highest mountains were in Asia.
22. I expect that when I am twenty-one, I will be in Omaha five years.
23. If he would have applied himself, he would have made the team.

24. Next Saturday my father and mother will be married twenty-five years.
25. He would have done better in college if he was better prepared in high school.

## *Having* with the Past Participle

**8f. In participial phrases, use *having* with the past participle to express action completed before another action.**

NONSTANDARD Being absent for the midterm exam, I was given a makeup test. [The present participle *being* is incorrectly used to express an action which had obviously been completed *before* the second action in the sentence.]

STANDARD **Having been** absent for the midterm exam, I **was** given a makeup test.

NONSTANDARD Making her decision, Gloria stuck to it. [The decision had to be made *before* she could stick to it.]

STANDARD **Having made** her decision, Gloria **stuck** to it. [This idea may also be properly expressed by using the word *after* before the present participle: **After** making her decision, Gloria stuck to it.]

## The Present and the Perfect Infinitives

**8g. Use the present infinitive (*to go, to see,* etc.) to express action following another action.**

NONSTANDARD The children were disappointed because they had hoped to have gone with us. [What had the children hoped, *to have gone* or *to go?* The present infinitive *to go* should be used because the action it expresses follows the action of the verb *had hoped.*]

STANDARD The children were disapppointed because they **had hoped to go** with us.

NONSTANDARD He intended to have written to all of us. [Was his intention *to have written* or *to write?*]

STANDARD He **intended to write** to all of us.

**8h. Use the perfect infinitive (*to have gone, to have seen,* etc.) to express action before another action.**

EXAMPLE **I am** glad **to have seen** that movie. [The action expressed by the perfect infinitive *to have seen* came before the time of the other verb *am.*]

**EXERCISE 17.** The sentences in this exercise contain errors in the use of tense and in the use of the present participle and the infinitive. Correct the sentences according to the rules you have just studied. You will not need to change more than one verb or verbal for each sentence. Discuss your corrections in class before doing Exercise 18.

1. Spending three hours on a review of chemistry, we then worked on irregular French verbs.
2. I should have liked to have met them.
3. I reread my book review that I typed yesterday.
4. We gained two hours when we flew from Missouri to California because the sun rose in the east.
5. We wanted to have avoided any controversy.
6. Sometime before the bus leaves, I will finish packing.
7. They already ate dinner when I stopped by.
8. We were hoping to have had a short-answer test in history instead of an essay exam.
9. If you told me you were going shopping, I would have gone with you.
10. By the time dinner was ready, I did all my math homework.

**EXERCISE 18.** The following sentences contain errors in the use of tense and in the use of the present participle and the infinitive. Correct the sentences.

1. I had hoped to have been a successful writer.

2. Working after school for the whole year, Nina did not work during the summer.
3. They were shocked to have learned that diamonds were merely a form of carbon.
4. If the team won, we would have celebrated.
5. Becoming ill during the morning, I went home at noon.
6. I hoped to have seen you on my trip to Chicago.
7. By Saturday I will be working here three weeks.
8. We should have liked to have met your sister.
9. If I didn't eat breakfast this morning, I'd have been on time.
10. By the time George returned my book, I already bought a new one.

## ACTIVE AND PASSIVE VOICE

A verb is in the *active* voice when it expresses an action performed *by* its subject. A verb is in the *passive* voice when it expresses an action performed *upon* its subject or when the subject is the result of the action.

ACTIVE VOICE The car hit a tree. [subject acting]

PASSIVE VOICE The tree was hit by a car. [subject acted upon]

All transitive verbs (those that take objects) can be used in the passive voice. Instead of the usual situation in which the verb expresses an action performed by the subject and affecting the object, a passive construction has the subject receiving the action. Compare the following sentences.

ACTIVE VOICE On the third strike the catcher (S) dropped (V) the ball (O).

PASSIVE VOICE On the third strike the ball (S) was dropped (V) by the catcher.

On the third strike the ball (S) was dropped (V).

As you can see, to form the passive construction, the object of the active sentence is moved ahead of the verb and becomes the subject. A form of *be* is added to the verb, and the subject of the active sentence is either expressed in a prepositional phrase or dropped.

Notice that in the passive voice the main verb is always a past participle and that the tense is expressed by an appropriate form of *be*.

ACTIVE Experienced pilots **fly** these planes.
PASSIVE These planes **are flown** by experienced pilots.

ACTIVE The sexton usually **rang** the church bell.
PASSIVE The church bell **was** usually **rung** by the sexton.

## The Retained Object

Active sentences that have direct objects often have indirect objects as well. When they do, either the direct or indirect object can become the subject in a passive construction:

S V IO O
ACTIVE The manager gave them free tickets.

S V
PASSIVE They were given free **tickets** (by the manager).

S V
PASSIVE Free tickets were given **them** (by the manager).

In both of the passive sentences above, one of the objects has been made the subject and the other continues to function as a complement of the verb. In the first sentence the direct object is retained as a complement; in the second it is the indirect object that is retained. The object that continues to function as a complement in a passive construction is called a *retained object.*

## Use of Passive Voice

The choice between the active or passive voice of any particular verb is usually a matter of taste, not of correctness. However, it is important to remember that a passive verb is usually less forceful than an active one and that a long succession of passive verbs usually produces an awkward and unpleasant effect.

AWKWARD PASSIVE At the beginning of his senior year, a secondhand typewriter was purchased by Bill, and a course in typing was signed up for by him.

ACTIVE At the beginning of his senior year, Bill purchased a secondhand typewriter and signed up for a course in typing.

WEAK PASSIVE The game was won when a home run was hit by Luis.

ACTIVE Luis won the game by hitting a home run.

WEAK PASSIVE An exciting game was expected by everyone, but a victory was predicted by no one.

ACTIVE Everyone expected an exciting game, but no one predicted a victory.

SUCCESSION OF PASSIVES We *were invited* by Dr. Rowland to see her famous collection of precious stones. A large table *had been placed* in the center of her study. The green cloth by which the table *was covered was removed* by Dr. Rowland, and a glittering collection of exquisite jewels *was revealed* beneath the glass top of the table. Although we *were delighted* by the display, there were so many precious stones that they *could* not *be* fully *appreciated* by us. It *was concluded* by all of us that we *would be* more *impressed* by one beautiful ruby than by a dozen.

**8i. Use the passive voice sparingly. Avoid weak and awkward passives. In the interest of variety, avoid long passages in which all the verbs are passive.**

There are, however, some qualifications of this general rule which should be mentioned. The passive voice is particularly useful in two common situations.

**(1) Use the passive voice to express an action in which the actor is unknown.**

EXAMPLE The door **had been closed** before we arrived.

**(2) Use the passive voice to express an action in which it is desirable not to disclose the actor.**

EXAMPLE A mistake **has been made** in issuing this order.

In some instances the passive voice is more convenient and just as effective as the active voice. The following passive sentences are entirely acceptable.

The laser **was invented** by an American.

We **were drenched** by the rain and **frozen** by the icy wind.

Miss Green, who **is** very well **liked** by the students, **has been invited** to act as chaperon.

Remember, however, that, in general, the active voice is stronger than the passive and less likely to get you into stylistic difficulties.

**EXERCISE 19.** Revise the following sentences by changing the passive verbs to active verbs wherever you think the change is desirable. If you think the passive is preferable, copy the sentence unchanged.

1. After the car had been washed by us, it was waxed and polished by the garage attendant.
2. We were held spellbound by Lieutenant Douglas as a number of his harrowing experiences in the Air Force were related by him.
3. A formal protest against the location of the new school building has been presented by the Student Council, which was urged on by the entire student body.
4. The rules of the school must be understood and followed by every student.
5. Since dinner had been prepared by the girls, the dishes were washed by the boys.
6. Gunpowder was invented by the Chinese long before its use was known in Europe.
7. Her new, high-heeled shoes were worn by her to the dance.
8. The new surprise play which had been taught to the team on Thursday was completely forgotten by them in the game on Saturday.

9. Janet Chen was known and liked by everybody.
10. Because proof of his accusations could not be provided by Mr. Brown, the case against the accused man had to be dropped by the FBI.

## THE SUBJUNCTIVE MOOD

Verbs may be in one of three moods: *indicative, imperative,* or *subjunctive.* Almost all the verbs you use are in the *indicative mood.* The *imperative mood* is used to express a request or a command.

IMPERATIVE **Draw** a circle around the verb phrase.
Please **reply** to this letter as soon as possible.

The only common uses of the subjunctive mood in modern English are to express a condition contrary to fact and to express a wish. These uses occur mainly in formal standard English and usually apply to only one verb form —*were.* The following partial conjugation of *be* will show how the subjunctive mood differs from the indicative.

| ***Present Indicative*** | | ***Present Subjunctive*** | |
|---|---|---|---|
| *Singular* | *Plural* | *Singular* | *Plural* |
| I am | we are | (if) I be | (if) we be |
| you are | you are | (if) you be | (if) you be |
| he is | they are | (if) he be | (if) they be |

The present subjunctive is used only in certain rather formal situations.

EXAMPLES I suggested that she **be** admitted to membership.
Mr. Black insists that I **be** reimbursed.
I move that she **be** reprimanded.

| ***Past Indicative*** | | ***Past Subjunctive*** | |
|---|---|---|---|
| *Singular* | *Plural* | *Singular* | *Plural* |
| I was | we were | (if) I were | (if) we were |
| you were | you were | (if) you were | (if) you were |
| he was | they were | (if) he were | (if) they were |

**8j. The subjunctive *were* is usually used in contrary-to-fact statements (after *if* or *as though*) and in statements expressing a wish.**

CONTRARY TO FACT If I **were** [not *was*] you, I'd save the money. [I am not you.]

If he **were** [not *was*] taller, he'd be a champion. [He is not taller.]

She talked as though she **were** [not *was*] my mother. [She is not my mother.]

WISH I wish it **were** [not *was*] true.

I wish she **were** [not *was*] my adviser.

**REVIEW EXERCISE A.** Some of the following sentences contain errors in the use of verbs. Others are correct. Number in a column on your paper 1–25. If the verbs in a sentence are correct, place a plus (+) after the corresponding number on your paper. If a verb is incorrect, write the correct form after the proper number.

1. If I was her mother, I'd speak to her sharply.
2. We lay logs under the boat and used them as rollers.
3. I had forgotten that Labor Day is a holiday.
4. Instead of working, I would have preferred to have gone to the game.
5. If he weren't so lazy, he'd be a good student.
6. When he entered the bank, the custodian discovered that the vault was opened during the night.
7. If you would have told the truth, you would have been forgiven.
8. The pilot of a search plane spotted wreckage laying at the bottom of a ravine.
9. As the warm air rises, the cool air pushes in beneath it.
10. If I was a year older, I could get a driver's license.
11. Survivors swum to the raft and pulled themselves up on it.
12. If you had taken your time, you would not have had an accident.
13. The driver did not see the second of the two children who run into the path of the car.

14. Would you have preferred to go to the movies?
15. When his new orders come through, Captain Martin was on his way overseas.
16. When I opened my locker, I discovered that somebody took my notebook.
17. Her mother found her lying at the foot of the stairs.
18. If he were a more liberal thinker, I'd vote for him.
19. I am not sure whether she seen us.
20. As we stepped through the door we realized that someone entered the house ahead of us.
21. I had just lain down when I heard the doorbell.
22. Ms. Stern told us that the Mississippi was the largest river in the United States.
23. If the judge would have listened to me, I'm sure she would not have fined me.
24. When we added our profits, we found we made more than a hundred dollars.
25. Was it Jean who give you the assignment?

**REVIEW EXERCISE B.** Some of the following sentences contain errors in the use of verbs. Others are correct. Number your paper 1–25. If the verbs in a sentence are correct, make a + after the proper number. If a verb is incorrect, write the correct form after the proper number.

1. Both armies laid down their arms willingly.
2. She couldn't remember where she had lain the book.
3. Several of us were setting on the steps.
4. I thought the sharp blow had broke my watch.
5. If I was Coretta, I'd let well enough alone.
6. The pond has not yet frozen over.
7. It wasn't until the third quarter that the team begun to play better.
8. If you would have called, we would have picked you up.
9. When I graduate from college, she will be married for three years.
10. He was still living in the house where he lived since 1970.
11. Please set the phonograph in the corner.

12. When I got to the station, I found the bus already left.
13. Were you at home when Tom come to the house?
14. I just laid down for a short nap when the phone rang.
15. Would you have preferred to have flown back?
16. If you had time, how would you have answered the question?
17. We laid a fire but did not light it.
18. The cost of living seems to raise every year.
19. We swum for an hour before lunch.
20. You should have lain there until help came.
21. I would like to have seen the performance.
22. As we were chasing him, he run into a man carrying a basket of feathers.
23. At the time you met her, she recently broke her leg and was using crutches.
24. We finally found our way back to the corner at which we made the wrong turn.
25. We found it laying at the foot of the stairs.

Chapter 9

# Correct Use of Modifiers

## Forms of Adjectives and Adverbs; Comparison

An adjective modifies a noun or a pronoun. An adverb may modify a verb, an adjective, or another adverb. These are familiar statements, but applying them to usage is sometimes difficult. Should you say "went quick" or "went quickly," "tastes strong" or "tastes strongly," "played good" or "played well"? These and other usage problems are discussed in this chapter.

### ADJECTIVE AND ADVERB FORMS

Before reviewing the usage of adjectives and adverbs, you should make sure that you are able to tell which is the adjective form of a word and which is the adverb form. The fact that most adverbs end in *-ly* (*clearly, happily, eagerly*) will be helpful if you understand that not *all* adverbs end in *-ly* and that a few common adjectives do end in *-ly*. Some words have the same form whether used as an adjective or as an adverb.

The list that follows includes a number of common adjectives and adverbs with identical forms. It also includes some adjectives ending in *-ly*. Remember that the *-ly* ending is not always a sign that a word is an adverb.

| ADJECTIVES | ADVERBS | ADJECTIVES ENDING IN –LY |
|---|---|---|
| a *fast* ball | She ran *fast.* | *daily* practice |
| a *slow* trip | Go *slow.* | *friendly* people |
| *hard* candy | She works *hard.* | *early* bird |
| a *tight* fit | Hold *tight.* | *kindly* gentleman |
| a *long* job | She worked *long.* | *lively* child |
| a *loud* noise | He sang *loud.* | *homely* dog |
| a *late* train | He came *late.* | *lovely* island |
| a *low* bridge | Swing *low.* | *elderly* person |
| a *straight* road | Go *straight.* | *lonely* feeling |

**9a. Linking verbs, especially the verbs of sense (*taste, smell, feel,* etc.), are often followed by an adjective. Action verbs are often followed by an adverb.**

EXAMPLES The dinner tasted **delicious.** [The adjective *delicious* is correct after the linking verb *tasted.* It modifies the subject *dinner.*]

Everyone felt **happy.** [The adjective *happy* is correct after the linking verb *felt.* It modifies the subject *everyone.*]

Some verbs may be used as either linking or action verbs. When they are used as action verbs, the modifier which follows modifies the verb rather than the subject and is, therefore, an adverb; for example, *looked* may be used as a linking verb and as an action verb.

EXAMPLES She looked **sleepy.** [After the linking verb *looked,* the adjective *sleepy* is correct. It modifies *she.*]

She looked **sleepily** in my direction. [After the action verb *looked,* the adverb *sleepily* is correct. It modifies *looked.*]

When you are in doubt as to whether a verb is a linking verb or not, try substituting for it a form of *seem,* which is always a linking verb. If the substitution can be made without greatly changing the meaning of the sentence, the verb is a linking verb and should be followed by an adjective.

EXAMPLES She looked sleepy. [*She seemed sleepy* gives about the same meaning; hence *looked* is a linking verb.]

She looked sleepily in my direction. [*She seemed sleepily in my direction* does not make sense; hence *looked* is not a linking verb in this sentence.]

**9b. In making a choice between an adjective and an adverb, ask yourself what the word modifies. If it modifies a noun or pronoun, choose the adjective. If it modifies a verb, choose the adverb.**

PROBLEM We built a raft (strong, strongly) enough to hold us.

SOLUTION We built a raft **strong** enough to hold us. [The adjective *strong* modifies the noun *raft*.]

PROBLEM Has he been studying math (regular, regularly)?

SOLUTION Has he been studying math **regularly?** [The adverb *regularly* modifies the action verb *has been studying*.]

**EXERCISE 1.** Number your paper 1–20. Select the correct one of the two words in parentheses in each sentence and write it after the proper number. If the word modifies the subject, select the adjective; if it modifies the verb, select the adverb. Remember that a linking verb is followed by an adjective.

1. The sled's runners slid (smooth, smoothly) over the ice.
2. The weather outside looks (miserable, miserably).
3. Plan your outline as (careful, carefully) as possible.
4. The official explanation of the budget cut sounds (incredible, incredibly).
5. Why was she looking at me (suspicious, suspiciously)?
6. This apple tastes (peculiar, peculiarly) to me.
7. Don't feel (glum, glumly) about missing the game.
8. You can watch (contented, contentedly) from the sidelines.
9. Dawn goes jogging (regular, regularly).
10. He disappeared (quiet, quietly) behind the curtain.
11. The conference room smelled (stuffy, stuffily).
12. At the end of the first act, we all applauded (enthusiastic, enthusiastically).

13. The stage manager appeared (sudden, suddenly).
14. She spoke (serious, seriously) to the audience.
15. "The leading lady in the play," she said, "is feeling (sick, sickly)."
16. "She is resting (comfortable, comfortably) backstage."
17. "Her understudy will take over the lead (temporary, temporarily)."
18. The understudy seemed (nervous, nervously) to the audience.
19. After a while she was saying her lines (easy, easily).
20. The audience felt (happy, happily) for the understudy.

## *Bad* and *Badly*

*Bad* is an adjective modifying nouns and pronouns. *Badly* is an adverb, modifying verbs, adjectives, and adverbs. Since the verbs of sense—*feel, smell, taste, sound*—are followed by an adjective (not an adverb) modifying their subjects, it is standard English to say *feel bad, smell bad,* etc.

She feels very bad about her failure.

The stockyards smell bad.

The common expression *feel badly,* however, has, through usage, become acceptable English, although ungrammatical. Used with other verbs of sense, *badly* is not yet standard. Do not say *smell badly, taste badly,* etc.

## *Well* and *Good*

*Well* may be used as either an adjective or an adverb. As an adjective, *well* has three meanings.

1. *To be in good health:*

   He feels **well.**[1] He seems **well.**

2. *To appear well-dressed or well-groomed:*

   She looks **well** in that dress.

[1] *He feels* GOOD is also correct, though its meaning is not limited to health. Example: He feels GOOD about the new job offer.

3. *To be satisfactory:*

   All is **well.**

As an adverb, *well* means to perform an action capably.

> She sang very **well.**

*Good* is always an adjective. It should never be used to modify a verb.

| | |
|---|---|
| NONSTANDARD | The team played good today. |
| STANDARD | The team played **well** today. |
| NONSTANDARD | They work very good together. |
| STANDARD | They work very **well** together. |

### *Slow* and *Slowly*

*Slow* is used as both an adjective and an adverb. *Slowly* is an adverb. Except for the expressions *Drive slow* and *Go slow,* which have become acceptable because of their wide use on highways signs, *slow* should be used only as an adjective.

**EXERCISE 2.** Number your paper 1–25. If the *italicized* modifier in a sentence is correct, write a + after the proper number on your paper. If it is incorrect, write the correct form, and after the correct form write the word it modifies.

1. The old car held up fairly *good.*
2. We were surprised to find the patient looking so *well.*
3. I always do my homework as *speedy* as I can.
4. Some of the food tasted *bad.*
5. Work *slow,* and you will make fewer mistakes.
6. Jean appeared quite *happy.*
7. I can do these errands *easy.*
8. Was George feeling very *bad?*
9. Her clothes never fit her very *good.*
10. The family felt *bitterly* about Aunt Fran's will.
11. Drive *careful.*
12. Nancy looks *well* in blue.

13. I was afraid you had been hurt *bad.*
14. Their voices blended *beautiful* with one another.
15. We couldn't hear very *good* because of the storm.
16. Isn't it possible for you to drive *slowly?*
17. She looked *hopefully* in my direction.
18. The prisoners said they had been treated very *unfair.*
19. If the food smells *bad,* throw it away.
20. Each of us wrote the assignment down *separate.*
21. Before the game, things looked *badly* for our team.
22. She speaks French too *rapid* for me.
23. Ms. Ames always speaks *sharp.*
24. I crept *cautiously* up the stairs.
25. The class had been behaving very *bad.*

## COMPARISON OF ADJECTIVES AND ADVERBS

**9c. *Comparison* is the name given to the change in the form of adjectives and adverbs when they are used to compare the degree of the qualities they express. There are three degrees of comparison: *positive, comparative,* and *superlative.***

| POSITIVE | COMPARATIVE | SUPERLATIVE |
|---|---|---|
| big | bigger | biggest |
| anxious | more anxious | most anxious |
| cheaply | more cheaply | most cheaply |
| fast | faster | fastest |
| easily | more easily | most easily |

### Comparative and Superlative Forms

**(1) Most adjectives and adverbs of one syllable form their comparative and superlative degrees by adding *–er* and *–est.***

| POSITIVE | COMPARATIVE | SUPERLATIVE |
|---|---|---|
| long | longer | longest |
| hard | harder | hardest |
| cold | colder | coldest |

**(2) Some adjectives of two syllables form their comparative and superlative degrees by adding *–er* or *–est;* other adjectives of two syllables form their comparative and superlative degrees by means of *more* and *most.***

When you are in doubt as to how a word is compared, consult an unabridged dictionary.

| POSITIVE | COMPARATIVE | SUPERLATIVE |
|---|---|---|
| happy | happier | happiest |
| eager | more eager | most eager |

**(3) Adjectives of more than two syllables and adverbs ending in *–ly* usually form their comparative and superlative degrees by means of *more* and *most.***

| POSITIVE | COMPARATIVE | SUPERLATIVE |
|---|---|---|
| capable | more capable | most capable |
| rapidly | more rapidly | most rapidly |

**(4) Comparison to indicate less or least of a quality is accomplished by using the words *less* and *least* before the adjective or adverb.**

| POSITIVE | COMPARATIVE | SUPERLATIVE |
|---|---|---|
| bright | less bright | least bright |
| excited | less excited | least excited |
| willingly | less willingly | least willingly |

## Irregular Comparison

Adjectives and adverbs that do not follow the regular methods of forming their comparative and superlative degrees are said to be compared irregularly.

| POSITIVE | COMPARATIVE | SUPERLATIVE |
|---|---|---|
| bad | worse | worst |
| good, well | better | best |
| many, much | more | most |

**EXERCISE 3.** Write the comparative and superlative forms of the following words. Use a dictionary.

1. tall
2. beautiful
3. few
4. short
5. graceful
6. satisfactory
7. ill
8. little
9. industrious
10. bravely
11. bad
12. casually
13. reckless
14. clear
15. good
16. humble
17. dear
18. stealthy
19. diligently
20. small

## Use of Comparatives and Superlatives

**9d. Use the comparative degree when comparing two things; use the superlative degree when comparing more than two.**

COMPARISON OF TWO THINGS

Although both Laura and Ted wrote on the same topic, Laura's paper was **longer** [not *longest*].

The doctors tried both penicillin and sulfanilamide; the penicillin proved to be the **more** [not *most*] **effective** drug.

Gail is the **more** capable one of the twins.

COMPARISON OF MORE THAN TWO THINGS

I chose this book because it was the **shortest** [not *shorter*] of the **three.**

One of the **three** branches of the armed services, the Air Force has been the **most** [not *more*] **favored** in recent years.

Which of the **twenty-eight** flavors is the **most** popular?

▶ **USAGE NOTE** Rule 9d describes a practice generally observed by writers of formal English. In informal speech and writing, however, the superlative is often used for emphasis, even though only two things are being compared:

INFORMAL Which book did you like best, *Moby Dick* or *The Scarlet Letter?* [formal: *better*]

Of the two readings of *Hamlet,* Gielgud's interpretation is the most interesting to me.

**9e. Include the word *other* or *else* when comparing one thing with a group of which it is a part.**

NONSTANDARD At the end of World War II, the United States was stronger than any country in the world. [Since the United States is one of the countries in the world, this sentence says illogically that it was stronger than itself.]

STANDARD At the end of World War II, the United States was stronger than any **other** country in the world.

NONSTANDARD He has better marks than anyone in his grade. [He is a member of his grade; he cannot have better marks than himself.]

STANDARD He has better marks than anyone **else** in his grade.

**9f. Avoid double comparisons.**

A double comparison is one in which the degree is formed incorrectly by adding *-er* or *-est* in addition to using *more* or *most.*

NONSTANDARD She is a more prettier girl than I.

STANDARD She is a **prettier** girl than I.

NONSTANDARD She is the most happiest child I know.

STANDARD She is the **happiest** child I know.

**EXERCISE 4.** Number your paper 1–25. For each correct sentence, write a + after the proper number; revise each incorrect sentence and write the sentence correctly.

1. Speak to her gentle.
2. I played as good as she did.
3. Bill works harder than any boy in his group.
4. Whatever she does, she does well.
5. If negotiations proceed too slowly, the work will not be completed this year.
6. Since there were two recommended procedures, the committee had to decide which one would be best.
7. To our palates the highly seasoned food tasted strangely.
8. Try to speak as convincingly as you can.
9. Chloe arrived unexpectedly and took charge of the meeting.

10. His greeting was more friendlier than hers.
11. When the tide is in, the water is many feet more deep.
12. Although he writes badly, his books are popular.
13. *Gone with the Wind* sold better than any American novel.
14. The judges were given ten manuscripts and asked to select the best one.
15. Eat moderate, and you will lose weight.
16. The tiger rushed menacing toward me.
17. I found Mrs. Trumbull the most cooperative of the two women.
18. Has she been working regular?
19. The entire menu looked good to us.
20. Three jobs faced us, and we did the easier one first.
21. Pine Lake has the most clearest water.
22. I didn't believe she could act as stubborn as that.
23. She makes up her mind too slow.
24. Jean is a lot truthfuller than her brother.
25. When she ran out of money, she felt too proudly to borrow.

# Chapter 10

# Glossary of Usage

Chapters 6 through 9 of this book describe the conventions of standard English usage observed by most careful users of the language in matters of agreement, and in verb, pronoun, and modifier usage. In addition to vocabulary, these are the major areas in which standard English differs from nonstandard English.

There are, however, a number of special usage problems which require separate treatment. These are presented here in the glossary.

## SUMMARY: LEVELS OF USAGE

### *Standard English*

| | |
|---|---|
| Informal | The everyday language of people who observe the conventions of English usage, suitable for all but the most formal occasions. |
| Formal | The language of most serious speakers when they take special pains to say the correct thing; appropriate for all serious writing and speaking, but suitable in any situation. |

### *Nonstandard English*

Idiomatic usages and dialects identifiably different from standard English; most often less appropriate than standard English for widespread communication. Sometimes suitable for special, but not general, purposes.

If you are not sure of these terms after reading the brief summary, review Chapter 5, in which they are discussed in detail.

In doing the exercises in this chapter, as well as those in other parts of the book, follow the conventions of standard formal English.

The items in this glossary are arranged in alphabetical order, with exercises interspersed. Problems of spelling such as the difference between *already* and *all ready* and similar words often confused are taken up on pages 661–69, included in the chapter on spelling.

**accept, except** *Accept* is a verb; it means "to receive." *Except* as a verb means "to leave out"; as a preposition it means "excluding."

We **accept** your invitation with pleasure.

If you **except** her freshman grades, she has a good scholastic average.

My grades are satisfactory in every subject **except** English.

**adapt, adopt** *Adapt* means "to change in order to fit or be more suitable, to adjust." *Adopt* means "to take something and make it one's own."

To survive, an animal must **adapt** to its environment.

Some long novels have been **adapted** for young readers.

They **adopted** their physician's suggestion and **adopted** a baby.

**affect, effect** *Affect* is usually a verb; it means "to impress" or "to influence (frequently the mind or feelings)." *Effect* as a verb means "to accomplish, to bring about." *Effect* as a noun means "the result of some action."

How did the defeat **affect** the team?

A number of improvements were **effected** [brought about] by the new student council.

**Effects** [results] of the strike were felt everywhere.

**all the farther, all the faster** Used informally in some parts of the country to mean "as far as, as fast as."

DIALECT I did not know that was all the faster the car would go.

STANDARD I did not know that was **as fast as** the car would go.

**allusion, illusion** An *allusion* is a reference to something. An *illusion* is a mistaken idea.

Her writing is full of classical **allusions.**

In spite of the evidence, she clung to her **illusions.**

**alumni, alumnae** *Alumni* (pronounced ə·lum′nī) is the plural of *alumnus* (male graduate). *Alumnae* (pronounced ə·lum′nē) is the plural of *alumna* (female graduate). The graduates of a coeducational school are referred to (as a group) as *alumni.*

All of my sisters are **alumnae** of Adams High School.

I attended a reunion of Boys' High School **alumni.**

Every high school should keep track of its **alumni.**

**amount, number** Use *amount* to refer to a singular word; use *number* to refer to a plural word.

A large **amount** of money (singular) **was** in the drawer.

A large **number** of coins (plural) **were** in the drawer.

**and etc.** Since *etc.* is an abbreviation of the Latin *et cetera,* which means "and other things," you are using *and* twice when you write "and etc." The *etc.* is sufficient.

STANDARD We carry a complete stock of newspapers, magazines, stationery, school supplies, tobacco, candy, **etc.** [not *and etc.*]

**and which, but which** The expressions *and which, but which* (*and who, but who*) should be used only when a *which* (or *who*) clause precedes them in the sentence.

NONSTANDARD The public was shocked by the council's revelations and which the commissioner had tried to suppress.

STANDARD The public was shocked by the revelations **which** the council published **and which** the commissioner had tried to suppress.

STANDARD The public was shocked by the council's revelations **which** the commissioner had tried to suppress.

**anywheres, everywheres, nowheres** Use these words and others like them *without* the final *s*.

We looked **everywhere,** but the children were **nowhere** in sight; they could not be found **anywhere.**

**at** Do not use *at* after *where.*

NONSTANDARD Where were you staying at?

STANDARD **Where** were you staying?

**EXERCISE 1.** The sentences in this exercise contain usage problems presented on the preceding pages in the glossary. Number your paper 1–20. Write after the proper number on your paper the standard one of the two words in parentheses.

1. Some pets find it hard to (adapt, adopt) to city life.
2. This new product has had a harmful (affect, effect) on some people.
3. Does this poem contain any (allusions, illusions) to Homer's *Odyssey?*
4. Jane and Nina are (alumni, alumnae) of our school.
5. I own a large (number, amount) of campaign buttons.
6. During my travels in Europe, I met Americans (everywheres, everywhere).

7. Everyone likes peanut butter (accept, except) you.
8. One of the two lines looks longer because of an optical (allusion, illusion).
9. We all (adapted, adopted) the resolution to have a class picnic.
10. A fund-raising letter went out to all (alumni, alumnae) of the state university.
11. This is (all the farther, as far as) I can run.
12. How does humidity (affect, effect) the speed of sound?
13. Everyone (accept, except) Janet and me applied there.
14. I hope that at least one college will (accept, except) me for admission next year.
15. Ms. Benchley is an (alumna, alumnus) of Reed College.
16. Were any crops (affected, effected) by this year's dry spell?
17. The quiz-show contestant won a large (amount, number) of points by correctly answering questions on geography.
18. The expression "lock, stock, and barrel" is an (allusion, illusion) to the parts of a flintlock rifle.
19. Please (accept, except) my congratulations.
20. The ending of the movie had a great emotional (affect, effect) on the audience.

**bad, badly** See page 164.

**because** The use of *because* after *reason is* ("The reason is because . . .") is common in informal English, but it is generally avoided in formal writing. In a sentence beginning "The reason is . . .," the clause following the verb is a noun clause used as a predicate nominative. A noun clause may begin with *that* but not with *because,* which usually introduces an adverb clause.

ACCEPTABLE The reason she refused to go was **that** [not *because*] she had no money.

BETTER She refused to go **because** she had no money.

**being as, being that** Nonstandard English when used for *since* or *because.*

NONSTANDARD Being as my mother was away, I had to do the housework.

STANDARD **Because** my mother was away, I had to do the housework.

**beside, besides** *Beside* means "by the side of" someone or something. *Besides* means "in addition to."

Who sits **beside** you in English class?

**Besides** my homework, I have an errand to run.

**between, among** The distinction in meaning between these words is usually observed in formal English. Use *between* when you are thinking of two items at a time, regardless of whether they are part of a group of more than two.

The ball went **between** Karen and her.

Do you know the difference **between** a Pomeranian, a Pekingese, and a Chihuahua? [*Between* is correct because the speaker is thinking of one dog and another dog—*two at a time.*]

What is the difference **between** the four plans?

Use *among* when you are thinking of a group rather than of separate individuals.

She is never at ease **among** strangers.

Petitions were circulated **among** the voters.

We had ten dollars **among** the five of us.

**bring, take** Use *bring* when the meaning is to convey something *to the person speaking.* Use *take* when the meaning is to convey something *away from the person speaking. Bring* is related to *come; take* is related to *go.*

When you **come** back, **bring** your textbooks, pencils, and paper.

Will you please **take** [not bring] this note to your parents when you go home?

**can't hardly, can't scarcely** See *Double negative* (pages 190–91).

**can't help but** See *Double negative* (page 191).

**could of** Sometimes carelessly written for *could have.* Do not write *of* for *have.* Similar expressions frequently written incorrectly are *ought to of, might of, must of.*

NONSTANDARD She could of warned me about the dangerous roads.

STANDARD She could **have** warned me about the dangerous roads.

**credible, creditable, credulous** Sometimes confused because of their similarity, these words have quite different meanings.

*Credible* means "believable."

Such a ridiculous story is hardly **credible.**

*Creditable* means "praiseworthy."

For a beginner, she gave a **creditable** performance.

*Credulous* means "inclined to believe just about anything."

Being **credulous,** she is often fooled by practical jokes.

**data** The plural form of the Latin *datum.* In standard informal English, *data* is frequently used, like a collective noun, with a singular pronoun and verb.

INFORMAL This data was collected by the committee.

However, since *data* has only recently become acceptable as a singular word, you will be safer if, in your writing, you use the word as a plural. See **phenomena.**

FORMAL **These data were** collected by the committee.

**discover, invent** Do not use *invent* to mean "discover." *Invent* means "to make something not known before, to bring something into existence." *Discover* means "to find something which has been in existence but unknown."

Edison **invented** the electric light.

Astronomers **are** still **discovering** new stars.

**done** Not the past form of *do*. *Done* always needs a helping verb: *has done, was done, will be done,* etc. The past form of *do* is *did.*

NONSTANDARD The doctors done all they could.

STANDARD The doctors **did** all they could.

STANDARD The doctors **had done** all they could.

**don't** A contraction of *do not, don't* should not be used with a singular noun or the third person of singular pronouns (*it, he, she*). Use *doesn't.* See page 97.

NONSTANDARD It don't matter to me.

STANDARD It **doesn't** matter to me.

**effect, affect** See **affect, effect.**

**emigrate, immigrate** *Emigrate* means "to go from a country" to settle elsewhere. *Immigrate* means "to come into a country" to settle there.

Residents of crowded countries have been advised to **emigrate** from their homelands to less crowded regions.

Her parents **immigrated** to this country in 1910.

**etc.** See **and etc.**

**except, accept** See **accept, except.**

**famous, notorious** Learn the specific meanings of these words. *Famous* means "well and widely known." *Notorious* means "widely known" but is used in an unfavorable sense.

Katharine Hepburn and Bette Davis are among the most **famous** American film actresses.

Jesse James is probably America's most **notorious** outlaw.

**farther** See **all the farther.**

**fewer, less** In standard formal English *fewer* (not *less*) is used before a plural noun. *Less* is used before a singular noun.

There were **fewer** [not *less*] guests at the last party.

We took in **less** money tonight.

**good, well** See pages 164–65.

**EXERCISE 2.** The sentences in this exercise contain usage problems explained on pages 175–79. Double negatives and the listed items explained elsewhere in this text are not covered. Number your paper 1–25. Write after the proper number the correct one of the two words in parentheses.

1. You can fool him easily because he is so (credulous, credible).
2. (Beside, Besides) the excellent meals, the hotel provides superb recreational facilities.
3. (Bring, Take) your cousin with you when you come to my house tonight.
4. I'll (take, bring) your letters to the post office when I go downtown.
5. It took courage to (emigrate, immigrate) from an established home and settle in the American wilderness.
6. There are (fewer, less) students enrolled here this year than last year.
7. Do you intend to divide the work (among, between) the four of us?
8. (Being that, Because) father was tired, I did the driving.
9. We have (fewer, less) honor classes this year.
10. In what year was the transistor (invented, discovered)?
11. (Among, Between) the six of us we could raise the money.
12. Please (bring, take) this card to the library when you go.

13. Has anyone (beside, besides) you heard José Feliciano?
14. You have (fewer, less) friends than she.
15. We (done, did) the lessons according to instructions in the textbook.
16. Cold weather (don't, doesn't) bother him very much.
17. To me this is not a (credulous, credible) tale.
18. With better equipment they could (of, have) completed the job sooner.
19. Our government found it necessary to discourage (immigration, emigration) into this country.
20. Will you please (take, bring) these books to Miss Barrett when you go to see her?
21. Eisenhower became (famous, notorious) as commander of the Allied forces.
22. Who (discovered, invented) the telephone?
23. (Being as, Since) they are identical twins, people frequently mix them up.
24. Shakespeare is the most (famous, notorious) dramatist ever to write in English.
25. She was promoted because of the (creditable, credible) job she had done as an administrative assistant.

**EXERCISE 3.** This exercise covers all usage items explained in the glossary to this point. Number your paper 1–33. If a sentence does not contain a usage error, write a + after the proper number on your paper. If it does contain a usage error, write the correct form. You do not have to copy whole sentences.

1. He has less friends than his brother.
2. Being as the mayor was going away, she appointed an assistant to handle emergencies.
3. How will the new laws affect the school?
4. Besides my teachers, my parents have been making me study.
5. The reason for the failure of our campaign was because we didn't work hard enough.
6. Ms. Standish threatened to sue the newspaper because of its unflattering allusions to her private life.

7. We asked directions of a very helpful police officer and who advised us to take Route 4.
8. Both of the women on the platform are alumni of a famous women's college.
9. The reward money was divided between the four women.
10. Is that all the faster you can work?
11. Please take this briefcase to your mother.
12. Mrs. Corbin hunted everywheres for her lost book.
13. In the confusion no one knew exactly where she was at.
14. Doctors are studying the effects of this new drug.
15. I found the people full of allusions about the real causes of the strike.
16. I am sure I could of done better on my test if I had had more time.
17. Without family or a job, Francis had no other choice than to emigrate.
18. I hope you will take your family when you come to Illinois this summer.
19. As you grow older, you will encounter less opportunities to change jobs.
20. He excepted our gifts with thanks.
21. Leslie expected us to use the camera which she had given us but which we had lost.
22. The amount of push-ups that he can do is incredible.
23. There is growing dissatisfaction among the students.
24. With three jobs offered to her, Paula could not decide which one to except.
25. The dance on June 20 was sponsored by the high school alumni.
26. She complains about everything: health, taxes, government, weather, children, and etc.
27. I found the new statistics almost incredible.
28. The animals seemed unable to adapt to their new environment.
29. The librarian complained about the amount of books that students had lost.
30. She made a fortune by discovering a new type of automatic transmission.

31. A notorious and widely admired athlete, she represented her country three times in the Olympic Games.
32. Anyone so credulous can be easily duped by swindlers.
33. Being as it is supposed to be a democratic country, it should have free elections.

**had of** The *of* is superfluous.

NONSTANDARD If I had of known her better, I'd have spoken to her.
STANDARD If I **had known** her better, I'd have spoken to her.

**had ought, hadn't ought** Do not use *had* with *ought.*

NONSTANDARD You had ought to read more carefully.
STANDARD You **ought** to read more carefully.

NONSTANDARD You hadn't ought to stay out so late.
STANDARD You **ought not** to stay out so late.

**he, she, they,** etc. Do not use unnecessary pronouns after a noun. This error is sometimes called the *double subject.*

NONSTANDARD My aunt she lives in California.
STANDARD My aunt lives in California.

**hisself, theirselves** These words are sometimes incorrectly used for *himself, themselves.*

NONSTANDARD He did the work hisself.
STANDARD He did the work **himself.**

**illusion, allusion** See **allusion, illusion.**

**immigrate, emigrate** See **emigrate, immigrate.**

**imply, infer** *Imply* means "to suggest something." *Infer* means "to interpret, to get a certain meaning from a remark or an action."

The speaker **implied** that she was a friend of the President's.

I **inferred** from the speaker's remarks that she was a friend of the President's.

**in, into** In standard formal usage observe the difference in meaning between these words. *In* means "within"; *into* suggests movement from the outside to the inside.

FORMAL At two o'clock we walked **into** [not *in*] the principal's office.

INFORMAL We threw some pennies in the well and made a wish.

FORMAL We threw some pennies **into** the well and made a wish.

**invent, discover** See **discover, invent.**

**kind, sort, type** In standard formal usage the adjectives *this, these, that, those* are made to agree in number with the words *kind, sort, type: this kind, these kinds; that sort, those sorts.*

I like **that kind** of oranges.

I like **those kinds** of oranges.

**kind of, sort of** In standard formal usage, avoid using these expressions to mean "rather" or "somewhat."

INFORMAL I feel kind of tired.

FORMAL I feel **rather** [*somewhat*] tired.

**kind of a, sort of a** The *a* is superfluous.

What **kind of** [not *kind of a*] pen are you using?

**lay, lie** See page 135.

**learn, teach** *Learn* means "to acquire knowledge." *Teach* means "to dispense knowledge."

I **learn** more when she **teaches** [not *learns*] me.

**leave, let** *Leave* (*left*) means "to go away." *Let* means "to allow, to permit."

NONSTANDARD Leave me work by myself.
STANDARD **Let** me work by myself.

NONSTANDARD You should have left him go.
STANDARD You should have **let** him go.

The expressions "Leave me alone" and "Let me alone" are both correct and are commonly used interchangeably. Strictly speaking, "Leave me alone" suggests that you want somebody to go away, leaving you by yourself. "Let me alone" suggests that you want somebody to stop bothering you.

**less, fewer** See **fewer, less.**

**liable** See **likely, liable.**

**lie, lay** See page 135.

**like, as** *Like* is a preposition and introduces a prepositional phrase. *As* is usually a conjunction and introduces a subordinate clause.

She walks **like her mother.** [prepositional phrase]
She walks **as her mother does.** [subordinate clause]

*Like* as a conjunction is commonly heard in informal speech, but it is unacceptable in formal English.

INFORMAL She cooks spaghetti like the Italians do.
FORMAL She cooks spaghetti **as** the Italians do.

**like, as if** *Like* should not be used for *as if* or *as though,* which are conjunctions used to introduce clauses.

INFORMAL The girls acted like they were tired.
FORMAL The girls acted **as if** [*as though*] they were tired.

**likely, liable** These words are used interchangeably in standard English, but some writers of standard formal

English prefer to observe the following distinctions:

*Likely* is used to express simple probability.

She is **likely** to answer your letter promptly.

*Liable* is used to express probability with a suggestion of harm or misfortune; it is also used to mean "responsible" or "answerable."

If you swim here, you are **liable** to be attacked by sharks.

Is a mother **liable** for her daughter's debts?

**myself, ourselves** Most careful writers of English avoid using pronouns ending in *-self, -selves* as subjects. See page 118.

Karen and **I** [not *myself*] almost always do our homework together.

**EXERCISE 4.** The sentences in this exercise cover usage problems explained in the part of the glossary that follows Exercise 3. Number your paper 1–20. If a sentence contains no error in usage, write a + after the proper number; if it contains an error, write a 0.

1. In his address to Congress, the President implied that an economic reversal might occur soon.
2. Without any warning, the cat jumped from the chair and leaped in my arms.
3. The children helped themselves to more turkey.
4. When you have time, will you learn me to sew?
5. Leave me figure this problem out by myself.
6. We had ought to have been more considerate.
7. Your room looks as if a tornado had been through it.
8. What am I to imply from your sarcastic remarks?
9. Ben did all the work himself.
10. If you had asked me, I would of told you.
11. What can you infer from the closing couplet of this sonnet?
12. You hadn't ought to complain so much.

13. Why doesn't he get his work done like he's supposed to?
14. Jane and myself are the editors of our yearbook.
15. We implied from the principal's announcement that our school's administration is becoming stricter.
16. I asked my boss if he would let me have Saturday afternoon off.
17. Some people they're always making a fuss about nothing.
18. Are you implying that I can't read music?
19. Leave them stay if they don't want to join us.
20. We cheered like we never cheered before.

**nauseated, nauseous** These words do not mean the same thing. *Nauseated* means "sick." *Nauseous* means "disgusting, sickening."

After riding on the roller coaster, the child became **nauseated.**

The **nauseous** odor of dead fish overwhelmed us.

**none** *None* may be either singular or plural. See page 88.

**notorious, famous** See **famous, notorious.**

**number** *The number* takes a singular verb. *A number* takes a plural verb. (See page 98, Rule 6s.)

**The number** of candidates **was** surprising.

**A number** of candidates **were nominated** by the committee.

**number, amount** See **amount, number.**

**of** Do not use *of* unnecessarily. See **could of, had of.**

**off of** The *of* is unnecessary.

Never jump **off** [not *off of*] a moving train.

Do not use *off* or *off of* for *from.*

NONSTANDARD I got some money off them.

STANDARD I got some money **from** them.

NONSTANDARD I borrowed the book off of my English teacher.

STANDARD I borrowed the book **from** my English teacher.

**or, nor** Use *or* with *either;* use *nor* with *neither.*

**Either** Lois **or** Helen is mistaken.

**Neither** Lois **nor** Helen is mistaken.

**ought** See **had ought.**

**persecute, prosecute** Distinguish between these words, which have quite different meanings. *Persecute* means "to attack or annoy someone," often for a person's beliefs. *Prosecute* means "to bring legal action against someone for unlawful behavior."

Hitler **persecuted** people who opposed the Nazi government.

The district attorney **will prosecute** anyone caught looting.

**phenomena** If you use this word, use it correctly. *Phenomena* is the plural form of the word *phenomenon.* Do not use it as a singular noun.

**These** [not *this*] natural **phenomena are** [not *is*] most interesting.

**This** natural **phenomenon** is most interesting.

**politics, mathematics, athletics** For the number of these words and other similar words, see pages 96–97.

**reason is because** See **because.**

**respectfully, respectively** *Respectfully* means "with respect" or "full of respect." *Respectively* means "each in the order given."

Although hostile, the audience listened **respectfully.**

*Jane Eyre, Emma,* and *Adam Bede* were written by Charlotte Brontë, Jane Austen, and George Eliot, **respectively.**

**Reverend, Honorable** These titles should never be used with a person's last name alone. In addition, the word *the* commonly precedes the titles.

NONSTANDARD Reverend Hiller, the Reverend Hiller, Honorable Hawkins.

STANDARD the Reverend Kenneth Hiller, the Reverend K. H. Hiller, the Reverend Mr. Hiller, the Reverend Dr. Hiller, the Honorable Paula Hawkins.

**rise, raise** See page 140.

**same, said, such** Avoid such artificial uses of these words as the following:

The crew worked all day on the boat and had *same* ready to sail by sundown.

We spent our summers at my aunt's ranch, and we became very fond of *said* aunt.

Jerry always wants me to let him copy my homework, but I don't approve of *such.*

**says** Commonly used incorrectly for **said.**

NONSTANDARD Jane stopped me and says, "I know where you're going."

STANDARD Jane stopped me and **said,** "I know where you're going."

**scarcely** See *Double negative* (page 190).

**shall, will** The old distinction between these words is no longer observed by most people. *Shall,* which was once considered the only correct form for the expression of the simple future in the first person, has been replaced by *will* in the speech and writing of most people.

STANDARD I **shall** consider your offer.

I **will** consider your offer.

In a few expressions *shall* is the only form ever used and so presents no usage problem: *Shall we go? Shall*

*I help you?* To use *will* in these expressions would change the meaning. With the exception of these special uses, *will* is as correct as *shall.*

**sit, set** See page 139.

**slow, slowly** See page 165.

**so** Because this word is usually overworked, avoid it in your writing whenever you can.

POOR The weather cleared, so we put up the sail and headed out to sea.

BETTER When the weather cleared, we put up the sail and headed out to sea.

BETTER Since the weather had cleared, we put up the sail and headed out to sea.

**some, somewhat** Use *somewhat* rather than *some* as an adverb.

FORMAL The rate of inflation in Europe has slowed **somewhat** [not *some*].

**take, bring** See **bring, take.**

**this here, that there** The *here* and the *there* are unnecessary.

NONSTANDARD This here book is easy to read.

STANDARD **This** book is easy to read.

**these kind, those kind** See **kind, sort, type.**

**ways** Sometimes used informally for *way* in referring to distance.

INFORMAL Although Silver Peak seemed close enough to touch, it was actually a long ways off.

FORMAL Although Silver Peak seemed close enough to touch, it was actually a long **way** off.

**well, good** See pages 164–65.

**when, where** Do not use *when* or *where* in writing a definition.

NONSTANDARD A pop foul is when the batter hits a high, short fly ball into foul territory.

STANDARD A pop foul is a high, short fly ball that is hit into foul territory.

NONSTANDARD A paradox is where a statement contradicts itself.

STANDARD A paradox is a self-contradictory statement.

**where** Do not use *where* for *that.*

NONSTANDARD I read where you are going to move away.

STANDARD I read **that** you are going to move away.

**where . . . at** See **at.**

**which, that, who** *Which* should be used to refer to things only. *That* may be used to refer to either things or people. *Who* should be used to refer to people only.

This is a book **which (that)** you would enjoy.

There is a girl **who** [not *which*] has talent.

There is a girl **that** has talent.

**who, whom** See page 112.

## The Double Negative

A double negative is a construction in which two negative words are used where one is sufficient. Formerly, double negatives were quite acceptable, but now they are considered nonstandard.

**can't hardly, can't scarcely** The words *hardly* and *scarcely* are negatives. They should never be used with negative *not.*

NONSTANDARD I can't hardly tell the difference between this year's cars and last year's.

STANDARD I **can hardly** tell the difference between this year's cars and last year's.

NONSTANDARD There wasn't scarcely enough food for everyone.

STANDARD There **was scarcely** enough food for everyone.

**can't help but** In standard formal English avoid this double negative.

FORMAL **I cannot help admiring** [not *can't help but admire*] his courage.

**haven't but, haven't only** In certain uses *but* and *only* are negatives. Avoid using them with *not*.

FORMAL We **had** [not *hadn't*] **but** a few cents in our pockets.
We **had** [not *hadn't*] **only** a few cents in our pockets.

**no, nothing, none** Not to be used with another negative word.

NONSTANDARD Haven't you no ticket?
STANDARD **Haven't** you a ticket?
STANDARD **Have** you **no** ticket?

NONSTANDARD She hasn't nothing to do.
STANDARD She **has nothing** to do.
STANDARD She **hasn't anything** to do.

NONSTANDARD He didn't give me none.
STANDARD He **gave** me **none.**
STANDARD He **didn't give** me **any.**

**EXERCISE 5.** The sentences in this exercise cover usage problems explained in the section of the glossary that follows Exercise 4. Number your paper 1–20. Write after the proper number the correct one of the two words in parentheses.

1. You may disagree with your teachers if you do so (respectfully, respectively).
2. You (can, can't) hardly afford to go to the movies every week.

3. Prospects for peace looked (some, somewhat) better.
4. Julio lives only a little (way, ways) from here.
5. Throughout history certain minorities have been cruelly (prosecuted, persecuted).
6. After she had heard our side of the story, she (says, said) we were all wrong.
7. We (haven't, have) no reason to question your honesty.
8. Neither the steamship (or, nor) the railroad has been outmoded yet.
9. We were only a little (ways, way) from home when the accident happened.
10. (This, These) strange phenomena puzzled the geologists.
11. The refugees (could, couldn't) hardly find food and shelter.
12. She insists that she (has, hasn't) done nothing wrong.
13. I (have, haven't) only a short time for my homework.
14. The French Club and the German Club will meet in rooms 41 and 525, (respectively, respectfully).
15. She would neither let me tell her the right answer (or, nor) let me give her any other help.
16. We (had, hadn't) but one choice to make.
17. I acquired a great respect for the Romans (whom, which) we studied in Latin class.
18. The superintendent said there wasn't (any, no) reason for closing school.
19. An hour after dinner I felt (nauseous, nauseated).
20. The boys insisted they (had, hadn't) nothing to do with the practical joke.

**REVIEW EXERCISE.** The sentences in this exercise cover problems explained in the entire glossary. Number your paper 1–33. If a sentence does not contain a usage error, write a + on your paper after the proper number. If a sentence does contain a usage error, write a 0. Your teacher may ask you to write the correct form after each 0.

1. Bring a camera with you when you go to the city.
2. Maria has a large amount of friends.

3. War usually results from causes such as greed and selfishness and which the world seems powerless to remove.
4. The applause showed how deeply the music had affected the audience.
5. There are less reasons for alarm now than there were a year ago.
6. I can't hardly read your writing.
7. The trustees did not accept her resignation.
8. You would of had a bad time driving in the mountains without snow tires.
9. Good speakers adapt their addresses to their audiences.
10. Her talk implied that she favored the honor system.
11. As soon as you graduate, you are one of the alumni.
12. Unfortunately, we cannot except your invitation.
13. There are many different forms of poetry, such as the ballad, the sonnet, the ode, the elegy, the simple lyric, and etc.
14. I have little sympathy with that kind of people.
15. Leave me give you a little good advice.
16. Beside having a great interest in photography, Sally is an enthusiastic artist.
17. In my opinion, her explanation was entirely credible.
18. Forty miles an hour is all the faster his car will go.
19. The volcano had been acting like it might erupt.
20. Everywhere the queen went she was welcome.
21. Dichotomy is when there is a division into two parts.
22. What effect will the new law have on taxes?
23. There isn't nothing else to do.
24. The mayor's speech inferred that the water shortage was serious.
25. Being as the winter is nearly over, the stores are having sales on heavy apparel.
26. He resented his parents' frequent allusions to his poor grades.
27. The girls invented a new route through the swamp, which no one had ever known about.
28. They asked her less questions than she had expected.
29. These phenomena, of course, are most unusual.

30. The committee members which I talked with were pessimistic.
31. The district attorney prosecuted three gamblers last year.
32. You will be disappointed if you try to borrow money off Sue.
33. An overpopulated country will place strict limitations on emigration.

# Composition: Sentence Structure

## PART THREE

Chapter 11

# Sentence Completeness

## Fragments and Run-on Sentences

Two kinds of sentence errors sometimes persist even in the writing of high school seniors. The first is the writing of part of a sentence, a *fragment,* as though it were a whole sentence, able to stand by itself with a capital letter at the beginning and a period at the end. The second kind of error is the writing of two or more sentences as though they were one sentence. The writer makes the mistake of using a comma, or no punctuation at all, between the sentences. You may think of these two sentence errors as opposites. The fragment is not complete; the run-on sentence is more than complete.

### SENTENCE FRAGMENTS

*A group of words is a complete sentence when it has a subject and a verb and expresses a complete thought.*

COMPLETE After the flood the barn roof lay in the yard.

INCOMPLETE After the flood the barn roof in the yard

INCOMPLETE After the flood the barn roof lying in the yard

Because they lack a verb, the last two examples do not express a complete thought. Words ending in *-ing,* like *lying,* are not verbs when they are used alone. Such words may, of course, be used with a *helping verb* to form a verb phrase (see page 13). Unless a word ending in *–ing* does have a helping verb, it cannot be used as the verb in a sentence.[1]

| | |
|---|---|
| NO VERB | the barn roof lying in the front yard |
| VERB PHRASE | The barn roof **was lying** in the front yard. |
| NO VERB | Amy competing in the marathon. |
| VERB PHRASE | Amy **will be competing** in the marathon. |

**11a. A *sentence fragment* is a group of words that does not express a complete thought. Since it is part of a sentence, it should not be allowed to stand by itself, but should be kept in the sentence of which it is a part.**

## The Phrase Fragment

A phrase is a group of words acting as a single part of speech and not containing a verb and its subject.

There are many kinds of phrases (participial, gerund, appositive, prepositional, infinitive) but regardless of their kind, they all have one important characteristic – they are parts of a sentence and must never be separated from the sentence in which they belong. When a phrase is incorrectly allowed to stand by itself, it is called a fragment.

Study the way in which the unattached phrase fragments in the following examples are corrected.

FRAGMENT Last Saturday I saw Gloria. Riding her new ten-speed bicycle. [This participial phrase fragment modifies the word *Gloria*. It should be included in the sentence with the word it modifies.]

FRAGMENT CORRECTED Last Saturday I saw Gloria **riding her new ten-speed bicycle.**

[1] The following helping verbs may be used with words ending in *–ing* to form a verb phrase:

| | | |
|---|---|---|
| am | were | can (may) be |
| are | will (shall) be | could (would, should) be |
| is | has been | will (shall) have been |
| was | had been | might have been |

FRAGMENT The largest sailing ship afloat is the Soviet frigate *Kurstan*. Used by the Soviet Union as a training ship. [This participial phrase fragment modifies the word *frigate*. It should be included in the sentence with the word it modifies.]

FRAGMENT CORRECTED The largest sailing ship afloat is the Soviet frigate *Kurstan*, **used by the Soviet Union as a training ship.**

FRAGMENT We pitched our tent on the north side of the lake. At the edge of a grove of pine trees. [This prepositional phrase fragment modifies the verb *pitched*, telling where we pitched our tent. This sequence of phrases belongs in the sentence.]

FRAGMENT CORRECTED We pitched our tent on the north side of the lake **at the edge of a grove of pine trees.**

FRAGMENT My parents finally gave me permission. To go with Gail to the game at West Point. [Here an infinitive phrase fragment has been separated from the word *permission*, which it explains. It should be included in the same sentence with the word it explains.]

FRAGMENT CORRECTED My parents finally gave me permission **to go with Gail to the game at West Point.**

FRAGMENT Aunt Deborah came bearing gifts. A wrist watch for Jean and a ring for me. [This appositive phrase fragment belongs in the sentence preceding it, separated by a comma from *gifts*, the word to which it refers.]

FRAGMENT CORRECTED Aunt Deborah came bearing gifts**, a wrist watch for Jean and a ring for me.**

## The Subordinate Clause Fragment

A second type of fragment is the subordinate clause that is incorrectly separated from the sentence in which it belongs. A clause is a group of words containing a subject and predicate and used as a part of a sentence. A subordinate clause does not express a complete thought and should not stand alone.

FRAGMENT The orchestra played "A Night in the Tropics." Which Louis Gottschalk wrote in 1859.

FRAGMENT CORRECTED The orchestra played "A Night in the Tropics," which Louis Gottschalk wrote in 1859.

**11b. Do not separate a phrase or a subordinate clause from the sentence of which it is a part.**

**EXERCISE 1.** Some of the items in this exercise consist of one or two completed sentences; others contain sentence fragments. Number your paper 1–20. If all the parts of an item are complete sentences, write *C* after the proper number. If an item contains a fragment, rewrite it to include the fragment in the sentence.

1. Elizabeth Blackwell was born in 1821. And died in 1910.
2. When, in 1832, her parents could no longer tolerate the social and political situation in Bristol, England, where Mr. Blackwell was a leading member of the business community. They immigrated with their eight children to New York.
3. After six years of adventures—some profitable, some unhappy—in the East, the family decided to move to Cincinnati. Where they hoped to prosper.
4. For a while things looked bright for the family. Despite the growing realization that some of them missed England.
5. But tragedy struck in 1832. Mr. Blackwell died.
6. Elizabeth established a school for girls. Feeling depressed by the economic plight of her family, which now consisted of her mother, four sisters, and four brothers.
7. By 1839 this school, staffed by several members of the family, had become quite successful. But Elizabeth was beginning to feel dissatisfied with teaching.
8. A woman friend, dying of cancer, suggested that Elizabeth, who loved to study, become a doctor. At first, Elizabeth totally rejected this suggestion.
9. In spite of herself, the idea of being a doctor plagued Elizabeth. Leading her to inquire into the possibility of a woman studying medicine.
10. When told that it would be impossible for a woman to become

a doctor, she became determined to follow her dying friend's advice. Not certain how she should proceed against the forces of prejudice.

11. Elizabeth Blackwell's conviction to study and practice medicine must be seen as courageous. Since matrimony was the only respectable career for a woman in the 1840's.
12. Her insistence on finding a place and a way to study medicine took Elizabeth Blackwell to North Carolina, where she received private instruction from two doctors. And taught music in boarding schools.
13. She then applied to and was rejected from medical schools in Philadelphia, the seat of medical education in America at that time. After which Elizabeth applied to schools around the country.
14. Finally, in 1847, the Medical Institution of Geneva College in northern New York State accepted Elizabeth Blackwell. Now known as Hobart College.
15. She graduated in 1849 at the head of her class. A young woman convinced that she was right and determined to change ideas about education.
16. She was not content with being the first woman in the United States to gain an M.D. degree from a medical school. Elizabeth Blackwell spent the next two years doing graduate work in Europe.
17. Once she was back in America, Elizabeth Blackwell led a life marked by an enthusiasm to encourage her sister Emily and a passion to practice medicine. Combined with an interest in helping the poor.
18. In 1857 Elizabeth Blackwell established the New York Infirmary for Indigent Women and Children, a hospital staffed by women. She decided to open the hospital on May 12, the birthday of her friend Florence Nightingale.
19. Because of Elizabeth's and Emily's breakthroughs in medicine and the social pioneering of the three other sisters, the Blackwell women are important in American history. Even though we may not hear their names very often.
20. Two women who married into the family, Antoinette Brown and Lucy Stone, also fought for women's rights and battled against social injustices. Besides the impressive women born into the Blackwell family.

## RUN-ON SENTENCES

When a comma (instead of a period, a semicolon, or a conjunction) is used between two complete sentences, the result is referred to as a "run-on sentence." One sentence is permitted to "run on" into the next. In high school writing, this type of sentence error is more common than the fragment error. Usually it results from carelessness in punctuation rather than from lack of understanding. Because the error involves the misuse of a comma—to separate sentences—it is sometimes referred to as the "comma fault." A worse, but less common, kind of run-on sentence results from omitting all punctuation between sentences.

**11c. Avoid the run-on sentence. Do not use a comma between sentences. Do not omit punctuation at the end of a sentence.**

RUN-ON SENTENCE The choice of a camera is difficult, there are many good ones on the market.

These two sentences should be either separated by a period or joined into one sentence by a conjunction or a semicolon. There are four ways of correcting the error:

1. The choice of a camera is difficult**.** There are many good ones on the market.
2. The choice of a camera is difficult**, for** there are many good ones on the market.
3. The choice of a camera is difficult **because** there are many good ones on the market.
4. The choice of a camera is difficult**;** there are many good ones on the market.

As you grow older and do more and more writing, you develop a "sentence sense," which is the ability to recognize at once whether a group of words is or is not a complete sentence. Reading your compositions aloud, so that your ears as well as your eyes can detect completeness, will help you find any run-on sentences in your own writing.

▶ **NOTE** Do not be surprised, after being warned against sentence fragments and run-on sentences, if you find them being used occasionally by writers in the best newspapers and magazines. Professional writers (who have a strong sentence sense, or they would not be professionals) do at times write fragments and use the comma between sentences, especially when the ideas in the sentences are very closely related. Leave this use of the comma and the use of the fragment to the experienced judgment of the professional.

**EXERCISE 2.** The items in this exercise are run-on sentences. Copy after the proper number on your paper the final word in the first sentence in each item and follow it with the first few words of the second sentence. Indicate how you would eliminate the faulty comma. You may use a semicolon, a comma and conjunction, or a period and a capital letter, or other appropriate punctuation. Do not be satisfied with using a period and a capital letter in every case; to make clear the relationship between ideas, some of the items should be corrected in other ways.

EXAMPLE 1. Flo didn't hear about the party until Thursday, she had to change her plans.
1. *Thursday; therefore she had . . .*

1. In social studies this year we are studying about ways to solve our major national problems, so far we have covered poverty, unemployment, inflation, and pollution.
2. We have a pet lovebird at home, its call is as harsh and shrill as the screech of chalk on a chalkboard.
3. Lovebirds are comical creatures, they are always busy rearranging objects in their cage.
4. Ynes Mexia, the botanical explorer, discovered rare tropical plants on her expeditions to Mexico and South America, these discoveries were of great value to science.
5. Juan took an art elective and discovered he had talent, now he spends his afternoons in the art room.
6. At an advanced age she began to write the story of her colorful life, at least she thought her life had been colorful.

7. The astounding scientific developments of one generation are accepted commonplaces in the next generation, the computer and the cassette recorder, for instance, are taken for granted by everyone today.
8. A new club is being formed for the study of social behavior, instead of just reading, students will do research and conduct interviews outside the school.
9. A large suggestion box has been placed in the hall just outside the principal's office, students can, by this means, express their pet peeves about the school, names should not be signed to the suggestions.
10. First try to do the assignment by yourself, if you can't do it, ask your teacher for help.

**EXERCISE 3.** The following exercise contains sentence fragments and run-on sentences. Prepare to explain to the class how you would eliminate the sentence errors. Use the chalkboard when giving your explanation.

1. I have never known anyone who was a better worker than Paula. Who always did her homework in half the time I took, she usually had it done twice as well, too.
2. Concentration was the secret of her success. Although she undoubtedly had a keen mind.
3. I asked Paula to help me with my math once. When I was particularly desperate, I hadn't been getting good grades for several weeks.
4. She could do the problems easily, and she could explain them to me. So that I could understand them, anyway, I didn't ask her again.
5. Mr. Rehman urges all musicians to continue to study their instruments in high school. Because he knows that as they get busier and busier, many students stop taking lessons, sports and other activities cut in on their practice time.
6. A mammoth crane was brought here to lift into place the steel girders. Huge orange-colored beams that were easily set into place. Almost as though they were matchsticks.
7. The time when a radio station may broadcast is determined by its license, some stations must go off the air at sundown.

8. Everyone was asking me about Stacey. Where she was and what she was doing, wild rumors had been circulating.
9. The city's water supply has been threatened. Very little rain or snow having fallen during the past weeks.
10. I learned to like poetry when I read Kipling, his poems appealed to me. Because of their strong rhythm and their rhyme.
11. I have learned to recognize several kinds of customers. Especially the kind that likes to argue about the merchandise, when I see one of these coming, I duck out of sight, they take too much time, rarely buy anything, and invariably make me angry.
12. Some teen-agers spend an allowance foolishly, they don't know the value of money. Until they have to work for it.
13. Women's colleges were established in America in the nineteenth century. During the Victorian period. When girls were considered frail flowers to be kept safe and separate.
14. Audiences appeared to enjoy the play, the reviews in the papers, however, were unfavorable.
15. A back-to-school night for parents convinced the taxpayers of the inadequacy of our building, consequently the bond issue for a new building was passed by a large vote. When it was presented later in the year.

Chapter **12**

# Coordination and Subordination

## Relationship Between the Ideas in a Sentence

## COORDINATE IDEAS

When a sentence contains more than one idea, the ideas may be equal in rank or unequal in rank. Ideas that are equal in rank are *coordinate*. (*Co–* means "equal"; *–ordinate* means "ordered" or "ranked"; hence *coordinate* means "of equal order or rank.")

COORDINATE IDEAS Mrs. Carter is an architect, **and** Mrs. Murphy is a contractor.

We tried everything that we could think of, **but** nothing worked.

The writer of the preceding sentences considered the two ideas in each sentence of equal rank; he gave them equal emphasis by expressing them in independent clauses. The clauses are coordinate clauses.

### Clear Relationship Between Coordinate Ideas

The relationship between coordinate ideas (equal in rank) is made clear by means of the word used to connect the two ideas. Different connectives may be used to express different relationships. The common kinds of relationship between coordinate clauses are *addition, contrast, choice,* and *result.*

### *Addition*

The following connectives are used to indicate that what follows is supplementary to what precedes.

EXAMPLE I wrote to her, **and** she wrote to me.

| | |
|---|---|
| also | furthermore |
| and | likewise |
| besides | moreover |
| both . . . and | then |

### *Contrast*

The following connectives are used to introduce an idea that in some way conflicts or contrasts with what has gone before.

EXAMPLE I wrote to her, **but** she did not write to me.

| | |
|---|---|
| but | still |
| however | yet |
| nevertheless | |

### *Choice*

The following connectives are used to introduce an alternate possibility.

EXAMPLE You write to her, **or** I will write to her.

| | |
|---|---|
| either . . . or | or, nor |
| neither . . . nor | otherwise |

### *Result*

The following connectives are used to state a result or consequence of the preceding statement.

EXAMPLE I wrote to her; **therefore** she wrote to me.

| | |
|---|---|
| accordingly | hence |
| consequently | therefore |

**12a. Make clear the relationship between the ideas in coordinate clauses by using connectives which express the relationship exactly.**

A good writer chooses connectives carefully, making certain that the connectives chosen will express exactly the relationship intended between the ideas in the sentence. In order to avoid a monotonous style you should always use a variety of connectives.

If the wrong connective is used, the relationship between the ideas will not be clear. The connectives in the following *not-clear* sentences were poorly chosen.

NOT CLEAR Mrs. Bothwell took a long vacation, and her health did not improve.

CLEAR Mrs. Bothwell took a long vacation, **but** her health did not improve. [contrast]

NOT CLEAR The veterans spent a year in the hospital, but they emerged entirely well.

CLEAR The veterans spent a year in the hospital; **consequently**, they emerged entirely well. [result]

► NOTE When used to join coordinate clauses, the words *and, but, yet, or, nor* are usually preceded by a comma.

When used to join coordinate clauses, the words *besides, likewise, furthermore, moreover, however, nevertheless, otherwise, consequently, therefore, accordingly* are usually preceded by a semicolon.

**EXERCISE 1.** Number your paper 1–20. Read each sentence thoughtfully. Determine the logical relationship between the two clauses and write after the proper number on your paper what this relationship is: *addition, contrast, choice,* or *result.* Then write an appropriate connective selected from the lists above—the word which will make unmistakably clear the relationship between the clauses. Use a variety of connectives. Give the correct punctuation mark with each connective.

EXAMPLE 1. The demand exceeded the supply prices remained the same.

1. *contrast ; nevertheless*

1. The student body was dismissed at one o'clock nobody went home.
2. Bea was seriously injured in yesterday's practice she will not be able to play in the game today.
3. Jimmy played right end I played left end on the varsity.
4. Deliver the shipment by Friday I will cancel my order!
5. Math has always been my hardest subject I have never failed a math test.
6. In an auditorium of this size, you must speak louder your audience will not be able to hear you.
7. This magazine publishes the best literary criticism it is a financial failure.
8. Some of the best TV courses are offered at 6:30 a.m. they reach only a small audience of early-rising intellectuals.
9. The American economy has long depended on a high level of military spending some people fear the economic consequences of ending the arms race.
10. The oil burner had stopped during the night the house was cold when we awoke.
11. We had heard the assignment we hadn't understood it.
12. We were to be marked for neatness we took greater pains than usual.
13. We returned late; the rented canoe was a wreck the lifeguard said she'd like to see us after swim period.
14. We thought we were not to blame we braved her wrath and didn't say a word.
15. We had planned on going to town that afternoon we were slightly annoyed at being kept in camp.
16. The head counselor warned us to take better care of the property of others she said she would send our parents a bill.
17. The bill which my parents received was quite unexpected it took them some time to recover from the shock.
18. Sue's parents also received a bill they were just as surprised as my parents.

19. They were all amazed at the high price of canoes they paid the bills promptly.
20. Parents can be put to a great deal of trouble and expense by their children they are usually patient and generous with us.

## SUBORDINATE IDEAS

When ideas in a sentence are unequal in rank, the ideas of lower rank are subordinate. (*Sub–* means "under" or "lower.") If the idea of lower rank is expressed in a clause, the clause is a *subordinate* clause.[1] The main idea of the sentence is expressed in an *independent* clause.

EXAMPLES The pilot, who was a veteran flyer, brought her crippled plane down safely. [Independent clause–greater emphasis: *The pilot brought her crippled plane down safely;* subordinate clause–lesser emphasis: *who was a veteran flyer.*]

Because each of them was politically ambitious, the council members rarely supported one another's proposals. [Main clause–greater emphasis: *the council members rarely supported one another's proposals;* subordinate clause–lesser emphasis: *Because each of them was politically ambitious.*]

### Adverb Clauses

**12b. Make clear the relationship between subordinate adverb clauses and independent clauses by selecting subordinating conjunctions which express the relationship exactly.**

The relationship between the idea in a subordinate adverb clause and the idea in an independent clause is made clear by the subordinating conjunction that introduces the subordinate clause. The common kinds of relationship between subordinate adverb clauses and independent clauses are *time, cause* or *reason, purpose* or *result,* and *condition.*

[1] For a more detailed explanation of subordinate clauses see pages 53–64.

Some of the conjunctions can be used in more than one way and therefore appear in more than one list.

*Time*

The following subordinating conjunctions introduce clauses expressing a time relationship between the idea in the subordinate clause and the idea in the independent clause.

EXAMPLE Several guests arrived **before** we were ready.

| | | | |
|---|---|---|---|
| after | before | until | whenever |
| as | since | when | while |

***Cause or Reason***

The following subordinating conjunctions introduce clauses expressing the cause or reason for the idea expressed in the independent clause. The subordinate clause tells *why*.

EXAMPLE We stopped **because** the light was red.

| | |
|---|---|
| as | since |
| because | whereas |

***Purpose or Result***

The following subordinating conjunctions introduce clauses expressing the purpose of the idea in the independent clause or the result of the idea in the independent clause.

PURPOSE Astronauts undergo the most rigorous training **so that** they will be able to handle any emergency. [The subordinate clause states the purpose of training described in the independent clause.]

RESULT Extreme differences of opinion developed in the committee **so that** agreement seemed unlikely. [The subordinate clause states a result of the committee's differences of opinion.]

that in order that so that

***Condition***

The following subordinating conjunctions state the condition or conditions under which the idea in the independent clause is true. Think of *although, even though, though,* and *while* as meaning "in spite of the fact that." They introduce a condition in spite of which the idea in the independent clause is true.

EXAMPLES **Although** (in spite of the fact that) it was raining, we went to the game. [The clause states the *condition* under which we went to the game.]

**If** you pass the examination, you will pass the course. [The clause states under what condition you will pass the course.]

| | | | |
|---|---|---|---|
| although | though | provided | if |
| even though | while | unless | |

**EXERCISE 2.** Number your paper 1–20. From the preceding lists choose a subordinating conjunction to fill the blank in each sentence and write it after the proper number on your paper. Make sure the conjunction you choose fits the meaning of the sentence. After the conjunction, tell what relationship it expresses: *cause* or *reason, condition, purpose* or *result, time.*

1. —— you buy a rare manuscript, make certain of its authenticity.
2. There is a good chance of being swindled, —— you fail to do this.
3. —— it is the oldest of rackets, all sorts of con men continue to forge works of the great masters.
4. It seems to work again and again, —— there are enough gullible people in the market.
5. William Henry Ireland was one of the most successful forgers, —— he was only a teen-ager at the height of his exploits.
6. Ireland began forging Shakespeare manuscripts, —— his father had a keen interest in them.
7. —— his first efforts were difficult, he continued his questionable work with zeal.
8. There seemed to be no sort of forgery beyond his reach, —— he had the necessary equipment.

9. —— many scholars greeted his work with enthusiasm, others were less easily persuaded.
10. —— he forged a document, Ireland had to do careful research on the proper details such a document would require.
11. Nothing he forged could be shown to others —— the ink had long since dried.
12. Special blends of ink were required —— the age would be properly deceptive.
13. —— his motives and methods were questionable, his work possesses a certain unique attractiveness.
14. Ireland's father published a collection of his son's forgeries, —— he considered his son worthy of complete confidence.
15. The skepticism of scholars increased enormously, —— it became impossible to answer their objections.
16. Ireland published a truthful confession —— the documents were agreed to be fraudulent and his father's health became endangered.
17. —— he tried to ease his father's disappointment, the older man died in disgrace at the height of the furor.
18. His ill health was hardly surprising, —— real disgrace is a difficult burden to bear.
19. —— a love letter with a lock of hair enclosed was his masterpiece, Ireland also forged leases, contracts, notes, poems, and whole plays.
20. —— Ireland himself died in 1835, the art of forgery obviously did not die with him.

**EXERCISE 3.** Number your paper 1–20. From the lists of subordinating conjunctions on pages 211–12, choose an appropriate subordinating conjunction to fill the blank in each sentence and write it after the proper number on your paper. Notice that when an adverb clause begins a sentence, it is followed by a comma.

1. —— peace was declared, the citizens of the small country rejoiced in the streets.
2. —— the proper preparations are made, the children will be ready for the hike.
3. —— the doctor was at home, we decided to pay her a visit.
4. —— the barometer fell, weather warnings were sent out.

5. —— we had eaten a delicious meal, we sat around the fireplace and told ghost stories.
6. —— she had not slept well the night before, Melissa did not run as well as her coach had expected.
7. We waited for the hurricane —— we had closed the windows and bolted the door.
8. The players started scrimmage —— the coach blew her whistle.
9. Many people take courses in painting —— they want to express their creativity.
10. You will solve this math problem —— you take one step at a time.
11. —— Van Gogh is now considered a great painter, his work was not appreciated in his lifetime.
12. You are welcome to stay here —— you wish.
13. I bandaged my cut —— it would not become infected.
14. —— you arrived so late, you will have to sit at the back of the auditorium.
15. —— I had ordered two pairs of gloves, the mail-order company sent me two pairs of pants instead.
16. You may register to vote —— you are a legal resident.
17. —— the defense attorney made her final plea, the prisoner sat stiffly in a chair.
18. The doctor administered the new antibiotic —— no further complication would arise.
19. Many people fail to enjoy music —— they do not know how to listen properly.
20. —— the soldiers reached the clearing, they made camp.

**EXERCISE 4.** Rewrite each of the following sentences by adding a subordinate clause at the beginning or at the end of each sentence. Vary your choice of subordinating conjunctions.

EXAMPLE 1. The fans filed out of the stadium.

1. *After the game was over, the fans filed out of the stadium.*

1. The heat became unbearable.
2. We started jogging in the afternoons.

3. Arturo agreed to come with us.
4. Lauren began clapping enthusiastically.
5. You will not have enough time to finish the composition.

## Adjective Clauses

The subordinate clauses in the preceding exercises are *adverb* clauses. Subordinate *adjective* clauses are especially helpful in making clear the relationship between sentence ideas because they permit a writer to emphasize one idea above another.[1] A writer may, for instance, wish to express the following ideas in one sentence: *Sacajawea acted as interpreter for explorers of the West. She was a Lemhi Indian.* To emphasize that Sacajawea acted as interpreter, the writer places this information in an independent clause and subordinates the other idea by placing it in an adjective clause.

**Sacajawea,** who was a Lemhi Indian, **acted as interpreter for explorers of the West.**

On the other hand, for a different purpose, the writer may wish to change emphasis from one of these ideas to the other. This can be done by reversing the positions of the ideas.

**Sacajawea,** who acted as interpreter for explorers of the West, **was a Lemhi Indian.**

**12c. Make clear the relative emphasis to be given ideas in a complex sentence by placing the idea you wish to emphasize in the independent clause and by placing subordinate ideas in subordinate clauses.**

**EXERCISE 5.** Change the emphasis in each of the following sentences by placing in the independent clause the idea which is now in the subordinate clause and by placing in the subordinate clause the idea which is now in the independent clause.

[1] Adjective clauses may begin with *who, whom, whose, which, that,* and *where*.

1. *Z,* which is a voiced alveolar fricative, is the last letter of the English alphabet.
2. Dictionary listings, which end with words beginning with *z,* proceed alphabetically.
3. A word that comes from an ancient Greek word meaning "to boil," *zeal,* is one of the more familiar words found there.
4. *Zero,* which can mean a symbol, a mark on a scale, a temperature, a gunsight setting, a location in space, or nothing at all, is also a verb.
5. Applying zinc to something, which sounds rather complicated, is called "zincifying."
6. Zinjanthropus, who is having a complicated time just being a two-million-year-old fossilized forerunner of modern human beings, is nicknamed "Nutcracker Man."
7. The word *zodiac,* which comes from an old adjective meaning "having to do with animals," is much younger than Zinjanthropus.
8. Human beings, who are not regarded as edible themselves, are nevertheless quite zoophagous in that they eat other animals.
9. Animal lovers, though they may not welcome the name, can be called "zoophiles."
10. *Zymurgy,* which means "the chemistry of fermentation," results in good wine and ends at least one dictionary.

## CORRECTING FAULTY COORDINATION

Faulty coordination occurs when two unequal ideas are placed in coordinate clauses as though they deserved equal emphasis.

FAULTY COORDINATION The Governor was a native of Ohio, and she was elected for a third term. [ideas of unequal rank]

The two ideas in this sentence are vastly different. It is unlikely that a writer would wish to give them equal rank. The faulty coordination can be corrected by placing one of the ideas in a subordinate position. Which idea the writer puts in the subordinate clause will depend on the purpose.

FAULTY COORDINATION CORRECTED **The Governor,** who was a native of Ohio, **was elected for a third term.**

*or* **The Governor,** who was elected for a third term, **was a native of Ohio.**

## 12d. Faulty coordination may be corrected by placing ideas of lesser emphasis in a subordinate position. An idea may be given less emphasis by being expressed in a subordinate clause or a modifying phrase or an appositive.[1]

### (1) Subordination may be accomplished by means of a subordinate clause.

FAULTY COORDINATION The books are on the new-book shelf, and they may be borrowed for a week.

CORRECTED BY AN ADJECTIVE CLAUSE The books **that are on the new-book shelf** may be borrowed for a week.

CORRECTED BY AN ADVERB CLAUSE **If the books are on the new-book shelf,** they may be borrowed for a week.

**EXERCISE 6.** Clarify the relationship between ideas in the following examples of faulty coordination by placing one of the ideas in a subordinate clause, either an adverb clause or an adjective clause. Choose carefully the subordinating conjunctions which introduce your adverb clauses.

1. I am taking a course in bookkeeping this year, and I will have a better chance of getting an office job this summer.
2. The material is tan with thin red stripes, and it will be used to make slipcovers for a couch and a chair.
3. Mr. and Mrs. Davis have donated a hundred books to our school's library, and they own a large bookstore in town.
4. The answer had to be a whole number, and so I knew that my answer of 6.33 was wrong.

[1] For the use of subordination in achieving sentence variety, see page 273. For the use of subordination in correcting stringy sentences and choppy sentences, see page 286.

5. Columbia College was originally named King's College, and it was established by King George III of England.
6. Mosquitoes and gnats buzzed around our heads, and we still had an enjoyable picnic in the park.
7. The rain had soaked the playing field, and it did not let up until the next day.
8. I am going to play baseball this Saturday, and the infield is still wet.
9. Nora and I heard that a course in photography would be given in the spring, and we signed up for it.
10. Our school marching band will be performing in the statewide semifinals in the middle of October, and it has a hundred members.

**(2) Subordination may be accomplished by means of a modifying phrase.**

FAULTY COORDINATION The house is at the end of the street, and it is very modern in design.

CORRECTED BY A MODIFYING PHRASE The house **at the end of the street** is very modern in design.

**(3) Subordination may be accomplished by means of an appositive.**

An appositive is a word, with or without modifiers, which follows a noun or pronoun and helps to explain it.

FAULTY COORDINATION Ms. Fitch is the manager of the store, and she is tall and handsome.

CORRECTED BY AN APPOSITIVE Ms. Fitch, **the manager of the store,** is tall and handsome.

**EXERCISE 7.** Correct the faulty coordination in the following sentences in the ways prescribed.

Correct by a subordinate clause:

1. Next Monday is a legal holiday, and my boss expects me to report for work.
2. Bessie Smith sang the blues in the 1920's and 1930's, and she had a strong influence on many younger jazz singers.

3. The hurricane was first spotted in the Caribbean, and it was heading northwest toward the Gulf Coast.
4. The department store had shoes in my size at a greatly reduced price, and I bought two pairs.
5. I saw myself on the six o'clock news, and I called all my friends to tell them to watch.

Correct by a modifying phrase:

6. The call was to abandon ship, and it came from the captain.
7. I need to find a recent magazine article, and it should be about the process of digital recording.
8. The woman was playing the accordion, and she had a repertoire of hundreds of folk songs.
9. Neal hit a line drive to left field, and it happened with two out and runners on first and third.
10. The bottle was of household ammonia, and it fell onto the kitchen floor and spilled.

Correct by an appositive:

11. Mr. Miller is the custodian of our building, and he came to this country only three years ago.
12. The new ruler is a woman of great experience in government, and she should be able to reconcile the factions in the country.
13. The violin was an instrument with a beautiful tone, and it belonged to my grandfather.
14. This passenger plane is the fastest one in the world, and it will take you to Europe in record time.
15. Her new book is a volume of poetry, and it received very favorable reviews.

### SUMMARY

(1) Make clear the relationship between ideas in a sentence by using connectives that express the relationship exactly.

(2) Correct faulty coordination by placing ideas of lesser emphasis in a subordinate position. Use a subordinate clause or a modifying phrase or an appositive.

**EXERCISE 8.** The relationship between ideas in the following sentences is not clear: the conjunctions used are not exact, or the sentences contain faulty coordination. Rewrite the sentences. Some may be improved in more than one way.

1. The Bay Challenge Cup represents the highest achievement in sailing, and it was first put up for competition in 1903.
2. The principle that government employees shall not strike has been recently challenged, and it applies to both federal and state employees.
3. High school graduates are better educated today than ever before, and they have a hard time finding jobs.
4. The final chapters of this book outline a constructive program dealing with the problem, and they are the most important.
5. Every business has several ambitious competitors, and no business can afford to stand still.
6. The new regulations call for the opening of school at 7:30 every morning, and they are unpopular with both students and teachers.
7. Mr. Greenberg was a high school coach for many years, and he is now coaching college teams in Ohio.
8. Representatives came from more than fifty countries, and they met in the United Nations Building in New York City.
9. The title of the book was very interesting, and the book itself was very dull.
10. Because their principal crop was potatoes and the potato season was poor, the farmers managed to avoid going into debt.
11. Miss Lang had not directed many plays, and she knew how to manage an inexperienced cast.
12. Helen may go to Wellesley next year, and she may go to Barnard.
13. Carl has taken piano lessons for only three years, and he is already a good pianist.
14. Mr. Stark has never paid back the money he borrowed, and he wants me to lend him more.
15. We waited on the corner for an hour, and the bus didn't come.
16. The Commercial High School is a large stone building on

Market Street, and it is attended by students from all over the city.

17. Stewart Harrison was a famous detective, and he could not solve the arsenic murder case.
18. Miss Armstrong has been selling advertising for many years, and she has been made advertising director of the *Herald.*
19. I am going to the airport to meet a friend, and she is coming from Chicago.
20. Professor Drake has been head of the chemistry department for twenty years, and she died yesterday.

Chapter 13

# Clear Reference

## Pronouns and Antecedents

The meaning of a pronoun is clear only when you know what it refers to. The word to which a pronoun refers is its antecedent. For example, the sentence, "He was talking with them," has little meaning unless you know to whom the pronouns *he* and *them* refer. Similarly, the pronoun *it* is meaningless in the sentence, "It chased me all the way home," unless you know to what *it* refers—a dog or a monster, for example.

In the following sentences, arrows connect the pronouns and their antecedents.

I asked Mr. Jordan for the answer but he didn't know it.

The Potters have a new sailboat on which they intend to cruise.

Handing George the coat, the salesclerk said, "Try this on for size."

**13a. A pronoun must refer clearly to the right antecedent. Avoid *ambiguous* reference, *general* reference, and *weak* reference.**

One simple way of testing pronoun reference is to substitute the antecedent for the pronoun.

Charlie is always thinking about cars. *It* [*cars?*] is his only interest. [The antecedent cannot be substituted; the reference is faulty.]

Charlie is always thinking about cars. They [*cars* ] are his only interest. [The antecedent fits.]

## AMBIGUOUS REFERENCE

**(1) Avoid *ambiguous reference.* Ambiguous reference occurs when a pronoun refers confusingly to two antecedents so that the reader does not know at once which antecedent is meant.**

AMBIGUOUS The President appointed Senator Moore as chairman because he was convinced of the importance of the committee's work.

Here the pronoun *he* can refer to either the President or Senator Moore. The context in which such a sentence appears will ordinarily provide readers with the clues they need to identify the antecedent. Occasionally, however, the use of a pronoun that can refer to more than one antecedent causes momentary confusion. Such ambiguous reference can usually be avoided by rephrasing the sentence.

CLEAR The President, convinced of the importance of the committee's work, appointed Senator Moore as chairman.

CLEAR Because Senator Moore was convinced of the importance of the committee's work, the President appointed him as chairman.

Occasionally, the only way to avoid ambiguity is to replace the pronoun with the appropriate noun:

AMBIGUOUS The partnership between Jones and Potter ended when he drew the firm's money from the bank and flew to Brazil.

CLEAR The partnership between Jones and Potter ended when Jones drew the firm's money from the bank and flew to Brazil.

**EXERCISE 1.** Find the ambiguous pronoun in each of the following sentences. Make the sentence clear either by revising it or by replacing the pronoun with a noun.

1. As soon as the students had left the classrooms, the custodians cleaned them.
2. Fay was arguing with Jane, and she looked unhappy.
3. One of the passengers told the bus driver that she didn't know the route very well.
4. We unpacked our dishes from the barrels and then returned them to the moving company.
5. Right after the accountant sent in a report to the treasurer, she became very much alarmed.
6. Pilar noticed that the principal was smiling in an odd way as she came into the office.
7. Raise the viewfinder to your eye, turning it slowly to the right until it is focused.
8. Our job was to remove the labels from the old bottles and wash them.
9. Mrs. Miller did a beautiful chalk drawing of our cat and then sprayed it with fixative.
10. International good will is essential to successful international trade. It will help to make a peaceful world.

## GENERAL REFERENCE

**(2) Avoid *general reference*. General reference occurs when a pronoun refers confusingly to a general idea that is only vaguely expressed.**

The pronouns *which, this, that,* and *it* are commonly used in a general way.

GENERAL The boys wore ski boots to their classes which the principal disapproved of.

In this sentence the pronoun *which* refers to the general idea, *the wearing of ski boots to class;* furthermore, the pronoun is so placed that it appears to refer to *classes*. The writer did not mean that the principal disapproved of the classes. The sentence can be corrected by revision.

CLEAR The principal disapproved of **the boys' wearing** ski boots to their classes.

In the following example, the pronoun *this* does not have a clear antecedent.

GENERAL The trip to town was strenuous. The car broke down; a tire blew out; and Father sat on the basket of eggs. This put us in a poor frame of mind.

The pronoun *this* should be replaced with a definite noun, making clear the reference to a number of misfortunes.

CLEAR These **misfortunes** put us in a poor frame of mind.

In the next example, the pronoun *it* does not have a clear antecedent. A definite noun makes the meaning clear.

GENERAL Great ships were moving slowly up the harbor; tugs and ferryboats scurried in and out among them; here and there a white cabin cruiser sliced sharply through the blue water under the suspension bridge. It was thrilling to a young farmer.

CLEAR The **sight** was thrilling to a young farmer.

Although you can sometimes correct general reference by merely substituting a noun for the unclear pronoun, you will often find it necessary to revise the entire sentence.

GENERAL In her act Maria told jokes, did impersonations, and sang comic songs. This amused her audience.

CLEAR Maria amused her audience by telling jokes, doing impersonations, and singing comic songs.

**EXERCISE 2.** The following sentences contain examples of general, or vague, reference of pronouns. Revise the sentences or replace the unclear pronouns with nouns.

1. The Chinese were bitter when Russia withdrew its technical assistance; they said it would harm the Chinese economy.
2. Macbeth's mind was constantly imagining horrible things, and that frightened him.
3. He is a conscientious, hard-working man with an engaging personality, but it doesn't make him any richer.
4. A number of people gathered around the speaker and her microphone, which was due to curiosity.

5. I enjoyed the author's style and the type of characters she wrote about. It made me want to read her other books.
6. Rabbi Meyer came to the house daily, from which a sturdy friendship grew.
7. A great deal of effort went into planning the expedition, hiring the right sort of men, and anticipating every emergency, which accounts for the success of the undertaking.
8. Chicago stretches along the shore of Lake Michigan, which makes a beautiful shore drive possible.
9. School gymnasiums will be open every Saturday during the winter, and school playgrounds will be supervised during the summer months. Other school facilities, such as the shops and the little theater, will be available to hobbyists. This will cost money, but the Board of Education thinks the public will be glad to meet the expense.
10. Even students with season tickets had to pay admission to the postseason games. We thought it wasn't fair.

## WEAK REFERENCE

**(3) Avoid *weak reference.* Weak reference occurs when the antecedent has not been expressed but exists only in the writer's mind.**

WEAK We spent the day aboard a fishing boat, but we didn't catch a single one.

In this sentence there is no antecedent of the pronoun *one.* The adjective *fishing* is not the antecedent, since it is fish, not fishing, that *one* refers to. The writer meant the pronoun to stand for the noun *fish.*

CLEAR We spent the day aboard a fishing boat, but we didn't catch a single **fish.**

CLEAR We spent the day aboard a fishing boat trying to catch some **fish,** but we didn't catch a single **one.**

In other words, the antecedent of a pronoun should be a noun. When the antecedent is "hidden" in a modifier or a verb form, the reference is weak.

WEAK The people want honest public servants, but that has not always been a virtue of politicians.

In this sentence the antecedent should be the noun *honesty,* but the noun is "hidden" in the adjective *honest.* Correct the sentence by replacing the weak pronoun with a noun.

CLEAR The people want honest public servants, but **honesty** has not always been a virtue of politicians.

In the next sentence, the antecedent of *it* should be the noun *writing,* which is "hidden" in the verb *wrote.*

WEAK Lois wrote whenever she could find the time, but none of it was ever published.

CLEAR Lois wrote whenever she could find the time, but none of **her writing** was ever published.

In the next sentence the pronoun *they* does not have an antecedent. The writer had *witches* in mind as the antecedent, but the word does not appear at all.

WEAK She is a great believer in witchcraft, but she doubts that they ride on broomsticks.

CLEAR She is a great believer in **witches,** but she doubts that **they** ride on broomsticks.

CLEAR She is a great believer in witchcraft, but she doubts that **witches** ride on broomsticks.

Correct weak references by replacing the weak pronoun with a noun, or by giving the pronoun a clear antecedent.

**EXERCISE 3.** Correct the weak reference in each of the following sentences.

1. I take many pictures with my camera and consider it an enjoyable hobby.
2. Before you start painting the house, be sure to stir it thoroughly.
3. Being neighborly is important because you may need their help someday in an emergency.
4. The salesperson in the television store showed us some that cost thousands of dollars.

5. She was a virtuoso violinist, but she never owned a valuable one.
6. After reading about the private detective's exciting adventures, I decided that I too would someday be one.
7. She is highly intelligent, but she hides it from people she doesn't know well.
8. I telephoned him all day, but it was always busy.
9. She knows many Nigerian legends but has never visited it.
10. Our guide said the Pueblo village was well worth seeing, but it would take three hours.

## INDEFINITE USE OF PRONOUNS

**13b. In writing avoid indefinite use of the pronouns *it, they,* and *you.***

The indefinite use of these pronouns in sentences like the following occurs in ordinary conversation but is not acceptable in writing.

INDEFINITE In the final chapter it implies that the hero died a martyr's death.

BETTER **The final chapter** implies that the hero died a martyr's death.

INDEFINITE On this flight to California, they serve meals without charge.

BETTER On this flight to California, **meals** are served without charge.

INDEFINITE In some countries, you don't dare express political views openly.

BETTER In some countries, **the people** don't dare express political views openly.

► NOTE The expressions *it is raining, it seems, it is late* are, of course, entirely correct.

**EXERCISE 4.** The sentences in this exercise contain examples of ambiguous, general, and weak reference. There are some examples of the indefinite use of *it, they,* and *you.*

Correct the sentences either by replacing a faulty pronoun with a noun, or by revising the sentence. Make the meaning unmistakably clear.

1. Western farmers today can produce more because of machines and the many people working under them.
2. Nancy rode home from school with Suzie, but she didn't tell her anything.
3. We had a long assignment, an inadequate library, and insufficient time, which was very frustrating.
4. Golf wouldn't cost me so much if I didn't lose so many in the rough.
5. The radiator was leaking badly; it ran all over the garage floor.
6. In the cabin he checked the fuel. In those days this might mean the difference between life and death.
7. She overcame her hip injury which doctors had said was impossible.
8. Her spelling and sentence structure are not good, but most of it is due to carelessness.
9. Ruth saw Julie when she was in town last week.
10. In yesterday's editorial, it says the mayor has failed to live up to his campaign promises.
11. We talked with the other passengers as though we had had years of flying experience, but we had never been up in one before.
12. If the prospective buyer learns that the heating system in the house is unsatisfactory, he had better not buy it.
13. The witness testified that she had seen the accused when she was eating dinner in the dining car, which convinced the jury of her presence on the train.
14. The library does not have enough copies of some of the books in greatest demand by students writing research papers, which makes it hard for you.
15. In Washington they are skeptical about the success of the new farm program.

Chapter 14

# Placement of Modifiers

## Misplaced and Dangling Modifiers

A sentence may be confusing for one of two quite different reasons. It may be confusing because the ideas, although clearly stated, are hard to understand. This kind of sentence does not represent faulty writing. But a sentence may also be confusing because of the clumsiness of the writer in arranging the modifiers in the sentence. A modifier should clarify or make more definite the meaning of the word it modifies. If the modifier is placed too far from this word, the effect of the modifier may be either lost or diverted to some other word.

## MISPLACED MODIFIERS

**14a. Place phrase and clause modifiers as near as possible to the words they modify.**

A misplaced modifier may force the reader to reread the sentence in order to be sure of what it says. Sentences like the following examples may be clear on first reading; on the other hand, because of a misplaced word or group of words, they may mislead the reader or force a second look.

CONFUSING Two meetings have been held to make arrangements for a return bout in the office of the State Athletic Commission.

Although most readers know that the return bout is not likely to be held *in the office of the State Athletic Commission,* they may be momentarily distracted by this interesting thought. Placing the phrase next to *held,* the word it modifies, makes the sentence clear.

CLEAR Two meetings have been held in the office of the State Athletic Commission to make arrangements for a return bout.

CONFUSING I bought a small computer for the accounting staff which gave everyone a great deal of trouble.

The reader of this sentence will probably assume that the computer, not the staff, gave everyone trouble. Nevertheless, the clause *which gave everyone a great deal of trouble* should be next to *computer,* which it modifies.

CLEAR I bought the accounting staff a small computer which gave everyone a great deal of trouble.

CONFUSING The thief decided to make a run for it when he saw the police officer, abandoning the stolen car and dashing into the woods.

This sentence would be clearer if on first reading it did not give the impression that the police officer was abandoning the stolen car and dashing into the woods. Moving the adverb clause *when he saw the police officer* to the beginning of the sentence makes it clear that the thief, not the police officer, ran away.

CLEAR When he saw the police officer, the thief decided to make a run for it, abandoning the stolen car and dashing into the woods.

The usual way to clarify a sentence containing a misplaced modifier is to move the modifier next to the word it modifies. Some sentences, however, cannot be clarified so easily. In the sentence above, for example, moving the participial phrases next to *thief,* the word they modify, changes the meaning of the sentence: The thief, abandoning the car and dashing into the woods, decided to make a run for it when he saw the police officer.

Often, you can improve a sentence by moving an adverbial modifier (in this instance *when he saw the police officer*) to the beginning of the sentence. Indeed, regardless of how it may fit elsewhere in the sentence, an adverbial modifier is often better placed at the beginning.

The point of this discussion of the placement of modifiers is that you recognize the importance of making yourself clear at first reading. Do not try to hide behind the weak explanation, "You know what I mean."

**EXERCISE 1.** The following sentences may be confusing on first reading because of a misplaced phrase or clause. Improve the sentences by placing modifiers near the words they modify. You may find that placing an adverbial modifier first often improves the sentence. Doing the exercise orally in class will save time.

1. The students deserved the severe reprimand they received for their misbehavior in the cafeteria in the principal's office on Monday.
2. Commander Richardson was decorated for his action, but he was haunted by the memory of the men he had had to sacrifice for years after.
3. The company is now running a late bus for skiers leaving at 6:15.
4. The big schooner was steered through the narrow channel by a daring skipper without running lights or motor about midnight.
5. One of our observers sighted a plane through binoculars that she could not identify.
6. The minister announced that next Sunday's sermon would be an explanation of the nature of sin, in which he hoped the congregation would take great interest.
7. The causeway has a drawbridge to permit the passage of fishing boats from which all fishing is prohibited.
8. The mystery has been solved after ten years of the missing portrait.
9. The community center was built by Mrs. Borden, who later became Mrs. Gruber, at a cost of $800,000.

10. The suspect tried to make the police believe that he had found the wallet in his car that didn't belong to him.
11. Detectives narrowed down the number of the houses where the robbers might strike by deduction.
12. Myra almost made the mistake one afternoon of running and diving when the pool was empty into the deep end.
13. I'll check the manuscript when you finish for accuracy.
14. He worked hard in his fields, raising crops that would bring in money without complaint.
15. At the meeting on Tuesday, the mayor discussed the enormous cost of filling in the Buskill Swamp with city council members.
16. If what the directions say is true on the package, this is a powerful insecticide.
17. Father bought a gadget for his new car from a fast-talking salesclerk that was guaranteed to reduce gas consumption.
18. She wore a straw hat on the back of her head which was obviously too small.
19. Ms. Steinberg, the explorer, described her trips through the jungle in our social studies class.
20. Uncle Jim brought a new carriage for the baby that was named "Boodle Buggy."

## DANGLING MODIFIERS

**14b. A modifying phrase or clause must clearly and sensibly modify a word in the sentence. When there is no word that the phrase or clause can sensibly modify, the modifier is said to dangle.**

DANGLING MODIFIER Carrying a heavy pile of books, her foot caught on the step.

An introductory participial phrase modifies the noun or pronoun following it. In this example, the phrase *carrying a heavy pile of books* appears to modify *foot.* Since a foot could not carry a pile of books, the phrase cannot modify it sensibly. In fact, there is no word in this sentence which can be sensibly modified by the introductory phrase. The phrase, therefore, is a dangling modifier. The sentence can be corrected in two ways:

1. By adding a word that the phrase can sensibly modify.

   Carrying a heavy pile of books, **she** caught her foot on the steps.

2. By changing the phrase to an adverb clause.

   **While she** was carrying a heavy pile of books, her foot caught on the steps.

Study the following examples of dangling modifiers and the ways in which they have been corrected.

DANGLING MODIFIER Representing the conservative point of view, the liberals rebutted her.

CORRECTED Representing the conservative point of view, she was rebutted by the liberals.

CORRECTED Since she represented the conservative point of view, the liberals rebutted her.

DANGLING MODIFIER After standing up well under the two-year exposure test, the manufacturers were convinced that the paint was sufficiently durable.

CORRECTED After the paint had stood up well under the two-year exposure test, the manufacturers were convinced that it was sufficiently durable.

DANGLING MODIFIER To win the baseball championship this year, Luis and Oscar should join our team.

CORRECTED If we are to win the baseball championship this year, Luis and Oscar should join our team.

CORRECTED To win the baseball championship this year, we should get Luis and Oscar to join our team.

It is only fair to point out that examples of dangling modifiers may sometimes be found in the works of the best authors. These examples, however, are either so idiomatic as to be entirely acceptable, or they are so clear that no possible confusion can result. The following are not objectionable:

Relatively speaking, the cost of living has remained static for several years.

To be perfectly frank, the rate of inflation is still too high.

It is important, however, that you realize the absurd meanings into which danglers can lead you so that you will avoid them in your own writing.

**EXERCISE 2.** Each of the following sentences contains a dangling modifier. Remove the danglers by revising the sentences.

1. Coming up the front walk, the bouquet in the picture window looked beautiful.
2. Left alone in the house, the thunderstorm terrified him.
3. Enormous and architecturally striking, everyone is impressed by the new building.
4. When selecting a college, the social life seems to interest some students more than education.
5. After considering the proposal for several hours, it was rejected by the council.
6. While talking with friends recently, the topic of dentistry came up.
7. After spending Saturday morning working in the library, a feeling of righteousness possessed me.
8. After flying in darkness for two hours, the moon rose, and navigation became less difficult.
9. To keep the guacamole dip from turning brown, its surface should be covered with a thin layer of mayonnaise.
10. Living in this coastal town for many years, the fishing boats and their skippers were well known to him.
11. After working in the fields all day, little strength was left for social activities.
12. When only a youngster in grade school, my father instructed me in the art of boxing.
13. Yielding to the temptation to look at a classmate's paper, the proctor caught them cheating.
14. While working in California, her family was living in New York.
15. To understand many of the allusions in modern literature, a knowledge of Greek and Roman myths is essential.

16. Having promised to be home by midnight, the family was annoyed when I came in at two o'clock.
17. While playing in the highchair, I was afraid the baby would fall out.
18. Riding in the glass-bottomed boat, hundreds of beautiful tropical fish could be seen.
19. Being very shy, strangers frighten my little sister.
20. After being wheeled into the operating room, a nurse placed a mask over my nose.

## TWO-WAY MODIFIERS

A third way in which a careless writer sometimes confuses the reader is by placing a modifier in such a way that it may be taken to modify two words. As a result, the reader cannot be sure which of the two possible meanings is intended. Such a modifier is called a *two-way,* or a *squinting,* modifier.

EXAMPLE Mary said *during the meeting* Jo acted like a fool.

Since the phrase *during the meeting* may be taken to modify either *said* or *acted,* this sentence is not clear. Did Mary say this during the meeting, or did Jo act like a fool during the meeting? The sentence should be revised to make it say one thing or the other.

CLEAR **During the meeting** Mary said Jo acted like a fool.

CLEAR Mary said Jo acted like a fool **during the meeting.**

Study the following examples of two-way modifiers:

NOT CLEAR Mrs. Stewart asked us *before we left* to call on her.

CLEAR **Before we left,** Mrs. Stewart asked us to call on her.

CLEAR Mrs. Stewart asked us to call on her **before we left.**

NOT CLEAR Tell Fred *when he comes home* I want to see him.

CLEAR **When he comes home,** tell Fred I want to see him.

CLEAR Tell Fred I want to see him **when he comes home.**

**EXERCISE 3.** The sentences in this exercise contain misplaced, dangling, and squinting modifiers. Revise each sentence so that its meaning will be clear on first reading.

1. The Simpsons gave a toy robot to one of their children with a bullet-shaped glass head and flashing red eyes.
2. Pounding the piano keys with all her might, the chords of the prelude resounded through the concert hall.
3. The waiter brought us ice cream in glass bowls which started melting almost immediately.
4. We saw a herd of sheep on the way to our hotel.
5. To succeed in college, a great deal of time must be spent studying.
6. When only five years old, my father took me to see my first baseball game.
7. Topped with mounds of whipped cream, most people love strawberry shortcake.
8. While trying to get ready for school, the doorbell suddenly rang.
9. Elaine told Joanne after the first act the drama gets more exciting.
10. By practicing a foreign language daily, great fluency can be gained.
11. While watching the ball game, Sue's horse ran away.
12. A tarantula was shown to me by the museum's curator that had eight legs and a huge hairy body.
13. Preferring the mountains to the seashore, the Great Smokies were chosen as our vacation spot.
14. After working in Washington for twenty years, the methods of lobbyists were familiar.
15. This bank approves loans to reliable individuals of any size.
16. Did you know when you were in Chicago I was living in Highland Park?
17. While tuning the radio, the car swerved dangerously toward a telephone pole.
18. Being completely untamed, Anita warned us that the animals were dangerous.
19. One can see more than a hundred lakes, flying at an altitude of several thousand feet.

20. Jack bought a book of shorthand lessons along with his new typewriter which he read and studied diligently.
21. Living constantly under the eyes of the police, her nervousness increased.
22. Plans for a new road have finally been approved after three years of red tape to stretch across the valley.
23. Ramón wanted to know before the game began what the referees said to the two captains.
24. Believing that freedom was more important than security, homes, relatives, and countries were abandoned by these emigrants.
25. Rounding a sharp curve, a detour sign warned us of danger.

Chapter 15

# Parallel Structure

## Structures of Equal Rank; Correcting Faulty Parallelism

Parallelism in sentence structure exists when two or more sentence elements of equal rank are similarly expressed. Stating equal and closely related ideas in parallel constructions often adds clarity and smoothness to writing.

## KINDS OF PARALLEL STRUCTURE

**15a. Express parallel ideas in the same grammatical form.**

There are three sentence elements which commonly require parallel treatment: coordinated ideas, compared and contrasted ideas, and correlative constructions. A sentence reads smoothly when the writer has taken the trouble to put parallel ideas in the same form.

### Coordinate Ideas

Coordinate ideas are equal in rank. They are joined by coordinate connectives. The coordinate connectives most often used in parallel structure are *and, but, or, nor.*

To express parallel ideas in the same grammatical form, pair one part of speech with the same part of speech, a verbal with the same kind of verbal, a phrase with a phrase, a clause with a clause. Do not pair unlike grammatical forms.

FAULTY The committee studied all aspects of the problem—humane, political, and cost. [The adjectives *humane* and *political* are paired with the noun *cost*.]

PARALLEL The committee studied all aspects of the problem—**humane, political,** and **financial.** [All three coordinate elements are adjectives.]

FAULTY The math exam tested our knowledge of exponential functions, the quadratic formula, and solving linear equations. [two nouns paired with a phrase]

PARALLEL The math exam tested our knowledge of exponential **functions,** the quadratic **formula,** and linear **equations.** [three nouns]

FAULTY According to my teacher, my composition revealed exceptional creative ability but that I make too many spelling errors. [noun paired with clause]

PARALLEL According to my teacher, my composition revealed exceptional creative **ability** but too many spelling **errors.** [noun paired with noun]

PARALLEL According to my teacher, my composition revealed **that I have exceptional creative ability** but **that I make too many spelling errors.** [clause paired with clause]

## Compared or Contrasted Ideas

FAULTY Water-skiing no longer interests me as much as to go scuba diving. [gerund *water-skiing* paired with infinitive *to go*]

PARALLEL **Water-skiing** no longer interests me as much as **scuba diving.** [gerund paired with gerund]

PARALLEL **To water-ski** no longer interests me as much as **to scuba dive.** [infinitive paired with an infinitive.]

FAULTY Her novel was praised more for its style than for what it had to say. [noun paired with a clause]

PARALLEL Her novel was praised more for its **style** than for its **ideas.** [noun paired with a noun]

## Correlative Constructions

Correlative constructions are formed with the correlative conjunctions *both . . . and, either . . . or, neither . . . nor, not only . . . but (also).*

FAULTY At the gate they tried both persuasion and to force their way in. [noun paired with an infinitive]

PARALLEL At the gate they tried both **persuasion** and **force.** [noun paired with a noun]

FAULTY The new clerk soon proved herself to be not only capable but also a woman who could be trusted. [adjective paired with a noun]

PARALLEL The new clerk soon proved herself to be not only **capable** but also **trustworthy.** [adjective paired with an adjective]

# COMPLETED PARALLELISM

### 15b. Place correlative conjunctions immediately before the parallel terms.

NONSTANDARD Mrs. Sayers is not only president of the National Bank but also of the Chamber of Commerce. [*Not only . . . but also* should precede the parallel terms *of the National Bank* and *of the Chamber of Commerce,* not the word *president.*]

STANDARD Mrs. Sayers is president **not only** of the National Bank **but also** of the Chamber of Commerce.

NONSTANDARD The team both felt the satisfaction of victory and the disappointment of defeat.

STANDARD The team felt **both** the satisfaction of victory **and** the disappointment of defeat.

### 15c. In parallel constructions repeat an article, a preposition, or a pronoun whenever necessary to make the meaning clear.

Note that the omission or inclusion of a word in the paired sentences below changes the meaning.

> Before the meeting I talked with the secretary and treasurer. [The sentence may mean that I talked with one person who holds the double office of secretary and treasurer.]
>
> Before the meeting I talked with the secretary and **the** treasurer. [This sentence indicates that I talked with two persons.]
>
> The weather was a greater handicap to the invading army than their enemy. [This sentence means that the invaders would rather fight the enemy than the weather.]
>
> The weather was a greater handicap to the invading army than **to** their enemy. [This sentence means that the invaders had the harder job.]
>
> We feel certain that she is capable, she will succeed, and you will be proud of her. [In a series of parallel *that* clauses, the meaning is usually clearer if the introductory word is repeated in each clause. Omission of the introductory *that* from the clauses may give the impression that this is a run-on sentence, the first sentence ending with *capable*.]
>
> We feel certain that she is capable, **that** she will succeed, and **that** you will be proud of her.

**EXERCISE 1.** Improve the following sentences by putting parallel ideas into the same grammatical form. Correct any errors in the placement of correlatives and in the omission of a necessary article, preposition, or pronoun.

1. Its large size, simple structure, and how readily available it is, make the common cockroach convenient to study.
2. Cockroaches have smooth leathery skin, long thin antennae, and they have a body that is thick and flat.
3. They are not only found in urban areas but in the tropics.
4. The Oriental cockroach is short-winged, while cockroaches from America have full wings.
5. North America boasts about sixty species, but only two in Great Britain.
6. Cockroaches may be dark brown, pale brown, or of a green color that is delicate.

7. Cockroach eggs are laid in small cases, carried on the female body, and then they deposit them in hidden crevices.
8. A typical cockroach lives as a nymph for about a year, and as an adult its life lasts about half a year.
9. The odors that attract cockroaches are sweet, but they emit disagreeable odors.
10. Cockroaches will eat anything, but they especially like sweet foods and foods that are starchy.
11. What a cockroach soils is far more than it consumes.
12. By day the average cockroach is quietly lazy, but busily energetic describes how it is by night.
13. We might not only view the cockroach with disgust but also interest.
14. The cockroach both is the most primitive living winged insect and the most ancient fossil insect.
15. We have as much to learn from the cockroach's evolution as there is to gain from extinguishing it.

**15d. Include in the second part of a parallel construction all words necessary to make the construction complete.**

Occasionally in your haste you may fail to include in one part of a parallel construction all the words necessary to make the construction complete.

INCOMPLETE Linda always chose topics that were more difficult than the other students.

COMPLETE Linda always chose topics that were more difficult than **those of** the other students.

In the first of these sentences you feel that something has been omitted because the sentence compares *topics* with *students*.

**EXERCISE 2.** Correct the parallelism in each of the following sentences by inserting the words that have been omitted.

1. Ms. Connor's lectures are easier to comprehend than Ms. Moore.

2. She is busy the entire day, since she gives half of each day to her work and to team practice.
3. A modern director's interpretation of *Hamlet* is very different from a nineteenth-century director.
4. A dog's ability to hear high-pitched sounds is much keener than humans.
5. How do your grades in English compare with science?
6. New cars this year are smaller than last year.
7. The biographical information in the encyclopedia is more detailed than the dictionary.
8. People have been more interested in reading the book than the movie version.
9. The view from the World Trade Center is even more spectacular than the Empire State Building.
10. The rate of interest paid by the Amalgamated Bank is higher than the Security Bank.
11. Radio reception on the top floor is usually clearer than the ground floor.
12. The strength in my left hand is greater than my right hand.
13. Some birds like to eat fruit as much as insects.
14. The damage caused by this year's natural disasters is greater than last year's.
15. For the past month the price of gold has risen more sharply than silver.

**EXERCISE 3.** The following sentences contain faulty parallelism. Rephrase the sentences so that the parallelism will be correctly and logically expressed. You will do well to review the various kinds of faulty parallelism before doing the exercise.

1. One of the accident victims suffered a broken arm, several broken ribs, and one of her lungs was punctured.
2. She not only was industrious, but she could be depended on.
3. As we were leaving the harbor, the radio weather report predicted gale-force winds, heavy rain, and that tides would be abnormally high.
4. A cloudy day is better for a game than sunshine.

5. She spoke about her experience in Australia and several predictions about the country's future.
6. To the unthinking person, war may be a romantic adventure, but a foolish and dirty business is the way the wise person regards it.
7. The unexpected cooperation of China was a greater surprise to Russia than the United States.
8. The skipper had a harsh voice, a weatherbeaten face, and was very stocky in build.
9. We were not sure that our request for a raise was fair or it would be granted.
10. The speech of cultivated Britishers is not so different as it used to be from Americans.
11. The public's attention has been centered on the need for more teachers, adequate classrooms, and there isn't enough new equipment.
12. This was a much harder assignment for me than Luis.
13. The ambassador did not know whether the President had sent for him or the Secretary of State.
14. Her friends not only were shocked by her failure but they felt a great disappointment.
15. The players were annoyed not so much by the decisions of the officials as the hostile crowd.
16. The company announced a bonus for all five-year employees and that deserving new employees would be given additional benefits.
17. The headmaster insisted that all of us return by ten o'clock and the housemasters must check us in.
18. High school programs have been accused of being too closely tied in with college education and that they neglect the average teen-ager.
19. Pioneers came with hopes of being happy and free and to make their fortunes in the new world.
20. All delegates to the convention were advised that on their return they would both have to make a written and oral report.

Chapter 16

# Unnecessary Shifts in Sentences

## Awkward Changes in Subject and in Verb Forms

Within a sentence a shift is a change from one subject to another or from one verb to another. Often shifts are acceptable because they are necessary to express the meaning the writer intends.

ACCEPTABLE SHIFT The trials of peace are great, but the dangers of war are greater. [The shift in subject from *trials* to *dangers* is a natural one.]

The smoothness of a sentence is sometimes seriously affected, however, by an unnecessary and awkward shift.

AWKWARD A student should choose books from the reading list so that you can be sure of their being acceptable to the teacher. [The unnecessary shift from *student* to *you* is awkward and confusing.]

ACCEPTABLE A **student** should choose books from the reading list so that **he** can be sure of their being acceptable to the teacher.

AWKWARD Pam did her math homework, and then her composition was written. [The shift from active to passive voice and the resulting shift in subject is unnecessary and awkward.]

ACCEPTABLE Pam **did** her math homework, and then she **wrote** her composition.

## 16a. Avoid unnecessary shifts from one subject to another.

UNNECESSARY SHIFTS

*Fishers* from many states visit the Ontario lakes where *fish* are found in abundance and, in the cool, crisp air of the North woods, a welcome *relief* from summer heat is enjoyed. *Planes, trains,* or *automobiles* bring the fishers to the edge of the wilderness. From there *boats* are used to penetrate the remoter waters where *trout, bass, pickerel, perch,* and freshwater *salmon* are caught.

SHIFTS AVOIDED

*Fishers* from many states visit the Ontario lakes where *they* find fish in abundance and, in the cool, crisp air of the North woods, enjoy a welcome relief from summer heat. After coming by plane, train, or automobile to the edge of the wilderness, the *fishers* use boats to penetrate the remoter waters, where *they* catch trout, bass, pickerel, perch, and freshwater salmon.

## 16b. Avoid unnecessary shifts from one verb form to another within one sentence.

### (1) Avoid unnecessary shifts in the voice of verbs.

Unnecessary shifts from one subject to another are often the result of a shift from active to passive voice.

When the subject of a verb is acting, the verb is in the *active voice.* When the subject of a verb is acted upon, the verb is in the *passive voice.*[1]

S ⟶ V

ACTIVE VOICE Jane **won** both events. [subject acting]

S ⟵ V

PASSIVE VOICE Both events **were won** by Jane. [subject acted upon]

Note that a shift in voice results in a shift in subject.

UNNECESSARY SHIFT Volunteers made [active verb] the dangerous journey after dark, but no wolves were encountered [passive verb].

[1] A fuller treatment of voice will be found on pages 153–57.

SHIFT AVOIDED Volunteers **made** [active verb] the dangerous journey after dark but **encountered** [active verb] no wolves.

UNNECESSARY SHIFT Since she knew the ability to speak well before a group is important, a course in public speaking was taken by her.

SHIFT AVOIDED Since **she knew** the ability to speak well before a group is important, **she took** a course in public speaking.

**(2) Avoid unnecessary shifts in the tense of verbs.**

Changing without reason from one tense to another within a sentence creates an awkward and confusing effect. Stick to the tense you start with unless there is an excellent reason for changing.

UNNECESSARY SHIFT At this point the President reads [present tense] a prepared statement but refused [past tense] to answer any questions.

SHIFT AVOIDED At this point the President **read** [past tense] a prepared statement but **refused** [past tense] to answer any questions.

SHIFT AVOIDED At this point the President **reads** [present tense] a prepared statement but **refuses** [present tense] to answer any questions.

UNNECESSARY SHIFT She caught [past tense] the puck and weaves [present tense] between two defenders.

SHIFT AVOIDED She **caught** [past tense] the puck and **wove** [past tense] between two defenders.

SHIFT AVOIDED She **catches** [present tense] the puck and **weaves** [present tense] between two defenders.

In correcting unnecessary shifts in subject and verb, you will often find the best method is to omit the second subject. This can usually be done by using the second verb in the same voice as the first and making the verb compound.

UNNECESSARY SHIFT A good driver has complete control of the car at all times, and allowance is made for the carelessness of other drivers.

SHIFT AVOIDED A good **driver has** complete control of the car at all times **and makes** allowances for the carelessness of other drivers. [The use of the compound active voice for both verbs corrects the awkward shift.]

**EXERCISE 1.** Most of the following sentences contain unnecessary shifts from one subject to another or from one verb form to another. By revising these sentences orally in class, show how these shifts may be avoided. Two of the sentences are acceptable. Identify these.

1. If one wants to try a delicious recipe from Puerto Rico, you should make rice with pigeon peas.
2. To start, sauté three tablespoons of diced salt pork until the fat has melted.
3. A chopped onion and two minced cloves of garlic should be added to the skillet, and then add two chopped green peppers.
4. After you have peeled two tomatoes, chopping them comes next.
5. The tomatoes, too, should be placed into the skillet, and you should cook the entire mixture for five minutes.
6. A tablespoon of capers goes in next, and you should follow this with a teaspoon of salt, two cups of uncooked long-grain rice, and three cups of water.
7. After you stir the rice, a pound of cooked pigeon peas needs to be added.
8. A tablespoon of achiote should not be forgotten to be included, since this spice imparts a lovely golden color to the food.
9. When the liquid comes to a boil, cover the skillet, the flame should be reduced, and simmer the mixture until the water has been absorbed.
10. Stir the mixture occasionally to keep the rice from sticking, and continue cooking until the rice is dry and fluffy.

**EXERCISE 2.** In the following passage the tense of the verbs is frequently shifted from past to present and from present to past. Decide in what tense (past or present) it should be written. Prepare to read aloud in class, changing the verb forms to remove the unnecessary shifts in tense.

Mr. Sampson, who had been for ten years the faculty adviser of the high school annual, sat calmly at his desk after school, watching the autumn sun light the empty room, while he waited for the first meeting of the new yearbook staff. A veteran like Mr. Sampson could hardly be expected to show much emotion over the repetition of an event he had taken part in so many times. He is not particularly disturbed when the door opens and Jane Billings led a noisy group of students into his room.

Following a general falling over desks and slumping into seats, Jane called the meeting to order. This year, she explains, the staff would produce the finest yearbook East High has ever had. Someone wanted to know, first of all, what kind of cover the book would have. A great preference is expressed for a thick and heavy leather cover, suitably embossed, and bearing the seal and colors of the school. Mr. Sampson smiles, for he had never yet known a new staff that did not begin with a discussion of the cover.

Complete agreement about the cover having been so quickly reached, Sue Thompson wants to know why last year's book was so dull. Here Mr. Sampson smiles again. Everything's going to be just fine, he thought, remembering that no staff in the past had ever had a good word to say for its predecessors. "Let's have twice as many pictures, a bigger sports section, not so much writing that nobody ever reads." These weighty matters agreed upon, everyone wanted to know whether the seniors aren't entitled to more space in the book. "How about three or four instead of ten senior pictures to a page? After all, it's our book."

Mr. Sampson listened and said nothing. He is quietly thinking about next January, when the supply of snapshots will be disappointingly small, when the budget will be alarmingly inadequate, when compromise after compromise will be frantically made in order to get a yearbook out at all. But he doesn't say much. He knows it is better for the staff to find out for itself why last year's book and all the books before it had been such complete "failures."

**EXERCISE 3.** The sentences in this exercise are awkward because of unnecessary shifts in the subject and in the verb. Revise the sentences to eliminate these shifts.

1. Adolescents naturally rebel against authority, but the authority of the law must be respected by them.
2. Lonely students might participate in an extracurricular activity so that new friendships can be made.
3. A senior must not only pass his courses and graduate, but also plans for your future must be made before the year is over.
4. My brother frequently procrastinates, and a tendency toward laziness is occasionally shown.
5. My father has some amusing peculiarities which are not recognized by him.
6. The union's demands were unacceptable even though some concessions were contained in them.
7. If a teacher wants to be liked, you must treat students impartially.
8. Coach Martin always insisted on long practice sessions and strict training, but her winning teams justify her methods.
9. The Vice-President flew to the Paris Conference, but few concrete results were accomplished by him.
10. A good student can win a college scholarship, and thus his parents are relieved of part of the cost of his college education.
11. When you buy a car, a person should be sure he can afford the upkeep.
12. In the end Robert stays with his mother, and the girl he loves is lost to him forever.
13. The cement and sand are first mixed thoroughly; then add the water.
14. The experienced boat operator is aware of the danger of fire, and when filling the gas tank, great precautions are taken not to spill gasoline in the bottom of the boat.
15. As a young district attorney he successfully handled the Tammany Hall cases, and the backing of the Republican Party was won.
16. As the bus careens toward the edge of the road, we thought our time had come, and we grab our seats in desperation.
17. Many doctors recognize the value of health insurance, but the particular kind we should have is something they could not agree on.

18. Searching for the right words, Livia composed her closing sentence, and another essay was brought to its logical conclusion.
19. Sammy had just finished his bitter denunciation of all teachers and of one chemistry teacher in particular, when he turns around and Ms. Lerner was seen in the laboratory doorway.
20. An explorer must study maps very carefully so that you will be able to plan your trip efficiently.

Chapter **17**

# Sentence Conciseness

## Avoiding Wordiness and Overwriting

It is a mistake to believe that the more words a theme contains the better. Professional writers who are paid according to the number of words they write may find wordiness profitable, but they would never claim that it improves their articles. Most good writing is effective because it is not cluttered with unnecessary words.

Do not think, however, that wordiness appears only in long compositions. A long piece of writing may contain no superfluous words, whereas a short piece may be full of them. Studying the principles in this section and doing the exercises will make you aware of wordiness in writing and help you to avoid it in your own compositions.

## SUPERFLUOUS WORDS AND UNNECESSARY REPETITION

The following example of wordiness was the opening paragraph of a high school student's composition about an overnight hike. Lines have been drawn through the superfluous words.

When ~~in the course of human events, when~~ a woman finds it necessary to rest her weary bones, she packs up and goes on what is inappropriately called a vacation. Last summer I had the good fortune to go ~~during the summer~~ to a mountain camp in ~~the~~

~~mountains of~~ eastern Pennsylvania. On the day that I arrived, ~~when I got to camp~~, I found that the camp had been quarantined because of the measles that one of the younger campers had brought in, ~~and no one who was in the camp could leave~~. After we had spent a week in camp, the prospect of an overnight hike in the mountainous wilds looked especially good to us campers who had been so long confined ~~to camp by the quarantine~~.

## 17a. Avoid wordiness by eliminating superfluous words and the unnecessary repetition of ideas.

WORDY The game is played with tiny, little round balls, which, in my opinion, I think are made of steel.

BETTER The game is played with tiny balls, which, I think, are made of steel.

WORDY After descending down to the edge of the river, we boarded a small raft which was floating there on the surface of the water.

BETTER After descending to the edge of the river, we boarded a small raft.

WORDY The first story in the book is a masterpiece in itself and quite a story.

BETTER The first story in the book is a masterpiece.

**EXERCISE 1.** Revise the following sentences, eliminating superfluous words.

1. We watched the big, massive black cloud rising up from the level prairie and covering over the sun.
2. Far away in the distance, as far as anything was visible to the eye, the small, diminutive shapes of the campers' tents were outlined in silhouette against the dark sky.
3. Modern cars of today, unlike the old cars of yesterday, can be driven faster without danger than the old ones.
4. When what the speaker was saying was not audible to our ears, I asked her to repeat again what she had said.
5. It was in this mountain wilderness that the explorers found there the examples of wildlife for which they had been looking.
6. During this year's current baseball season, all home games

and many away games in other cities may be watched at home on your television screen as they are brought to you over station WPIX.

7. The mediator said that if both parties would give in a little that a satisfactory settlement could be reached that would satisfy both parties.
8. In spite of the fact that the danger was neither tangible to the touch nor visible to the eye, it was very real to all the dwellers and inhabitants of the village in the foothills which circled around the base of Mt. Wilson.
9. The drive over to Cross Village follows and winds along the top of a great, huge bluff above the lake.
10. When at last the pounding finally began to stop, I stretched myself out prone upon the bed and attempted to try to go to sleep.
11. The world in its present state of affairs today is in great and dire need of great leaders who will work hard to prevent the recurrence again of a disastrously destructive world war.
12. During the hours in the morning before noon, there is a variety of radio programs of different kinds to which you may listen to.
13. As you continue on in the book a little further, you will be surprised and amazed by the clever skill of the writer of the book in weaving in together the many previously unrelated threads of his story.
14. At the final end of the picture, the villain abruptly and suddenly does an about-face and changes completely into a good person with admirable characteristics.
15. His mental thought processes puzzled his school teachers and made them despair of his future success in the years after his graduation from school.
16. I am always as a rule surprised to find out that a currently popular hit tune was also a popular number years ago in the past when my parents were both going to high school.
17. She was firmly determined to combine together both of the two divisions of the firm in order to achieve a stronger company eventually in the long run.
18. Circling around his adversary with a menacing look on his face, Broadhurst bided his time and waited for an opening through which he could connect up with his mighty right.

19. The President's struggle with Congress ended up in a victory for the President when the public voted at the November election to reelect him again to the Presidency for another term of four years.
20. The final conclusion of the novel on which she had been working on for more than five years was disappointing to everyone who read the manuscript, and she decided to revise and change the story.

**EXERCISE 2.** Revise the following wordy paragraphs. Eliminate all unnecessary words but keep the ideas of the paragraphs clear.

1

When we were two hundred yards away from our objective, which was a small little grove of pine trees on the sloping side of a hill, we were confronted by a vast, wet swamp. I remembered that during the last two weeks we had had, out of fourteen days, ten days of rain, and decided in my own mind to send out a few scouts who might discover a way by means of which we could reach the grove without getting our feet wet. Then, when the scouts reported back that their efforts to try to find a dry path through the swamp had been unsuccessful, we gave up and resigned ourselves to sloshing knee-deep through the muddy water.

2

When, after eight years of education in school, the student enters the ninth grade and becomes a freshman, then he begins to find out what seniors are really like. Up until this point, seniors have been heroes to him, admired from a respectful distance away as though they were gods, unless he has happened to know one personally, of course. But now, however, his conception undergoes a change. The senior becomes an ogre whose one and only purpose in life seems to the freshman to be to make life as miserable as possible for each and every freshman. Every way the freshman turns in the school corridors, a senior hall cop, with a great big letter on his chest, grabs him with huge talons and tells him with hot and fiery breath that he cannot go down an up stairway. He is enticed into joining clubs which are ruled over and presided over by seniors who use him mainly for the performance of unpleasant errands beneath the dignity of a senior. Whenever the freshman cannot be of use, he is ignored. His former ambition to be a senior fades out and wanes until one day he begins to think thoughts of getting his revenge. In his frenzied brain the idea dawns on him if he is patient, he, too, will someday enjoy the privilege of molding the lives and characters of ninth-graders. This idea accounts for the fanatic fixed stare which is to be seen in the eyes of so many freshmen.

## CONCISENESS THROUGH REDUCTION

The opposite of wordiness is conciseness. In your effort to write well, you will profit from studying some ways to make your writing more concise. Of course, there is a danger in being too economical in your use of words; writing which is too concise will not be clear and will not achieve its intended effect. Nevertheless, the following rule will call to your attention some helpful methods of avoiding wordiness.

**17b. Avoid wordiness by reducing clauses to phrases, and phrases to single words. This process is known as *reduction.***

***1. Clauses reduced to participial, gerund, or infinitive phrases***

CLAUSE When they were trapped by a cave-in, the miners waited for the rescue team.

PARTICIPIAL PHRASE **Trapped by a cave-in,** the miners waited for the rescue team.

CLAUSE Because we had found no one home, we left a note in the mailbox.

PARTICIPIAL PHRASE **Having found no one home,** we left a note in the mailbox.

CLAUSE **If you leave at noon,** you can get to Chicago at three o'clock.

GERUND PHRASE **Leaving at noon** will get you to Chicago at three o'clock.

CLAUSE We decided **that we would get an early start.**

INFINITIVE PHRASE We decided **to get an early start.**

### *2. Clauses reduced to prepositional phrases*

CLAUSE The teams **which had come from Missouri** were not scheduled to play the first day of the tournament.

PHRASE The teams **from Missouri** were not scheduled to play the first day of the tournament.

CLAUSE **When the sun sets,** the streetlights come on.

PHRASE **At sunset** the streetlights come on.

CLAUSE **After you have graduated,** you will be looking for a job.

PHRASE **After graduation,** you will be looking for a job.

CLAUSE My cousin **who lives in Mexico** speaks Spanish fluently.

PHRASE My cousin **in Mexico** speaks Spanish fluently.

### *3. Clauses reduced to appositives*

CLAUSE Dr. Brown, **who is the chief surgeon,** will operate.

APPOSITIVE Dr. Brown, **the chief surgeon,** will operate.

CLAUSE Her two dogs, **one of which is a collie and the other a spaniel,** perform different duties on the farm.

APPOSITIVE Her two dogs, **a collie and a spaniel,** perform different duties on the farm.

### *4. Clauses and phrases reduced to single words*

CLAUSE The dance classes **that have been canceled** will be rescheduled.

WORD The **canceled** dance classes will be rescheduled.

CLAUSE Laura is a runner **who never tires.**

WORD Laura is a **tireless** runner.

CLAUSE We met a woman who dances in the ballet.

WORD We met a **ballerina.**

PHRASE Her career **in the movies** was brief.

WORD Her **movie** career was brief.

PHRASE She greeted everyone **in a cordial manner.**

WORD She greeted everyone **cordially.**

From these examples of reduction you can see how to make your own writing more concise. Usually the time for such reduction is during revision of your papers. Revising the sentences in the following exercises will give you practice in writing more concisely.

**EXERCISE 3.** The following sentences can be made more concise by reducing the italicized groups of words according to the directions given. Rewrite each sentence according to the directions.

1. (a) *Since she is an automobile dealer,* Mrs. Holmes has promised her children a car as a gift (b) *when they reach their seventeenth birthday.*
   [(a) Reduce clause to an appositive; (b) reduce clause to a prepositional phrase.]
2. After (a) *he had looked* everywhere for an old place (b) *that he could renovate,* Mr. Dayton bought the house (c) *that was deserted* on the edge of town.
   [(a) Reduce *he had looked* to a gerund (*–ing*); (b) reduce clause to an infinitive phrase (*to* + verb); (c) reduce *that was deserted* to an adjective.]
3. The orchard (a) *of apple trees* which stood (b) *in the area behind the house* yielded no fruit during his first year there, but it bore much fruit (c) *when the second season came.*
   [(a) Reduce phrase to an adjective; (b) reduce to one prepositional phrase; (c) reduce clause to a prepositional phrase.]
4. (a) *Since we were sitting in seats* (b) *which were near first base,* we were able to judge the accuracy of the decisions (c) *of the umpire.*
   [(a) Reduce clause to a participle (*–ing*), omitting *in seats;* (b) reduce clause to a prepositional phrase; (c) reduce phrase to a possessive.]
5. (a) *Because it was necessary for her to be away from home* (b) *in the afternoon and in the evening* for many days, Mrs. Stein, (c) *who is the president of the Parent-Teacher Association,* hired a succession of baby-sitters (d) *who were to take care of her children* (e) *while she was absent.*
   [(a) Reduce clause to a participial phrase (*Having to be . . .*); (b) reduce two phrases to two words telling when; (c) reduce clause to an appositive; (d) reduce clause to an infinitive phrase (*to* + verb); (e) reduce clause to a prepositional phrase.]

**EXERCISE 4.** The italicized clauses and phrases in the following sentences can be reduced. Revise the sentences, reducing the clauses to phrases or appositives or single words, and the phrases to single words. You may omit unnecessary words, and you may occasionally need to change the word order.

1. We decided to wait for the bus *in order that we might save money.*
2. After I had finished the assigned reading, I read three novels *which were written by Virginia Woolf.*
3. This small hotel, *which is situated in Connecticut,* is patronized mainly by *people from Boston.*
4. *After he lost a leg in an accident which occurred while he was hunting,* Monty Stratton, *who was a pitcher for the White Sox,* made a comeback in professional baseball *which was amazing.*
5. Our seats *in which we sat at the Army-Navy game* were almost on the forty-yard line, *and they were at the top of the stadium.*
6. The poetry *of Blake* has had an influence *which is notable* on the poetry *of Yeats.*
7. *While he was inspecting his new house, which is in the suburbs,* Mr. Doyle stumbled over a piece of flooring and fell down the stairs *leading to the cellar.*
8. Our days *that we spent in the north woods* would have been perfect if it had not been for the mosquitoes *that were enormous and hungry.*
9. Inez, *who is an ambitious young actress,* found that the acting *that she did in a stock company in the summer* gave her the experience *which she needed.*
10. The most common complaint *that is made by students* is that every teacher chooses Friday *on which to give examinations.*

**EXERCISE 5.** Revise the following wordy paragraphs. Eliminate all unnecessary words and reduce clauses to phrases or appositives or single words. You may change the word order, but you must keep the ideas of the paragraphs clear.

1

As a result of the nation's energy shortage, the nation's government spends literally thousands of dollars in money each and every year making energy-saving improvements in selected homes in order to demonstrate to its citizens that energy-saving improvements can result in huge money savings on gas and electric bills. Despite such efforts, many people do not bother to take the advice of the government and to make the improvements to their own homes. According to a number of social scientists who are studying the problem of motivating people to conserve energy, homeowners do not always and everywhere respond to government planning and policy making in the way that government would like them to respond. As far as saving energy is concerned, many people wonder why they should make any improvements at all if they are able to afford the higher price of energy with the money they have. Furthermore, people desire convenience and comfort in the home and this desire affects their decisions about their homes just as much as their desire to save energy or to save money. Therefore, if the government is to be more successful in convincing people to conserve energy, it must, by way of example, show people that a home with weatherstripping, for example, is or can be more enjoyable or more comfortable than a home without weatherstripping. According to social scientists, unless the government takes a different approach to the needs and wants of its citizens, its program to conserve energy in homes around the country may not succeed as well as could be expected.

2

Needless to say, I am not one of those who are members of the senior class who believe that the senior lounge should be closed during the week of exams. It goes without saying that seniors need a place which is quiet and relaxing in order for them to escape the pressures which accompany exam week. If the lounge is closed during this time, it would mean that seniors would be forced to use the cafeteria, which is crowded, or the auditorium, which is noisy, for the purpose of relaxation. Furthermore, the use of the senior lounge during exam week is by this time one of the few privileges that seniors are still able to enjoy here at East High; not long ago the right of seniors to park cars in the parking area reserved for members of the faculty was recently taken away by the Student-Teacher Council. If more privileges are taken away, the morale of seniors will weaken.

## THE OVERWRITTEN STYLE

In their efforts to write impressively, high school students sometimes produce writing that is so artificial, flowery, and cumbersome as to be absurd. Such a style results from the mistaken notion that big words, unusual words, and figures of speech, no matter how commonplace, are "literary." Unlike mistakes made through carelessness or laziness, a mistake of this kind is made by trying too hard to sound like a great writer. The resulting style is said to be "overwritten."

**17c. Avoid an overwritten style. Write naturally without straining after a "literary" effect.**

The following example of overwriting will make you aware of the fault. Doing the exercise which follows this will also help you correct overwritten passages in your own work.

HARBOR FOG

The fog slowly crept in and covered the metropolis with its sinister cloak of impressive quietude. An entire day of heavy rain had drenched the surrounding municipality, forming puddles in the thoroughfares which reflected the shimmering images of the gleaming street lights and the illumination emanating from multitudes of office windows.

As I stood on the magnificent span which arched above the swirling waters, the mournful warnings of the anchored ships pierced the dense fog. The constant beat of the harbor bell buoys and the gentle lapping of the murky water on the piling of this bridge combined to permeate the night air with a mystic tenseness.

The harbor boats moved tediously through the night, and their wakes left grotesque trails which slowly dissolved and enveloped themselves in the depths of the blackness.

Although it was late, the never-ceasing rumble of activity from the nearby city could still be apprehended. The penetrating night air was heavy with moisture and with each soft puff of breeze the salt of the sea could be detected.

During World War II, Representative Maury Maverick, of Texas, became impatient with the overwritten style of some government writing and branded this sort of writing with the descriptive term "gobbledygook." Here is an example of the gobbledygook that troubled Mr. Maverick: "Illumination is required to be extinguished upon vacating these premises." You can see how much more effective would be, "Turn out the lights when you leave."

**EXERCISE 6.** Each of the following sentences represents the fault of overwriting. In simpler words write your version of the idea which is here expressed in a forced and unnatural style.

1. In a vast explosion of frozen precipitation, Jan shot through the feathery drift, maintaining without apparent effort her equilibrium upon the fragile strips of ash strapped to her pedal extremities.
2. My exploration of the intriguing heights of the science of economics left me with the firm conviction that *Homo sapiens* is powerless when it comes to exerting any detectable influence on the fundamental operation of supply and demand.
3. The bitterest irony of our fevered time is the oft-repeated concept that only by creating more magnificent and more deadly instruments of explosive destruction can human beings bring to this whirling planet the era of tranquillity for which it has longed since the beginning of time.
4. The sharp impact of wood upon the little white sphere was followed by a sudden emanation of sound, like an explosion, from the throats of the assembled multitude in the tiered stands as the soaring pellet arched over the greensward and came to rest beyond the masonry in the left field.
5. Nothing so impresses one with the warm security and pleasing restfulness of one's native surroundings as extensive peregrinations into foreign realms and among the exotic areas on the surface of our world.
6. Following our educational endeavors of the day, several of us conscientious seekers after knowledge relaxed our weary cerebrums by lending our ears to the latest discs at Jacobsen's music emporium.
7. Laying aside for the nonce the tomes of wisdom, I selected from the periodical rack the current issue of my favorite pictorial publication and, elongated upon the resilient daven-

port, slowly perused the photographic narrative of the week's outstanding occurrences.

8. In order to forestall the embarrassment of a refusal, I preceded my request for Helen's company upon an excursion to the local cinema by inquiring of her nearest of kin as to what Helen's social calendar held for the Friday evening in question.
9. Bent upon a week's exploration of our nation's vast regions of tranquil pristine wilderness, I bade a fond farewell to my anxious mater and, with my earthly possessions ensconced in a commodious rucksack, embarked upon my great adventure via public interstate omnibus.
10. Lifting the pigskin from the water-soaked gridiron with his trusty toe, Harvey booted it with mathematical precision directly between the white uprights silhouetted against the setting sun.

Chapter 18

# Sentence Combining and Revising

## Variety, Interest, and Emphasis

## SENTENCE COMBINING

Good writers avoid the choppy style caused by using too many short, subject-first sentences. Study how the following paragraph, written in a choppy style, has been revised to achieve a more fluent, more mature style. The revised version uses subordination, coordination, apposition, and other devices to indicate clearly the relationship between ideas.

The sinking of the *Titanic* was a great disaster. The *Titanic* weighed 42,000 metric tons. It was the largest ship of its time. It was the most luxurious ship of its time. The sinking was one of the worst maritime disasters in history. The *Titanic* was on its maiden voyage. The ship struck an iceberg. The iceberg was off the Grand Banks of Newfoundland. The accident happened on the night of April 14, 1912. The night was clear. The night was cold. The captain had received iceberg warnings. He had chosen to pass through a perilous ice field. The rate of speed was 42 kilometers per hour. He wished to reach New York ahead of schedule. The *Titanic*'s hull had sixteen watertight compartments. The iceberg punctured five compartments. The ship's designers thought no accident could puncture more than four compartments. The ship sank in less than three hours. Over 1500 of the 2220 passengers and crew drowned. Another ship, the *Californian*, lay stopped in the water. It was less than eighteen kilometers away. It did not respond to the distress signal. The radio operator was off duty. The *Carpathia* was ninety kilometers away. It reversed course. It sped through the ice floes. It picked up the survivors. By the time it arrived, many lives had been lost. The *Titanic* disaster quickly led to the reform of maritime safety laws.

The sinking of the 42,000-metric-ton *Titanic,* the largest and most luxurious ship of its time, was one of the worst maritime disasters in history. On the clear, cold night of April 14, 1912, the ship, on its maiden voyage, struck an iceberg off the Grand Banks of Newfoundland. Although the captain had received iceberg warnings, he had chosen to pass through a perilous ice field at 42 kilometers per hour in order to reach New York ahead of schedule. The iceberg punctured five of sixteen watertight compartments in the ship's hull, one more than the ship's designers had thought possible in any accident, and the ship sank in less than three hours, with the loss of over 1500 of the 2220 passengers and crew. Another ship, the *Californian,* lay stopped in the water less than eighteen kilometers away, but it did not respond to the distress signal because its radio operator was off duty. The *Carpathia,* which was ninety kilometers away, reversed course, sped through the ice floes, and picked up the survivors, but by then many lives had been lost. The *Titanic* disaster quickly led to the reform of maritime safety laws.

Sentence-combining exercises provide useful practice in improving your writing style. As you combine short, choppy sentences in the exercises that follow, you will be making choices with regard to sentence structure and emphasis. This experience will enable you to achieve a more fluent style, richer in variety and interest.

## 18a. Combine short, related sentences by inserting adjectives, adverbs, and prepositional phrases.

Note how the following three sentences have been rewritten as one sentence by eliminating unnecessary words.

THREE SENTENCES The Prime Minister closed the session.
The Prime Minister felt weary.
He closed the session with the Cabinet.

ONE SENTENCE The **weary** Prime Minister closed the session **with the Cabinet.**

There may be more than one correct way to combine short sentences.

THREE SENTENCES The plane moved slowly.
The plane moved along the runway.
The plane moved toward the hangar.

ONE SENTENCE **Slowly,** the plane moved **along the runway toward the hangar.**

*or*

**Along the runway,** the plane moved **slowly toward the hangar.**

There are other correct ways in which these sentences could have been combined. Although you often have some degree of choice in combining short, related sentences, you may find that some combinations do not read smoothly, such as, *Along the runway toward the hangar slowly the plane moved.* You should avoid these combinations as well as those that change the meaning of the original short sentences.

**EXERCISE 1.** Combine each group of short, related sentences by inserting adjectives, adverbs, or prepositional phrases into the first sentence and by eliminating unnecessary words. Add commas where they are necessary.

EXAMPLE 1. Peregrine falcons soar.
They soar gracefully.
They soar in the air.
1. *Peregrine falcons soar gracefully in the air.*

1. The peregrine falcon adapts to varying climates.
It adapts quickly.
It adapts easily.
2. The falcon dives on its victims and kills them.
The falcon is bluish-gray.
It kills its victims by the force of the impact.

3. Peregrine falcons inhabit areas where birds are often plentiful.
The areas are open.
The areas are rocky.
The areas are near water.
4. Peregrines nest on the sides of cliffs.
They usually nest there.
They nest high on the cliffs.
They nest in small ledges.
5. Peregrine falcons became scarce.
They became extremely scarce.
They became scarce in the United States.
They became scarce because of the pesticide DDT.
6. No breeding pairs remained.
No pairs remained east of the Mississippi.
No pairs remained by 1970.
No pairs of falcons remained.
7. Scientists are reintroducing falcons.
The scientists are from Cornell University.
The falcons are wild.
The scientists reintroduce falcons under controlled conditions.
The scientists reintroduce falcons to the eastern United States.
8. The ban on DDT has helped the falcons.
The ban was effective.
The ban has helped considerably.
The falcons have been endangered.
9. Peregrines are hatching eggs.
These peregrines are in the Eastern wilderness.
They are hatching eggs for the first time.
It is the first time since the 1950's
10. Peregrine falcons prefer nesting in cities.
They prefer nesting in large cities.
Some peregrines prefer this.
They prefer nesting on high skyscrapers.
They prefer the cities because of a supply of pigeons.
The supply of pigeons is abundant.

## 18b. Combine closely related sentences by using participial phrases.

Participial phrases—phrases containing a participle and any complements or modifiers it may have—help you add concrete details to nouns and pronouns in sentences. In the following example, the participial phrases are printed in bold-faced type. Notice how they describe the subject of the sentence, the noun *ship*.

> **Badly damaged by high winds** and **deserted by half its crew,** the ship finally reached a safe harbor.

Participial phrases are often a useful way to combine sentences and to express ideas concisely. The following two sentences can be combined by using a participial phrase.

TWO SENTENCES The colors were orange, red, and blue.
The colors were painted on the ceiling.

ONE SENTENCE The colors **painted on the ceiling** were orange, red, and blue.

The second sentence has been turned into a participial phrase, *painted on the ceiling,* and attached to the first sentence. Unnecessary words have been deleted.

A participle or participial phrase must always be placed close to the noun or pronoun it modifies. Otherwise the sentence may confuse the reader.

MISPLACED Wrapped in silver paper, the bride accepted the wedding present.

IMPROVED The bride accepted the wedding present **wrapped in silver paper.**

**EXERCISE 2.** Combine each of the following pairs of sentences into one sentence by turning either the first sentence or second sentence of each pair into a participial phrase and inserting it into the remaining sentence. Punctuate the combined sentences correctly.

EXAMPLE 1. The employee asked for a raise.
The employee found out about the boss's temper.
1. *Asking for a raise, the employee found out about the boss's temper.*

1. Tomb robbers searched inside a crypt.
Tomb robbers found gold.
2. The pitcher concentrated on the batter.
The pitcher forgot about the base runner.

3. The index in this book is very long.
   It contains every topic found on every page.
4. The student did not hand in her paper.
   The student realized that two pages were missing.
5. We held back our cheers.
   We waited for the speech to end.
6. The van failed to stop at the red light.
   It narrowly missed another car.
7. I left the bread in the oven too long.
   I burned the crust.
8. Our counselor was stung by a bee.
   Our counselor yelled angrily.
9. The teacher was pleased with the test results.
   The teacher congratulated the class.
10. The hurricane swept across the ocean.
    The hurricane demolished every boat in its path.

**18c. Combine short, related sentences by using appositives or appositive phrases.**

Appositives and appositive phrases add definitive detail to nouns and pronouns in sentences by helping to identify or explain them. Note how the appositive phrase in the following sentence helps identify the noun *captain*.

> The captain of the swim team, **holder of six school records,** won a full athletic scholarship.

Two sentences can often be combined through the use of an appositive or an appositive phrase.

TWO SENTENCES Many students in the school play lacrosse. Lacrosse is the national summer sport of Canada.

ONE SENTENCE Many students in the school play lacrosse, **the national summer sport of Canada.**

**EXERCISE 3.** Combine the following pairs of sentences by turning one of the sentences into an appositive or an appositive phrase. Punctuate the combined sentence correctly. Answers may vary.

EXAMPLE 1. Elizabeth Bowen was born in Ireland.
She is one of the leading fiction writers in England since World War I.
1. *Elizabeth Bowen, one of the leading fiction writers in England since World War I, was born in Ireland.*

1. In *The Death of the Heart* the protagonist is a sensitive person, ill at ease with the world.
   *The Death of the Heart* is one of Bowen's best-known novels.
2. Bowen was a nurse and an air-raid warden during World War II.
   Bowen wrote about the psychological effects of war on civilians.
3. Nadine Gordimer is a South African writer.
   She published her first stories at the age of fifteen.
4. Many of Gordimer's stories are set in South Africa.
   Many of Gordimer's stories are accounts of modern-day social tensions.
5. In *Going Home* Doris Lessing writes about a return visit to Rhodesia.
   *Going Home* is an autobiographical narrative.
6. Doris Lessing is a sensitive observer of social and political struggles.
   She describes people attempting to find meaning in life.
7. Katherine Mansfield is a modern master of the short story.
   She died of tuberculosis at the age of thirty-four.
8. Revealing the influence of Anton Chekhov, her stories focus more on character, atmosphere, and language than on plot.
   Chekhov was a great Russian writer.
9. *A Room of One's Own* is a book of essays by Virginia Woolf.
   *A Room of One's Own* is a short defense of women's rights.
10. Virginia Woolf was a member of the Bloomsbury Group.
    This group was a circle of British intellectuals.

**18d. Combine short, related sentences by using compound subjects or verbs or by writing a compound sentence.**

Compound subjects and verbs and compound sentences are common in writing. Writers, however, often overuse compound constructions by loosely stringing together ideas that belong in separate sentences (see page 286). You should not only learn the appropriate function of various connectives but should also avoid the overuse of *and* or *so* in your writing.

Compound subjects and verbs are joined by conjunctions such as *and, but,* and *or* and by correlative conjunctions such as *either–or, neither–nor,* and *both–and.*

EXAMPLES **Either** Mr. Sanderson **or** one of his students will bring the slide projector.
We watched the game this afternoon **and** cheered our team to victory.

Independent clauses are joined into a compound sentence by conjunctions such as *and, but, for,* and *or* and by other connectives such as *furthermore, yet, however, therefore, either–or,* and *neither–nor.* The relationship of the independent clauses determines which connective works best.

EXAMPLES Two cats were stranded in the tree, **and** no one could rescue them.
The police officer questioned him; **however,** he refused to answer. [Note the use of the semicolon.]

Ideas in separate sentences can be combined by using the appropriate connecting words. See page 207 for a complete list of connecting words.

TWO SENTENCES Rain had soaked the playing field.
Practice was canceled.

ONE SENTENCE Rain had soaked the playing field; **therefore,** practice was canceled.

**EXERCISE 4.** Most of the following items consist of two closely related ideas. Combine these ideas into a single sentence, using the appropriate connectives. (Consult the list of connectives on page 207 if necessary.) Certain items contain unrelated ideas. In such instances, write *Unrelated* on your paper to show that the ideas are better expressed in two separate sentences.

EXAMPLE 1. The Congress will approve this bill.
The President will veto it.

1. *The Congress will approve this bill, but the President will veto it.*

1. The basketball team has played well all season.
   It will probably win the championship.
2. Frank worked hard on his homework.
   His friend had given him the wrong assignment.
3. America must learn to use less energy.
   There will be a more severe energy shortage in a few years.
4. Acid rain is a problem in the Northeast.
   This problem is due to air pollution.
5. The student account is empty.
   We shall have to raise some money.
6. The prospects are bleak for new gym equipment.
   The student council will continue to recommend this important purchase.
7. The atmosphere on Mars is very thin.
   The planet is smaller than Earth.
8. School spirit sometimes wanes during the winter months.
   The seniors have organized a carnival in December.
9. The class elections are in three weeks.
   Everyone voted last year.
10. Sue is a well-qualified candidate.
    Most of her class support her.

## 18e. Combine short, related sentences into a complex sentence by putting one idea into a subordinate clause.

Subordination allows you to express the relationship between two unequal ideas within a single sentence. Methods for subordinating ideas include the use of an adjective clause, an adverb clause, and a noun clause. Mastering these methods of subordination will improve the variety and clarity of your writing.

### (1) Use an adjective clause to combine sentences.

Adjective clauses, like adjectives, modify nouns or pronouns. In the following sentence, the adjective clause is printed in bold-faced type.

The detective **who solved the case** was a master at logical thinking.

To combine sentences by using an adjective clause, you must first decide which idea to emphasize (see page 210). Then you must choose the correct relative pronoun to join the sentences.

RELATIVE PRONOUNS who, whom, whose, which, that

The adjective clause must always be placed close to the word or words it modifies.

| | |
|---|---|
| TWO SENTENCES | The story has an intricate plot.<br>I found the plot hard to follow. |
| ONE SENTENCE | The story has an intricate plot **that I found hard to follow.** |
| TWO SENTENCES | The woman heads the delegation.<br>I met her yesterday. |
| ONE SENTENCE | The woman **whom I met yesterday** heads the delegation. |

**EXERCISE 5.** Combine the following pairs of sentences by subordinating one idea in an adjective clause. Punctuate your sentences correctly.

EXAMPLE 1. Martin Luther King, Jr., married Coretta Scott.
He met her while studying at Boston University.
1. *Martin Luther King, Jr., married Coretta Scott, whom he met while studying at Boston University.*

1. My uncle is an experienced traveler.
He has recently returned from the Grand Canyon.
2. Richard prefers trout fishing.
It requires more patience than deep-sea fishing.
3. This blanket is too heavy for the summer.
It should be kept in the closet.
4. Pedro drove the truck.
Pedro has just received his driver's license.
5. He gave me the rest of the money.
He owed the money.
6. Melissa is about to begin her project.
You can reach her after eight this evening.
7. Mr. Partridge coaches our basketball team.
I introduced him to you.

8. Antique chairs lined the corridor.
   Each of them had a price tag on the arm.
9. I forgot the notebook.
   It was lying on the sofa.
10. The elephant sprayed water on passers-by.
    The elephant was standing near the fence.

**(2) Use an adverb clause to combine sentences.**

Adverb clauses can express a relationship of time, cause, purpose, or condition between two ideas within a single sentence.[1]

EXAMPLE **Although you present a convincing argument,** I will not change my mind.

To combine sentences by using an adverb clause, you must first decide which idea should become subordinate. You must then decide which subordinating conjunction best expresses the relationship between the two ideas.

TWO SENTENCES Elsie received the reply in the mail.
She tore open the envelope impatiently.

ONE SENTENCE **When Elsie received the reply in the mail,** she tore open the envelope impatiently.

TWO SENTENCES Injuries would decrease.
People would be more careful.

ONE SENTENCE **If people would be more careful,** injuries would decrease.

**EXERCISE 6.** Combine each pair of sentences by subordinating one idea in an adverb clause. (Consult the list of subordinating conjunctions on page 211 if you need to.) Punctuate the combined sentences correctly.

EXAMPLE 1. Sally did her best.
She was unable to win the prize.
1. *Although Sally did her best, she was unable to win the prize.*

1. It is true that you learn to do by doing.
   It is obvious that you learn to write by writing.

[1] See page 211 for a list of common subordinating conjunctions.

2. You should not make up your mind.
   You have studied all the evidence.
3. Money is undoubtedly important.
   It has never made anyone happy.
4. All students should learn standard English.
   They will never be embarrassed by their usage.
5. This critic recommends a new book.
   The book becomes a best seller.
6. She will invest her money with you.
   You can prove that the investment is safe.
7. We raised our prices.
   Our business increased.
8. She wanted to graduate in January.
   She could join the Navy.
9. You train rigorously.
   You will be able to do well in cross-country.
10. She was ill.
    She insisted on going ahead with the show.
11. The committee members could not agree.
    The whole matter was referred to the president.
12. The president took the responsibility.
    She wanted to settle the matter herself.
13. She decided to bring the issue before the entire club.
    Everyone could express an opinion.
14. There was a great deal of talk.
    Nothing was decided.
15. A decision is reached today.
    The donors will not give us the money.
16. The City Council offered to give us money for a clubhouse.
    We would let the public use it.
17. We had never admitted the public to our meetings.
    We didn't want to admit them to our clubhouse.
18. We would not lose the chance for a new clubhouse.
    Some of us favored admitting the public.
19. I agreed with those in favor of admitting the public.
    I sympathized with the others.
20. No agreement was reached.
    The money went to another club.

### (3) Use a noun clause to combine sentences.

A noun clause is a subordinate clause used as a noun. Read the following examples of noun clauses and note where they appear in the sentences.

> **Whoever buys that car** will be sorry. [noun clause as subject]
>
> Yesterday we learned **what Napoleon had accomplished.** [noun clause as direct object]
>
> We can spend the money for **whatever we like.** [noun clause as object of preposition]

A noun clause can also be used as a predicate nominative and as an indirect object. Noun clauses are usually introduced by *that, what, whatever, why, whether, how, who, whom, whoever,* or *whomever.*

Noun clauses are sometimes used without the introductory word *that.*

EXAMPLE My sister said the trip would take three days.

**EXERCISE 7.** Combine each of the following pairs of sentences by turning the italicized sentence in each pair into a noun clause. Use one of the introductory words listed above.

EXAMPLE 1. *They thought that they did not need help.*
This was a very foolish idea.
1. *That they did not need help was a very foolish idea.*

1. The new senator promised.
*The state would get more aid.*
2. *Could they endure the debate?*
This was uncertain.
3. *They might succeed.*
This was the incentive that kept them working.
4. The odor of smoke convinced the family.
*They should call the fire department.*
5. The attorney asked a question.
*He asked how the defendant had found the money.*

**REVIEW EXERCISE A.** Using the sentence-combining methods you have practiced thus far, combine each group of sentences into one smooth, well-written sentence. You may omit unnecessary words and change the word order, but you may not change the meaning of the original sentences. Punctuate your combined sentences correctly.

EXAMPLE 1. Hugo Gernsback began publishing *Amazing Stories.*
He began in 1926.
*Amazing Stories* was the first science-fiction magazine.
1. *In 1926 Hugo Gernsback began publishing* Amazing Stories, *the first science-fiction magazine.*

1. Science fiction ranges.
It ranges from projection to speculation.
The projection is careful.
The speculation is outlandish.
Science fiction usually requires the appearance of credibility.
2. *Frankenstein* is an early example of science fiction.
*Frankenstein* is a novel by Mary Shelley.
*Frankenstein* describes the scientific creation of human life.
3. There is another early example of science fiction.
The example is H. G. Wells's *The Time Machine.*
*The Time Machine* entertains.
*The Time Machine* offers social criticism.
*The Time Machine* predicts the future.
4. Some critics did not accept science fiction as serious literature.
These critics did not accept it easily.
Writers often included science fiction in their works.
These writers were major twentieth-century authors.
5. Today science fiction has supporters.
Science fiction has many active supporters.
They hold annual conventions.
They present Hugo and Nebula awards.
These awards are for the year's best writing.

**REVIEW EXERCISE B.** Combine the short, choppy sentences in the following paragraph into longer, smoother sentences. Be sure that the sentences you write add variety to the paragraph. Punctuate the paragraph correctly.

Mount St. Helens erupted in May, 1980. It is near Vancouver, Washington. The eruption was sudden. The force was over five hundred times that of an atomic bomb. The explosion was caused by pressure from gas and molten rock. It tore the top off the mountain. It threw ash high into the air. The explosion and subsequent mudslides caused many deaths. More than thirty people died. The destruction left many homeless. The force of the blast leveled huge trees. The area was wide. The mud killed hundreds of deer and elk. The mud turned Spirit Lake into a mudhole. The lake was formerly picturesque. Much of the ash fell to earth within a few days. A cloud of dust remained in the stratosphere. This cloud was over much of the Northern Hemisphere. People saw spectacular sunrises and sunsets. This continued for two years. The sunrises and sunsets were rose-colored. The sunsets were due to solar rays. They struck microscopic particles of ash. Scientists suspect that intermittent showers will continue. The showers will consist of volcanic ash. They will continue for the next two decades.

**REVIEW EXERCISE C.** Follow directions for Review Exercise B.

Several reported incidents indicate that extrasensory perception, or ESP, may exist. Several controlled laboratory experiments indicate that extrasensory perception, or ESP, may exist. ESP is usually divided into three kinds. These kinds are telepathy, precognition, and clairvoyance. Telepathy supposedly allows people to communicate by "reading minds." Telepathy is also known as thought transference. No conclusive scientific evidence for telepathy exists. Many people are convinced it works. For example, a retail store manager hired a man. This man was paid to identify shoplifters by reading their minds. He read their minds as they entered the store.

Another kind of ESP is precognition. Precognition is the ability to perceive things. These are things that are about to happen. For example, a mother had a dream. In the dream a heavy light fixture fell on her child's crib. She awakened from the dream. She immediately removed the child from the crib. Minutes later a storm developed. High winds shook the house. A chandelier fell on the crib.

The third kind of ESP is clairvoyance. Clairvoyance is the ability to see objects or events. These objects or events are distant or hidden. For example, a clairvoyant person is given the latitude and longitude of any spot on earth. Then this person can supposedly describe the features of that place accurately. No scientific theory adequately explains ESP. No scientific proof of it has been universally accepted. Many dedicated people are studying the subject.

### 18f. Experiment with the length and structure of your sentences to achieve greater interest and variety.

Sentences in English—both spoken and written—begin with the subject. Any piece of writing in which most of the sentences needlessly depart from this normal order will strike a reader as artificial. However, an unbroken sequence of subject-predicate sentences may result in another stylistic fault—monotony. Such a sequence of sentences is monotonous because it lacks the logical connections and special emphasis that variations in sentence structure can provide. For example, the following sentences are perfectly clear:

> The two friends quarreled violently over a matter of slight importance.
>
> They never spoke from that time on.

But a closer connection can be made between these two sentences by moving the adverb phrase, which refers to the quarrel, up to the beginning of the second sentence:

> The two friends quarreled violently over a matter of slight importance.
>
> **From that time on** they never spoke.

Similarly, an important idea expressed by a modifier can be emphasized:

> Sue was not impressive in the classroom.
>
> **On the tennis court,** however, she came into her own.

The contrast is less striking when the second sentence begins with its subject:

Sue was not impressive in the classroom.
She came into her own, however, on the tennis court.

The normal order of sentences should not be shunned merely for the sake of variety. However, it is a good idea to remember that beginning a sentence with an important modifier may sometimes increase the force and clarity of your thought as well as provide a pleasing variation.

The exercises that follow are intended to give you practice in using different kinds of sentence openers. Used sparingly, these devices will improve your writing.

## AVOIDING MONOTONY

**(1) Begin some of your sentences with a transposed appositive or with one of these modifiers: single-word modifier; phrase modifier; clause modifier.**

*Appositives*

The human brain, an enormously complex mechanism, contains about ten billion nerve cells. [subject first]

**An enormously complex mechanism,** the human brain contains about ten billion nerve cells. [transposed appositive first]

*Single-word Modifiers*

The book is long and badly written, and it failed to hold my interest. [subject first]

**Long and badly written,** the book failed to hold my interest. [single-word modifiers first]

A number of changes have been made here recently. [subject first]

**Recently,** a number of changes have been made here. [single-word modifier first]

The house was deserted and dilapidated and made a depressing picture. [subject first]

**Deserted and dilapidated,** the house made a depressing picture. [single-word modifiers first]

### *Phrase Modifiers*

She was almost unbeatable on the tennis court. [subject first]

**On the tennis court,** she was almost unbeatable. [prepositional phrase first]

Joe tired rapidly during the second set and decided to save his strength for the third set. [subject first]

**Tiring rapidly during the second set,** Joe decided to save his strength for the third set. [participial phrase first]

Wendy Hsi worked late every night to win the essay prize. [subject first]

**To win the essay prize,** Wendy Hsi worked late every night. [infinitive phrase first]

### *Clause Modifiers*

Investigators of the cause of the crash had to depend on evidence found in the wreckage because there were no survivors or witnesses. [subject first]

**Because there were no survivors or witnesses,** investigators of the cause of the crash had to depend on evidence found in the wreckage. [clause first]

Our leading lady, when she heard the orchestra playing the overture, suffered a severe attack of stage fright. [subject first]

**When she heard the orchestra playing the overture,** our leading lady suffered a severe attack of stage fright. [clause first]

**EXERCISE 8.** This exercise will give you practice in beginning sentences in a variety of ways. Revise each sentence according to the instructions.

1. The Marine Historical Society has recreated a nineteenth-century coastal village at Mystic, Connecticut. [Begin with a prepositional phrase.]
2. Traveling, eating, and shopping with credit cards seems wonderfully easy until you receive your bill at the end of the month. [Begin with a subordinate clause.]
3. Some people are selfish and materialistic and are never happy with what they have. [Begin with single-word adjective modifiers.]

4. José worked part-time at a gas station during his senior year in high school and managed to save a thousand dollars toward his college expenses. [Begin with a participial phrase: *Working . . .*]
5. The most glamorous of all the new professions created by the space age is that of the astronaut. [Begin with a prepositional phrase.]
6. Belmer, one of the oldest players in professional football, makes up in experience what he lacks in speed. [Begin with a transposed appositive.]
7. The college president stated at the alumni luncheon the immediate financial needs of the college. [Begin with a prepositional phrase.]
8. A university's primary responsibility is to its resident students, although it should encourage educational programs for its alumni. [Begin with a subordinate clause.]
9. This seems to be a highly technical book, to the casual reader. [Begin with a prepositional phrase.]
10. The first ships of the expedition will sail in October, if present plans are approved. [Begin with a subordinate clause.]
11. Navy divers expertly and rapidly repaired the damaged hull. [Begin with single-word adverb modifiers.]
12. The firm lacked funds for expansion and so attempted to borrow money. [Begin with a participial phrase: *Lacking . . .*]
13. The skin on the average adult weighs 8.8 pounds and occupies an area of 20 square feet. [Begin with a participial phrase.]
14. The expedition was led by Colonel Walter H. Wood of New York and spent several weeks at its camp on Seward Glacier. [Begin with a participial phrase.]
15. One can see at first glance that modern office furniture uses more metal than wood. [Begin with a prepositional phrase.]

**EXERCISE 9.** Rearrange each sentence so that it will begin with a single-word, phrase, or clause modifier or an appositive.

1. A bowling team was formed this winter for the first time in the history of the school.
2. A sinister figure stepped cautiously into the dark room.

3. Candidates for a driver's license must take a written examination to prove their knowledge of traffic regulations.
4. The children, when both parents are working, are cared for in nursery schools.
5. The audience, tired and hot, soon became impatient.
6. We were frightened by the explosion and dared not move from our places.
7. More than half of the 90,000 acres under cultivation had been ruined by the recent drought.
8. Jim, a merchant sailor for ten years, knew every important port in the world.
9. The new houses, although they look exactly alike from the outside, have very different interiors.
10. Competition has been growing more and more intense in the transportation industry.
11. A small boy, sobbing bitterly, ran toward me.
12. Music is to me an excellent tranquilizer when it is soft and rhythmic.
13. A person, when striving for the highest spiritual goals, will frequently become discouraged.
14. More and more people are rushing to local gymnasiums and health clubs either to reduce their weight or to improve their physical fitness.
15. Nothing is more satisfying than producing your own music, even if you cannot play an instrument well and are not musically inclined.

**(2) By means of subordination, vary the structure of your sentences. Avoid the exclusive use of simple and compound sentences.[1] Skillful use of the complex sentence is an indication of maturity in style.**

**REVIEW EXERCISE D.** By using various means of subordination (participial phrase, appositive, subordinate clause, etc.), combine the short sentences in each group into one long, smooth sentence.

[1] For a review of subordination, see pages 210–19. For an explanation of the kinds of sentences, see pages 65–67.

1. Alma Gropius Mahler Werfel, the "widow who married the arts," first married Walter Gropius, the architect.
   Then she married Gustav Mahler, the composer.
   Then she married Franz Werfel, the novelist.
2. Amelia Earhart made her first solo crossing of the Atlantic in 1932.
   Five years later she attempted a round-the-world flight.
   She became a major figure of concern when her plane lost radio contact on the second of July.
3. Gwendolyn Brooks is a poet, the author of *A Street in Bronzeville.*
   She has won the Pulitzer Prize.
   She has taught poetry in several Chicago colleges.
4. A year after Simon and Garfunkle first recorded "Sounds of Silence," a studio engineer dubbed in additional background.
   Newly edited, the song became a national hit.
   It launched their successful career.
5. Time is an odd thing.
   It does not exist all by itself.
   It is a name we give to one of our ways of experiencing our lives.
6. Eleanor Roosevelt was both versatile and talented.
   She wrote some very important books.
   One of them was *On My Own.*
   She was twice a delegate to the United Nations.
7. The Pulaski Highway in Maryland and the Pulaski Skyway in New Jersey were named after General Casimir Pulaski.
   He was an exiled Polish count.
   He served under Washington in the Revolution.
8. The Shakespeare Memorial at Stratford-on-Avon houses a theater.
   Stratford-on-Avon is the birthplace of Shakespeare.
   The Memorial also contains a gallery and a library.
9. When spirits are distilled, the parts of a solution are separated by heating.
   The part of the solution that escapes first when heated is called the distillate.
   Cognac is the distillate of grape wines from the Charente region in France.
10. On March 10, 1876, Alexander Graham Bell spoke through the first electromagnetic telephone.

He spoke to Watson, his assistant.
He said, "Mr. Watson, come here; I want you."

## AVOIDING "STRINGY" STYLE

**18g. Give variety to your writing by avoiding the "stringy" style which results from the overuse of *and* and *so*.**

In everyday conversation we tend to string our ideas out, one after another, by means of the simple conjunctions *and* and *so*. In writing, however, this sort of thing appears childish and monotonous. As you can see from the following examples, "stringiness" is an obvious fault which can be easily corrected. There are three ways to correct it.

**(1) Correct a stringy sentence by subordination of ideas.**

STRINGY SENTENCE College admission standards continue to rise, *and* tension and anxiety build to a ridiculous point in college preparatory seniors, *and* this spoils their final year in high school.

IMPROVED As college admission standards continue to rise, tension and anxiety build to a ridiculous point in college preparatory seniors, spoiling their final year in high school. [One *and* has been removed by means of the beginning subordinate clause. The other has been removed by means of the participial phrase, *spoiling their final year in high school.*]

The use of *so* as a conjunction is considered poor form. Its use can be avoided almost always by using a subordinate clause or a phrase expressing cause or reason.

POOR USE OF SO Maria Martinez believed in tradition, *so* she experimented with ancient Pueblo pottery techniques.

IMPROVED Believing in tradition, Maria Martinez experimented with ancient Pueblo pottery techniques.

*or*

Because she believed in tradition, Maria Martinez experimented with ancient Pueblo pottery techniques.

STRINGY USE OF <u>SO</u> We heard the static on the radio, *so* we were afraid of a thunderstorm, *so* we decided not to go out in the boat.

IMPROVED Fearing a thunderstorm when we heard the static on the radio, we decided not to go out in the boat.

**(2) Correct a stringy sentence by dividing it into two sentences.**

STRINGY SENTENCE I am very fond of foreign films, and so I go to the Celtic Theater more than to the other theaters, and we get only the best foreign films in this country, so I not only learn a lot, but I see better pictures.

IMPROVED Being very fond of foreign films, I go to the Celtic Theater more than to the other theaters. Since we get only the best foreign films in this country, I not only learn a lot, but I see better pictures. [stringiness corrected by subordination and by division into two sentences]

**EXERCISE 10.** Revise the sentences by one or more of the following methods: subordination, division into more than one sentence, and reduction. Get rid of the monotonous use of *and* and *so*. You may add a few words of your own if the words will help you to improve the sentences.

1. Tom Sawyer made Becky Thatcher jealous by talking to Amy Lawrence, and then Becky became very upset, so she invited everyone except Tom and Amy to her picnic, and then spent recess with Alfred, and she pretended not to notice Tom.
2. Tom and Becky continued to be angry with each other for a while, and then eventually they made up, and Tom looked forward to going to Becky's picnic.
3. Mrs. Thatcher set the day for the picnic and Tom and Becky visited the cave called "McDougal's Cave" with the rest of the company, and played hide-and-seek after exploring the more familiar wonders of the cave.
4. They followed a little stream of water and Tom played the role of a discoverer and Becky thought that was fun and followed him.

5. They wound down through the cave this way and that and crept from cavern to cavern and found a spring-fed pool.
6. In one cavern the ceiling was completely lined with bats, and the bats swarmed down when Tom and Becky entered the cavern with their candles and one of them almost snuffed Becky's candle out with its wings.
7. Soon the stillness of the caves dampened Tom and Becky's spirits, and they realized that they had gone some distance from the others, and suddenly they were afraid that they might be unable to get back.
8. They started back, and indeed they had become lost, and there was no way Tom could remember which route they had followed, and they had only one piece of cake and a few candle-stumps.
9 After several false starts through the various tunnels their candles gave out and they were left in total darkness and Becky wept and they both thought they were certain to die in the pitch-black cave.
10. Leaving Becky alone, Tom took a length of rope and traced his way through the tunnels looking for an exit and soon saw a candle, so he shouted at the top of his voice and the next thing he knew a familiar face was there in front of him.

# Chapter 19

# Effective Diction

## Appropriate Choice of Words

The quality of the words you select to express your ideas is just as important in composition as the quality of your sentence structure. The words you choose constitute your diction. For years, your teachers have urged you to enlarge your vocabulary. A large vocabulary is indeed a great asset in both reading and writing. But the acquisition of a large vocabulary, acquiring control of a number of big words, is only one way to improve your diction. It is not a guarantee of effective expression, because the effectiveness of a word does not depend on the number of its syllables or its rareness. The best word to use is always the one that conveys the exact meaning you intend. Careful attention to the instruction given in this chapter will help you to select your words wisely.

## TRITE EXPRESSIONS

### 19a. Avoid trite expressions.

Trite expressions, sometimes called *clichés,* are expressions which have grown stale through too frequent use. Originally fresh and effective, they have been used so much that they have lost any freshness and originality they once had. No doubt, the first time someone described the sensation of stage fright as "butterflies in my stomach," the description was strikingly apt, but overuse has made it too commonplace to be arresting. Similarly, such basically effective comparisons as *blanket of snow, busy as a bee, on the fence,* while still generally used in conversation, are so well known that they make writing dull rather than bright. Clichés suggest laziness and a lack of originality in the writer who uses them. They come to mind so easily when you are writing that unless you consciously guard against them, they will seriously weaken your style. The simple, straightforward statement of an idea is preferable to the use of a worn-out expression.

| TRITE | SIMPLE, STRAIGHTFORWARD |
| --- | --- |
| bury the hatchet | stop fighting, make peace |
| at loose ends | disorganized |
| on speaking terms | friendly |
| fair and square | completely honest |
| at death's door | near death |

You have probably noticed that some clichés are comparisons (*busy as a bee*), while others are simply commonplace ways of stating an idea (*fair and square*). Study the following far-from-complete list of clichés. Reading it will make you sensitive to trite expressions. You and your classmates can add to the list.

TRITE EXPRESSIONS

a good time was had by all
accidents will happen
add insult to injury
after all is said and done
at death's door
at loose ends
beat a hasty retreat
beauty is skin-deep
beyond the shadow of a doubt
bite off more than you can chew
blushing bride
break the ice
brown as a berry
budding genius
bury the hatchet

busy as a bee
by the sweat of one's brow
calm before the storm
clear as crystal
depths of despair
diamond in the rough
discreet silence
doomed to disappointment
each and every
easier said than done
eternal triangle
fair sex
Father Time
few and far between
fond parents

gala occasion
green with envy
hale and hearty
in no uncertain terms
in this day and age
irony of fate
last but not least
long arm of the law
make a long story short
none the worse for wear
on speaking terms
on the fence
out of the frying pan into the fire
point with pride
quick as a flash
ripe old age
sadder but wiser
silence reigned
straight and narrow path
supreme sacrifice
to the bitter end
trials and tribulations
view with alarm
viselike grip
white as a sheet
word to the wise

**EXERCISE 1.** Rewrite each of the following sentences, substituting simple, straightforward language for the trite expressions.

1. After our sumptuous repast, we agreed that a good time had been had by all.
2. In this day and age, political figures who remain on the fence when burning questions are argued will be doomed to disappointment on Election Day.
3. Although warned not to bite off more than I could chew, I signed up for six courses with the result that after all was said and done I was a sadder but wiser woman.
4. To make a long story short, I failed two courses, and to add insult to injury, my parents sent me to summer school.
5. Among the novel's characters are two members of the fair sex who wander from the straight and narrow path and are eventually embraced by the long arm of the law.
6. In the depths of despair, each and every one of us maintained a discreet silence.
7. Sensing that Mr. Stern's pleasant greeting was only the calm before the storm, I tried to beat a hasty retreat, which was nipped in the bud as, with a viselike grip, he led me into his office.
8. Busy as a bee in her ripe old age, Grandmother always pointed with pride to the beautiful garden she had made by the sweat of her brow.
9. Having known the agony of defeat as well as the dizzying

heights of success, Jim was determined to fight to the finish in this tennis match, which seesawed back and forth, continually swaying the balance.

10. Green with envy, Ira watched from the sidelines as Fred kicked up his heels and danced up a storm.

## JARGON

### 19b. Use a vocabulary that is free of jargon.

Jargon has two meanings. First, it means "the technical language used by specialists in the same profession." An engineer may use engineering jargon in a report to other engineers. An educator may use educational jargon in an article in a teacher's magazine. Jargon of this kind is an expected and usually acceptable feature of the style of a specialist writing for other specialists in the same field. There is always the danger, however, that a writer may carry the use of jargon to such an extreme that it will obscure rather than clarify meaning, even for members of the same profession. When this happens, professional jargon becomes a stylistic fault. The specialist should, whenever possible, use simple, everyday language rather than professional jargon. As a high school student you may encounter the specialist's jargon in your reading, but you will not be likely to use it in your writing.

EXAMPLE OF PROFESSIONAL JARGON

> Both equalitarianism and achievement are dominant values intimately articulated in existing institutional structures. Though they manifest certain contradictory features, neither value seems likely to cease playing a significant role. It is strange that in an age in which all the empirical evidence demonstrates that there is more upward social mobility than at any time in our history—in which large numbers of workers respond to a reduction of the work week by taking second jobs, in which more married women continue their careers after marriage on both the working-class and middle-class level, and in which the advertising industry, which most typifies an America oriented to mass consumption, demands and

secures a prolonged work week from its creative personnel—it is strange that in such an age men see the norms of hard work and achievement as dead. A systematic examination of the available evidence suggests, as we shall see, that both equalitarianism and achievement have remained the dominant values in most existing institutional structures. Actually, a study of the available evidence bears most eloquent testimony to the thesis that America was and has remained a revolutionary country, more equalitarian in manners and opportunity than anyplace else in the world.[1]

The second meaning of jargon is "vague, puffed-up, pretentious language that tends to confuse the reader." The writer of this kind of jargon uses words so general in meaning that they mean practically nothing. Examples of words dear to the writer of jargon are *case, factor, field, aspect, matter, concept,* etc. Vague and unnecessary phrases like the following usually characterize jargon: *as for the fact that, under the circumstances pertaining, along the line of, in the case of, relative to the matter, as to whether, with reference to,* etc. Perhaps these examples show why jargon has been called "fuzzy language."

Writers of jargon usually overwrite. They prefer the big word to the simple word, the unusual word to the ordinary one. To them, knives are cutlery; table napkins are napery; dogs are canines; a trailer truck is a behemoth of the highways; they rarely start or begin—they initiate or commence. In short, the "jargonist," in using a vague, wordy, overwritten language, not only obscures meaning but also confuses and irritates the reader.

EXAMPLE OF COMMON JARGON

In spite of the fact that government aviation agencies were not in agreement with respect to the question of the cause of the accident at Kennedy Airport, the court decided

[1] From "Trends in American Society" by Seymour M. Lipset from *An Outline of Man's Knowledge of the Modern World,* edited by Lyman Bryson. Published by Nelson Doubleday, Inc., Garden City, New York. Reprinted by permission of the publisher.

that one of the contributing factors was a propeller that had been structurally weakened.

REWRITTEN WITHOUT JARGON

Although government aviation agencies disagreed on the causes of the accident at Kennedy Airport, the court decided that one cause was a structurally weakened propeller.

**EXERCISE 2.** In the following passage, the meaning is somewhat obscured by jargon. Read the passage several times until you are sure what the writer was trying to say. Then write a jargon-free revision.

Owing to the fact that a number of social factors along the line of unemployment and dislocation follow consequentially from the automation of industry, government, as well as labor and management, must concern itself with the implementation of the processes of adjustment of affected persons.

## FIGURATIVE LANGUAGE

### 19c. Use figures of speech to make writing interesting and vivid.

In reading literature, especially in your study of poetry, you encounter many figures of speech. Those most commonly found are metaphor, simile, and personification. In each of these, the writer draws a comparison. Two things are compared which are not really alike, but which are similar in at least one respect. By making the comparison, the writer is able to express meaning more clearly, vividly, and convincingly than could be done by writing a literal description or explanation.

D. H. Lawrence describes a row of distant houses on a ridge at night: "The homes stood . . . black against the sky, *like wild beasts glaring curiously with yellow eyes down into the darkness.*" Lawrence knows, of course, that houses and beasts are literally quite unlike, but the houses with lighted windows suggest to his imagination beasts with yellow eyes. This figurative description makes you see the scene as he saw it and as he thought of it. It is more arresting than would be a literal statement—"The lighted houses were black against the sky."

Note the striking effect of the four figures of speech used by Pearl Buck in describing a suddenly revealed handful of precious jewels: "There were such a mass of jewels as we had never dreamed could be together, jewels *red as the inner flesh of watermelons, golden as wheat, green as young leaves in spring, clear as water trickling out of the earth.*"

## Simile

**19d. A *simile* is a comparison between things essentially unlike, expressed directly through the use of a comparing word such as *like* or *as*.**

EXAMPLES Her hair was **like** silk.
He was thin **as** a stick.

If the things compared are really alike, the comparison is not a figure of speech, not a simile.

NOT A SIMILE He wore a hat like mine.
SIMILE He wore a hat **like an overturned pail.**

NOT A SIMILE Her sister was like her mother.
SIMILE Her sister was **like an angel.**

## Metaphor

**19e. A *metaphor* is a comparison between things essentially unlike, expressed without a comparing word such as *like* or *as*. The comparison is implied rather than directly stated.**

EXAMPLES The silver lace of the branches above the river. . . .
The road was a ribbon of moonlight.—NOYES

## Personification

**19f. Personification is a figure of speech in which the characteristics of a human being are attributed to an animal, a thing, or an idea.**

EXAMPLES But, look, **the morn in russet mantle clad**
**Walks** o'er the dew of yon high eastern hill.
— SHAKESPEARE

Only through the rusty hinges and swollen sea-moistened woodwork certain airs, detached from the **body of the wind** (the house was ramshackle after all) **crept** round corners and **ventured** indoors.[1]
— VIRGINIA WOOLF

► NOTE Other figures of speech which you will find more useful in literary appreciation than in composition are *antithesis, apostrophe, hyperbole, irony, paradox,* and *metonymy.* The dictionary will give you definitions of these.

**EXERCISE 3.** Copy the figures of speech from the following passages. After each tell whether it is simile, metaphor, or personification. Be prepared to explain the figure and to evaluate its effectiveness. You should find fifteen figures.

1. When Alma went down into the audience room, in the midst of the chattering singers, who seemed to have descended like birds, from song flights to chirps, the minister approached her. — MARY E. WILKINS FREEMAN
2. The silence is cloven by alarm as by an arrow. — JAMES JOYCE
3. Spring was a very flame of green. — D. H. LAWRENCE
4. The edge of the colossal jungle, so dark green as to be almost black, fringed with white surf, ran straight, like a ruled line, far, far away along a blue sea whose glitter was blurred by a creeping mist. — JOSEPH CONRAD
5. Are there no water-lilies, smooth as cream
   With long stems dripping crystal? — ELINOR WYLIE
6. I felt like a small bubble on the surface of a mighty thing like the sea. — ROBERT P. TRISTRAM COFFIN

[1] From *To the Lighthouse* by Virginia Woolf. Reprinted by permission of Harcourt Brace Jovanovich, Inc., the Literary Estate of Virginia Woolf, and The Hogarth Press Ltd.

7. Night's candles are burnt out, and jocund day
Stands tiptoe on the misty mountain tops. — SHAKESPEARE
8. The exhilarating ripple of her voice was a wild tonic in the rain. — F. SCOTT FITZGERALD
9. The farm was crouched on a bleak hillside, whence its fields, fanged with flints, dropped steeply to the village of Howling a mile away. — STELLA GIBBONS
10. Maternally the great tree protected us, sighing and groaning, as she lowered her arms to shield us from the storm.

**EXERCISE 4.** Select five of the following that you think you can suggest by using simile, metaphor, or personification. For each write a sentence with the figure of speech.

1. hot August scene on a city street
2. sensations while walking in a hurricane or a blizzard
3. a person's reaction to sudden fear
4. a fruit tree in bloom
5. cars in bumper-to-bumper traffic
6. emerging from a stuffy room into a cold, clear night
7. stubbornness
8. a drink of cool water after hours of thirst
9. birds sitting on a telephone wire
10. a plane taking off

## Hazards of Figurative Language

### 19g. Avoid strained or commonplace figures of speech.

The habit of thinking metaphorically, of seeing life in terms of comparisons, can help a writer — in prose as well as in poetry — to enliven style and clarify meaning.

A writer, however, must be aware of three pitfalls that lie in wait for the glib or careless user of figurative language. The first is the use of similes and metaphors which, though much used, have become so commonplace that they weaken style. Such figures are clichés: *clear as crystal, ran like the wind, silence reigned, clear as day,* etc. The second pitfall is the use of figures which are strained. They give the reader the feeling that the writer is trying too hard. They attract attention because they are inappropriate or farfetched: "Like a boiling lobster, the dawn turned from black to red." This fault, more common in verse than in prose, need not concern you much in your attempts to use the figures of speech. As a young writer, you are quite likely to show evidence of trying too hard, and you may be forgiven for a few strained metaphors.

The third pitfall, however, is one which you can easily avoid provided you understand it. This is the error of mixing your figures of speech.

### 19h. Avoid mixed figures of speech.

A mixed figure of speech—sometimes referred to as a "mixed metaphor"—is one in which the writer starts with a comparison and then shifts to another comparison that is not consistent with the first. A few examples will make clear how a careless writer mixes metaphors.

MIXED Flailing both wings, Mr. McCall flew to the platform and barked for silence. [The first metaphors compare Mr. McCall to a bird, and the last to a dog.]

BETTER Flailing both wings, Mr. McCall **flew** to the platform and **screeched** for silence.

MIXED Her face reddened as mountainous waves of embarrassment broke over her, all but drying up the little confidence she had. [Mountainous waves suggest water; they would hardly "dry up" anything.]

BETTER Her face reddened as mountainous **waves** of embarrassment broke over her, all but **washing away** the little confidence she had.

**EXERCISE 5.** Seven of the following sentences contain mixed figures of speech. Revise the sentences to remove the mixed figures. If the figure is consistently maintained, write + after its number on your paper.

1. After enduring an hour of Carl's insane driving, we ordered him into the asylum of the back seat.
2. The senator told the investigators that he would lay his cards on the table, since his life was an open book with no skeletons in the closet.
3. Bionics researchers are on a small island of knowledge in the midst of a sea of ignorance, but, like corals, they are building reefs, extending their knowledge in all directions.
4. Unfortunately the speaker did not know that he was flying too high over the heads of his audience until their general restlessness made him realize that he had better get out of the depths into the shallower water where they were.
5. In college, she changed course abruptly, and instead of foundering on the submerged rocks of low grades and expulsion from school, she got on the beam, which eventually led her to a safe landing.
6. Elisa dived into her studies, afraid that she would never reach the top of the heap, but determined not to give up before the final whistle blew.
7. The productive field of psychiatry, once considered a pseudoscience, has now achieved respectability and may become a most important branch of medical research.
8. Every morning a chorus of starlings in the trees outside her window awakened her, their dissonances and harsh voices jangling her nerves unbearably.
9. She spent the morning of her career groping through the dark halls of obscurity until the publication of her third novel thrust her above the surface of the black waters into the brilliant noonday sun.
10. Unless the mayor sets a new course, our city is likely to be buried beneath a mound of debt.

**EXERCISE 6.** Each item in the following exercise contains a figure of speech and a space where a portion of the sentence has been omitted. Beneath the sentence four wordings are suggested for this space, one of which is preferable if the figure of speech is to be consistently maintained. After the proper number, write the letter of the wording which best fits the blank space.

1. Mr. Gross, who was up to his neck in debt, . . . when his company went on strike.
   a. collapsed
   b. nearly went under
   c. was caught off base
   d. suffered a setback

2. Her path was strewn with serious problems which threatened . . .
   a. to drop on her with crippling effect.
   b. to engulf her completely.
   c. to trip her up at every step.
   d. to wreck her career.

3. The book is a treasure chest of wisdom in which you will find . . .
   a. a rich supply of bonbons to sweeten your speech.
   b. a greenhouse of rare flowers to decorate your speech.
   c. new clothes to dress up your speech.
   d. a hoard of verbal gems to adorn your speech.

4. Heavy income taxes, which exert a stranglehold on the economy, have . . . sources of new investment capital.
   a. crippled
   b. choked off
   c. tied up
   d. destroyed

5. Like a person tenderly raking leaves from a new lawn, we must always be careful that in removing the old and unwanted, we do not . . . the new.
   a. uproot
   b. bury
   c. undermine
   d. drown out

6. Mr. Browne behaves in the classroom like a tough top sergeant, . . .
   a. shouting from his pulpit and frightening even the most devout worshipers.
   b. calling all plays and carrying the ball himself.
   c. shouting out orders and brutally exaggerating the details of discipline.

d. beating his slaves with the lash of long assignments and low grades.

7. In the character of Willie Stark, fiction has been draped about the bones of fact, and, in places . . .
   a. the truth emerges.
   b. one can recognize the original.
   c. the skeleton shows through.
   d. the model becomes clear.

8. The moon had just risen, very golden, over the hill, and like a bright, watching spirit . . . the bars of an ash tree's naked boughs.
   a. towered above
   b. rolled behind
   c. obscured
   d. peered through

9. The characters weave the pattern of the book, . . . of motives and cross-purposes, that looks like a triangle, but is really a quadrangle.
   a. an edifice
   b. a vehicle
   c. a fabric
   d. a structure

10. After bounding around the bases like a frightened kangaroo, Mills was . . . at home plate by Smith's shot from center field.
   a. winged
   b. snared
   c. pinned
   d. dropped

## SLANG AND INFORMAL ENGLISH

**19i. Use diction that is appropriate to the kind of composition you are writing—avoid slang in written composition; use extremely informal English sparingly in formal writing.**

## Slang

Slang consists of new words, or old words in new uses, that have made their way into the language because they are vivid or colorful. High school and college students enjoy adopting the latest slang. Most slang is short-lived. It enjoys a brief popularity and then is forgotten. Therefore, it is always difficult to compile an illustrative list of slang terms which will be meaningful even a year later. The expressions in the following list were current a short while ago. How many of them do you recognize. Are any of them still in use?

SLANG

| | |
|---|---|
| cool it | it's not my bag |
| groovy | heavy |
| uptight | nuts (crazy) |
| it's a drag | oddball |
| goof off | square |
| dig it | far out |

Occasionally a slang expression makes its way up the usage ladder and becomes acceptable even in formal writing, whereupon, of course, it is no longer slang. Slang should rarely be used in writing, and only when a special purpose is being sought, as in reproducing dialogue.

## Informal English

As explained in Chapter 5, there are two kinds of standard English—formal and informal. Informal English is good English. We use it in all our conversation and in most of our writing. Within the general category of informal English, however, there are degrees of informality. Expressions typical of the most extreme degree of informality are never "bad" English, but they are sometimes inappropriate English. Because it is light in tone and sometimes very close to slang, extremely informal English should be carefully limited in serious composition.

TYPICAL INFORMAL EXPRESSIONS

| | |
|---|---|
| in a jam | out on a limb |
| kid (child) | highbrow |

Although dictionaries label words *informal* or *slang,* you cannot rely on their arbitrarily drawn distinctions as a means of deciding whether a word is appropriate to your composition. You need to understand the basic point that any word which is inappropriate to the general *tone* of your composition should not be used, regardless of its dictionary label. You should control your natural tendency to rely too much on informal English. The deciding factor is, of course, the degree of formality of your composition, which, in turn, determines the appropriateness of the words used. In a research paper extremely informal English should be used very sparingly. In an informal essay, it may be used as frequently as in conversation.

Read the following sentences taken from formal compositions and note the inappropriateness of the italicized words.

> In any eighth-grade classroom where *kids* of the same chronological age are grouped together, we expect to find a physiological age range of six or seven years.
>
> There is a grave danger that we may expose far too many students of only medium ability to the long course of professional study in our universities. The employment situation in some professional areas, we must admit, is *not so hot.*
>
> Dickens's *bag* was to reveal the social evils of the day so that they could be destroyed one by one.

**EXERCISE 7.** Point out the words and expressions in the following passage which are slang or so informal as to be inappropriate to the general tone.

While it is true that the students in the top ten percent of any grade are capable of doing good work in the grade above them, to undertake a general upward transfer of these students would produce more socially maladjusted kids than you could shake a stick at. Efforts to meet the problem by cutting out the arbitrary division of a school into grades have been successful in small schools, where the need to classify and control has not been great and where parents couldn't care less what grade their children are in. Today the schools which allow children to go at their own speed, with a child doing sixth-grade work in one subject and third- or fourth-grade work in another, are considered pretty far out. Eventually this method of school organization may become general practice.

## MEANING AND CONNOTATION

**19j. Use a vocabulary which is specific. Select words with due regard for their varied meanings and their connotations.**

A word is a symbol. A word has no meaning for you unless you know what it stands for. The thing or idea that a word stands for, or refers to, is known as its *referent*. You are able to understand a word only if you know what its referent is. The referent of a word should be the same for the person using the word as for the person reading or hearing it. When two persons each have in mind a different referent for the same word, the word is useless for communication between them until they recognize the problem and agree on the same referent.

If your teacher says, "Please give me the chalk," you immediately understand the request. You know what action *give* refers to, whom *me* refers to, and what the symbol *chalk* refers to. Had your teacher said, "Please give me the *glub*," however, you would have been confused. *Glub,* which looks and sounds like a word, is not customarily used to refer to anything. Since for you it has no referent, it is not, so far as you are concerned, a word at all.

### Concrete Words and Abstract Words

Words may be divided into two groups—*concrete* words and *abstract* words. A concrete word is one whose referent can be touched or seen: *book, cloud, car, chalk.* An abstract word is one whose referent is an idea, something which cannot be touched or seen: *peace, need, love, freedom.*

**(1) For clearness in description, choose the concrete word with the most specific referent.**

Concrete words vary in definiteness. For example, the word *vehicle,* while its referent is something which can be seen and touched, is not at all specific. You probably do not have a clear mental picture of a *vehicle.* The word *car* is more specific; the word *station wagon* is still more specific. "John was driving a dilapidated vehicle" will not convey as clear a picture as "John was driving a dilapidated station wagon." As description, the second sentence is clearer. In all your writing, whenever you are considering several different words to express a particular meaning, select the most specific one.

**EXERCISE 8.** Arrange the words in each group so that the word with the least specific referent will come first, and the word with the most specific referent will come last.

1. seat, desk chair, chair, furniture, swivel chair
2. quadruped, creature, mammal, spaniel, dog
3. fruit juice, drink, lemonade, juice, liquid
4. storm at sea, typhoon, occurrence, storm
5. laborer, carpenter, employee, human being, woman

**EXERCISE 9.** For each of the following general words, list three words which have a more specific referent:

| | | |
|---|---|---|
| 1. food | 3. elevation | 5. educational institution |
| 2. boat | 4. punishment | 6. restaurant |

## Synonyms

**(2) For clearness, choose the synonym that expresses your meaning exactly.**

Synonyms are words which are similar, but rarely identical, in meaning. Careful writers select the words which have the exact referents they have in mind. For example, the words *disciple, partisan,* and *satellite* are synonyms in that each refers to a person who is a *follower* of a leader. Yet each has its own meaning somewhat different from the others. *Follower,* the most general in meaning, may be used in place of any of the other three, but for the writer who has a specific kind of follower in mind, it lacks exactness. A writer who has in mind the followers of a professor or a religious leader, for instance, would probably use the word *disciples.* If the writer wishes to refer to the blindly devoted followers of a political or military leader, the word *partisans* might be preferable. To refer to the kind of followers who continuously and obsequiously circulate about a powerful leader, perhaps in hope of favors, the word *satellites* could be used. Do not always be satisfied with the first synonym that occurs to you.

**EXERCISE 10.** Without using the dictionary, explain the difference in meaning of the words in each group. Describe a situation in which each word would be properly used.

1. highway, road, street, boulevard, expressway, path, trail
2. compel, coerce, force, constrain
3. reveal, divulge, tell, betray
4. repulsive, obnoxious, abhorrent, distasteful
5. laughing, giggling, snickering, guffawing

## Exact Meaning of Abstract Words

**(3) Make clear the referent of an abstract word by definition or example.**

Abstract words, which usually refer to general ideas, must always be used with care. A great many misunderstandings are caused by abstract words which have not been carefully defined. Unless two persons agree on the meaning (referent) of an abstract word, communication between them may break down. An abstract word may have many referents.

The word *freedom,* for example, has only a very vague referent until you define it. To a prisoner behind bars, *freedom* means getting out of jail. To Mr. Barnes, who resents the neighbors' criticism of his noisy family, *freedom* means the right of his family to make as much noise as they wish. Franklin D. Roosevelt defined the freedoms in which America believes as freedom of speech, freedom of worship, freedom from want, and freedom from fear. Each of these definitions provides a more specific referent for the word *freedom,* and each, in turn, could be more narrowly defined.

Sometimes an example will help to clarify the meaning of an abstract word. In the following passage the meaning of *quality* in the context "a man of quality" is made clear by an example.

> Mansfield was a man of quality. Although he never pushed himself forward or tried to assert his superiority, you could tell by his bearing, his quiet sense of humor, and his manner of speaking that he was a superior person.

**EXERCISE 11.** Without using a dictionary, write a one- or two-sentence definition of each of the following words. Compare your definitions with those of your classmates. In discussion, you may find it helpful to clarify your meaning by means of an example.

| | | |
|---|---|---|
| 1. fairness | 3. success | 5. skill |
| 2. beauty | 4. failure | 6. happiness |

**(4) In reading and writing, distinguish between the denotative and the connotative meanings of a word.**

Compare the meaning of the following sentences:

> Nan's persistence surprised everyone.
>
> Nan's stubborness surprised everyone.

Of course, the meaning of the two sentences may be the same. *Persistence* is another word for *stubbornness,* the quality of not giving up easily. This is the *denotative* meaning of the words. But the *effect* of the words on reader or listener is very different. *Stubbornness* suggests that Nan is unreasonable, narrow-minded, unwilling to listen to others. This *suggestive* meaning of a word is its *connotation,* or *connotative* meaning. Most words have connotations. There is nothing wrong in choosing a word for its connotations, but you must be aware of the connotations lest you say or write something you did not intend.

**EXERCISE 12.** Write the numbers 1–20 in a column. As you read each word in the following list, write *F* after its number if the word has favorable, pleasing connotations for you. Write *U* if it has unfavorable connotations. Write *N* if the connotations are neutral—that is, if the word does not stir any feeling in you. Compare your answers with those of your classmates.

1. liberal
2. propaganda
3. mother
4. tavern
5. atheist
6. home
7. church
8. bureaucrat
9. saloon
10. stars and stripes
11. conservative
12. communism
13. bar and grill
14. police
15. grand opera
16. organized labor
17. welfare
18. protest
19. Pentagon
20. rebel

## Loaded Words

A word which, through its connotations, carries strong feelings is said to be "loaded." The propagandist, the newspaper columnist, the political speaker are likely to use loaded words. They are trying to appeal to the emotions of people. When used deliberately, loaded words are a form of persuasion which clear thinkers disapprove of.

**EXERCISE 13.** Compare the following reports of the same speech. Both reports contain loaded words. One is loaded against Senator Blank; the other is loaded in his favor. List the loaded words and compare them with their counterparts in the other report.

1

Senator Blank today blasted opponents of the highway expansion program in a blistering attack from the Senate floor. In a long-winded tirade, the aging politician made a desperate bid for support but succeeded in frightening only a few senators into backing the program.

2

Senator Blank today criticized opponents of the highway expansion program in a powerful statement from the Senate floor. In a thorough discussion, the venerable legislator made another strong bid for support, which apparently convinced several senators that they should back the program.

**EXERCISE 14.** Discuss with your classmates and teacher the connotations of the following words.

1. plump, fat, pot-bellied, stout
2. visionary, crackpot, idealist
3. crowd, gang, mob, assemblage
4. aging, venerable, senior, mature, graying
5. determined, persevering, dogged, resolute, relentless, tenacious

Chapter 20

# Exercises in Sentence Revision

This chapter contains exercises only. The exercises will help you in two ways: (1) they will test your understanding of sentence correctness, clearness, and smoothness; (2) they will give you practice in repairing faulty sentence structure. The theory behind the inclusion of exercises in any textbook is that if you learn to criticize and revise the awkward sentences in the book, most of which have been taken from student compositions, you will be able to criticize and revise your own awkward sentences.

Use the exercises in this chapter to "keep your hand in" the skills of good writing. The exercises are of various kinds, and every exercise is devoted to more than one kind of skill.

## Identifying and Correcting Errors

**EXERCISE 1.** Immediately following the directions you will find a list of errors in sentence structure. Each faulty sentence in the exercise illustrates one of these errors. Some of the sentences are correct. You are to do two things: (1) write *before* the number of the sentence on your paper the letter of the error illustrated in the sentence; (2) write *after* the number of the sentence a revision which eliminates the error. How you remove the error is not important, provided your sentence is correct, clear, and smooth.

If the sentence is correct as it stands, write a + before its number.

- A Lack of agreement (subject and verb, or pronoun and antecedent)
- B Incorrect case of pronoun
- C Dangling modifier
- D Lack of parallelism or faulty parallelism
- E Unclear reference of pronoun (ambiguous, general, weak)

EXAMPLE 1. Do you know whom it was?
*B* 1. *Do you know who it was?*

1. People may disapprove of laws, but that doesn't prove they are good or bad.
2. Human behavior is complicated and difficult, not only to analyze but for evaluation.
3. The law is society's tested system of behavior, and they would have even worse problems without it.
4. Unless two individuals observe the same laws, the more powerful can always take advantage of the weaker.
5. Any wise judge, as well as the more experienced citizens, can appreciate that.
6. The fundamental principle behind all laws are the same.
7. It is that the rights of others limit the rights of any individual.
8. The law has many arms, touching all of us, and to prescribe the limits proper to us in all our different roles.
9. It governs you as a student and I as a writer.
10. Hoping for order in our social dealings with one another, the fact that legality requires judicial decision often makes us impatient.
11. The complexity of judicial decisions reflects how complex is law itself.
12. When a law is carelessly formulated or improperly applied, a judge can cut them down to size.
13. The presiding judge in an American court of law is a person whom scholars agree has no counterpart in other nations.
14. Making every effort to avoid the "tyranny" of politics, the Constitution was written by men who knew how the law can be twisted to the selfish interests of those in power.

15. In the Constitution, legislative and executive power is restricted to a greater degree than they are in other national systems of government.
16. Facing one practical question after another, this restriction was less a matter of design than it was the result of many difficult decisions individually reached.
17. If the writers of the Constitution had not given the powers they did to the courts, they would have been subject to one of the other branches of government.
18. The mood of an executive and the whim of a legislator consequently does not determine one's fate in a court of law.
19. Instead, the acts of executives and the laws of legislatures all become subject, when necessary, to the judgment of a judge.
20. Abuse and violation of the existing law is the last resort of any loyal citizen.

**EXERCISE 2.** Follow the directions for Exercise 1.

A Sentence fragment

B Run-on sentence

C Incorrect tense or verb form

D Misplaced modifier

E Unclear relationship between sentence ideas (lack of subordination, faulty coordination)

1. Our camp, which lays at the north end of the lake, is overshadowed by the cliffs which raise steeply above it.
2. Team teaching offers teachers at least one important advantage, it enables each teacher on the team to teach his specialty.
3. Since it has a full squad of seasoned players, this year's football team should win the championship.
4. The car was driven by a stunning girl with whitewall tires.
5. The band in its new uniforms and the high-stepping majorette with her twirling baton as well as the stirring music.
6. A compromise is a settlement of differences reached by mutual concessions between two parties.
7. Secret police with hidden cameras that were trying to take pictures at the meeting were physically ejected by angry students.

8. She had intended to have gone to the dance with her brother.
9. At home we suffer the constant interference of our parents, at college we will be free to make our own decisions.
10. Tickets for matinees will cost $3.50, and matinees will be given on Wednesdays and Saturdays.
11. These experiences will be valuable in my career as a social worker, and it is a career in which I shall work with people from all walks of life.
12. At the beginning of my junior-level Spanish course, the teacher reviewed the material I had the year before.
13. During negotiations between labor and management, work in the factory continued as usual.
14. The five junior high school buildings will cost eight million dollars, and they were approved by the taxpayers in yesterday's balloting.
15. We found several of the students in the shop very busy. Learning how to take a motor apart and put it together again.
16. The senator denied the many charges that had been made against her briefly and categorically.
17. In high school I have been unable to take some courses I wanted and have been required to take others I did not want.
18. Twenty percent of the students said they were satisfied with their own study habits, fifty-four percent said they wished they knew how to study more effectively.
19. If you would have come earlier, you could have seen the first act.
20. The demand for good television material exceeds the supply, and some of the best material, important news events, is not being fully used, and the reason is that news telecasts are not profitable.

## Selecting the Best Expression

**EXERCISE 3.** Number your paper 1–25. After each of the following sentences, the italicized part of the sentence is rephrased in two ways. If you consider one of these rephrasings an improvement, write the letter of the better one (*a* or *b*) after the proper number on your paper. If you consider the sentence correct as it stands, write +.

1. Behind one of the doors waits a tiger, *and the other has a beautiful lady behind it.*

   a. . . . and behind the other waits a beautiful lady.
   b. . . . and a beautiful lady waits behind the other.

2. If you go on a trip, *it will give you an excellent chance to practice your camera technique.*

   a. . . . you will have an excellent chance to practice your camera technique.
   b. . . . an excellent chance to practice your camera technique will be yours.

3. When developing films, *a darkroom will be needed.*

   a. . . . one thing you will need is a darkroom.
   b. . . . you will need a darkroom.

4. A deep-sea fisher needs an outboard motor much larger *than a fisher who fishes in sheltered waters.*

   a. . . . than that used by a fisher who fishes in sheltered waters.
   b. . . . than one fishing in sheltered waters.

5. This discovery had a bad effect on the mind of *Usher, he thought he had buried his sister alive.*

   a. . . . Usher, for he thought he had buried his sister alive.
   b. . . . Usher. He thought he buried his sister alive.

6. Although they listen to several news broadcasts each day, *most people continue to buy a daily paper.*

   a. . . . a daily paper continues to be bought by most people.
   b. . . . the buying of a daily paper by most people continues.

7. It had been stated earlier in the press that representatives of union and management *would either meet around the clock until they reached an agreement or accepted government arbitration.*

   a. . . . would meet around the clock until either they reached an agreement or government arbitration was accepted by them.
   b. . . . would meet around the clock until they either reached an agreement or accepted government arbitration.

8. During the winter *Angela both developed her skill in skiing and ice-skating.*

a. . . . Angela developed her skill in both skiing and ice-skating.
b. . . . Angela developed both her skill in skiing and in ice-skating.

9. *Pat and him told Mike and I* the answers to the homework problems.
   a. Pat and him told Mike and me . . .
   b. Pat and he told Mike and me . . .

10. Ever since the accident, *driving past that spot,* the whole experience has returned.
    a. . . . while driving past that spot, . . .
    b. . . . as I have driven past that spot, . . .

11. The Governor sent her budget message to the legislature yesterday, conferred with the director of the budget this morning, *and a conference with the press was held this afternoon.*
    a. . . . and held a conference with the press this afternoon.
    b. . . . and this afternoon held a conference with the press.

12. *Was it he who* you thought stole the money?
    a. Was it he whom . . .
    b. Was it him whom . . .

13. When one of the girls *have completed their report, ask them* to bring it to me.
    a. . . . has completed their report, ask them . . .
    b. . . . has completed her report, ask her . . .

14. Don't expect *Jane and I to be as good as her* in English.
    a. . . . Jane and me to be as good as she . . .
    b. . . . Jane and I to be as good as she . . .

15. Plans for the P.T.A. party *include not only dancing but also* a floor show and a buffet supper.
    a. . . . not only include dancing but also . . .
    b. . . . include not only dancing, but also the guests will enjoy . . .

16. Jim had been in jail for safecracking *but because of good behavior was paroled.*
    a. . . . but because of good behavior had been paroled.
    b. . . . but had been paroled for good behavior.

17. To my complete surprise the students *accepted the new type of examination which the teachers had prepared without a complaint.*
    a. . . . accepted the new type of examination without a complaint, which the teachers had prepared.
    b. . . . accepted without a complaint the new type of examination which the teachers had prepared.

18. The mayor's economy committee *has been investigating street-cleaning costs, and it has published a report on its findings.*
    a. . . . , which has been investigating street-cleaning costs, has published a report on its findings.
    b. . . . has been investigating street-cleaning costs, and a report has been published on its findings.

19. The two causes of "college neurosis" are trying to get into college *and then you try to stay there.*
    a. . . . and then to try to stay there.
    b. . . . and then trying to stay there.

20. *The students received the new yearbook,* which came out on the last day of school, *with enthusiasm.*
    a. The students received with enthusiasm the new yearbook . . .
    b. The students with enthusiasm received the new yearbook . . .

21. *The telegram reached me too late advising against going to Washington.*
    a. Too late the telegram advising against going to Washington reached me.
    b. The telegram advising against going to Washington reached me too late.

22. *It is not the cost of a gift but its appropriateness that matters.*
    a. The cost of a gift does not matter, but the appropriateness of it does.
    b. It is not the cost that matters of a gift, but its appropriateness.

23. After being reprimanded twice, *the teacher, for further punishment, sent Ann to the principal.*

a. . . . by the teacher, Ann was sent to the principal for further punishment.
b. . . . the teacher sent Ann to the principal for further punishment.

24. Public figures must learn to take *the reporters' questions and the jostling of photographers calmly.*
    a. . . . the questions of reporters and the jostling of photographers calmly.
    b. . . . calmly the questioning of reporters and the jostling of photographers.

25. *Driving through the mountains, we were impressed by the engineering achievements of road builders.*
    a. We were impressed by the engineering achievements of road builders, driving through the mountains.
    b. We were impressed by the engineering achievements, driving through the mountains, of road builders.

## Revising Awkward Sentences

**EXERCISE 4.** This exercise is composed of awkward sentences which you are to rewrite. The sentences may be rearranged in any way that will make them clearer and smoother. Your purpose is to express the same idea in a better way. The faults in a sentence may not always be specific errors; they may be generally clumsy constructions. You may add words or omit words wherever you wish, provided you do not alter the meaning. Remove wordy passages. Eliminate errors in usage. Each problem can be handled in a single sentence, but your teacher may allow you to divide some of the problems into two sentences.

1. She tried to find out the boy's name that she was to invite.
2. Featherbedding is one result of automation, which is the practice of keeping workers on the job, which is unnecessary, because the job has been made obsolete by machines.
3. The dean was more impressed by the candidate's scholastic record than his athletic record impressed him.

4. There are many persons who have jobs part of the year, and a job is not held by them the rest of the year, being among the unemployed.
5. There is a great deal of Franklin's philosophy which certainly everyone who reads it can benefit from in his *Autobiography.*
6. Soon many families will have helicopters just like cars today and able to go from place to place much more easier than by car since there will be a direct route and the traffic will be much less.
7. Since we hadn't no tire repair kit, the motorcycle was pushed to the nearest gas station where we had a patch put on it.
8. Tammy was an optimist, easygoing, and nothing ever seemed to trouble her no matter what happened.
9. Opening the curtain, an empty stage was revealed, but the stage crew arrived a moment later and, busily working and talking, the set was soon up for the first act.
10. In a child a negative attitude may come from the natural desire for recognition and independence, but when an adult shows a negative attitude, it may be a symptom of neurosis.

**EXERCISE 5.** Follow the directions for Exercise 4.

1. Mrs. Turnbull is a good author and through experience has found out what a reader wants and has given them it in this book.
2. From my own standpoint, gardening, whether flowers or vegetables, is a lot of fun, good exercise, and the experience it provides is valuable.
3. There are many ways to show loyalty to a friend that you can use, and one of these is not to talk about them behind their back.
4. In some countries the biggest problem of the people is getting enough food, but the biggest problem of some people in America is dieting which is when you keep yourself from eating too much food.
5. Psychologists have proved that a child's mind is often more active than an adult, and they are usually eager to learn.
6. The mechanic working for the airline that failed to check the

landing gear was not only guilty of negligence, but, in effect, he was a murderer as well.

7. After the dances in the gymnasium, of which we have a reasonable amount, many couples go to some eating place which is not too far away to have a bite to eat.
8. I found out that shopping quickly weakens a friend's patience when I went to a department store with Dolores one day.
9. The clash between East and West of ideals were blocking world unity at a time when war might be led to if unity could not be achieved.
10. By the time you have got the children into bed, you are so exhausted that all ambition to study has been lost by you, and television is all that is left as the only entertainment until the return of the parents is made.
11. A single goal may dominate an individual so that it is the only thing they live for and they work so hard that they miss the fun in life and are never satisfied.
12. Being the first author to make a strong case for complete independence from England, Paine's book was a big seller, and it was about American independence.
13. Going even further into the effects of not having any more petroleum would have on the world is the realization that the thousands of factories in the world which use oil would have to close down.
14. After graduating from high school the learning we have attained may be lost or become hazy in a year of military training and it also adds another year to the time we will graduate from college to get a job.
15. There should be required by the school a pre-season physical examination, and there should be enforced a law to prevent anyone from playing football with a history of heart abnormalities.

# Composition: Paragraphs and Longer Papers

PART FOUR

# Chapter 21

# The Paragraph[1]

No matter how long an essay is, it really consists of a series of short compositions. Each of these helps to develop the essay, at the same time developing its own topic. These short compositions are paragraphs.

**21a. A *paragraph* is a series of sentences developing one topic.**

In your review of paragraph writing in this chapter, you will practice techniques that are applicable to all writing. In many ways a paragraph is a complete composition on a small scale. It deals with one subject which it introduces, develops, and concludes. The ideas in a paragraph, like those in a longer piece of writing, must be arranged according to a definite plan and should follow one another clearly and smoothly. The topic of the paragraph must be fully developed. In other words, the planning and writing of one-paragraph themes give you excellent practice in important techniques of composition.

## THE TOPIC SENTENCE

**21b. The topic of a paragraph should be stated in a sentence somewhere in the paragraph.**

In the sample paragraph which follows, the topic sentence is the opening sentence, printed in bold-faced type. The

[1] The student should realize that the rules for paragraph organization and development given here do not apply to the paragraph in novels and short stories or in very informal personal essays or in news writing.

author, a native American, develops the idea in this sentence by listing supporting details. Most paragraphs are developed in this way.

> **The widespread use of cloth brought on many new variations to women's dresses.** One popular style used a cape, decorated with beadwork and shells, which could be worn over any plain calico dress. Some capes were actually the decorated remnants of worn-out cloth dresses. Some cloth dresses were decorated with buckskin additions that were fringed. Some dresses were made of velvet, with decorations of ribbons and metal sequins. The most valuable dresses had their tops covered with elk teeth or cowrie shells.[1]

### 21c. In general, place the topic sentence at or near the beginning of the paragraph.

A topic sentence may be placed at any point in a paragraph, but the most effective position for it in most paragraphs is at or near the beginning. Placing the topic sentence at the beginning helps readers by giving them a clear idea of what is going to be said; it helps writers by requiring them to formulate clearly the main point before going on to develop it.

In a composition of several paragraphs it would, of course, be unwise to begin every paragraph with the topic sentence; to do so might give a monotonous effect.

Experienced writers are skilled enough to *imply* the topic of a paragraph without stating it. But practice is required to develop this skill. At first, you should practice writing a clear topic sentence for every paragraph.

#### *Paragraph with the Topic Sentence in the Middle*

Occasionally, the topic sentence will appear in or near the middle, as in the following paragraph.

> The economic drain [that] children now represent adds to the new economic pressures on families. Since most children

[1] From p. 231 in *The Ways of My Grandmothers* by Beverly Hungry Wolf. Copyright © 1980 by Beverly Hungry Wolf. Reprinted by permission of William Morrow & Company, Inc.

now use family income for seventeen to twenty-five years and few yield significant income in return, the years of child-rearing are the years of greatest financial stress on families. **That stress helps push women out into paid jobs to maintain the family standard of living.** This is particularly true of single-parent families headed by a woman; her work is a necessity if the family is to avoid welfare and the stigmas that accompany it. Many families are above the poverty line not because wages have kept abreast of needs and inflation, but because wives have gone to work to make up the difference. Mothers work outside the home for many reasons, but one of them is almost always that their families need their income.[1]

*Paragraph with Topic Sentence at the End*

Sometimes the topic sentence comes at the end, where it serves as the climax to the series of details that lead up to it.

Convinced that he had identified "the African," about whom his grandmother had spoken, [Alex] Haley searched through shipping records in London and Annapolis to trace Kunta Kinte's arrival in America in 1767 and his sale to the Waller family of Spotsylvania County, Virginia. After that line was established, his job was largely a matter of working through census records to trace the family's migrations from Virginia to North Carolina and, after emancipation, to Tennessee. ***Roots* is Haley's account of seven generations of his family, from Africa to America, from freedom to slavery and on to freedom again.**[2]

## The Concluding, or Clincher, Sentence

At the end of a paragraph, particularly a long one, a writer will sometimes summarize by restating, in different words, the topic sentence used at the beginning. A concluding sentence of this kind is often called a "clincher" sentence because it clinches the point made in the paragraph.

[1] From *All Our Children: The American Family Under Pressure* by Kenneth Keniston and The Carnegie Council on Children. Published by Harcourt Brace Jovanovich, Inc. Reprinted by permission of the Carnegie Corporation of New York.

[2] From "Family Chronicle" by David Herbert Donald. Copyright © 1976 by the American Jewish Committee. Reprinted from *Commentary*, December 1976, by permission.

You should be warned against overuse of the clincher sentence and against tacking it on artificially when it is not of any value. Avoid such weak and unnecessary concluding sentences as "Those are the three reasons why I like baseball" or "Now I have told you why I like baseball." It is better not to attempt a clincher sentence than to write one that is ineffective. In the following example both topic and concluding sentences are in bold-faced type.

> **The interpretation of words is a never-ending task for any citizen in modern society.** We now have, as the result of modern means of communication, hundreds of thousands of words flung at us daily. We are constantly being talked at, by teachers, preachers, salesmen, public officials, and moving-picture sound tracks. The cries of the hawkers of soft drinks, soap chips, and laxatives pursue us into our very homes, thanks to the radio—and in some houses the radio is never turned off from morning to night. Daily the newsboy brings us, in large cities, from thirty to fifty enormous pages of print, and almost three times that amount on Sundays. The mailman brings magazines and direct-mail advertising. We go out and get more words at bookstores and libraries. Billboards confront us on the highways, and we even take portable radios with us to the seashore. **Words fill our lives.**[1]

**EXERCISE 1.** Each of the following subjects can be treated in a paragraph. Select three subjects from the list; think through your ideas on each of the three, and write a topic sentence you could use to introduce a paragraph on it. You will write three topic sentences.

1. Self-discipline
2. Immature behavior
3. An important decision
4. A recent invention
5. Ads on television
6. Handling money wisely
7. My favorite place
8. Unsafe driving
9. Health foods
10. A good book

[1] From *Language in Action* by S. I. Hayakawa. Copyright © 1941 by Harcourt Brace Jovanovich, Inc. Reprinted by permission of the publisher.

**EXERCISE 2.** Develop one of the topic sentences written for Exercise 1 into a paragraph of approximately 150 words.

## Adequate Development of the Topic Sentence

**21d. Develop a paragraph by giving additional, detailed information in support of the idea expressed in the topic sentence.**

Since a paragraph is the development of an idea, it must give enough details to make the idea clear and convincing. A common fault in one-paragraph compositions, such as those you are writing in your study of this chapter, is the failure to provide enough information. Although there can be no strict rule as to paragraph length, a one-paragraph composition of only two sentences or of less than 100 words is likely to be thin. Because most students have difficulty in developing rather than in limiting their paragraphs, it is hardly necessary to set a maximum number of words; but if you find your paragraph running above 300 words, you are taking the risk of destroying its unity. Long paragraphs are likely, in other words, to contain details not closely related to the topic sentence.

**21e. In developing a paragraph, supply enough information to insure adequate development. Avoid the thinness which results from merely repeating in different words the idea in the topic sentence.**

*Paragraph Lacking Sufficient Development*

> **Every student should engage in some extracurricular activity.** A student needs experience in such an activity for success in life. If you include athletics, there are enough activities to provide everyone with something to do in addition to the regular schoolwork. No student should leave school every day when the final bell rings and have no definite interest to follow in the after-school hours. Everyone can benefit educationally and socially by extracurricular work. No one should think of school as solely a matter of subjects to study.

### *Adequately Developed Paragraph*

**Every student should engage in some extracurricular activity because from extracurricular work you learn a great many valuable things that you won't learn in a classroom.** School is not just a matter of learning the difference between *lie* and *lay* or the causes of the Civil War; it is learning to live and work with others. You learn to work and play with others harmoniously, to give and take, win and lose. When, as a member of a club, you are given a job to do, you learn to assume responsibility and to work unselfishly for the good of the group. In a radio club or a photography club you get additional knowledge which may be more valuable in the long run than the knowledge you get from doing homework or attending classes. Furthermore, if you work hard in dramatics or in musical organizations, you will develop talents which will be satisfying to you all your life, talents which might never have been discovered had you thought of school as confined to the hours of the daily schedule. Finally, extracurricular activities broaden your circle of acquaintances. No amount of ordinary schoolwork can take the place of friends acquired in the informal familiarity of activities.

## UNITY IN THE PARAGRAPH

**21f. A paragraph should be unified. Unity is achieved by discussing only one topic in a paragraph, the topic stated in the topic sentence.**

**EXERCISE 3.** The unity of the paragraphs which follow has been weakened by inclusion of ideas not closely related to the topic of the paragraph. The topic sentences are in bold type. Point out which sentences in each paragraph should be omitted because they do not deal with the topic.

1

**Because in most cities and towns all the water we need gushes forth at the mere touch of a faucet and because water is cheap, we Americans use it lavishly.** New York City alone consumes one and a half billion gallons a day. Every day each of us draws about 83 gallons: 24 for flushing, 32 for bathing, laundry, and dishwashing, and 25 for such other uses as swimming pools, lawn watering, and the mere 2 gallons we use for drinking and cooking. These figures are surprising enough, but they do not cover the much greater daily consumption in agriculture and industry. In 75 percent of the world, cities and towns lack any municipal supply of pure water. The facts about our consumption of water should make us wonder how long our supply will last if we continue to drain it so recklessly.

2

**From the standpoint of suitability and adaptability, English has thoroughly proven itself as a world language.** It is precise and concise for commercial use, at the same time that it is capable of infinite distinction of shades of meaning for literary purposes. Its vocabulary is not only the most abundant in the world, but also the most international of all existing major national languages—more international, in fact, than that of Esperanto. Its speakers are more numerous than those of any other tongue save Chinese, and widely and strategically distributed over the earth's surface. French was once considered the language of diplomacy. English is *par excellence* the language of science and technological progress. Its popularity among non-English speakers is such that if it came to a vote today it would undoubtedly gather more second-choice votes than any other national language.[1]

3

**A dishonest newspaper may warp the day's news either by hiding a story or by slanting headlines.** A paper with a strong political bias may hide a story favorable to the opposing party by placing it in an inconspicuous position. On the other hand, it may give large headlines and a front-page position to news favorable to its own party. Although newspapers do not change the facts in the stories which come to them, they may, if it serves their political purpose, change the total effect of a story by giving it a headline which is deliberately misleading or slanted. Headlines are written by those highly skilled in their jobs. Once

[1] From *The Story of the English Language* (Revised Edition of *The Story of English*) by Mario Pei, copyright © 1952, 1967 by Mario Pei. Reprinted by permission of Harper & Row, Publishers, Inc. and George Allen & Unwin Ltd.

the drudges of the newspaper office, these newswriters in recent years have been accorded greater respect as reflected in easier hours and higher pay. A headline may be made misleading simply by means of the kinds of words used. MAYOR JONES REPLIES TO CRITICS gives a quite different impression from MAYOR JONES CRACKS DOWN ON CRITICS.

4

**Restaurant work is the kind of work most likely to be available to teen-agers seeking employment at a summer resort.** This kind of employment has one major disadvantage and several advantages. The disadvantage is that only the low-paying restaurant jobs are available to persons under eighteen: dishwashers, porters, kitchen maids, and buspersons. These behind-the-scene jobs sometimes pay less than the minimum wage because members of the better-paid dining-room staff are expected to share their tips with those in the more menial jobs, but the generosity of waiters and waitresses is often uncertain. Other summer jobs, low-paying but pleasant, are the outdoor jobs of lawn mower, lifeguard, and camp counselor. It is possible to find work as a salesperson, a stock clerk, or a bag packer in a supermarket. But even the menial restaurant jobs have some advantages. If you are lucky enough to work evenings only, you have the daytime for the beach and outdoor activities. Friendships with fellow workers frequently develop and add to your summer fun. There is, too, the daily fringe benefit of a free meal.

**EXERCISE 4.** Select one of the following topic sentences and develop it into a paragraph of approximately 150 words. Insure adequate development of the topic by (1) gathering enough ideas, (2) avoiding commonplace ideas, and (3) resisting the tendency to restate the topic sentence again and again in different words. Insure unity by including only ideas which support the topic sentence.

1. Our school's athletic program puts too much (too little) emphasis on competition.
2. Jogging offers several benefits.
3. A good novel has three important qualities.
4. A person's little mannerisms may bother others.
5. Growing up in the inner city, you learn some valuable lessons.

6. Judged by any standard, —— is an excellent team sport.
7. Three qualities characterize the good citizen.
8. The established industrial nations should do more to help the developing nations.
9. For several reasons I have chosen —— as my lifework.
10. My favorite piece of music is ——.

# COHERENCE IN THE PARAGRAPH

## Arrangement of Details

A paragraph is coherent when its sentences are logically and clearly related to one another and their total effect is the clear development of the paragraph topic. One way of achieving coherence is by arranging the details in a paragraph in a clear and logical order.

**21g. To insure that the details in a paragraph will follow one another logically and smoothly, arrange them in order according to some definite plan.**

Four plans, or orders, for the arrangement of the details in a paragraph are *chronological order, spatial order, the order of importance,* and *the order required to bring out a comparison or contrast.*

**(1) The details in a paragraph may be arranged in *chronological* order.**

*Chronological order,* the order of time, is followed in two kinds of paragraphs. It is followed in the *narrative* paragraph, in which events are given in the order in which they happened; and it is followed in the *expository* paragraph in which a *process* is described from beginning to end. The paragraph on page 351, about how luck is sometimes the deciding factor in a game, illustrates chronological order in a narrative paragraph. The following paragraph illustrates chronological order used in explaining a process.

All the products of erosion which reach the coast finally settle down on the sea floor, but rivers also deposit in their beds a great deal of the material they bring down from the mountains. What usually happens **first** is that frost and rain conspire to wash in the sides and form a valley, and the vast bulk of rock disintegrated by these agents is carried away as mud, sand, and pebbles by the stream at the bottom. **As the valley gets older,** it grows wider and may **presently** be so wide in its lower reaches as to have a virtually level bottom, over which the river slowly winds toward the sea. The river has **now** lost speed, and begins to distribute its mud and sand over its widened valley floor. **Once a river begins** to flow in a curve, a cycle of events is started which results in a steady and systematic covering of the whole valley floor with sediment. The water naturally moves most rapidly round the outside of the curve, where its increased speed causes it to remove a quantity of mud from its bank. It may actually scoop out a little cliff for itself. But on the inside of the curve the water is moving extra slowly, and because mud settles down in still water it is here that some of the mud it is already carrying is deposited. **As the river goes on** scooping out mud from one bank and depositing it on the other, so it moves sideways across its valley, leaving a carpet of alluvium in its trail.[1]

**(2) The details in a paragraph may be arranged in *spatial* order.**

*Spatial order,* the order of position, is frequently followed in descriptive writing. A word picture is clear and coherent when the writer shows exactly where the various items in the picture are located. Usually this is done by setting up and following a logical plan which takes the reader smoothly and naturally from one part of the scene to another. The writer also may make effective use of such expressions as "in the foreground," "to the left," "in the distance," etc. It is not necessary to describe methodically from left to

[1] Adapted from *Science Marches On* by Walter Shepherd. Reprinted by permission of Harcourt Brace Jovanovich, Inc. and George G. Harrop & Company Ltd.

right or top to bottom as though "panning" a scene with a moving-picture camera. Such slavish adherence to spatial order may produce an artificial style. But it is advisable to follow some plan which will make clear in an orderly fashion exactly how the parts of the picture are related spatially.

In describing the Van Tassel farmhouse, Washington Irving follows a clear plan. He first gives a general impression of the house as an approaching visitor would see it. The porch or piazza is logically next, then the hall, or living room, and through the door beyond, a view of the parlor. Notice the frequent use of expressions which give the location of the things described.

> It was one of those spacious farmhouses with high-ridged but low-sloping roofs, built in the style handed down from the first Dutch settlers, the low projecting eaves forming a piazza **along the front** capable of being closed up in bad weather. **Under this** were hung flails, harness, various utensils of husbandry, and nets for fishing in the neighboring river. Benches were built **along the sides** for summer use, and a great spinningwheel **at one end** and a churn **at the other** showed the various uses to which this important porch might be devoted. From this piazza the wondering Ichabod entered the hall, which formed the center of the mansion and the place of usual residence. Here rows of resplendent pewter, **ranged on a long dresser,** dazzled his eyes. **In one corner** stood a huge bag of wool ready to be spun; **in another** a quantity of linsey-woolsey just from the loom; ears of Indian corn and strings of dried apples and peaches hung in gay festoons **along the walls,** mingled with the gaud of red peppers; and **a door left ajar gave him a peep into the best parlor,** where the clawfooted chairs and dark mahogany tables shone like mirrors; andirons, with their accompanying shovel and tongs, glistened from their covert of asparagus tops; mock-oranges and conch-shells decorated **the mantelpiece;** strings of various-colored birds' eggs were suspended **above it;** a great ostrich egg was hung from **the center of the room,** and a corner cupboard, knowingly left open, displayed immense treasures of old silver and well-mended china.[1]

[1] From "The Legend of Sleepy Hollow" by Washington Irving.

**(3) The details in a paragraph may be arranged in the *order of importance*.**

*Order of importance* usually means proceeding from the least important to the most important. This order may be profitably followed in any paragraph which presents evidence in support of an opinion or an argument. For instance, in the following example, the author, after stating his opinion that oil tankers are the dominant vessels of the age, gives reasons to support this opinion. You will note that the reasons are given in the order of importance, the least important coming first, the most important last.

> **Oil tankers, a once obscure and largely unremarked race of ships, have established themselves during the past fifteen years as the dominant vessels of the age and, arguably, of all time.** They qualify in both respects merely on grounds of size. They are the biggest ships that have ever been, their dimensions being one of the technological audacities of the century. Most of all, however, they qualify because no other ships have ever been so universally important, none more political. They were the harbingers of that new manifestation of global strategy and national self-interest, the energy crisis; it was to keep them moving that Britain and France landed their troops at Suez in 1956. Much broader and more subtle implications now rest upon their safe voyaging. They have become indispensable to so much more of the world than at the time of Suez that they are now pivotal to global peace and economic survival to a degree that could not have been easily visualized even then.[1]

**(4) The details in a paragraph may be arranged to bring out a *comparison* or a *contrast*.**

Occasionally a writer wishes to use a paragraph to compare or contrast two things or ideas. Naturally details will be arranged in such a way as to bring out clearly the nature of the comparison or contrast.

In bringing out a comparison or a contrast, a writer may follow one of two arrangements: (1) details supporting one point of view may be presented first, followed by details

[1] From *Supership* by Noel Mostert. Copyright © 1974 by Noel Mostert. Reprinted by permission of Alfred A. Knopf, Inc.

supporting the opposite point of view; (2) details of similarity or difference may be compared or contrasted one by one, rather than being grouped into two complete parts as in the first method. These two arrangements are illustrated by the following paragraphs.

There are many advantages and some disadvantages involved in working part-time while you are in school. On the one hand, part-time work can offer you an interesting experience that contributes to your education. It helps you to be more independent of your family. For many students, a job provides needed spending money and helps cover many of the hidden costs of a high school education. Thus part-time work helps many students to remain in school. The experience that you gain through part-time work may be of great help to you in making a decision as to the type of occupational career you would like to follow. On the other hand, you may gain temporary advantages at the expense of values that are more important from the long-range point of view. For example, you may lose time needed for sleep, rest, study, club activities, and play. As a result, you may find it hard to adjust to what the school expects from you as well as to what your employer has a right to expect. It is obvious that, if you work five hours a day in school and five or six hours a

topic sentence

advantages

disadvantages

day on the job, you are carrying too much of a load. Work experience is most desirable—but you have to strike a balance between school and the job.[1]

concluding sentence

In several respects, living in an apartment building is easier than living in a house. There is no outside work to do. Apartment dwellers can forget those chores that keep householders busy, like mowing the lawn, cleaning the sidewalk, and repairing the porch. The responsibility for heat, water, and electricity falls on the building superintendent, not on the occupants of the apartments. When a sink is stopped up or a short develops in an electrical circuit, house dwellers are responsible for repairs, and they usually try to solve such problems themselves to save the cost of a plumber or an electrician. An apartment is easier to clean because normally it has fewer and smaller rooms than a house. When apartment dwellers leave home, whether for an hour or a month, they have only one door to lock. House dwellers may have as many as three doors to lock and perhaps three times as many windows to secure.

topic sentence

contrast 1

contrast 2

contrast 3

contrast 4

**EXERCISE 5.** Each of the following items suggests a com-

[1] From *Points for Decision* by Harold J. Mahoney and T. L. Engle. Published by Harcourt Brace Jovanovich, Inc. and reprinted by permission of the authors.

parison or contrast that can be developed into an interesting paragraph. Select one and fashion a topic sentence stating your point. Using one of the two methods of arranging material in a paragraph of this kind, write a paragraph of about 150 words which will bring out clearly the point in the topic sentence. You will be developing a paragraph by means of comparison or contrast.

1. A novel or book of short stories (your preference and why)
2. Two families of neighbors or two neighbors
3. A school you formerly attended and the one you attend now
4. Women's and men's gymnastics
5. Indoor and outdoor soccer
6. A novel and its movie or TV version
7. Two kinds of fishing
8. Romantic and realistic views of life
9. Chinese and Japanese cooking
10. Mysteries by Dorothy Sayers and Agatha Christie
11. Celsius and Fahrenheit temperature scales
12. Democrat and Republican

## Linking Expressions and Connectives[1]

**21h. Strengthen the coherence of a paragraph by using linking expressions and connectives which help the reader to follow the line of thought from one idea to the next.**

The linking expressions are usually pronouns which refer to words or ideas in the preceding sentences. They serve to carry the reader back to what has just been said. The pronouns commonly used in this way are *she, he, it, they* (and their objective and possessive forms) and *this, that, these, those*. When used as adjectives, the words *this, that, these,* and *those* serve as linking expressions just as well as when they are used as pronouns.

[1] Methods of making smooth transitions from one paragraph to another are further described on pages 365–68.

### (1) Keep the thought of a paragraph flowing smoothly from sentence to sentence by using pronouns which refer to words or ideas in preceding sentences.

> One final effect of radio and TV on the language must be noted. There is no doubt that **these** great media of information have cut down considerably the time that used to be devoted to reading, both of newspapers and of books. **This** means in turn that while radio and TV may enhance the spoken language (if indeed they do) they also tend to make of us a nation of functional illiterates, absorbing our language through the ear rather than the eye. Some may view **this** as a return of language to its original form and function; others may consider it a reversal, pure and simple, to the semi-literate Middle Ages.[1]

### (2) Keep the thought of a paragraph flowing smoothly from sentence to sentence by the use of connectives.

The second kind of transitional device is the word or expression which *connects* what has preceded with what is to follow. Devices of this kind may be referred to simply as *connectives*. Judicious use of connectives makes writing coherent, but you must not overuse them, for too many will make your writing artificial and cumbersome.

Study the following list of common connectives. Notice that some express spatial relationship (*above, beyond*); some express chronological order (*first, finally*); and others indicate a logical relationship of ideas (*accordingly, on the contrary*). With a few exceptions, connectives are equally useful in all kinds of discourse: description, narration, exposition, persuasion.[2]

[1] From *The Story of the English Language* (Revised Edition of *The Story of English*) by Mario Pei. Copyright 1952, © 1967 by Mario Pei. Reprinted by permission of Harper & Row, Publishers, Inc. and George Allen & Unwin Ltd.

[2] For work on the careful selection of the proper connective, see pages 206–08, 210–12.

### *Connectives*

above
accordingly
across from
adjacent to
again
also
although
another
as a result
at last
at the same time
before me
below me
beside me
besides
beyond
consequently
equally important
finally
first
for example
for instance
further
furthermore
hence
here
if this be true
in addition
in fact
in short
in the distance
likewise
moreover
nearby
nevertheless
next
next to
on my left
on my right
on the contrary
on the other hand
opposite to
otherwise
second
similarly
such
then
then too
therefore
thus
to sum up
to the left
to the right
whereas

**EXERCISE 6.** Select one of the following topics and write a paragraph of approximately 150 words. Begin with your topic sentence. Then develop it, paying special attention to such matters as having enough details to develop the idea adequately, sticking to the subject, following a definite arrangement, and using pronouns and connectives to keep the thought running smoothly.

1. An educational TV program
2. Overcoming a personal handicap
3. Characteristics of high school students' speech
4. Homemaker and/or career woman
5. Privileges and responsibilities
6. Some decisions a senior must make
7. My ecological efforts
8. A good friend and a bad friend
9. Ways to waste spending money
10. Causes of injury in sports
11. Comparison of two sonnets (two by Elizabeth Barrett Browning, for example, or by two different poets)

12. A new source of energy
13. Pictorial art and abstract art
14. Regional differences in the United States
15. The meaning of fair play
16. Ways to entertain children
17. The appeal of movies
18. The theme of a play (for example, Lillian Hellman's *Watch on the Rhine*)
19. Irony in *Macbeth* (or another work)
20. A great person

## FOUR TYPES OF PARAGRAPH

**21i. Learn to write the four common types of paragraphs: expository, descriptive, narrative, persuasive.**

Like longer forms of writing (which you will study in later chapters) paragraphs can be classified into four types: the expository paragraph, the descriptive paragraph, the narrative paragraph, and the persuasive paragraph. The type of paragraph you write may often depend upon your purpose in writing. If, for example, your purpose is to relate an incident, then you choose the narrative paragraph, for it develops its topic sentence by telling a brief story. The following presentation of the four types of paragraphs will familiarize you with the ways in which paragraphs may differ according to their purpose.

### The Expository Paragraph

The expository paragraph is by far the most common kind of paragraph. Its primary purposes are to give information or to explain something or to define the meaning of something. Sometimes a single expository paragraph will both inform and explain.

**(1) An expository paragraph may be developed by *facts*.**

The following informative paragraph is developed by facts. The facts support the statement made in the topic sentence.

Basic to all the Greek achievement was freedom. The Athenians were the only free people in the world. In the great empires of antiquity–Egypt, Babylon, Assyria, Persia–splendid though they were, with riches beyond reckoning and immense power, freedom was unknown. The idea of it never dawned in any of them. It was born in Greece, a poor little country, but with it able to remain unconquered no matter what manpower and what wealth were arrayed against her.[1]

topic sentence

facts

The following paragraph is explanatory. It is developed by facts.

> **Condensation trails, usually called contrails or vapor trails, are visible artificial clouds of water droplets or ice crystals that form in the wake of an airplane.** They form because the water in the exhaust of aircraft engines condenses in the cool air. For a contrail to form, the air around the plane must be colder than –60° C. If the air is warmer, the warmth will prevent condensation of the moisture coming from the engines, and no contrail will form. Jets, which fly in the very cold upper layers of the atmosphere, are the planes most likely to produce contrails.

**(2) An expository paragraph may be developed by *examples*.**

Sometimes an expository paragraph may be developed by an example or a few examples. An example is one kind of fact. It may name names–persons, places, events. Frequently it is preceded by the expression *for example*. The

[1] From *The Ever-Present Past* by Edith Hamilton. Copyright © 1964 by W. W. Norton & Company, Inc. Reprinted by permission of the publisher.

topic of the following paragraph is the differences you will see in old buildings as you travel from north to south. The writer develops the paragraph by giving examples of these differences. The examples are given in chronological order as the trip progresses from north to south.

**If you travel over regions where the buildings were made in earlier times, you will notice great differences from north to south.** In the north the roofs are steep to shed the snow, the windows small to keep out the cold, the building materials often easily worked soft woods provided by the abundant nearby forests. The ceilings are low to conserve heat, the chimneys numerous or large, the doors and windows arranged to baffle chilling drafts, and the hearth is the focus of the dwelling. As you move south the roofs flatten, the windows grow larger, the ceilings rise, so that houses on the steamy James River, in Virginia, for example, have very high ceilings and also a through hall to permit easy cooling of the rooms. As you near the tropics the woods become harder to work and more vulnerable to dampness and insects. The roofs may get still flatter unless the rainfall is torrential, in which case they steepen again as in Celebes. The patio usually replaces the hearth, and the walls of adobe or stone become thicker in order to preserve coolness; now the windows are small and deeply recessed to keep the hot direct sun from penetrating the interiors. All these practical arrangements were worked out empirically long ago.[1]

The facts or examples in an expository paragraph may be arranged to bring out a comparison or contrast. The following paragraph is developed by contrasting the various lengths of days and years on the planets.

**An inexhaustible variety distinguishes the various worlds from one another.** On the Moon, for example, there are only twelve days and twelve nights in a year, although the length of the year is the same as ours, and ours is divided into 365 days. On Jupiter, which actually does not all spin in one piece but at a rate that varies with latitude, the year is nearly twelve times longer than ours, while the day is shorter by over a half; so that on Jupiter there are over 10,500 days in a year. On

[1] From "Architecture and Building" by John Burchard from *An Outline of Man's Knowledge of the Modern World,* edited by Lyman Bryson. Published by Nelson Doubleday, Inc., Garden City, New York. Reprinted by permission of the publisher.

Saturn, which also does not spin as one piece, the disproportion is even greater, for its year is twenty-nine times longer than ours and has nearly 25,000 days in it. And what should we say of Neptune, where each year lasts over a century and a half, or 165 of our short years; or of Pluto, whose year is 249 of ours, two centuries and a half?[1]

**(3) An expository paragraph may be developed by *definition*.**

Sometimes in the course of a composition we need to define terms, to make clear to our reader the meaning of a word or a phrase as we understand it. Usually a quick one-sentence definition is not adequate, and we find ourselves devoting a paragraph to the definition. Writing such as definition may involve explanations and description; it may require development by the citing of examples.[2]

Developing a paragraph by definition should produce a clear and useful statement of the author's idea of the meaning of a term.

In the following paragraph the writer defines romantic fiction. He gives his definition in a general way in the first sentence, the topic sentence. Then he develops it by giving a great many facts and examples which clarify the phrase "escape from reality."

> **Romantic fiction is primarily the kind which offers the reader an escape from reality.** It often deals with distant lands and times. The things that happen in it are more exciting or mysterious or adventurous or strange than the things that happen in real life. Often it deals with such things as tournaments and besieged castles and perilous journeys through hostile country. Sometimes its characters have long journeys to go alone through forests, . . . are besieged in lonely old houses, or are shut up on islands in the midst of faraway lakes, or lie in hushed hiding while a mortal foe treads close by. Sometimes there are pirates, hidden treasures, shipwrecks, thrilling flights from a close-pursuing enemy, last-minute rescues, ominous prophecies, missing heirs, disguised princes,

[1] From *The Flammarion Book of Astronomy* by Cammille Flammarion, translated by Anabel and Bernard Pagel. 

[2] For more detailed discussion of how to write a definition, see pages 376–79.

intrigue, murder, breathless suspense. Again, romance is often pervaded by an atmosphere of strange things about to be revealed; often it deals with places and people now changed or forgotten or long since passed away. In short, romance shows life not just as it is, but as we like to imagine it to be.[1]

**(4) An expository paragraph may be developed by a combination of methods.**

When you are practicing paragraph writing, you may wish to decide ahead of time which of the several methods will best develop your topic sentence. This concentration on one method at a time is excellent training. You should realize, however, that a paragraph need not be developed in only one way. In fact, experienced writers do not try to limit themselves to one method—facts or examples or definitions; they simply use any combination of methods that will be effective. Combining various methods does not mean that the writing is poor. The important point to remember is that the topic of the paragraph must be fully and effectively developed; the method is incidental. The following paragraph is developed by facts and by examples.

We have become more dependent on *things* than rational beings should be.

topic sentence

In some societies this dependence is already causing people to degenerate physically. Men and women who live all their lives in centrally heated homes and offices, and go in the car to post a letter and collect the children from school, and have labor-saving devices for every conceivable purpose (including electric toothbrushes and carving knives)—such people have become so sensually unaware and so unresponsive to physical

factual statement supported by examples

[1] From *The Enjoyment of Literature* by Ralph P. Boas and Edwin Smith. Reprinted by permission of Harcourt Brace Jovanovich, Inc.

challenges that they are only half alive.
If they cannot soon escape from Afflu-
ence and Technology, some very odd
biological mutations seem likely within
the next few generations. The urge to    fact
effect this escape, of course, underlay
what was vaguely known as the Hippy
Movement. But few hippies realized that    examples
their routine of quitting the rat race,
seeking a guru, going vegetarian and
growing a lot of hair was no substitute
for training their bodies to do what in
previous generations any healthy young
body could do.[1]

**EXERCISE 7.** Read carefully each of the following expository paragraphs. Find the topic sentence in each and write it on your paper. After each topic sentence indicate by the numbers—(1), (2), (3), (4)—the method by which the paragraph is developed:

(1) facts
(2) examples (one or more)
(3) definition
(4) combination of methods

1

In learning a second language, you will find that vocabulary is comparatively easy, in spite of the fact that it is vocabulary that students fear most. The harder part is mastering new structures in both content and expression. You may have to free yourself from the bondage of thinking of everything as either singular or plural. Perhaps the new language will organize content into singular, dual, and plural (here meaning "three or more"). Or perhaps the new language will not give routine consideration to the matter. English speakers can never make a statement without saying something about the number of every object mentioned. This is

[1] From *Wheels Within Wheels* by Dervla Murphy, published by Ticknor & Fields. Copyright © 1979 by Dervla Murphy. Reprinted by permission of Houghton Mifflin Company and John Murray Publishers Ltd.

compulsory, whether it is relevant or not. In Chinese, objects are noted as singular or plural only when the speaker judges the information to be relevant. The Chinese experience suggests that it actually seldom is, for that language operates with only occasional references to number.[1]

2

In 1976 [Barbara] Jordan delivered the keynote address at the Democratic National Convention. She thrilled the meeting with a ringing call for "a national community" where everyone is equal. "We cannot improve on the system of government handed down to us by the founders of the Republic," she said, "but we can find new ways to implement that system and realize our destiny." Her own role that night, she asserted, showed "that the American dream need not forever be deferred." Jordan was the first black and the first woman ever to be the Party's keynoter.[2]

3

Since the Second World War, the American people have come to accept the poetry reading as a legitimate and frequently satisfying kind of artistic performance. Prior to the 1940's there were, to be sure, a few vivid or beloved figures to whom our audiences were glad to listen: Robert Frost, with his New England wit and accent; Carl Sandburg, with his guitar; Edna Millay in her white dress; Vachel Lindsay, with his camp-meeting style and his tambourines. But the public attitude toward the verse recital has now so matured that any poet, whether or not he qualifies as a platform personality, is likely to find himself on a platform several times a year. Sometimes it will be in a university auditorium, sometimes in an art gallery or community center, sometimes in a nightclub or coffeehouse. The audience may be ten or twenty; or it may be hundreds, even thousands; what matters is that it is now there.[3]

4

We remain happily unaware of the countless little seizures,

[1] From *An Introduction to Descriptive Linguistics,* Revised Edition, by H. A. Gleason, Jr. Reprinted by permission of Holt, Rinehart and Winston, Inc.

[2] From *Profiles of an Era: The Nixon Ford Years,* edited by Eleanora Schoenbaum. © 1979 Facts on File, Publications, Inc. Reprinted by permission of the publisher.

[3] From "On My Own Work" in *Responses* by Richard Wilbur. Copyright © 1976 by Richard Wilbur. Reprinted by permission of Harcourt Brace Jovanovich, Inc.

but the big ones strike terror. In between, there are degrees of earthquakes less than dangerous but quite noticeable enough to cause lively conversation. A relative scale was devised by Charles Richter of the California Institute of Technology in 1956 so you may know just how much earthquake you are enduring. The degrees of intensity go from 1 to 12. (Below 1 the tremor can only be detected by seismographs.) Number 1 on the Richter scale can be felt by very few people. Number 2 is apparent to people at rest on upper floors. A number 3 earthquake makes people indoors aware something is happening. Hanging objects swing. During 4, hanging objects swing more noticeably. Vibrations are felt such as those caused by heavy trucks. Windows, dishes, and doors rattle. Glasses clink. Some houses begin to creak. Number 5 on the Richter scale can be felt outdoors. Little objects fall over. Doors move, open and close. Pendulum clocks behave erratically. Number 6 earthquakes make themselves heard. People run outside. Glasses, dishes, and windows break. Books fall out of bookshelves and pictures fall from the walls. Furniture moves or topples over. Plaster walls begin to crack. Small bells in steeples begin to ring. Trees and bushes shake. During a scale 7 earthquake it is difficult to stand. Weak chimneys tumble. Loose bricks, tile roofs, architectural ornaments shake loose. Large bells ring. At 8 it becomes very difficult to steer an automobile. Ordinary masonry collapses. The best built masonry resists. By 9 on the scale there is probably panic. Many buildings crumble or at least move from their foundations. Reservoirs are endangered. Pipes underground are destroyed. Large cracks are seen in the ground. The worst modern earthquakes have not registered beyond 9 on the Richter scale, but it is interesting to note that at 12 the damage is nearly total. The scenery is moved about very significantly. Things are even thrown into the air.[1]

5

Many think that Braille is merely conventional letters, figures, and symbols raised so that they can be perceived by the fingers. It isn't; it is quite unlike any conventional alphabet, consisting rather of raised dots bearing no physical resemblance to actual letters or figures. When "written" by hand, the dots

[1] "Earthquake: The Richter Scale" from Chapter VIII, "Why Does the Earth Quake?" in *Mysteries of Our World* by Peter Briggs, David McKay Company, Inc., Copyright © 1969 by Peter Briggs. Reprinted by permission of McIntosh & Otis, Inc.

are punched out on stiff paper with the help of a template and a small tool resembling an awl. Because it would be virtually impossible to punch out the dots from underneath, Braille is written backwards so that for most European languages it can be "read" with the fingers in normal left-to-right order when the page is turned over.[1]

**EXERCISE 8.** Choose one sentence from the following list (or make up a sentence of your own) and develop it into an interesting expository paragraph of about 150 words. Whether your purpose is to inform or to explain or to define, give coherence to your writing by arranging the details according to a definite plan—chronological order, or comparison and contrast—and by using linking expressions and connectives.

1. I now realize that there are some serious gaps in my education.
2. Part-time jobs have given me valuable experience.
3. The eye (hand) is a remarkable organ.
4. People-watching is fun.
5. What is courtesy?
6. In any sport, equipment is important.
7. Our football coach and our basketball coach are different in personality and methods.
8. What does it mean to be well-groomed?
9. The greatest influence on teen-agers is other teen-agers.
10. Some parental restrictions do more harm than good.

## The Descriptive Paragraph

Description is the means by which a writer helps the reader to share an experience fully. Description appears in all kinds of writing: expository, narrative, and persuasive. Since passages of description do not usually stand by themselves but are woven into the other forms of discourse, whole paragraphs consisting solely of description are not common. Nevertheless, writing a paragraph-length descrip-

[1] From pp. 26–27 in *More Misinformation* by Tom Burnam. (Lippincott and Crowell, Publishers). Copyright © 1980 by Tom Burnam. Reprinted by permission of Harper & Row, Publishers, Inc.

tion permits you to concentrate on this kind of writing and gives you practice in a very important writing skill.

In the following paragraph, the writer describes part of a German city. Her description is intended to let us see the city as Italian immigrants saw it when they came to find work there during the industrial recovery of Germany following World War II. You will find here two of the elements of effective description: an abundance of details and the use of figurative language: "modest skyscrapers act as bookends for lower structures," "potbellied trucks," "gingerbread eyebrows."

> Closer to the center of town a few dusty trees break the linear bleakness. Then on a boulevard, divided in the middle by a row of trees that meet overhead with trees on either curb to form two leafy tunnels, the traffic begins to swirl, dragging you mercilessly on, past a park into the unfinished glass and chrome and concrete world of the city. Modest skyscrapers act as bookends for lower structures, furniture showrooms and stores of electronic equipment. Vast windowless walls of concrete, some studded, some quilted for texture, loom over garages, amusement arcades, record shops, restaurants, and potbellied trucks dribbling their premixed concrete near the hoardings of a would-be skyscraper. At the end of a short street, drab with two-story buildings, rooming houses, and dejected shops, squats a miniature station, its newly painted gingerbread eyebrows giving it a sullen expression. Half-defiant, half-apologetic, a remnant of the past, it looks out on the wrong century.[1]

The details in a descriptive paragraph may be given in either spatial or chronological order. In the preceding example, the author organizes her description spatially—starting with the "few dusty trees" near the center of the town, moving along the boulevard, and finally reaching "the unfinished glass and chrome and concrete world" of the downtown city. In the following example, the author uses chronological order to describe a scene. Details are given in the order in which the woman in the paragraph comes upon them.

[1] From *Strangers and Pilgrims: The Last Italian Migration* by Ann Cornelisen. Copyright © 1980 by Ann Cornelisen. Reprinted by permission of Holt, Rinehart and Winston, Publishers.

She went out into the soft yellow light that fell from the windows and that lay upon the ground and the pile of wood. She knelt down and picked up the cold, hard lengths of wood and laid them in the crook of her arm. They were sharp and seamed at the ends where the axe had shaped them like pencil points, and they smelled of resin. When again she stood, she inadvertently touched the handle of the axe; it was stiff and immovable in the block, and cold. She felt with the soles of her feet the chips of wood which lay all about on the ground, among the dark stones and weeds. The long black rim of the canyon wall lay sheer on the dark, silent sky. She stood, remembering the sacramental violence which had touched the wood. One of the low plateaus, now invisible above her, had been gutted long ago by fire, and in the day she had seen how the black spines of the dead trees stood out. She imagined the fire which had run upon them, burning out their sweet amber gum. Then they were flayed by the fire and their deep fibrous flesh cracked open, and among the cracks the wood was burned into charcoal and ash, and in the sun each facet of the dead wood shone low like velvet and felt like velvet to the touch, and left the soft death of itself on the hands that touched it.[1]

**EXERCISE 9.** Select from your experience a scene, a place, an event, an object, or a person that you can describe clearly in a paragraph of 100–150 words. Plan your paragraph. Begin with an introductory sentence stating in a general way the subject of the description. Decide in what order you will give the descriptive details. If possible, appeal not only to the reader's sense of sight but also to other senses: hearing, smelling, feeling.

## The Narrative Paragraph

A narrative is a story. A narrative paragraph, then, is a paragraph in which the topic sentence is supported by a story—an incident or an anecdote. Most narrative paragraphs are arranged chronologically, in the order in which events occur in time.

[1] From p. 35 in *House Made of Dawn* by N. Scott Momaday. Copyright © 1966, 1967, 1968 by N. Scott Momaday. Reprinted by permission of Harper & Row, Publishers, Inc.

In the following paragraph, the writer develops the idea in the topic sentence by telling a story of a particular baseball game. The story is an example of the idea expressed in the opening sentence.

> **Luck is sometimes the deciding factor in a game.** In the eighth inning of the deciding game of the World Series of 1924, the Giants were leading the Senators by the fairly comfortable margin of 3–1. A hard-hit ground ball struck a pebble, bounded over the head of third baseman Fred Lindstrom, and two runs came in, tying up the game. The contest went into extra innings. In the last of the twelfth, the Giant catcher, about to dash for a pop fly behind the plate, caught his foot in his mask and, to free himself, missed an easy out. The batter, given another chance, then doubled. The next man up hit another grounder toward third base. The ball again struck a pebble, soared over the third baseman, and the game and series were won by the Senators.

The writer of the following paragraph tells a story to illustrate her point that artists, writers, and even such great philosophers as Arthur Schopenhauer expect others to recognize their greatness.

> **Artists, writers, even great philosophers, are sometimes quite ingenuous about their powers, indignantly surprised when someone does not recognize them for what they are.** One of the stories I like best is about Schopenhauer, not an endearing character, certainly, but hardly one to ignore. Apparently Schopenhauer ate, quantitatively, like an elephant. One day a young man, an admirer, came to lunch, and sat marveling at the philosopher's capacity. The young man stayed for supper, and the sage went at it as if he had not been fed in a week. Finally the young man said, "Sir, why do you eat so much?" "I eat a great deal," Schopenhauer replied, "because I am a great man."[1]

**EXERCISE 10.** Select one of the following topic sentences (or make up a topic sentence of your own) and develop it into a narrative paragraph of about 150 words.

1. Some "work" is fun, and some "fun" is work.

[1] From "The Nature of the Artist" by Catherine Drinker Bowen in *119 Years of the Atlantic,* edited by Louise Desaulniers. Copyright © 1961 by Catherine Drinker Bowen. Reprinted by permission of Harold Ober Associates, Inc. as agents for the estate of Catherine Drinker Bowen.

2. I learned the importance of obeying rules.
3. A fool and his money are soon parted.
4. Practicing may be dull, but it pays off.
5. "Bad luck" is a bad excuse.
6. —— is smarter than you think.
7. Fearlessness is not always commendable.
8. I found out I wasn't as good as I thought I was.
9. I had always been impatient until ——.
10. Jumping to conclusions is dangerous.

## The Persuasive Paragraph

When expressing an opinion, especially when engaged in an argument, you attempt to persuade someone that you are right. A persuasive paragraph is a paragraph written in support of an opinion or in an effort to persuade someone to follow a certain course of action. A persuasive paragraph is developed with reasons based on facts.

In the following persuasive paragraph, the writer is attempting to convince us that Queen Victoria, who was queen of England from 1837 to 1901, was a more cultivated woman than has been commonly supposed. His reasons for this opinion are based on the facts he gives.

> Victoria was considerably more cultivated than some of her biographers have allowed. She spoke perfect German, excellent French, and adequate Italian; she was well-read in literature and history; she sketched charmingly, and she had a trained ear for music. Because as queen she was uncomfortable in the company of scientists of whose fields she was ignorant, it is sometimes assumed that she was less well-educated than she was. But few men of her era, let alone women, received any training at all in the sciences. Victoria was almost a bluestocking by modern standards.[1]

[1] From *Persons of Consequence: Queen Victoria and Her Circle* by Louis Auchincloss. Copyright © 1979 by Louis Auchincloss. Reprinted by permission of Random House, Inc.

Reasons in a persuasive paragraph may be given in the order of importance. In general, it is better to begin with the least important reason and build up to the most important ones, thus achieving a vigorous conclusion, as in the paragraph on page 334. In some situations, however, especially when the writer may have one very important reason and several less important ones, it may be appropriate to do just the reverse—to give the most important reason first and then support it with the less important details. Whether the writer chooses one order or the other, the reader must be able to distinguish important from less important details in a persuasive paragraph.

The writer of the following paragraph has organized her reasons by saving the most important reason for last.

> **Although cooking is generally destructive to nutrients, we should not forget that it also has advantages.** It softens and breaks down the cellulose or fibrous coverings which enclose many plant nutrients, making their starch, protein, and vitamins available to us. Some nutrients, which are in a bound form in raw food, such as the niacin and trytophan in cornmeal, are released when the food is heated. Finally, cooking destroys toxic substances in some foods (like soybeans) and makes palatable other foods which we would otherwise not even eat.[1]

**EXERCISE 11.** Select a controversial subject that has become an issue in your school or community, in the nation, or even just among your friends. Write a topic sentence stating your opinion on the subject and develop it into a persuasive paragraph by giving the reasons for your opinion. The reasons, of course, should be based on facts.

[1] From *Laurel's Kitchen: A Handbook for Vegetarian Cookery and Nutrition* by Laurel Robertson, Carol Flinders, and Bronwen Godfrey. Copyright 1976 by Nilgiri Press, Petaluma, California, 94953. Reprinted by permission of the publisher.

Chapter 22

# Expository Writing

## The Whole Composition

The literal meaning of *compose* is "to form by *putting together.*" A composition is a piece of writing formed by putting together the ideas you have on a subject. This suggests two important points about writing a composition. The first is that you must have some ideas on the subject about which you are going to write. The second is that you must be able to put these ideas together in such a way that they will form an effective whole. In your study of Chapter 21, you had a good deal of practice in composing paragraphs. In this and the chapters immediately following, you will gain practice in writing longer compositions.

The emphasis will be on expository writing. In general, the purpose of expository writing is not primarily to amuse or entertain (although it may do both), but to enlighten and instruct. Its essential quality is clarity. Most of the writing you are required to do in school—tests, reports, essays—is expository, and most of the writing you will do after you leave school will be of this kind.

No matter what you are writing about, the basic steps involved in writing are almost always the same. They should become so familiar that you will follow them habitually whenever you write.

## PLANNING THE COMPOSITION

The steps in writing a composition fall into two main stages: planning and writing. Planning includes the first three steps: selecting and limiting the subject, assembling materials, and organizing (outlining).

### Selecting and Limiting the Subject

**22a. Select a subject that can be adequately treated within the limits of your composition.**

Unless your teacher specifies what you are to write about, your first problem is the choice of a subject. Of course, you will choose one in which you are interested. You will choose one, too, on which you either have or can find enough information to make a worthwhile composition. You should know before you select your subject how long your composition is going to be. On this basis you must limit your subject so that you will be able to cover it adequately in the space at your disposal. Study the following examples of how a subject may be limited for treatment in compositions of different length.

| | |
|---|---|
| NOT LIMITED | Energy |
| SLIGHTLY LIMITED | The Energy Problem Today |
| MORE LIMITED | Renewable Sources of Energy |
| FURTHER LIMITATIONS | How a Solar-Energy Cell Works |
| | Growing Trees for Fuel |
| | Building a Backyard Windmill |

Limiting your subject must always be done with reference to your purpose. The purpose of your composition, in fact, determines its scope. Your teacher may ask you to precede your composition with a statement of your purpose or, at least, to state the purpose in the introductory paragraph. In any event, for your own benefit you will do well to write the purpose in a one-sentence statement so that you will be able to keep it clearly before you as you plan and write:

"My purpose in this composition is to explain my objections to some TV commercials."

## Assembling Materials

**22b. List all the ideas you may wish to use in your composition.**

Some compositions can be written "out of your head" without recourse to the library or to the opinions of others. Many compositions, however, will send you on a hunt for information.[1] In both instances Step 2 is the same. It is the listing of the ideas you think you can use in your paper. In this step, it does not matter in what order you list the ideas; the important thing is to get them down where you can look at them, evaluate them, and arrange them.

In order to illustrate the steps in planning and writing a composition, the next few pages are devoted to showing you, through a specific example, how the steps should be followed.

Imagine that you have been asked to write as a composition assignment a critical essay on some aspect of modern living. You have decided to write about TV commercials. For a long time, the common commercials have bothered you, and so you will use this writing assignment to state why. Writing your criticisms is the best way to clarify them. Since the materials for this composition are your own, you begin by searching your mind for them. You do not need to go to the library or to consult other people. You begin Step 2 by making a list of things you might include in your essay.

When you have jotted down your ideas in the order and form in which they occur to you, you will end up with a list like the following:

necessity for commercials
interrupt programs too often
no commercials in some other countries*
some good commercials*

[1] For a detailed discussion of writing a long research paper, see Chapter 26.

irritating ads
too much repetition
singing commercials
romantic touch
sexist commercials
cure-all medicines
my favorite TV programs
meaningless terms
tiresome slogans
meaningless testimonials
insulting ads
dangerous ads
15-second ads*
misleading
false impressions of life
emphasize luxuries
no reasons given why product is best
dramatic*
banks and finance companies
cold cereals
detergents
cosmetics
pretty women and handsome men
keeping up with the Joneses
false scientific*
magazine ads*
applies to radio, too*
children (box tops, etc.)*

After the list has been completed, you should go over it carefully and remove any items that, on second thought, seem unrelated to the subject, or that, if included, would make the composition too long. For example, in going over this list, you decide to eliminate certain items (marked by an asterisk). The total absence of TV advertising in some other countries does not seem essential to a composition about American television. There seems little point in singling out the 15-second commercial or the commercials on children's programs because they have the same characteristics as all the others. To discuss the good commercials would lead away from your subject. Proceeding in this way, you reduce your list until you think it is manageable. You next perform the all-important step of organizing the ideas—putting them together according to a plan.

## Organizing Materials—Outlining

**22c. Group related ideas together. Arrange the groups in a logical order. Make an outline.**

As you group the related ideas, you are really making an outline. In making an outline, you must make major decisions concerning the content and the organization of your composition. It is no exaggeration to say that more than half the work on a composition has been done when the outline has been completed.

### *The Topic Outline*

Two kinds of outline are in common use: the topic outline and the sentence outline. In a topic outline each item is merely a topic to be discussed in the paper; it is not a sentence. For most of the outlining that you will do, the topic outline will be adequate; in fact, it will be preferable because it is easier to make and is clear enough to serve its purpose. The following outline of the first part of the essay on TV commercials is of this kind.

I. Necessary
  A. To pay costs of a TV program
  B. To sell sponsors' products
II. Irritating
  A. Repetitious
  B. Frequent

### *The Sentence Outline*

There are some occasions, however, when you may prefer to use the sentence outline, which is always clearer because it gives in more detail the exact meaning of each topic. A sentence outline is the better kind if you are outlining for someone else who may not grasp the full meaning of the short headings in a topic outline. A comparison of the sentence outline below with the topic outline above will indicate the advantage of the sentence form.

I. Commercials are necessary.
  A. The money a sponsor pays to a station to air commercials during a TV program pays for the production costs of that program.
  B. It is the commercials that sell the sponsors' products.
II. Commercials are irritating.
  A. The constant repetition is irritating.
  B. The too-frequent interruption of programs is irritating.

## Outline Form

**22d. Observe rules for form in making an outline.**

**(1) Place the title above the outline. It is not one of the numbered or lettered topics.**

**(2) The terms *Introduction, Body, Conclusion* should not be included in the outline. They are not topics to be discussed in the composition. They are merely organizational units in the author's mind.**

**(3) Use Roman numerals for the main topics. Subtopics are given letters and numbers as follows: capital letters, Arabic numerals, small letters, Arabic numerals in parentheses, small letters in parentheses.**

*Correct Arrangement of Numbers and Letters*

```
I.
    A. } subtopics of I
    B. }
        1. } subtopics of B
        2. }
main topics     a. } subtopics of 2
                b. }
                    (1) } subtopics of b
                    (2) }
                        (a) } subtopics of (2)
                        (b) }
II.
```

**(4) Indent subtopics so that all letters or numbers of the same kind will come directly under one another in a vertical line.**

**(5) Begin each topic and subtopic with a capital letter; otherwise, capitalize only proper nouns and proper adjectives.**

**(6) In a topic outline do not follow topics with a period.**

**(7) There must never be, under any topic, a lone subtopic; there must be either two or more subtopics or none at all. Subtopics are divisions of the topic above them. A topic cannot be divided into fewer than two parts.**

**(8) As a rule, main topics should be parallel in form, and subtopics under the same topic should be parallel in form. If in a list of topics the first topic is a noun, the others should be nouns; if it is an adjective, the others should be adjectives, and so on. Topics in the form of phrases should not be mixed with topics in the form of nouns or a noun and its modifiers. Subtopics need not be parallel with main topics.**

The second half of the outline for the composition on television commercials is given below to show parallelism of topics.

parallel main topics—adjectives

III. Insulting
- A. Implied virtues of product
- B. Meaningless testimonials
- C. Catchy tunes

(adjectives and nouns)

IV. Dangerous
- A. Create demand for luxuries
  - 1. Dissatisfied family
  - 2. Debt-ridden parents

  (adjective and noun)
- B. Promote phony cure-alls

parallel subtopics—verb and object

A violation of the parallelism of topics is illustrated by the following part of the outline, incorrectly phrased.

FAULTY PARALLELISM

IV. Dangerous
- A. Create demand for luxuries [verb and object with modifying phrase]
  - 1. Dissatisfied family [adjective and noun]
  - 2. Parents in debt [noun and phrase]
- B. Promotion of phony cure-alls [noun and phrase]

**(9) Do not mix the topic and sentence forms of outline.**

MIXED FORMS

IV. Dangerous [topic]
  A. Commercials create a demand for luxuries. [sentence]
    1. The family becomes dissatisfied without all the advertised products. [sentence]
    2. Debt-ridden parents [topic]
  B. People are misled by phony cure-alls. [sentence]

**(10) For each number or letter in an outline there must be a topic. Never place an *a*, for instance, next to *1* like this: *1a*.**

The complete outline for the composition on TV commercials is given below. Note that all ten points about correct outlining have been carefully observed. Note also the number of main topics. For a 500-word composition, you should not have more than five main topics. A minimum of three is a sound general rule but an outline with two main topics is sometimes acceptable.

Compare this outline with the original list of topics on pages 356–57. You can see how the writer was able to group the desirable topics under four main topics. The changes in wording are necessary to make the outline clear and consistent in form.

### *Television Commercials*

I. Necessary
  A. To pay costs of a TV program
  B. To sell sponsor's products

II. Irritating
  A. Repetitious
  B. Frequent

III. Insulting
  A. Unexplained virtues of the product
  B. Meaningless testimonials
  C. Catchy tunes

IV. Dangerous
   A. Create demand for luxuries
      1. Dissatisfied families
      2. Debt-ridden parents
   B. Promote phony cure-alls

**EXERCISE 1.** Demonstrate that you understand the rules on pages 359–61 by correcting the following faulty outline. Make parallel the main topics and subtopics under the same main topic. Change sentences to topics, and be sure there are no isolated subtopics. Omit topics if necessary. Write the outline with proper alignment and number-letter designations.

***How to Study***

I. The conditions for studying must be right.
   1. You should allow enough time
   2. Quiet Place
   3. Proper Equipment
      a. textbooks
      b. reference books

II. The Techniques
   A. Assignments that are mainly reading
      a. How to take notes
      b. Memorizing
   B. Writing Assignments
      1. Term papers

III. Conclusion

**EXERCISE 2.** Arrange the items in the following list in a correct topic outline. Begin by placing the title, which is included in the list, at the top of your paper. Then group related topics and find a main topic for each group. The topics are correctly phrased so that if properly grouped, they will be parallel. Finally, place and letter the subtopics correctly and copy the outline neatly in perfect arrangement.

counselor at summer camp
indoor work
from tips
summer jobs
heavy work
assures an outdoor life
making extra money
shelf stocker in a supermarket
requires an interest in children
waiter at a summer hotel
confines one to camp
from baby-sitting for guests
enjoying hotel's social life
close to home

## WRITING THE COMPOSITION

If you have completed the planning stage carefully, you will have already solved many of the problems involved in the actual writing. The writing stage begins with composing the first draft and includes all of the revisions needed for achieving a satisfactory final draft.

### The First Draft

**22e. With the outline before you, write the first draft of your composition. Include an introduction and a conclusion. Pay careful attention to the division into paragraphs.**

#### The Introduction

Before you present the first point in your composition, you will introduce the subject. Whether or not the introduction is a separate paragraph depends upon the length of the entire paper. In a composition of 500 words or more, you will probably devote the first paragraph to introducing the subject.

**(1) Write an introduction which will make clear the purpose of your composition and arouse the interest of the reader.**[1]

A good introductory paragraph should make clear the purpose of the composition. It may give facts that will ex-

[1] Additional suggestions on how to make an introduction interesting will be found on pages 403–07.

plain the choice of subject, and it may give information necessary to the understanding of the subject. It should, if possible, arouse the interest of the readers so that they will want to read further. The following is the final form of the introductory paragraph in the composition on TV commercials.

> Restore happiness to your marriage by using Whiteshirt laundry detergent. Your husband will love you for it. End those lonely Saturday nights—use Bretheen mouthwash. Only Aloha Sealines Super-duper jets will fly you upside down to Hawaii! Thus the barrage of TV commercials continues day and night in almost every American home. I think most of the commercials are irritating or insulting or dangerous. I believe they can be improved so that they will be not only less offensive to the public but also more effective as advertisements.

Write your first draft rapidly. Do not worry unduly about details of punctuation and sentence structure. These can be taken care of later in your revision.

## Paragraphing

**(2) Paragraph a composition in such a way that the various phases of the subject will stand out clearly.**

As you write the first draft, you must decide at what points new paragraphs begin. When you begin a paragraph, you notify the reader that you are taking up another phase of your subject. In a brief composition you may find it advisable to devote one paragraph to each of the major (Roman numeral) topics in your outline. For example, if you have three main topics, you will have three main paragraphs. Add to these an introductory paragraph and a concluding paragraph and you will have a five-paragraph composition. In the sample composition on pages 371–76, which is written from an outline with four major topics, there are eight paragraphs. Two of these are the introductory paragraph and the concluding paragraph. The six others are necessary because two of the four major topics require two paragraphs each for proper development.

In a longer paper—a research paper, for instance—you cannot follow a simple formula for paragraphing; indeed, you may wish to devote several paragraphs to a subtopic.

**(3) Avoid the overlong and the very short paragraph.**

When paragraphing your writing, bear in mind that your reader will be able to follow you more easily if your paragraphs are not too long. Paragraphs of 300 words are probably too long for high school writers to handle effectively. On the other hand, a number of paragraphs of less than 100 words may indicate poor planning. Such paragraphs show that the writer is not taking time to support the topic sentence, and they give the composition a broken-up appearance which is confusing because it does not emphasize the major ideas.

## Transitions Between Paragraphs

**(4) Make the transition between paragraphs clear and smooth by using a transitional device at the beginning of a paragraph.**

Because the beginning of a paragraph signifies a shift to another phase of your subject, you should make your train of thought clear to the reader by showing the relationship between this new phase and the phase discussed in the preceding paragraph. There are several devices for accomplishing this transition between paragraphs. These devices help to keep the thought flowing smoothly from paragraph to paragraph in the same way that linking words and connectives (see the section beginning on page 337) keep the thought flowing from sentence to sentence.

Some frequently used transitional devices are explained and illustrated on the following pages.

### *Pronouns as Transitional Devices*

A pronoun that refers to a person or an idea mentioned in the preceding paragraph often provides a smooth transition between paragraphs. The pronouns most commonly used in this way are *he, they, this, that, these, those, them, it.* These words carry the reader back to their antecedents, helping to bridge the gap between the two paragraphs. *This, that, these, those,* when used as adjectives, are employed in the same way.

> Yet if you *didn't* nose down during the approach, you could, with a small misjudgment of your gliding angle, arrive over the edge of the airport with 200 feet of altitude and "overshoot" the whole field! Or again, in trying to avoid these errors, you could fall into their opposites: instead of overshooting, you could "undershoot"; instead of floating you might "pancake."
>
> All *this* is now wiped out. With the new gear, you can slobber it on anyhow; it makes no difference: there is no bounce. The moment the wheels touch the ground, the airplane assumes a level, no-lift attitude and clings to the ground.[1] [The pronoun *this* in the sentence *All this is now wiped out* accomplishes the transition between paragraphs.]

Each of the following sentences is the opening sentence of a paragraph. Note how the word in bold-faced type (a pronoun or an adjective) reflects something in the preceding paragraph.

> And **that's** still not all.
>
> What is **this** new formula?
>
> A day or so later, **they** began to notice that a number of rather valuable objects were missing.
>
> And just at **that** instant there came the sound of fifty cannons firing a lethal barrage of cannon balls.
>
> You will understand **this** better, perhaps, if I give you some familiar examples.
>
> Some of **these** feelings may lead to practical follies, but that is not the point.

[1] From "The Revolution in Small Plane Flying" by Wolfgang Langewiesche from *Harper's Magazine,* August 1960, copyright 1960 by Harper's Magazine. Reprinted by permission of Paul R. Reynolds, Inc.

### *Repetition of a Key Word or Term*

By repeating in the first sentence of a paragraph a key word or term used in the preceding paragraph, you help the reader over the gap between paragraphs.

1

In short, then, if civilization does survive intact into the next century, it will be because there will be a kind of global organization, a kind of international cooperation, that will consider global problems, weigh possible solutions, decide on the most useful, enact them and enforce them. I don't know what to call this except **"world government."**

The concept of **world government** is not popular anywhere on earth except in the case of occasional ivory-tower idealists like myself.[1] [Repeating the term *world government* helps to link the paragraphs.]

2

. . . They are still wrestling with the limitations and ambiguities of mathematics, but they have been able to pin down with a fair degree of certainty what their **uncertainties** are.

One of the most basic of the **uncertainties** was introduced by Einstein's theory of relativity.

### *Direct Reference*

A preceding idea may be referred to directly, often in summary form.

1

. . . This congressional committee literally worked itself out of existence by accomplishing efficiently the job for which it had been appointed.

**How the committee accomplished its job so efficiently** makes an interesting story. . . .

2

. . . Today a computer, sorting checks and printing figures faster than the eye can follow, can handle a whole day's work for one of the bank's thirty branches in fifteen minutes.

[1] From *Life and Time* by Issac Asimov. Copyright © 1978 by Issac Asimov. Reprinted by permission of Doubleday and Company, Inc.

**But the incredible efficiency of computers** and their remorseless logic, based on pure mathematics, may be eliminating jobs as well as problems.

### *Connectives*

Most of the connectives listed for use in linking sentences (see pages 338–39) may also serve as transitional expressions between paragraphs. The following connectives are commonly used in this way:

| | | |
|---|---|---|
| accordingly | for example | on the other hand |
| also | for instance | otherwise |
| another | furthermore | similarly |
| as a result | however | such |
| at last | in fact | then |
| consequently | likewise | therefore |
| finally | moreover | thus |
| | nevertheless | |

1

. . . To the writer, writing is more than communication. It is the revelation, to oneself as writer, of things that have been hidden, now forced into expression.

**On the other side,** the side of the reader, it is the revelation of one person to another, a personal communication in an impersonal world.

2

. . . It predicts a population of 50 billion (the highest estimate of the population-carrying capacity of the globe ever calculated by a responsible scholar) in less than 200 years.

The United Nations estimates of future world population, **moreover,** indicate even further acceleration in the rate of world population growth during the remainder of this century.

**EXERCISE 3.** Regard each of the following sentences as the opening sentence of a paragraph. Point out the device or devices used in each sentence to effect a transition from what had been discussed in the preceding paragraph.

1. In this vast domain, obviously, the planet Earth is insignificantly small.

2. Wherever such networks have been established, systems which do not yet belong to the networks—even systems as large as solar systems—are regarded as primitive.
3. Easing the inevitable tensions, therefore, is not merely desirable: it is quite necessary for survival.
4. As a result, it is difficult to describe those microscopic forms of life with the unaided eye.
5. In sophisticated regions, too, the same conclusions apply.

**EXERCISE 4.** Examine a daily newspaper or a current magazine to find further examples of transitional devices used by professional writers. Copy onto your paper five paragraph openings which contain such devices. Underline the transitional expressions.

## The Transitional Paragraph

Sometimes, especially in a long paper, you may wish to let your reader know that you have completed your discussion of one phase of the subject and are now about to take up another. A brief paragraph will easily accomplish this purpose. Such a paragraph is called a transitional paragraph.

1

So much, then, by way of proof that the method of establishing laws in science is exactly the same as that pursued in common life. Let us now turn to another matter (though really it is but another phase of the same question), and that is, the method by which, from the relations of certain phenomena, we prove that some stand in the position of causes toward the others.[1]

2

The entries in an unabridged dictionary such as the Webster's *Third New International Dictionary,* however, differ in

[1] From "The Method of Scientific Investigation" by Thomas Henry Huxley.

some respects from the entries in a college dictionary. Let us consider these differences.

3

Whereas at the beginning of *Pride and Prejudice* the reader sees Elizabeth as confident, even headstrong, in her opinions, later in the novel her self-assurance begins to falter. Take, for example, her meeting with Darcy at Rosings.

### The Conclusion

**(5) Write a conclusion which will summarize or reemphasize the major point of the composition.**

A whole paragraph of summary or conclusion may not be necessary. But you should make an effort to remind the reader at the end of the composition what it is that you have said. In a short paper one or two concluding sentences will usually be enough. Read on page 376 the concluding paragraph in the sample composition.

## Revising the First Draft

**22f. Read over the first draft. Eliminate or add ideas; change the order of ideas if advisable; revise sentences to improve their structure; check spelling and punctuation.**

The revision of your first draft is extremely important. Students who lazily choose to hand in this draft as a completed composition are doing themselves a great injustice. Professional writers are thorough revisers. They are rarely satisfied with the first draft of their work. A student should not claim an ability which an experienced writer would never claim.

A study of the first draft may reveal faults in the original outline. Do not hesitate, in such a case, to change the outline. *No aspect of the composition should be considered unchangeable until the final draft has been completed.*

**REVISION CHECKLIST**

As you revise your composition, ask yourself the following questions:

1. Have I made my purpose clear at the start?
2. Is the paragraphing correct? Does it reveal the major points in the composition? Is each paragraph unified and coherent? Are the paragraphs clearly related to one another by transitional devices?
3. Are the sentences varied in structure? Can more complex sentences be used?
4. Is the style wordy? What expressions can be eliminated?
5. Are all words spelled correctly?
6. Where is punctuation needed to make the meaning clear?

## Preparing the Final Draft

**22g. When the revision has been completed, copy the composition neatly. Type this copy if it is possible to do so.**

The final draft of the composition you have seen taking shape throughout this chapter is given below. Read it through, noting the general organization, the adherence to the outline (pages 361–62), the paragraphing, the transitions, the introduction, and the conclusion.

TELEVISION COMMERCIALS

Restore happiness to your marriage by using Whiteshirt laundry detergent. Your husband will love you for it. End those lonely Saturday nights—use Bretheen mouthwash. Only Aloha Sealines Super-duper jets will fly you upside down to Hawaii! Thus the barrage

introduction

of TV commercials continues day and night in almost every American home. I think most of the commercials are irritating or insulting or dangerous. I believe they can be improved so that they will be not only less offensive to the public but also more effective as advertisements.

statement of purpose

Even while I am registering my objections to commercials, I recognize that commercials are necessary. Without them we would have no television programs, for it is the sponsor who pays the bill. Since the money which pays for a TV program comes from the sale of the sponsor's products, the sponsor must have air-time in which to advertise. Americans must put up with the hourly brainwashing, and they must buy the sponsor's products if they want to enjoy television. They should not, however, have to endure the kind of advertising that accompanies most of the programs.

transition – key words

(compare outline: I, A and B)

This advertising is objectionable, first, because it is irritating. The two sources of irritation are the endless repetition of the same commercial and the too frequent interruption of programs. I suppose that once advertisers have a slogan that has proved effective, they are reluctant to give it up, but if they realized how meaningless the familiar words become after a thousand repetitions, maybe

transition – direct reference

they would find that an occasional change would be effective. My parents say that some of the ads commonly heard today, like "a combination of medically proved and tested ingredients," were used in radio advertising in the forties. The truth is that no one pays any attention to the worn-out slogans, and everyone is irritated rather than interested when the familiar lines begin.

(compare outline: II, A)

I think, too, that advertisers lose more than they gain when they insist on interrupting a program every ten minutes to plug their wares. Irritation of the viewer-buyer is surely not the way to sell anything. Just as the bad guys are about to destroy the good guys—for the first time in television history—the picture stops, and you are taken into a sparkling kitchen to observe the wonders of a floor wax or a detergent or a hand lotion, wonders you have already heard proclaimed night after night. As you are poised deliciously on the brink of disaster in an adventure film or carried away by the immortal lines of Shakespeare, the illusion is shattered by the shouted advice that only by banking at National can you end up a millionaire. If sponsors would all agree to confine commercials to the beginning and the end of programs, the public's appreciation would be reflected in its buying. If they would

transitional word

(compare outline: II, B)

realize how weary we get of the same old commercials, they might find an occasional change to be surprisingly effective.

Another kind of objectionable commercial is the kind that insults our mentality with its meaningless claims. Analyze the claims made by many TV commercials, and you will find yourself asking, quite logically, "Well, so what?" In our simple-minded way, we are expected to accept blindly the word of a cowpuncher or a water-skier as sure proof of the quality of a soft drink. Every Little Leaguer knows that the leading hitter in the American League has not really achieved his enviable record because of the breakfast food he eats. And parents know that not all family problems will be solved by downing a couple of headache pills. Even shy and desperate Danny doubts that a change in deodorant, shaving lotion, or mouthwash will make him irresistible to the prettiest models on TV. Claims that are completely without reason are insulting to thinking people. The writers of commercials should give their viewers credit for some brains.

transitional expression

(compare outline: III, A, B)

Finally, TV commercials can be dangerous. They can endanger the finances of the American family. The goal of advertisers is to create a demand if none exists. You should have the

transitional word

latest dishwasher, the newest electric hair dryer, a second car, and such status symbols as a backyard swimming pool and a winter vacation. To listen to the honeyed pleas of the handsome, suntanned, obviously happy announcers, you wonder how any of us can possibly live another minute without all the luxuries of a millionaire. But, then, the solution is so easy. Just apply for a personal loan—fast, courteous, no questions asked—and let the Easy Loan Finance Company pay all your bills at once. "We'll even write the checks." This lure could be irresistible to a young breadwinner trying to keep up with the standard of living fostered by the commercials the family watches every night as they try to catch a program in between.

(compare outline: IV, A, 1 and 2)

Commercials endanger our health as well as our budgets. Although the writers are careful to advise us to see our doctors "if the pain persists," they do strongly suggest that we ailing viewers can get the relief we want just as well by following the do-it-yourself patent-medicine approach. Hypochondriacs must go crazy after a day of television. They are presented with a sure cure for every ailment. They can fill their medicine cabinets until they are bursting with cure-alls, fill their objecting stomachs with pills, and cover their

transition-direct reference

(compare outline: IV, B)

bodies with creams until they are either dead or unrecognizable. Certainly the daily bombardment leads many people into a way of living that is dangerous to both pocketbook and health.

I have tried to make a case for the TV commercial which appeals to the intelligence of its audience. I have tried to show that commercials should be improved so that they will arouse the approval instead of the antagonism of the viewer. I myself run to the refrigerator every time I feel a commercial coming, and as a result I am getting dangerously fat!

conclusion

## SPECIFIC KINDS OF EXPOSITORY WRITING

The essential steps in preparing a composition apply to all kinds of writing with the possible exception of narration. You may find it helpful, however, to consider a few additional facts about expository writing. Planning an expository composition is affected by the particular kind of exposition being planned. In general, there are three kinds: exposition that defines, exposition that informs, and exposition that explains. Often one composition contains all three kinds, but for the sake of practice, try your hand at writing some compositions each of which will be devoted primarily to a different one of the three kinds. Follow the suggestions on the next few pages.

### Exposition That Defines

Planning a definition always involves two stages. First, you must place the subject, the term to be defined, in its general class. Second, you must differentiate it from other members of that class. This is the genus-species method familiar to you from your study of biology.

To make clear what a puffin is, a dictionary tells you first that it is a sea bird and then differentiates it from other sea birds by listing its distinguishing characteristics.

**puf·fin** (puf'in) *n.* [ME. *poffin* < ?: associated by folk etymology with PUFF, because of the enormous beak or blown-up appearance of the young] any of a number of related northern sea birds (genus *Fratercula*) black above and white below, with a short neck, ducklike body, and brightly colored triangular beak

PUFFIN
(to 13 1/2 in. long)



You follow this two-stage method also in defining an abstract term. Suppose, for example, that you wish to define *sportsmanship.* You must ask yourself first to what general class of things sportsmanship belongs. Is it an attitude, a belief, or a kind of conduct? If you should decide that it is an attitude, you must then show what kind of attitude it is by giving its differentiating characteristics which distinguish it from all other attitudes. In order words, in the general class *attitude,* sportsmanship has characteristics which make it unique, a particular kind of attitude.

**22h.** **Plan a definition in two stages: (1) classification; (2) differentiation.**

### *Limited Definition*

Limited definition is the kind represented by the definition of *puffin.* It is a dictionary-type definition—brief and readily usable in reading and writing. The ability to write a clear limited definition is important because vague or ambiguous words obscure meaning. One way to overcome the faults of vagueness and ambiguity is to define, whenever necessary, the important, or key words you use so that your reader will get from them the meaning you want to express. You may have been asked by your opponent in an argument to "define your terms." This is always a reasonable request, for you cannot communicate effectively unless both you and your listener or reader have the same meaning in mind.

**EXERCISE 5.** Select five of the words listed below and write a limited definition of each in two or three sentences. Decide the general class to which the subject belongs; then, giving more information, differentiate it from other members of the class. Try this first without a dictionary.

1. a mansion
2. a chapel
3. a vase
4. a dog
5. an optimist
6. a surgeon
7. a canoe
8. a dictionary
9. radar
10. golf

### *Extended Definition*

A really meaningful definition of an abstract term like *happiness, liberty,* or *democracy* may require a much more extensive piece of writing than a limited, dictionary-type definition. Writing such an extended definition is a valuable exercise because it requires careful planning and thinking and always serves to clarify your own thoughts. Most of an extended definition consists of a statement or description of the specific characteristics that differentiate the term from others in its class. When you have defined *happiness* as a state of mind, you have merely taken the first step. You have placed the word in its general class. The second step, differentiation, may be extended indefinitely as you give the distinguishing characteristics of happiness, perhaps by telling how it can be achieved, what it is not, how it can be recognized, and what its effects are. This kind of defining is sometimes called "descriptive definition." An extended definition may be as long as a book, but you will find that a fully developed paragraph (150 words) is often adequate.

**EXERCISE 6.** Select one of the following words and write an extended definition of approximately 200 words. Your definition may be a very personal one if you wish—that is, it may quite deliberately give your own concept of the meaning of the word rather than a dictionary-type concept which must give the meaning most generally accepted. Whenever possible, try to use examples and incidents to make your meaning clear.

1. integrity
2. loyalty
3. love
4. maturity
5. immaturity
6. generosity
7. wit
8. freedom
9. jealousy
10. charm

**EXERCISE 7.** Define one of the following in a full-length composition—400–500 words.

1. a good student
2. a poor student
3. a natural leader
4. a snob
5. a competent teacher (mechanic, coach, etc.)
6. a natural athlete
7. a friend
8. a suffragist
9. a novel
10. a poem

## Exposition That Informs

A common purpose of expository writing is to inform. Essay questions on an examination, reports on library reading, accounts of experiments and other research usually call for informational writing. In planning an informational composition, you do two things. First, you analyze your subject; that is, you take a careful overall look at it to see exactly what it consists of. As you analyze the subject, you will find that the information you have tends to break up into a number of fairly distinct parts or divisions.

Your second step, then, is to determine these logical divisions of the subject. When listed in order, they constitute the main topics in your outline. When you have completed the two steps—analysis and division—you have arrived at your basic plan. This process is the same as Steps 2 and 3 of the essential steps in the preparation of a composition, which you studied earlier.

**22i. Plan an informational composition in two stages: (1) analyze the subject; (2) divide the subject into its logical parts or divisions.**

To take a simple example of this analysis-division method, suppose that you are going to write an informational article on a place where you used to live, perhaps on one of the states you lived in for several years. Keeping in mind that your purpose is to inform others about a state they may not be familiar with, you analyze the subject, asking yourself what facts the members of your audience should learn. You recognize certain indispensable items of information: location, size, population, geography, climate, natural resources. Following the dictates of your purpose and your readers' interests, you may add other facts: industries, educational facilities, sociological characteristics, highways, recreational areas, political character, etc. Your analysis thus yields a number of divisions. If you find you have too many divisions, you can reduce the number of main topics by combining some of them, relegating some divisions to the status of subtopics.

**EXERCISE 8.** Select from the following list a subject upon which you can write an informational composition. Analyze the subject and divide it into a number of (4 or 5) logical divisions, or main topics. Write the composition in about 300–500 words.

1. The city in which you live
2. Your school's extracurricular program
3. A part-time job

4. A person you admire
5. A new type of car (plane, boat, rocket)
6. The new styles (clothing, hairdos, etc.)
7. An interesting animal
8. Facts about the moon (Mars, Venus, etc.)
9. An important event
10. A relatively unknown country (area of the world)

## Exposition That Explains

While exposition that defines and exposition that informs are common enough, a more common kind of exposition is that which explains. It is not often, of course, that these three kinds of exposition occur in a pure form. Usually you will use all three within one piece of expository writing. Thus, although your primary purpose in a piece of writing may be to explain, you will find that, in the course of the explanation, you must both define and inform.

### *Analysis and Division*

In planning an explanatory composition, you follow the same steps you follow in planning an informative composition. You (1) analyze your subject and (2) divide it or break it down into a number of divisions.

For example, in planning an explanation of the work done by the Student Council in your school, you begin by analyzing the Council. Your analysis reveals that the work of the Council is done by a number of standing committees. This fact is a clue to a possible plan for your essay. By describing the responsibilities and activities of each committee, you can give a clear explanation of the Council's functions. These committees, then, become the divisions of your composition.

In one school the Student Council has the following committees: Student Citizenship Board, Student Court, Handbook Committee, Activities Committee, Assembly Committee, Orientation Committee, Social Committee, Budget Committee, Student-Faculty Relations Committee.

A plan for a composition which would explain the Council's functions would have too many divisions if a separate section were devoted to each of these; therefore, the writer would probably combine some which are closely related: for instance, the Student Citizenship Board, which is primarily disciplinary, and the Student Court. Also, the Orientation and Social committees could be considered together since they are, at least in part, concerned with students' social adjustment and social activities.

Similarly, to explain how a jet engine works, you begin by analyzing the engine and dividing it into its important parts. Then, by explaining the functions of each part, you can cover the operation of the engine as a whole. Your plan, again, is achieved through analysis and division.

**EXERCISE 9.** Plan and write a composition (300–500 words) explaining one of the following:

1. How to drive (or any other appropriate activity)
2. Fundamental tactics in basketball (or any other sport)
3. A traffic plan to avoid tie-ups
4. The achievements of space exploration
5. Why we are prejudiced (have prejudices)
6. Why you like a particular novel (movie, etc.)
7. A concert band (symphony, musical group, etc.)
8. How an airplane flies
9. Why my allowance is insufficient
10. Causes of pollution
11. Directing a play
12. An efficiently designed kitchen
13. Weather forecasting
14. The medical risks of smoking
15. Causes of international dissension

## Explanation of a Process

A common kind of explanatory essay is that which explains or describes a process. This type of composition requires a different kind of plan. Because a process is a chronological thing, you divide your explanation according to the steps in the process and explain them in the order in which they occur.

**EXERCISE 10.** Choose one of the following topics and write a composition explaining the process in chronological order. Write 300–500 words.

1. How to develop photographs
2. How to make a dress
3. How to plant a new lawn
4. How to prepare a field for planting
5. How to train a dog
6. How to administer first aid
7. How to study
8. How to prepare a meal
9. How to redecorate a room
10. How to write a short story (poem, essay, etc.)

## SUGGESTED TOPICS FOR COMPOSITION

Put into practice the techniques described in this chapter as you write compositions assigned to you. If you are not assigned a definite subject on which to write, the topics in the following list may provide suggestions. Many will require limiting if you are to treat them in a composition of two or three pages. Many can be handled either informally or formally, humorously or seriously.

### *The Arts*

1. American music
2. A definition of jazz
3. The recording industry
4. The charm of folk music
5. Good music on the radio
6. Music as a form of social protest
7. Music and moods
8. The sculpture of Louise Nevelson (or of any other sculptor)
9. The art of Georgia O'Keeffe
10. How to judge a painting
11. Abstract painting
12. A comparison of media (oil, watercolor, pastel, etc.)

13. The work of a commercial artist
14. Effective poster making
15. My favorite artist (composer, singer, poet, etc.)
16. Modern furniture design
17. How to refinish furniture
18. Principles of home decoration
19. The ceramic process
20. Modern home architecture
21. How to arrange flowers
22. What poetry (music, art, etc.) means to me
23. Ballet or modern dance?
24. Designing and building a stage set

*Family and Social Life*

1. Making family decisions
2. Mistakes parents make
3. Discipline in the home
4. Teen-age marriage
5. Preserving the family
6. Television and family life
7. Should both parents work?
8. Living on a budget
9. On being the oldest (youngest)
10. On being an only child
11. Traveling with the family
12. Parents' responsibilities
13. Family customs
14. My family doesn't understand me.
15. What I want in marriage
16. Dates without money
17. Good manners
18. Definition of courtesy
19. Parents are the last to know.
20. On following the crowd
21. It's hard to be yourself
22. How to plan a party
23. A place to meet friends
24. The teen-age rebel
25. The price of popularity

***People***

1. A person who has influenced me
2. Student types
3. A good teacher
4. Our doctor (minister, priest, etc.)
5. The school politician
6. A great sports figure
7. Our neighbors
8. My parent(s)
9. An old friend
10. A funny person
11. A person prominent in recent news
12. A colorful character from history (fiction, drama, etc.)

***Personal***

1. Pressures that force conformity
2. Decisions I must make
3. A senior's worries
4. Traits I wish I didn't have
5. On being an outsider
6. On being average
7. Facing the truth about oneself
8. How to be unpopular
9. On being spoiled
10. Beliefs changed by experience
11. After-school jobs
12. Rules I could do without

13. My biggest mistake
14. My greatest success
15. Living up to or living down a reputation
16. The meaning of "well dressed"
24. Social classes in high school
25. Our student government

*School and Education*

1. Homework
2. Is the grading system fair?
3. College Board Examinations
4. What education ought to be
5. The extracurricular activity burden
6. Too many standardized tests
7. How to get a scholarship
8. Needed improvements in this school
9. Who should go to college?
10. Why we have drop-outs
11. Teaching as a career
12. The ideal teacher
13. Teachers' faults
14. Bookworm vs. socialite
15. Audio-visual instruction
16. How to choose a college
17. Large college vs. small college
18. Four-year college vs. junior college
19. Experiences with the Guidance Department
20. New educational techniques (devices)
21. Wasteful educational practices
22. Aid to education
23. Education and civil rights

*Social Studies*

1. America's image
2. A definition of communism
3. The importance of world government
4. Problems of a new century
5. A threat to planetary peace
6. Our dependence on other nations
7. If we had no Bill of Rights
8. A lesson of history
9. The importance of the minority
10. Propaganda techniques
11. The dangers of nationalism
12. Socialized medicine
13. Care of the aged
14. Urban renewal
15. Facts about the population of this community
16. The geography of this community
17. Population control
18. The importance of a free press
19. Cause and cure of juvenile delinquency
20. Why welfare?
21. How to vote intelligently
22. Characteristics of a good citizen
23. A significant news event of the past week
24. Government subsidies for farm price support
25. On world citizenship

26. Crime in the streets
27. Why such heavy military spending?

*Science*

1. A recent conservation project
2. Prevention of soil erosion
3. Science aids the hunter and angler.
4. New drugs and their uses
5. Pesticides and health
6. Smoking, cancer, and heart disease
7. Causes of heart disease
8. Scientific dieting
9. New uses of plastics
10. The scientist aids the detective.
11. Photography, a scientific tool
12. The scientist looks at cosmetics.
13. A scientist looks at the comics.
14. Wind storms
15. Chemical aids to agriculture
16. Predicting the weather
17. Effects of science on our amusements
18. Lengthening the life span
19. New knowledge about space
20. Moonshots and planet probes—traveling in space
21. Space stations
22. An electronic marvel
23. My research project
24. On science fiction
25. Correcting the world's water shortage
26. Weather prediction by satellite
27. Telemetry and space probes
28. Science and automation
29. An astronaut's capsule environment
30. Food from the sea
31. The atom as a source of energy
32. The uses and dangers of radioactivity
33. Human factors in space travel
34. Life in a drop of water
35. Wildlife management and preservation
36. Growing plants without soil (hydroponics)
37. Better plants and animals (breeding and heredity)
38. Unconquered fields in science

*Sports*

1. Women in professional sports
2. Professional vs. amateur sports
3. A great sports performance
4. Good teamwork
5. Bench warming
6. My best sports performance
7. Ice fishing
8. Hunting with a camera
9. Tennis tips (any sport)
10. Coaches' nightmares

11. My favorite team
12. A great sports figure
13. How to sail (any sport)
14. How to train
15. A brand-new sport

*General*

1. Keeping physically fit
2. The wise use of leisure
3. How to shop economically
4. Popular superstitions
5. Gifts
6. Experiences as a tourist
7. Living in the North vs. living in the South (or East vs. West)
8. Life in another country
9. On friendship
10. A definition of happiness
11. Why I prefer farm life (or city or suburban life)
12. What is success?
13. Vegetarianism
14. New trends in movies
15. My encounters with prejudice
16. My chosen vocation
17. Values of 4-H Club work (scouting, etc.)
18. The duties of the leader of a meeting
19. Qualities of a good salesperson
20. Causes of highway accidents
21. The teen-age driver
22. Considerations in buying a car
23. How to train a dog
24. How to judge a newspaper
25. Our dependence on machines
26. My life one year from now
27. Our changing fashions
28. High school slang
29. American speech mannerisms
30. Teen-age fads

## Literature

Literature offers an almost unlimited supply of ideas, characters, and technical matters to write about. Naturally, composition topics on specific literary works will be of no use to you unless you have read the particular works on which they are based. You can, however, choose a general subject and develop it by reference to works with which you are familiar. The following general subjects are intended merely to suggest the kinds of composition topics that can be drawn from your reading of literature.

1. A great novel and what makes it great
2. A social-problem play
3. The difference between theme and plot (specific examples)

4. A comparison of attitudes toward love (death, nature, war) in two poems (novels, plays, essays)
5. Three interesting characters portrayed by modern poets
6. Characterization or caricature in a novel (play)
7. A comparison of the style of two writers (fiction, poetry)
8. A comparison of two historical novels (plays) about the same period or the same person
9. Comparison of a novel and its movie version (play version or musical version)
10. The typical Western (detective story, romance, etc.)
11. The influence of the setting in a novel
12. The philosophy of a writer you know well
13. Irony in a piece of literature (short story, novel, play, poem)
14. Satire in a piece of literature
15. The use of symbols in a piece of literature

Although specific works and authors are mentioned in the following topics, a great many other works and authors may be substituted for them. You may wish to use the general idea in a topic but apply it to other literary works.

1. Shakespeare's *Julius Caesar* and modern politics
2. Some Shakespearean clowns
3. Recurrent themes in Virginia Woolf's novels
4. A comparison of *West Side Story* and *Romeo and Juliet*
5. The whale as a symbol in *Moby Dick*
6. Adolescent psychology in *The Red Badge of Courage*
7. American lifestyles in the stories of Edna Ferber
8. Irony in the poems of Emily Dickinson
9. Edith Wharton as a portrayer of character
10. Satire in the works of Phyllis McGinley
11. A comparison of *My Fair Lady* and *Pygmalion*
12. Aldous Huxley's *Brave New World* and George Orwell's *1984*
13. A comparison of Arthurian legends in Thomas Malory's *Morte d'Arthur* and T. H. White's *The Once and Future King*
14. The detective story—Edgar Allan Poe and Dorothy Sayers
15. The typical setting of Eudora Welty's novels

Chapter 23

# Making Writing Interesting

This chapter explains some of the ways reporters, columnists, and other authors of articles, features, essays, and reports make their writing interesting. While these professionals know that the first requirement for success is to have something to say, they also know that unless they can attract and hold readers, they will not long survive as writers, no matter how good their ideas or how important their information. You may have no aspirations toward a career as an author. But you can, by studying this chapter, learn to make your essays, articles, and reports more interesting by using some of the tricks of the journalist's trade.

## MAKING WRITING INTERESTING BY USING NARRATIVE

Everyone likes a story. The interesting conversationalist is the person who always has a good tale to tell and can tell it in an entertaining way. The interesting writer is the writer who, recognizing the high interest value of narrative, includes incidents—brief stories—that illustrate the ideas being presented. Using narrative in this way not only increases the reader's interest but also makes the writer's ideas easier to understand and to remember. Ministers and other public speakers know the great value of inserting a brief story in a sermon or an address. You have observed in church how quickly the congregation comes to life when the preacher starts to tell a story to illustrate a point in the sermon. Chances are that many in the congregation will remember the story first and the sermon second.

Keep in mind that using narrative to enhance a longer article does not involve simply reporting a story; it requires dramatizing the story. Also keep in mind that the narrative used to illustrate a point or to arouse the reader's interest must be related in some way to the rest of the article; the narrative cannot be extraneous.

In the following article about the training given by a counter-terrorist driving school in West Virginia, the writer shows he is well aware of the value of using narrative to arouse and hold the reader's interest in the article. As you read the article, note the ways in which the writer uses stories and dramatizes incidents in order to draw his reader into the article and to clarify several points. Here dramatization, or narrative, makes an interesting article even more interesting and exciting.

## DRIVE FOR LIFE

1. The night is balmy. The highway is lit by a full moon. Suddenly, as the car crests a hill, there it is, just 50 yards ahead, a terrorist roadblock: two small foreign cars parked across the pavement. With only a second to react, the driver lunges at the emergency brake to lock the rear wheels, then jams down hard on the brake pedal too. He jerks the steering wheel to the right. The rear of the car twists savagely in a 180° "bootleg" turn.

2. There is a horrible screeching and the hot stink of brake pads and burning tires. Heart pounding, the driver guns his motor, racing away from the barricade. But now another car pulls out of a dark side road to cut him off. Though half blinded by its headlights, he jams on the brakes again, and just as his car is shuddering

to a stop, he slams it into reverse and guns the engine. Seconds later he takes his foot off the gas and turns the steering wheel hard. Tires screaming, the car spins around once more, but is again facing the roadblock. There is no choice now but to pray, step on the gas and try to ram his way through.

3. He hits. But no deafening, jolting crash occurs. On impact, the two cars swing away easily, for they are on casters and covered with polyurethane foam pads. The terrorist threat was not for real, but still there is genuine sweat on the driver's palms. This is part of the final exam given at the BSR Counter-Terrorist Driving School. It is the culmination of a four-day course held at Summit Point, W. Va., about 80 miles west of Washington. Instructor Bill Scott, 42, a Yale Ph.D. in geology and an ex-champion Formula Super Vee race-car driver, started the course in 1976 after the Air Force asked him to provide driver training for some of its officers. Since then, Scott and three other instructors, backed by a team of mechanics, have trained hundreds of chauffeurs and corporation executives in how to foil attempts to kill or capture them on the road. The basic course, including films and lectures plus actual driving, costs $1,495.

4. Scott does not advertise. Many of his clients demand that their names be kept secret. Information about the course is passed along by word of mouth through an old boy network of corporate security chiefs and ex-CIA and Secret Service types. "Worldwide, attacks on cars happen every day," says Scott. "They don't even make news any more. About 90% take place in European suburbs. About 90% are successful."

5. There are six or eight drivers in most of Scott's classes. The first day is devoted to shooting up an old Buick with a 9-mm machine gun, an automatic pistol, and a 12-gauge shotgun, so that the students will be familiar with the firepower available to the "opposition." Most slugs easily penetrate the side of the car. Then four of the class put on crash helmets and seat belts for an initiation run around the track in one of

Scott's four new, high-performance Chevrolet Malibu police cars.

6. It's the white-knuckle express. Scott does straightaways at 110 m.p.h. and rarely corners at less than 65 m.p.h. The car seems to be flying out of control. Passengers are jerked around hard as Scott throws the Chevy into bootleg and J turns. Tires scream. Heads (and stomachs) spin. Everyone is scared witless. "This is hardball out here," shouts Scott in the understatement of the week, "but you'll be doing it in a few days." No way, each student groans to himself. But only 10% fail the course.

7. The next three days are a kind of Outward Bound for driving. At the speeds required (70 to 80 m.p.h.), students at first have no sense of how to control the car—or whether they have it in control at all. Many Americans are defensive drivers, quite content to putt around in an underpowered, six-year-old sedan, carefully navigating the maniacal freeway traffic that surrounds many cities. And every sensible and safe reflex built up for that kind of driving must be violated in Scott's course.

8. Skid control comes first, performed by going through a slalom course on an inch of loose gravel. The trick is to accelerate and brake and countersteer the car as the rear end skids violently. You must use the skid. It's like driving on ice. The best way to stop a car is to brake steadily and very hard, not to pump the brakes as many people believe. Next comes emergency braking and swerving to avoid objects at high speeds. Each student is ordered to drive absolutely flat out toward a sharp curve until the last possible second. Just when he is convinced that the car will shoot off the road, just when every instinct and a lifetime of conditioning demand that he brake and slow down, Scott shouts: "Gun it! Faster! Faster!"

9. "We want to jam you right into the middle of it," says Scott. "Whether you are normally cautious on the road or a hot-shot, it upsets nearly everyone. Especially the macho types. It's a heavy landing for them to find out they really can't drive and are nowhere near the limits of the car." For reassurance, the student looks at the special brake pedal installed on

the passenger side of Scott's Malibu for the instructor to use if a student panics and freezes.

10. The class learns to make fast, tight turns so the terrorist cannot get "inside" and force their quarry off the road. "Driving a car is a very sensuous thing," says Bruce Reichel, 33, one of Scott's instructors. "You have a lot of feedback from a car. Be aware of it."

11. The feedback from the car-ramming exercise is anything but sensuous. "Use the car as a weapon, if necessary," insists Scott. To learn what that means, students take turns driving a beat-up 1975 Cadillac into an old bronze Buick special. Proper technique: slow down, then slam on the brakes to make the terrorists think you are stopping. Then gun the car, aiming for the front or rear axle. At 30 m.p.h. this barely rattles the Cadillac. But it spins the Buick into a full 360° turn and produces a very satisfying roar, crumpling metal and shattering glass. The Cadillac is hardly dented, but anyone inside the Buick will be badly shaken up.

12. Ramming is almost the last alternative to consider. In an ambush the two basic maneuvers are the bootleg and J turns, which students practice for hours. The worst thing is to do nothing. During "confrontation and chase," a sort of mid-term exam on wheels, each student jockeys one Malibu around the track, trying to anticipate, and avoid, ambushes by "terrorist" instructors in three other cars.

13. In one pattern the student drives at 30 m.p.h., with two cars following. Over a hill and 50 yards ahead a barricade looms. At the same time one of the cars behind passes, distracting the student driver. He grows breathless, loses control, can't think. Can't do anything, in fact. Finally he just stops the car. "All you learned just dropped out of your head," Scott chides. The next try is much better. He spins the car into a good J turn, evading a suddden roadblock, and escapes. When Scott concedes that the move was a "reasonable reaction," the student feels as proud as a small boy the first time he manages to stay up on a two-wheeler. Fear turns into exhilaration. He can hardly wait for the next ambush.

14. Scott advises students "to be suspicious of any-

> thing unusual." In the Third World, for example, where official police roadblocks are common, it is not difficult for terrorists to get weapons and government uniforms. But it is hard for them to get police cars. "That could be the tip-off," Scott warns. "Look at the vehicle in the roadblock. In the Middle East or Italy, if a van, baby carriage, or wheelchair appears in front of you, you can be statistically assured you are being attacked."
>
> 15. To be useful, the reflexes of anti-terrorism must be instantaneous. And though they have saved several of Scott's graduates from trouble, on occasion they can be dangerous. A corporate chauffeur confronted by a man pushing a rack of clothes across a downtown street in Pittsburgh was suspicious enough to gun the car onto the sidewalk, smashing several parking meters in an escape attempt. It was not an attack. Luckily no pedestrians were injured. Though trying to drive around a roadblock is the worst thing to do—it exposes you to broadside fire—the chauffeur's startled boss gave him a $5,000 bonus and paid for the parking meters.[1]

The writer begins the article with narrative; he describes a terrifying experience in which a driver first avoids and then rams through a terrorist roadblock. This exciting account is specifically intended to arouse the reader's interest in the rest of the article. The writer immediately follows this story with an explanation (paragraph 3) of what the story shows. In paragraphs 4 and 5 he gives the reader some factual information about the counter-terrorist driving school. Then in paragraphs 6 through 12 the writer recounts what the students learn during four days of counter-terrorist driving classes. Note that the writer uses quotations from the driving instructors to dramatize the article at this point. These quotations give information in a colorful and exciting way, but they do not in themselves constitute narrative; they do not tell a story. In paragraph 13 the writer again uses narrative to dramatize one of the driving school exams and to show the reactions of a student during the exam. The use of narrative at this point in the article is not

[1] "In West Virginia: Drive for Life" by Robert C. Wurmstedt. Copyright 1980 by Time Inc. Reprinted by permission from *Time*, The Weekly Newsmagazine.

necessary to maintain the reader's interest, but it is the most effective means of communicating the information.

Whenever the writer uses narrative in the article, he attempts to dramatize the incident he writes about, just as a writer of fiction does. He knows that people in action are usually more interesting than ideas.

## Narrative as a Method of Paragraph Development

As you know, a well-constructed paragraph usually begins with a general statement expressing the main idea of the paragraph. This general statement is called the topic sentence. Having begun with the topic sentence, the writer then goes on to support it by giving additional details. These details may be examples of the truth expressed by the topic sentence. One kind of example is the incident, a brief story that supports the opening generalization. Telling an incident, or story, dramatizes the generalization and makes it more specific.

In the following paragraph, for example, Mr. Hayakawa makes the point that quoting a writer or speaker "out of context" is a vicious practice. A person's words should be judged, not in isolation, but in relation to the situation in which they were spoken and to the content before and after the quoted passage. Read the paragraph and note how effectively the author uses narrative in the form of an incident to illustrate his idea.

> It is clear, then, that the ignoring of contexts in any act of interpretation is at best a stupid practice. At its worst, it can be a vicious practice. A common example is the sensational newspaper story in which a few words by a public personage are torn out of their context and made the basis of a completely misleading account. There is the incident of a Veterans' Day speaker, a university teacher, who declared before a high school assembly that the Gettysburg Address was "a powerful piece of propaganda." The context clearly revealed that "propaganda" was being used, not according to its popular meaning,

> but rather, as the speaker himself stated, to mean "explaining the moral purposes of a war." The context also revealed that the speaker was a very great admirer of Lincoln's. However, the local newspaper, ignoring the context, presented the account in such a way as to suggest that the speaker had called Lincoln a liar. On this basis, the newspaper began a campaign against the instructor. The speaker remonstrated with the editor of the newspaper, who replied, in effect, "I don't care what else you said. You said the Gettysburg Address was propaganda, didn't you?" This appeared to the editor complete proof that Lincoln had been maligned and that the speaker deserved to be discharged from his position at the university. Similar practices may be found in advertisements. A reviewer may be quoted on the jacket of a book as having said, "A brilliant work," while reading of the context may reveal that what he really said was, "It just falls short of being a brilliant work." There are some people who will always be able to find a defense for such a practice in saying, "But he did use the words 'a brilliant work,' didn't he?"[1]

You will find another paragraph developed by an incident on page 351.

**EXERCISE 1.** Write a paragraph in which you use an incident (or two) to support your topic sentence. If you need suggestions, you may use one of the following as your topic sentence.

1. As graduation approaches, the star high school athlete is besieged by college coaches with fantastic offers.
2. Cheating on homework assignments and examinations sometimes backfires.
3. In summer we city children used the streets as our playground.
4. In northern climates, fishing in winter is rugged but fun.

[1] From *Language in Thought and Action* by S. I. Hayakawa, copyright © 1941 by Harcourt Brace Jovanovich, Inc. Reprinted by permission of Harcourt Brace Jovanovich, Inc. and George Allen & Unwin Ltd.

5. Nothing teaches a family the virtues of patience and consideration for others so well as a vacation tour in the car.
6. Some causes of friction between neighbors are ridiculous.
7. Getting accepted by the college of your choice involves more than submitting a good scholastic record.
8. A dog owner's personality is revealed by the way the dog behaves.
9. The prejudices of parents become the prejudices of their children.
10. Nonconformists are rarely popular.

## Narrative in Descriptive Writing—the Character Sketch

A kind of description that can be most effectively developed by narrative is the character, or personality, sketch. In a character sketch, your purpose is to show the reader the kind of person your subject is. Since a person's actions reveal character, you can often accomplish your purpose effectively by showing your subject in action. In other words, you tell a story.

In the following paragraphs taken from a longer profile of Woody Allen, the comic, the writer uses descriptions of actual events to convey the points she is making about Woody Allen's quixotic character.

> Woody Allen lay down in a commando position with a BB gun on one of his New York East Side terraces, outside a pair of French windows, and took potshots at some pigeons that fondly think he wants them there and that he emphatically does not. Feathery things seem to bother him: dowagers' fussy hats, bouffant hairdos, pigeons most of all. His penthouse duplex is a pigeon heaven, and nothing he tries seems to turn it into a purgatory for them. In his usual mood of seriousness about jokes, he once went to a Manhattan novelty shop and bought some coiled rubber snakes to frighten the pigeons off, but they treated the snakes as a welcome. Then he got some patent stuff to slather onto his terraces. It was supposed to

> rid one of pigeons. By "rid," he thought vaguely, the manufacturers meant that the pigeons would take umbrage at the smell. He went to bed. Next morning, he told me, he came down and the terraces were littered with pigeons stuck in the stuff. "I didn't know what to do," he said. "I was all alone. They were struggling. In the end, I had to *prize*[1] them off, *one by one,* with a *spatula.*" His brown eyes looked larger and more appalled than ever behind his black spectacles, which are like the headlamps of a beautiful prewar car and give him an authority that he feels obliged, being an honest recorder, to undermine.
>
> He wears saddle shoes, nice checked shirts with indescribable jeans, and, outdoors, a khaki fishing hat and a khaki battle jacket. "I have a tendency to wear clothes that don't match," he said mildly to me. The same day, when we had gone a long time without eating—the prospect of eating not being something that draws him much—his mind wandered to hospitality. "There's some chocolate pudding," he said, sitting on the floor in his drawing room. And then, lowering his voice like a spy, "I don't know how good it is." He paused, and whispered with restraint, "I hate the maid."[2]

**EXERCISE 2.** Write a character sketch (three or four paragraphs) of someone whose personality interests you. You may choose a relative, a friend, a public figure, or a teacher you had in either elementary or secondary school. In the course of your sketch, tell at least one incident to illustrate a personality trait.

## Narrative in Expository Writing

The principal purposes of expository writing are to inform and to explain. Both purposes can be accomplished by telling a brief story. For example, if your purpose in writing a composition is to explain how to handle a sailboat in

[1] ***prize:*** to raise or force with a lever.

[2] From "Guilty, with an Explanation" by Penelope Gilliatt; © 1974. Reprinted by permission, The New Yorker Magazine, Inc.

a severe squall, you might do this by telling the story of a personal experience in which, while sailing, you were caught in a squall. By telling exactly what you did and what happened, you would, in effect, be explaining what to do and what not to do in such circumstances. Narrative would make your explanation interesting.

In the excerpt below, the author is making the point that a harpsichord is a difficult instrument to keep in working condition. He supports his point by telling a story.

> Lemon or no, the harpsichord is the tetchiest instrument ever invented, bar none, and keeping one in working condition is a drain on anybody's time. Because it contains so many wooden moving parts, the instrument is extremely sensitive to changes in humidity and temperature. Once, as a reviewer, I attended one of those oh-so-important debut recitals where everything had to be just so, and for this occasion the artist had selected (that is, borrowed) a brand-new and magnificent Hubbard. It was an unseasonably hot night in October, and because the people were suffering, somebody opened a window, letting humanity off the hook but putting the harpsichord in a draft. When the harpsichordist tore into his opening Couperin group, he found his whole upper keyboard in the terminal stages of harpsichord pneumonia, with many of the notes more than a whole tone out of tune and one whistling away an octave and a half out of sight. The show was wrecked. Luckily, the man's career was not; but for all the labor that went into it, this recital did him no good.[1]

The kind of expository writing that relies most heavily on narrative is the informal essay. In an informal essay the writer expresses personal opinions and prejudices. The tone of the essay is light, often frivolous. Informal essayists recognize that narrative is entertaining. Some essays are nothing more than a series of incidents, often humorous, that support or explain the opinions of the writer.

[1] From "The Harpsichord Boom" by Robert Evett from *The Atlantic Monthly*, May 1970. Copyright © 1970, by The Atlantic Monthly Company, Boston, Mass. Reprinted by permission of the author.

The following is an informal essay. Note, as you read, how the author uses a story to make her point.

## HONESTY IS THE ONLY POLICY

I aim to pick a quarrel with an old and time-honored maxim, to wit: Honesty is the best policy.

That has been a high-sounding axiom ever since Cervantes set it down in *Don Quixote*. But it is fallacious, misleading, and deceitful, not to say a snare for the feet of the unwary.

Honesty is not the best policy: Honesty is the only policy, and the sooner the old saw is amended to this effect, the fewer public officials who will languish in durance vile[1]—perhaps. It is doubtful if even Madison Square Garden could hold all the public figures now convicted or serving time for lying.

If the maxim is eventually amended, I don't want any credit. It should go, posthumously, to Papa. He was a rugged individualist who faced up to Cervantes and the third-grade schoolteacher in Caldwell, Idaho, and rewrote the old saw for home consumption.

In those far-off days, they taught penmanship and high moral precepts by making us third graders copy in faltering script such varied truisms as "Sweet mercy is nobility's true badge" and "Poverty is no sin."

So one day when I was dragging my feet at my homework, Papa glanced over my shoulder and saw that I was writing, for the eighty-ninth time "Honesty is the best policy."

Papa insisted that I start all over again and write "Honesty is the only policy," and that began his private war with Miss Grant, the third-grade teacher. Because Miss Grant fired the paper right back at me and told me to copy the maxim as written: Honesty is the best policy.

That was when Papa marched up to the Lincoln School to confront Miss Grant, and the battle was joined. His argument went something like this:

"I do not want my child taught that honesty is

[1] **durance vile:** harsh imprisonment.

the best policy. I want it pounded into her thick little skull that honesty is the only policy.

"If you say that honesty is the best policy, it implies that there are other policies and that there is an element of choice in the matter. But there is no choice. Either you are honest or you aren't. You can't be a 'little bit honest' without being equally dishonest at the same time." In summing up, Papa delivered his coup de grâce.

"It's this way, Miss Grant," he said, "there is no such thing as 'a little garlic' or 'a little honesty.' Either you refrain from either or you go whole hog."

Miss Grant stuck by Cervantes, but Papa stuck by honesty, and eventually he wore her down. I was permitted to write "Honesty is the only policy." And so were my sister and my brother, when they made third grade.

"If they wind up in jail," Papa told Miss Grant, "it won't be your or my or Cervantes' fault. They'll have done it on their own."

At the risk of sounding not a little stuffy, let me point out that none of us has ever been in jail—although there is yet time. None of Papa's children has ever been caught lying to a grand jury, a congressional committee, or a duly constituted court. Or doctoring the books.

It would benefit all to see Papa's reform sweep the country, to wit: Honesty is the only policy. While the politicians and public officials are out back writing this truism a hundred times in their copy books, they could very well keep their ball-point pens poised for a hundred-time go at another of Papa's favorite saws: "Tell the truth and shame the devil." Nothing else will.[1]

**EXERCISE 3.** Write an informal essay (about 300 words) in which you give your personal opinions on a subject that is not of earth-shaking consequence. Although infor-

[1] "Honesty Is the Only Policy" from *Don't Just Stand There* by Inez Robb. Copyright by Inez Robb. Reprinted by permission of the Harold Matson Company, Inc.

mal essays are more likely to be humorous than serious, amusing rather than instructive, you need not strain to be funny. (Mrs. Robb's essay is amusing but completely serious.) You must, however, be interesting. To insure this, tell a few incidents in illustration of your opinions. If you need help in finding a suitable subject, read the list of suggested topics for composition on pages 383–87. Many of the topics can be treated informally.

## Narrative in Argumentative Writing

The kinds of discourse—narration, description, exposition, and argument—rarely appear in pure form. Description is an important part of narration and exposition; narration, as you have seen, can be an important feature of both description and exposition. Narration may also be used with good effect in argument. Suppose, for example, that a former player writes an article arguing against big-time college football because of its bad effects on those who play it. He could hardly do better than to support his views by relating some of his experiences as a varsity athlete. These, of course, would take the form of narratives.

The following is the concluding portion of an essay in which Phyllis McGinley argues in favor of the northeastern portion of the Eastern seaboard as an ideal place to live. She relates an incident. Miss McGinley knows that a single incident, one example, does not prove anything, but the brief story beautifully summarizes her argument and concludes the essay in an interesting way.

> Ungrudgingly, then, we admit to the Californian that he's a lucky fellow in the matter of weather. We tell the man from Alabama that we could certainly do with a few of those magnolias, and we agree with the Coloradan that he possesses some mighty elegant scenery. But we know that scenery is no substitute for conversation and art galleries and windows that open on the world. There are some of us who breathe more easily in a meadow full of daisies than on top of a mountain, and some of us who would rather

explore the jungles of Madison Avenue than the Carlsbad Caverns.

A friend of mine who lives in Honolulu is spending a year in the East while her professor husband takes his sabbatical leave from his university. Her family is numerous and they have lived cramped in a city apartment during one of the foulest of our recent winters. I asked her the other day if she was not longing for the return to Hawaii and its spacious amenities.

"Oh, no!" She sighed. "No, no, no. We're all so happy here. I suppose it's ungrateful of me not to miss Hawaii. But somehow I just don't want to go back to Paradise."

No, this is not Paradise or even close to it. But it is home for a certain kind of moderate heart. And while I wouldn't visit here if you gave me the place, it's a wonderful region just to live in.[1]

## MAKE WRITING INTERESTING WITH ATTRACTIVE INTRODUCTIONS

### Begin with a Story.

You have seen that narrative adds interest to any kind of writing. Because this is true, telling a story is an excellent way to attract your reader's attention at the beginning of a composition. Reread the beginning of the article on pages 390–94. Note how effectively the story he tells serves to introduce the article.

Vilhjálmur Stefánsson (1879–1962), the great arctic explorer, once wrote an article explaining that we can learn a great deal from the Eskimo about how to dress warmly in cold weather. He could have begun by stating this thesis and then gone on to explain how the Eskimo's clothing, although much lighter than our winter clothing, is also much warmer. But Mr. Stefánsson knew something about

[1] From "The Happy Exile" in *The Province of the Heart* by Phyllis McGinley. 

the interest value of narrative and began his article as follows:

> During the winter of 1909, an elderly woman of Flaxman Island, northern Alaska, went out to gather driftwood half a mile from her house. She was wearing only one coat or shirt, hair side turned in. With a sudden onslaught rare in the Flaxman country, a gale descended. She could not find her way home; she had to wait the storm out.
>
> Most Eskimos would have built themselves some sort of a shelter in such a blizzard, but our aged woman thought it too much bother. In the blinding storm, she felt around with her feet until she discovered a tiny knoll. Taking off her mittens, she placed them on the hillock and sat down, using them as insulation to keep her body heat from melting the snow beneath her. Like all good Eskimo garments, her jacket was so designed that she could slip her bare arms out of the sleeves to cross them within the coat upon her bare breast, thus warming them and using them as added radiators to warm the inside of her shirt. With her back to the wind, she settled herself to wait the gale out, leaning slightly forward with elbows on knees so as not to topple over when she fell asleep. Every now and then, stiffened from sitting, she would pick up her mittens and walk around in a small circle. When tired of this, she would sit down again on them and try to sleep. The gale lasted till late afternoon the next day.
>
> When the weather cleared, the old lady came home. She was not very hungry, because she had slept or rested most of the time. It was during the first day that she had been most hungry. No one thought anything of her experience, except that some argued that she should have taken the trouble to build a shelter.
>
> Had she known she was going to be caught out, she would have worn two coats, the entire costume weighing about ten pounds. What she wore weighed six or seven. A Minneapolis businessman going to his office in January would wear from twenty to thirty

pounds, and he wouldn't be planning to sit out a two-day blizzard. The difference in their clothing systems explains largely why the average Minnesotan is more eager to move to California than the average Eskimo. In our time, the Eskimo has been the sole possessor of a clothing system adequate in the sense that it permits in January a degree of mobility, efficiency, and comfort similar to that of July. We have taken a long time to understand how it works, and we are still a long way from making full use of its principles.[1]

## Begin with a Startling Statement—a Fact or an Opinion.

A good introduction attracts the reader's attention. One way to do this is to tell a story. A second way is to begin with such a startling statement that any reader will be intrigued or shocked enough to want to read further.

The following are the opening statements of five articles. It should be obvious that their authors were counting on their shock value to attract the reader's attention:

1. What we have to do, what at any rate it is our duty to do, is to revive this old art of lying.

OSCAR WILDE

2. In one comic book story, out of fifty-one pictures, no less than forty-five are scenes of violence and brutality.

FREDERIC WERTHAM

3. The past fifty years of what we call civilization have utterly ruined childhood.

PHILIP WYLIE

4. Europeans have made a cliché of saying that nothing is so sad as the sight of Americans having a good time.

BERNARD DE VOTO

[1] From "Clothes Make the Eskimo," by Vilhjálmur Stefánsson from *Natural History,* January 1955. © 1955 by American Museum of Natural History. Reprinted by permission of the publisher.

5. Never was there a stranger purpose than that which brought us together that June night in Euston Railway Station.

VIRGINIA WOOLF

## Begin with a Question.

Asking a question at the beginning of a composition offers two advantages. First, it is an easy way to make clear what the article is about. The reader assumes that in the article the author will answer the opening question. Second, a question stirs an immediate response in the reader. In wondering how to answer it, the reader is forced to think about the subject of the article, something that every author wants the reader to do. Here are examples of how two authors used the question in the introduction to an article.

> What is a tropical jungle like, not from distant generalities or sweeping surveys, but as seen by an ordinary human on a very usual walk?
>
> WILLIAM BEEBE

> What do college grades predict? Can you forecast from the record of a young man graduating from college now how successful he's likely to be a few decades from now?
>
> SYLVIA PORTER

The next example actually combines two kinds of openings—the startling statement and the question.

> According to the Nobel prize-winning chemist Dr. Wendell M. Stanley, the next century will find mankind able to control to a remarkable degree the hereditary traits of plants, animals, and humans. Hermann J. Muller, another Nobel laureate, has also predicted the guidance of human evolution. The notion that man may be able to manipulate his genetic endowment is at once exciting and troublesome: How

accurate are such predictions likely to be, and how desirable is the prospect of their fulfillment?[1]

LOUIS LASAGNA

**EXERCISE 4.** Thumb through a number of magazines, looking at the opening paragraphs of articles. Try to find an example of a narrative beginning, a startling-statement beginning, and a question beginning. Copy them and bring them to class to share with your classmates. Note other methods that writers use to attract a reader's attention in an introduction.

## MAKE WRITING INTERESTING BY USING SPECIFIC LANGUAGE

The content of a piece of writing is more important than its style. If what you have to say is not interesting, your manner of saying it, no matter how skillful, will probably not make it seem interesting to your reader. Still, given the same content for a piece of writing, one writer may produce an interesting article while another writer may produce a dull one. The difference may lie in their style of writing.

It is possible to list some of the qualities of an interesting style. You can, by studying these qualities and by trying to incorporate them into your own writing, make your writing more interesting.

### Interesting Writing Is Specific.

Writing is said to be specific when it contains a great many details and examples to support its general statements. The opposite of specific is vague or general. By comparing the expressions in each of the following pairs, you will learn what is meant by specific writing.

[1] From "Heredity Control: Dream or Nightmare" by Louis Lasagna from *The New York Times Magazine,* August 5, 1962. © 1962 by The New York Times Company. Reprinted by permission of the publisher.

VAGUE a beautiful day

SPECIFIC mountainous white clouds in a pale blue sky, crisp air, bright sunshine

VAGUE She bore a great burden.

SPECIFIC After her mother died, Sylvia helped raise her younger sisters and brothers and cared for her ill father.

VAGUE For several years Chris Evert Lloyd has been one of the most successful women's tennis players in the world.

SPECIFIC Between 1974 and 1980 Chris Evert Lloyd won the United States Open Tennis Championship in women's singles five times and the All-England Tennis Championship in women's singles four times.

As you compare the following three descriptions, note how, by means of additional details, the writing becomes less vague, more specific.

1. Some of the children on the outing seemed to be more interested than others in the planned activities.
2. The younger children at the Firefighter's Picnic could hardly wait for the games and races to begin. The older children, apparently indifferent toward sack races, the broad jump, and softball, stood around talking and watching the adults.
3. The younger children at the Firefighter's Picnic besieged Chief Barnard, jumping up and down as they circled him, clamoring for the games and races to begin. The older children, apparently indifferent toward sack races, the broad jump, and softball, stood in a group by themselves, talking and watching the adults, who were busily preparing food for everyone's lunch.

The second example is more specific than the first.

"The younger children" is more specific than "some of the children."

"Firefighter's Picnic" is more specific than "outing."

"The older children" is more specific than "others."

"Sack races, the broad jump, and softball" is more specific than "planned activities."

Comparing the third example with the second, what

details do you find that have been expressed more specifically in the third?

Read the following descriptions of the imperial train of Tsar Nicholas II, the last Russian Tsar. The one in the left-hand column is full of details. The one in the right-hand column, because it omits many of the specific details, is far less interesting. A comparison of the two passages should convince you of the importance of specific details in making writing interesting.

I

The Imperial train which bore the Tsar and his family on these trips across Russia was a traveling miniature palace. It consisted of a string of luxurious royal-blue salon cars with a double-eagled crest emblazoned in gold on their sides, pulled by a gleaming black locomotive. The private car of Nicholas and Alexandra contained a bedroom the size of three normal compartments, a sitting room for the Empress upholstered in mauve and gray, and a private study for the Tsar furnished with a desk and green leather chairs. The white-tiled bathroom off the Imperial bedroom boasted a tub with such ingeniously designed overhangs that water could not slosh out even when the train was rounding a curve.

Elsewhere in the train, there was an entire car of rooms for the four Grand Duchesses and the Tsarevich, with all the furniture painted white. A mahogany-paneled lounge car

II

The Imperial train which bore the Tsar and his family on these trips across Russia was a traveling miniature palace. It consisted of a string of luxurious cars, pulled by a gleaming black locomotive. The private car of Nicholas and Alexandra contained a bedroom, a sitting room for the Empress, and a private study for the Tsar. The bathroom boasted a tub with such ingeniously designed overhangs that water could not slosh out even when the train was rounding a curve.

Elsewhere in the train was an entire car of rooms for the four Grand Duchesses and the Tsarevich. A lounge car served as a gathering place for the ladies-in-waiting, aides-de-camp, and other members of the Imperial suite, each of whom had a private compartment. One car was devoted entirely to dining. It included a kitchen, a dining room, and a small anteroom, where before with deep rugs and damask-covered chairs and sofas served as a gathering place for the ladies-in-waiting, aides-de-camp and other members of the Imperial suite, each of whom had a private compartment. One car was devoted entirely to dining. It included a kitchen equipped with three stoves, an icebox, and a wine cabinet; a dining room with a table for twenty; and a small anteroom, where before every meal *zakuski* were served. Even while traveling, the Imperial suite observed the Russian custom of standing and helping themselves from a table spread with caviar, cold salmon, sardines, reindeer tongue, sausages, pickled mushroom, radishes, smoked herring, sliced cucumber, and other dishes. At dinner, Nicholas always sat at the middle of a long table with his daughters beside him, while Count Fredericks and other court functionaries sat opposite. With rare exceptions, the Empress ate alone on the train or had her meals with Alexis.[1]

every meal *zakuski* were served. Even while traveling, the Imperial suite observed the Russian custom of standing and helping themselves from a table spread with food. At dinner Nicholas always sat at the middle of a long table with his daughters beside him, while Count Fredericks and other court functionaries sat opposite. With rare exceptions, the Empress ate alone on the train or had her meals with Alexis.

Specific writing is not only more interesting than vague writing; it is also clearer. It is clearer because every general statement, every abstraction, is followed by an example, which clarifies what the writer means.

[1] From *Nicholas and Alexandra* by Robert K. Massie, copyright © 1967 by Robert K. Massie. Reprinted by permission of Atheneum Publishers, Inc. and Victor Gollancz Ltd.

For instance, the generalization in the first paragraph of the following selection is clarified by specific examples.

> The game of quote-catching is, of course, another form of one-upmanship and the pleasure one takes in it is, therefore, rather mean and unworthy. It is nonetheless gratifying. To the seasoned practitioner, the game provides many a private glow of satisfaction, however fleeting, and many a happy tingle of superiority, however unfounded. No wonder some play the game with a relish that seldom abates.
>
> Up there on the television screen is, say, Orson Welles. He is pontificating with all the massive authority of his massive person and, looking 20 million people straight in the eye, he is saying: "As Oliver Wendell Holmes said, 'When good Americans die, they go to Paris'."
>
> The quote catcher, if he is any good, pounces at once. "Come, come, Orson," he sneers. "That wasn't Oliver Wendell Holmes. It was Thomas Gold Appleton, the New England wit. That was the best line he ever got off, and he shouldn't be deprived of it." The quote catcher has chalked up another score.[1]

## Interesting Writing Is Rich in Images.

An image is usually a word picture. More accurately, it is anything that can be experienced through the senses: sight, hearing, touch, taste, and smell. "The law" is an abstraction; a police officer is an image. "Democracy" is an abstraction; a voter casting a ballot is an image. You cannot see the law or democracy, but you can see a police officer and you can see a voter casting a ballot. Abstract terms are necessary, but the interesting writer strives to give them specific equivalents as often as possible.

The more specific an image is, the more effective it is. "A police officer" is not so specific as "a heavy-set police captain, his gold badge glistening and his shoes highly polished."

[1] From "Quotesmanship" by Richard Hanser in the *New York Times Magazine,* August 10, 1980. © 1980 by The New York Times Company. Reprinted by permission.

## Use Adjectives to Create Specific Images.

Adjectives help us to make our images specific, but adjectives themselves may be specific in varying degrees. The phrase "pretty girl" is such a vague image that it is almost meaningless. "A slender redhead with startling blue eyes framed by long black lashes" is a far more meaningful and interesting message.

Compare the following two descriptions of the same scene. Evaluate the images.

1. From our vantage point on the mountainside, we could see several small towns scattered about the valley.
2. From the narrow rock ledge on which we stood high on the precipitous mountainside, we could see the white church spires of five tiny villages scattered across the green floor of the valley.

## Use Specific Active Verbs.

Writing becomes more vivid and therefore more interesting as its verbs become more specific and active. The forms of the verb *to be—am, is, are, was, were, be, being, been*—are totally colorless. Necessary and common as they are, they do nothing to enliven style. Vague verbs like *walk, act,* and *move* are weak in their image-making ability. You can think offhand of half a dozen more interesting substitutes for each of them.

Like nouns, verbs, if they are specific enough, do not need modifiers. When a reporter writes "The players *trotted* toward the sidelines," the verb *trotted* expresses the action so exactly that adverbs—*slowly, mechanically, dutifully,* for instance—while they may in a certain context be necessary, would in most contexts be superfluous.

**EXERCISE 5.** The following passage is an account of a high school student and his father, who is a high school teacher, leaving their farmhouse home for school early on a very cold winter morning. As you read the passage, copy onto your paper at least ten examples of the writer's use of specific details and images that make the experience real to the reader. Include the specific words, especially adjectives and verbs, that make the description clear and interesting. Discuss the style of the author with your classmates.

> It was a long, heavy car, and the cylinders needed to be rebored. Also it needed a new battery. My father and I got in and he pulled out the choke and switched on the ignition and listened, head cocked, to the starter churn the stiff motor. There was frost on the windshield that made the interior dim. The resurrection felt impossible. We listened so intently that a common picture seemed crystallized between our heads, of the dutiful brown rod straining forward in its mysterious brown cavern, skidding past the zenith of its revolution, and retreating, rejected. There was not even a ghost of a spark. I closed my eyes to make a quick prayer and my father got out and frantically scraped at the windshield frost with his fingernails until he had cleared a patch for the driver's vision. I got out on my side and, heaving together on opposite doorframes, we pushed. Once. Twice. An immense third time.
>
> With a faint rending noise the tires came loose from the frozen earth of the barn ramp. The resistance of the car's weight diminished; sluggishly we were gliding downhill. We both hopped in, the doors slammed, and the car picked up speed on the gravel road that turned and dipped sharply around the barn. The stones crackled like slowly breaking ice under our tires. With a dignified acceleration the car swallowed the steepest part of the incline, my father let the clutch in, the chassis jerked, the motor coughed, caught, *caught,* and we were aloft, winging along the pink straightaway between a pale green meadow and a fallow flat field. Our road was so little travelled that in the center it had a mane of weeds. My father's grim lips half-relaxed. He poured shivering gasoline into the hungry motor. If we stalled now, we would be out of luck, for we were on the level and there would be no more coasting. He pushed the

choke halfway in. Our motor purred in a higher key. Through the clear margins of the sheet of frost on our windshield I could see forward; we were approaching the edge of our land. Our meadow ended where the land lifted. Our gallant black hood sailed into the sharp little rise of road, gulped it down, stones and all, and spat it out behind us. On our right, Silas Schoelkopf's mailbox saluted us with a stiff red flag. We had escaped our land. I looked back: our home was a little set of buildings lodged on the fading side of the valley. The barn overhang and the chicken house were gentle red. The stuccoed cube where we had slept released like a last scrape of dreaming a twist of smoke that told blue against the purple woods. The road dipped again, our farm disappeared, and we were unpursued. Schoelkopf had a pond, and ducks the color of old piano keys were walking on the ice. On our left, Jesse Flagler's high whitewashed barn seemed to toss a mouthful of hay in our direction. I glimpsed the round brown eye of a breathing cow.

The dirt road came up to Route 122 at a treacherous grade where it was easy to stall. Here there was a row of mailboxes like a street of birdhouses, a STOP sign riddled with rusty bullet-holes, and a lop-limbed apple tree. My father glanced down the highway and guessed it was empty; without touching the brake he bounced us over the final hurdle of rutted dirt. We were high and safe on firm macadam. He went back into second gear, made the motor roar, shifted to third, and the Buick exulted. It was eleven miles to Olinger. From this point on, the journey felt downhill.[1]

[1] From *The Centaur* by John Updike. Copyright © 1962, 1963 by John Updike. Reprinted by permission of Alfred A. Knopf, Inc. and Andre Deutsch Limited, Publishers.

Chapter 24

# Language and Logic

## Propositions, Evidence, Reasoning

Argument is a familiar feature of your daily conversation. In class you argue about history, current events, literature. Essay-type examination questions often ask your opinion and expect you to support it with knowledge. People in all kinds of work—scientists, teachers, sales representatives, journalists, politicians, lawyers—know the importance of being able to argue convincingly.

In argumentative writing, your purpose is to persuade the reader to accept your views on a debatable subject. You try to prove that you are right. In its simplest form, argumentative writing is a statement of personal opinion backed up by facts and reasons. In its more elaborate form, it is a skillfully planned, tightly reasoned kind of writing frequently designed not only to convince an audience but also to persuade it to action. It may appeal to the emotions as well as to the reason.

### THE PROPOSITION

The statement of the point to be argued is called *the proposition*. It either states something as a fact or states that a particular course of action should or should not be followed. In either case, the proposition makes a definite assertion and is usually stated in a declarative sentence.

EXAMPLES My client is innocent.

The sums being spent on space exploration should be diverted to the solution of domestic problems.

Capital punishment does not deter crime.

All of the statements above can be believed, doubted, or disbelieved. The way each is stated causes us to expect reasons to be presented in support of the proposition. The reasons, or evidence, in support of a proposition are an essential part of argument. But before we consider them, we must understand what makes a good proposition and how it should be stated.

## The Arguable Proposition

### 24a. Formulate in a proposition the point to be argued.

While there is little likelihood of your writing an argumentative composition on an "unarguable" subject, you should be warned against two kinds of futile arguing that occur in our daily conversation.

One kind of futile argument is that in which the issue is a matter of verifiable fact. How familiar does the following argument sound?

"Mary is older than Bob." (Proposition)
"No, she isn't."
"Yes, she is. Her birthday is in April. Bob's is in July."
"But in different years."
"No, they were born the same year."
"They were not!"

These two people are getting nowhere at all. They are arguing instead of finding out the truth, something which they can easily ascertain. A statement of verifiable fact is not an arguable proposition.

Like verifiable facts, personal tastes are frequent, but poor subjects of argument. "Blue is a more beautiful color than red." "Tennis is more fun than golf." These are not sound propositions because, as matters of taste, they cannot be resolved by presenting evidence. To be sure, you could write an interesting composition in support of your taste, but no amount of arguing will ever establish a proposition of this kind as true or not true. A statement of personal taste is an expression of opinion, but it is not an arguable proposition.

## Stating the Proposition

A proposition should be so worded that its meaning is definite and its terms are not ambiguous. When the editor of the school newspaper begins an editorial with the proposition "Seniors with a B average should be excused from examinations," the editor is not writing with precision. The phrase "with a B average" is ambiguous. Does it mean an overall B average for all subjects, or does it mean seniors will be excused from examinations in only those subjects in which they have a B average? Also the word *examinations* is too general. The editor certainly does not mean all examinations given at the school but probably means only final examinations. Rewording the proposition will make it clear and get the editor's argument off to a better start: "Seniors should be excused from final examinations in courses in which they have a B average."

Sometimes a proposition, even though well phrased, requires explanation, or definition of some of its terms. These explanations and definitions can be given in the first paragraph of the composition.

A proposition should not in its wording assume the truth of something that has to be proved. Consider, for example, the proposition "This unfair tax should be repealed." The inclusion of the word *unfair* implies that everyone can, or should be able to, see that the tax is unreasonable, when in fact this is something that must be proved in the argument. Similarly, if you are setting out to prove that professional boxing should be outlawed because it is dangerous, it is not fair to state your proposition this way: "The *dangerous* sport of professional boxing should be outlawed." Making this kind of statement is called "begging the question."

To summarize, a proposition should be on a point that can sensibly be argued; it should be clearly stated; and it should not imply that the point to be proved is a foregone conclusion.

**EXERCISE 1.** Some of the following are sound, arguable propositions; others are not. Label each proposition *P* if it is both sound and arguable or *NP* if it is not both sound and arguable. Be able to explain your answers in class discussion.

1. Austen's novels are too old-fashioned to interest a modern reader.
2. In 1973 Rosemary Casals won the Family Circle tennis tournament by defeating Nancy Gunter in the final match.
3. Our high school should provide recreation rooms for seniors.
4. You should vote for Laura Tanaka for class president.
5. Solar energy research should receive more government funding.
6. Central should adopt the honor system for all examinations.
7. Marian Anderson was the recipient of numerous awards, including the Presidential Medal of Freedom, which she received in 1963.
8. Art is less satisfying than craft.
9. The school year should be extended to eleven months.
10. Our inadequate school library should be enlarged.

## Minor Propositions

**24b. List the points (minor propositions) you intend to use to support your proposition.**

Having set up your proposition, write down in order the points you will make in support of it. These points, many of which are themselves debatable, are sometimes called minor propositions.

For example, read the points listed as *minor propositions* below the following main proposition.

MAIN PROPOSITION Seniors should be excused from final examinations in courses in which they have maintained a B average.

MINOR PROPOSITIONS

1. B students have already shown that they know the material of the course.
2. Students will work harder to get a B if they have the inducement of being excused from examinations.
3. Since they will not be able to raise their course grade by getting a high mark on the final examination, students will study as they go instead of depending on cramming at the end of the semester.
4. Except in borderline cases, the examination is not weighted heavily enough to lower or raise the final grade.

## 24c. Prepare to answer arguments on the other side of the proposition.

While it is possible to write an argument without answering the points that will be made by a writer with opposite views, it is much better to refute those points in the course of your composition. Ignoring a major argument of the other side leaves you in a weak position. Your success in persuasion may depend entirely on how well you can answer opposing arguments. Therefore, in planning an argumentative article, consider carefully what can be said against your views, and prepare a strong reply.

A writer supporting the proposition about excusing seniors from examinations should list and try to answer the following points on the other side of the issue:

1. Examinations assure learning because they force the student to review material that may have been forgotten.
2. Examinations assure better learning because preparation for a final examination affords the student an overall view of the course.

3. Since even good students study only when they are forced to, removing the forcing power of the examination will encourage laziness.

**EXERCISE 2.** The following questions are arguable issues. Select one or use a subject of your own choosing and (1) state it in a clear proposition, (2) list at least three minor propositions in support, and (3) list at least two arguments that might be offered by someone arguing against the proposition.

1. Should high school students be allowed greater freedom in electing courses?
2. Should high school students be allowed to elect the teachers they want?
3. Should the intramural athletic program be expanded?
4. Should English courses emphasize modern literature more?
5. Should urban bicyclists be licensed?
6. Is homework necessary?
7. Should the sale of cigarettes be prohibited by law?
8. Should Americans tour the United States before touring abroad?
9. Should the state government give financial aid to private and parochial schools?
10. Should the state university charge tuition fees for students who are residents of the state?

## EVIDENCE

When you have formulated your proposition and listed points in support of both sides of it, you should turn to the problem of gathering the material you will use in support. This material is called *evidence.*

### 24d. Gather sufficient evidence to prove main and minor propositions and refute opposing views.

According to the dictionary, *evidence* is "that which tends to prove or disprove something." Hence it is the essence of argument. Two kinds of evidence are usually used to establish proof: (1) facts, (2) authoritative statements (testimony).

## Facts as Evidence

A fact is something that can be demonstrated to be true, or *verified.* That a certain number of births were recorded in the United States last year, that it was raining on a particular night at Kennedy Airport, that water boils at 212 degrees Fahrenheit—all these are facts that can be verified beyond a reasonable doubt. Obviously, the appropriate facts provide the strongest possible support for an argument.

Two cautions are to be observed in using facts as evidence. First, the facts must be accurate. Unfortunately, there can be dishonesty in argument, and the writer who does not check the facts carefully is dishonest. Second, the facts must be plentiful enough to be convincing. How many facts it takes to convince your reader will depend on the nature of the subject and the impressiveness of the facts themselves, but, in general, the more facts you have the stronger your argument will be.

Note the use of facts in the following paragraphs in which the writer proposes that the male skeleton is better suited to running than the female skeleton is.

> **The male skeleton gives men [runners] another built-in advantage.** With its wide shoulders and narrow hips and pelvis, it is more suited to running than a woman's wide-hipped, narrow-shouldered frame. A woman has more delicately constructed bones, muscles, tendons, and ligaments, and her wider pelvis creates a mechanical disadvantage for running because she must rock more from side to side to balance one step with the next. The sideward movement impedes her forward speed. Her wider hips also cause the quadriceps (the muscles which run from the pelvis down the front of the thigh) to angle in to their attachment at the knee, increasing the

chance of knee problems because of added torque[1] placed on the knee as it seeks a straight alignment. A lucky woman runner has small, narrow hips.[2]

## Authoritative Statements as Evidence

Important as facts are, we cannot depend exclusively upon them in argument. In the courtroom, for example, expert opinions may be admitted as evidence: a doctor may be asked to give an opinion about a matter relating to medicine; a handwriting expert may be asked to compare two letters, and so on. Of course it is always possible that the expert may be wrong; opinions are not verifiable in the same way that facts are. Yet, if a person is respected in a field and if it cannot be demonstrated that there is special interest in what is said on the matter at hand, the opinion should carry a good deal of weight.

The important question, then, is whether a particular authority is really an authority. There are no certain ways of telling, but caution and common sense will take us a long way. We may ask ourselves what obvious qualifications the person has. Doctors and lawyers display certificates showing they have attended a particular school and passed intensive examinations in their field. A scholar in another field is also likely to have degrees and is probably connected with a well-known college or university. A correspondent who has lived for years in India and has won journalistic honors for objective reporting, a technician working for a reputable testing company, a person with long experience in the training of horses—all of these people have qualifications that are easy to check and that tell us about which matters their opinions will be most reliable.

Note the use of an authority (U Thant, former Secretary General of the UN) in the following paragraph:

[1] ***torque:*** a twisting or wrenching effect.

[2] From *Sports Illustrated, Running for Women* by Janet Heinonen, published by Harper & Row, Publishers, Inc. Copyright © 1979 by Time Inc. Reprinted by permission of Sports Illustrated.

The gloomiest predictions made during the years since the establishment of the United Nations have not yet come true. The U.N. has been relatively feeble from the beginning—largely dependent upon the major nations, which often have failed to give that support. Yet the U.N. and related agencies—the World Health Organization, the Food and Agriculture Organization, the International Bank, UNICEF, the U.N. Development Fund, and many others—have helped to build the foundations for a community of man. U Thant has cited the process of decolonization that has "liberated nearly a billion people in less than a quarter of a century—a development on a scale that was inconceivable in 1945 and in which the U.N. has played a major role. . . . The obligation of the rich nations to assist the poor ones is now widely regarded as a normal feature of life and a new moral precept in the international community. And I think of the Universal Declaration of Human Rights, the effort to make it increasingly applicable, and the endless struggle against racism and discrimination in all their different forms that has been and is being waged at the United Nations."[1]

### The Testimonial

One kind of "evidence" loosely related to the authoritative statement is the *testimonial.* Some testimonials may be convincing. If you are considering the adoption of a merit system for good conduct in your school, you may be persuaded by the opinions of students in schools already using such a system. The testimonial as an advertising device, however, may be taken less seriously. Usually the actress who uses Glow face cream has been well paid for her testimonial and would have endorsed another product if paid enough money.

## REASONING

A common way to convince and persuade others is to reason with them. Reasoning must, of course, be logical;

[1] From "The Possibilities of Transformation" by Frank K. Kelly from *Saturday Review,* March 7, 1970. Copyright 1970 Saturday Review, Inc. Reprinted by permission of the publisher.

that is, the thinking must be clear. In the following pages you will study several common kinds of reasoning. Each has its pitfalls into which an unclear thinker may easily fall. Study the kinds of reasoning and note the pitfalls so that you can detect them in the arguments of others and avoid them in your own compositions.

## Inductive Reasoning

In inductive reasoning you begin with evidence—facts, statistics, instances, etc., and after studying the evidence, you arrive at a conclusion or generalization. For example, suppose that you have a box of chocolate creams all of which are identical in appearance. You bite into one of the chocolates and find it to be a peppermint cream. You taste a second and find it to be peppermint, too. You try a third, which is also peppermint. Now, reasoning inductively, you are about to say, "This box contains only peppermint creams." Of course, your generalization may be wrong because you have not tested every piece of candy in the box. The chances are, however, that you may be right. The more creams you sample, the more reliable your generalization becomes. You can easily see that the more evidence you have in favor of your generalization, the more likely it is that the generalization will be true.

### 24e. Avoid generalizations based on insufficient evidence.

*Hasty Generalization*

When you make a generalization based on insufficient evidence, you are committing a major error in reasoning. This error is called *hasty generalization.* All your life you will hear people make it.

An understandably angry motorist wrote the following letter to a newspaper:

> About midnight Saturday I was going through the intersection of Haven Boulevard and Elm Street on a green light

> when my car was rammed into at a right angle by a car which had obviously passed through the red light. The driver of this car was seventeen years old. He had six other teen-agers in the car with him, one of whom was badly injured in the collision. A month ago I was forced off the highway by a car driven by a high school student who insisted on passing even though there was not enough room to pass. To avoid a side-swipe, I drove into the ditch. These experiences have convinced me that teen-age drivers are a menace and that the driving age in this state should be raised to twenty-one.

The validity of this motorist's generalization is highly doubtful because the generalization is based on only two instances. It could be true, but it certainly has not been proved true by the evidence given.

Now suppose that a large insurance company decides to find out whether teen-age drivers, in proportion to their number, are involved in more accidents than are adult drivers. The insurance company has access to a vast amount of information. Its research department conducts an extensive investigation. If, after studying thousands of accident reports, the company finds that the percentage of teen-age drivers involved is greater than the percentage of adult drivers involved, the company may draw a generalization which will probably be true. There is always the possibility that further research may disprove the generalization, but until that happens, the company would be justified in making a generalization on the basis of its research.

### *Analogy*

Sometimes during an argument a person, in order to clarify a point, may use an *analogy*. An analogy is a comparison. Reasoning by analogy is the kind of reasoning that compares one situation with another. Suppose, for example, that the president of the Student Council of a school is impatient with the students for not cooperating with their student monitors, who are charged with keeping order in corridors, cafeteria, assembly, and at athletic events. In an address before the school, he tries, by drawing an analogy, to persuade the students to be more cooperative. He says that a school is like an army. Just as soldiers must obey their officers, students must obey their monitors. If soldiers ignore their officers' orders, the battle may be lost. If students ignore their monitors' orders, the school will not function smoothly and its educational and social programs will be affected. It is the function of an army to win battles; it is the function of a school to provide effective educational and social programs for its students. The success of a school, like the success of an army, depends upon good discipline and respect for authority. Like good soldiers, all students should obey orders.

By drawing this analogy between a school and an army, the speaker hopes to persuade his listeners to be more cooperative, more obedient. Since discipline is essential in both an army and a school, there is some point in the analogy, and this point may have been persuasive. However, you will recognize at once that the analogy is really very weak because there are many more dissimilarities than similarities between an army and a school. Is military discipline the kind we want in a school? Is the job of an army officer like that of a school monitor? Is winning a battle really much like furthering an educational program? The analogy grows weaker the longer you study it, a fact which is true of many analogies.

Nevertheless, analogies have their place in argument. If a good one occurs to you, use it for its clarifying effect. Almost invariably it will be interesting to your readers and will help them to understand your argument better. Be ready, of course, to have an analogy attacked by people of opposing views.

**24f. The soundness of an analogy depends upon the number of points in common between the things being compared.**

When an analogy will not stand careful examination, it is called a *false analogy*. In other words, when the points of similarity are found to be very few or even nonexistent, the analogy is false.

**EXERCISE 3.** Discuss the following examples of argument by analogy. How strong are the analogies?

1. A large vocabulary and the ability to use it with ease will not make you a great writer. Joseph Conrad said, "The gift of words is no such great matter; a man is not made a hunter or a warrior by the mere possession of a firearm."
2. As we know, a body of criticism stands ready to provide its [fiction's] solution, which is a kind of translation of fiction into another language. It offers us close analysis, like a head-phone we can clamp on at the U.N. when they are speaking the Arabian tongue.[1]
3. It is imperative for us to absorb the fact that we cannot know the nature of the universe by reason of what we know about our own planet. The whole cannot infallibly be known simply by the study of one of its smallest parts. Yet that is all our planet is: one of the smallest parts of the whole, which is the universe. How representative a part is it of that whole? We cannot say; we do not know. This will come as a disappointment to those who thirst for quick conclusions. But how can we claim to know the galaxies of suns and their relationships to each other from our very limited point of view? We would be putting ourselves in the position of city children, who think that every part of the big city they live in is like their own neighborhood.
4. Like the manager of a wild animal circus, the principal of a high school is engaged in the business of training animals. His success depends on the performance of his charges. He will not hold his position long if they fail standardized tests, just as an animal trainer will soon go out of business if his seals cannot bounce balls on their noses and his tigers won't leap through a fiery hoop. There is always the strain, too, of having to keep the animals under control. A school can no more permit students complete freedom than a circus can re-

[1] From *The Eye of the Story: Selected Essays & Reviews* by Eudora Welty. Reprinted by permission of Random House, Inc.

lease its wild animals. In both instances, the public would protest with equal vigor.

5. Although nuclear war is unthinkable, a country like ours must be prepared to wage it. In this preparedness, which accounts for the largest part of our national budget, lies the only sure deterrent we have. We have no choice. We are like a bank which must build a great vault with heavy steel doors, a combination time lock, and the best electrical alarm system engineers can devise. The banker regrets the enormous cost of this vault; he hopes never to have to use the alarm. But he knows the installation is the only deterrent to criminals. It would be unrealistic for a bank to reduce expenses by using a kitchen cupboard for the storage of money. It would be equally ridiculous for our country to cut its budget in half by abandoning all preparedness measures.

## Deductive Reasoning

You have seen that inductive reasoning works by assembling evidence and making a generalization about it. By this method we arrive at judgments that are *probably* true. Until the last item of evidence is in, we cannot be sure.

Deductive reasoning, on the other hand, starts out from a generalization that is assumed to be true and by logical steps leads to a conclusion about a particular situation.

### *The Syllogism*

A deductive argument can be stated in a three-part form called a *syllogism.* The first part is the generalization with which the argument begins. It is called the *major premise.* The second part states the particular situation to which the major premise is to be applied. It is called the *minor premise.* The third part states the *conclusion.*

SYLLOGISM All sweet apples are ripe. [major premise]
This apple is sweet. [minor premise]
(Therefore) This apple is ripe. [conclusion]

If the major and minor premises in this syllogism are true, the conclusion is sound. It is possible for a conclusion to be valid but not sound. A conclusion is valid if it is correctly reasoned regardless of its truth. For example, the reasoning in the following syllogism is perfectly correct, making the conclusion valid. No one, however, would accept the conclusion as sound because it is simply not true.

All two-legged animals are human beings.
A monkey is a two-legged animal.
A monkey is a human being.

If you grant the truth of the first premise and the minor premise, your conclusion follows with unquestionable logic – it is a *valid,* correctly reasoned conclusion. However, the first premise is not true: not all two-legged animals are human beings. Hence the conclusion is unsound, or false.

### *Testing a Syllogism*

There are many complicated ways of testing the soundness of a syllogism, but for ordinary purposes, you may test a syllogism by asking three questions.

## 24g. Test a syllogism by asking:

**(1) Are the premises true? That is, has the major premise been arrived at inductively from enough instances? And is the fact stated in the minor premise true?**

**(2) Does the major premise ignore any significant fact?**

**(3) Does the conclusion follow logically?**

### *False Syllogisms*

When you apply the three-question test to the following false syllogisms, you will see why they are false.

All ripe apples are sweet. [major premise]
This apple is ripe. [minor premise]
(Therefore) This apple is sweet. [conclusion]

This syllogism is false because it does not stand up under the test of the first question. It is not true that all ripe apples are sweet.

Red apples are ripe. [major premise]
This apple is green. [minor premise]
(Therefore) This apple is not ripe. [conclusion]

This syllogism can be shown to be false when the second test question is applied to it. The generalization (major premise) ignores a very significant fact, which is that some green apples are also ripe.

All sweet apples are ripe. [major premise]
This apple is ripe. [minor premise]
(Therefore) This apple is sweet. [conclusion]

The syllogism is false because it does not pass the test of the third question. The conclusion does not follow logically. It is based on a misunderstanding of what the major premise says. The major premise does not say that all ripe apples are sweet.

The falseness of these simple "apple" syllogisms is easy to understand. Yet deductive reasoning of the kind they illustrate is all too common. Have you ever heard arguments like this:

Communists believe in government ownership of natural resources.

Mrs. Doe believes in government ownership of the coal mines.

(Therefore) Mrs. Doe is a Communist.

Here the premises are true, but the major premise ignores the important fact that some people who are not Communists also believe in government ownership of coal mines.

An unsound deductive conclusion reached in this way is like a hasty generalization in inductive reasoning. It is too quickly arrived at. We call it "jumping to a conclusion," for the argument literally "jumps" over (ignores) an important fact.

**EXERCISE 4.** This exercise is a series of examples of both inductive and deductive reasoning. Number your paper 1–10. After studying each item, write after the corresponding number on your paper the kind of reasoning it represents (inductive or deductive). If the reasoning is valid, add a plus (+); if it is not valid, add a zero (0). Be able to explain your answers.

1. Only Caribou Airlines flies nonstop between here and Atlanta. Carl said he was coming from Atlanta on a nonstop flight, so he must be coming on Caribou.
2. Mom says she won't buy another station wagon because the last one we had developed too many rattles.
3. Look at the number of shining cars in college parking lots. Look at the number of college students who spend their winter vacations at ski resorts and their summers abroad. You can see that college students these days are a pretty rich group.
4. To commit a burglary, one has to be at the scene of the burglary. Roy Maxwell admits that he was at the scene. Roy Maxwell is the burglar.
5. Every girl I know who comes from a wealthy home is a spoiled brat. The children of rich people are always spoiled.
6. Socialists believe in socialized medicine. Mrs. Cross believes in socialized medicine. I guess Mrs. Cross is a Socialist.
7. The per pupil cost of education is greater in the high school than in the elementary school. In the future a greater proportion of pupils will be in high school than has been true in the past. The cost of education, therefore, is sure to increase.
8. In the long run machinery has improved our national economy. Since 1850, when the machine age began in earnest, our population has grown $7\frac{1}{2}$ times, but jobs have grown $8\frac{1}{2}$ times, and goods and services, 34 times. Apparently we really have no reason to fear automation.
9. When an hour-long interview with the President on the problems of the Presidency was broadcast in prime evening time, six million people watched it, while twenty-one million were watching a popular-song program on another network. The majority of the American people prefer entertainment to enlightenment.
10. Statistics compiled by the United Nations Fund for Population Activities (UNFPA) indicate that the worldwide birthrate has been dropping in recent years. Still, the lowest world population forecast offered for the year 2000 is 5.8 billion.

> More than 1.5 billion people will thus be added to a world where almost a billion of the people alive today do not have enough food to eat. The additional drain on the earth's resources and the human suffering from inadequate food supply is potentially catastrophic.

## Clear Thinking

We have already discussed some of the pitfalls in reasoning—the use of a dubious authority, hasty generalization, and the false analogy. These came up naturally in connection with the kind of reasoning in which they are most likely to occur. There are also some other important errors in reasoning that may come up in a variety of situations. Being aware of them will help you to be sure that your reasoning is clear and logical.

### *Cause and Effect*

The purpose of much of our discussion and writing is to find remedies and preventive measures for existing evils. As any physician knows, the first step in assigning a remedy for an illness is to find the cause, and it is important that the true cause be found. In our effort to explain an event or a situation, we naturally examine the events which preceded it. We look for the cause. In so doing, however, we must not make the mistake of assuming that just because one event preceded another, it caused the second event. A Latin phrase is commonly used to describe this kind of thinking: *post hoc, ergo propter hoc,* which means "after this, therefore because of this."

A simple form of this kind of error in thinking is the basis of our superstitions. For instance, you may slip on the stairs and sprain your ankle so badly that you are on crutches for weeks. Looking back on events preceding the accident, you recall that just before you slipped, a black cat crossed your path. You say to yourself, "Now that explains the accident. That cat was the cause of my bad luck."

**24h. The fact that an event or a condition follows another event or condition does not necessarily mean that the second was caused by the first. Before ascribing a result to a certain cause, consider other possible causes.**

Suppose that the basketball team at your school has won the regional championship and is therefore going to the state tournament, a day's journey away. The team travels by bus and must play its first tournament game the same night. It loses the game to a team which eventually wins the tournament. The sports columnist in your school paper, looking for the cause of the defeat, seizes upon the bus ride which preceded the game: "If the players hadn't been exhausted from the tiring trip, they would have won the game and the championship." Of course, the columnist could be right, but there were other factors which he should have considered before deciding on the cause of defeat. The winning team also made a long trip the day of the game. The winners won by a margin of 16 points. The winning team had a better season record than the losing team. Finally, they went on to win the tournament. In the light of these considerations, it looks as though the columnist was guilty of *post hoc, ergo propter hoc* thinking.

### *The Irrelevant Fact—"Off-the-Subject" Arguments*

The word *relevant* means "related to." A relevant argument is one which is related to the issue being argued. An *irrelevant* argument is one which is not related to the issue. When introduced into a discussion, irrelevant facts or arguments may throw the discussion "off the track." You have probably heard the leader of a discussion warn the participants about "getting off the subject." Clever but dishonest people may deliberately try to sidetrack a discussion when they find the argument going against them.

A common form of irrelevant argument is the one which attacks the person offering an argument rather than attacking the argument itself. For example, a nervous father advises his son at the wheel of the family car not to drive above the legal speed limit. The son's answer is that since he has often seen his father drive above the limit, it is all right for him to do so.

**24i. Do not let an argument or discussion be confused by an irrelevant point.**

An irrelevant point is one which simply has no bearing on the discussion. For example, a Democrat and a Republican are arguing the merits of their party platforms in an election year. The Republican says, "The American people have elected more Republican Presidents than Democratic Presidents." You can see, of course, that this statement, although true, is irrelevant so far as the merits of the current party platforms are concerned.

**EXERCISE 5.** A student-faculty committee is discussing the question, "Should students trying out for varsity sports be excused from last-period study halls?" Arguments presented by both sides are listed below. Study the arguments and identify those which are irrelevant, likely to lead the discussion off the subject.

*Arguments in favor of excusing the students:*

1. It will relieve locker room congestion after school.
2. Outdoor exercise is better for the students than studying in a stuffy classroom.
3. Recently four students on the varsity were sent to the office from last-period study because they created a discipline problem.
4. The students will have more time for practice. The more they practice, the better the varsity teams will be.
5. Study halls should be eliminated anyway so that the school day can be shortened.
6. Athletics are as important as studies.
7. Last year our teams were the worst in years.

*Arguments against excusing the students:*

1. The students would waste the extra time because the coaches cannot join them until after school.
2. Those who are excused would have an unfair advantage over those who have a class the last period.
3. Sometimes the weather is bad, and the students could not go outdoors.
4. It is better for students to study in school before practice because they will be too tired after practice to study at home.
5. We don't excuse students for other outdoor activities like fishing or playing golf, or playing outdoors at home.

### *Rationalizing*

When you fool yourself by attributing your behavior to reasons or motives which are not your true reasons or motives, you are rationalizing. All of us are guilty at times of rationalizing actions for which we cannot give a truly reasonable defense. The following paragraph illustrates the kind of reasoning by which a student explains his failure to make the honor roll. He is fooling himself. The truth probably is that he hasn't the ability, or he is too lazy, but he does not want to admit either of these.

> I could have made the honor roll if I had wanted to be called a brain or an overachiever. I'd rather be a normal person and enjoy life. The students who knocked themselves out to get on the honor roll aren't too popular. Who wants a brain for a friend? Lots of us are just as smart. We just don't want to spend our whole lives studying.

### *Wishful Thinking*

People sometimes argue that a thing is true or may become true simply because they wish it to be true. Their evidence may be weak, but they believe it because they want to believe it. This kind of thinking is called wishful thinking. A simple illustration is Henry, whose girlfriend has been dating Bill for several months. Henry says, "I can wait. Betty will get tired of him, and then she'll come back to me."

**EXERCISE 6.** Each of the following items illustrates an error in thinking. Number your paper 1–15. Analyze the thinking in each item. After its corresponding number write the letter of the kind of unclear thinking it represents.

A hasty generalization
B unsound deductive reasoning (false syllogism)
C unclear thinking about cause and effect
D weak or false analogy
E irrelevant (off-the-subject) argument
F rationalizing
G wishful thinking

1. Both Mary and Joe told me that Mr. Hilton is a hard marker. I need to raise my marks to get into college, and so I hope I don't get Mr. Hilton for English.
2. Lazy people use a great deal of slang. Jane's speech, which is full of slang, shows her to be lazy.
3. When asked about the cause of the fire, Chief Charles Waterman said he understood that the Slagles, in whose apartment the blaze started, had a habit of eating dinner by candlelight.
4. The President states that education must remain a matter of state and local control. But should a responsible federal government help pay the piper without being expected to call some of the tunes?
5. Someone is ill at the Hartmans' house. I saw a car with a doctor's license plates parked outside this morning.
6. When Ellen Smith appeared before the Student Court to answer to the charge of running in the halls, she pleaded not guilty because she said lots of other kids were running in the halls, too, and they didn't have to appear in court.
7. World War I, World War II, the Korean War, and the Vietnam War all came when the United States was governed by a Democratic administration. To avoid war, vote Republican.
8. Automobile mechanics do not need to know good English.

I intend to become an automobile mechanic. Teaching me correct English makes as much sense as teaching a polar bear how to catch an alligator.

9. Dr. Kimball advised me not to chew gum because, he said, it is bad for my teeth. I didn't pay any attention because I noticed that he chews gum all the time.
10. In the free competition of a capitalist society, business which cannot compete must be allowed to fail. In the United States the railroads have been unable to compete successfully with other modes of transportation. They should be abandoned, not subsidized by the federal government.
11. For a long time the West has based its attitude toward the East on the assumption that the fundamental goal of Russia and China is to force communism upon the entire world. Recent events in both countries, however, give us hope that their attitude has changed and that the East may be ready to join us in accepting détente as a permanent compromise.
12. Lila wrote a short story which her classmates selected as the best short story written during the school term. Allan objected to the vote on the ground that Lila's stories were always chosen as best. He said no one else ever had a chance.
13. People shouldn't work all the time. They need recreation to keep them fit and help them to do their work better. Although I have not finished my homework for tomorrow, I'm going bowling tonight with Sam and Jack. I've been working so hard that I need the change and recreation. I'll feel much more like working and do a better job after a night off.
14. People who are so conscientious that they always do more work than the teacher assigned make it hard for the rest of us to get good grades. If it weren't for these people, I'd be getting an A instead of a C in English.
15. At noon on Friday, Ms. Beatty, my science teacher, saw some students leaning on her car in the faculty parking lot. After school she was unable to start the car and discovered a battery cable had come loose. Ms. Beatty accused the students of detaching it.

**EXERCISE 7.** Using the propositions prepared for Exercise 2 (page 420), write an argumentative composition of 300–500 words incorporating these propositions, supporting your views with appropriate evidence: facts, authoritative statements, logical reasoning. Test your reasoning to be sure you have not fallen into any of the common pitfalls described on the preceding pages.

## Argument and Propaganda

When an organized group—a government, an institution, a business concern—embarks upon a program to win over the public, the ideas and arguments it uses in its favor are called propaganda. Thus we refer to political propaganda, communist propaganda, labor propaganda, advertising propaganda, etc. Propaganda is a kind of argument. Its purpose is to convince and persuade to action.

Nowadays the word *propaganda* has unpleasant associations. It suggests wily and deceitful means of swaying people's minds. But propaganda may be used for purposes we approve as well as for ones we disapprove. A physician who tries to persuade an audience to stop smoking cigarettes because there is a direct relationship between cigarette smoking and lung cancer is a propagandist, but is being unselfish in the attempt. The doctor is seeking a result which will be beneficial to others.

An individual or group that tries to influence others' opinions or actions for selfish ends is engaging in propaganda which may be harmful. Professional propagandists are promoting their own causes regardless of whether or not their effects on you are beneficial.

### *Recognizing Propaganda*

In your own argumentative writing, you probably will not be tempted to use the tricks of the propagandist. Nevertheless, you should, as part of your study of argument, learn to recognize and resist commonly used propaganda devices.

### 24j. Learn to recognize and evaluate propaganda.

Propagandists are skillful users of most of the kinds of faulty reasoning you have studied on the preceding pages.

They are given to frequent use of the hasty generalization; they jump to conclusions; they reason by analogy; they attribute an effect to the wrong cause; they divert you from the real issue by an irrelevant fact or an off-the-subject argument. Loaded words (see page 307) and doubtful testimonials (see page 423) are their stock in trade.

In addition to all of these, propagandists have other ways of trying to arouse your support. Some of the most common of these are described below.

### *Name-Calling*

This is a device by which a speaker attempts to defeat opponents not by rational arguments but by calling them names or smearing their reputations. Mudslinging of this sort is not worthy of anyone. Do not repeat a smear and do not believe it until the person under attack has had a full opportunity to reply or until you have examined the evidence.

### *Slogans*

Propagandists know the value of a slogan. It is simple, catchy, and easily remembered. An involved train of thought is hard to follow. A series of arguments is hard to remember. A slogan makes thinking unnecessary. It oversimplifies by reducing a chain of arguments to a few words.

Slogans play an important part in politics and advertising. When you hear a slogan, remember that it does not tell a complete story. It is a device to capture your attention and memory. Here are some examples of effective slogans:

> The life you save may be your own!
> Make the world safe for democracy.
> The right is more precious than the peace.
> Fight cancer with a checkup and a check.
> Liberty, equality, fraternity!

### *The Unproved Assertion*

Repetition is not proof. Unless the restatement is accompanied by reasons, statistics, examples, or the statements of competent and unprejudiced authorities, it is no stronger than the original utterance.

The following declaration seems to prove a point. Actually it does not because there is no evidence offered.

> My candidate is the best qualified of all. In character, experience, education, and intellectual ability she is superior to everyone who is running for this office. No one even remotely approaches her qualifications for the position. She stands head and shoulders above the other candidates. Everyone admits her superior merits. Therefore she deserves your vote.

### *The Bandwagon*

Most people like to do what others are doing and believe as others believe. Propagandists know and capitalize on this human tendency.

"Everybody is joining our cause," they say. "Come along or you'll find yourself alone."

It requires willpower and the ability to think for oneself, to resist hopping on the bandwagon. Do not be fooled into joining a movement simply because "others are doing it."

**EXERCISE 8.** Out of your experience as a reader or listener, give an example of five of the following propaganda devices or errors in thinking.

| | |
|---|---|
| Hasty generalization | Slogans |
| Unsound deduction | Name-calling |
| The wrong cause | The bandwagon |
| Weak analogy | The unproved assertion |
| Irrelevant argument | Wishful thinking |
| Loaded words | Rationalizing |

**EXERCISE 9.** As a form of propaganda, advertising uses many of the common propaganda devices as evidence. In

magazine advertisements and radio or television commercials find and report on examples of the following:

| | |
|---|---|
| Loaded words | Slogans |
| Testimonials | Bandwagon |

## SUMMARY

***In preparing an argumentative paper, observe the following:***

1. Formulate a proposition that is arguable and clear.
2. List supporting points—minor propositions.
3. Prepare to refute the arguments on the other side.
4. Gather sufficient evidence: facts, authoritative statements, logical reasoning.

**EXERCISE 10.** Select a controversial subject currently being argued in your school or community. State it in the form of a proposition. List minor propositions on both sides. Write a paper (300–500 words) using all the evidence you can gather. Watch for pitfalls in your reasoning.

**EXERCISE 11.** Select a controversial subject of national interest currently in the news—or in the news within the past two weeks. State your views in an argumentative essay (300–500 words). Support your views with evidence. Watch for the common pitfalls in reasoning.

**EXERCISE 12.** Select one of the following issues on which you have definite opinions. Limit the subject so that you can support one side (and refute the other) in an argumentative composition of 300–500 words. Prepare carefully, following the four steps discussed in this chapter. Supply plenty of evidence. Keep your reasoning sound.

1. Is the quality of television programs as high as it could practically be?
2. Are labor unions becoming too powerful?
3. Are the requirements for a driver's license in this state adequate?

4. Is life in the suburbs a good life?
5. Should high school reading be censored?
6. Should federal farm subsidies be continued?
7. Does modern fiction overemphasize violence?
8. Is foreign language study worthwhile?
9. Is modern advertising harmful?
10. Should the legal drinking age be raised? lowered?
11. Do we have true equality of opportunity in America?
12. Should college education, like elementary and secondary education, be free?
13. Should guided individual study replace classes in schools?
14. Do interscholastic athletics destroy sportsmanship?
15. Should the government assume the responsibility for care of the aged?
16. Are the advantages of living in a small town greater than the disadvantages?

Chapter 25

# Exercises in Composition

## The Précis, The Factual Report

The exercises in this chapter will provide valuable practice in composition. In many of them the subject matter for writing has been supplied for you so that you may concentrate entirely on the writing. Do not attempt to work straight through the chapter in one stretch of a few weeks, for that plan would soon grow tiresome. Use the exercises from time to time during the year as your teacher assigns them, working on one type of exercise for a while and then on another. This plan will afford regular reviews of writing skills.

Although it is quite possible that you may do well on these composition exercises without having studied other chapters in this book, you will certainly get more help from the practice they provide if you bring to the work an understanding of the composition principles presented in Chapters 11 through 19 and especially in Chapters 21 and 22.

The kind of writing required by these exercises is rather formal expository writing. This is the kind of writing you are most often expected to do in your other classes, and the kind expected of you in business and in college.

Since in doing these exercises every member of the class faces the same composition problems, you will find it to your advantage to compare papers and, in class discussion, to evaluate the various methods of solving these problems.

## THE PRÉCIS

A précis is a brief summary. Writing a précis is valuable training in composition. Since the writing requires you to be clear and concise, you must choose your words carefully and arrange them skillfully to get the maximum amount of meaning into the minimum space.

In addition to its value as a writing exercise, précis work is excellent reading practice. In order to summarize another's ideas in your own words, you must understand the ideas thoroughly.

In school and in life after school, there are many situations that call for the writing of a brief, accurate summary of your reading. You are frequently asked to prepare a summary of what you have read in your textbook or in the library. Answers on examinations often require a brief summary. People in business, in club work, and in social work must prepare short digests of articles and reports.

Study the following facts about a précis and the basic steps in précis writing.

**1. A précis is a *short* summary.** It is not a paraphrase, which merely says in different and simpler words exactly what the passage being paraphrased has to say. A paraphrase may be as long as the passage itself. A précis rarely is more than one-third the length of the original selection and may be only one-fourth as long.

**2. A précis gives only the "heart" of a passage.** It omits repetitions and such details as examples, illustrations, and adjectives unless they are of unusual importance.

**3. A précis is written entirely in the words of the person writing it, not in the words of the original selection.** Avoid the temptation to lift long phrases and whole sentences from the original.

**4. A précis is written from the point of view of the author whose work is being summarized.** Do not begin with such expressions as "This author says" or "The paragraph means." Begin as though you were summarizing your own writing.

In writing a précis proceed as follows:

1. Read carefully, sentence by sentence, the passage to be summarized. Try to grasp the writer's main point. Spotting the topic sentence will help. Look up in the dictionary any words whose meaning is not absolutely clear. As you read, take brief notes to be used in your writing.

2. When you have finally decided what the author's main point is, write it out in your own words. Do not use the wording of the original except for certain key words which you may find indispensable. If you cannot translate the ideas into language of your own, you do not understand them very well. Be especially careful not to rely too much on the topic sentence. Do not add any opinions or ideas of your own.

3. Revise your writing until you are sure that you have given an accurate summary.

4. Usually you will find your précis is too long—more than one-third the length of the original. Continue your revision until you have reduced the précis to the proper length. In this careful revision lies the principal value of the précis as a composition exercise. The work on "reduction" on pages 257–61 will be helpful to you in shortening your précis. Don't try to get the précis into a single sentence unless the passage is very short.

**EXERCISE 1.** Read the following paragraph two or three times. Then read the four précis of it given below. Each of them illustrates one major error in précis writing.

The first thing that strikes the critical minority, as it looks at the whole cultural picture, is that ours is a nation of new-rich people, well washed, all dressed up, rather pathetically unsure just what it is washed and dressed up for; a nation convinced that a multitude of material goods, standardized, furiously and expensively advertised by appeals to greed and vanity, will in themselves make life worth the living. Because we are new-rich, we overvalue possessions. Almost any individual who makes a great deal of money very rapidly supposes that mere possession of wealth is evidence of worth. He also is apt to imagine that with his means he can buy happiness. These mistakes usually seem folly to the old-rich, to one who was born to property, whose father and mother were bred with it. Such a one knows that merely because he or his friends have it, it is no sign that they are worth it, but quite commonly the contrary. He has learned through experience that money is not in itself very valuable stuff. Happiness, which is what all men desire, cannot be purchased; it is an illusive something not for sale. The old-rich know these things well enough, but the new-rich rarely discover them until they too have grown accustomed to possessions. So it seems to be with our society. We go in, almost without question and in all classes, for the sordid nonsense of supposing that externalities possessed ennoble the owners, that a full fist invariably indicates a fine spirit.[1] [255 words]

## FAULTY PRÉCIS

1. Ours is a nation of new-rich people convinced that material goods will in themselves make life worth the living. Any individual who makes a great deal of money rapidly supposes that wealth is evidence of worth. He imagines that with his means he can buy happiness. These mistakes seem folly to one born to property. He knows that because he or his friends have it, it is no sign that they are worth it. Happiness, which all men desire, cannot be purchased. We go in for the nonsense that a full fist indicates a fine spirit. [96 words]

phrases and sentences merely copied from original

2. On the whole we are a nation of new-rich people who are well washed and well dressed, but we don't know what we're washed and dressed for. Our material goods are all standardized

précis misses point of original and emphasizes unimportant points

[1] From *Crowd Culture* by Bernard Iddings Bell. Reprinted by permission of Harper & Row, Publishers, Incorporated.

and expensively advertised. Advertisers appeal to our greed and vanity. We think these material goods are the means to wealth and happiness. The old-rich know that their friends aren't worth the money they have, but the new-rich don't know this until they have been rich for a while. [81 words]

3. First, the critical minority says that we are a nation of new-rich people all dressed up with no place to go. We think the material goods advertised by appeals to our greed and vanity are what make life worth living. Anyone who makes a lot of money thinks his money shows his worth and believes that it will make him happy. The old-rich, however, think that these ideas are foolish. Born into a rich family with property, these people know that money and property don't make them any better people. They know that the opposite is frequently true. They know that money in itself isn't worth much and that it won't buy happiness, which is the thing everyone wants. The new-rich, however, don't know these things until they have been rich long enough to find them out. Almost everyone, regardless of social class, believes that possessions make their owners better, and the more you have the more worthy you are. This is nonsense. [163 words]

précis is too long—nearly two-thirds the length of original

4. The critical minority says we are a nation of new-rich people who are victims of newspaper, magazine, and television advertising which, by appealing to our greed and vanity, tries to convince us that all we need for happiness is a lot of possessions. We don't need most of the advertised stuff such as appliances, cars, and fur coats, but the rest of the world judges our worth by what we have. In many other countries, people don't have the material goods we have. We can't all be as lucky as the old-rich, who don't have to worry about money because they already have it. [104 words]

writer of précis has injected his own ideas

ACCEPTABLE PRÉCIS

Critics of American culture see us as a new-rich people who, because we are new-rich, think that material goods make life worth living. We think that money is an indication of worth and that wealth brings happiness. The old-rich know better. Born to property, they do not believe that just because they have it, they are worth it. They know that happiness cannot be bought. The new-rich, however, mistakenly believe that possessions indicate the worth of their owner. [78 words]

idea stated in précis writer's words

less than one-third of length of original

**EXERCISE 2.** As your teacher directs, use the following passages for practice in précis writing.

1

Rapidity in reading has an obvious direct bearing on success in college work, because of the large amount of reading which must be covered in nearly all college courses. But it is probably also a direct measure of the special kind of aptitude which I am calling bookish, because rapidity of reading usually correlates with comprehension and retention. Generally speaking, the more rapidly a reader reads, the more effectively he grasps and retains. The median reading speed of college freshmen has been found to be around 250 words a minute on ordinary reading matter, and a student who reads more slowly than that will certainly have difficulty in completing his college tasks within reasonable study periods. To be a really good college risk under this criterion one should readily and habitually cover not fewer than 300 words a minute on ordinary reading matter.[1] [143 words]

2

The major struggle between writer and subject is fought here, in the arena of reputation. A modern biographer may or may not choose to reveal the intimate, the amorous details of a life, but he must, if he is good at what he does, probe beneath its public, polished self. The doubts and vulnerabilities, the meannesses, ambitions, and private satisfactions that are hidden within a social personality yield him his greatest insights. Seeking to reveal what his subject filters out as unworthy or perhaps only as uninteresting, he becomes for him, we have seen, an adversary to be frustrated, coopted, or even outsmarted ("It will read charmingly in your biography," Jane Carlyle wrote bitingly of an insincere letter from her husband). A life taken only at its own crafted word is imperfectly and even unjustly rendered. Fine biography challenges the pose to find the personality.[2] [145 words]

3

Ever since a group of men first developed a government, there have been two opposing ideas of the relation between the state and its members. One view puts the state above the indi-

[1] From "Who Should Go to College?" in *Our Children*, edited by Sidonie Matsner Gruenberg, published by Viking Press.

[2] From "The Biographer Himself: An Introduction" in *Telling Lives: The Biographer's Art* by Marc Pachter. Copyright © 1979 by the Smithsonian Institution. Published by New Republic Books, Washington, D.C. Reprinted by permission of the publisher.

vidual. The individual has no existence except as a member of the community, carrying out its will, living for its welfare, ready to die in its service. He is not supposed to separate his identity or his personal profit from that of the nation. The community has a right to interfere in all of his affairs; he has no private life in which it is bound not to interfere. The state is more than the sum of its members. Its continuance must be assured at whatever cost to them. The state is a *totality* in which they are completely submerged. This view of the state is held by all absolute rulers, including modern dictators. We usually speak of it as *totalitarianism* or *fascism*. It prevails over a large part of the world.

The other view puts the individual above the state. The state exists for the individual, not the individual for the state. The government has no other purpose than to serve the people; they may alter its form or, if need be, revolt against it, should it fail to carry out their wishes. Public and private life are quite distinct. The state may not interfere with the individual's private life so long as he does no injury to others. The individual has numerous rights which the state may not restrict except to protect the rights of other individuals. This view came to be widely held in England and northern Europe in the 1600's and 1700's; from there it spread to the New World. It took shape in the democratic form of government.[1] [295 words]

4

What is strange about this new passivity, regarding both travel and broadcasting, is that not so long ago the reverse was considered normal; that is, flying was once a highly participatory activity—as was automobile driving, as was broadcasting. Thirty-five years ago, the driver of an ordinary car was intimately involved with the event of driving, by means of direct access to his steering wheel, brakes, transmission, and the outside environment. In the same period, a listener to Edward R. Murrow's broadcasts from London was directly involved with the event of broadcasting as well as the events of the Second World War that Murrow was describing. Since then, however, the automobile driver has given up his direct involvement in favor of power controls, auto-

[1] From *Our Changing Social Order* by Ruth Wood Gavian, A. A. Gray, and Ernest R. Groves. Copyright © 1964 by D. C. Heath and Company. No part of the material covered by this copyright may be reproduced in any form without written permission of the publisher. Printed in the United States of America. Reprinted by permission of the publisher.

matic transmissions, and sealed-in passenger interiors, while the television audience has largely given up its involvement with drama and news in favor of undemanding, mechanical entertainment and uninvolving news. Nowadays, only aggressive people insist on direct, or participatory, driving, by means of sports cars; at least they are owned by people who are willing to appear aggressive. And only an aggressive minority, perhaps of a different, cultural, nature, appears to prefer participatory television, such as the music and serious drama programs that now and then are shown on public television.[1] [215 words]

5

One of the most significant facts that came out of the atomic meeting at Geneva was the willingness of all nations, including the Soviet Union, to exchange knowledge and experience on the peaceful uses of atomic energy. This in itself promises to go a long way toward eliminating the danger of an atomic war, as it marks a big step forward toward the eventual international control of atomic energy. But the most significant fact of all for the future of mankind was the assurance that, for the first time in his existence on earth, man at last has at his disposal an unlimited supply of energy, a supply great enough to satisfy all his needs for all time.

In one scientific report after another, presented by world authorities in the field, it was made evident that the nightmare of a future without energy was a thing of the past. The highly industrialized countries need no longer worry about the exhaustion of coal and oil within a century or less. And the peoples of Asia, Africa and other underdeveloped countries need no longer worry about not being able to raise their standards of living. For the nuclear fuels, uranium and thorium—until recently believed to be rather rare—have now been found to be present in many parts of the world in relative abundance, enough to last thousands, and more likely millions, of years. And beyond that, scientists believe they will find in the relatively near future, possibly no more than twenty years from now, a way to tame the power of the hydrogen bomb for industrial power. When that day comes, and it will surely come long before the uranium and thorium supplies are exhausted, the waters of the oceans of the world will supply man with energy from their practically limit-

[1] From "Prufrock Before the Television Set" by Michael Arlen; © 1976. Reprinted by permission, The New Yorker Magazine, Inc.

less supply of the heavy variety of hydrogen, a store estimated by authorities to be great enough to last a billion years.

It thus became clear at the Geneva atomic conference that man was on the eve of the greatest industrial, social and economic revolution in the million years of his evolution on earth. From a civilization limited and controlled by scarcity, he is about to enter a new world based on peace, a world built to order with no limit to the realization of his vast potentialities, physically, intellectually and spiritually.[1] [395 words]

## THE ONE-PARAGRAPH FACTUAL REPORT

The two exercises which follow will give you practice in summarizing factual material in a brief and clear paragraph. The material is presented graphically. You are to study the graphs and write out the significant facts which they present. You must support convincingly whatever conclusions you draw.

To insure clear organization, make a brief outline of your paragraph before you write. Fashion a generalization and write a topic sentence expressing it. You will find it advisable to write two drafts of your paragraphs. In the first you will be primarily concerned with getting the supporting facts down on paper; in the second you will be concerned with matters of style. This kind of writing must be especially clear and concise.

**EXERCISE 3.** Study the graph 1 on page 453. It shows clearly the rise and fall of unemployment between the years 1965 and 1978. In a one-paragraph report (150 words) tell what trends the graph illustrates for unemployment for the years 1965–1969, 1970–1975, and 1975–1978.

Do not begin by saying "The graph shows. . . ." Begin with a generalization about employment trends, and then support the generalization by the facts shown in the graph.

[1] From *Men and Atoms* by William A. Laurence. Copyright 1946, © 1959 by William Laurence. Reprinted by permission of Simon and Schuster, a division of Gulf & Western Corporation, and Curtis Brown Ltd.

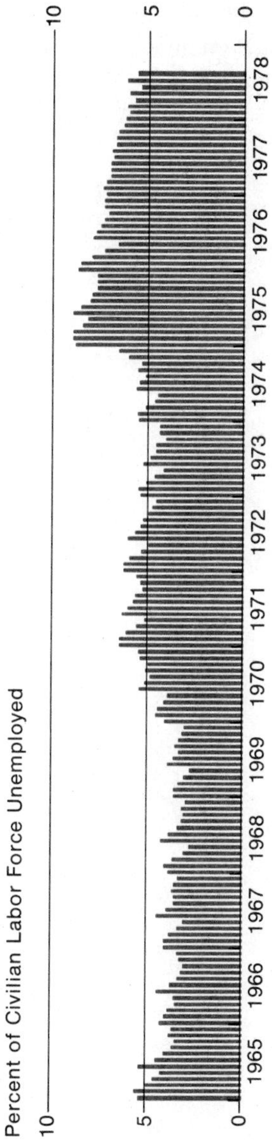


GRAPH 1

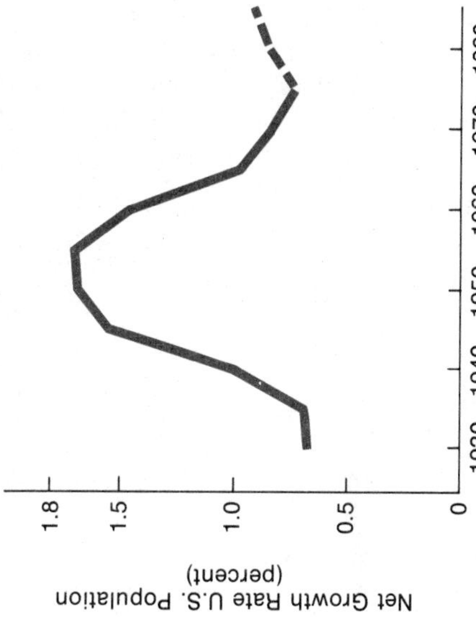


GRAPH 2

[1] From *Economics: Principles and Policy* by William J. Baumol and Alan S. Blinder. Copyright © 1979 by Harcourt Brace Jovanovich, Inc. Reprinted by permission of the publisher.

**EXERCISE 4.** Graph 2 on page 453 indicates some significant facts about population trends in the United States. These facts have enormous economic and political significance for your generation. In a one-paragraph report state the facts and your interpretation of them.

Chapter 26

# The Research Paper

## Research Techniques, The Formal Composition

A research paper is an extensive, formal composition giving information gleaned from reading in a number of sources. The purpose of research is to discover the facts about a subject. The research paper itself is a summary of the facts discovered.

Although many research papers are purely informational, some attempt to draw a conclusion from the facts they reveal. Typical of the purely informational kind would be a paper on medieval cathedrals or American folk music or rocketry. Typical of the paper that attempts to reach a conclusion would be a paper on a controversial subject, or one that seeks the answer to a question. For example: Should capital punishment be abolished? How will the world's population be fed? Have our federal spending policies been sound? Whether your purpose is merely to state the facts or to go a step further and draw a conclusion from the facts, your procedure is the same; in both instances, you must find out what the facts are.

Like any extensive undertaking requiring sustained concentration over a period of several weeks, the preparation of a research paper requires self-discipline. If you have good study habits, can stick to a schedule, and are not one who lets everything go until the last minute, you will find the job relatively easy; you may even enjoy it! If, on the contrary, you have not learned how to study efficiently and if you are a procrastinator, you may find the work frustrating. It is more than likely that the preparation of a research paper will do more to sharpen your study techniques and strengthen your self-discipline than any other single assignment of the year.

Plan to devote to your research paper enough time to insure that your work will be thorough and unhurried. Research work is careful work. Do not be satisfied with a paper that will merely "get by." Take pride in the amount of information you can give in approximately 2,000 words (or whatever length your teacher specifies); take pride in the accuracy of your work and in the neatness of its appearance.

Approach your subject with an open mind, especially if the subject is controversial. A research paper is the result of an attempt to find out the truth. Personal opinion and prejudice are completely out of place. You do not even use the pronoun *I*. Your paper can be completely impersonal.

The preparation of a research paper provides a valuable review of the following skills: using the library and reference tools, note taking, organizing and outlining, paragraphing, footnoting, compiling and writing a bibliography, writing correct, clear sentences. Before beginning work, study Chapters 32 and 33, which deal with the library and reference books.

From the experience of thousands of students, a standard method of preparing a research paper and a standard form for the paper have been developed. This method and this form are described on the following pages, which you should read through rapidly before starting work on your paper in order to get some idea of the nature and the proportions of the job ahead; then begin work, following this seven-step method:

**THE SEVEN STEPS IN WRITING A RESEARCH PAPER**

1. Selecting and limiting the subject
2. Preparing a working bibliography—a list of available sources
3. Preparing a preliminary outline
4. Reading and taking notes
5. Assembling notes and writing the final outline
6. Writing the first draft
7. Writing the revised final draft with footnotes and the bibliography

► **NOTE** The steps to be followed in writing a research paper are essentially the same as those for the whole composition (pages 354–71). The main difference is that in writing the research paper you must give more thought to research and the acknowledgment of sources.

## FINDING THE RIGHT SUBJECT

**26a. Select a subject which is interesting to you and suitable for research in the libraries at your disposal.**

Since you are to do a large amount of reading, you owe it to yourself to choose a subject you really want to know more about. In a small way, you are to become an authority on this subject; choose a topic which will hold your interest.

### Availability of Source Material

Other considerations are involved in the selection of a subject. The subject must lend itself to research in several sources, and the sources must be available in the libraries you use. Your autobiography would not be a suitable subject for a research paper because you could not look up material on it. It is not a research subject. Even the life of a famous person in whom you are interested would be of doubtful value for research because a complete life has probably already been published in one book, and you would tend to rely too much on just this one source. The best kind of subject is one on which information can be found in many different sources.

No matter how interesting to you a subject may be or how suitable for research, it will not be usable unless you can get the source material. If you find that your library does not have enough information on your chosen subject, you will have to choose another subject. Of course, the library is not the only source of material available to you. You may find that some excellent books on your subject are not in your school or public library but are available in inexpensive paperback editions. Government publications are also inexpensive. Students sometimes get information from personal interviews or correspondence with authorities on the subject. For example, if you were writing a history of your community, you could arrange to interview one of the older residents. If you were writing on conservation, you could interview a local conservation officer or write to the State Commissioner.

## Typical Areas for Research

The following lists suggest general areas in which high school research papers may be successfully written. The lists are intended to give you an idea of the kind of subject matter that is suitable for research. To be used, most of these subjects would have to be considerably limited.

**SOCIAL HISTORY** Superstition in primitive societies; the way of life in ancient Greece; medieval arms and armor; amusements in the Middle Ages; American colonial life; family life in the Victorian period in England; child labor in the nineteenth century; the 1890's; the Great Depression; the Prohibition era; the 1980 United States census and its importance; American fashions in the 1980's; immigrants to America in the 1980's; the growth of spectator sports in the United States; changing societies in modern Africa; native American social customs.

**POLITICAL OR MILITARY HISTORY** Early invaders of England; the Crusades; the French Revolution; the pioneer in American history; the Monroe Doctrine in American history; early history of the Republican party; the Lincoln–Douglas debates; Pan-Americanism; the League of Nations; the United Nations; the European Common Market; socialism; communism; third parties in America; the Electoral College; the birth of an African nation; the SALT treaties

**LITERARY HISTORY** Shakespearean playhouses; satire in eighteenth-century literature; Puritanism; the frontier in literature; transcendentalism; Brook Farm; romanticism and realism; existentialist drama; World War II novels; modern experimental poets; censorship; movies—yesterday and today; science fiction in the 1980's; contemporary themes in women's literature

**MODERN PROBLEMS** Juvenile delinquency; food supply; conservation of natural resources; urban renewal; nuclear proliferation; robots in industry; foreign relations and human rights; capital punishment; crime in the suburbs; Social Security; health care for the poor; health care for the aged; equal opportunity for minorities; equal opportunity for the handicapped; the United States' image abroad; the worldwide energy crisis; OPEC; aid to developing nations; inflation

**SCIENCE** Medieval medicine; history of anesthesia; advances in surgery; progress in the fight against cancer; diet and health; exercise and health; prolonging life; physical therapy; nuclear energy; solar energy; the uses of the laser; microcomputers; digital recordings; the space shuttle; exploring distant planets; plate tectonics; recent archaeological discoveries; controlling the weather

**ART** Gothic architecture; the Pre-Raphaelite painters; abstract art; modern sculpture; modern architecture; composing music with the help of computers; salsa; music and art in advertising

## Limiting the Subject

It should be obvious that your subject must be sufficiently limited to enable you to treat it adequately within the scope of your paper. Your paper will be a better piece of work if you go deeply into a narrow subject rather than treat a broad one superficially. The following examples show how a subject may be limited.

Education
Federal aid to education
Federal aid to nonpublic schools
Should federal aid be given to nonpublic schools?

Parapsychology
Extrasensory perception
Clairvoyance
Scientific studies of clairvoyance

## RESEARCH

### 26b. Use library tools to look up available sources of information. Prepare a working bibliography on cards.

When you have selected a subject for your research paper, limited it, and had it approved by your teacher, you are ready to look over the field. You begin by equipping yourself with a package of 3 × 5-inch cards.

### The Working Bibliography

With index cards in hand, you go to the card catalogue, the *Readers' Guide,* the vertical file, and appropriate reference books, and compile a list of all books and articles in the library which promise to be useful to you. Record each book or article on a card—one source to a card. For reasons which will be clear later you must write on the card *complete* information about the source. For books, this information can be obtained from the card catalogue; for magazines, it can be obtained from the *Readers' Guide.* For other sources (pamphlets, newspapers), you must get the information from the source itself.

BOOKS

1. Call number in upper left-hand corner
2. Author or editor, last name first for alphabetizing later. (Indicate editor by placing *ed.* after the name.) If a book has two or more authors, only the name of the first author is given last name first. The names of the others are given first name first.

3. Title, underlined (volume, if necessary). Pamphlets only: series and number, if any, in parentheses
4. Place of publication
5. Publisher
6. Year of publication (or date for some pamphlets)

MAGAZINE, NEWSPAPER, AND ENCYCLOPEDIA ARTICLES

1. Author (unless article is unsigned)
2. Title of article, enclosed in quotation marks
3. Name of magazine, newspaper, or encyclopedia, underlined
4. For magazines: volume and page numbers as in *Readers' Guide*. For newspapers: page number. For encyclopedias: volume and page numbers
5. For magazines and newspapers: date. For encyclopedias: place of publication, publisher, year of publication

While the card catalogue will give you, for a book, all the information you need for your working bibliography card, it will not tell you much about the contents of the book. One way to examine quickly a number of possibly useful books is to go to the shelf in the library where, according to its call number, a book on your subject will be found. Since nonfiction books are classified by subject, you will also find on this and neighboring shelves most of the books the library has on your subject. A glance at the table of contents and the index in these books will tell you how useful the books will probably be.

If you were writing on Shakespeare's Globe Theater, for example, and you found listed in the table of contents a chapter on the Globe or a chapter on Elizabethan theaters, including the Globe, you would list the book in your working bibliography. Even if the table of contents does not reveal information on your subject, such information may still be in the book. Look in the index and judge the usefulness of the book by the number of pages devoted to your subject. A listing like "Globe Theater, 250–275," for instance, would certainly suggest that the book would be worth including in your working bibliography.

At the conclusion of Step 2, you will have a stack of cards—a working bibliography—representing the sources

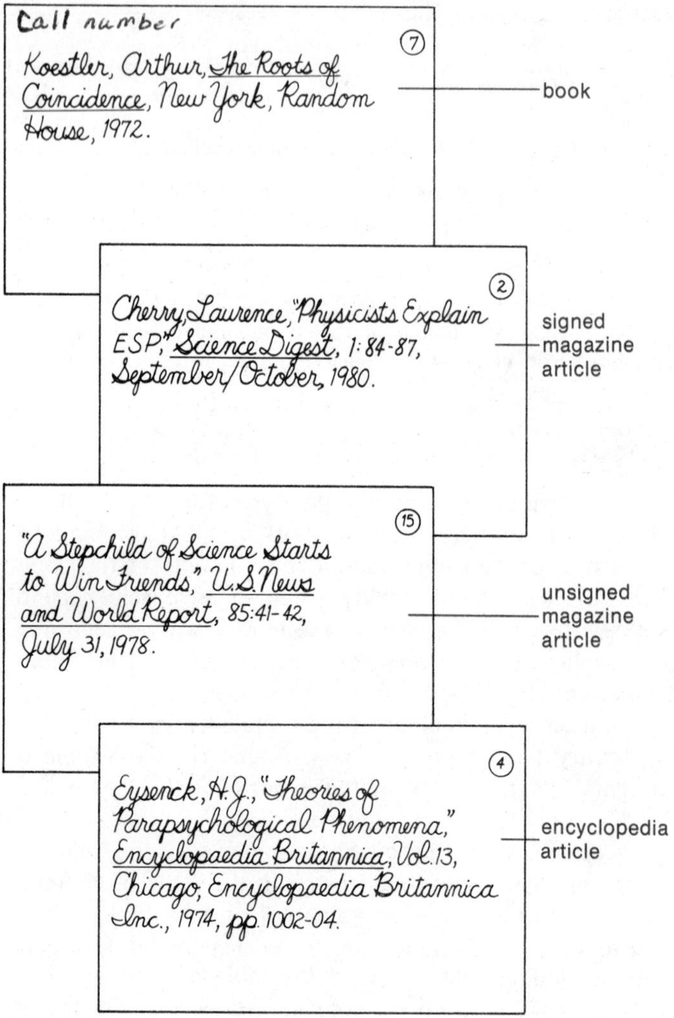


**Cards in a Working Bibliography**

you plan to read. *Number the cards clearly in the upper right-hand corner.* The card numbers will be used later when you are taking notes, saving you the task of identifying the source in detail for each note you take.

## The Preliminary Outline

### 26c. Prepare a preliminary outline to guide you in note-taking.

Before you can take notes in an organized way, you must have some idea of the topics on which you will need information. To formulate a list of such topics, begin your reading with a few general articles which give an overall survey. If your subject is treated in an encyclopedia, the article there will be excellent for this purpose. Another way to approach such an outline is to try to anticipate the important questions your paper will have to answer. Jot down what seem to be the major divisions of the subject.

The preliminary outline is not an outline of your paper as it will finally be organized. It is, rather, a guide for use in your reading and note-taking. It represents the topics which, at this point in your work, you think you will want to cover. As your reading suggests new topics, insert them in the outline; as you find some topics cannot or should not be treated in your paper, remove them from the outline.

SCIENTIFIC STUDIES OF CLAIRVOYANCE

I. Definition of clairvoyance
II. Scientific approach to clairvoyance
III. Experiments with clairvoyance
    A. Studies by J. B. Rhine
    B. Studies by Rhine's followers
IV. Objections to experiments
V. Future of clairvoyance studies

## The Note Card

### 26d. Read and take notes on cards.

With a package of ~~4 × 6~~ 9x8 index cards, your working bibliography, and your preliminary outline, you are ready to turn to the major task of reading your sources. The note cards should be larger than the working bibliography cards for two reasons: first, the cards will accommodate more notes; and second, you will be able to distinguish them from your smaller bibliography cards. Since you will be working with both kinds of cards at the same time, it is important that you be able to distinguish them at a glance.

***At the top of a note card write the topic the notes deal with.*** The notes you take will fall under one or another of the topics in your preliminary outline. As you can see in the outline above, these topics will be very broad at the start of your reading. As you read further, you will find new topics or subtopics for your outline, and these, in turn, will be used as headings for your note cards. At the top of each note card write the outline topic with which the notes deal. This topic is called a *slug*. (See the sample note card below.)

***Use a separate card for each source.*** In the upper right-hand corner of the card, write the number of the source as you have indicated it on the card in the working bibliography. You will find that several sources will provide information on the same topic; hence you will have several cards with the same heading, each card representing a different source.

Always write the page number either before or after every idea you jot down. You will need this number for the footnotes in your paper.

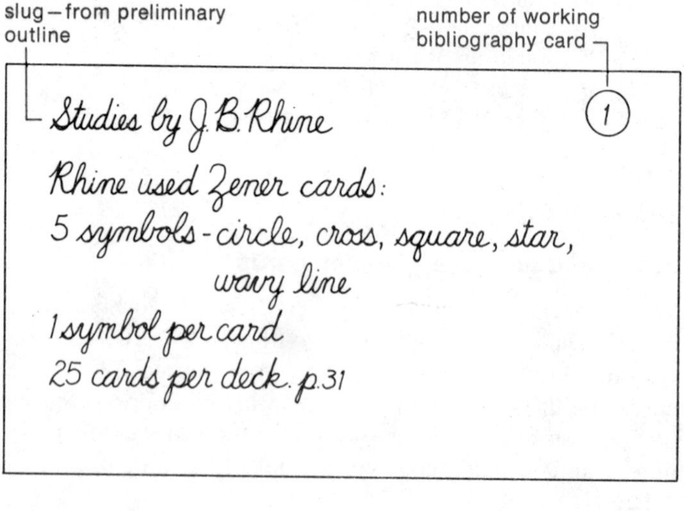

***Take notes in your own words.*** The best way to acquire skill in note-taking is to start right in taking down information which you think may be usable. As you progress, you will develop judgment as to what you are likely to use. You will develop judgment, too, as to when you should copy word-for-word from your sources and when you should write the information in your own words. In general, you should do very little copying. A research paper should not consist of a mere list of quotations. You are expected to gather facts and ideas from your sources, digest them thoroughly, and write them in your own words. Quote verbatim only when the words of the source are especially important and especially well chosen.

Develop your own shorthand to save time in note-taking. Common ways of getting ideas down quickly are (1) abbreviate as many words as you can without affecting the clarity of your notes, (2) use symbols for short words—& for *and,* for example, (3) write phrases rather than whole sentences. Always write legibly, for if you do not use your notes for a week or two, you will find that penmanship that was perfectly clear to you when you wrote it has become surprisingly baffling.

***Acknowledge your sources.*** No fault is more common and more serious in high school research papers than the use of quotations without acknowledgment of the sources. Teachers are quick to detect quotations that are not enclosed in quotation marks, and they are impatient with papers written not in your own style, but in the style of your sources. The danger here is that, in spite of good intentions, you may be led into copying the style of your sources without realizing that you are doing so. A "derived" style results from copying word for word everything you place on your note cards. The cure for this fault is always to take notes in your own words. Don't copy unless you intend to quote exactly. The use of the words of others as though they were your own is called *plagiarism,* and it is a serious offense. When you do copy, be sure to copy accurately, without abbreviating, and to enclose the copied material in quotation marks.

***Learn to judge the reliability of your sources.*** You should develop a critical attitude toward your sources, especially when you are writing on a controversial subject. Ask yourself these questions: What do I know about the author? Is the author recognized as an authority? Is there any ulterior motive behind the writing? When was this book or article published? If you are working on a current topic which forces you to rely largely on newspaper stories and magazine articles, which vary widely in quality, you should be especially alert to distinguish the truly dependable from the mere potboilers or the biased.

## The Final Outline

### 26e. Assemble your notes and write the final outline.

When you are satisfied that you have enough notes to insure adequate treatment of your subject, your next job is arranging the notes in the order in which you will use them. Since each note card has a slug, your first step is to assemble in one pile all cards bearing the same slug. This simple mechanical task actually carries you a long way toward the organization of your paper. You will have before you a number of piles of information, each pile treating one division of your subject as represented in the preliminary outline. You now have to consider such matters as the order of topics in your paper and the possibility of various subdivisions of the slug topics.

You will find it necessary at this point to prepare your final outline in rough form. This final outline will take shape readily as you skim through your note cards. Before writing the outline, review the techniques of outlining described on pages 359–61. Follow your teacher's instructions as to whether you are to write a sentence or a topic outline. You will find that many of your slugs will become subtopics, while others may become major topics. Some may be discarded. You should probably have no more than six major topics. Using too many of these Roman numeral divisions suggests poor organization.

# WRITING THE RESEARCH PAPER

## 26f. Write the first draft.

The writing of your paper, toward which all your work has been directed, should go smoothly if you have followed directions. With your outline to guide you and your notes on each topic conveniently arranged, you are ready to write.

### The First Draft

The first draft of your paper is a step in the whole process of creating a research paper; it is for your use only, not for anyone else to read. Do not worry unduly over details of style and mechanics. Do not delay your work trying to think of a clever introduction. You may start anywhere you wish; the important thing is to make a start, to put your ideas on paper, even though eventually you may revise extensively.

As you incorporate in your paper the ideas on your note cards, be careful to indicate the source on your manuscript *whether you are giving the ideas in your own words or quoting the words of the source.* You do not need to give the source of information which is a matter of general knowledge. For instance, it would not be necessary to give a source for the fact that the abbreviation ESP stands for "extrasensory perception" or that Duke University, where ESP research takes place, is in North Carolina. In writing this rough draft it will be sufficient to indicate the source of material by simply writing down after each idea the source number from the working bibliography card, and the page number. You need not bother to copy long quotations from your note cards into this rough draft; merely jot down enough information to help you find the quotation later when writing your final draft. Copying long quotations from your note cards will exhaust you and, of course, is unnecessary. Write rapidly.

## The Final Draft

### 26g. Write the revised final draft with footnotes and a bibliography.

If you have planned your work so that you are not pressed for time, the writing of the final draft should be relatively easy. Having solved troublesome problems of organization and expression, you are now concerned primarily with form. The following matters must be carefully handled.

*Style*

Having studied the chapters on usage and sentence structure in this textbook, you should apply what you have learned to your own sentences. Revise them just as you revised the exercise sentences in the chapters on correct, clear, and smooth sentences. Also check your mechanics: capital letters, punctuation, and spelling.

*Appearance*

Allow ample margins on both sides and at the top and bottom of each page. If you are typing your paper, type it double spaced and on only one side of the paper. Long quotations (five or more lines) should be typed single spaced and set off by wider margins than the rest of the paper.

*Transitions*

Use transitional devices to keep the thought moving smoothly from paragraph to paragraph and from one major division to another. See pages 365–68. An occasional transitional paragraph will help the reader to follow your organization. See pages 369–70.

Do not divide your paper into chapters. Chapter divisions in a 2,000-word paper tend to break it up and destroy its unity. The paper becomes five or six research papers instead of one.

*Footnotes*

To avoid constantly interrupting your paper with the citation of sources, you use footnotes. To the right and above the final word in a quotation or an idea taken from one of your sources, you will write a number. Write number 1 for the first source, 2 for the second, etc. These numbers refer the reader to their counterparts at the foot of the page, where the source is given. Follow your teacher's instructions as to whether you are to renumber footnotes with each page or number them consecutively straight through the paper. A footnote is followed by a period. Each page must be so planned that there will be enough space at the bottom to accommodate the footnotes for sources cited on that page.[1]

You must give footnotes for all ideas taken from sources even though the ideas are, as they should be, written in your own words. Do not make the mistake of using footnotes only for quoted matter.

*Footnote Form*

The footnote for a book or a pamphlet gives the name of the author (first name first), the title of the book (underlined), and the page number. Underlining in a manuscript is the equivalent of italicizing in print. Since you will have a complete bibliography (list of sources used) at the end of your paper, you need not give facts about publication in the footnotes.

The footnote for a magazine or newspaper article gives the author (unless the article is anonymous), the title of the article (in quotation marks), the name of the magazine or newspaper (underlined), the volume (for magazines only), date, and page number. All items in a footnote are separated by commas. The following are sample footnotes taken from a variety of research papers.

[1] The footnotes may instead appear together at the conclusion of the paper, on a separate page immediately preceding the bibliography. In this style, footnotes are called *endnotes*. Follow the style specified by your teacher.

[1]Doris Lessing, A Small Personal Voice: Essays, Reviews, Interviews, p. 47. [book by one author]

[2]Cleanth Brooks and Robert Penn Warren, Modern Rhetoric, Fourth Edition, p. 179. [book by two authors]

[3]Virginia Woolf, The Diary of Virginia Woolf, Vol. 2, p. 115. [one volume in multivolume work]

[4]Robert Coles, Eskimos, Chicanos, Indians, Vol. 4 of Children of Crisis, p. 12. [one volume in multivolume work with different titles]

[5]Virgil, Aeneid, trans. Allen Mandelbaum, p. 92. [translation]

[6]Maxwell Perkins, "Thomas Wolfe" in Thomas Wolfe: A Collection of Critical Essays, ed. Louis Rubin, Jr. p. 80. [one article in a collection of articles by different authors]

[7]S. A. Halper and R. W. Fontaine, "Birth of Zimbabwe," New Leader, 62, December, 1979, p. 5. [article in magazine]

[8]"Antibodies," Sciquest, 53, January, 1980, p. 25. [unsigned magazine article]

[9]"Navahos Upheld on Land Claims," New York Times, June 30, 1970, p. 20. [unsigned newspaper article]

[10]Hildegarde Thompson, "Education of the Indians," Encyclopedia Americana, 1965 Edition, Vol. 15, p. 60. [signed encyclopedia article]

[11]Interview with Florence Wright, Principal, Elgin High School, September 4, 1980. [interview]

[12]"Music in the Age of Shakespeare," PBS, September 17, 1980. [television interview]

## *Ibid.*

When two or more consecutive footnotes refer to the same source, writers use the Latin abbreviation *Ibid.* for footnotes after the first. *Ibid.* represents the Latin word *ibidem,* meaning "in the same place." The use of *Ibid.* is efficient because it makes it unnecessary to repeat the same author, title, etc., for a footnote which has been given immediately before. Suppose, for example, that you have referred three times in succession to the same source; you have, however, referred to a different page each time. Your footnotes will appear as follows:

> [1]Doris Lessing, A Small Personal Voice: Essays, Reviews, Interviews, p. 47.
> [2]Ibid., p. 52.
> [3]Ibid., p. 60.

Notice that *Ibid.* must be underlined and followed by a period. If the reference is to the same page as that referred to by the preceding footnote, the comma and page number are not necessary.

When a footnote reference to another source comes between two references to the same source, you do not use *Ibid.* to avoid repetition because *Ibid.* always refers to the footnote immediately preceding. Instead of *Ibid.*, you use the last name of the author of the work already footnoted earlier in your paper and follow it with the page number. If the source is anonymous, you repeat the title only and follow it with the page number. For instance, had the footnotes listed above been separated by a footnote referring to a different source, the result would appear as follows:

> [1]Doris Lessing, A Small Personal Voice: Essays, Reviews, Interviews, p. 47.
> [2]Paul Schlueter, The Novels of Doris Lessing, p. 3.
> [3]Lessing, p. 52.
> [4]Ibid., p. 60.

Of course, if you have referred previously in your paper to more than one work by the same author, you must, in addition to giving the author's last name, give the title followed by the page number.

> [3]Lessing, A Small Personal Voice: Essays, Reviews, Interviews, p. 52.

### *Footnoting "Second-hand" Quotations*

The question may arise as to how to footnote a quotation or an idea which the author you were reading had, in turn, taken from another author. The following sample shows how to give credit to both sources.

[1]Frederic McDowell, "Recent British Fiction: Some Established Writers," Contemporary Literature, 2, Summer, 1970, quoted in Schlueter, Paul, The Novels of Doris Lessing, p. 75-76.

### *The Explanatory Footnote*

The principal use of footnotes is to cite sources. Occasionally, however, they are used for comments by the author or for additional, interesting information which is not of first importance and which, if included in the paper itself, would constitute a confusing interruption. This kind of footnote, while sometimes useful, should be sparingly used.

**EXERCISE 1.** Each of the following items contains complete information for a footnote. Write the footnotes in correct form in the order in which they are given.

1. A magazine article entitled Psychic Research. Written by W. Stuckey. Appeared in Science Digest for October, 1976, vol. 80, page 32.
2. The same article as above, same page.
3. Book by Carl Murchison entitled The Case for and Against Psychical Belief, page 60.
4. Article in Science News for November 18, 1978, volume 114, page 343. No author. Title of article: No EM Detected in ESP Study.
5. Same as item 3 above, page 74.
6. An article by Rex Stanford in Psychic Exploration: A Challenge for Science, ed. by John White, pages 133–34. Title of article: Clairvoyance.

### *The Bibliography*

In order to give the reader complete information as to your sources, you must attach to your paper a bibliography, a list of the sources you used. This final bibliography differs from the working bibliography, which you prepared first, in that it includes only the books and articles you actually used. The bibliography is an important part of a research paper. Prepare it with great care. Be sure that it is complete, accurate, and consistent in form. Observe the following details of form:

1. Items are arranged in alphabetical order according to the last names of authors. Hence, unlike footnotes, which are not arranged alphabetically, bibliographical items give the author's last name first. This applies only to the first author if the book has more than one author. The names of a second and third author are written first name first. It is not necessary to number the items. Anonymous items are placed alphabetically by the first word of their titles, unless the first word is *the, an,* or *a,* in which case the second word determines the alphabetical position. Alphabetizing can be done easily by arranging the working-bibliography cards in alphabetical order.

2. If the bibliography includes more than one work by the same author, it is not necessary to repeat the author's name with each. Use a long dash in place of the name in all listings after the first.

3. When an item occupies more than one line, the second line should be indented so that the names of authors will stand out on the page.

4. Commas are used between all parts of a bibliographical item. A period at the end is optional.

5. Type your bibliography entries single space, but leave a double space between entries.

Study the following examples of bibliographic entries. The items were selected to illustrate the correct form for various kinds of listings. The entries are not in alphabetical order because most of them are drawn from different bibliographies. For a complete bibliography in alphabetical order, see pages 485–86.

Lessing, Doris, A Small Personal Voice: Essays, Reviews, Interviews, New York, Knopf, 1974.
[book with one author]

——, Stories, New York, Knopf, 1978. [book by the author of the previous entry]

Brooks, Cleanth and Robert Penn Warren, Modern Rhetoric, Fourth Edition, New York, Harcourt Brace Jovanovich, 1979. [book with two authors]

Woolf, Virginia, The Diary of Virginia Woolf, Vol. 2, New York, Harcourt Brace Jovanovich, 1978. [one volume in multivolume work]

Coles, Robert, Eskimos, Chicanos, Indians, Vol. 4 of Children of Crisis, Boston, Atlantic Monthly Press and Little Brown, 1978. [one volume in multivolume work with different titles]

Virgil, Aeneid, trans. Allen Mandelbaum, Berkeley, University of California Press, 1971. [translation]

Perkins, Maxwell, "Thomas Wolfe" in Thomas Wolfe: A Collection of Critical Essays, ed. Louis Rubin, Jr., Englewood Cliffs, Prentice Hall, 1973. [one article in a collection of articles by different authors]

Halper, S. A. and R. W. Fontaine, "Birth of Zimbabwe," New Leader, 62: 5-7, December, 1979. [magazine article]

"Antibodies," Sciquest, 53:25, December, 1980. [unsigned magazine article]

"Navahos Upheld on Land Claims," New York Times, June 30, 1970, p. 20. [unsigned newspaper article]

Thompson, Hildegarde, "Education of the Indians," Encyclopedia Americana, Vol. 15, New York, Americana Corporation, 1965. [signed encyclopedia article]

Wright, Florence, Principal, Elgin High School, interview, September 4, 1980. [interview]

"Music in the Age of Shakespeare," PBS, September 17, 1980. [television program]

**EXERCISE 2.** Each of the items in this exercise gives complete bibliographical information about a book or an article. Revise the items so that they are correct in form and in the proper order and arrangement for a bibliography.

1. Magazine article by Charles Tart entitled Psychic Lessons. Article in Human Behavior, volume 7, February 1978, page 51.

2. Magazine article, unsigned, entitled Science, the Media, and the Paranormal. It appeared in Science News, volume 112, August 20, 1977, page 118.
3. A book, The ESP Experience: A Psychiatric Validation by Jan Ehrenwald, published by Basic Books, New York, 1978.
4. A book by Naomi Hintze and J. Gaither Pratt entitled The Psychic Realm: What Can You Believe? published by Harper and Row, New York, 1975.

### *Charts, Diagrams, and Illustrations*

Charts and diagrams may be included in your paper where they are of real value. Always give with each the source from which you copied it. Illustrations cut out from sources may be looked upon with suspicion as attempts at padding, or as evidence of vandalism in the treatment of source material.

## CHECKLIST FOR RESEARCH PAPER

1. ***Cover.*** Give your research paper a stiff cover, bearing the title of the paper. Make it attractive.
2. ***Title page.*** The title page should give the title, your name, the name of the course, and the date. The first two will occupy the center of the page; the last two will be placed at the bottom, centered or at the right.
3. ***Final outline.*** This, in its revised form, is the outline you followed in writing your paper.
4. ***The paper itself.*** All material taken from your sources must be footnoted unless it is common knowledge. Check footnotes for accuracy and correct form.
5. ***The bibliography.*** Check for accuracy and correct form, including punctuation.

## ABBREVIATIONS USED IN SOURCE MATERIALS

**c or ©** *copyright;* used before a copyright date (c1935) to indicate when copyright was obtained. (The circled *c* is the international copyright symbol.)

**c., ca.** *about* (from the Latin *circa, circum*); used with dates—"*c.*" or "*ca.*" 1732 means "about" 1732.

**cf.** *compare* (from the Latin *confer*); "*cf.* the Atlantic Treaty" means "compare with the Atlantic Treaty."

**ed.** *editor, edited, edition*

**e.g.** *for example* (from the Latin *exempli gratia*)

***et al.*** *and others* (from the Latin *et alii*): also *and elsewhere* (from the Latin *et alibi*)

**f., ff.** *following page, pages;* "p. 25f." means "page 25 and the following page"; "p. 25ff." means "page 25 and the following pages."

***ibid.*** *in the same place* (from the Latin *ibidem*)

***id.*** *the same* (from the Latin *idem*)

***i.e.*** *that is* (from the Latin *id est*)

**l., ll.** *line, lines*

***loc. cit.*** *in the place cited* (from the Latin *loco citato*). This is used to refer again to a page or paragraph already cited in a previous footnote.

**ms., mss.** *manuscript, manuscripts*

***N.B.*** *note well* (from the Latin *nota bene*)

**n.d.** *no date;* publication date not given in book

***op. cit.*** *in the work cited* (from the Latin *opere citato*). This is used to refer to the *title* of a work previously cited.

**p., pp.** *page, pages*

***q.v.*** *which see, whom see* (from the Latin *quod vide*)

***sic*** *thus* (from the Latin); when a writer quotes a passage containing an error (wrong date, misspelling, etc.) and wishes to make clear that the original was copied accurately, [*sic*] is inserted beside the error.

***vide*** *see* (from the Latin)

CLAIRVOYANCE: INVESTIGATING A "SIXTH SENSE"

Michael Davis

[The following are sample pages from a high school student's research paper. Use them as a model in preparing your own paper.]

Psychology

Ms. Baker

April 8

## OUTLINE

I. Definition of clairvoyance
   A. Comparison with other types of extrasensory perception
   B. Examples of clairvoyant ability

II. Scientific approach to clairvoyance
   A. Need for valid evidence
   B. Need for extensive evidence

III. Experiments with clairvoyance
   A. Studies by J. B. Rhine
      1. Method of card-guessing
      2. Interpretation of data
      3. Favorable results of studies
   B. Studies by Rhine's followers
      1. Use of separate rooms
      2. Use of categories for subjects
      3. Use of random-number generator
      4. Use of remote locations
      5. Use of hypnosis

IV. Objections to experiments
   A. Possibility of fraud
   B. Lower scores from tighter controls
   C. Variable results from repeated efforts

V. Future of clairvoyance studies

Clairvoyance: Investigating a "Sixth Sense"

Have you ever had a hunch or made a wild guess which proved correct? Your sudden insight, some scientists claim, may have been a form of extrasensory perception called clairvoyance. According to the findings of some research that this paper will examine, the clairvoyant mind can "see" objects or events without the use of the senses. [statement of purpose]

Clairvoyance, say scientists, is one of four categories of extrasensory perception: (1) telepathy--reading the thoughts of another, (2) precognition--sensing future events, (3) psychokinesis--affecting objects by thinking about them, and (4) clairvoyance--perceiving objects or events that are impossible to perceive by the normal senses.[1] The category of clairvoyance includes such acts as guessing the unknown contents of a sealed envelope or describing the location of a lost child.

In one account of supposed clairvoyant ability, a young woman was driving home at night with her husband. They came to a roadblock, where a police officer told them about an accident a half-mile ahead. After they had made a detour and had continued driving for a few minutes, the woman began to tremble and cry. She told her husband that her sister was lying dead on the road they had just left! Forty-five minutes after they had arrived home, the phone rang. A local doctor called to tell the woman that her sister was dead. She had been killed instantly in a car

---

[1]Laurence Cherry, "Physicists Explain ESP," Science Digest, 1, September/October, 1980, p. 84.

accident, the same accident the couple had heard of an hour before.[2]

Was the woman's sudden knowledge an example of clairvoyance? Montague Ullman, a leading researcher of extrasensory perception, warns, "Scientifically, of course, such cases don't prove anything, because they can be called coincidence, unconscious self-deception, or deliberate hoaxes."[3] [direct quotation]

Ullman and other investigators insist that clairvoyance exists; yet in order to prove their claim, they recognize the need for reliable data. Accordingly, clairvoyance has been the focus of experiments based upon careful controls. Following the scientific method, scientists gather evidence from these experiments and use the evidence as the basis of proof.

During experiments, subjects may guess at hidden cards, locations, numbers, or a variety of other items. If enough of these guesses are correct, then scientists can be certain that more than mere luck is at work. However, as an added precaution against lucky guesses, scientists require extensive evidence, drawn from thousands of experiments. They may even repeat a particular experiment with one person hundreds of times before accepting its results.

This experimental research is relatively new. It began during the 1930's, when Dr. J. B. Rhine conducted experiments

---

[2]Louisa E. Rhine, "Psychological Processes in ESP Experiences: Part 1, Waking Experiences," Journal of Parapsychology, 26, June, 1962, pp. 95-96.

[3]Montague Ullman, "Can You Communicate with Others in Your Dreams?" in The Psychic Scene, ed. John White, p. 17.

for all four categories of extrasensory perception.[4] In his earliest attempts, he found clairvoyance the most suitable for research. He stated:

> Clairvoyance experiments are the easiest of all to conduct. ...Not only is it easier to control against the more common experimental errors, but it is also easier to eliminate any alternative hypothesis that might be applied to the data.[5] [extended quotation]

Enthusiastically, Dr. Rhine performed hundreds of experiments, testing the clairvoyant powers of ordinary people. His method was surprisingly simple; in fact, with patience and accurate record-keeping, anyone can imitate it.

Rhine used a pack of cards called Zener cards, which contained five symbols: a star, a circle, a cross, a square, and a wavy line. One of these symbols was printed on each card. In the deck there were twenty-five cards, five of each symbol.

After shuffling the cards, the experimenter placed the deck on a table. Behind an opaque screen which concealed the experimenter and the cards at all times, the subject either wrote down or called out in order the symbols in the deck.[6] By pure chance, one would expect five correct guesses out of twenty-five in a single run-through of cards. Any consistent scoring higher than five correct guesses, Rhine concluded, was evidence of clairvoyance.[7]

---

[4] Norma Bowles and Fran Hynes, PsiSearch, p. 27.

[5] J. B. Rhine and J. G. Pratt, Parapsychology: Frontier Science of the Mind, p. 53.

[6] Bowles and Hynes, p. 31.

[7] Daniel Cohen, ESP: The Search Beyond the Senses, p. 76.

*[The paper goes on to discuss Dr. Rhine's interpretation of his data, the favorable results of his studies, and the experiments of Dr. Rhine's followers. The following paragraphs make a transition from this section of the paper to the objections against clairvoyance experiments.]*



The most recent development in clairvoyance research involves hypnosis. In tests, two groups of people perform Dr. Rhine's card-guessing experiment. One group is awake, while the other group is under hypnosis. The group under hypnosis has scored a significantly greater number of correct guesses than the other group. Although researchers find these results encouraging, they are performing further tests to measure the effect of hypnosis.[15]

As research into clairvoyance continues, however, opponents refuse to accept the findings. Critics cite three overwhelming problems in the studies: first, that researchers do not guard enough against fraud; second, that they get lower scores as they improve their testing methods; and third, that they cannot get the same results every time they repeat an experiment.

[transitional paragraph]

*[The next section of the paper discusses each objection. The paper concludes as follows on the next page.]*

---

[15]Carl L. Sargent, "Hypnosis as a Psi-Conducive State," Journal of Parapsychology, 42, December, 1978, pp. 264-67.

Defenders, meanwhile, claim that scientific standards, such as requiring similar results each time an experiment is repeated, need not apply to research into the human mind. Arthur Koestler writes, "[The standard of] repeatability [is] valid in the physical sciences, but less so in the frontiers of medicine and even less in those branches of psychology which involve unconscious processes . . . ."[21]

Although Koestler and others claim that clairvoyance "is a hard reality,"[22] many disagree, and the future of clairvoyance studies is uncertain. Philip H. Abelson, editor of the authoritative journal Science, sums up the controversy when he states that "these extraordinary claims require extraordinary evidence. Findings that question the basic laws of nature must be subjected to rigorous scientific scrutiny."[23] Many like Mr. Abelson believe that statistical evidence charting an unknown power at work gives insufficient reason for abandoning assumptions about the way the mind works. Remarks D. O. Hebb, professor of psychology at McGill University, "I do not accept ESP for a moment, because it does not make sense."[24]

Skeptics like Mr. Abelson and Dr. Hebb may be unfairly dismissing the positive results of clairvoyance studies, which, compared with many other fields, are still very new. By demand-

---

[21]Arthur Koestler, The Roots of Coincidence, p. 29.

[22]Ibid., p. 23.

[23]"A Stepchild of Science Starts to Win Friends," U.S. News and World Report, 85, July 31, 1978, pp. 41-42.

[24]D. O. Hebb, "The Role of Neurological Ideas in Psychology," Journal of Personality, 20, September, 1951, p. 45.

ing "extraordinary evidence" that extrasensory perception exists, they may be overlooking much of the evidence this paper has discussed.

On the other hand, scientists who claim that clairvoyance is a fact of life are exaggerating, for many questions remain. H. J. Eysenck, professor at the University of London, calmly states the crux of the issue:

> . . . very intriguing demonstrations have been given that suggest the existence of something outside the purview of physics and psychology, but no one has yet succeeded in bringing this something under adequate experimental control.[25]

Until scientists can present a reasonable explanation for clairvoyance, Mr. Eysenck contends, "it would be unwise to claim any more."[26]

---

[25] H. J. Eysenck, "Theories of Parapsychological Phenomena," Encyclopaedia Britannica, 1974 ed., Vol. 13, p. 1004.

[26] Ibid.

# BIBLIOGRAPHY


Bowles, Norma and Fran Hynes, PsiSearch, New York, Harper & Row, 1978.

Cherry, Laurence, "Physicists Explain ESP," Science Digest, 1:84-87, September/October, 1980.

Cohen, Daniel, ESP: The Search Beyond the Senses, New York, Harcourt Brace Jovanovich, 1973.

Eysenck, H. J., "Theories of Parapsychological Phenomena," Encyclopaedia Britannica, Vol. 13, Chicago, Encyclopaedia Britannica, Inc., 1974.

Hansel, C. E. M., ESP: A Scientific Evaluation, New York, Charles Scribner's Sons, 1966.

Hebb, D. O., "The Role of Neurological Ideas in Psychology," Journal of Personality, 20:40-52, September, 1951.

Koestler, Arthur, The Roots of Coincidence, New York, Random House, 1972.

Puthoff, Harold E. and Russell Targ, "Remote Viewing: New Research Frontier," in The Signet Handbook of Parapsychology, ed. Martin Ebon, New York, New American Library, 1978.

Rhine, J. B., The Reach of the Mind, New York, Peter Smith, 1972.

______ et al., Extrasensory Perception After Sixty Years: A Critical Appraisal of the Research in Extrasensory Perception, Boston, Bruce Humphries, 1966.

______ and J. G. Pratt, Parapsychology: Frontier Science of the Mind, Springfield, Illinois, Charles C. Thomas, 1972.

Rhine, Louisa E., Hidden Channels of the Mind, New York, William Sloane Associates, 1961.

______, "Psychological Processes in ESP Experiences: Part 1, Waking Experiences," Journal of Parapsychology, 26:88-111, June, 1962.

Sargent, Carl L., "Hypnosis as a Psi-Conducive State," Journal of Parapsychology, 42:264-67, December, 1978.

"A Stepchild of Science Starts to Win Friends," U. S. News and World Report, 85:41-42, July 31, 1978.

Taylor, John, Science and the Supernatural, New York, E. P. Dutton, 1980.

Ullman, Montague, "Can You Communicate with Others in Your Dreams?" in The Psychic Scene, ed. John White, New York, New American Library, 1974.

Chapter 27

# The Business Letter

## Standard Practice in Business Correspondence

### FORMAL COMMUNICATIONS

When you wrote your first friendly letters in elementary school, you probably made use of the advice given you by your teachers. You tried to make your letters to your friends interesting, and you probably followed the instructions given you about details of form, standard practice regarding neatness, use of stationery, and so on. At this stage, however, there is little point in attempting to lay down rules for what is obviously a gesture of friendship, and essentially personal.

Formal business correspondence, however, has little to do with friendship, and is fairly conventionalized. The reasons for this are plain. It is not the purpose of a business letter to say hello and express concern for your correspondent's continued health and happiness. It is often the case that the mail brings business letters to a desk rather than a person and, as often as not, to a person who has replaced the person originally addressed. A business letter is always intended merely to convey the required amount of information as efficiently and clearly as possible, with as little delay and distraction as possible. Today there are many designed preprinted forms in use, precisely to avoid unnecessary detail and inaccuracy.

There is, therefore, a great deal of value in learning the conventional methods of business correspondence, since all of us need from time to time to engage in it. It is also helpful for those who will be engaged in secretarial duties to master the general conventions involved. This can save valuable time later, for example, and allow you to devote more attention to the other aspects of secretarial work, which become more and more complicated by the year.

This chapter considers the general form of a business letter and its different parts, concludes with a discussion of the different kinds of business letters, and supplies models of them.

## Form in Business Letters

Whether formal or informal in tone, the business letter is always written according to a standard form.

### 27a. Observe standard practice in the writing of business letters.

#### (1) Use appropriate stationery.

Standard business stationery comes in two sizes, either of which is subject to slight variations by individual firms. The larger of the standard sizes is $8\frac{1}{2} \times 11$ inches; the smaller is $5\frac{1}{2} \times 8\frac{1}{2}$ inches, used for very short letters.

#### (2) Make an attractive "letter picture."

The "letter picture" is the overall picture a letter presents to the reader at first glance. People in business insist that their letters make a favorable impression. To make the picture attractive, you must center the letter on the page, leaving equal margins on the sides and at the top and bottom—the margins are the frame around your "picture"; space the letter parts carefully; follow consistently a standard pattern of indention and punctuation; and make the letter absolutely free of strikeovers, erasures and other marks which mar its appearance.

FertiGlobe, Inc.
655 Third Avenue
New York, New York 10017
Telephone: 212-599-0338

Telex: WUI-668628 FER GLO
Telex: WUD-645475 FER GLO
TWX: 7105815213
Cable: FERTIGLOBE

FertiGlobe

March 22, 1980

Mr. Paul Bruno
Sales Manager
Balzac Bag Company
555 South Monroe Street
Baltimore, Maryland 21224

Dear Mr. Bruno:

Thank you for your letter of February 4, 1980, and enclosed pricelist. We would like to order the following items:

| | | |
|---|---|---|
| 1. | 5,000 woven polypropylene bags with polyethylene liners, 22½" x 35", delivered to Tampa latest April 20th, and marked "DAP - M/V Catherine P", @ $0.55 per bag: | $2,750.00 |
| 2. | 4,500 woven polypropylene bags with polyethylene liners, 23" x 39", delivered to Tampa latest May 10th, and marked "URA - M/V Miss Calvi", @ $0.62 per bag: | $2,790.00 |
| | Total: | $5,540.00 |

All bags should be delivered to the warehouses of Manley Stevedoring, Inc., 710 Kings Road, Port Authority Complex, Tampa, Florida.

As always, it is a pleasure to do business with Balzac.

Yours truly,

*Jeanette Hudson*

Jeanette Hudson
Operations

CABLE ADDRESS "ELHEIR"

(212) [illegible]-4400

JOHN M. RIEHLE & CO.
INCORPORATED
*Complete Insurance Service*
SINCE 18[illegible]
757 THIRD AVENUE
NEW YORK, N.Y. 10017

February 4, 1981

Miss Margaret Scanlon
651 East 78th Street
New York, NY 10089

Re: Homeowner's Insurance
Plymouth Insurance Company
Policy No. 88HO4297721

Dear Miss Scanlon:

Enclosed please find your Homeowner's Insurance policy No. 88HO4297721 issued by Plymouth Insurance Company for the period March 1, 1981 through March 1, 1982.

The annual premium, as indicated on the enclosed invoice, is $150.00.

Please return payment at your earliest convenience. A self-addressed envelope has been provided. If you have any questions, please do not hesitate to call.

Sincerely,

*M. A. Roberts*

M. A. Roberts
Account Executive

MAR/dg

Enclosures

MT. KISCO, NEW YORK • NEW CANAAN, CONNECTICUT • MASSAPEQUA, NEW YORK

On page 489 two business letters have been reproduced in miniature. Note that the text of the letters is carefully centered on the stationery. The side margins are equal, and the top and bottom margins are equal. Two popular styles are represented: the block style without paragraph indentions and the block style with paragraph indentions. Note also that the text of the letters is placed attractively in relation to the letterhead. In general, the overall appearance is important here, not exact measurement.

**(3) Follow standard practice in continuing a letter on a second page.**

A business letter should be as short as possible without being abrupt or confusing. However, if a letter must be continued on a second page, use a second sheet; never write on the reverse side of a page. If a letter is to run over, you must anticipate the fact and arrange the material so that at least three lines can be written on the second page. Never complete a letter on one page and put just the leave-taking and signature on the next.

The first line on the second page of a business letter on $8\frac{1}{2} \times 11$-inch stationery should be about two inches from the top. The page number should be centered about four lines above the first line of writing.

## Parts of a Business Letter

**(4) Make the six parts of the letter conform to standard practice.**

While you are studying the following descriptions of the six parts of a business letter, refer frequently to the model letter on page 494.

### The Heading

Business firms use stationery bearing their letterhead, so that the writer does not need to supply anything but the date in the heading. When you write a business letter without a letterhead, you must give a complete heading: street address on the first line; city, state, and zip code on the second line with a comma between the city and state; date on the third line with a comma between the day and the year. If you use abbreviations, use them consistently.

## The Inside Address

In the inside address you must give the name of the person or the firm (or both) to whom you are writing and the address with the usual comma between city and state. Business firms file copies of the letters they write. Since the copies are filed under the name of the person or firm to which they are written, it is necessary to have an inside address on each letter. Ordinarily the inside address is placed four typewriter spaces below the heading or date and flush with the left-hand margin. If you wish to include the title or position of the person to whom you are writing, you may give the person's title after the name on the same line or, if the title is too long, on a separate line below.

EXAMPLES Ms. Lucinda Green, Principal
Westbend High School
Westbend, Iowa 50597

Mr. James Moore
Plant Supervisor
King Products, Inc.
1420 Havens Blvd.
Chicago, Illinois 60636

## The Salutation

The salutation, or greeting, is placed below the inside address (two spaces on the typewriter) and flush with the left-hand margin. It is always followed by a colon. The salutation varies with the nature of the inside address as follows:

**1.** If you are writing to a firm or a group, not to any specific individual, the traditional salutation is *Gentlemen:* (*Ladies:* or, rarely, *Mesdames:* for an exclusively female concern).

EXAMPLES Soundcraft Corporation
10 East 52nd Street
New York, New York 10022

Gentlemen:

When you use the traditional salutation (*Gentlemen:*), it is understood that the group you are writing to may be composed of both men and women. (You may instead use an impersonal salutation such as *Editors:* or *Personnel Department:* if you are addressing a specific group within a firm.)

**2.** If you are writing to a specific person but know only the official position and not the name, the traditional salutation is *Dear Sir:* (or *Dear Madam:*).

EXAMPLE Personnel Manager
Airborne Instruments Laboratories, Inc.
160 Old Country Road
Mineola, New York 11501

Dear Sir:
*or*
Dear Madam:

(You may instead use an impersonal salutation such as *Personnel Manager:* if you wish.)

**3.** If you are writing to a man and have included his name in the inside address, the proper salutation is *Dear Mr.——:*

EXAMPLES Mr. D. H. White, Manager
Eastern Oil Company
60 East 42nd Street
New York, New York 10017

Dear Mr. White:

When writing to a woman who does not identify herself as *Miss* or *Mrs.,* you may use *Ms.* in the salutation. You may also address a man or woman by using both first and last names in the salutation.

EXAMPLES Dear Ms. Alvarez:
Dear Jane Alvarez:
Dear Philip Wright:

In an address always use a title with a person's name. Permissible abbreviations are *Mr., Messrs., Mrs., Ms., Dr., Hon.* Others should be spelled out: *Professor* Grace Tamura, *Reverend* Thomas E. Haupt, etc.

**4.** High government officials may be addressed as follows:

THE PRESIDENT

The President
The White House
Washington, D.C. 20015

Dear Mr. President:

SENATOR

The Honorable Nancy Landon Kassebaum
United States Senate
Washington, D.C. 20015

Dear Senator Kassebaum:

REPRESENTATIVE

The Honorable Charles Rangel
House of Representatives
Washington, D.C. 20015

Dear Mr. Rangel:

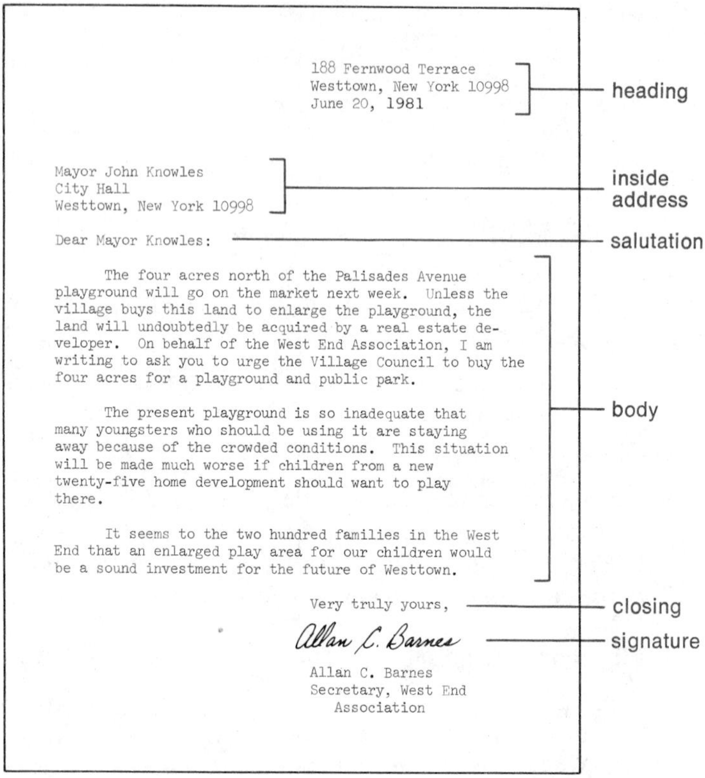

188 Fernwood Terrace
Westtown, New York 10998
June 20, 1981

Mayor John Knowles
City Hall
Westtown, New York 10998

Dear Mayor Knowles:

The four acres north of the Palisades Avenue playground will go on the market next week. Unless the village buys this land to enlarge the playground, the land will undoubtedly be acquired by a real estate developer. On behalf of the West End Association, I am writing to ask you to urge the Village Council to buy the four acres for a playground and public park.

The present playground is so inadequate that many youngsters who should be using it are staying away because of the crowded conditions. This situation will be made much worse if children from a new twenty-five home development should want to play there.

It seems to the two hundred families in the West End that an enlarged play area for our children would be a sound investment for the future of Westtown.

Very truly yours,

Allan C. Barnes

Allan C. Barnes
Secretary, West End
Association



**Model Business Letter**

GOVERNOR

The Honorable William O'Neill
Governor of Connecticut
Hartford, Connecticut 06115

Dear Governor O'Neill:

MAYOR

The Honorable Edward Koch
Mayor, New York City
New York, New York 10007

Dear Mayor Koch:

## The Body

There is no room for chat and discursiveness in business letters, but there is room for courtesy. Use simple language, clearly and directly phrased. The following trite phrasings, once in common use, are no longer considered good form: *Yours of the 5th inst. received and contents noted; beg to advise* (*remain, state, etc.*); *please be advised that; thanking you in advance.* For discussion of the contents of particular kinds of letters, see the treatment of the order letter, the letter of inquiry, the adjustment letter, and the letter of application on pages 498–503.

The first line of the body of a business letter is placed two typewriter spaces below the salutation. It may be indented either the usual five spaces of a typed manuscript or as far as the length of the salutation. In the pure block style, indentions are not used. Subsequent paragraph indentions will be uniform with the first one (see the letter pictures on page 489).

## The Closing

In a business letter the standard form for the closing, or leave-taking, is *Yours truly* or *Very truly yours.* Less formal but frequently used is *Sincerely yours.* In writing to high government and church officials, you may use *Respectfully yours,* but avoid this in ordinary correspondence.

The closing is begun just to the right of the middle of the page and is followed by a comma. Note that only the first word is capitalized.

## The Signature

The signature is written in ink immediately below the closing and flush with it. Directly below the signature the writer's name should be typewritten, a wise custom in the light of the illegibility of many signatures. This typewritten repetition of the writer's name may be accompanied by his or her official position.

EXAMPLE Very truly yours,
*James MacPherson*
James MacPherson
President

When writing to a stranger, a single woman may choose to place *(Miss)* in parentheses before her signature. A married woman may write her full married name in parentheses beneath her signature.

EXAMPLES Very truly yours,
*(Miss) Virginia Shaw*

Very truly yours,
*Elizabeth Blake*
*(Mrs. Henry G. Blake)*

In general, however, do not put a title before a signature.

EXAMPLES Very truly yours,
*Thomas Strong* [not *Mr.* Thomas Strong]

Very truly yours,
*Sally Blake* [not *Ms.* Sally Blake]

**(5) Make the envelope conform to standard practice.**

The addresses on the envelope should conform with the addresses used in the letter itself. Your own name and address are placed in the upper left-hand corner of the envelope. The name and address of the person to whom the letter is going are placed just below the middle of the envelope and slightly to the right, so that they occupy the lower right-hand quarter in a neat fashion with generous margins. Avoid crowding the edge of the envelope; if a particularly long line is necessary, as occasionally happens when you are writing the name of a lengthy organization, use a second line and indent it a few spaces from the left margin of the address. The name of the person you are addressing should be preceded by the proper title (*Mr., Dr., Ms.*, etc.). Always include the initials or the first name: *Ms.*

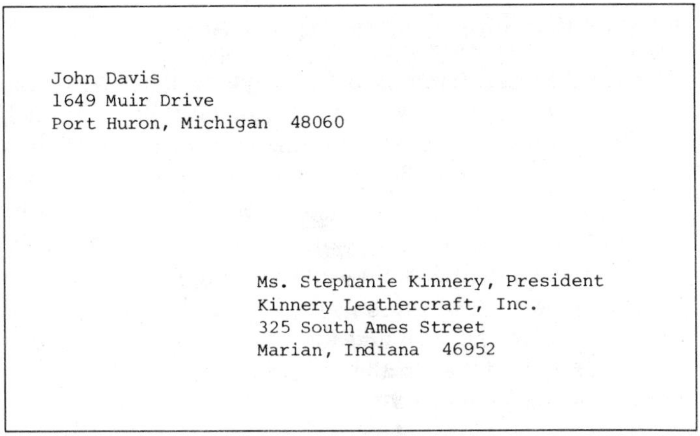
John Davis
1649 Muir Drive
Port Huron, Michigan  48060
Ms. Stephanie Kinnery, President
Kinnery Leathercraft, Inc.
325 South Ames Street
Marian, Indiana  46952

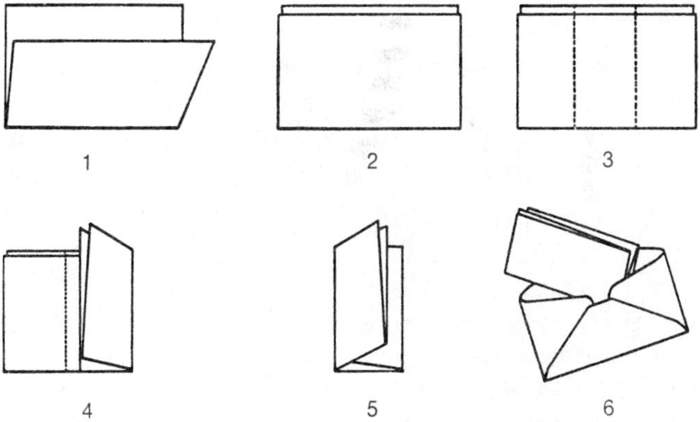
1
2
3
4
5
6

*Georgia V. Bryce,* or *Ms. G. V. Bryce,* not *Georgia Bryce* or *Ms. Bryce.* Your own name in the return address need not be accompanied by a title. The stamp is always placed in the upper right-hand corner.

**(6) Fold the letter according to standard practice.**

The folding of a letter is determined by the size of the envelope. If a letter written on standard $8\frac{1}{2} \times 11$-inch stationery is to be placed in a long envelope, the letter is folded twice: up from the bottom about a third of the way, then down from the top so that when unfolded it will be right side up. If it is to be placed in a small envelope, the letter should be folded up from the bottom to within a quarter of an inch of the top; then the right side is folded over a third of the way and the left side folded over that fold. Insert the letter in the envelope with the fold at the bottom of the envelope.

## Kinds of Business Letters

**27b. Learn the requirements for various types of business letters.**

A busy office will turn out in a single day a dozen different kinds of business letters, but the average person, in carrying on private affairs, will have occasion to write only three or four types of letters. You will almost certainly have need at some time for the four types described on the following pages: the order letter, the letter of inquiry or request, the letter of adjustment or complaint, and the letter of application.

### The Order Letter

The order letter is being outmoded by the prevalent use of printed order forms. However, there are occasions when it is necessary to write out an order in letter form. Study the model order letter on page 499 and the four requirements which follow.

21 Cranberry Road
Harmon, Illinois 61042
November 20, 1981

New Fashions Shop
187 Main Street
Castleton, Illinois 61426

Gentlemen:

Please send me the following articles advertised in the Journal for November 19.

| | |
|---|---|
| 1 Heatherland tweed skirt, size 24 waist | $29.95 |
| 2 prs. Slimfit slacks, gray, size 10 long @ $22.95 | 45.90 |
| 1 Hemper blouse, white, Style A, size 34 | 19.95 |
| Total | $95.80 |

I am enclosing a money order for $97.35 to cover the order and parcel post charges of $1.55.

Very truly yours,

*Judy Abbott*

Judy Abbott

**"Model Order Letter"**

**1.** Set the list of ordered items off from the rest of the letter in a column arrangement.

**2.** Include all appropriate details as to quantity, catalogue number, size, style, and price. The symbol @ means *each* or *apiece:* 3 boxes @ $1.25 = $3.75. It is usually wise to specify from what advertisement (magazine or paper and date) you have taken the information for your order.

**3.** Indicate how you are paying for the order: by check, money order, C.O.D., or charge account. Include money for postage if you think it is expected.

**4.** If you wish the merchandise sent to an address different from the address in the heading, give the address in the letter.

A simple kind of order letter is that in which only one type of thing is ordered—theater tickets, a book, or a pen, for example. Such a letter is illustrated below.

```
                                  345 Graham Road
                                  Bellmore, New York  11710
                                  October 10, 1981


Box Office
Majestic Theater
245 West Forty-fourth Street
New York, New York  10018

Gentlemen:

      Please send me three tickets @ $16.00 for the
matinee performance of Hamlet on Saturday, November
28.  Acceptable alternate dates are November 21,
December 5.

      I am enclosing a check for $48.00 and a self-
addressed, stamped envelope.

                                        Very truly yours,

                                        Albert Armstrong

                                        Albert Armstrong
```

## The Letter of Inquiry or Request

Occasionally you may require information which can be obtained only by writing a letter. Writing for material to use in a research paper, for facts about travel in a certain locality, for a college catalogue, etc., are common situations of this kind. Be brief and direct. Make clear immediately what you wish; then stop.

## Model Letter of Inquiry

348 Converse Avenue
Masonville, Iowa 50654
February 15, 1981

Bonar Plastics Corporation
1835 Washington Street
St. Louis, Missouri 63110

Gentlemen:

For my Chemistry II class I am writing a research paper on the manufacture of plastics. I should appreciate very much your sending me any literature on this subject that you may have for free distribution.

Very truly yours,

*Mary Robinson*

Mary Robinson

118 Mountain Road
Kingston, New York 12401
April 17, 1981

School of Agriculture
Cornell University
Ithaca, New York 14850

Gentlemen:

Please send me your general catalogue and any additional literature you have on admission to the School of Agriculture and courses in dairy farming.

Very truly yours,

*Walter Owen*

Walter Owen

## Model Letter of Request

## The Letter of Adjustment or Complaint

When you write to a business firm to ask for correction of an error or to register a complaint of any kind, you will get better results if you restrain your annoyance and adopt a courteous tone. This is true also when you write to a government official complaining about poor service being given by municipal, state, or government employees.

14 Oklahoma Avenue
Tulsa, Oklahoma 74106
May 24, 1981

Guerber's Sports Company
85 Court Street
Maysville, Oklahoma 73057

Gentlemen:

On May 14 I sent you an order which included two white T-shirts, No. 86, size 36, @ $3.00. When the shipment arrived, I found that you had neglected to send the shirts. I assume that this was merely an oversight in packing and will appreciate your sending me the shirts.

Very truly yours,

*Ralph Gray*

Ralph Gray

**Model Adjustment Letter**

## The Letter of Application

The letter of application is most important for you who are about to leave high school. Whether you seek a permanent job or temporary employment for the summer months,

321 Fifth Street
Riverside, Missouri 64168
March 2, 1981

Personnel Director
Central Insurance Company
41 Bank Street
Riverside, Missouri 64168

Dear Sir:

Please consider me an applicant for the secretarial position advertised in Sunday's <u>Herald</u>.

I am eighteen years old and graduated last June from Riverside High School. Since then I have completed a six-months' course in secretarial training at the Clarkson Business Institute. In high school I completed two years of courses in shorthand and typing and worked as a student assistant for two years in the office. At Clarkson I studied office practice, business machines, business English, and bookkeeping.

For the past two summers I was employed as a fill-in stenographer by the Moore Trucking Company, where I did filing and billing as well as regular stenographic work. I feel at home in a business office and enjoy being given extra duties and responsibilities.

The following people have given me permission to use their names as references:

Miss Catherine Greenberg
Head of the Commercial Department
Riverside High School

Mr. Stanley Williams
Moore Trucking Company
Riverside, Missouri 64168

I shall be glad to come for a personal interview at your convenience. My telephone number is 592-3107.

Very truly yours,

Jane Parkman

Jane Parkman

**Model Letter of Application**

you will want to make a favorable impression with your letter. Since the letter will undoubtedly be one of many received by your prospective employer, you must make sure that it is correct in every detail and sufficiently convincing to make the reader consider your application further. It should, if possible, be typewritten.

There are certain clearly definable requirements for a good letter of application.

1. Begin by naming the position for which you are applying. Mention how you learned about it.

2. State all the facts an employer would certainly want to know: your age, education, experience.

3. Indicate, if you can do so naturally, that you are familiar with the requirements of the position and explain why you believe you can meet them.

4. Give references (three, if possible) with addresses. If you have held other jobs, be sure to include among your references one of your former employers. Include also an older person who is acquainted with you and your family. Since you are still in school, a recommendation from a member of the faculty is appropriate. Before giving someone's name as a reference, ask permission.

5. Request an interview at the employer's convenience.

6. Be especially careful with all the details of letter form, neatness, spelling, grammar, etc. You would not wish to lose a good position simply because you were too lazy to look up the spelling of a word or to copy your letter a third or fourth time to ensure its being perfect.

**EXERCISE 1.** ***The letter picture.*** Following the models on pages 489 and 494, lay out on a piece of typewriter paper a perfectly arranged business letter, using neatly drawn lines for the body of the letter. Use your own address and the present date in the heading. Make up an inside address. Be sure the salutation is proper.

**EXERCISE 2.** ***The inside address and salutation.*** The following inside addresses are mixed up. Rewrite them in correct block form. Beneath each, write the proper salutation.

1. Fred Emerson, a professor at Columbia University, West 116th Street, New York City 10027
2. Miami University, Dean of Admissions, Oxford, Ohio 45056
3. 10 East 53rd Street, Harper & Row, New York City 10022
4. Representative from your district in the House of Representatives in Washington, D.C., Robert E. Thomas
5. Personnel Director of the Bradley Company, Cass City, 82–84 South Avenue, Illinois 61016, Carol T. Brooks

**EXERCISE 3.** ***Order letters.***

1. Write a letter to the Board in Control of Intercollegiate Athletics, Yost Field House, Ann Arbor, Michigan 48103, ordering two tickets for the Michigan–Minnesota game on November 7. The tickets cost $6.00 each.

2. Write to any firm you wish, ordering at least three different articles advertised in a magazine or newspaper. Order more than one of some of the articles. Follow the model order letter on page 499.

**EXERCISE 4.** ***Request letter.*** Write a letter to the Dean of Admissions of any college or university stating that you wish to apply for admission at a certain date and requesting an application blank and other necessary forms.

**EXERCISE 5.** ***Adjustment letter.*** Write a letter to a business firm asking why you have received a bill for an order for which you have already paid C.O.D. Give all important details, dates, etc.

**EXERCISE 6.** ***Letters of application.***

1. Using your local newspaper, select a help-wanted advertisement and answer it with a letter of application. Clip the advertisement to your letter when you hand it in.

2. Write to the manager of a summer camp, applying for a position as a counselor on the camp staff during the coming summer.

3. If you are going to work immediately upon graduation from high school, you probably have in mind the kind of position you intend to apply for. Write an imaginary letter of application for such a position.

► NOTE The United States Postal Service recommends the use of two-letter codes for states, the District of Columbia, and Puerto Rico. The service also recommends the use of nine-digit zip codes. When you use these codes, the address on business correspondence should look like this:

EXAMPLE Ms. Ann Washington
405 Vera Park Drive
Orlando, FL 32804–4335

The two-letter code is in capital letters and is never followed by a period. The following is a list of two-letter codes.

Alabama AL
Alaska AK
Arizona AZ
Arkansas AR
California CA
Colorado CO
Connecticut CT
Delaware DE
District of Columbia DC
Florida FL
Georgia GA
Hawaii HI
Idaho ID
Illinois IL
Indiana IN
Iowa IA
Kansas KS
Kentucky KY
Louisiana LA
Maine ME
Maryland MD
Massachusetts MA
Michigan MI
Minnesota MN
Mississippi MS
Missouri MO
Montana MT
Nebraska NE
Nevada NV
New Hampshire NH
New Jersey NJ
New Mexico NM
New York NY
North Carolina NC
North Dakota ND
Ohio OH
Oklahoma OK
Oregon OR
Pennsylvania PA
Puerto Rico PR
Rhode Island RI
South Carolina SC
South Dakota SD
Tennessee TN
Texas TX
Utah UT
Vermont VT
Virginia VA
Washington WA
West Virginia WV
Wisconsin WI
Wyoming WY

# Mechanics

# PART FIVE

Chapter 28

# Manuscript Form

## Standard Practices in Preparing and Revising Compositions

A neat, properly prepared manuscript is the mark of a careful writer. While it is possible that a sloppy, hard-to-read manuscript may show evidence of thorough research and good thinking, it is not very likely. A writer who has gone to the work of doing research and writing a good composition is usually willing to go to the extra pains of making the work presentable to a reader. By following the simple procedures described in this chapter you can make sure that the form of your manuscript is clear and acceptable.

### THE MANUSCRIPT

***Paper and ink.*** Write compositions on standard size ($8 \times 10\frac{1}{2}''$) lined paper. Use black, blue, or blue-black ink. Write on only one side of the paper.

If you type, use standard size ($8\frac{1}{2} \times 11''$) white typewriter paper. Double-space and use only one side of the paper.

***Labeling and numbering pages.*** Follow the school policy concerning labeling and numbering of pages. The common practice is to write your name, the subject (English IV), and the date in that order, one below the other, in the upper right-hand corner of the first page. Number all pages, except the first, with Arabic numerals in the upper right-hand corner. It is a good plan to write your name beneath the page number on each sheet.

***Margins.*** Leave a margin of at least one and a quarter inches at the left and one inch at the right side of the paper. The left-hand margin must be even; the right-hand margin may be slightly uneven. In typewritten manuscripts, place the first line of all pages after the first at least one inch below the top of the paper and leave a one-inch margin at the bottom of all pages.

***The title.*** Place the title of the composition in the center of the first line of a ruled page, and skip a line between the title and the first paragraph. The title of a typewritten composition should be placed about two inches below the top of the page. Composition titles should not be underlined or placed in quotation marks, except in rare instances when the title is itself a quotation.

***Indention.*** Indent the first line of every paragraph the same distance—about one inch in handwritten papers; five spaces in typewritten papers.

Long quoted passages may be made to stand out by indenting the entire passage. In typescript such indented passages are single-spaced and written without quotation marks.

***Neatness.*** Do not mar the appearance of a composition by cross-outs, insertions between lines, and afterthought additions in the margins. If changes must be made in the final copy, make them neatly or rewrite the entire page. Strike-overs and messy erasures mar the neatness of typewritten work.

Never begin any line with a comma, dash, or other punctuation mark, with the exception of opening quotation marks.

## REVISING THE FIRST DRAFT

All compositions should be written at least twice. The first draft of a composition is your own copy and need not conform to the manuscript standards noted above. Mark up this first draft with your revisions and corrections. When you are satisfied that you have made all necessary changes, write your final draft to be handed to your teacher.

Revision is an extremely important step in the composition process. You should look upon each theme, whether written for English or for any other class, as an attempt at perfection. Revision of a first draft should be done in three steps: (1) Evaluate the general organization of the whole composition. (2) Eliminate badly constructed sentences and poorly chosen words. (3) Check the mechanics.

Use the following checklist each time you revise the first draft of a composition.

### CHECKLIST FOR REVISION

***Evaluate:***

Quality of material (effectiveness, relevance, interest, etc.)
General organization (sequence of ideas)
Division into paragraphs (topic sentences)
Transitions (within and between paragraphs)
Variety of sentence structure

***Eliminate:***

Errors in grammatical usage
Sentence fragments and run-on sentences
Awkward sentences
Confusing sentences
Wordy passages
Clichés

***Check:***

Spelling
Punctuation (Don't forget the apostrophe!)
Capital letters
Hyphenated words at the ends of lines

## Abbreviations

**28a. In compositions do not use abbreviations except in certain special instances in which abbreviations are customary.**

NONSTANDARD One cold Mon. A.M. in Feb., as I was crossing a downtown st., a man rushed from a bldg. directly ahead of me and leaped into a car bearing a Cal. license.

STANDARD One cold **Monday morning** in **February,** as I was crossing a downtown **street,** a man rushed from a **building** directly ahead of me and leaped into a car bearing a **California** license.

**(1) The following abbreviations are customary before a name: *Mr., Messrs., Mrs., Ms., Dr., Rev., St.* (Saint). The following are abbreviated after a name: *Jr., Sr.,* and the college degrees *A.B., Ph.D.,* etc. With the exception of the college degrees, these abbreviations are used only with a name.**

NONSTANDARD We called a Dr. for the sr. member of the firm.

STANDARD We called a doctor for John Parsons, Sr.

**(2) The following abbreviations are acceptable when used with numbers: *A.D.* (*A.D.* 485); *B.C.* (271 *B.C.*); *A.M.* (before noon); *P.M.* (after noon). The following are acceptable in all writing: *etc.* (and so forth); *i.e.* (that is); *e.g.* (for example). Abbreviations for government agencies are acceptable: *FBI, NLRB.* Periods are not used with abbreviations of this kind.**

**(3) Do not use the symbol & or + for *and.***

## Numbers

**28b. Do not begin a sentence with a numeral.**

NONSTANDARD 8 students crowded into the car.

STANDARD **Eight** students crowded into the car.

**28c. Numbers of more than two words should be written in numerals.**

EXAMPLES 1,450,280; $125.75; 1981
two dollars; forty cents; thirty-three
Expenditures on roads and highways rose to over a billion dollars.

Be consistent in your use of words and numerals.

NONSTANDARD My brother makes forty dollars a week, but I make only $35.00.

STANDARD My brother makes **forty** dollars a week, but I make only **thirty-five.**

► **NOTE** Rule 28c applies to ordinary writing. In mathematical, scientific, and statistical writing, most numbers are written as numerals, not spelled out.

Never spell out the year or spell out page numbers following the word *page*.

### 28d. Hyphenate all compound numbers from *twenty-one* to *ninety-nine* and fractions used as adjectives.

EXAMPLES She spent **twenty-three** days in the hospital.
a **two-thirds** majority, but **two thirds** of the people

### 28e. Write out numbers like *second, twenty-fifth,* etc., instead of writing them as numerals with letter endings: *2nd, 25th,* etc.

EXAMPLE I was standing **tenth** (not 10th) in the **third** (not 3rd) line.

The number of the day when given with the month is not used with the letter endings *st, nd, rd, th.* The name of a street, however, may be written with these endings.

EXAMPLES On June **25** we sail for Europe, and on August **21** we return.
133 West **34th** Street (also 34 Street or Thirty-fourth Street)

## Dividing Words at the End of a Line

Division of words at the end of a line in order to maintain an even margin should be avoided but is sometimes necessary. A hyphen is used between parts of words divided in this way. Words should be divided between syllables, but accurate division of words into syllables is a technical matter. When you are in doubt, consult the dictionary. A few simple rules may help you to decide where to place the hyphen.

**28f. Divide a word at the end of a line between pronounceable parts only. One-syllable words should never be divided.**

NONSTANDARD stay-ed [one-syllable word]
STANDARD **stayed**

NONSTANDARD underst-and [parts not pronounceable]
STANDARD **under-stand**

**28g. A word having double consonants should be divided between the consonants.**

EXAMPLES hap-py
recom-mend

Words like *bill-ing* and *toss-ing* are exceptions. See rule 28i regarding prefixes and suffixes.

**28h. Do not divide a word so that a single letter stands alone. Try to avoid dividing a word so that only two letters are carried over to the next line.**

NONSTANDARD e-normous, priva-cy
STANDARD enor-mous, pri-vacy

**28i. Words having prefixes and suffixes should usually be divided between the prefix and the root of the word or between the root of the word and the suffix.**

EXAMPLES pre-heat, happi-ness, jump-ing, call-ing

# CORRECTING COMPOSITIONS

The marking symbols and other corrections your teacher writes on your composition will teach you little unless you do something about them. What you are to do about each marking symbol, or marked error, is explained in the list of symbols below.

All errors requiring rewriting of one or more sentences should be numbered (①, ②, etc.) in the margin where the symbol occurs and then rewritten, marked with the same number, on a separate "correction sheet" or, if there is space, on the final page of your composition. As the instructions below indicate, errors which do not require rewriting a whole sentence are to be corrected on the composition at the place where the error appears.

Study the marked and corrected passages on pages 516–17.

## *Correction Symbols with Instructions*

***ms*** *error in manuscript form or neatness*
Rewrite the sentence or paragraph neatly on correction sheet.

***cap*** *error in use of capital letter*
Cross out the incorrect letter and write the correct form above it.

***p*** *error in punctuation*
Insert punctuation, remove it, or change it as required.

***sp*** *error in spelling*
Cross out the word; write the correct spelling above it; write the word five times correctly spelled on your correction sheet.

***frag*** *sentence fragment*
Correct it by changing punctuation and capital or by rewriting on correction sheet.

***rs*** *run-on sentence*
Correct it by inserting the necessary end mark and capital.

**ss** *error in sentence structure*
Rewrite the sentence on your correction sheet.

**k** *awkward sentence or passage*
Rewrite the sentence or passage on your correction sheet.

**nc** *not clear*
Rewrite the sentence or sentences on your correction sheet.

**ref** *unclear reference of pronoun*
Cross out the error and write the correction above it.

**gr** *error in grammar*
Cross out the error and write the correct form above it.

**w** *error in word choice*
Cross out the word and write a better one above it.

**¶** *Begin a new paragraph here.*
This will not be corrected but should be carefully noted.

**t** *error in tense*
Cross out the error and write the correct form above it.

**∧** *You have omitted something.*
Insert omitted words above the line.

## COMPOSITION PASSAGE MARKED BY THE TEACHER

p     A repertory company, with it's com-
gr   mand of a number of plays, are quite
sp   different from a cast which preforms
      only one play for a run and then breaks
cap up. The usual company on broadway con-
      sists of actors brought together to pro-
w ref duce one thing. If it is a success, the
      actors repeat the same roles night after
p     night. A repertory company, on the other
r-s  hand produces a number of plays, it may

produce three or four different plays
frag in the course of one week. Each actor
thus playing a different role each night.
k At any time a repertory company is able
to revive an old play with as many as
twenty-five plays in its repertoire.
nc The parts are all ready and the scenery,
properties, and costumes.

PASSAGE CORRECTED BY THE STUDENT

p A repertory company, with it's com-
gr mand of a number of plays, ~~are~~ is quite
sp different from a cast which ~~preforms~~ performs
only one play for a run and then breaks
cap up. The usual company on ~~b~~Broadway con-
sists of actors brought together to pro-
w ref duce one ~~thing~~ play. If ~~it~~ the play is a success, the
actors repeat the same roles night after
p night. A repertory company, on the other
rs hand, produces a number of plays. ~~i~~It may
produce three or four different plays
in the course of one week, ~~E~~each actor
frag thus playing a different role each night.
At any time a repertory company is able
(1) k to revive an old play with as many as
twenty-five plays in its repertoire.
The parts are all ready and the scenery,
(2) nc properties, and costumes.

CORRECTION SHEET ATTACHED TO COMPOSITION

perform, perform, perform; perform, perform

① A repertory company, with as many as twenty-five plays in its repertoire, is able to revive an old play at any time.

② The actors are familiar with their parts; and the scenery, properties, and costumes are ready in the company's storeroom.

Chapter 29

# Capitalization

## Standard Uses of Capital Letters

Capital letters serve many purposes. They indicate the beginnings of sentences, an important aid to the reader; they distinguish names, titles, etc., from the rest of the sentence (*The Black River divides Port Huron*); they show respect (*the worship of God*). On the other hand, many uses of capital letters are merely conventions; i.e., they are usages customarily observed by educated people for no other reason than that they are customary. Readers expect capital letters to be used according to rules established by custom; in other words, according to *standard usage*. Writers should follow the conventional usage expected of them just as they follow the conventions of correct spelling, grammatical usage, and punctuation.

In the use of capital letters, as in all matters pertaining to language usage, variations and inconsistencies are common. In standard usage, for instance, the names of the seasons are not capitalized, but some newspapers do capitalize them. Newspapers may also adopt what they call the "down style" of capitalization in which words like *street, high school, club* are not capitalized as they are in standard usage when used with a particular name.

| STANDARD USAGE | "DOWN STYLE" |
| --- | --- |
| Twenty-first Street | Twenty-first street |
| Bellmore High School | Bellmore high school |
| Hunting and Fishing Club | Hunting and Fishing club |

The usage described in this book is standard ("up style")

usage, which is followed in books and magazines. Review the rules and do the exercises so that you will be able to check accurately the capitalization in your own writing.

## 29a. Capitalize the first word in any sentence.

If failure to use a capital letter at the beginning of a sentence is one of your faults, you should review Chapter 11, because the error is almost invariably due to failure to recognize the end of one sentence and the beginning of the next.

**(1) Capitalize the first word of a formal statement following a colon.**

EXAMPLE The following statement was released to the press: For reasons of national security, details of the defense program cannot be given to the general public at this time.

**(2) Capitalize the first word of a resolution following the word *Resolved.***

EXAMPLE Resolved: That American aid to developing nations should be increased.

**(3) Capitalize the first word of a direct quotation.**

EXAMPLE Ms. Jackson said, "Your sister is her own worst enemy."

Do not capitalize the first word of a quoted sentence fragment.

EXAMPLE I agree with Ms. Jackson's remark that my sister is "her own worst enemy."

**(4) Capitalize the first word of a statement or question inserted in a sentence without quotation marks.**

EXAMPLE Our problem is, How can we get somebody to help us?

► **NOTE** Traditionally, poets capitalize the first word in a line of poetry. This use of capitals, while by no means as common today as it once was, is still often found.

## 29b. Capitalize the pronoun *I* and the interjection *O*.

You will probably have little use for the interjection *O*, which is used only in such rare expressions as "O happy day, come soon!" The common interjection *oh* ("Oh, what a beautiful morning!") is capitalized only when it appears at the beginning of a sentence. *Oh* is usually followed by a mark of punctuation, but *O* is rarely followed by punctuation.

EXAMPLES Help us, **O** mightiest of all!
He said he was sorry, **oh,** so sorry!

## 29c. Capitalize proper nouns and proper adjectives.

A proper noun is the name of a particular person, place, thing, or idea. The opposite of a proper noun is a common noun, which is not capitalized.

| PROPER NOUNS | COMMON NOUNS |
|---|---|
| Denise Tseng | woman |
| Canada | country |
| Mohawk River | river |

► **NOTE** Words which name a kind or a type (*spaniel, sloop, sonnet*) are not capitalized. Names given to individuals within the type are proper nouns and are capitalized (Fido, ***W**ave-**R**ider,* "Sonnet XXI").

A proper adjective is an adjective formed from a proper noun.

| PROPER NOUNS | PROPER ADJECTIVES |
|---|---|
| England | English |
| Europe | European |

Study the following classification of proper nouns.

### (1) Capitalize the names of persons.

Before writing names beginning with *Mc* or *Mac* (meaning "son of"), find out whether or not the person spells the name with two capitals. Custom varies: **McDonald, MacNutt, Macdonald, Macmillan, Macbeth,** etc. Names beginning with *O'* (meaning "of the family of") usually contain two capitals: **O'Reilly, O'Neill.**

The abbreviations *Sr.* and *Jr.* following a name are capitalized: Henry Morgan, Sr.; Martin Luther King, Jr.

**(2) Capitalize geographical names.**

*Cities, townships, counties, states, countries, continents* Garden City, Hempstead Township, Dade County, New Mexico, United States of America, North America

*Islands, peninsulas, straits, beaches* Sea Island, Iberian Peninsula, Strait of Gibraltar, Silver Beach

*Bodies of water* Arrowhead Lake, Lake Superior, Red River, Atlantic Ocean, Baltic Sea, Cedar Pond, Peconic Bay

*Mountains* Rocky Mountains, Pikes Peak

*Streets* Washington Avenue, Whitehall Boulevard, Dover Parkway, Pennsylvania Turnpike, Forty-second Street [In a hyphenated street number, the second word begins with a small letter.]

*Parks, forests, canyons, dams* Yosemite National Park, Belmont State Forest, Grand Canyon, Hoover Dam

*Recognized sections of the country or world* the South, the Northwest, the Far East

► **NOTE** Do not capitalize *east, west, north,* and *south* when they indicate directions. Do capitalize them when they refer to recognized sections of the country.

EXAMPLES Turn east at the next corner, and you will see the church on the north side of the street.

To understand America, visit the Middle West.

We were going south, and the car that hit us was going east.

We are going South for the winter.

The modern tendency is to write nouns and adjectives derived from *East, West, North,* and *South* without capital letters (a *southerner, southern* hospitality, *northern* cities, *middle-western* customs, *western* clothes), but in the light of conflicting authorities, the capitalization of such words is also correct.

Adjectives specifying direction are not capitalized unless they are part of the name of a country: southern Ohio, eastern Russia, but West Germany, South Korea.

In spite of their origin, some nouns and adjectives derived from proper names are not capitalized: mackintosh, macadam, morocco leather, china dishes. Most words of this nature, however, may be written with or without capital letters: roman (Roman) numerals, plaster of paris (Paris), venetian (Venetian) blinds, turkish (Turkish) bath, gothic (Gothic) style, etc. When you are in doubt about the capitalization of words of this kind, refer to your dictionary.

**EXERCISE 1.** Number your paper 1–25. In each of the following items you are to choose the correct one of two forms. After the proper number on your paper, write the letter of the correct form (*a* or *b*). In two of the items, both forms are correct; write both *a* and *b*.

1. a. the Amazon river
   b. the Amazon River
2. a. She said, "Wait for me."
   b. She said, "wait for me."
3. a. strait of Magellan
   b. Strait of Magellan
4. a. Oxford boulevard
   b. Oxford Boulevard
5. a. I heard him say he was "tired of being good."
   b. I heard him say he was "Tired of being good."
6. a. Norwegian settlers
   b. Norwegian Settlers
7. a. Aegean sea
   b. Aegean Sea
8. a. an American Citizen
   b. an American citizen
9. a. Westchester County roads
   b. Westchester County Roads
10. a. north of the barn
    b. North of the barn
11. a. the Malay peninsula
    b. the Malay Peninsula
12. a. Twenty-Third Street
    b. Twenty-third Street
13. a. Grand Coulee Dam
    b. Grand Coulee dam
14. a. William Winter, Jr.
    b. William Winter, jr.
15. a. people of the Far East
    b. people of the far east
16. a. the Verrazano Bridge
    b. the Verrazano bridge

17. a. a French poodle
    b. a French Poodle
18. a. Clearwater Beach
    b. Clearwater beach
19. a. valley of the Ohio
    b. Valley of the Ohio
20. a. Grand Teton national Park
    b. Grand Teton National Park
21. a. Go south for three miles.
    b. Go South for three miles.
22. a. Jericho Turnpike
    b. Jericho turnpike
23. a. Western Pennsylvania
    b. western Pennsylvania
24. a. Kara O'neill
    b. Kara O'Neill
25. a. Seventy-ninth street
    b. Seventy-ninth Street

**EXERCISE 2.** Copy the following, using capital letters wherever they are required; or, prepare to write them from your teacher's dictation.

1. essex county
2. an african village
3. dallas, texas
4. latin america
5. two miles west
6. pioneering in the west
7. thirty-fourth street
8. great salt lake
9. glacier national park
10. the indian ocean
11. the catskill mountains
12. a city like san francisco
13. a popular british composer
14. an english bulldog
15. mackinac island
16. german composer
17. farragut boulevard
18. elmore county
19. the canadian wilderness
20. george o'connor, jr.

**(3) Capitalize names of organizations, business firms, institutions, and government bodies.**

*Organizations* Spanish Club, League of Women Voters, Veterans of Foreign Wars

*Business firms* American Airlines, Minnesota Mining and Manufacturing Company, General Motors Corporation, Barclay Hotel, Plaza Theater

*Institutions* Princeton University, Arizona State College, Franklin High School, Ford Foundation, First Methodist Church, English Department

*Government bodies* Congress, House of Representatives, Securities and Exchange Commission, Department of Defense

► **NOTE** The names of government bodies are capitalized when they are exact names. Do not capitalize such general names as the following: *the state legislature, the latest department meeting.*

► **NOTE** Do not capitalize such words as *hotel, theater, church, high school, college,* and *university* unless they are part of a proper name.

| | |
|---|---|
| Onondaga Hotel | a hotel in Syracuse |
| University of Michigan | a university in Michigan |
| Emerson High School | a high school textbook |
| United States Post Office | the local post office |

### (4) Capitalize the names of historical events and periods, special events, and calendar items.

*Historical events* Battle of the Coral Sea, Middle Ages, French Revolution, World War II

*Special events* National Open Golf Championships, World Series, American Legion Convention, Junior Prom

*Calendar items* Sunday, November, Christmas Eve, Labor Day, Book Week

► **NOTE** Names of the seasons are not capitalized unless personified.

a late spring
Spring in her green dress

### (5) Capitalize the names of nationalities, races, and religions.

EXAMPLES Caucasian, Semitic, Roman Catholic, Baptist, Belgian, Australian, Afro-American

### (6) Capitalize the brand names of business products.

EXAMPLES Coca-Cola, Chemstrand, Tostitos

► **NOTE** The common noun which often follows a brand name is not capitalized except in advertising displays.

Tip-Top bread, Royal typewriter, Toyota station wagon

**(7) Capitalize the names of ships, planes, monuments, awards, and any other particular places, things, or events.**

EXAMPLES the *Constitution* (ship), Lincoln Memorial, Purple Heart

► **NOTE** Do not capitalize the names of school subjects, except for languages and for course names followed by a number.

EXAMPLES English, French, German, Latin, Italian, math, art, chemistry, home economics, Chemistry II, History III, Art 102

► **NOTE** Schoolrooms and other nouns followed by a numeral or letter are usually capitalized.

EXAMPLES Room 31, Parlor B, School District 18, Chapter 4

► **NOTE** Names of school classes may or may not be capitalized, but the modern tendency is to capitalize them; however, the words *senior, junior, sophomore, freshman* are not capitalized when used to refer to a student.

A freshman attended the meeting of the Senior Class.

**EXERCISE 3.** Number your paper 1–25. Copy after the proper number all items to which capitals must be added. Write *C* after the number of a correct item.

1. cambridge university
2. room 134
3. a neighborhood theater
4. parkview high school
5. She is a sophomore.
6. the french people
7. an underwood typewriter
8. summer vacation
9. the arcade theater
10. geometry
11. interstate commerce commission
12. biology II
13. the shafer hotel
14. memorial day
15. science department
16. skippy peanut butter
17. five college freshmen
18. bureau of internal revenue
19. *metroliner* (train)

20. members of the department
21. the american revolution
22. the battle of bunker hill
23. the kentucky derby
24. fairview country club
25. a swedish restaurant

**EXERCISE 4.** This exercise covers all capitalization rules presented to this point. List in proper order the words which should be capitalized in each sentence. When the capitalized words belong in one phrase, write them as a phrase: *Sunrise Highway, Jefferson Memorial Library.* Indicate in which sentence each word or word group appears.

EXAMPLE 1. As a child in montclair, new jersey, I used to play in anderson park.

1. *Montclair, New Jersey*
   *Anderson Park*

1. Mrs. glenn, our science teacher, took her sophomore biology classes to willow creek to collect specimens for the high school laboratories.
2. This winter, in social studies III, we have been studying about the pioneers who settled in the west during the years following the civil war.
3. The university of wisconsin is situated on lake mendota in madison, the capital of the state.
4. Residents of five school districts in shannon county voted to build a new high school and junior college as recommended by the state department of education.
5. In washington, d.c., during the annual spring trip of the senior class, those seniors who are members of the art club visited the national gallery of art, where they saw many famous paintings and sculptures.
6. In 1754 columbia college, then called king's college, stood next to trinity church in lower manhattan, near the corner of broadway and wall street.
7. Mr. frank mills, jr., is faculty adviser to the upper classes and is personally acquainted with every junior and senior in the high school.
8. One mile north of the village of turnerville, the lincoln highway crosses salt creek near the entrance to cameron state park.

9. The state theater and the park hotel on the corner of bay avenue and twenty-third street will be torn down to make room for the approach to the new marlborough bridge.
10. Fiona mcdonald, who has a highland scottish accent, read some of robert burns's poems to our english class on monday afternoon.
11. Samantha gardner, owner of the gardner baking company, makers of tasty crust bread and pastries, endowed the city's new hospital, which will be built in avon park and known as the gardner general hospital.

## 29d. Capitalize titles.

**(1) Capitalize the title of a person when it comes before a name.**

EXAMPLES Superintendent Williams, Dean Marsh, Chairman Mao, President Drake

**(2) Capitalize a title used alone or following a person's name only if it refers to a high government official or someone else to whom you wish to show special respect.**

EXAMPLES Dr. Jana Williams, superintendent of schools; Ms. Marsh, dean of women; Tina Drake, president of our class; *but* DeWitt Clinton, Governor of New York; Thurgood Marshall, Justice of the Supreme Court [titles of high government officials]
the Senator, *but* the work of a senator; the General's orders, *but* the insignia of a general; the Chief Justice, the Secretary of Agriculture, the Prince of Wales

► NOTE When used to refer to the head of a nation, the word *president* is usually capitalized. Two capitals are required in *vice-president* when it refers to the vice-president of a nation. The words *ex-* and *-elect* used with a title are not capitalized: *ex*-President, Governor-*elect*.

► NOTE When a title is used in place of a person's name, it is usually capitalized.

Hello, Doctor.
I'll find out, Coach.

**(3) Capitalize a word showing family relationship when the word is used with a person's name but *not* when it is preceded by a possessive (unless it is part of the name).**

EXAMPLES Uncle Manuel, Cousin Pam, my cousin Pam, your mother, Judy's sister, *but* my Aunt Mary (when "Aunt Mary" is considered her name)

► NOTE Words of family relationship are usually, but not always, capitalized when used in place of a person's name.

Someone told Mother.

**(4) Capitalize the first word and all important words in titles of books, periodicals, poems, stories, articles, documents, movies, paintings and other works of art, etc. [The important words are the first and last words and all other words except the articles (*a, an, the*), coordinating conjunctions, and prepositions of fewer than five letters.]**

EXAMPLES *A Tale of Two Cities, Newsweek,* "The Force That Through the Green Fuse Drives the Flower," Treaty of Paris, *Winter in New England* [painting]

► NOTE The words *a, an, the,* written before a title, are capitalized only when they are part of the title. Before the names of magazines and newspapers, they are not capitalized.

*The Last of the Mohicans, An Island Voyage* [*The* and *An* are part of the title.]

Have you read the *First Principles* of Herbert Spencer? [*The* is not part of the title.]

the *Reader's Digest,* the *Los Angeles Times*

**(5) Capitalize words referring to the Deity.**

God, the Almighty, Lord

Pronouns referring to God (*he, him* and, rarely, *who, whom*) are often capitalized.

EXAMPLE Sarah said she was sure that God would make His wishes known to her.

The word *god,* when used to refer to the gods of ancient mythology, is not capitalized.

EXAMPLE Achilles' mother asked the gods to help her son.

**EXERCISE 5.** Number your paper 1–25. Copy after the proper number all items to which capitals must be added. Write *C* after the number of a correct item.

1. captain Blake
2. a senator rose to speak
3. Ms. Goldberg, the librarian
4. our class president
5. the club secretary
6. the vice-president of the United States
7. Father Casey, an Army chaplain
8. ex-president Ford
9. the leader of the guerrillas
10. a captain in an army
11. The lord in his wisdom
12. aunt Louise
13. senator Kennedy
14. mayor Gibson of Newark
15. Willa Thompson, one of the principals
16. *down and out in paris and london* [book title]
17. the *new republic* [magazine]
18. the monroe doctrine
19. Carl Stokes, a former mayor of Cleveland
20. your aunt
21. the *Washington post* [newspaper]
22. responsibilities of a senator
23. god, whom we worship for his goodness
24. Mildred Zaharias, former national champion
25. "the world is too much with us"

**REVIEW EXERCISE.** This exercise covers all capitalization rules in the chapter. List in order the words which should be capitalized in each sentence as you did in Exercise 4.

1. The rotary club of edgemont county has established an office in the Roosevelt hotel.
2. In their english classes this term the juniors have read *giants in the earth,* a novel about the norwegian immigrants who settled in the dakotas.
3. According to professor Schwartz, Tennyson's *idylls of the king* was published in 1859, the same year that saw the pub-

lication of Darwin's *origin of species,* Fitzgerald's translation of the *rubáiyát of omar khayyám,* and Dickens' *a tale of two cities.*

4. The president went to Dulles international airport to bid farewell to the secretary of state, who was taking off for europe on an important mission.
5. Since he is not a high school graduate, Russell is taking courses at Springfield vocational school to prepare for a position with the Bowman electronics company, manufacturers of stayput remote control modules.
6. After spending several winters in the northwest, my parents sought a warm climate and moved to the south, finally entering the real estate business in madeira beach, florida, on the east side of the gulf of mexico.
7. The early christian missionaries to north America worked among american indians who worshiped many gods.
8. Dr. Eugene Walker, jr., principal of the high school, explained why all sophomores are required to take history II and biology.
9. The treaty of versailles, which followed world war I, specified that germany should lose its colonies, the african colonies being made french and english mandates under the league of nations.
10. The site proposed for the new high school is on the shore of clear lake about two miles north of here on highway 101.
11. My grandmother, who grew up in the south, cooks southern fried chicken much better than my mother does.
12. Mary Mckay, who is president of the riding club, owns a beautiful horse, which she keeps at the Johnson farm on River road to the west of town.
13. The vice-president of the United States automatically takes over if the president dies in office.
14. Most of the girls in my cabin at camp this summer were from junior high schools in suburban communities outside New York and Boston and a few other large cities in the east.
15. Shea stadium, which was built near the site of the New York world's fair, is the home of the mets, the national league team in New York.

## SUMMARY STYLE SHEET

| | |
|---|---|
| Mexico **C**ity | a **c**ity in Mexico |
| Ocala **N**ational **F**orest | our **n**ational **f**orests |
| **T**wenty-ninth **S**treet | across the **s**treet |
| **H**oughton **L**ake | a shallow **l**ake |
| **N**orth America | **n**orthern Wisconsin |
| the Explorers' **C**lub | a **c**lub for explorers |
| Ford Motor **C**ompany | an automobile **c**ompany |
| Central **H**igh **S**chool | a new **h**igh **s**chool |
| Pomona **C**ollege | four years in **c**ollege |
| the American **R**evolution | a successful **r**evolution |
| the Wrigley **B**uilding | a Chicago **b**uilding |
| the **F**ourth of July | the **f**ifth of July |
| the **S**enior **B**all | a **b**all given by **s**eniors |
| the **F**reshman **C**lass | **f**reshman **c**lasses |
| **E**nglish, **F**rench, **L**atin | **s**ocial **s**tudies, **p**hysics, **a**rt |
| **H**istory II | a course in world **h**istory |
| **W**inter's frosty breath | **s**pring, **s**ummer, **w**inter, **f**all |
| **P**rincipal Langley | Mrs. Langley, the **p**rincipal |
| the **P**resident (U.S.) | the **p**resident of our club |
| **G**overnor **S**mith | a **g**overnor's duties |
| **G**od made **H**is will known. | tribal **g**ods of the Cherokees |
| the **S**outh | a mile **s**outh (**n**orth, **e**ast, **w**est) |
| Don't tell **M**other (or **m**other). | Don't tell my **m**other. |
| **U**ncle Bill | my **u**ncle |
| **I**vory **s**oap | |
| a **P**resbyterian, a **S**wede | |
| *The **L**ast of the **M**ohicans* | |
| the *__R__eader's __D__igest* | |

Chapter 30

# Punctuation

## End Marks and Commas

Punctuation is used to make the meaning of a sentence clear to the reader. Some marks of punctuation indicate in writing the pauses and stops which the voice makes in speaking. They indicate not only where a pause should come but also how long the pause should be—the comma standing for a slight hesitation, the period for a longer one. Other vocal inflections are conveyed by the question mark and the exclamation point.

A complete statement of the correct uses of all punctuation marks is provided in this chapter and the one that follows, together with exercises to help you fix these uses in your mind. Punctuating exercises is at best an artificial activity, however, and you must be very careful to carry over into your writing the punctuation principles you have learned. Since punctuation is so closely related to meaning, you probably should punctuate as you write, for while you are writing, you continually use punctuation to group certain ideas together and to separate other ideas from each other. On the other hand, many writers prefer to concentrate first on getting their ideas onto paper; then they go back over what they have written and insert whatever punctuation is necessary to make the writing clear to others and conventionally correct. This latter process, known as proofreading, is a very important part of writing. Proofread all of your writing carefully.

Do not overpunctuate. Use a mark of punctuation for only two reasons: (1) because meaning demands it, or (2) because conventional usage requires it.

# END MARKS

### 30a. A statement is followed by a period.

EXAMPLE Summer vacation begins June 26.

### 30b. An abbreviation is followed by a period.[1]

EXAMPLES Ave. Dec.
A.D. Dr.

► **NOTE** Abbreviations in the metric system are often written without periods.

### 30c. A question is followed by a question mark.

**(1) Distinguish between a statement containing an indirect question and a sentence which asks a question directly.**

EXAMPLES She wants to know what the assignment is. [statement containing an indirect question—followed by a period]

Do you know what the assignment is? [a direct question—followed by a question mark]

**(2) Polite requests in question form (frequently used in business letters) may be followed by a period; a question mark would, of course, be perfectly correct.**

EXAMPLES Will you please ship this order three weeks before Christmas.

Will you please ship this order three weeks before Christmas?

**(3) A question mark should be placed inside quotation marks when the quotation is a question. Otherwise, it should be placed outside the quotation marks.**

EXAMPLES Hector asked, "Have you heard from Ellen?" [The quotation is a question.]

[1] For fuller discussion of abbreviations see page 512.

Did you say, "Meet me at eight o'clock"? [The quotation is not a question. The whole sentence, however, is a question.]

**30d. An exclamation is followed by an exclamation point.**

EXAMPLES What a beautiful dress!
How expensive!
You're joking!
Congratulations!

**(1) Many exclamations begin either with "What a . . ." or "How . . ." as in the first two of the preceding examples. When you begin a sentence with these words, check your end mark carefully.**

**(2) An interjection at the beginning of a sentence is usually followed by a comma.**

CUSTOMARY Ah, there you have me!
RARE Ah! There you have me!

**(3) An exclamation point should be placed inside quotation marks when the quotation is an exclamation. Otherwise, it should be placed outside the quotation marks.**

EXAMPLES "What a game that was!" exclaimed Nadine as she entered the cafeteria.
How foolish of him to say in the fifth inning, "The game is won"!

**30e. An imperative sentence may be followed by either a period or an exclamation point, depending upon the force intended.**

EXAMPLES Please reply by return mail.
Block that kick!

**EXERCISE 1.** Many periods and all exclamation and question marks have been omitted from the following passage. Copy in a column on your paper all words which you think should be followed by end marks. After each word write the end mark required. If a new sentence should begin after the end mark, write the first word of the sentence, giving it a capital letter. Before each word write the number of the line in which it appears.

EXAMPLE "What an exciting picture" exclaimed my companion as we left the theater wasn't it too bad I couldn't agree with him the picture had been . . .

1. *picture!*
2. *theater. Wasn't*
3. *him? The*

Janet Smith, M D, Director of the Carla S Lewis clinic, stopped her car behind a truck "Whew" she sighed. "What a lot of traffic" Presently the cars at her right moved forward, but not the truck ahead although in a hurry, she accepted the fact that Sixth St at this hour was an overcrowded thoroughfare, and she decided to be patient. The taxi driver behind her, however, had a different idea he honked his horn the sound startled Dr. Smith, but what could she do anyone could see the truck was blocking her way. "How stupid some drivers are" she thought. The insistent honking continued, and Dr Smith became annoyed when the truck moved on, she deliberately made a slow start and felt rewarded when the horn behind her broke into a deluge of noise.

When the light turned green at the next corner, she was about to press the accelerator when another horn, of deeper tone but just as unpleasant, broke out in the rear "All right All right" she exclaimed. "Hold your horses" When, after a number of similar incidents, she turned into her own drive, she was thoroughly sick of horns and ill-mannered drivers.

That evening, as Dr Smith settled down to her favorite television program, her calm was shattered again by a too familiar sound. "Good heavens" she exclaimed. "Will I never have any peace" Looking across the front lawn, she saw Hal Jordan's jalopy at the curb Hal was calling for Jimmy Smith. "Jimmy," she shouted, "come here at once" Jimmy stopped short in the second of his usual two leaps from stairway to door. "Jimmy, you tell that Hal Jordan he is never to honk that horn in front of this house again can't he walk up to the door and ask for you" Her words were drowned by Hal's obliging repetition of the two long and three short blasts Jimmy escaped, leaving his mother still talking but inaudible.

"Cut it out" she heard him yell "Do you love the sound of that horn"

When Mr Smith came in from his work, his wife gave him an account of her experience with hornblowers "I will propose to the Governor tomorrow morning," she said, "that auto horns be made inoperable when the car is not in motion wouldn't that be a good law" Mr Smith agreed with his wife.

## THE COMMA

The comma—the most frequently used mark of punctuation—is used mainly to group words that belong together and to separate those that do not. Some other uses have little to do with meaning but are simply customary ways of punctuating sentences.

### Items in a Series

**30f. Use commas to separate items in a series.**

EXAMPLES She was formerly on the staff of the embassies in Moscow**,** Berlin**,** Vienna**,** and Madrid.

There were books on the desk**,** posters on the wall**,** and clothing on the floor.

► **NOTE** Do not place a comma before the first item or after the last item in a series.

INCORRECT During the summer the workers had installed, a new gymnasium floor, an improved heating system, and green chalkboards, in the high school building.

CORRECT During the summer the workers had installed a new gymnasium floor**,** an improved heating system**,** and green chalkboards in the high school building.

It is permissible to omit the comma before the *and* joining the last two items in a series if the comma is not needed to make the meaning clear. There are some constructions in which the inclusion or omission of this comma affects the meaning of the sentence.

> American folk songs may be classified in the following categories: marching songs, work songs, ballads, hymns, and spirituals. [five categories]
>
> American folk songs may be classified in the following categories: marching songs, work songs, ballads, hymns and spirituals. [four categories]

► NOTE Words customarily used in pairs are set off as one item in a series: *bag and baggage, pen and ink, hat and coat, pork and beans, bread and butter,* etc.

> For lunch they served a fruit cup, macaroni and cheese, salad, ice cream and cake, and coffee.

**(1) If all items in a series are joined by *and* or *or,* do not use commas to separate them.**

EXAMPLE The weather forecaster predicted rain or sleet or snow.

**(2) Independent clauses in a series are usually separated by a semicolon. Short independent clauses, however, may be separated by commas.**

EXAMPLE We walked, we played, we ate, and we gained weight.

## 30g. Use a comma to separate two or more adjectives preceding a noun.

EXAMPLES She is an alert, vivacious girl.

We patiently sat through a long, dull, amateurish performance.

**(1) Do not use a comma before the final adjective in a series if the adjective is thought of as part of the noun.**

INCORRECT It was a cold, raw, dark, November day.

CORRECT It was a cold, raw, dark November day. [*November day* is considered as one word, one item. The adjectives modify *November day,* not *day.*]

CORRECT She is a bright, charming, talented young woman. [*Young woman* is thought of as one word.]

**(2) If one of the words in a series modifies another word in the series, do not separate them by a comma.**

EXAMPLE He wore a bright blue blazer.

## Comma Between Independent Clauses

**30h. Use a comma before *and, but, or, nor, for, yet* when they join independent clauses, unless the clauses are very short.**

EXAMPLES Saturday's Council meeting was unusually harmonious, for no one raised any objections.

The first two acts were slow-moving, but the third act was full of action and suspense.

You go ahead and I'll follow. [independent clauses too short to require punctuation]

When the conjunction joins two verbs, not two main clauses, a comma is not used.

EXAMPLES I gave some good advice to Geraldo and got some from him in return. [The conjunction joins the verbs *gave* and *got*.]

I gave some good advice to Geraldo, and he gave me some in return. [The conjunction joins two independent clauses.]

► **NOTE** You are allowed some freedom in the application of this rule. Many writers use the comma before these conjunctions —as they use the comma before *and* between the last two items in a series—only when necessary to keep the meaning clear.

NOT CLEAR I carved the turkey and the family watched.

CLEAR I carved the turkey, and the family watched.

NOT CLEAR I didn't know whether or not to wait longer for the letter carrier had brought no word from you.

CLEAR I didn't know whether or not to wait longer, for the letter carrier had brought no word from you.

As you can see from the preceding examples, a reader may easily be confused if the comma is omitted. This is especially true of the comma before the conjunction *for,* which should always be preceded by a comma when it means *because.*

**EXERCISE 2.** The following sentences cover rules 30f–h. Number your paper 1–15. Copy after the proper number the words in each sentence which should be followed by a comma, placing the comma after the word. Since the meaning of some sentences may be determined by the punctuation, you should be prepared to explain the punctuation you use.

1. The police searched everywhere but there were no fingerprints to be found.
2. Mr. Feinstein asked the waiter for coffee beans and ham and eggs.
3. States included in the Japanese beetle area are New York New Jersey Maryland and Delaware.
4. I played the melody on the guitar and the electric bass provided the rhythm.
5. Everyone turned to watch the large pale yellow moon.
6. This policy covers medical expenses iron-lung rental hospitalization and transportation to a center of treatment.
7. The train pulled out and left me in a strange town without my luggage hat and coat or credentials.
8. The school administration is responsible for these disciplinary problems stem from rules made in the office.
9. This poet did not use capital letters and her punctuation was frequently unconventional.
10. The wagon train was approaching lonely wild country.
11. The wind froze us the rain soaked us and the waves tossed us.
12. We are learning more and more about space through our new and stronger telescopes our huge radar installations and our instrument-packed space probes.
13. She found that it was a friendly unsophisticated little town that she had chosen for her home.
14. Soldiers were stationed at frequent intervals along the curb and the sidewalks behind them were jammed with onlookers.
15. She is pretty tall and blonde; her sister is small and dark and beautiful.

## Nonessential Elements

**30i. Use commas to set off nonessential clauses and nonessential participial phrases.**

A nonessential (nonrestrictive) clause is a subordinate clause that is not essential to the meaning of the sentence but merely adds an idea to the sentence.

NONESSENTIAL Joan Thomas, **who was offered scholarships to three colleges,** will go to Mt. Holyoke in September.

The basic meaning of this sentence is *Joan Thomas will go to Mt. Holyoke in September.* The subordinate clause does not affect this basic meaning; it merely adds an idea to the sentence. It is a nonessential clause because it does not limit in any way the word it modifies—*Joan Thomas.* Clauses which modify proper nouns are nearly always nonessential.

The opposite of a nonessential clause is an essential (restrictive) clause.

ESSENTIAL Joan Thomas is the only senior **who won scholarships to three colleges.**

Here the subordinate clause is essential to the sentence, for without it the sentence would mean something else: *Joan Thomas is the only senior.* The subordinate clause limits the meaning of *senior—senior who won scholarships to three colleges.*

Study the following examples of essential and nonessential clauses until you understand the terms. Note the punctuation: *essential—no punctuation; nonessential—set off by commas.*

ESSENTIAL The city **which interests me most** is Hollywood.

NONESSENTIAL Bismarck, **which is the capital of North Dakota,** is in the south-central part of the state.

ESSENTIAL The man **who spoke to me** is my science teacher.

NONESSENTIAL Mr. Orban, **who is my science teacher,** spoke to me.

Sometimes a clause may be interpreted as either essential or nonessential. In such instances the writer must decide which interpretation to give to the clause and punctuate it accordingly.

> Dave took his problem to the librarian who is an authority on reference books. [interpreted as essential]
>
> Dave took his problem to the librarian, who is an authority on reference books. [interpreted as nonessential]

We may assume from the first sentence, which contains an essential clause, that there is more than one librarian. Dave chose the one who is an authority on reference books.

From the second sentence we may assume that there is only one librarian and that the librarian is an authority on reference books.

> My aunt who works at the Union Trust Company lives in New Jersey. [I have several aunts, and this is one of them.]
>
> My aunt, who works at the Union Trust Company, lives in New Jersey. [I have only one aunt, no others.]

**EXERCISE 3.** Some of the sentences in this exercise contain essential clauses; others contain nonessential clauses. Number your paper 1–20. If the italicized clause is essential, write *E* after the proper number; if it is nonessential, write *Commas* to indicate that you would use commas in this sentence.

1. Friends *who do favors for you* may expect you to do favors for them.
2. The Welcoming Committee *who made us feel at home in a strange school* helped us through the first confusing days of the term.
3. Our new Buick *which my parents bought in Detroit* is a four-door model.
4. The Buick *which Mr. Burton drives* is like the one we saw on television.
5. She is wearing the sweater *that she received for Christmas.*
6. Her new sweater *which was a Christmas gift* is two sizes too large.

7. People *who are nervous* do not make good drivers.
8. Men *who are sometimes thought to be the stronger sex* cannot stand pain as well as women.
9. American cities *that are outwardly very much alike* may show distinctive characteristics on more intimate acquaintance.
10. Cities *that have great financial problems* levy a sales tax.
11. The Sault Sainte Marie Canals *which connect Lake Superior and Lake Huron* would be a prime target in wartime.
12. I do not like people *who litter public parks.*
13. These antiquated tariffs *which were necessary during the depression* are shutting off foreign markets from American manufacturers.
14. Many people *who settled America* came to escape tyranny.
15. The Hudson's Bay Company *which is one of the oldest trading firms in the world* was founded in 1670.
16. Leontyne Price *who is well-known for her role as Cleopatra* is one of the world's leading sopranos.
17. The book *that I have read for this report* is a novel about World War II.
18. On my return I found that the people *that I had expected to see* had moved away.
19. Lucy French *who does her own gardening* says she exhausts herself trying to get rid of weeds.
20. All the tickets *that had been sold* were recalled.

A participial phrase is a group of related words containing a participle (see page 42). Present participles end in *-ing;* past participles of regular verbs end in *-ed* or *-d.*

Like a nonessential clause, a nonessential participial phrase is set off by commas because it is not necessary to the meaning of the sentence.

NONESSENTIAL My little brother**,** **playing in the street,** was struck by a car.

ESSENTIAL A child **playing in the street** may be struck by a car.

NONESSENTIAL Our dog**,** **frightened by the thunder,** hid in a closet.

ESSENTIAL Animals **frightened by thunder** often try to hide.

NONESSENTIAL The crowd broke up suddenly, **dispersing rapidly in all directions.**

ESSENTIAL I watched the crowd **dispersing rapidly in all directions.**

**EXERCISE 4.** This exercise covers all comma rules given up to this point in the chapter. After the proper number write all words in the sentence which should be followed by a comma. Write the comma after each word. Be prepared to explain your answers.

1. Any student who wishes to join the gymnastics team will have to excel in floor exercises on the balance beam and on the uneven parallel bars.
2. The sophomores decorated the gym and the juniors provided the refreshments.
3. Anyone taking the basic photography course will learn how to shoot close-ups portraits and still lifes.
4. The judge leaving her chambers stopped to talk to some court reporters who had gathered around her.
5. We got encouragement from everyone but our parents helped us most of all.
6. Careful writers distinguish between *uninterested* which means "indifferent" and *disinterested* which means "unbiased."
7. Any student wishing to sing act or perform on Class Day should sign up before tomorrow which is the deadline.
8. Governor Quigley whose speeches are filled with clichés appeared on television last night asking people to "tighten their belts bite the bullet pull their own weight and give till it hurts."
9. A sad-looking mongrel which had followed me halfway home suddenly trotted up to me and staring at me soulfully started to lick my hand.
10. A story which appeared in yesterday's newspaper was about the Toronto Maple Leafs which is my favorite hockey team.

## Introductory Elements

**30j. Use a comma after certain introductory elements.**

**(1) Use a comma after words such as *well, yes, no,* and *why* when they begin a sentence.**

EXAMPLES Yes, you were elected.
Oh, I wouldn't be too sure about that.
Why, the entire argument is false!

**(2) Use a comma after an introductory participial phrase.**

EXAMPLE **Behaving like a spoiled child**, he pouted and sulked.

► NOTE Do not confuse a gerund ending in *-ing* and used as the subject of the sentence with an introductory participial phrase.

EXAMPLES **Washing and polishing the car** is fun. [gerunds used as subjects—not followed by a comma]

**Washing and polishing the car**, I developed sore muscles. [introductory participial phrase—followed by a comma]

**(3) Use a comma after a succession of introductory prepositional phrases.**

EXAMPLE **At the edge of the deep woods near Lakeville in Cumberland County**, they built a small log cabin.

► NOTE A single introductory prepositional phrase need not be followed by a comma unless it is parenthetical (*by the way, on the contrary,* etc.) or the comma is necessary to prevent confusion.

EXAMPLES By the way, I had a letter from Edith Yen.
With the weak, competition is unpopular.
In the morning I am never wide awake.

**(4) Use a comma after an introductory adverb clause.**

EXAMPLE **While Mario put the costume on**, the accompanist played "Deep Purple."

An adverbial clause at the end of a sentence is not usually set off:

The accompanist played "Deep Purple" **while Mario put the costume on.**

**EXERCISE 5.** This exercise covers all comma rules to this point in the chapter. Number your paper 1–10. Copy after the proper number the words in each sentence which should be followed by a comma, placing a comma after each word.

1. One look at the assignment is not enough for most students will need to study it carefully.
2. When we had finished playing the piano was rolled offstage to make room for the next act.
3. On the afternoon of the first day of school the halls were still filled with lost confused or frightened freshmen.
4. Well if you need help please don't hesitate to ask me or Mrs. Seil or Mrs. Faust.
5. In the second half of the third period Johnson evaded the defense caught a twenty-yard pass and raced into the end zone.
6. Speaking in assembly yesterday Katy Stover urged students to obey the new rules governing conduct in the cafeteria the school corridors and the parking lot.
7. Having studied the tax proposals of both political parties Governor Ross who was not satisfied rejected both proposals and then presented a new plan.
8. Marchers in the long orderly picket line appeared to have the support of everyone in the crowd but the police carrying out their orders broke up the demonstration.
9. Legitimate theaters are prospering in many American cities but the New York stage is still the goal of young actors dancers and musicians.
10. When Bill was driving our truck lurched unexplainably and we wondered whether he was falling asleep at the wheel.

## Interrupters

### 30k. Use commas to set off expressions that interrupt the sentence.

To set off an expression takes two commas unless the expression comes first or last in the sentence.

**(1) Appositives and appositive phrases are usually set off by commas.**

An appositive is a word—with or without modifiers—that follows a noun or pronoun and identifies or explains it. An appositive phrase consists of an appositive and its modifiers.

EXAMPLE A syndicated column by Bernice Silverman, **the noted writer**, will appear in the *Times-News*, **a local paper.**

When an appositive is so closely related to the word it modifies that it appears to be part of that word, no comma is necessary. An appositive of this kind is called a restrictive appositive. Usually it is one word.

EXAMPLES Her cousin Raquel
The novel *Windswept*
Your friend Jean
Catherine the Great
The conjunction *and*

**(2) Words used in direct address are set off by commas.**

EXAMPLES I don't know, **Alice**, where your brother is.
**Sam**, please come here.
Your grades are disappointing, **my friend.**

**(3) Parenthetical expressions are set off by commas.**

The following expressions are commonly used parenthetically: *I believe* (*think, know, hope,* etc.), *I am sure, on the contrary, on the other hand, after all, by the way, incidentally, in fact, indeed, naturally, of course, in my opinion, for example, however, nevertheless, to tell the truth.*

EXAMPLES My parents will, **I am sure**, let me have the car tonight.
The weight of the car, **of course**, determines the price of the license.
**On the contrary**, jogging is relaxing.
Jenkins was doing things the hard way, **naturally.**

Knowledge of the above rule and of the expressions commonly used parenthetically is helpful in punctuating, but you should understand that your intention is what determines the punctuation that you use. If you wish the reader to pause, to regard an expression as parenthetical, set it off; if not, leave it unpunctuated. Sometimes, however, the placement of the expression in the sentence determines the punctuation. Study the following examples, noting in which ones the comma is a matter of choice and in which ones the placement of expression governs the punctuation. All the examples given illustrate standard usage.

This is **indeed** a great piece of news.

This is**, indeed,** a great piece of news.

**Indeed,** this is a great piece of news. [comma required by placement]

We **therefore** agreed to sign the petition.

We**, therefore,** agreed to sign the petition.

We agreed**, therefore,** to sign the petition. [comma required by placement]

**I hope** this raise in salary will relieve your financial distress. [no comma because of placement]
This raise in salary will**, I hope,** relieve your financial distress. [comma required by placement]

**EXERCISE 6.** The following exercise covers all comma rules to this point in the chapter. Number your paper 1–20. Copy after the proper number the words in each sentence that should be followed by a comma, placing a comma after each word. Write *C* if the item is correct.

1. The final act a general free-for-all had the first-night audience a dignified crowd holding their sides.
2. Indeed if I knew the answer my friend I would not be asking you for it.
3. The authors of this book a volume of bitter criticism have in my opinion been most unfair.
4. This painting Betty is by Emilio Sanchez an artist born in Cuba.
5. Russian artists on the other hand must promote Communist doctrines for everyone in Russia works for the state.

6. Our plan I knew would have to succeed for there would be no second chance.
7. The nineteenth-century book *El Jíbaro* which was written by Manuel A. Alonso is by the way considered the first Puerto Rican classic.
8. Imprisoned without warning or explanation the two reporters were held if I remember correctly for two months in spite of efforts by England France and the United States to effect their release.
9. If you are prompt in getting your order in our office will guarantee delivery before Christmas which is only ten days off.
10. You should understand my good friend that much as I should like to do so I cannot give money to every organization that thinks it needs help.
11. Passengers riding in the front of the wrecked bus were the ones who were most severely injured.
12. This school composed largely of students from farm homes must offer courses in agriculture the occupation that most of the students will enter.
13. Looking for a sports car at a bargain price Henry who is car-crazy spent the day hanging around the North Country Motor Company which buys sells and services all makes of foreign cars.
14. Lauren and Jim left alone in the house immediately raided the refrigerator which was full of tasty items for the party that Kay's mother was giving the next day.
15. Napoleon's brothers Joseph and Lucien tried to prevent him from selling Louisiana but Richard Livingston and James Monroe the American representatives succeeded in making the purchase.
16. Well having tried all morning to reach me the girls delivered the message and I gave them a written reply which I hoped would be satisfactory.
17. In spite of their parents' warning Amy and Joan who should have known better stayed up reading the night before the test and didn't get to sleep they admitted until two o'clock.
18. Taking an afternoon stroll in the park my little sister Sally befriended a retriever a spaniel and a mutt that followed her home.

19. Before you start taking anything apart Maria I hope you will be sure that you can if necessary put it together again.
20. When Jimmie had finished the cake and pie were all gone and left untouched were the steak potatoes and salad.

## Conventional Uses

### 30l. Use a comma in certain conventional situations.

**(1) Use a comma to separate items in dates and addresses.**

EXAMPLES Our sentimental idea was to hold a class reunion on June 20**,** 1980**,** at the old high school.

Address me at 222 Twin Oaks Road**,** Akron**,** Ohio**,** after the first of March.

Their baby was born on Monday**,** May 3**,** 1976**,** in Baltimore**,** Maryland.

▶ NOTE When only the month and day are given, no punctuation is necessary.

It was on May 10 that we began work.

When the items are joined by a preposition, do not use commas.

She lived at 331 Main Street in Passaic, New Jersey.

**(2) Use a comma after the salutation of a friendly letter and after the closing of any letter.**

EXAMPLES Dear Rhonda**,** Sincerely yours**,**

**(3) Use a comma after a name followed by *Jr., Sr., Ph.D.,* etc.**

EXAMPLES Frank Lehman**,** Jr. Hazel Sellers**,** Ph.D.

## Unnecessary Commas

### 30m. Do not use unnecessary commas.

Commas are not to be sprinkled about in a composition as if they were salt, merely to add flavor. The tendency of modern writers is to use commas sparingly. You should be able to show either that the commas you use help the reader to understand what you have written or that they are required by custom—as in a date or address, for example. Using commas just for the fun of it is as bad as not using them when they are necessary. Your teacher will surely question your competence if you use them when they cannot be justified.

**REVIEW EXERCISE.** This exercise covers end marks and all comma uses. Copy the sentences, inserting punctuation and capitalization where necessary.

1. Trapped on a sand bar by the incoming tide the amateur clam diggers Pete and Don who could not swim had to be rescued.
2. In the first semester the following courses in homemaking will be offered: cooking sewing interior decoration baby care and feeding.
3. Our house at 2125 Northern Boulevard Flushing New York was sold and we moved to 433 West Thirty-fourth Street New York City.
4. John Carr Jr the only Eagle Scout in the troop organized the parade selected the flag-bearers hired the band and generally substituted for the troop leader.
5. In 1935 putting the *Herald Tribune* on microfilm was begun and we now have on microfilm copies of every issue of the *Tribune* from April 19 1841 up to its last issue.
6. When Josie who was driving tried to show off her friend Lucille fearing an accident threatened never to ride with her again.
7. In a gesture of good will Laura who owns a car missed the dance on Friday and drove to see Jan her girlfriend who had been hospitalized with pneumonia.
8. When the general called Stackpole a major in the RAF and an official of the British government were standing at the table watching an experiment.
9. Some of the workers were eating some were clearing away debris and the sheriff was conferring with the troopers who had just arrived to assist in the cleanup.
10. Our company which has a branch in your area will gladly submit designs for a ranch-type split-level or colonial house.
11. Maria had moved to Tampa Florida on November 19 1975 and in 1976 she moved again to Columbia Ohio.

12. Our research papers on which we had worked for weeks were destroyed in the fire at school, how disappointed we were to find that Ms. Walker had not yet read them.
13. When the school on the one hand had refused us the use of a bus and our parents on the other hand had refused us their cars what other solution was open to us.
14. In an address delivered on Friday March 5 in Miami Florida she said that the way to peace is through international economic cooperation political understanding and disarmament.
15. Although the crossbar had trembled as she passed over the judges declared she had not touched it and declared her the winner.

## SUMMARY OF USES OF THE COMMA

30f. Use commas to separate items in a series.

30g. Use a comma to separate two or more adjectives preceding a noun.

30h. Use a comma before *and, but, or, nor, for, yet* when they join independent clauses, unless they are very short.

30i. Use commas to set off nonessential clauses and nonessential participial phrases.

30j. Use a comma after certain introductory elements.
- (1) After words such as *well, yes, no, why,* etc., when they begin a sentence
- (2) After an introductory participial phrase
- (3) After a succession of introductory prepositional phrases
- (4) After an introductory adverb clause

30k. Use commas to set off expressions that interrupt the sentence.
- (1) Appositives
- (2) Words in direct address
- (3) Parenthetical expressions

30l. Use a comma in certain conventional situations.
- (1) To separate items in dates and addresses
- (2) After the salutation of a friendly letter
- (3) After a name followed by *Jr., Sr., Ph.D.,* etc.

30m. Do not use unnecessary commas.

# Chapter 31

# Punctuation

## Other Marks of Punctuation

Although the marks of punctuation treated in this chapter are used less frequently than the period and comma, they are often important. Just as you have learned to follow certain conventions in grammar and usage and spelling, you should observe the conventional uses of the punctuation marks described in this chapter.

### THE SEMICOLON

**31a. Use a semicolon between independent clauses not joined by *and, but, or, nor, for, yet.***

EXAMPLES Representatives of 130 nations attended the spring meeting of the General Assembly**;** they remained in session from April 5 to May 18.

Take with you only indispensable things**;** leave behind all heavy and bulky items.

A writer must have some basis for deciding whether to use two independent clauses with a semicolon between them, or two sentences with a period (and capital letter). In most writing, the division into sentences is preferable. A semicolon is used only when the ideas in the two clauses are so closely related that a period would make too distinct a break between them.

**31b. Use a semicolon between independent clauses joined by such words as *for example, for instance,***

***that is, besides, accordingly, moreover, nevertheless, furthermore, otherwise, therefore, however, consequently, instead, hence.***

EXAMPLES Holiday traffic has always been a menace to safety; **for instance,** on one Fourth of July weekend, four hundred persons were killed in traffic accidents.

Tension rose rapidly during yesterday's meeting; **nevertheless,** most of the Council members remained calm.

Matters involving Egypt and Israel were discussed; **therefore** representatives from these countries were invited to attend the preliminary planning sessions.

When the connectives mentioned in this rule are placed at the beginning of a clause, the use of a comma after them is frequently a matter of taste. When they are clearly parenthetical (interrupters) they are followed by a comma. The words *for example, for instance,* and *that is* are always followed by a comma. The word *however* is almost always followed by a comma.

EXAMPLES The foreign situation was deteriorating rapidly; **that is,** governments could find no basis for agreement.

The foreign situation was deteriorating rapidly; **however,** all governments remained optimistic. [. . . all governments, *however,* remained optimistic.]

Most of the words listed in this rule, however, are rarely used at the beginning of a clause. They are usually placed later in the clause.

EXAMPLE Matters involving Egypt and Israel were discussed; representatives from these countries were **therefore** invited to attend.

**31c. A semicolon (rather than a comma) may be needed to separate independent clauses if there are commas within the clauses.**

EXAMPLE The Canby, the new theater on Bank Street, announced programs of Westerns, gangster pictures, and re-releases of horror and blood-and-thunder movies; and the crowds, surprisingly enough, were enormous.

► **NOTE** As suggested in Rule 31c by the words "may be needed," you are allowed considerable leeway in applying this rule. When there are only one or two commas in the independent clauses, the semicolon is not needed. It is required when there are so many commas, as in the example above, that the sentence would be confusing without the semicolon because the reader could not immediately see where the first clause ended.

**31d. Use a semicolon between items in a series if the items contain commas.**

EXAMPLE The following are members of the new committee: Jan Bates, president of the Student Council; Allan Drew, president of the Senior Class; Helen Berger, vice-president of the Honor Society; and James Green, who, as a member of the Student Council, proposed that the committee be formed.

## THE COLON

**31e. Use a colon to mean "note what follows."**

**(1) Use a colon before a list of items, especially after expressions like *as follows* and *the following*.**

EXAMPLES The car trunk was large enough for everything: rackets, golf clubs, fishing supplies, suitcases, a picnic basket, and heavy clothing.

You will probably have to answer the following questions: How long have you been unemployed? Why did you leave your last position? What experience have you had? [list introduced by "the following"]

► **NOTE** When a list comes immediately after a verb or a preposition, do not use a colon.

EXAMPLES Foreign-aid organizations **sent** food, clothing, medical supplies, toys, and books. [list follows the verb *sent*]

He has always had an interest **in** snakes, lizards, mice, and other small animals. [list follows the preposition *in*]

**(2) Use a colon before a long, formal statement or quotation.**

EXAMPLE Dr. Stoddard made the following observation**:** The time is coming when a general college education will be as common as a high school education is today . . . [Note that a formal statement like this need not be enclosed in quotation marks.]

**(3) Use a colon between independent clauses when the second clause explains or restates the idea in the first.**

EXAMPLE These seat covers are the most durable kind**:** they are reinforced with double stitching and covered with a heavy plastic coating.

## 31f. Use a colon in certain conventional situations.

**(1) Use a colon between the hour and the minute when you write the time.**

EXAMPLE 4**:**30 P.M.

**(2) Use a colon between chapter and verse in referring to passages from the Bible.**

EXAMPLE John 3**:**16

**(3) Use a colon between volume and number or between volume and page number of a periodical.**

EXAMPLES *Harper's* 198**:**12 [volume and number]

*Harper's* 198**:**68–74 [volume and page numbers]

**(4) Use a colon after the salutation of a business letter.**

EXAMPLES Dear Ms. Green**:** Gentlemen**:**

## UNDERLINING (ITALICS)

**31g. Use underlining (italics) for titles of books, periodicals, works of art, ships, etc.**

EXAMPLES The Ox-Bow Incident

the Louisville Courier-Journal, or the Louisville Courier-Journal

the Reader's Digest

the Blue Boy, Humoresque, The Thinker

the Mayflower, the Chief, the City of Houston

The use of quotation marks for titles is now generally limited to short compositions such as short stories and short poems and to parts of publications; the titles of the publications themselves are underlined. (Compare page 562.)

EXAMPLE Read Chapter 39, "Americans in the Second World War (1941–1945)," from Rise of the American Nation

► NOTE When set in type, underlined words are italicized.

*The Ox-Bow Incident* the *Reader's Digest*

The words *a, an, the,* written before a title, are underlined only when they are part of the title of a book, article, etc. Before the names of magazines and newspapers, they are not underlined within a composition.

EXAMPLE I took a few ideas from my history text, The World's History, and some others from the latest issue of the Atlantic.

**31h. Use underlining (italics) for words, letters, and figures referred to as such and for foreign words.**

EXAMPLES The commonest English word is the; the most frequently used letters are e and t; frequently confused numbers are 7 and 9.

I had to look up the meaning of such Latin terms as carpe diem and caveat emptor.

**EXERCISE 1.** This exercise covers semicolons, colons, and italics. Number your paper 1–10. After the proper number copy from the sentence words and numbers that should be followed by a semicolon or a colon and write the punctuation after each. Copy and underline all words that should be italicized.

1. Today, fewer than 10 percent of Americans work on farms one hundred years ago, a majority of Americans worked on farms.
2. The following band members can play two instruments. Tony Winch, cornet and trumpet Sallie Davis, saxophone and clarinet and Sara Petterson, drums and marimba.
3. The Daily Blade often devotes its front page to sensational stories murders, robberies, catastrophes, kidnappings, and juicy scandals.
4. The Ten Commandments are in the Old Testament, Exodus 20 1–17 however, the Beatitudes are in the New Testament, Matthew 5 3–11.
5. Our sailing party, which consisted of three women and four men, went aboard the Sealark at 8 30 but we had to wait until 9 30 before our skipper, the wind, and the tides would permit us to sail.
6. Ms. Graham frequently gives assignments in current magazines for example, a typical assignment would run as follows the Atlantic, 210 41–6 Senior Scholastic, 78 4 Commonweal, 74 17.
7. According to an editorial in the Times-News, the election indicates a change in the public's attitude toward tariffs the candidate who favored protective tariffs was defeated.
8. Mrs. Johnson had me revise my composition three times first, to correct the spelling second, to revise some sentences third, to remove all so's and and so's.
9. The smaller colleges are in a difficult position their income has been cut, but their expenses have increased.
10. At the bookstore I bought the following gifts a book of essays by Joan Didion for my father, a framed Mary Cassatt print, entitled Mother and Child, for my mother and for my sister, a new album called Folksong Favorites.

## QUOTATION MARKS

**31i. Use quotation marks to enclose a direct quotation — a person's exact words.**

DIRECT QUOTATION Mother said, "I have heard Martina Arroyo sing at the opera."

Do not use quotation marks to enclose an indirect quotation — one that does not give a person's exact words.

INDIRECT QUOTATION Mother said she has heard Martina Arroyo sing at the opera.

*Enclose* means to place quotation marks at both the beginning and the end of a quotation. Omission of quotation marks at the end of a quotation is a common error.

**(1) A direct quotation begins with a capital letter.**

EXAMPLE I heard her say, "Complete the lesson at home."

Exception: If the quotation is only a fragment of a sentence, do not begin it with a capital letter:

EXAMPLE One critic called the book "an appalling waste of paper."

**(2) When a quoted sentence is divided into two parts by an interrupting expression such as *he said* or *Mother asked,* the second part begins with a small letter.**

EXAMPLES "Go home," he pleaded, "**b**efore you cause more trouble."

"Have you," she asked, "**b**een working this summer?"

If the second part of a broken quotation is a new sentence, it begins with a capital letter.

EXAMPLE "Drive carefully," he warned. "Recklessness is the cause of most accidents."

**(3) A direct quotation is set off from the rest of the sentence by commas or by a question mark or an exclamation point.**

EXAMPLES She said, "We can reach them by telephone."
"What did you say about me?" she asked.

► **NOTE** If the quotation is only a phrase, do not set it off by commas.

EXAMPLE Apparently he does not believe in government "of the people, by the people, for the people."

**(4) Other marks of punctuation when used with quotation marks are placed according to the following rules:**

1. *Commas and periods are always placed inside the closing quotation marks.*

EXAMPLE "I know," he said, "that we can finish the job today."

2. *Semicolons and colons are always placed outside the closing quotation marks.*

EXAMPLES "Ellen," my grandmother said, "you should stop being a burden on your family"; then she suggested that I finish school and get a job.
The following are what Jane Sims describes as "highbrow reading": Homer, Shakespeare, Levertov, and Dickinson.

3. *Question marks and exclamation points are placed inside the closing quotation marks if the quotation is a question or an exclamation; otherwise they are placed outside.*

EXAMPLES "Are the players ready?" asked the referee.
"How trying you are sometimes!" she exclaimed.
Were you surprised when he said, "Pull over"?
How disappointing it was to hear him say, "Your train has left"!

No more than one comma or one end mark is used at the end of a quotation.

INCORRECT Did you ask Mrs. Regan who said, "Life is a flight of uncarpeted stairs."? [two end marks, period and question mark]

CORRECT Have you asked Mrs. Regan who said, "Life is a flight of uncarpeted stairs"?

INCORRECT Did you ever ask yourself, "Where will I be ten years from now?"?

CORRECT Did you ever ask yourself, "Where will I be ten years from now?"

**(5) When you write dialogue, begin a new paragraph every time the speaker changes.**

EXAMPLE "Hi, guys. Have you heard about Sandra and Bob?" Betty and I knew it was Sally Howe with some more gossip, and we also knew Sandra was on the other side of the row of lockers.

"Hi, Sally. How'd you like that French exam?" Betty was trying to change the subject fast.

"Oh, who cares about French?" she said. "Have you heard about Sandra and Bob?"

"Sally," I said in a feeble attempt to sidetrack her, "where did you get that sweater? I've never seen one like it."

"Say, what goes on here?" Sally persisted. "I'm trying to tell you a story I heard about Sandra and that Bob Sharp and—oh, hello, Sandra. I didn't know you were here!"

"Serves you right, you gossip!" Sandra approached menacingly. "Now what's that story?"

**(6) When a quoted passage consists of more than one paragraph, place quotation marks at the beginning of each paragraph and at the end of the entire passage, not at the end of each paragraph.**

► **NOTE** Usually such a long quotation will be set off from the rest of the paper by indention and single spacing. In such a case, no quotation marks will be necessary.

**(7) Use single quotation marks to enclose a quotation within a quotation.**

EXAMPLE Her exact words were, "For tomorrow read Frost's poem 'Mending Wall.' "

**31j. Use quotation marks to enclose titles of chapters, articles, short stories, poems, songs, and other parts of books and periodicals.**

EXAMPLES Read Chapter 37, "Victorian Poetry."

I enjoy Pauline Kael's column, "The Current Cinema," in the *New Yorker.*

► **NOTE** Book titles and names of magazines are indicated by underlining (italics) (see page 557).

**31k. Use quotation marks to enclose slang words, technical terms, and other expressions that are unusual in standard English.**

Use this device sparingly.

EXAMPLES I heard him characterized as a "loony" and a "weirdo."

These units of speech are referred to by linguists as "phonemes."

Because his first name was Fiorello, Mayor La-Guardia was known as the "little flower."

**EXERCISE 2.** Copy the following sentences, inserting quotation marks and other required punctuation.

1. How many of you Mrs. Martinez asked have studied a foreign language for more than two years.
2. Nice try Donna was what the coach said.
3. We should have started our homework earlier said Beth we have answered only three questions so far.
4. Where have you been she asked.
5. Someone once asked Bernard Shaw how old he was, and he answered I'm as old as my tongue and a few years older than my teeth.
6. To whom was Stendhal referring asked Mrs. Ross when he dedicated his novels to the happy few.
7. Was it Elizabeth Browning said Sandra who wrote the poem Shall I Compare Thee to a Summer's Day?
8. Cast off shouted the captain we're bound for Rio.

9. Would you let us hand in our research papers next week Ms. Lewis we asked none of the books we need are in the library.
10. Alice whispered thank you for lending me the article Is There Life on Other Planets? Barbara.

## THE APOSTROPHE

**31l. To form the possessive case of a singular noun, add an apostrophe and an *s*.**

EXAMPLES Glenda's opinion
Kay's coat
Gus's hat

In words of more than one syllable which end in an *s*-sound, it is permissible to form the singular possessive by adding the apostrophe without the *s*. This is done to avoid too many *s*-sounds.

EXAMPLES the Furness' car
the princess' wedding
Odysseus' travels

► NOTE Since writers vary in the use of the apostrophe, it is not possible to make a hard and fast rule about the apostrophe in singular words ending in *s*. Thus *Hughes' poetry* and *Hughes's poetry* are equally acceptable. Punctuate according to pronunciation. If you say "Hugheses" or "McCullerses," write "Hughes's" and "McCullers's." If you say "Hughes" poems or "McCullers" novels, write "Hughes' " and "McCullers'."

**(1) To form the possessive case of a plural noun ending in *s*, add only the apostrophe.**

EXAMPLES girls' gymnasium
the Joneses' tennis court

► NOTE The few plural nouns that do not end in *s* form the possessive by adding the apostrophe and an *s* just as singular nouns do.

EXAMPLES women's fashions
children's games

**(2) Personal pronouns in the possessive case (*his, hers, its, ours, yours, theirs,* and the relative pronoun *whose*) do not require an apostrophe.**

INCORRECT I thought the scarf was her's.
CORRECT I thought the scarf was **hers.**

INCORRECT You have seen baseball at it's best.
CORRECT You have seen baseball at **its** best.

INCORRECT Do you know who's book this is?
CORRECT Do you know **whose** book this is?

**(3) Indefinite pronouns (*one, everyone, everybody,* etc.) in the possessive case require an apostrophe and an *s*.**[1]

EXAMPLES **Everyone's** prediction was wrong.
She objected to **everybody's** getting a prize.

**EXERCISE 3.** Number your paper 1–10. After the proper number, write both the singular and plural possessive of the italicized word.

EXAMPLE 1. *citizen* privilege
1. *citizen's, citizens'*

1. *city* water supply
2. *girl* dresses
3. *friend* opinions
4. *deer* horns
5. *laborer* wages
6. *man* neckties
7. *dog* collars
8. *fox* tricks
9. *student* books
10. *church* doctrines

**EXERCISE 4.** Number your paper 1–20. If the possessive case in each item in the list has been correctly formed, write a + after the proper number. If it has been incorrectly formed, write the correct form.

1. everyone's friend
2. bus' brakes
3. children's toys
4. this school's reputation
5. spectacles' rims
6. Is this your's?
7. a girl's or a boy's bike
8. made it's way to port
9. tree's trunk
10. Victory is our's.

[1] Note the correct form of such words used with *else:* everyone *else's;* somebody *else's.* Note that there is no apostrophe in *oneself.*

11. a street of worker's homes
12. in the Brown's yard
13. that nation's business
14. women's objections
15. broke it's back
16. travelers' passports
17. marines bravery
18. did its best
19. babie's bottles
20. the actors' roles

**(4) In hyphenated words, names of organizations and business firms, and words showing joint possession, only the last word is possessive in form.**

| | |
|---|---|
| EXAMPLES | **Mother-in-law'**s visit |
| | **commander-in-chief'**s order |
| ORGANIZATIONS | the **Food and Agriculture Organization'**s work |
| | **Dun and Bradstreet'**s publications |
| | **Proctor and Gamble'**s products |
| JOINT POSSESSION | **Dorothy and Ann'**s room |
| | **Jack and Tom'**s responsibility |

EXCEPTION: When the second word is a possessive pronoun, the first word is also possessive.

| | |
|---|---|
| INCORRECT | Dorothy and my room |
| CORRECT | **Dorothy's and my** room |
| INCORRECT | her friend and her reasons |
| CORRECT | her **friend's and her** reasons |

**(5) When two or more persons possess something individually, each of their names is possessive in form.**

EXAMPLE **Jack'**s and **Tom'**s sweaters

**(6) The words *minute, hour, day, week, month, year,* etc., when used as possessive adjectives, require an apostrophe. Words indicating amount in cents or dollars, when used as possessive adjectives, require apostrophes.**

EXAMPLES a minute's work, five minutes' work
a day's rest, three days' rest[1]
one cent's worth, five cents' worth

[1] Also correct: a three-day rest, etc.

**EXERCISE 5.** In the following list, the possessive relationship is expressed by means of a phrase. Change each so that the possessive case of the noun or pronoun will be used to express the same relationship. Write your answers.

EXAMPLE 1. a vacation of two weeks
1. *a two weeks' vacation*

1. gloves of Gail and Pat
2. locker room of the boys
3. home of my sister-in-law
4. personality of a person
5. boat of Carlos and Bob
6. opinion of the editor in chief
7. worth of three dollars
8. store of Barton and McLean
9. research of Charles Drew
10. top of it
11. fears of the witnesses
12. a delay of a week
13. worth of ten cents
14. events of the day
15. wraps of the ladies
16. authority of the sergeant-at-arms
17. car of Tina and Jill
18. a wait of ten minutes
19. rays of the moon
20. films of Abbott and Costello

**31m. Use an apostrophe to show where letters have been omitted in a contraction.**

A contraction is a word made up of two words combined into one by omitting one or more letters.

EXAMPLES For *do not* the contraction is **don't.** [the letter *o* *omitted*]
For *it is* the contraction is **it's.** [the letter *i* omitted]
For *they are* the contraction is **they're.** [the letter *a* *omitted*]

► **NOTE** The most common error in the use of the apostrophe in a contraction (except the failure to use it at all) comes from the confusion of *it's,* which means *it is,* with the possessive form *its* (*its* appearance), which has no apostrophe. Another common error, probably the result of carelessness, is the insertion of the apostrophe in the wrong place: *ca'nt* for *can't, does'nt* for *doesn't,* etc. Also note especially that *let's* in such an expression as "Let's go!" is a contraction of *let us* and requires an apostrophe for the omitted *u.*

**31n. Use the apostrophe and *s* to form the plural of letters, numbers, and signs, and of words referred to as words.**

EXAMPLES Mississippi is spelled with four *s*'s, four *i*'s, and two *p*'s.

Instead of a *3* and an *8* he had written two *3*'s.

How many +'s in this exercise?

Count the number of ***and***'s in that paragraph.

**EXERCISE 6.** Number your paper 1–25. Copy the following, inserting apostrophes where they are needed and changing the phrasal possessives to the possessive case. Some of the items are correct.

1. girls locker room
2. guns of a man-of-war
3. Its quite true, isn't it?
4. wind in its rigging
5. Lets find out whats up.
6. Ive found cryings no use.
7. firm of Stengel and Ford
8. mens shoes
9. Whats its meaning?
10. a days fun
11. football of Fred and Herb
12. Whos in Jeans car?
13. this chains links
14. Im sure its early.
15. Theyll play if he lets them.
16. Her parents opinions are the same as hers.
17. Arent there two *r*s in *embarrass?*
18. womens handbags
19. boys magazine
20. Her numbers two *3*s and two *0*s.
21. publications of Bennett and Osborne
22. One works by oneself.
23. office of the boss
24. notebooks of Rosa and Maria
25. Lets see whos here.

## THE HYPHEN

**31o. Use a hyphen to divide a word at the end of a line.**

Division of words at the end of a line in order to maintain an even margin should be avoided, but it is sometimes necessary. For rules that will help you in deciding where to place the hyphen see "Manuscript Form," pages 513–14.

**31p. Use a hyphen with compound numbers from *twenty-one* to *ninety-nine* and with fractions used as adjectives.**

EXAMPLES **thirty-three** students
a **two-thirds** majority, *but*
**two thirds** of the students

**31q. Use a hyphen with the prefixes *ex–, self–, all–,* with the suffix *–elect,* and with all prefixes before a proper noun or proper adjective.**

| | | |
|---|---|---|
| EXAMPLES | ex▪president | un▪American |
| | self▪imposed | anti▪Russian |
| | all▪star | pro▪British |
| | governor▪elect | Pan▪American |

**31r. Hyphenate a compound adjective when it precedes the word it modifies.**

| | |
|---|---|
| a second▪story room | a room on the second story |
| an after▪school meeting | a meeting after school |
| dark▪colored glasses | glasses of a dark color |
| door▪to▪door selling | selling from door to door |
| well▪planned program | The program was well planned. |

► NOTE Do not use a hyphen if one of the modifiers is an adverb ending in *–ly*.

EXAMPLES beautifully made table
quietly prepared meal

**31s. Use a hyphen to prevent confusion or awkwardness.**

EXAMPLES re▪collect [prevents confusion with *recollect*]
re▪form [prevents confusion with *reform*]
anti▪icer [avoids the awkwardness of *antiicer*]
semi▪invalid [avoids the awkwardness of *semiinvalid*]

## THE DASH

**31t. Use a dash to indicate an abrupt break in thought.**

EXAMPLES He might—and according to plans, should—have reinforced the Second Division.

The title—if, indeed, the poem had a title—has escaped me.

**31u. Use a dash to mean *namely, in other words,* or *that is* before an explanation.**

EXAMPLE The referees had it in their power to prevent the fracas—they could have stopped the game at any time. [dash means *that is*]

In this use the colon and the dash are frequently interchangeable.

EXAMPLE The referees had it in their power to prevent the fracas: they could have stopped the game at any time.

## PARENTHESES

**31v. Use parentheses to enclose incidental explanatory matter which is added to a sentence but is not considered of major importance.**

EXAMPLES Representative Chisholm (New York) is a member of the committee.

The results of the recent election affected the stock market (see Diagram A) only temporarily.

► NOTE For setting off incidental matter, commas, dashes, and parentheses are frequently interchangeable. Commas and dashes are more common than parentheses.

**(1) Be sure that any material within parentheses can be omitted without changing the basic meaning or structure of the sentence.**

IMPROPER USE OF PARENTHESES

Lena had been working (in a bookstore) for many years. [The idea in parentheses is too important to the meaning of the sentence to be placed in parentheses.]

**(2) Punctuation marks are used within parentheses when they belong with the parenthetical matter. Punctuation marks which belong with the main part of the sentence are placed after a closing parenthesis.**

EXAMPLES Mr. Baker asked him **(**What a tactless question**!)** whether he had been fired.

If the petition is signed by Alison **(**Does she spell her name that way**?),** others will probably sign it.

## BRACKETS

In ordinary composition you will have practically no use for brackets. Commas, dashes, and parentheses are preferable as means of setting off parenthetical matter.

**31w. Use brackets to enclose explanations within parentheses or in quoted material when the explanation is not part of the quotation.**

EXAMPLES The following is a quotation from Mrs. Gray's address of acceptance: "I am honored by it **[**the appointment**]**, but I am also aware of the responsibilities which accompany it."

The court of appeals upheld the lower court's decision by a vote of 3–2. (See the explanation on page 217 **[**Chart B**]** of the system of *lower* and *higher courts.)*

**REVIEW EXERCISE.** Most of the necessary punctuation and capital letters have been omitted from the following passages. When a passage is assigned, copy it, making it as mechanically perfect as you can. The only changes you need to make in paragraphing are those required by dialogue. Some of the punctuation is incorrect, but in most instances you need only *add* punctuation and capitals. When you are in doubt as to a particular punctuation or capitalization problem, don't guess. Look up the rule.

1

In any discussion of the thrilling unbelievable deeds of Americas sports immortals the feats of Ty Cobb the georgia peach are sure to play a prominent part. In his twenty three years in the major leagues Cobb scored more runs made more hits and stole more bases than any other player in history. His lifetime batting average the highest ever made was .367 he finished three seasons with an average better than .400 won the american league batting championship twelve times a feat never equaled and stole ninety-six bases in one season 1915 more than entire teams now steal. To increase his speed Cobb used to wear heavy shoes in training so that his playing shoes would feel light he was the first player to swing three bats while warming up pitchers who usually walk dangerous hitters didn't dare walk Cobb he was too dangerous on the bases, he played twenty-one years with the Detroit tigers taking time out in 1918 to join the chemical warfare division of the army. He was the first of baseballs heroes to be represented when in 1939 the baseball hall of fame was opened in Cooperstown New York.

2

At 9 30 A M on lincolns birthday which isnt a holiday here a fire broke out in the chemistry laboratory of emerson high school the big new fireproof brick building on the north side of oxford boulevard. The third period chemistry II class which is composed of seniors happened to be in the laboratory displaying a seniors presence of mind the students seized their chemistry notes their english texts and their french notebooks and shouting with glee hurled them into the flames. It was Jerry Montague I believe who at this exciting moment appeared in the doorway carrying one of the schools fire extinguishers. wow what a splendid conflagration he exclaimed whats cooking as he prepared to warm himself at the literary bonfire someone I am sure it was an accident knocked a bottle of sodium into a sink which was full of water. During the ensuing weeks the principals squad of detectives did its duty but didnt succeed in finding the pyromaniac who had caused all the excitement.

3

I was sitting in the front row of the bleachers Wednesday afternoon waiting for the start of the fifth inning of our game with plainfield high. These are Ann Wrights books Sue, she asked me to keep them while she went back to the high school for a minute but Ive got to go home. Will you watch them until she gets back This unexpected outburst from Jan Cunningham was accompanied by the arrival in my lap of a pile of literature science math and French textbooks a notebook and a pencil case I wondered why some girls carry so many books home. I dropped Anns library under the seat and turned back to the game. Someones voice bellowed in my ear knock the cover off it Meg, Meg you know is our best hitter. I forgot everything but the game at 8 30 that night Jan telephoned she wanted to know what Id done with Anns books. Anns books I asked vaguely oh yes I guess I left them there. where did you leave them Jan sounded desperate. Under the bleachers, Ann didnt come for them I said. Yes she did Jan explained, she looked for me and when she couldnt find me she thought Id taken the books home now she hasnt her books and its pouring outside.

I was sorry when I saw the books the next morning they had been swollen by the rain to twice their normal size, Jan said Ann and she were angry but it wasnt my fault was it.

# Aids to Good English

## PART SIX

Chapter 32

# Information in the Library

## Arrangement and Resources of the Library

Libraries are sufficiently alike so that when you have become familiar with one library, you can easily find your way in others. You should understand the following:

1. The arrangement of books in the library
2. The uses of the card catalogue
3. The names and functions of the parts of a book
4. The use of the *Readers' Guide*
5. The use of the vertical file
6. The location of items in your library

## ARRANGEMENT OF BOOKS IN THE LIBRARY

### 32a. Learn the arrangement of books.

#### Fiction

Books of fiction (novels and stories) are usually arranged on the shelves alphabetically by authors. By this time you know where in your library the books of fiction are located. It is a simple matter, if you know the author of a book, to go directly to the book on the fiction shelves.

You can find out whether the library owns a certain book by looking it up in the card catalogue (page 578). If the book you want is listed in the catalogue but is not on the shelf, ask the librarian about it. It may be "out" in circulation, or it may be "on reserve." Possibly, the librarian will reserve the book for you by placing your name on the waiting list. When your name comes up, the librarian will notify you.

## Nonfiction: The Dewey Decimal System

The arrangement of nonfiction books is accomplished through an amazingly efficient system developed by Melvil Dewey, an American librarian.[1] Although only librarians need to know all the details of the Dewey system, every user of a library should understand the principle on which the system is based.

In the Dewey system, every nonfiction book receives a number. The number, which is written on the spine of the book, is determined by the particular classification of the book in the system. There are ten subject classifications, and any book can be fitted into one of them.

Within these broad divisions there can be an unlimited number of subdivisions. Since a decimal point plays an important part in the numbering of books, the plan is called the Dewey decimal system. A valuable feature of this system is that all books on the same subject are given the same number and may be placed together on the library

[1] The Library of Congress system of cataloguing, used in many public libraries but not commonly used in high school libraries, classifies all books, both fiction and nonfiction. Each general subject category (Philosophy, Science, etc.) is assigned a code letter. For example, the letter *H* at the beginning of a call number designates Social Science. In addition, whole categories are often subdivided by adding a second code letter to the first. Thus letter *P* (which designates Literature) may be followed by the letter *S* to specify American literature. Call numbers include the letter codes, followed by a series of numbers that identify specific books within a category. For example, the book *Responses: Prose Pieces 1953–1976*, by Richard Wilbur, an American author, has the Library of Congress call number PS 3545. A complete schedule of Library of Congress categories and their letter codes is usually available in the reference section of any library using this system.

shelves. Once you have learned the class number of the subject you are interested in, you can find most of the books in the library on this subject grouped in one place.

| | |
|---|---|
| 000–099 | General Works (encyclopedias, periodicals, etc.) |
| 100–199 | Philosophy (includes psychology, conduct, etc.) |
| 200–299 | Religion (includes mythology) |
| 300–399 | Social Sciences (economics, government, law, etc.) |
| 400–499 | Language (dictionaries, grammars, etc.) |
| 500–599 | Science (mathematics, chemistry, physics, etc.) |
| 600–699 | Technology (agriculture, engineering, aviation, etc.) |
| 700–799 | The Arts and Recreation (sculpture, painting, music, photography, sports, etc.) |
| 800–899 | Literature (poetry, plays, orations, etc.) |
| 900–909, 930–999 | History |
| 910–919 | Travel |
| 920–929 | Biography (arranged alphabetically by name of subject of biography) |

Books having the same class number may be distinguished from one another by the author's name. For instance, all books on aviation are given the number 629.1. This number appears on the spine of the book. With the number appears the first letter of the author's name: if the author is Hood, the book's complete number is $\frac{629.1}{\text{H}}$. This number, including the first letter of the author's name, is known as the book's *call number.* To find the call number of a book, you look up the book in the card catalogue.

## LOCATING INFORMATION IN THE LIBRARY

### The Card Catalogue

Undoubtedly you have used the card catalogue in your school or town library. You may not, however, know as much about it as you need to know in order to get the most help from it.

## 32b. Learn the uses of the card catalogue.

The card catalogue is a cabinet containing drawers filled with alphabetically arranged cards. In most libraries, the catalogue holds at least three cards for each book in the library: at least one *author card,* the *title card,* and at least one *subject card.*

### The Author Card

The *author card* has the name of the author at the top. When there is joint authorship, there is a card for each author. You may look up any book in the library by looking under the author's last name. Since the cards for all books by an author are placed together, you have the additional advantage of being able to find out what other books by the author the library owns. Cards for books *about* an author follow the cards for books *by* an author.

### The Title Card

The *title card* has the book's title at the top. The quickest way to find a book in the catalogue is to look it up under its title. Cards for books whose titles begin with *a, an,* or *the* are arranged alphabetically by the second word in the title. For example, the title card for a book entitled *The Writing of Fiction* would be found under *Writing of Fiction, The.*

### The Subject Card

The *subject card* has at the top the subject with which the book deals. Subject cards are invaluable when you wish to find a number of books on a subject but do not know specific titles or authors. Under the subject heading "Political parties—United States" for instance, you will find a card for every book in the library on this subject. In fact, you may find a card for every book that contains as little as one article or chapter on United States political parties, so thoroughly is the cataloguing done.

### Information Given on a Catalogue Card

Brief study of the sample catalogue cards reproduced on page 578 will show you that a complete card gives a great deal of information. In addition to giving the title, author, and call number of a book, the card may give the following information:

1. *Facts about authorship:* full name of the author; names of joint authors and illustrators, if any.
2. *Facts about publication:* the place of publication; the name of the publisher; the date of publication.
3. *Facts about the book:* number of pages; whether the book contains illustrations, diagrams, etc.; height of the book in centimeters.

### "See" and "See Also" Cards

An important feature of a complete card catalogue is the cross-reference cards which it contains. These are of two kinds—"see" cards and "see also" cards. The "see" card refers you to a subject heading under which you will find the material you wish. Suppose, for instance, that you wish to look up some books on World War I. You look under "World War I" in the card catalogue. The card headed "World War I," however, says "see European War 1914–1918." This means that books on World War I are catalogued under the heading "European War 1914–1918." The "see" card tells you, in effect, "There is nothing here. You will find what you want under this other heading."

A second type of cross-reference card is the "see also" card, which refers you to places in the catalogue where you may find additional titles on your subject. For instance, if you are looking for books about detectives and have found some listed under the subject heading "Detectives," you may find a "see also" card advising you to look also under the subject headings "Police" and "Secret Service." A "see also" card says, "There is more material in these places."

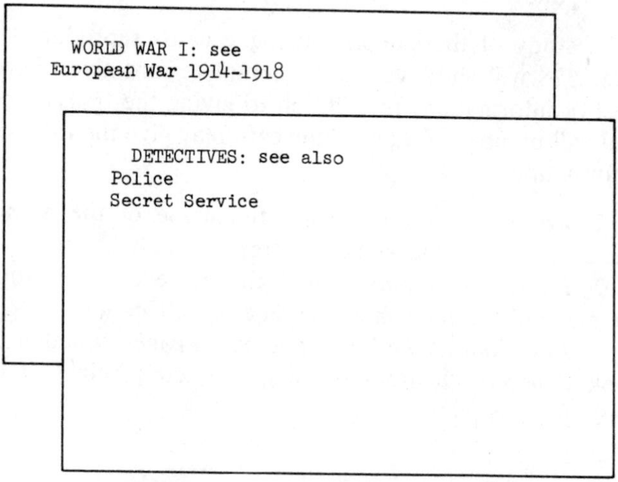


**Sample Cross Reference Cards**

## SUMMARY

The card catalogue is a valuable library tool which may be used for the following purposes:

(1) To find the call number of a book
(2) To find out whether a certain book is owned by the library
(3) To find out what books by a certain author are in the library
(4) To find out what books on a certain subject are in the library
(5) To find out such facts about a book as may be given on a catalogue card: facts about authorship, publication, number of pages, illustrations, etc.

**EXERCISE 1.** Using the card catalogue in your library, find the title, author, and call number of the following. Write them on your paper.

1. A history of American literature
2. A book about South America
3. A book by Edith Wharton
4. A book giving information about Edith Wharton
5. A book about baseball

Using the card catalogue, find answers to the following questions. Write the answers.

6. Does the library own any books by Willa Cather? If so, give the title and call number of one of them.
7. Give the title, author, publisher, and publication date of a book about George Washington Carver.
8. Does the library own the complete plays of Shakespeare in one volume? If so, give the exact title and the publisher of the book.
9. Give the title, author, and date of publication of a book of American poetry.
10. Does the library own a copy of Charlotte Brontë's *Jane Eyre*? If so, give the publisher.

## The Parts of a Book

Once you have found the right book, you should be able to take advantage of the various aids that the author and publisher have provided. To do so, you need to know the important parts of a book and the uses of each.

**32c. Learn the names and functions of the parts of a book.**

### The Frontispiece

The frontispiece is a full-page illustration. If the book has a frontispiece, it faces the title page.

### The Title Page

The first important page in a book, the title page gives the complete title, the subtitle, if there is one, the name of the author or editor (sometimes an affiliation, especially in a textbook), the name of the publisher, and the place of publication.

### The Copyright Page

The reverse side of the title page is the copyright page. Here you find the year in which the book was copyrighted; i.e., registered in the government copyright office in Washington. Before publishers release a new book, they send two copies to the United States Copyright Office along with certain required information. The office then issues a copyright, which gives to the copyright owner exclusive right to print the book or any part of it during the lifetime of the author and for a period of fifty years after the author's death. Sometimes publishers secure a copyright in their own name, sometimes in the name of the author. The purpose of the copyright is to protect the author and publisher, who have invested their work and money in the book. Reprinting copyrighted materials without the permission of the copyright owner is a criminal offense.

Often you will find more than one date listed on the copyright page: "Copyright 1946, 1949, 1955." This means that the first edition of the book was copyrighted in 1946. In 1949 and 1955 new material was added and a new copyright secured to cover the new material. In books published since September, 1957, the international copyright symbol is used: © 1980. The date of copyright is very important when you wish to know whether the material in a book is sufficiently up-to-date to be reliable.

Publishers sometimes indicate on this page which printing of the book this particular volume represents. Note the distinction between a new copyright date and a new printing date. The former tells when the book was last revised; the latter, when it was merely reprinted.

## The Preface, Foreword, Introduction

These terms are now used interchangeably to refer to matter at the beginning of a book in which the author, editor, or publisher explains the purpose and scope of the book, gives information which aids the reader in understanding the book, acknowledges indebtedness, etc.

## The Table of Contents

The table of contents appears at the front of the book and consists of a list of the chapters and subdivisions with their page numbers. It provides a quick view of the content and organization of the entire book.

The table of contents may tell you how much information the book contains on a particular topic, but the index is a more reliable guide for this purpose. For example, a book on the history of aviation may or may not have a chapter title referring to fighter planes of World War I, but some mention of this topic is almost certain to be included in such a book. If it is, you will find it listed in the index.

## List of Illustrations (Maps, Diagrams, Charts, etc.)

A list of illustrations with page numbers is sometimes included in books that give a prominent place to illustrations. Such a list would be of obvious value in an atlas, a history of art, or a book on fashions, for example.

## The Appendix

The appendix contains additional material which the author did not wish to include in the body of the book. It may include long quotations from other works on the subject, lists, diagrams and tables, etc.

## The Glossary

A glossary is usually a list of definitions of technical words used in the book. It is placed near the close of the book.

## The Bibliography

The bibliography is a list of books consulted by the author in writing a book or recommended to the reader who wishes more information.

## The Index

The index is an alphabetical list of topics treated in the book, given with page numbers. It is much more detailed than the table of contents. The index lists every reference to a topic and tells you exactly how many pages are devoted to it. When you have found a book that seems likely to provide information on your topic, the index will tell you how much information there is and exactly where to find it.

## The End Papers

The pages pasted inside the front and back covers of the book are the end papers. Sometimes they are used for a map or an illustration or to give a kind of summary of the contents.

**EXERCISE 2.** Write answers to the following questions. You will notice that the last 6 items refer to this book.

1. List the parts of a book of nonfiction that you would not find in a book of fiction.
2. In a sentence or two, distinguish between printing date and copyright date.
3. Explain the purpose of a glossary.
4. Distinguish between a table of contents and an index.
5. Write the date when this book was copyrighted.
6. In which years was new material added?
7. By what firm was this book published?
8. Where is this firm located?
9. Skim the preface of this book and in a sentence or two state its primary purpose.
10. How many pages are there in the index of this book?

## The *Readers' Guide*

A large part of the library reference work you will do in high school will deal with subjects of a contemporary rather than a historical nature. The best source of information, indeed very often the only source of information on truly current subjects, is the magazine. Without some sort of guide, you would have to spend hours hunting through magazines in search of articles on a subject. However, the *Readers' Guide to Periodical Literature* solves this problem for you.

### 32d. Learn how to use the *Readers' Guide to Periodical Literature.*

In the *Readers' Guide,* articles from some 170 magazines are indexed alphabetically by subjects and by authors. You may look up the subject in which you are interested and

**BALL, George Wildman**
Options on Iran. por Newsweek 95:43 Ap 7 '80
Question of oil [interview by R. Christopher] por Macleans 93:50 Ja 7 '80
*about*
Mr. Ball's world. E. N. Luttwak. New Repub 182:12-14 Ap 5 '80 •
**BALL, Leslie D.** See Waldron, D. jt auth
**BALLANTINE, H. Thomas, Jr**
Role of government in health-care delivery in the 1980s [address, January 16, 1980] Vital Speeches 46:258-60 F 15 '80
**BALLANTINE, Ian**
Uses and abuses of enchantment. D. Weinberger. il Macleans 93:45-5 Ja 28 '80 •
**BALLERINAS.** See Dancers
**BALLET**
*See also*
Choreography
Cleveland Ballet Company
Dance Theatre of Harlem
Houston Ballet Company
Joffrey Ballet
Maryland Ballet
Merce Cunningham & Dance Company
Metropolitan Opera Ballet
Motion pictures—Dance films
New York City Ballet
Pittsburgh Ballet Theatre
Television broadcasting—Dance programs
Dance. J. Maskey. See issues of High fidelity and Musical America
Domestic reports: news and views from across the country. See issues of Dance magazine
Editor's log. W. Como. See issues of Dance magazine
Opera ballet:
Taming the two-headed monster. B. Laine. Dance Mag 54:51-3 F '80
Presstime news. See issues of Dance magazine
Reviews:
Ballet Metropolitan of Columbus. A. Barzel. Dance Mag 54:51-3 F '80
Dance Ring. A. Barzel. Dance Mag 54:44-6 F '80
Louisville Ballet. A. Barzel. Dance Mag 54:50-1 F '80
Ohio Ballet. W. Salisbury. Dance Mag 54:116+ F '80
Tulsa Ballet Theatre: old world style for a new frontier. J. Pikula. il pors Dance Mag 54:62-5 F '80

**Bibliography**

Dance, books. il Dance Mag 54:106+ Ja; 121 F; 121 Mr '80

**Directories**

Dance directory. See issues of Dance magazine

**International aspects**

Foreign reports: news and views from around the world. See issues of Dance magazine

**Study and teaching**

Education briefs [ed by M. Pierpont] See issues of Dance magazine

**Australia**

Dance in Australia. A. Brissenden. il Dance Mag 54:12 F '80

**Canada**

*See also*
National Ballet of Canada

- author entry
- article by author
- article about author
- "see" cross reference to joint author
- title of article
- title and issue of magazine
- subject entry
- "see" cross reference
- volume number
- page reference
- date of issue
- description of article
- secondary subject heading
- "see also" cross reference

find the articles that have been written on it and the magazines in which they appeared.

Magazine stories are listed by title and by author; the complete entry is given with the author listing only. Poems and plays are listed by author.

Articles *about* moving pictures and plays are listed under the subject headings MOVING PICTURE PLAYS and DRAMAS, beneath the subheading **Criticisms, plots, etc.**

The *Readers' Guide* is published in paperbound pamphlets twice a month from September to June and monthly in July and August. Occasionally during the year a cumulative issue is published including the articles listed in preceding months as well as those for the current month. At the end of a year, a large volume is published containing all entries for the year, and every two years a volume covering a two-year period is published.

You must remember, however, that the usefulness of the *Readers' Guide* is limited by the availability to you of the magazines to which it refers you. When you are taking down references from the *Readers' Guide,* you should know what magazines your library has. You should know, too, whether the library has kept back issues of all these magazines or only of certain ones, and for how many years back it has the magazines.

A sample excerpt from the *Readers' Guide* is reproduced on the left. You can probably understand the many abbreviations used, but if you cannot, you will find them explained in the front of the *Readers' Guide* itself.

**EXERCISE 3.** Write answers to the following questions.

1. Is there in your library a list of the magazines to which the library subscribes? Does the list give the dates of back numbers on file? If so, for what years does the library have back numbers of either the *Atlantic* or *Harper's Magazine?*
2. Where are the back numbers of magazines stored in your library? How do you get the particular number you want?
3. What is the date of the latest *Readers' Guide* in your library? What period does it cover?

4, 5, 6. Select one of the following subjects, look it up in the *Readers' Guide,* and list on your paper three articles *that you could get in your library* on the subject. Give the complete listing for each, as shown in the *Readers' Guide.* Show that you understand the abbreviations by spelling out all of them.

| | | |
|---|---|---|
| Housing | Aviation | Photography |
| Education | Taxation | Labor |

7. Select a prominent person of today and look for an article about the person in the *Readers' Guide.* Give the complete listing.
8. Find and copy a "see" reference from the *Readers' Guide.*
9. Copy from the *Readers' Guide* the complete listing of a review of a motion picture.
10. Copy from the *Readers' Guide* the complete listing of a review of a play.

## The Vertical File

**32e. Learn the nature and proper use of the vertical file.**

Useful information on current topics is often to be found in pamphlets, usually paperbound. They are published by government agencies, industrial concerns, museums, colleges and universities, radio stations, welfare organizations, etc. The librarian files pamphlets in a special cabinet, usually referred to as the vertical file, and can help you find material on your subject, especially if it is of contemporary interest.

In the vertical file the librarian also stores interesting pictures and significant clippings from newspapers.

## Microfilm Projectors

To save space, many libraries today store certain publications, such as newspapers and government publications, on microfilm. Each small spool of microfilm can contain hundreds of pages, reduced photographically to microscopic size. To use the film, one must thread it into a projector that enlarges each microscopic image to a size suitable for reading. A librarian can provide assistance in operating microfilm projectors.

**32f. Learn the location of items in your library.**

Your use of a library will be more efficient if you know the exact location of the principal items you may wish to use. If you will remember the information the following exercise calls for, you will save both the librarian and yourself a great deal of time.

**EXERCISE 4.** Be prepared to state where each of the following is located in your school or public library.

1. The desk where books are charged out
2. The card catalogue
3. The *Readers' Guide*
4. The magazine rack and the newspaper rack
5. The pamphlet file
6. The fiction shelves
7. The encyclopedias
8. The biography shelves
9. The unabridged dictionaries
10. The reserved-book shelf or the new-book shelf

Chapter 33

# Reference Books

## Special Sources of Information

Some libraries have bigger collections of reference books than others, but almost any library will have most of the standard reference books described here. It may surprise you to find how quickly and easily you can put a finger on needed facts, once you know that a reference book specifically made to supply them is in a nearby library. Familiarity with a library's reference books will increase your efficiency in looking up information.

Just reading the descriptions that follow here will not be enough. Familiarity comes from direct contact. Go to the library and spend a few minutes with each book. Look at the table of contents, locate the index, and sample enough text to see how it works.

Each of you might be asked to concentrate on one particular reference work listed here and to report on it later to the entire class.

All of you, however, should carefully study the descriptions of the books discussed here and do the exercises that end the chapter. Even though a reference work is not available here and now, you should know that it exists and you should know what to expect from it.

## ENCYCLOPEDIAS

**33a. Get acquainted with encyclopedias: their plan, content, and indexes.**

You have probably been using an encyclopedia in your schoolwork for some time. You know that it is a collection of articles in alphabetical order on nearly all fields of knowledge. Articles are written by experts, and the level of factual accuracy is high.

When you were younger, you may have believed an encyclopedia article contained all anyone needed to know about a subject. By now, however, you realize that an encyclopedia article gives an overall view. It cannot go into detail or show evidence on debatable points. It is a useful introduction, but for study in depth fuller treatment is necessary. For example, an encyclopedia article of less than five pages on Franklin Delano Roosevelt cannot give you as much information as James MacGregor Burns does in his biography of more than twelve hundred pages.

The index is important. If you looked in the *Encyclopedia Americana* under the entry "Olympic Games," you would find an article several columns long. But in the index, you would find the volumes and page numbers of more than twenty other entries with information about the games. If you had not used the index, you would not have known about these other entries.

This has been the usual plan. In 1974, the *Encyclopaedia Britannica* introduced a new plan. It expanded to thirty volumes. The first is an introduction to the rest of the encyclopedia. The remaining twenty-nine volumes are divided into a ten-volume *Micropaedia* and a nineteen-volume *Macropaedia*. The *Micropaedia* contains shorter articles, and the *Macropaedia* contains longer ones. Of course, there are far more articles in the *Micropaedia;* but the *Macropaedia* contains, in its smaller number of articles, extremely long, detailed, and in-depth treatment of the topics covered. Many of the *Macropaedia* articles are much longer than full-length books. In using the new *Britannica,* you would usually turn first to the *Micropaedia,* which includes complete cross-referencing, and then follow up the cross-referencing as far as you like. Whether this new approach to planning an encyclopedia will prove more popular or more helpful in dealing with today's vast amount of information remains to be seen.

Encyclopedias are kept up-to-date in three ways. First, a completely new edition can be prepared. Second, before a new printing some revisions can be made to keep up with new knowledge or developments. Third, encyclopedias publish yearbooks, which contain statistics, important events, and developments in every field pertaining to the year just preceding.

## Encyclopedias in Many Volumes

***Collier's Encyclopedia***

24 volumes
Bibliography and Index in Volume 24
Publishes *Collier's Yearbook*

***Encyclopedia Americana***

30 volumes
Index in Volume 30
Publishes the *Americana Annual*

***Encyclopaedia Britannica***

30 volumes
Cross-referencing throughout *Micropaedia*
Publishes the *Britannica Book of the Year*

***Encyclopedia International***

20 volumes
Index in Volume 20
Publishes the *Encyclopedia International Yearbook*

***World Book Encyclopedia***

22 volumes
Research Guide and Index in Volume 22
Publishes an annual supplement

### One- and Two-Volume Encyclopedias

Very often a brief, handy account of a subject is enough. For this purpose, a one- or two-volume "desk" encyclopedia is adequate. There are three well-known works of this kind. The *New Columbia Encyclopedia* and the *Random House Encyclopedia* are arranged alphabetically like dictionaries. The *Lincoln Library of Essential Information* has two volumes arranged in broad fields of knowledge with many subdivision articles and an index. Typical of the big fields covered are "The English Language," "Literature," and "History."

## GENERAL REFERENCE BOOKS

### Almanacs and Yearbooks

Although almanacs come out annually to cover a one-year period, many of their statistics include data for preceding years. Remember that an almanac tells about the year before its date: data for 1980 should be sought in the 1981 issue.

#### *World Almanac and Book of Facts*

Most popular of the handy annual reference books on the world today, the *World Almanac* gives facts and figures that are needed very often. Typical items are census tables, production quantities, export and import figures, election results, officeholders, sports records, Nobel and other prizewinners, and a summary of notable events. A full index is in the front.

#### *Information Please Almanac*

This almanac covers much of the same ground as the *World Almanac,* but in a different arrangement. Its full index is in the back. The *Information Please Almanac* covers fewer subjects, but its informal style is easy to follow and its articles are sometimes fuller.

***The International Yearbook and Statesmen's Who's Who***

*The International Yearbook and Statesmen's Who's Who* includes up-to-date information on international organizations and political, statistical, and directory information about each country of the world. A biographical section gives sketches of world leaders in government, church, commerce, industry, and education.

***Statesman's Year-book***

The *Statesman's Year-book* calls itself a "statistical and historical annual of the states of the world," with information useful to diplomats, officials, journalists, and scholars dealing with international affairs. Starting with international organizations (such as the UN) it goes on to individual nations, giving facts about each under these heads: government, area and population, religion, education, welfare, justice, defense, finance, production, communications, currency and banking, and diplomatic representatives. The index is in the back.

## Atlases

Don't think of an atlas as just a collection of maps. It contains information of many kinds: climate, rainfall, crops, topography, population, some history, etc.

There are many fine atlases. Find out which ones your library has and where they are kept. Because our day is marked by amazing numbers of new nations, new unions, and secessions, an atlas even a few years old may not show from ten to perhaps twenty or thirty nations as they now are. To find out how up-to-date an atlas is, check its copyright date in the opening pages.

A few of the atlases that are reliable (if you use a recent edition) are listed here.

***General Atlases***

*Hammond Contemporary World Atlas*

*National Geographic Atlas of the World*
*New York Times Atlas of the World*

Along with atlases showing the world as it is now are atlases showing it, or a region of it, as it was in one or more past periods. These historical atlases help us to visualize history.

***Historical Atlases***

*The American Heritage Pictorial Atlas of United States History*
*Rand McNally Atlas of World History*
Shepherd, William, *Historical Atlas*

## BIOGRAPHICAL REFERENCE BOOKS

**33b. Learn to use these handy biographical reference tools.**

Many of the biographical reference works discussed here are likely to be on your library's reference shelves. Since their functions differ, be sure to find out what each can do for you.

### General Biography

***Biography Index* (1946 to date)**

This work, as its name implies, is not a collection of biographies, but an index that tells you where to find material on the life of nearly anyone about whom a book or an article has been published. It indexes current biographical books written in English and biographical material in more than 1500 periodicals, in much the same manner as the *Readers' Guide.*

Like the *Readers' Guide,* the *Biography Index* is published regularly and in cumulative editions. It appears quarterly (in November, February, May, and August), with an annually published bound volume including all the year's listings. Arrangement is of two kinds: (1) straight alphabetical listing of persons written about, and (2) alphabetical listing of names under broad divisions by profession or occupation. Remember that this book is an *index* to biographical books and articles, not a book of biographies.

***Dictionary of American Biography***

This monumental work provides authoritative articles on the careers of hundreds of notable Americans no longer living, from the earliest historical times virtually to the present. Individual articles are more detailed than those in any encyclopedia, and there are more of them. The complete set of fifteen volumes includes a one-volume index, as well as separate supplementary volumes that keep the set up-to-date.

***Dictionary of National Biography***

From the long course of British civilization, this famous work selects notable Britishers no longer living, and covers their careers. It preceded our *Dictionary of American Biography* and was something of a model for it.

***The New Century Cyclopedia of Names* (3 volumes)**

As the title may imply, this work deals with proper names of all sorts, including real, legendary, and mythological persons, places, and events, as well as literary works and characters and works of art—100,000 in all. Names hard to find elsewhere are often at hand in it, and historians commend its accuracy.

***Webster's Biographical Dictionary***

In this book, over 40,000 concise biographies appear in alphabetical order. Care has been taken to give the correct pronunciation of each name. Information given is somewhat fuller than that shown in a general dictionary. Though it offers some details, it is not intended to provide the complete life of any person. The biography of Abraham Lincoln, for example, occupies less than one column.

### *Who's Who, Who's Who in America,* and *The International Who's Who*

These standard books, found in most libraries, give essential facts about notable *living* persons. Note that these are books of *facts;* they do not summarize the subject's life in any detail. Typical entries list parentage, place and date of birth, names of members of family, educationl background, positions held, important achievements, writings and their dates, awards, clubs or societies, religious and political affiliations, and present address.

*Who's Who* gives information about notable British persons and some famous persons in other countries. It comes out yearly.

*Who's Who in America* gives facts about notable Americans. It comes out every two years. Although persons listed in *Who's Who in America* are dropped out after they die, entries for the most important persons thus dropped are preserved in a volume entitled *Who Was Who in America.*

*The International Who's Who* might prove useful to you in locating material on persons not listed in the above-mentioned sources. Well-known educators, artists, diplomats, etc., from various parts of the globe are included here. However, due to space limitations, many of the lesser-known figures do not appear.

### *Current Biography*

Like the *Who's Who* books above, this monthly serial is concerned with *living* people. Each issue contains short, informal biographies of those currently prominent in the news. A picture of the person is often included. The scope is international.

Annually, articles in the 12 issues are put in alphabetical order in one bound volume. Currently, its cumulative index locates articles from 1971 on. A separate index covers those from 1940 through 1970. Biographies are also indexed by professions.

## Books About Authors

Although the lives of authors are included in all biographical reference books and in the encyclopedias, the following books treat authors only. *The Writers Directory* briefly lists 18,000 of today's writers. It comes out every two years. Articles in the others are informal, longer, and include authors' pictures.

***American Authors 1600–1900*** by Kunitz and Haycraft
***British Authors Before 1800*** by Kunitz and Haycraft
***British Authors of the Nineteenth Century*** by Kunitz and Haycraft
***Contemporary Authors: First Revision***
***The Writers Directory,*** St. James Press, London/St. Martin's Press, N.Y.

Magill's *Cyclopedia of World Authors* is a popular reference that includes authors from all over the world. It gives biographical facts for each author and a critical sketch characterizing his or her works.

# LITERATURE REFERENCE BOOKS

### 33c. Develop the habit of using reference books on literature.

You were just introduced to some standard reference books on authors. For information on literary works and their plots, characters, sources, quotations, etc., the following books are useful.

## General

**Benét's *The Reader's Encyclopedia***

This book describes itself aptly as "an encyclopedia of all the things you encounter in reading." It does have great variety: plots and characters, summaries of poems, allusions to myths and to the Bible, and descriptions of works of art, music, and so on. Though the Second Edition best meets today's interests, either is good.

## Books of Quotations

At one time or another everybody wants to find the source or exact wording of a quotation. There are many books of quotations. Your library may have several. Because they differ in arrangement, you need to learn how to find what you want in the one you are using.

### Bartlett's *Familiar Quotations*

Bartlett's is probably the best known. It can provide four kinds of information: (1) the author of a quotation; (2) the book or speech which is its source; (3) its exact wording; (4) some famous lines by any author.

To find the author or source of a quotation, turn to the big index in the back of the book. This index lists important words alphabetically as keys to quotations. For example, *cat, gloves,* and *mice* are key index words to the quotation:

"The cat in gloves catches no mice."

Since quotations come under authors, who are listed in chronological order, you can find a number of quotations from a famous writer by looking in the author index for the page where quotations from the author's work begin, and turning to it.

### Stevenson's *Home Book of Quotations* and *Home Book of Proverbs, Maxims, and Familiar Phrases*

Using a different type of arrangement, these books group quotations according to subject matter, not by author. This plan is convenient when you want quotations on a particular subject—success, love, duty, etc.

### H. L. Mencken's *New Dictionary of Quotations*

The choice of numerous quotations marked by epigrammatic wit or satire makes this collection unusual.

## Indexes and Collections of Poetry

### Stevenson's *Home Book of Verse* and *Home Book of Modern Verse*

When you want to find a popular poem, it is a good idea to look for it first in these two big anthologies. The poems are arranged by subjects: for example, Poems of Youth and Age; Love Poems; Poems of Nature; Familiar Verse; Poems, Humorous and Satiric; etc. Since the books are indexed in three ways—by author, by title, and by first line—you should have no trouble finding the poem you want if it is in either book.

### *Granger's Index to Poetry* (sixth edition)

When you want to find a particular poem, *Granger's Index* can lead you quickly to a collection that includes it. It has three listings for each poem: by author, by title, and by first line. Whichever you use will give you the same information as the other two do.

Suppose you want to read "Casey at the Bat." Under that title you will find a number of abbreviations, each standing for an anthology containing the poem. A table in the front of the *Index* spells out the titles for which the abbreviations stand.

Now use the library's card catalogue to find one of the books the *Index* lists for "Casey at the Bat." This is the whole process.

Remember that the *Index* does not print any whole poems, but its listings are quick poem-locators for almost any poem you want to find.

# OTHER REFERENCE BOOKS

Your teacher may ask members of your class to report on those of the following reference works which are in your library. A report should include author or editor, title, number of volumes or supplements, publication date, scope and arrangement of material, and principal uses.

***Literature***

*American Authors and Books* by W. J. Burke and W. D. Howe, augmented and revised by Irving Weiss
*Book Review Digest*
*Bulfinch's Mythology*
*Cambridge History of American Literature*
*Cambridge History of English Literature*
*Guide to Great Plays* by J. T. Shipley
*The New Century Classical Handbook*
*Oxford Companion to American Literature*
*Oxford Companion to English Literature*
*Oxford Companion to French Literature*
*Oxford Companion to Classical Literature*
*Oxford Companion to the Theatre*

***Grammar and Usage***

The *Careful Writer: A Modern Guide to English Usage* by Theodore M. Bernstein
*A Dictionary of Contemporary American Usage* by Bergen and Cornelia Evans

***History and Social Studies***

*Cambridge Modern History*
*Dictionary of American History* by J. T. Adams
*The Dictionary of Dates* by Helen R. Keller
*Encyclopedia of American History* by R. B. Morris
*Encyclopedia of the Social Sciences*
*Encyclopedia of World History* by W. L. Langer
*Statistical Abstract of the United States*
*Webster's New Geographical Dictionary*

***Science and Mathematics***

*Chambers Dictionary of Science and Technology*
*McGraw-Hill Encyclopedia of Science and Technology*

***Music and Art***

*Encyclopedia of the Arts,* edited by Herbert Read

*The Harvard Dictionary of Music,* first edition, edited by Willi Apel. (The second edition contains additional and updated entries but abbreviates the first listings considerably. A paperback edition is also available, abridged: *The Harvard Brief Dictionary of Music.*)

*The International Cyclopedia of Music and Musicians*

*The McGraw-Hill Encyclopedia of World Art*

*The New College Encyclopedia of Music,* edited by J. A. Westrup and F. L. Harrison (the handiest and best one-volume popular work)

*Vasari's Lives of the Painters, Sculptors, and Architects,* new edition in four paperback volumes

***Colleges and Universities***

*American Universities and Colleges,* American Council on Education

*Barron's Profiles of American Colleges*

*Comparative Guide to American Colleges,* edited by James Cass and Max Birnbaum

*Lovejoy's College Guide*

**EXERCISE 1.** Be able to explain the principal uses of each of the following, their advantages and their limitations.

An encyclopedia

Yearbooks

*World Almanac and Book of Facts*

*Information Please Almanac*

*The International Yearbook and Statesmen's Who Who*

*Statesman's Yearbook*

*Americana Annual*

*Britannica Book of the Year*

*Collier's Yearbook*

An atlas

Biographical reference books

*Biography Index*

*Current Biography*

*Dictionary of American Biography*

*Dictionary of National Biography*

*Webster's Biographical Dictionary*

*New Century Cyclopedia of Names*
*Who's Who, Who's Who in America, Who Was Who in America,* and *The International Who's Who*
*British Authors Before 1800*
*British Authors of the Nineteenth Century*
*American Authors 1600–1900*
*European Authors 1000–1900*
*Contemporary Authors: First Revision*
*Cyclopedia of World Authors*

Literature reference books
Bartlett's *Familiar Quotations*
Benét's *The Reader's Encyclopedia*
Stevenson's *Home Book of Quotations*
Stevenson's *Home Book of Proverbs, Maxims, and Familiar Phrases*
Stevenson's *Home Book of Verse* and *Home Book of Modern Verse*
*Granger's Index to Poetry*

**EXERCISE 2.** Answer in writing the following questions.

1. Distinguish between *Who's Who* and *Who's Who in America.*
2. Explain the difference between the *Biography Index* and *Current Biography.*
3. Distinguish between a world atlas and a historical atlas.
4. Name three important differences between the *Dictionary of American Biography* and *Who's Who in America.*
5. List four books that contain information about events of the past year.
6. Which literature reference book would you use to find the author of a poem whose title you know?
7. Which literature reference book would you use to find the title of a book containing a poem you want?
8. Arrange the following titles in order according to the length of their biographical articles, listing the one with the longest articles first: the dictionary, *Dictionary of American Biography, Webster's Biographical Dictionary.*
9. Arrange the following titles in order according to the frequency of their publication, listing the most frequently pub-

lished first: *Readers' Guide, Biography Index, Who's Who in America, Who's Who, Current Biography.*

10. Contrast the arrangements of Bartlett's *Familiar Quotations* and Stevenson's *Home Book of Quotations.*

**EXERCISE 3.** Number your paper 1–18. From the books and reference works given in brackets, select the one you would use to get the specified information. Write the title after the proper number on your paper. Be prepared to explain your choices.

1. Names of the senators in Congress from your state. [encyclopedia, *Who's Who in America, World Almanac*]
2. Quotations on the subject of love. [Bartlett's *Familiar Quotations,* Stevenson's *Home Book of Quotations*]
3. Books in your library about reptiles. [*Readers' Guide,* card catalogue, vertical file]
4. A description of the present government of France. [encyclopedia, *Statesman's Year-book*]
5. The life of Abigail Adams. [*Biography Index, The Reader's Encyclopedia, Dictionary of American Biography*]
6. A list of magazine articles on education published during the past few months. [*World Almanac, Readers' Guide,* card catalogue]
7. Life of the Secretary-General of the United Nations. [*Current Biography, Dictionary of American Biography, Webster's Biographical Dictionary*]
8. Which book would probably contain Lowell's poem "Patterns"? [*Granger's Index,* Bartlett's *Familiar Quotations,* Stevenson's *Home Book of Verse*]
9. A description and history of the rubber industry. [*Britannica Book of the Year, World Almanac,* encyclopedia]
10. International records in track events. [*Information Please Almanac, Statesman's Year-book, Readers' Guide*]
11. The source of the common expression "All the world's a stage." [Stevenson's *Home Book of Verse, Webster's Dictionary of Synonyms,* Bartlett's *Familiar Quotations*]
12. Titles and authors of biographies of the President. [*Biography Index, Who's Who in America, Webster's Biographical Dictionary*]

13. A quotation about youth. [Bartlett's *Familiar Quotations, World Almanac,* Stevenson's *Home Book of Quotations*]
14. The copyright date of any book in your library. [encyclopedia, card catalogue, *Readers' Guide*]
15. The body of water into which the Suwannee River flows. [*Statesman's Year-book, World Almanac,* atlas]
16. A picture of an author who came into prominence during the past six months. [encyclopedia, *Current Biography, Who's Who*]
17. Leaflets recently published by the National Safety Council. [card catalogue, *Readers' Guide,* vertical file]
18. Educational background of the president of an American university. [*Who's Who, Biography Index, Who's Who in America*]

**EXERCISE 4.** Which library tool or reference book, including the encyclopedia, would you use to find the following items of information?

1. Titles of recent magazine articles on the latest fashions in dress
2. The special power that the mythological character Clotho had
3. The title of a book, owned by your library, on conservation
4. An account of the climate of Tahiti
5. The life of the author of a best-selling first novel, recently published
6. The pronunciation of the name of the prime minister of Kenya
7. Biographies (books and articles) of a famous person in today's world
8. The latest magazine articles about automobile accidents
9. An article on the life and work of a Latin American author
10. The native state of the Vice-President of the United States
11. The publisher and copyright date of a book in the library
12. The ten most populous cities in the United States
13. An illustrated article on the Navajo Indians
14. A history of the past year in sports
15. Pamphlets published by the Foreign Policy Association
16. Any books the library may have on stamp collecting

17. Officials of the present government of Pakistan
18. An illustrated article on Italian art
19. The name of the novel in which Eustacia Vye is a character
20. A picture of Lillian Hellman, modern dramatist

Chapter 34

# The Dictionary

## Content and Uses of Dictionaries

Dictionaries vary greatly in size, purpose, and reliability. From the unabridged dictionaries with upwards of 300,000 entries to the smallest pocket-sized ones, dictionaries offer a range of possibilities that calls for judgment on the part of the user.

Although dictionaries differ from one another in number of entries and method of presenting information, they all provide a report on the way language is used. Dictionary makers do not by themselves decide what words mean or how they should be pronounced and spelled. As a result of careful scientific research, dictionary makers are able to record the way the majority of educated people uses the language: the meanings such people apply to words and the ways they pronounce and spell words.

To people who want to make themselves understood and who wish to understand what they read, such a reliable report on language practice is of obvious value. No speaker of English knows all the words. Everyone needs help sometimes with the meaning, spelling, pronunciation, and use of a particular word. The dictionary records the customary language practice of other literate speakers and writers.

## KINDS OF DICTIONARIES

### 34a. Know the kinds of dictionaries.

Excluding the many special dictionaries—dictionaries of scientific terms, foreign language dictionaries, etc.—there are two main kinds of dictionaries with which you should be familiar: the large *unabridged* dictionary, which you will probably use mainly in libraries; and the "college-size" dictionary, which you should have at hand when you study.

You should be warned against the small, often pocket-sized, dictionaries sold in book, stationery, and drugstores for a few dollars. While these books may help you with common word meanings and spellings, they should be taken for what they are intended to be—inexpensive condensations for quick, general reference; they are not dependable as scholarly, complete, up-to-date works.

### College Dictionaries

The most practical dictionary for everyday use is the college dictionary, which usually has from about 100,000 to about 160,000 entries. Material in the front and the back often includes guides to punctuation, usage, preparing research papers, and may contain other information useful to students. Because it is frequently revised, a college dictionary, when purchased, is likely to be more nearly up-to-date than an unabridged.

The four listed alphabetically below are well known and kept reasonably up-to-date.

***The American Heritage Dictionary of the English Language,*** Houghton Mifflin Co., Boston

***The Random House College Dictionary,*** Random House, New York, N.Y.

***Webster's New Collegiate Dictionary,*** G. & C. Merriam Co., Springfield, Mass.

***Webster's New World Dictionary of the American Language,*** *Second College Edition,* William Collins Publishing Co., Cleveland, Ohio

### Unabridged Dictionaries

The largest dictionaries—containing over 300,000 entries—are called *unabridged* dictionaries. *Unabridged* in this context means only "not cut down from a bigger one." (The common idea that it means "containing the whole language" is mistaken, not to say impossible.) Out of the now small number presently available, three (two American and one British) are listed below:

***The Random House Dictionary of the English Language,*** Random House, New York, N.Y.

***Webster's Third New International Dictionary,*** G. & C. Merriam Co., Springfield, Mass.

***The Oxford English Dictionary,*** Oxford University Press, New York, N.Y.

An unabridged dictionary has two to three times the number of entries in a college dictionary. Many entries are likely to be more detailed and to give more facts. An unabridged dictionary is more likely to contain a rare or very old word, a dialect or regional word. *Webster's* and the *Oxford* use many actual quotations from named writers to show words in certain senses. An unabridged dictionary, though unwieldy, does make available information a college dictionary cannot.

## CONTENT AND ARRANGEMENT OF DICTIONARIES

**34b. Familiarize yourself with the kinds of information in your dictionary and learn where and how each kind is given.**

Although people most commonly use the dictionary to look up the spelling and meaning of words, to use it only for these purposes is to miss the many other kinds of information it has to offer.

Before making a detailed study of the treatment of individual words in the body of the dictionary, find out the other sources of information a good dictionary offers. The following study materials and exercises will help you discover the full resources of your dictionary and may lead you to refer to it more often and more efficiently.

Although all good dictionaries contain essentially the same facts, material may be arranged and handled quite differently. For example, some list items such as notable persons and places in the main alphabetical listing; others put them in separate sections. The location of abbreviations and foreign phrases may also differ. Get to know your dictionary.

**EXERCISE 1.** Using the dictionary with which you have been provided, write the answers to the following questions. Use the table of contents whenever it is helpful.

1. What is the full title of your dictionary?
2. Who is the publisher?
3. What is the latest copyright date? (Look on the back of the title page.)
4. Where does the complete key to pronunciation appear?
5. Is there a shorter key on each page? On every other page?
6. On what page do the explanatory notes on pronunciation begin?
7. On what page does the introductory article describing and explaining the dictionary begin?
8. What special articles are there on the history of the language, grammar, etc.?
9. On what page does your dictionary list the abbreviations used in the dictionary?
10. Are other abbreviations, such as A.D., C.O.D., and UNESCO, explained in the body of your dictionary or in a separate section at the back?
11. Are guides to spelling, punctuation, and capitalization given? If so, list the page on which each begins.
12. Is there a section giving the meaning of commonly used signs and symbols? If so, give the page it begins on.
13. Are the names of important people and places listed in the body of your dictionary or in a separate section?

14. Does your dictionary provide derivations of words? If so, do they appear near the beginning or at the end of an entry?
15. Are the names of literary, mythological, and Biblical characters listed in the body of your dictionary or in a special section? To find out, look up Hamlet, Poseidon, and Deborah.

**EXERCISE 2.** Look up in your dictionary the answers to the following questions and write the answers in a column on your paper. *After each answer write the page number on which you found it.* If any of the items are not in your dictionary, write the number of the question and leave a blank space.

1. What does the abbreviation LL.D. mean? Give the English translation.
2. What is the population of Londonderry?
3. What was the occupation of Maria Mitchell?
4. Who was Europa?
5. Give the meaning of the French phrase *comme il faut.*
6. Give the spelling rule for retaining the silent final *e* on a word when you add a suffix.
7. Where should commas and periods be placed with relation to quotation marks—inside the quotation marks or outside?
8. Give the meaning of the sign ℞ used in medical prescriptions.
9. In what play is Iago the villain?
10. Where is Prince Edward Island?

## A DICTIONARY'S INFORMATION ABOUT A WORD

### *Definitions*

The main function of a dictionary is to give the meanings of words. Since a single word may have many meanings, an entry covering it must have a matching number of definitions. In some dictionaries, all definitions are simply numbered in sequence. In others, small subdivisions of meaning within a numbered definition are headed by letters in sequence.

Some dictionaries still put definitions in historical order, the earliest meaning first, the latest last. Others base order on frequency of use, the most common meaning first, the least common last. The first entry below shows historical order; the second, frequency of use.

**mas·ter·piece** \ˈmas-tər-ˌpēs\ *n* **1 :** a piece of work presented to a medieval guild as evidence of qualification for the rank of master **2 :** a work done with extraordinary skill; *esp* **:** a supreme intellectual or artistic achievement <the three motion pictures that most critics consider his ~*s* —*Current Biog.*>



**mas·ter·piece** (mas′tər pēs′, mä′stər-), *n.* **1.** a person's most excellent production, as in an art. **2.** any production of masterly skill. **3.** a piece made by a journeyman or other craftsman aspiring to the rank of master in a guild or other craft organization as a proof of his competence. [MASTER + PIECE, modeled on D *meesterstuk,* G *Meisterstück*]



A label usually shows the part of speech of the word being defined. For example, *n.* stands for noun, *v.* for verb, and so on. (Abbreviations used are explained in a dictionary's front matter.) In older dictionaries, a word used as more than one part of speech was given a new entry for each one. Now these once-separate entries are usually gathered into one main entry, with definitions still grouped and labeled by part of speech—noun definitions together, verb definitions together, etc. Definition numbers commonly start over for each new part of speech. College-size and bigger dictionaries cling to these practices.

When you look up a word's meaning, read all its definitions. Unless you do, you can't be sure that the meaning you select best fits the context in which the word is used.

Even though you have looked up the meaning, you should be wary of using a word you have encountered only once. As any foreigner will tell you, a great many English words not only have more than one meaning, but they also have *implied,* or *connotative* meanings, which are not given in a dictionary. Furthermore, there may be idiomatic uses of which a young student speaker or writer is not aware. Until you have had several contacts with a word and have had a chance to observe just how it is used, you will be wise not to try to use it solely on the basis of its dictionary definition.

For example, suppose you did not know the meaning of the verb *transpire*. Looking it up, you find that it has four meanings. The first two are technical meanings in the field of physiology. The third is "to become known," and the fourth, marked *informal,* is "to happen." Now suppose that you try to use this verb in place of "happen" in the sentence "The police happened along just in time to catch the thieves." You will not make any sense if you say, "The police transpired along just in time to catch the thieves."

### *Spelling*

The bold-faced word at the very beginning of a dictionary entry tells you the accepted spelling. When there are two or more acceptable spellings, the various spellings are given. Any spelling given has enough standing to justify use of it if you prefer it.

EXAMPLE **cat·a·log** *or* **cat·a·logue**

If grammatical change in the form of a word is likely to raise spelling problems, *inflectional* forms are given. (These are forms of a word resulting from its habitual usage, like the principal parts of verbs or the comparative and superlative forms of adjectives.) A dictionary is the best reference work to consult if you are uncertain about doubling a consonant, changing an *i* to a *y,* and so on.

The dictionary tells you that *bases* is the plural of *basis,* and *solos* is the plural of *solo,* although *heroes,* with the *e,* is the plural of *hero*. It also tells you that *refer* doubles its *r* when it is inflected (*referred, referring*) while *care* does not (*cared, caring*). Both the principal parts of irregular verbs you may have difficulty remembering, and the spelling of frequently misspelled words (like *misspell*), can be found in any good dictionary. In general, you should think of the dictionary as the place to find the proper spelling (and forms) of:

a. the plural of a word, if the plural is formed irregularly
b. the feminine form of a foreign word: **alumnus; alumna,** *fem.*
c. the principal parts of an irregular verb
d. comparative and superlative forms of irregular adjectives and adverbs
e. case forms of pronouns: **who;** *possessive* **whose;** *objective* **whom**

### *Syllable Division*

When a word must be divided at the end of a line, it should be divided between syllables. Syllable division is indicated in the bold-faced entry word and often in inflectional forms. The break is usually shown by a centered dot (**bas·ket**). In some dictionaries it is shown by a space (**bas ket**). Look at the various sample entries throughout this chapter to see the different ways each dictionary shows syllable division.

### *Capitalization*

Proper nouns and adjectives, commonly written with initial capital letters, are entered in most dictionaries with the usual capitals. *Webster's Third,* however, prints the entry word in small letters followed by a brief note such as: *usu cap* or *often cap,* short for *usually capitalized* or *often capitalized.*

Sometimes a word not capitalized in most of its meanings should be capitalized when used in one sense, or perhaps more than one. The abbreviation *cap.* following a definition number indicates that the word is capitalized when used in that sense.

EXAMPLE

> **cap·i·tol** \ˈkap-ət-ᵊl, ˈkap-tᵊl\ *n* [L *Capitolium,* temple of Jupiter at Rome on the Capitoline hill] **1 a :** a building in which a state legislative body meets **b :** a group of buildings in which the functions of state government are carried out **2** *cap* **:** the building in which the U.S. Congress meets at Washington

### *Pronunciation*

Ordinary spelling cannot show the sounds of words precisely. Dictionary pronunciations respell each word, using one fixed symbol for each of the 42 or 43 common sounds of English. New, made-up symbols might have been used. Most of the symbols actually used look like ordinary letters of the alphabet, some with special marks added, but they work differently: each one stands exclusively and consistently for only one sound.

In different dictionaries symbols may differ, too. For the vowel in *burn* one may show /û/ and another /ə/. The sound is, of course, the same. Each dictionary explains its symbols in a key, usually in the front of the book, and also prints a shortened key at the foot of each pair of facing pages. The key shows each symbol tied to its sound *as heard in one or two familiar words*. To understand the respellings in a particular dictionary, you must familiarize yourself with what its symbols mean.

After each entry word, these symbols "spell" its sounds in order, divided into syllables as needed.

EXAMPLE **cap·tain** /ˈkap-tən/
(kap′tən, kap′tin)

In long words, one syllable, or sometimes more than one, may be spoken with more stress or force than the others. This stress is shown by accent marks: heaviest stress by a heavier mark, lighter stress by a lighter mark. The marks may be either slanted or straight, either above or below the line of type, and either before or after the syllable involved.

EXAMPLES **tax·i·cab:** tak′ se kab′
ˈtak se ˌkab
ták se kăb

When a word has more than one recognized pronunciation, all of the pronunciations are given. You will have to study your dictionary's way of giving pronunciations, since each of the most available dictionaries differs from the others in the system it uses.

## *Etymologies, or Word Histories*

Most dictionaries indicate the history of a word. They show, by means of abbreviations and symbols, what language the word originally came from, and what its original meaning was. English is unusual among languages for the vast number of words it has taken from other languages. During their history, many words have undergone interesting changes in form or meaning. The source of recently coined words, such as *quark,* is explained in a dictionary. Knowing the source and original meaning of a word is often a great help in understanding the word's present meaning and correct use.

The abbreviations used to indicate the languages from which words derive are explained in front of your dictionary. The following examples show how dictionaries vary in where they position an etymology within an entry. The symbol < means "from," like the abbreviation *fr.*

> [1]**book** \'bůk\ *n* [ME, fr. OE *bōc;* akin to OHG *buoh* book, OE *bōc* beech; prob. fr. the early Germanic practice of carving runic characters on beech wood tablets — more at BEECH]

From *Webster's New Collegiate Dictionary,* © 1974 by G. C. Merriam Co., Publishers of the Merriam-Webster Dictionaries. Reprinted by permission of the publishers.

> **an·ec·dote** (an′ik dōt′), *n.* a short narrative concerning an interesting or amusing incident or event. [earlier *anecdota* (pl.) < ML < Gk *anékdota* things unpublished, neut. pl. of *anékdotos* = *an-* AN-[1] + *ékdotos* given out, ptp. of *ekdidónai* to give out, publish (*ek-* EC- + *didónai* to give)]

From *Random House College Dictionary,* published by Random House, Inc., copyright © 1971, 1970, 1969, 1967 by Random House, Inc. Reprinted by permission of the publisher.

## *Restrictive Labels*

Most of the words defined in a dictionary are part of the general vocabulary. Some, however, have to do with a special field or are used almost exclusively in a single region or are used at only one level of usage.

Dictionaries use restrictive labels—*subject labels* such as *Law, Med.* (medicine), *Chem.* (chemistry), etc.; *area labels* such as *southwest U.S.;* and *usage labels* such as *informal, slang,* or *dialect.*

*Area label:* **corn pone** *n, South & Midland* : corn bread often made without milk or eggs and baked or fried

By permission. From *Webster's New Collegiate Dictionary.* © 1980 by G. & C. Merriam and Company, publishers of the Merriam-Webster Dictionaries.

*Usage label:*

**goon** (go͞on) *n.* **1.** *Informal.* A thug hired to commit acts of intimidation or violence. **2.** *Slang.* A stupid or oafish person. [From dialectal *gooney, gony*†, fool; popularized by the comic-strip character Alice the *Goon,* created by E.C. Segar (1894–1938).]



*Usage note:*

**fi·nal·ize** (fī′nə-līz′) *tr.v.* **-ized, -izing, -izes.** To put into final form; to complete.
***Usage:*** *Finalize* is closely associated with the language of bureaucracy, in the minds of many careful writers and speakers, and is consequently avoided by them. The example ***finalize plans for a class reunion*** is termed unacceptable by 90 per cent of the Usage Panel. In most such examples a preferable choice is possible from among ***complete, conclude, make final,*** and ***put in final form.***



Usage labels provide a good general guide to usage, but all writers must learn to make judgments about these matters on the basis of their own observation. Assigning a label such as *slang* or *informal* is necessarily a subjective judgment on the part of the definer, and not all dictionaries agree about labeling the same word. Your knowledge of the connotations of a word and the situation in which you want to use it should be your guide in choosing or rejecting a particular word or meaning. If you are not sure of the appropriateness of a word without looking it up, you will do well not to use it until you know it better.

### *Synonyms and Antonyms*

Dictionaries often list other words of similar meaning (synonyms) and sometimes also words of opposite meaning (antonyms) at the end of an entry. At times they also append a slightly longer note comparing two or more words with similar meanings, showing fine shades of difference as well as similarity.

In the following example, synonyms (SYN) are discussed in detail, and antonyms (ANT) are also given.

**brave** (brāv) ***adj.*** [Fr. < It. *bravo*, brave, bold, orig., wild, savage < L. *barbarus*, BARBAROUS] **1.** willing to face danger, pain, or trouble; not afraid; having courage **2.** showing to good effect; having a fine appearance **3.** fine, grand, or splendid [a *brave* new world] —***n.*** **1.** any brave man ☆**2.** [< 17th-c. NAmFr.] a North American Indian warrior **3.** [Archaic] a bully —***vt.*** **braved, brav'ing** **1.** to face with courage **2.** to defy; dare **3.** [Obs.] to make splendid, as in dress —***vi.*** [Obs.] to boast —**brave'ly** ***adv.*** —**brave'ness** ***n.***
***SYN.***—**brave** implies fearlessness in meeting danger or difficulty and has the broadest application of the words considered here; **courageous** suggests constant readiness to deal with things fearlessly by reason of a stout-hearted temperament or a resolute spirit; **bold** stresses a daring temperament, whether displayed courageously, presumptuously, or defiantly; **audacious** suggests an imprudent or reckless boldness; **valiant** emphasizes a heroic quality in the courage or fortitude shown; **intrepid** implies absolute fearlessness and esp. suggests dauntlessness in facing the new or unknown; **plucky** emphasizes gameness in fighting against something when one is at a decided disadvantage —***ANT.*** **craven, cowardly**



## Encyclopedic Entries

Besides giving information about words, the college dictionaries listed in this chapter (but not some unabridged dictionaries) give facts about many people and places. These may appear as entries in the body of the dictionary or in special sections in the back.

### *Important Persons*

A dictionary usually covers these items about a person:

1. *Name:* spelling, pronunciation, and given names
2. *Date of birth (and death if deceased)*
3. *Nationality (and country of birth if different)*
4. *Why famous*

Note how a typical entry covers all four:

**Er·ics·son** (er'ik sən) **1. Leif,** fl. 1000; Norw. explorer & adventurer: discovered VINLAND, believed to be part of N. America: son of ERIC THE RED: also sp. **Er'ic·son** **2. John,** 1803–89; U.S. naval engineer & inventor, born in Sweden: builder of the *Monitor*



Dictionary information about contemporaries soon goes out of date. It may be safer to refer to *Who's Who* or *Who's Who in America* for up-to-date facts.

*Important Places*

In treating a geographical entry, a dictionary usually gives the following information:

1. *Name:* spelling, pronunciation
2. *Identification:* city, nation, lake, river, etc.
3. *Location*
4. *Size:* population, as of a city; area, as of a state, body of water, etc.; length, as of a river; height, as of a mountain
5. *Political importance:* If a city is capital of a state or nation, the fact will be noted, and the city may be named in the entry for the state or nation.
6. *Historical or other interest:* as Yorktown, site of surrender of the British
7. *Controlling country:* as in Guam, a United States possession

Be sure that a dictionary uses the latest census for its (undated) population figures before you trust them. Old data can be seriously misleading.

## SPECIAL DICTIONARIES

### 34c. Learn the use of special dictionaries.

Along with general dictionaries, there are dictionaries of the special vocabularies of law, medicine, slang, and so on.

Books of synonyms are useful to people who do much writing. They help you to vary your choice of words and to find the exact word needed. Their use is opposite to that of a dictionary. Instead of looking up a word you *mean to use,* you look up one you *mean to avoid* in order to find a substitute for it.

***Roget's Thesaurus of English Words and Phrases***

This is the classic book of synonyms, over a century old. Originally, its words were grouped by classes and subclasses of meaning, with a huge index attached. Some recent editions (including new words) retain this ingenious format. Others (at least one in paperback) put the material in dictionary form—straight alphabetical order.

Fernald, James C., ***Funk and Wagnalls Standard Handbook of Synonyms, Antonyms, and Prepositions***

This is also a standard book, listing in alphabetical order most of the words you might want to use and giving synonyms and antonyms for them.

***Webster's Dictionary of Synonyms***

This is valued especially for its able discussion of distinctions between words of similar meaning.

**EXERCISE 3.** This exercise is designed to test your knowledge of the information given about a word in the dictionary. With your dictionary before you, begin work at the teacher's signal. Look up the answers to the following questions. While your speed indicates to some degree your efficiency in using the dictionary, accuracy is the more important consideration.

1. Which is the more usual spelling: *judgment* or *judgement?*
2. In the first pronunciation for *research,* is the accent on the first or second syllable?
3. Copy the correct pronunciation of the word *comely,* using the respelling and symbols.
4. Are the comparative and superlative forms of *comely* shown to be *more comely* and *most comely,* or *comelier* and *comeliest?*
5. Copy the word *automatic,* dividing it correctly into syllables.
6. How many different meanings are given in your dictionary for the word *run* as an intransitive (*v.i.*) verb?
7. What restrictive label, if any, is given the word *swell* when used to mean *first-rate?*
8. What restrictive label is given the word *shank* when used in the expression "the shank of the evening"?
9. What are the past and past participle forms of the irregular verb *burst?*
10. Distinguish between the meaning of *councilor* and *counselor.*

11. What restrictive label is given to the adverb *erstwhile?* What does the label mean?
12. What restrictive label is given to the verb *gyp?*
13. What is the origin of the word *candidate?*
14. In what literary work does the character Mrs. Malaprop appear? For what was she noted?
15. Tell the story of Hero and Leander as given in your dictionary.

**EXERCISE 4.** Like the preceding exercise, this exercise will test your knowledge of the information given in a dictionary and your familiarity with the location of this information in the dictionary. At the teacher's signal look up the answers to the following questions. Accuracy is more important than speed, but speed is important.

1. Find two synonyms for the word *cowardly.*
2. Write the plural of *analysis.*
3. Write the comparative and superlative forms of *ill.*
4. What city is the capital of Burma?
5. What is the population of Dallas, Texas?
6. When did Queen Victoria reign?
7. For what is Johann Gutenberg famous?
8. What was George Eliot's real name?
9. What is the meaning of the abbreviation RSVP?
10. In the first pronunciation for *hospitable,* is the accent on the first or second syllable?
11. What is the meaning of the symbol $\overline{A}\overline{A}$ used by a doctor in writing a prescription?
12. Write two acceptable plurals of *octopus.*
13. Should you or should you not use a comma before the *and* joining the last two items of a series?
14. Give the rule for the formation of the plural of nouns ending in *o* preceded by a vowel. Give two examples.
15. What is the meaning of the Latin phrase *caveat emptor?*

# Chapter 35

# Vocabulary

## Meaning Through Context and Word Analysis

Although it is likely that this may be your last year of systematic vocabulary study, the number of English words you know and are able to use will continue to be important throughout your life. Most immediately, you will see that a good vocabulary will help you to succeed in college or at a job. More important, however, your general knowledge or your knowledge of a specific field cannot be very deep or impressive unless you have a considerable stock of words at your command. The number of words you know is one indication of the pride you take in your mind. You owe it to yourself to have a vocabulary that fairly reflects your interests and abilities.

### Diagnostic Test

Number your paper 1–25. After the proper number, write the letter of the word or expression that comes closest to the meaning of the italicized word.

| | | |
|---|---|---|
| 1. to *augment* the budget | a) increase<br>b) examine closely | c) reduce<br>d) disapprove of |
| 2. to *ascertain* the facts | a) cover up<br>b) review | c) find out<br>d) testify to |
| 3. a king known for his *avarice* | a) wisdom<br>b) vanity | c) deceitfulness<br>d) greed |

4. a *biennial* event
a) twice yearly
b) every two weeks
c) every two years
d) twice daily

5. a *blithe* mood
a) bitter
b) proud
c) angry
d) carefree

6. an offer to *capitulate*
a) confer
b) mediate
c) compromise
d) surrender

7. a suspicion of *collusion*
a) robbery
b) foolishness
c) mistrustfulness
d) agreement to deceive

8. to *conjecture* about the facts
a) talk
b) lie
c) guess
d) conceal the truth

9. to *corroborate* testimony
a) testify about
b) confirm
c) deny
d) question

10. to act under *duress*
a) compulsion
b) misunderstanding
c) difficulties
d) bribery

11. an imposing *edifice*
a) natural wonder
b) manner
c) speech
d) building

12. wholesome *environment*
a) nourishment
b) outlook
c) surroundings
d) diet

13. a leader's *foible*
a) weakness
b) habit
c) example
d) follower

14. an *interminable* show
a) worthless
b) endless
c) tedious
d) difficult to describe

15. to *intimidate* a witness
a) make disappear
b) make fearful
c) bribe
d) coach

16. to *nurture* a child
a) neglect
b) give medicine to
c) scold
d) feed and bring up

17. a sign of *opulence*
a) poverty
b) health
c) wealth
d) generosity

18. a *prosaic* sight
a) commonplace
b) solemn
c) stirring
d) peaceful

19. a *prudent* action
a) unexpected
b) ill-mannered
c) sensible
d) foolish

20. good-natured *raillery*
a) scuffling
b) boisterousness
c) competition
d) banter

21. a well-deserved *reproof*
a) promotion
b) reprimand
c) apology
d) recognition

| | | |
|---|---|---|
| 22. an act showing *sagacity* | a) experience<br>b) feebleness | c) good judgment<br>d) old age |
| 23. a *sanguine* outlook | a) hopeful<br>b) pessimistic | c) quarrelsome<br>d) depressing |
| 24. the *travail* of the artist | a) illness<br>b) oppression | c) bad luck<br>d) toil |
| 25. a *volatile* temperament | a) changeable<br>b) disagreeable | c) sluggish<br>d) easygoing |

## CONTEXT CLUES

### 35a. Find clues to meaning in context.

Occasionally we encounter words in isolation—mainly in crossword puzzles and other word games—but most of the time a word that we read or hear is closely connected with other words that help to make its meaning clear. The words that surround a particular word in a sentence or paragraph are called the *verbal context* of that word. Consider this sentence, for example:

> Although she continued to predict victory, Captain Winters was really not *sanguine* about her team's prospects.

If you are not sure of the meaning of *sanguine*, the rest of this sentence provides some important clues. The first part suggests that there is something contradictory about the captain's predicting victory when she is not sanguine about her team's chances. From the whole sentence, you may reasonably conclude that *sanguine* must mean "hopeful" or "optimistic." Sometimes, of course, such reasoning will lead you into a wrong guess; but more often than not you will be right.

In addition to the other words, the situation itself often provides clues to the meaning of a word. In the example above, you would expect a captain to be concerned about her team's success. Thus, you would not suppose that *sanguine* meant "bored" or "disinterested." Clues provided by the situation being discussed often help in deciding between two very different meanings of the same word or of words that have the same spelling. For example, if you are reading about an argument, *retort* is likely to mean "a ready and effective reply." In a description of a scientific experiment, on the other hand, *retort* would probably mean "a vessel used in distilling."

**EXERCISE 1.** Number your paper 1–10. After each number, copy the italicized word in the sentence and write a short definition based on the clues you find in context. You may check your definitions with the dictionary later.

1. After listening to a good deal of coaxing, the mother finally *acceded* to her children's request.
2. After a *hectic* year in the city, George was glad enough to return to the peace and quiet of the country.
3. Although the risks were great, the dissatisfied officers met and formed a *cabal* against the commander-in-chief.
4. The last two lines of the poem are so *cryptic* that no two readers can agree about what they mean.
5. Any person who was not entirely *devoid* of honor would have been outraged at the suggestion.
6. A person on a reducing diet is expected to *eschew* most fatty or greasy foods.
7. A large constrictor grabs its prey in its mouth and quickly coils itself around the victim to *immobilize* it. The harder the animal struggles, the tighter the snake constricts.
8. Eventually, the criminal *expiated* this murder and many other crimes on the gallows.
9. According to Bacon, scientists should learn about nature through *empirical* observations based on experiments and on careful study of the greatest possible amount of evidence.
10. Despite the awesome *fecundity* of certain species of fish, the balance of nature limits the population.

**EXERCISE 2.** Number your paper 1–10 and copy the corresponding italicized word after each number. After each word write a short definition based on your understanding of the context. When you have completed the exercise, check your definitions against your dictionary.

Science gets most of its information by the process of (1) *reductionism,* exploring the details, then the details of the details, until all the smallest bits of the structure, or the smallest parts of the mechanism, are laid out for counting and (2) *scrutiny.* Only when this is done can the investigation be extended to (3) *encompass* the whole organism or the entire system. So we say.

Sometimes it seems that we take a loss, working this way. Much of today's public anxiety about science is the (4) *apprehension* that we may forever be overlooking the whole by an endless, obsessive (5) *preoccupation* with the parts. I had a brief, personal experience of this (6) *misgiving* one afternoon in Tucson, where I had time on my hands and visited the zoo, just outside the city. The designers there have cut a deep pathway between two small artificial ponds, walled by clear glass, so when you stand in the center of the path you can look into the depths of each pool, and at the same time you can regard the surface. In one pool, on the right side of the path, is a family of otters; on the other side, a family of beavers. Within just a few feet from your face, on either side, beavers and otters are at play, underwater and on the surface, swimming toward your face and then away, more filled with life than any creatures I have ever seen before, in all my days. Except for the glass, you could reach across and touch them.

I was (7) *transfixed.* As I now recall it, there was only one sensation in my head: pure (8) *elation* mixed with amazement at such perfection. Swept off my feet, I floated from one side to the other, swiveling my brain, staring astounded at the beavers, then at the otters. I could hear shouts across my (9) *corpus callosum,* from one hemisphere to the other. I remember thinking, with what was left in charge of my consciousness, that I wanted no part of the science of beavers and otters; I wanted never to know how they performed their marvels; I wished for no news about the (10) *physiology* of their breathing, the coordination of their muscles, their vision, their endocrine systems, their digestive tracts. I hoped never to have to think of them as collections of cells. All I asked for was the full hairy complexity, then in front of my eyes, of whole, intact beavers and otters in motion.[1]

[1] From "The Tucson Zoo" in *The Medusa and the Snail* by Lewis Thomas. Copyright © 1974–1979 by Lewis Thomas. Originally appeared in *The New England Journal of Medicine.* Published in Great Britain by Allen Lane, 1980. Reprinted by permission of Viking Penguin Inc. and Penguin Books, Ltd.

## Common Clues to Meaning

Although a sentence may provide clues to the meaning of a word in a variety of ways, there are three kinds of context clues that are particularly helpful.

### Words Similar in Meaning

In the sentence "The loud, *raucous* laughter of the troop irritated the lieutenant," you can guess at the meaning of *raucous* because you know the word *loud*. (*Raucous* means "harsh of voice, coarse.")

### Words Used in Contrast

Contrasts often supply clues to meaning by pairing an unfamiliar word against a known one. In such a situation, you can usually assume that the unfamiliar word is more or less the opposite of the one you know.

EXAMPLES This accidental development did not *vitiate* the theory; it strengthened it. [*Vitiate* is contrasted with *strengthened*. It probably means "weakened" or "robbed of force."]

The defendant claims he had no intention of breaking into the apartment, but the state contends that in his possession were found burglar tools and a floor plan of the apartment, indicating *premeditation*. [The prosecutor must mean that the defendant had previously planned to commit the crime; *premeditation* must mean "planning beforehand."]

Contrasts are often signaled by such words as *but, although,* and *however*. Sometimes *or* indicates a contrast, but you cannot assume that it always does. In the first sentence below, two antonyms are joined and contrasted. In the second example, however, two synonyms are joined by *or* and no contrast is indicated.

CONTRAST *Rich* or *poor*, the people resented the tax.

NO CONTRAST No one thought her behavior *servile* or *subservient*.

In the second example, *servile* and *subservient* mean essentially the same thing: "slavish, overly submissive." Contrasts offer many helps to meaning, but for certainty you had better find other clues that confirm your guess or look the word up.

## Supplied Definition

When writers anticipate that their readers may not know the meaning of an important word, they often provide a definition. They may introduce the definition with an expression such as *in other words,* or *that is,* or they may slip it in without calling attention to it. The definitions or explanations in the following examples are italicized, and the words defined are in bold-faced type.

> The painting clearly shows the **aegis,** or *shield,* of Athena.
>
> A word is often defined by a **synonym**—that is, *a word of similar meaning.*
>
> His *observation* was *too obvious to mention*—a **truism.** [Notice that the explanation comes before the word defined in this example.]
>
> Since the days of the early Greek philosophers, the word **atom** has designated *the smallest and last unit of matter that would be reached if a given body were divided into smaller and smaller parts.*

People do not go to the trouble of explaining things unless they want to be understood. Be on the lookout for definitions of difficult words.

**EXERCISE 3.** Number your paper 1–10 and after each number copy the italicized word. Give a brief definition in your own words, based on the context.

1. Along with the discovery of the properties of poisons came the discovery of substances that had properties of combating the effects of poisons. These early *antidotes* were strange mixtures.
2. The border rebellion, *quiescent* during the winter months, broke out in renewed violence in the spring.

3. To the rest of us, the outlook just then seemed more ominous than *propitious*.
4. Most snakes are meat eaters, or *carnivores*.
5. The *salutary* effect of the new drug was shown by the rapid improvement in the patient's condition.
6. *Subterranean* temperatures are frequently higher than those above the surface of the earth.
7. Because the official could not attend the meeting herself, she had to send a *surrogate*, or deputy.
8. The method of reasoning from the particular to the general—the *inductive* method—has played an important role in science since the time of Francis Bacon.
9. If the leaders felt any *compunction* about planning and carrying out unprovoked attacks on neighboring countries, they showed no sign of it.
10. Formerly, a doctor who found a successful cure often regarded it as a trade secret and refused to *divulge* it to others.

**EXERCISE 4.** Read the following passage and then write your own definitions for the italicized words. Consult your dictionary only after you have written your own definitions from context.

Most of the doctors who had treated cases of the peculiar disease were almost certain by then that the characteristic initial (1) *lesion* was the bite of some (2) *minute* creature, but they had little reason to suspect mites of being the guilty parties. At the time, it was generally believed that mites could transmit only two serious (3) *febrile* diseases—Japanese river fever and endemic typhus. Both of these are rarely found in the United States, and anyway both had been eliminated from consideration in this instance by laboratory tests. Moreover, the mouse, unlike the rat, had never been proved to be a reservoir for disease-bearing parasites. Mr. Pomerantz admits that hitting upon the mouse as the probable (4) *host* was largely intuitive. He is persuaded, however, that in singling out mites as the carriers—or (5) *vectors*, as such agents are known—of the disease he was guided entirely by (6) *deduction*.

Mites are insectlike organisms, closely related to ticks. Both are members of the Arachnida, a class that also includes spiders and scorpions. Compared to a tick, a mite is a minute animal. A mite, when fully (7) *engorged,* is about the size of a strawberry seed. In that state, it is approximately ten times its usual, or unfed, size. So far, science has classified at least thirty families of mites, most of which are vegetarian and indifferent to man and all other animals. The majority of the (8) *parasitic,* blood-sucking mites have to feed once in every four or five days in order to live. Most mites of this type attach themselves to a host only long enough to engorge, and drop off, (9) *replete,* after fifteen or twenty minutes. No one ever feels the bite of a mite—or of a tick, either, for that matter—until the animal has dropped off. Entomologists believe that both creatures, at the instant they bite, (10) *excrete* a fluid that anesthetizes a small surrounding area of the body of the host. Mites are only infrequently found in this country and until recently were practically unknown in New York City. Consequently, very few Americans, even physicians and exterminators, have ever seen a mite. Mr. Pomerantz is one of those who have. He came across some in line of duty on three occasions in 1945.[1]

## 35b. Look up unfamiliar words in your dictionary.

For those words that context does not make sufficiently clear, the dictionary will provide you with the help you need. But here, too, context is important. Most words have a number of different meanings. To find the one you want, you will need to keep in mind the context in which you originally encountered the word. Once you have found the meaning you want, you will do well to read on through the whole definition. Most words have a range of different meanings; to know the word well, you should know more than one of its meanings. Moreover, learning the pronunciation, the derivation, and related forms of the word will help you to remember it. Once you take the trouble to go to the dictionary, you may as well get as much information as possible from it.

[1] From "The Alerting of Mr. Pomerantz" in *Eleven Blue Men and Other Narratives of Medical Detection* by Berton Roueché. Copyright 1947 by the New Yorker Magazine, Inc.; renewed 1975 by Berton Roueché. Reprinted by permission of Harold Ober Associates, Inc.

**35c.** **Keep a vocabulary notebook.**

Having learned a new word, you should not stop there. To insure that the word will become a permanent part of your vocabulary, write it in your notebook. Follow it with its pronunciation, the sentence in which you first found it, and its definition. Whenever you learn a new word, enter it in your notebook in this way; and review your list from time to time. You will find that keeping a special section of your notebook for new words will result in noticeable vocabulary growth.

## WORD ANALYSIS

**35d.** **Use your knowledge of prefixes, suffixes, and roots.**

In general, English words are of two kinds: those that can be analyzed into smaller parts (*unworkable, impolitely*) and those that cannot (*stone, money, winter*). The words of the first kind, those that can be divided, are made up of parts called prefixes, roots, and suffixes. Because these parts have broad, general meanings that remain essentially the same in different words, knowing something about word analysis can help you figure out the meaning of an unfamiliar word. However, there are some difficulties that make it unwise to depend entirely on word analysis for clues to meaning. It is not always easy to tell whether a particular group of letters is really the prefix or suffix it appears to be. The *-er* in *painter* is a suffix, but the *-er* in *winter* is not. To be certain, you have to know something about the origin of the word. Moreover, the original force of a combination of word parts may no longer have much to do with the modern meaning of a word. For these and other reasons, absolute dependence on word analysis would lead you to make as many bad guesses as good ones.

There are, however, some good reasons for having a general knowledge of the way English words are formed. Word analysis helps you to understand the peculiarities of

English spelling and the connection between the related forms of a particular word. (Knowing about related forms often enables you to learn four or five new words as easily as one.) Also, word analysis gives you useful practice in taking a close look at words. In reading, you pass very quickly over words, hardly noticing more than their general shape. This is all very well for words you know well, but close examination is called for with unfamiliar ones. Most important of all, word analysis offers the key to the origin of English words. The fact that many different cultures have contributed to the vocabulary of English is one of its particular strengths. Educated people should know something about the history as well as the use of their words. After all, building a vocabulary is a kind of collecting, differing from the collection of stamps or coins in being less expensive and more useful. No collector worthy of the name is content to possess a specimen and know nothing about it. Word analysis will tell you a great deal about the words you add to your collection.

## How Words Are Divided

Words that can be divided have two or more parts: a core called a *root* and one or more parts added to it. The parts that are added are called *affixes*—literally, "something fixed or attached to something else." An affix added before the root is called a *prefix;* one added after the root is called a *suffix.* A word may have one or more affixes of either kind, or several of both kinds. A root with no affixes at all is incapable of being divided. A word consisting of a root only is one like *stone* or *money,* to which word analysis does not apply.

The following table shows some typical combinations of affixes (prefixes and suffixes) and roots.

| PREFIX[ES] | ROOT | SUFFIX[ES] | EXAMPLE |
|---|---|---|---|
| un– | work | –able | unworkable |
| post– | –pone | | postpone |
| | friend | –ly | friendly |
| | fright | –en, –ing | frightening |

| PREFIX[ES] | ROOT | SUFFIX[ES] | EXAMPLE |
|---|---|---|---|
| il– | –leg– | –al | illegal |
| under | take | –er | undertaker |
| | truth | –ful | truthful |
| | child | like | childlike |

Some of the affixes and roots in English are recognizable as complete words in themselves (*fright* in *frighten; child* and *like* in *childlike*). Most other affixes and roots were also once separate words, though the original words may no longer exist in our modern language. For example, *post* in *postpone* was a Latin word meaning *after,* and *pone* (*pono, ponere*) was the Latin word for *put.*

## The Origins of English Words

In the lists that appear later in this chapter, prefixes and roots are grouped according to the language in which they originated: Old English, Latin (or Latin-French), and Greek. Although it is not possible here to give a detailed account of the contribution of these three sources to modern English, a brief discussion of word borrowing will make the lists more useful.

### Old English

Old English, or Anglo-Saxon, is the earliest recorded form of the English language. It was spoken from about A.D. 600 until about A.D. 1100, and most of its words had been part of a still earlier form of the language. Many of the common words of modern English, like *home, stone,* and *meat* are native, or Old English, words. Most of the irregular verbs in English derive from Old English (*speak, swim, drive, ride, sing*), as do most of our shorter numerals (*two, three, six, ten*) and most of our pronouns (*I, you, we, who*). Many Old English words can be traced back to Indo-European, a prehistoric language that was the common ancestor of Greek and Latin as well. Others came into Old English as it was becoming a separate language.

As the speakers of Old English became acquainted with Latin, chiefly through contact with Christianity, they began to borrow Latin words for things for which no native word existed. Some common words borrowed at this time were *abbot, altar, candle, temple, fever,* and *lettuce.*

Many other Latin words came into English through French. In 1066, toward the end of the Old English period, the French under William the Conqueror invaded England and defeated the Anglo-Saxons under King Harold. For the next three hundred years, French was the language of the ruling classes in England. During this period, thousands of new words came into English, many of them words relating to upper-class pursuits: *baron, attorney, ermine, luxury.* English has continued to borrow words from French right down to the present, with the result that over a third of our modern English vocabulary derives from French.

Many words from Greek, the other major source of English words, came into English by way of French and Latin. Others were borrowed directly in the sixteenth century when interest in classic culture was at its height. Directly or indirectly, Greek contributed *athlete, acrobat, elastic, magic, rhythm,* and many others.

In the modern period, English has borrowed from every important language in the world. The etymologies in your dictionary trace the origins of words, often providing insights into their present meanings and into history as well.

**EXERCISE 5.** Find out from your dictionary the origins of each of the following words. (For help in interpreting the etymology, see page 616 of this book.)

| | | |
|---|---|---|
| abscond | demon | quart |
| air | legal | tyrant |
| chase | loyal | votary |

## Prefixes

English borrowed not only independent words from Greek, Latin, and French, but also a number of word parts from these languages for use as affixes and roots. These sources are indicated in the following list of prefixes and in the list of roots on pages 642–44.

Prefixes have broad general meanings like *not, under,* and *against,* and a particular one of them may appear in hundreds of different words. In general, a knowledge of prefixes will help you to know when to double consonants in such words as *misspell* and *overrun*. Many prefixes have several different spellings in order to fit with various roots.

| PREFIX | MEANING | EXAMPLES |
|---|---|---|
| *Old English* | | |
| a– | in, on, of, up, to | afoot, awake |
| be– | around, about, away | beset, behead |
| for– | away, off, from | forsake, forget |
| mis– | badly, poorly, not | mismatch, misspell |
| over– | above, excessively | oversee, overdo |
| un– | not, reverse of | untrue, unfold |
| *Latin* and *Latin-French* | | |
| ab–, a–, abs– | from, off, away | abduct, absent |
| ante– | before | antedate |
| bi– | two | bimonthly, bisect |
| circum– | around | circumnavigate |
| com–, co–, col–, con–, cor– | with, together | compare, coexist, collide, convene |
| contra | against | contradict |
| de– | away, from, off, down | defect, desert |
| dis–, dif– | away, off, opposing | dissent, differ |
| ex–, e–, ef– | away from, out | excise, efface |
| in–, im– | in, into, within | impose, induct |
| in–, il–, im–, ir– | not | incapable, illegal, impious |
| inter– | among, between | intercede, intersperse |
| intro–, intra– | inward, to the inside, within | introduce, intravenous |
| non– | not | nonentity, nonessential |
| post– | after, following | postpone, postscript |
| pre– | before | prevent, preclude |
| pro– | forward, in place of, favoring | proceed, pronoun, pro-American |
| re– | back, backward, again | revoke, recede, recur |

| PREFIX | MEANING | EXAMPLES |
|---|---|---|
| *Latin* and *Latin-French* (continued) | | |
| retro– | back, backward | retroactive, retrospect |
| semi– | half | semiannual, semicircular |
| sub–, suf–, sum–, sup–, sus– | under, beneath | subjugate, suffuse, summon, suppose, suspect |
| super– | over, above, extra | supersede, supervise |
| trans– | across, beyond | transfuse, transport |
| ultra– | beyond, excessively | ultramodern, ultraviolet |
| *Greek* | | |
| a– | lacking, without | amorphous, atheistic |
| anti– | against, opposing | antipathy, antithesis |
| apo– | from, away | apology, apocrypha |
| cata– | down, away, thoroughly | cataclysm, catastrophe |
| dia– | through, across, apart | diameter, diagnose |
| eu– | good, pleasant | eulogy, euphemism |
| hemi– | half | hemisphere, hemiplegic |
| hyper– | excessive, over | hypercritical, hypertension |
| hypo– | under, beneath | hypodermic, hypothesis |
| para– | beside, beyond | parallel, paradox |
| peri– | around | periscope, perimeter |
| pro– | before | prognosis, program |
| syn–, sym–, syl–, sys– | together, with | synchronize, sympathy, syllable, system |

**EXERCISE 6.** Divide the following words into prefix and root, putting a slant line (/) at the point of division. Then give the meaning of the English word. Be ready to explain the connection between the meaning of the prefix and the present meaning of the word.

EXAMPLE 1. amnesia
1. *a/mnesia* (*loss of memory*)

1. absolve
2. amorphous
3. antipodes
4. biennial
5. circumspect
6. compunction

7. excise
8. hypodermic
9. impolite
10. subordinate

**EXERCISE 7.** Find and write on your paper two words that contain each of the following prefixes: *ad–*, *de–*, *dia–*, *dis–*, *eu–*, *im–*, *ir*, *mis–*, *post–*, *pro–*, *re–*, *sub–*, *trans–*, *syn–*, *ultra–*.

## Suffixes

Suffixes, you will recall, are affixes added after the root, or at the end of a word. There are two main kinds of suffixes: those that provide a grammatical signal of some kind but do not greatly alter the basic meaning of the word and those that, by being added, create new words. The endings *–s*, *–ed*, and *–ing* are suffixes of the first kind; by adding them to *work* (*works*, *worked*, *working*) we indicate something about number and tense, but we do not change the essential meaning of the word. This kind of suffix is a *grammatical* suffix.

Grammatical suffixes are important in grammar, but in vocabulary we are more concerned with the second kind of suffixes—those that make new words. By adding *–ful* to *thank*, we get a different word: *thankful*. Adding *–hood* to *girl* gives us *girlhood*, again a different word. Suffixes that change meaning in this way are called *derivational* suffixes. Notice in the following examples that the addition of a derivational suffix often gives a new part of speech as well as a new meaning.

| ROOT | DERIVATIONAL SUFFIX | RESULT |
| --- | --- | --- |
| acid (n. or adj.) | –ity | acidity (n. only) |
| free (adj.) | –dom | freedom (n.) |
| accept (v.) | –ance | acceptance (n.) |

Since derivational suffixes so often determine the part of speech of English words, we can conveniently classify them according to parts of speech. The meanings given for the suffixes are very broad. Often they have little connection with the meaning of the resulting word.

| NOUN SUFFIXES | MEANING | EXAMPLES |
|---|---|---|
| *Old English* | | |
| –dom | state, rank, condition | freedom, wisdom |
| –er | doer, maker | hunter, writer, thinker |
| –hood | state, condition | childhood, statehood |
| –ness | quality, state | softness, shortness |
| *Foreign (Latin, French, Greek)* | | |
| –age | process, state, rank | passage, bondage |
| –ance, –ancy | act, condition, fact | acceptance, vigilance, hesitancy |
| –ard, –art | one that does (esp. excessively) | coward, laggard, braggart |
| –ate | rank, office | delegate, primate |
| –ation | action, state, result | occupation, starvation |
| –cy | state, condition | accuracy, captaincy |
| –ee | one receiving action | employee, refugee |
| –eer | doer, worker at | engineer, racketeer |
| –ence | act, condition, fact | evidence, patience |
| –er | doer, native of | baker, westerner |
| –ery | skill, action, collection | surgery, robbery, crockery |
| –ess | feminine | waitress, lioness |
| –et, –ette | little, feminine | cigarette, islet, majorette |
| –ion | action, result, state | union, fusion, action |
| –ism | act, manner, doctrine | baptism, barbarism, socialism |
| –ist | doer, believer | monopolist, socialist |
| –ition | action, state, result | sedition, expedition |
| –ity | state, quality, condition | paucity, civility |
| –ment | means, result, action | refreshment, disappointment |
| –or | doer, office, action | elevator, juror, honor |
| –ry | condition, practice, collection | dentistry, jewelry |
| –tion | action, condition | creation, relation |
| –tude | quality, state, result | fortitude, multitude |
| –ty | quality, state | novelty, beauty |
| –ure | act, result, means | culture, signature |
| –y | result, action, quality | jealousy, inquiry |

| ADJECTIVE SUFFIXES | MEANING | EXAMPLES |
|---|---|---|
| *Old English* | | |
| –en | made of, like | wooden, golden |
| –ful | full of, marked by | thankful, masterful |
| –ish | suggesting, like | childish, devilish |
| –less | lacking, without | helpless, hopeless |
| –like | like, similar | childlike, dreamlike |
| –ly | like, of the nature of | friendly, cowardly |
| –some | apt to, showing | tiresome, lonesome |
| –ward | in the direction of | backward, homeward |
| –y | showing, suggesting | hilly, sticky, wavy |
| *Foreign* | | |
| –able | able, likely | capable, affable |
| –ate | having, showing | animate, separate |
| –escent | becoming, growing | obsolescent, quiescent |
| –esque | in the style of, like | picturesque, statuesque |
| –fic | making, causing | terrific, soporific |
| –ible | able, likely, fit | edible, possible, divisible |
| –ose | marked by, given to | comatose, bellicose |
| –ous | marked by, given to | religious, furious |

| ADJECTIVE OR NOUN SUFFIXES | MEANING | EXAMPLES |
|---|---|---|
| –al | doer, pertaining to | rival, animal, autumnal |
| –an | one belonging to, pertaining to | human, European |
| –ant | actor, agent, showing | servant, observant |
| –ary | belonging to, one connected with | primary, adversary, auxiliary |
| –ent | doing, showing, actor | confident, adherent |
| –ese | of a place or style, style | Chinese, journalese |
| –ian | pertaining to, one belonging to | barbarian, reptilian |
| –ic | dealing with, caused by, person or thing, showing | classic, choleric |
| –ile | marked by, one marked by | juvenile, servile |
| –ine | marked by, dealing with, one marked by | marine, canine, divine |

| ADJECTIVE OR NOUN SUFFIXES | MEANING | EXAMPLES |
|---|---|---|
| –ite | formed, showing, one marked by | favorite, composite |
| –ive | belonging or tending to, one belonging to | detective, native |
| –ory | doing, pertaining to, place or thing for | accessory, contributory |

| VERB SUFFIXES | MEANING | EXAMPLES |
|---|---|---|
| *Old English* | | |
| –en | cause to be, become | deepen, darken |
| *Foreign* | | |
| –ate | become, form, treat | populate, animate |
| –esce | become, grow, continue | convalesce, acquiesce |
| –fy | make, cause, cause to have | glorify, fortify |
| –ish | do, make, perform | punish, finish |
| –ize | make, cause to be | sterilize, motorize |

Some of the words in the above lists make independent sense without the suffix (*employee, employ*). Others, however, do not (*delegate, deleg–*).

Because the English language has been exposed to so many different influences, the pattern of adding suffixes to form related words is often inconsistent. Things made of wood are *wooden,* but things made of stone are not *stonen.* We do have some regularities: verbs ending in *–ate* usually have a related noun ending *–ation* (*prostrate, prostration*). We have such regular patterns as *differ, difference, differential, exist, existence, existential,* etc., but we have many other examples that are not so systematic. This irregularity is one reason why it is so important to learn related forms of the new words you add to your vocabulary. You cannot derive the noun form of *reject* (*rejection*) by knowing the noun form of *accept* (*acceptance*). You have to learn it separately. In a sense, you do not really know a word until you know its important related forms.

**EXERCISE 8.** What nouns, if any, are companion forms of the following verbs? Write the noun after the proper number. Do not use gerunds.

EXAMPLES 1. convene 2. decode
1. *convention* 2. *decoder*

1. cavil
2. collate
3. demur
4. disburse
5. intercede
6. intervene
7. prescribe
8. proscribe
9. stultify
10. verify

**EXERCISE 9.** Number your paper 1–10. Give a related verb for each noun below if there is one. If there is no verb form, write 0 after the proper number.

1. asperity
2. austerity
3. complaisance
4. defection
5. notation
6. raillery
7. remission
8. remuneration
9. turpitude
10. verification

**EXERCISE 10.** Number your paper 1–10. Give a related adjective for each of the following nouns and verbs.

1. austerity
2. complaisance
3. deduce
4. increment
5. environment
6. essence
7. excess
8. prescience
9. prescribe
10. vituperate

## Roots

A root is the core of a word—the part to which prefixes and suffixes are added. To find the root, you have only to remove any affix there may be. For example, removal of the affixes *a–* and *–ous* from *amorphous* leaves us with *–morph–*, a root meaning "form or shape." The root *–clysm,* meaning "falling," remains after we remove the prefix *cata–*, meaning "down," from *cataclysm.*

Roots have more specific and definite meanings than either prefixes or suffixes and appear in fewer different words. The following list contains some of the common foreign roots in English words.

| ROOT | MEANING | EXAMPLES |
|---|---|---|
| *Latin* | | |
| –ag–, –act– | do, drive, impel | agitate, transact |
| –agr– | field | agriculture, agrarian |
| –am–, –amic– | friend, love | amatory, amicable |
| –aqu– | water | aquatic, aqueduct, aquarium |
| –aud–, –audit– | hear | audible, auditorium |
| –ben–, –bene– | well, good | benefit, benediction |
| –brev– | short, brief | abbreviate, breviary |
| –cand– | white, glowing | candor, incandescent |
| –capit– | head | capital, decapitate |
| –cent– | hundred | century, centennial |
| –cid–, –cis– | kill, cut | suicide, regicide, incision |
| –clin– | bend, lean | decline, inclination |
| –cogn– | know | recognize, cognizant |
| –cred– | belief, trust | incredible, credulity |
| –crypt– | hidden, secret | crypt, cryptic |
| –culp– | fault, blame | culpable, exculpate |
| –duc–, –duct– | lead | educate, conductor |
| –equ– | equal | equation, equanimity |
| –err– | wander, stray | erratic, aberration |
| –fac–, –fact–, –fect–, –fic– | do, make | facile, manufacture, defective, efficient |
| –fer– | bear, yield | transfer, fertile |
| –fid– | belief, faith | fidelity, perfidious |
| –fin– | end, limit | final, indefinite |
| –frag–, –fract– | break | fragment, fracture |
| –fus– | pour | transfuse, effusive |
| –gen– | birth, kind, origin | generate, generic |
| –jac–, –ject– | throw, hurl, cast | adjacent, eject |
| –junct– | join | junction, disjunctive |
| –jud– | judge | prejudice, adjudicate |
| –jug– | join, yoke | conjugal, conjugate |
| –jur– | swear, plead | adjure, perjury |
| –leg–, –lig–, –lect– | choose, read | eligible, legible, lectern |
| –loc– | place | locus, locale |

| ROOT | MEANING | EXAMPLES |
|---|---|---|
| –loqu–, –loc– | talk, speech | colloquial, locution |
| –magn– | large | magnitude, magnify |
| –mal– | bad | malady, malevolent |
| –man–, –manu– | hand | manicure, manual |
| –mit–, –miss– | send | remit, emissary |
| –mor–, –mort– | die, death | mortuary, immortal |
| –omni– | all | omnipotent, omniscient |
| –ped– | foot | pedal, quadruped |
| –pend–, –pens– | hang, weigh | appendix, suspense |
| –pon–, –pos– | place, put | postpone, interpose |
| –port– | carry, bear | transport, importation |
| –prim– | first, early | primitive, primordial |
| –punct– | point | punctuation, punctilious |
| –reg–, –rig–, –rect– | rule, straight, right | regent, incorrigible, rectangular |
| –rupt– | break | rupture, interrupt |
| –sang– | blood | sanguine, consanguinity |
| –sci– | know, knowledge | omniscient, prescience |
| –scrib–, –script– | write | inscribe, proscribe, manuscript |
| –sent–, –sens– | feel | presentiment, sensitive |
| –sequ–, –secut– | follow | sequel, persecute |
| –son– | sound | consonant, sonorous |
| –spir– | breath, breathe | expire, inspiration |
| –string–, –strict– | bind tight | constrict, stricture |
| –tract– | draw, pull | traction, extractor |
| –uni– | one | unity, uniform |
| –verb– | word | verbal, verbiage |
| –ven–, –vent– | come | intervene, supervene |
| –vid–, –vis– | see | evident, television |
| –vit– | life | vitality, vitamin |

*Greek*

| | | |
|---|---|---|
| –anthrop– | man | anthropology, misanthropic |
| –arch– | ancient, chief | archaeology, monarch |
| –astr–, –aster– | star | astronomy, asterisk |
| –auto– | self | automatic, autonomy |

| ROOT | MEANING | EXAMPLES |
|---|---|---|
| *Greek* | | |
| -bibli- | book | bibliography, bibliophile |
| -bio- | life | biology, autobiography |
| -chrom- | color | chromatic, chromosome |
| -cosm- | world, order | cosmos, microcosm |
| -cycl- | wheel, circle | cyclone, bicycle |
| -dem- | people | democracy, epidemic |
| -gen- | kind, race | eugenics, genesis |
| -geo- | earth | geography, geology |
| -gram- | write, writing | grammar, epigram |
| -graph- | write, writing | orthography, geography |
| -hydr- | water | hydrogen, dehydrate |
| -log- | word, study | epilogue, theology, logic |
| -micr- | small | microbe, microscope |
| -mon- | one, single | monogamy, monologue |
| -morph- | form | amorphous, metamorphosis |
| -neo- | new | neologism, neolithic |
| -orth- | straight, correct | orthodox, orthography |
| -pan- | all, entire | panorama, pandemonium |
| -path- | feeling, suffering | apathy, pathology, sympathy |
| -phil- | like, love | philanthropic, philosophy |
| -phon- | sound | phonology, euphony |
| -poly- | many | polygon, polygamy |
| -proto- | first | prototype |
| -psych- | mind | psychology, psychosomatic |
| -soph- | wise, wisdom | philosophy, sophomore |
| -tele- | far, distant | telegram, telepathy |
| -zo- | animal | zoology, protozoa |

**EXERCISE 11.** List two English words (other than those given as examples above) containing each of the following roots.

EXAMPLE 1. -verb-
1. *adverb, verbose*

1. -aud- (hear)
2. -crypt- (hidden, secret)
3. -duc- (lead)
4. -fin- (end, limit)
5. -junct- (join)
6. -man-, -manu- (hand)
7. -mor-, -mort- (death)
8. -port- (carry)
9. -vid-, -vis- (see)
10. -vit- (life)

**EXERCISE 12.** Follow the instructions for Exercise 11.

1. -arch- (chief)
2. -auto- (self)
3. -bio- (life)
4. -chron- (time)
5. -cycl- (wheel, circle)
6. -dem-, -demo- (people)
7. -gram- (write, writing)
8. -hydr- (water)
9. -mega- (large)
10. -poly- (many)

**REVIEW EXERCISE A.** Using slanting bars (/) to mark each separation, divide the following words into their parts. Then, referring to the preceding lists of prefixes, suffixes, and roots—or, if necessary, to your dictionary—write a brief definition for each. Be prepared to explain how the parts produce the total meaning.

EXAMPLE 1. zoology
1. *zoo/log/y (study of animals)*

1. achromatic
2. autonomy
3. bibliophile
4. cosmic
5. cryptogram
6. deduction
7. evoke
8. extortion
9. geology
10. ineligible
11. incapable
12. infidel
13. judicious
14. lucid
15. nominee
16. proponent
17. pseudonym
18. subsequent
19. transmission
20. vociferous

## Limitations of Word Analysis

Knowing something of the way in which prefixes, suffixes, and roots combine to form words provides insights into the history of our words and into their meanings. However, it would be misleading to suggest that the original meanings of the parts are always clearly reflected in a modern word.

It may happen that following the method of word division will lead you to a meaning that is so far from the modern one as to be of little help. For example, the words *admonition* and *monetary* have an element (*-mon-*) in common. The first means "warning" and the second "pertaining to money." What is the connection? There is one, but it is remote: in ancient Roman times, money was coined in or near a temple of Juno, a goddess known as "the warner." This is interesting, but not much of a clue if you do not already know the meaning of both words. Word analysis can often help you to make a plausible guess at what a word may mean; it can rarely be absolutely depended upon.

## Semantic Change

One obvious reason that word analysis does not always work as a way of finding meaning is that words change their meanings. This change in meaning—called *semantic change*—is extremely common.

There are several ways in which this change comes about. Sometimes a word that has had a general meaning comes to have a specific meaning. The word *starve* once meant "to die." It only later took on the special meaning of "to die for lack of food." In Old English, any crawling creature—including the dragon in *Beowulf*—could be called a *worm*. Now the word is used only to mean earthworms and the like.

Words also take on new meanings in the opposite way—from specific to general. Originally *barn* meant "a storage place for barley," and *lord* meant "loaf guard or bread keeper."

When a word acquires a new meaning, it may lose the old meaning, as *worm, starve,* and *lord* have. When this situation takes place, the word has become detached from the root meaning, although it retains the original root form. The *-jure* of *adjure* is related to *jury* and originally had to do with swearing in a legal sense. But usually the word now means "to entreat," and the meaning connection with the root has been lost.

*Auspices* literally means "looking at birds." The ancient Romans believed that they could tell from studying the entrails of sacrificial birds whether or not an enterprise would be successful. The word came to be used for any combination of favorable signs and then, as it is now, for a combination of protection, guidance, and patronage.

Sometimes both old and new meanings are retained. Indeed, often it works out that a word will have six, eight, or ten meanings. Some of these meanings may be close to the original meanings of the word elements; some may vary from them considerably. The word *aegis* meant originally a shield or breastplate, especially one associated with the goddess Athena; then it came to mean also "protection" and "patronage, sponsorship." Depending on the context, it can mean any of these things in modern English. As a result, we may say that a lecture or exhibit is held under either the auspices—originally, bird watching—or the aegis—originally, shield—of a certain group. *Insular* means "pertaining to an island," but it has also come to mean "isolated, detached" and also "narrow, provincial." *Sanguine* may retain the root meaning and indicate "bloody," but it is more likely to mean "quite optimistic." Because there are so many situations involving semantic change, careful use of context clues or steady use of the dictionary is likely to give a more accurate sense of word meanings than word analysis alone.

**EXERCISE 13.** List the following words and write after each its original meaning as given in the dictionary: *abeyance, challenge, derive, detriment, dirge, farce, glamour, knave, lampoon, melancholy, monster, pedigree, sabotage, scandal, vegetable.*

## Synonyms

Word borrowing, word derivation by affixes and roots, semantic change, and other processes keep going on all the time, making English rich in synonyms. Synonyms are words that may be interchanged in given contexts. We can say "a hard task" or "a difficult task," because *hard* and *difficult* are synonyms. We can say that New York is a large city or a metropolis, and *city* and *metropolis* are therefore synonyms.

It is often said that there are very few pairs of words in English that are entirely interchangeable, because there are usually slight but important differences between synonyms. Sometimes one synonym is noticeably more learned than another; *edifice* is more learned and pretentious than *building, domicile* more so than *home* or *residence. Daily* is the ordinary English word, *diurnal* and *quotidian* quite learned. Sometimes one of a pair of synonyms is noticeably informal; *smidge* or *smidgeon* is less formal than *particle.* Often learned words are rather specific in their suggestions; the sphere in which they can be used is narrow. It is possible to analyze both *terrestrial* and *mundane* as "pertaining to the world." But *terrestrial* is likely to suggest contrast between our world and other heavenly bodies, described by words like *lunar* and *solar,* and *mundane* carries with it suggestions of the practical, routine, everyday affairs of this world, as contrasted with more spiritual matters. Synonyms may differ, too, in expressing value judgments; to be *resolute* is a virtue; to be *determined* expresses no value judgment; and to be *obstinate* is a fault.

The wealth of synonyms in English gives us a variety of ways of expressing ourselves, but challenges us to decide on the most appropriate of them.

**EXERCISE 14.** Find three synonyms apiece for each of the following words. Use your dictionary if necessary. Be prepared to discuss differences between your synonyms.

1. sick
2. expensive
3. pleasant
4. hard
5. dangerous
6. talk
7. walk
8. see
9. dislike
10. work
11. enjoyment
12. knowledge

**EXERCISE 15.** Be prepared to discuss in class differences between the following pairs of synonyms.

1. donation, gift
2. venomous, toxic
3. reverent, pious
4. lean, gaunt
5. meditate, ruminate
6. vapid, inane
7. void, vacuum
8. gracious, cordial
9. congenital, hereditary
10. handle, manipulate

Early in this chapter, you were advised to keep a vocabulary notebook in which to list new words and their meanings. If you have done so, your notebook should contain a number of new words drawn from this chapter and from the word list that follows it. Do not be content, however, to have these words in your notebook. Listen for them, and watch for them in your reading. Observing how a new word is used is the best way of learning to use it yourself. Your vocabulary notebook is like the address books people use to remind them of the names and addresses of people they don't encounter often. No one needs such a book for close acquaintances. Get into the habit of making old friends of new words.

**REVIEW EXERCISE B.** Number 1–20. After the proper number, write the letter of the word or expression that comes closest to the meaning of the italicized word.

| | | |
|---|---|---|
| 1. *amorphous* clouds | a) formless<br>b) romantic | c) jar-shaped<br>d) commonplace |
| 2. under the *auspices* of the state | a) protests<br>b) sponsorship | c) opposition<br>d) observation |
| 3. struggle for *autonomy* | a) fair treatment<br>b) self-esteem | c) survival<br>d) self-rule |
| 4. the last chance to *capitulate* | a) turn the tide<br>b) surrender | c) negotiate<br>d) compromise |
| 5. *circumspect* behavior | a) improper<br>b) cautious | c) surprising<br>d) praiseworthy |
| 6. to *collate* two documents | a) preserve<br>b) seal up | c) duplicate<br>d) compare |
| 7. feeling no *compunction* | a) satisfaction<br>b) ambition | c) remorse<br>d) pride |
| 8. to *conjecture* about a motive | a) guess<br>b) mislead | c) lie<br>d) find out |
| 9. the soldier's *defection* | a) weakness<br>b) decoration | c) desertion<br>d) wound |
| 10. not daring to *demur* | a) whisper<br>b) appear | c) object<br>d) tell the truth |

11. *devoid* of sympathy
a) full
b) without a trace
c) deserving
d) undeserving

12. without *divulging* the answer
a) guessing
b) revealing
c) suspecting
d) peeking at

13. to *expiate* a crime
a) profit from
b) witness
c) atone for
d) facilitate

14. a *judicious* choice
a) illegal
b) required by law
c) wise
d) laughable

15. a *minute* creature
a) short-lived
b) quickly moving
c) very small
d) very young

16. *mundane* concerns
a) worldly
b) tedious
c) religious
d) dishonest

17. *parasitic* followers
a) loyal
b) living off others
c) disloyal
d) fanatical

18. a *propitious* start
a) proper
b) false
c) sudden
d) favorable

19. an unusual *pseudonym*
a) last name
b) antonym
c) pen name
d) honorary title

20. an act of *temerity*
a) cowardice
b) rage
c) uncertainty
d) foolish daring

## *Word List*

The 240 words in the list below may be used as the basis of your vocabulary study this year. In many of them you will recognize the Old English, Latin, and Greek word parts you have just studied. Make it a habit to learn unfamiliar words from this list regularly; ten each week is a practical number. When you consult a dictionary for the meaning of an unfamiliar word, make sure you find the meaning that fits the context you have in mind; or ask your teacher to verify the meaning.

abdicate
abeyance
abscond
accede
accessory
accost

acquisition
acrimonious
adjudge
adjure

aegis

aesthetic
allay
amorphous
antipathy
antipodes
apostasy

apposite
archives
ascertain

ascetic
ascribe
asperity
auspices
austerity
autonomy
biennial
bucolic
cabal
calumny

capricious
cataclysm
cavil
chicanery
chimerical
cognizant
collateral
complaisance
compunction
conjecture

conjugal
consanguinity
contravene
contrive
conversant
cosmic
cosmopolitan
coterie
couplet
covet

credible
credulous
cryptic
decorum
deduction

defection
demure
denizen
derive
derogatory

desiccate
desist
deteriorate
detriment
devoid
differentiate
dilatory
dirge
disburse
discursive

disparity
dissent
diurnal
divulge
doggerel
dogma
drastic
dupe
duress
dynamic

effete
eject
elegant
elite
elixir
elocution
elude
emissary
emolument
empirical

enormity
entomology
environment

ephemeral
epicurean
equanimity
eschew
essence
ethereal
eulogy

euphony
evanescent
evoke
excise
exhort
expiate
facile
febrile
fecundity
foible

fortuitous
frivolous
gratuitous
humdrum
hyperbole
immutable
inane
inanimate
incarcerate
incompatible

increment
inculcate
induction
ingenuous
iniquity
insular
intercede
intervene
invidious
irony

laity

lampoon
loquacious
microcosm
modicum
mundane
nefarious
nemesis
nonentity
omniscient

opulence
panegyric
parasitic
patron
perfidious
perspicuity
pertinent
platitude
pleasantry
plebeian

plebiscite
politic
predilection
prescience
presumptuous
primordial
priority
proffer
prognosis
proletarian

propitiate
propitious
proponent
proscribe
prospective
protagonist
protégé
prototype

proxy
pseudonym

pun
punctilious
purport
pusillanimous
querulous
quiescent
raillery
raucous
reactionary
recalcitrant

reciprocate
redundant
regale
regimen
remission
remuneration
repartee
replete
repository
repugnance

residual
restitution
retroactive
retrospect
revelation
rostrum
rotund
sagacity
salient
saline

salutary
sanguine
sardonic
scapegoat

schism
scurrilous
sedentary
sedulous
solstice
somnolent

sonorous
sortie
specious
stereotype
stipend
strident
stultify
subservient
subsidiary
subterfuge

superannuate
surreptitious
synchronize
syndicate
temerity
tenable
tenuous
tenure
truism
unprecedented

venal
verify
vernacular
virulent
vitiate
vituperate
vociferous
volatile
voluminous
votary

# Chapter 36

# Spelling

## Improving Your Spelling

This chapter suggests a number of things you can do to improve your spelling:

1. Be careful.
2. Use the dictionary.
3. Keep a list of your own spelling errors.
4. Learn to spell words by syllables.
5. Learn a few helpful spelling rules.
6. Learn to distinguish between words that sound alike.
7. Learn lists of commonly misspelled words.

## GOOD SPELLING HABITS

1. *Be careful.* Care in writing and in proofreading your compositions will eliminate errors in the spelling of simple words like *to, there, its,* which account for so many of the teacher's corrections on students' themes.

2. *Use the dictionary.* Some students apparently think themselves allergic to the dictionary. They would rather take a chance on guessing than expose themselves to the truth. But the only sure way to find out how to spell a word is to look it up.

3. *Keep a list of your own spelling errors.* We do not all misspell the same words. Although it is a difficult habit to establish, the habit of recording in your notebook the words

you misspell in your compositions will pay you a large return on the investment of a little time and patience.

4. *Learn to spell words by syllables.* This is the "divide and conquer" technique used with success by invading armies. It is equally effective in attacking a long and troublesome word. Dividing a long word into syllables gives a number of short parts. Short parts are simpler to spell than long ones; hence you can simplify your spelling problem by acquiring the habit of dividing words into syllables and spelling them part by part.

Two common causes of spelling mistakes are the omission of a letter or syllable and the addition of an extra letter or syllable. A student who spells *probably* as though it were *probaly* has made the first kind of mistake. If you spell *lightning* as though it were *lightening,* you have made the second kind. Errors like these are errors in pronunciation which, in turn, are the result of not knowing the exact syllables in the word.

Dividing a word into its pronounceable parts (syllables) will help you to pronounce and to spell the word correctly.

**EXERCISE 1.** Write each of the following words in syllables —place a hyphen between syllables. When you have completed the exercise and studied the words, take a test on them from dictation. Whether your divisions correspond exactly with the dictionary syllabication is not important, provided the words are divided into pronounceable parts and all letters are included and no letters are added.

| | | |
|---|---|---|
| 1. modern | 5. privilege | 9. representative |
| 2. similar | 6. perspiration | 10. entrance |
| 3. library | 7. boundary | 11. lightning |
| 4. surprise | 8. candidate | 12. accidentally |

**EXERCISE 2.** Follow directions for the preceding exercise.

| | | |
|---|---|---|
| 1. athletics | 5. equipment | 9. sophomore |
| 2. disastrous | 6. temperament | 10. quiet |
| 3. government | 7. recognize | 11. mischievous |
| 4. undoubtedly | 8. business | 12. curiosity |

## SPELLING RULES

5. *Learn a few helpful spelling rules.* Although some spelling rules are hopelessly complicated, a few are simple enough and important enough to justify the effort required to master them. Study the following rules and apply them whenever possible in your writing.

### *ie* and *ei*

**36a. Write *ie* when the sound is $\bar{e}$, except after *c*.**

EXAMPLES believe, thief, fierce, ceiling, receive, deceive
EXCEPTIONS seize, either, weird, leisure, neither

**Write *ei* when the sound is not $\bar{e}$, especially when the sound is $\bar{a}$.**

EXAMPLES freight, neighbor, weigh; height
EXCEPTIONS friend, mischief

**EXERCISE 3.** Write the following words, supplying the missing letters (*e* and *i*) in the correct order. Be able to explain how the rule applies to each.

| | | |
|---|---|---|
| 1. for . . . gn | 9. p . . . ce | 17. s . . . ge |
| 2. br . . . f | 10. rec . . . ve | 18. s . . . ze |
| 3. rel . . . ve | 11. retr . . . ve | 19. bel . . . ve |
| 4. conc . . . ve | 12. sl . . . gh | 20. w . . . rd |
| 5. v . . . l | 13. ach . . . ve | 21. rec . . . pt |
| 6. n . . . ce | 14. handkerch . . . f | 22. bel . . . f |
| 7. c . . . ling | 15. perc . . . ve | 23. f . . . nd |
| 8. gr . . . f | 16. th . . . f | 24. l . . . sure |

### *–cede, –ceed,* and *–sede*

**36b. Only one English word ends in *–sede: supersede;* only three words end in *–ceed: exceed, proceed, succeed;* all other words of similar sound end in *–cede.***

EXAMPLES precede, recede, secede, accede, concede

## Adding Prefixes

A *prefix* is one or more than one letter or syllable added to the beginning of a word to change its meaning.

**36c. When a prefix is added to a word, the spelling of the word itself remains the same.**

il + legal = **illegal**
in + elegant = **inelegant**
im + movable = **immovable**
un + necessary = **unnecessary**
un + excused = **unexcused**
a + moral = **amoral**
mis + understood = **misunderstood**
mis + spell = **misspell**
re + commend = **recommend**
over + run = **overrun**
over + eat = **overeat**

## Adding Suffixes

A *suffix* is one or more than one letter or syllable added to the end of a word to change its meaning.

**36d. When the suffixes *-ness* and *-ly* are added to a word, the spelling of the word itself is not changed.**

EXAMPLES mean + ness = **meanness**
final + ly = **finally**

EXCEPTIONS Words ending in *y* usually change the *y* to *i* before *-ness* and *-ly:* ready—**readily**; heavy—**heaviness**; happy—**happiness.** One-syllable adjectives ending in *y,* however, generally follow Rule 36d: dry—dryness; shy—shyly.

**EXERCISE 4.** Spell correctly the words indicated.

1. *rate* with the prefix *over*
2. *habitual* with the suffix *ly*
3. *agree* with the prefix *dis*
4. *green* with the suffix *ness*
5. *material* with the prefix *im*
6. *appoint* with the prefix *dis*
7. *apprehend* with the prefix *mis*
8. *practical* with the suffix *ly*
9. *abated* with the prefix *un*
10. *casual* with the suffix *ly*
11. *natural* with the prefix *un*
12. *stubborn* with the suffix *ness*
13. *legible* with the prefix *il*
14. *appropriate* with the prefix *in*
15. *appear* with the prefix *dis*

16. *movable* with the prefix *im*
17. *construct* with the prefix *re*
18. *animate* with the prefix *in*
19. *similar* with the prefix *dis*
20. *keen* with the suffix *ness*
21. *spell* with the prefix *mis*
22. *use* with the prefix *mis*
23. *avoidable* with the prefix *un*
24. *merry* with the suffix *ly*

**36e. Drop the final *e* before a suffix beginning with a vowel.**

EXAMPLES care + ing = caring use + able = usable

EXCEPTIONS Keep the final *e* before *a* or *o* if necessary to retain the soft sound of *c* or *g* preceding the *e*: noticeable, courageous

**36f. Keep the final *e* before a suffix beginning with a consonant.**

EXAMPLES care + ful = careful care + less = careless

EXCEPTIONS true + ly = truly argue + ment = argument
acknowledge + ment = acknowledgment [more usual spelling]

**36g. With words ending in *y* preceded by a consonant, change the *y* to *i* before any suffix not beginning with *i*.**

EXAMPLES funny—funnier; hurry—hurried; hurry—hurrying

**36h. Double the final consonant before a suffix that begins with a vowel if both of the following conditions exist: (1) the word has only one syllable or is accented on the last syllable; (2) the word ends in a single consonant preceded by a single vowel.**

EXAMPLES plan + ing = planning [one-syllable word]
forget + ing = forgetting [accent on last syllable; single consonant and single vowel]
cancel + ed = canceled [accent not on last syllable]
prefer + able = pref′erable [accent shifts; not on last syllable]

**EXERCISE 5.** Write correctly the words formed as follows:

1. defer + ed
2. defer + ence
3. hope + ing
4. approve + al
5. benefit + ed
6. nine + ty
7. prepare + ing
8. profit + ing
9. write + ing
10. propel + ing
11. desire + able
12. control + ed
13. hope + less
14. move + ing
15. true + ly
16. run + ing
17. singe + ing
18. fame + ous
19. name + less
20. red + est

## The Plural of Nouns

**36i. Observe the rules for spelling the plural of nouns.**

**(1) The regular way to form the plural of a noun is to add *s*.**

EXAMPLES chair, chairs    book, books

**(2) The plural of some nouns is formed by adding *es*.**

The *e* represents the extra sound heard when *–s* is added to words ending in *s, sh, ch,* and *x*.

EXAMPLES dress, dresses    bush, bushes
birch, birches    box, boxes

**(3) The plural of nouns ending in *y preceded by a consonant* is formed by changing the *y* to *i* and adding *es*.**

EXAMPLES fly, flies    lady, ladies
enemy, enemies    salary, salaries

**(4) The plural of nouns ending in *y preceded by a vowel* is formed by adding an *s*.**

EXAMPLES monkey, monkeys    donkey, donkeys

**(5) The plural of most nouns ending in *f* or *fe* is formed by adding *s*. The plural of some nouns ending in *f* or *fe* is formed by changing the *f* to *v* and adding *s* or *es*.**

EXAMPLES Add *s:* roof, roofs dwarf, dwarfs
chief, chiefs

Change *f* to *v* and add *s* or *es:*

knife, knives calf, calves
loaf, loaves wharf, wharves
leaf, leaves

**(6) The plural of nouns ending in *o preceded by a vowel* is formed by adding *s*. The plural of nouns ending in *o preceded by a consonant* is formed by adding either *s* or *es*.**

EXAMPLES *o* following a vowel:

rodeo, rodeos radio, radios

*o* following a consonant:

hero, heroes potato, potatoes
mosquito, mosquitoes

EXCEPTIONS Words of Italian origin ending in *o* that refer to music form the plural by adding *s*: piano, pianos; soprano, sopranos; solo, solos.

**(7) The plural of a few nouns is formed by irregular methods.**

EXAMPLES child, children ox, oxen
mouse, mice woman, women
tooth, teeth goose, geese

**(8) The plural of compound nouns written as one word is formed by adding *s* or *es*.**

EXAMPLES cupful, cupfuls
leftover, leftovers
strongbox, strongboxes

**(9) The plural of compound nouns consisting of a noun plus a modifier is formed by making the noun plural.**

In the following examples, the phrases *in-law* and *of-war* and the adjectives *martial, general,* and *by* are all modifiers. It is the nouns modified by them that are made plural.

EXAMPLES mother-in-law, mothers-in-law
man-of-war, men-of-war
court martial, courts martial
secretary-general, secretaries-general
passer-by, passers-by

**(10) The plural of a few compound nouns is formed in irregular ways.**

EXAMPLES drive-in, drive-ins
tie-up, tie-ups
six-year-old, six-year-olds

**(11) Some nouns are the same in the singular and the plural.**

EXAMPLES sheep, deer, trout, species, Chinese

**(12) The plural of some foreign words is formed as in the original language.**

EXAMPLES alumnus (*man*), alumni (*men*)
alumna (*woman*), alumnae (*women*)
datum, data
crisis, crises

**(13) The plural of other foreign words may be formed either as in the foreign language or by adding *s* or *es*.**

EXAMPLES index, indices *or* indexes
appendix, appendices *or* appendixes

► NOTE In certain words the English plural is the preferred one, for example, *formulas* not *formulae*. Whenever there is any doubt about which plural to use, consult the dictionary.

**(14) The plural of numbers, letters, signs, and words considered as words is formed by adding an apostrophe and an *s*.**

EXAMPLES If you think there are ten 5's in that column, you'd better count again.
There are two *s*'s in *necessary*.

My last paper was full of 0's, not +'s.

Don't use too many *I*'s in writing your paper.

**EXERCISE 6.** Write the plural form of each of the following nouns. Be able to explain your spelling on the basis of the rules.

1. candy
2. sheep
3. piano
4. valley
5. alumnus
6. cameo
7. torch
8. chief
9. tomato
10. gas
11. fly
12. alto
13. brother-in-law
14. shelf
15. bench
16. editor in chief
17. spoonful
18. hero
19. knife
20. goose

**EXERCISE 7.** By referring to the rules on the preceding pages, explain the spelling of each of the following:

1. regretted
2. receive
3. illegible
4. coming (*e* dropped)
5. conferring
6. niece
7. contraltos
8. misstate
9. stubbornness
10. peaceable
11. ladies
12. conference
13. alumnae
14. leisure
15. occurred
16. writing (*e* dropped)
17. roofs
18. weigh
19. disappear
20. naturally

## WORDS THAT SOUND ALIKE

6. *Learn to distinguish between words that sound alike.* These words present problems because they sound alike but have different meanings and different spellings. You have probably had trouble distinguishing between *principle* and *principal, capital* and *capitol,* and other such pairs. Most of the paired words in the following lists sound alike. Some pairs, however, are confused even though they are not pronounced exactly alike.

**already** *previously*
I had *already* seen the movie twice.

**all ready** *all are ready* (or *wholly ready*)
Give the signal when you are *all ready*.

**all right** [This word really does not belong in this list, but it is included here because many persons think there is a word spelled *alright*, as though *all right* did have a homonym. There is no word *alright*. The correct spelling is always *all right*.]

---

**altar** *a table or stand in a church* or *a place for outdoor offerings*
The priest was standing beside the *altar*.

**alter** *to change*
If we are late, we will *alter* our plans.

---

**altogether** *entirely*
She doesn't *altogether* approve of me.

**all together** *everyone in the same place*
We were *all together* at Christmas.

---

**born** *given birth*
When were you *born?*

**borne** *carried*
He has *borne* his hardships bravely.

---

**brake** *device to stop a machine*
A defective *brake* caused the accident.

**break** *to fracture, shatter*
Try not to *break* any dishes.

---

**capital** *city;* also as an adjective, *punishable by death* or *of major importance*
Washington is the *capital* of this country.
Killing a police officer is a *capital* offense.
That is a *capital* idea.

**capitol** *building*
The *capitol* faces a park.

---

**cloths** *pieces of cloth*
Try the new cleaning *cloths*.

**clothes** *wearing apparel*
Her *clothes* are expensive.

**EXERCISE 8.** Number your paper 1–20. Write after the proper number the correct one of the words given in parentheses in the sentences below.

1. The damage has (already, all ready) been done.
2. Mother was (all together, altogether) too surprised to protest.
3. Events have (born, borne) out my predictions.
4. Pete is an (altar, alter) boy at St. Anne's Church.
5. If you (brake, break) a window, you will pay for it.
6. When you are (already, all ready) I will help you.
7. Belgrade is the (capital, capitol) of Yugoslavia.
8. If you will (altar, alter) the neckline, I will buy the dress.
9. My mother was (born, borne) in France.
10. Was her work (alright, all right)?
11. We polished the car with (cloths, clothes).
12. We will (altar, alter) the building to suit tenants.
13. The dome on the (capital, capitol) is illuminated at night.
14. The club members have been (all together, altogether) only once.
15. Cars are (born, borne) across the river on a ferry.
16. Herbert was wearing his best (cloths, clothes).
17. When did the Supreme Court strike down (capital, capitol) punishment?
18. I applied the (brakes, breaks) immediately.
19. Are you feeling (all right, alright)?
20. The family were (all together, altogether) on my birthday.

**coarse** *rough, crude*
He wore a suit of *coarse* cloth and used *coarse* language.

**course** *path of action; part of a meal; a series of studies*
The golf *course* is outside of town.
Soup was the first *course*.
I am taking a *course* in cooking.

---

**complement** *something that completes or makes perfect*

The *complement* of 50° is 40°. [*completes* a 90° angle]

His part of the job *complements* mine. [Together they *complete* the job.]

**compliment** *a remark that says something good about a person; to say something good*

I am pleased by your *compliment.*

She *complimented* me on my backhand.

---

**consul** *representative of a foreign country*

The American *consul* in Quito helped us during our visit.

**council, councilor** *a group called together to accomplish a job;* a member of such a group is a *councilor*

The *council* met to welcome a new *councilor.*

**counsel, counselor** *advice; the giving of advice;* one who gives advice is a *counselor*

I accepted the wise *counsel* of my *counselor.*

---

**des'ert** *a dry region*

We flew across the *desert.*

**desert'** *to leave*

She *deserted* her friends in their time of need.

**dessert'** *the final course of a meal*

The *dessert* was ice cream.

---

**formally** *conventionally* or *properly, according to strict rules*

She spoke *formally* and with great dignity.

**formerly** *in the past, previously*

I was *formerly* a member of that club.

---

**its** [possessive]

The village is proud of *its* school.

**it's** *it is*

*It's* a long way.

---

**later** *more late*

We will arrive *later.*

**latter** *the second of two*
When given the choice of a football or a tennis racket, I chose the *latter*.

**lead** [present tense] *to go first*
You *lead* and we will follow.

**led** [past tense]
She *led* the team to victory.

**lead** [pronounced **lĕd**] *a heavy metal;* also *graphite in a pencil*
The industrial uses of *lead* are many.

EXERCISE 9. Number your paper 1–20. Write after the proper number the correct one of the words given in parentheses in the sentences below.

1. Our (consul, counsel) in Romania has returned to Washington.
2. I enjoyed the dinner but not the (dessert, desert).
3. Avoid (course, coarse) language.
4. Mr. Abrams was (formally, formerly) vice-president of the bank.
5. No (councilor, counselor) may serve more than three years on the council.
6. I do not enjoy parties conducted as (formally, formerly) as this one.
7. The walls of the room were papered but (its, it's) ceiling had been painted.
8. Some people are distrustful of (compliments, complements).
9. We are not sure which (course, coarse) to follow.
10. (Desert, Dessert) soil is often fertile if irrigated.
11. Are you sure (its, it's) not too late?
12. I spent five summers working as a camp (councilor, counselor).
13. A golf (course, coarse) requires continual care.
14. I spoke to the mayor and the superintendent; the (later, latter) was more helpful.

15. I can't recall his ever giving me a (complement, compliment) on my writing.
16. The soldiers who (deserted, desserted) were finally caught.
17. The guidance (councilor, counselor) advised me to take the test.
18. During his senior year, Albert (lead, led) the team to a championship.
19. Have you finished your (course, coarse) in hygiene?
20. These supplies will (complement, compliment) those you already have.

---

**loose** *free, not close together*
The animals broke *loose.*
They stumbled in the *loose* sand.

**lose** [pronounced **lo͞oz**] *to suffer loss*
When did you *lose* your books?

---

**miner** *worker in a mine*
A *miner's* job is sometimes dangerous.

**minor** *under legal age; less important*
A *minor* cannot marry without a parent's or guardian's consent.
They raised only *minor* objections.

---

**moral** *good;* also *a lesson of conduct*
His good conduct showed him to be a *moral* person.
The class understood the *moral* of the story.

**morale** *mental condition, spirit*
The *morale* in our school is excellent.

---

**passed** *verb*
The Fiat *passed* me at the finish line.

**past** *noun* or *adjective* or *preposition*
Some persons prefer to live in the *past* (n.) because *past* (adj.) events seem more interesting than present ones.
I went *past* (prep.) your house without realizing it.

---

**peace** *opposite of strife*
Everyone prefers *peace* to war.

| | |
|---|---|
| **piece** | *a part of something*<br>They ate every *piece* of cake. |
| **personal** | *individual*<br>He gave his *personal* opinion. |
| **personnel** | *a group of people employed in the same place*<br>The *personnel* of the company ranged in age from 16 to 64. |
| **plain** | *not fancy;* also *a flat area of land;* also *clear*<br>She lives in a very *plain* home.<br>We crossed the *plains* in two days.<br>Our problem is *plain.* |
| **plane** | *a flat surface;* also *a tool;* also *an airplane*<br>*Plane* geometry is a study of imaginary flat surfaces.<br>The carpenter used a *plane.*<br>A *plane* circled the airport. |
| **principal** | *head of a school;* also *the main one of several things*<br>They went to the *principal's* office.<br>The *principal* cause of accidents is carelessness. |
| **principle** | *a rule of conduct;* also *a main fact* or *law*<br>The judge accused the criminal of having no *principles.*<br>She understands the *principles* of mathematics. |
| **quiet** | *still, silent*<br>A study hall should be *quiet.* |
| **quite** | *completely, wholly;* also *to a great extent or degree*<br>I had *quite* forgotten her advice.<br>Angela is *quite* tall. |

**EXERCISE 10.** Number your paper 1–20. Write after the proper number the correct one of the words given in parentheses in the sentences below.

1. My troubles this year have been (miner, minor) ones.

2. Winning three games in a row boosted our basketball team's (moral, morale).
3. All three nations signed a (peace, piece) treaty.
4. Do these printed instructions seem (plain, plane) to you?
5. This store's sales (personal, personnel) are very helpful.
6. The assistant (principal, principle) will make the announcement.
7. The (principal, principle) of solar energy is easy to understand.
8. If you (loose, lose) your concentration, you might (loose, lose) the tennis match.
9. Suddenly the room became very (quiet, quite).
10. D. H. Lawrence often wrote about coal (miners, minors).
11. Can you tell the (principal, principle) parts of the verb "to shrink"?
12. I had a (peace, piece) of pumpkin pie for dessert.
13. One of the bolts was (loose, lose).
14. I filled out a job application form in the (personal, personnel) department.
15. Students have been requested to remain (quiet, quite) during a study period.
16. We (passed, past) through Indiana on our way to Illinois.
17. Does every fable have a (moral, morale)?
18. On my way to school I always walk (passed, past) the bakery.
19. If you are old enough to vote, you are officially no longer a (miner, minor).
20. She is a person who always tries to live up to her (principals, principles).

---

**stationary** *in a fixed position*
The classroom desks are *stationary.*

**stationery** *writing paper*
I received three boxes of *stationery* at Christmas.

---

**than** [a conjunction]
I am stronger *than* she.

**then** adverb meaning *at that time*
Wear a green hat; *then* I'll recognize you.

---

**there** *a place;* also used as an expletive (see page 26)
We were *there* at two o'clock.
*There* were four of us.

**their** [possession]
The pupils bring *their* own lunches.

**they're** *they are*
*They're* going with us.

---

**to** [a preposition or part of the infinitive form of a verb]
Give the book *to* me, please.
We will have *to* leave early.

**too** adverb meaning *also* or *too much*
George is a sophomore, *too.*
It is *too* late to go now.

**two** *one plus one*
We had only *two* dollars.

---

**waist** *middle part of the body*
She wore a wide belt around her *waist.*

**waste** *unused material;* also *to squander*
Pollution can be caused by industrial *wastes.*
Don't *waste* your time.

---

**who's** *who is, who has*
*Who's* coming?
*Who's* been here?

**whose** [possessive]
*Whose* coat is this?

---

**your** [possessive]
Is this *your* coat?

**you're** *you are*
*You're* a true friend.

---

**EXERCISE 11.** Number your paper 1–20. Write after the proper number the correct one of the words given in parentheses in the sentences below.

1. They had neglected to lock (there, their) lockers.
2. I wanted to go to camp, (to, two, too).
3. Tie the rope around your (waist, waste).
4. The platform, we discovered when we tried to move it, was (stationary, stationery).
5. No one could remember (whose, who's) name had been drawn first.
6. This year's annual will be larger (than, then) last year's.
7. Where do you think (your, you're) going?
8. Some students regard the class as a (waist, waste) of time.
9. The work was (to, too) strenuous for me.
10. I used school (stationary, stationery) for my letters.
11. When (you're, your) homework has been finished, call me.
12. I do not know (whose, who's) going to solve the problem.
13. As soon as (their, they're) printed, we will ship the books.
14. Write your letters on business (stationary, stationery).
15. (Your, You're) lucky to have such a good job.
16. I cannot do any more (then, than) I have done.
17. In only a few minutes we had already earned (to, two, too) dollars.
18. I'd like to know (who's, whose) responsible for this mess.
19. I was surprised at (you're, your) taking that attitude.
20. Chemistry has converted many (waste, waist) products into valuable commodities.

**REVIEW EXERCISE.** Number your paper 1–40. After the proper number write the correct one of the words in parentheses in the sentences below.

1. Columbia is the (capital, capitol) of South Carolina.
2. Everything seemed to be (alright, all right).
3. Mrs. Starkey (complemented, complimented) me on my English grade.
4. Have you discussed this problem with your guidance (councilor, counselor)?
5. We were blown several miles from our (course, coarse).
6. The letters have (all ready, already) been mailed.

7. The amount of vegetation in the (dessert, desert) surprised us.
8. Mrs. Crane (formally, formerly) taught here.
9. Every nation must conserve (its, it's) resources.
10. My companion (lead, led) me down a dark passage.
11. We were (all ready, already) to start before dawn.
12. Try not to (lose, loose) your keys.
13. Success is the best (moral, morale) builder.
14. Their (coarse, course) manners were not amusing.
15. We had been told not to ask for a second (piece, peace) of pie.
16. The new (altar, alter) is made of white marble.
17. I have read all of Murdoch and Spark, and I prefer the (later, latter).
18. You must go to the (principal, principle) to get a working permit.
19. (Its, It's) time to think about getting a job.
20. There was (all together, altogether) no truth in the accusations.
21. Members of the (counsel, council) are elected annually.
22. A (capital, capitol) offense will cost you your freedom.
23. Everyone is (all ready, already).
24. (Course, Coarse) wood absorbs more paint than fine-grained wood.
25. My red tie (complements, compliments) my blue suit.
26. Jack (past, passed) the ball to Joe.
27. When you are (all together, altogether), I'll take a group picture.
28. The mission was accomplished without loss of (personal, personnel).
29. The company embarked on the strongest advertising campaign in (its, it's) history.
30. What are the (principal, principle) products of Puerto Rico?
31. Some teachers prefer (stationary, stationery) seats in their classrooms.
32. There's a student (whose, who's) going to succeed.
33. His performance was not outstanding, but it was (alright, all right).
34. She always uses (plain, plane) stationery.

35. When we had cleaned our lockers, the (waistpaper, wastepaper) littered the floor.
36. The (principals, principles) of democracy have always been attacked.
37. Do you know (they're, their, there) new address?
38. Why didn't the campers follow their (counselor's, councilor's) instructions?
39. (Who's, Whose) pen is this?
40. Mrs. Smith gave us (complimentary, complementary) tickets.

## COMMONLY MISSPELLED WORDS

7. *Learn lists of commonly misspelled words.* Frequent short spelling tests are an effective means of fixing correct spellings in your mind. On the following pages you will find a list of 300 commonly misspelled words. Taking no more than twenty at a time, have these words dictated to you. Study the ones you miss and record them in your list of spelling errors. When you have studied them (divided them into syllables and practiced writing each word several times), write them again from dictation. Spelling tests should be written, not oral.

### *Three Hundred Spelling Words*[1]

abundant
academically
accelerator
accessible
accidentally
acclimated
accommodation
accompaniment
accomplishment
accuracy

acknowledge
acquaintance

adequately
admittance
admission
adolescent
advantageous
aerial
allege
allegiance

alliance
allotting
annihilate
anonymous

apologetically
apparatus
apparent
arousing
arrangement
atheistic

attendance
awfully
ballet
bankruptcy
barbarian
basketball

[1] The list does not include the homonyms listed on pages 662–69.

beggar
behavior
beneficial
bibliography

biscuit
blasphemy
boulevard
bracelet
buffet
bureaucrat
burial
calculation
camouflage
capitalism

carburetor
caricature
catalogue
catastrophe
cellar
cemetery
changeable
chassis
Christianity
circumstantial

colossal
communist
comparative
competition
complexion
conceivable
connoisseur
conscientious
consciousness
consistency

controlling
controversy
cruelty
curriculum
debacle

decadent
deceitful
deference
descendant
desirable

despair
detrimental
devastation
devise
dilemma
diligence
disastrous
disciple
discrimination
diseased

dissatisfied
division
ecstasy
efficiency
embarrassment
emperor
emphasize
endeavor
enormous
entertainment

enthusiastically
entrance
environment
espionage
exhaustion
exhibition
exhilaration
expensive
exuberant
familiarize

fascination
fascism
feminine
financier

fission
forfeit
fulfill
fundamentally
gaiety
galaxy

gauge
grammatically
guidance
harassment
hereditary
hindrance
horizontal
hospital
hygiene
hypocrisy

ideally
idiomatic
incidentally
independent
indispensable
inevitable
influential
ingenious
initiative
innocent

inoculate
institution
intellectual
interference
irrelevant
irresistible
kerosene
laborious
larynx
leisurely

license
livelihood
liquor

luxurious
magistrate
magnificence
maintenance
malicious
manageable
maneuver

marriageable
martyrdom
materialism
meadow
mediocre
melancholy
melodious
metaphor
miniature
mischievous

misspelled
mortgage
mosquito
municipal
mysterious
naive
necessity
neurotic
noticeable
novelist

nucleus
nuisance
nutritious
obedience
occasionally
occurrence
omitting
opportunity
orchestra
outrageous

pageant
pamphlet
paralysis
parliament
pastime
peasant
pedestal
penicillin
perceive
permanent

permissible
persistent
perspiration
phenomenon
physician
picnicking
playwright
pneumonia
politician
precede

presence
presumption
prestige
prevalent
privilege
procedure
propaganda
propagate
prophesy
prove

psychoanalysis
pursue
quietly
rebellion
receive
recommendation
reference
referred
rehearsal
relieve

reminiscent
remittance
representative
resources
responsibility
reveal
safety
seize
separation
sergeant

siege
significance
souvenir
specimen
sponsor
statistics
strategic
stubbornness
succeed
succession

summed
superintendent
supersede
suppress
surroundings
susceptible
symbolic
symmetrical
symphonic
synonymous

tariff
temperament
temperature
tendency
theoretical
tolerance
tomorrow
tortoise
traffic

tragedy

transcend
transparent
tried
twelfth
tyranny
undoubtedly
universal
unmistakable
unnatural
unnecessary
unscrupulous
vaccine
vacuum
valedictory
variation
vaudeville
vehicle
vengeance
versatile
vigilance

villain
vinegar
visage
welcome
whisper
whistle
withhold
yacht
yawn
yield

# College Entrance and Other Examinations

PART SEVEN

Chapter 37

# College Entrance and Other Examinations

## Tests of Vocabulary, Reading, and English Composition

No matter what your plans for the years following high school, it is more than likely that you will be asked to "take some tests." Many of the most commonly administered tests include measures of verbal fluency, reading comprehension, and/or grammar and composition.

Among the tests of this type used for college entrance, the best known are probably the *Scholastic Aptitude Test – Verbal,* or SAT-V (including the *Test of Standard Written English*), and the *English Composition Test,* or "English Achievement" test. Both of these tests are administered by the College Entrance Examination Board, or CEEB. Another well-known test is the American College Testing Program (ACT) Assessment Test.

Many schools and colleges do *not* require tests for admission but do administer tests for placement in courses and for guidance purposes after you have registered. The military and other employers may also, on occasion, administer tests of English vocabulary, reading, or grammar when such skills can be shown to be important to success in the job.

Tests with the word *aptitude* in their titles are used mainly to predict future success, whether in school or on the job. They do not, on the whole, measure what you have learned in particular courses. They measure the

English language skills which you have been developing all your life through your habitual listening, reading, and speaking.

*Achievement* tests, on the other hand, concentrate on specific skills and understandings which you have learned in the courses taken to complete your academic program.

Cramming is *not* an appropriate or helpful way to prepare for tests of this nature. There are, however, a number of good test-taking practices which will help you to do your best on any examination. These may be summarized as follows:

## SUMMARY OF TEST-TAKING PRACTICES

**1. *Take a positive approach to the test.***

a. Try to do your best even though you may be nervous. Don't panic.

b. Regard lapses of memory as normal. If you "block" on a certain question, go on and come back to it later if you can.

c. Don't expect to answer every question correctly. Some of the tests we are discussing are built so that the average student will answer only about half the questions correctly.

**2. *Use your time wisely.***

a. Look over the test before you start to work. Get a feel for its length and difficulty.

b. Plan your time. If you have a time limit of 20 minutes for a 40-question test, check that you are on or beyond question 21 after 10 minutes. But don't be an excessive clock-watcher. Clock-watching uses up your time and heightens anxiety.

c. Work rapidly but carefully. Answer the easy questions first. If you don't know an answer right away, leave it and go on. Easy questions "count" just as much as hard ones.

d. If you have time after finishing the test, try some of the questions you left out the first time. (On the ACT, you are not penalized for guessing.)

***3. Avoid careless errors.***

a. Pay close attention to directions. Do the sample questions even though you're sure you understand the task.

b. Read each question carefully. Be sure you know exactly what it is asking you to do.

c. Look at all the choices before you answer. In many cases the correct answer is not *absolutely* correct; it is the *best* among the choices you have been given. Be sure to compare all the choices before picking the one you believe to be the best answer.

d. Avoid careless mistakes in marking the answer sheet. Keep it lined up with the booklet if possible. Be sure you make your mark in the correct manner in the correct row for the question. The scoring machine can't tell when you were "off" by one question or one row.

e. If you change an answer, be sure you erase the first answer thoroughly. If the machine "reads" both marks, it will count the question as unanswered.

One of the best ways to prepare for any test is to become familiar with the types of tasks you will be asked to perform. Many test questions will be similar to those on tests you have taken before. Others may be new to you. The purpose of this chapter is to show you some of these question types. When any test you take makes use of them you will, in a sense, be on familiar ground.

## TESTS OF WORD KNOWLEDGE OR VOCABULARY

Vocabulary tests measure your understanding of the meanings of words, either in isolation or in context. Often, the relationships among words—the way they are related in meaning—will be tested. Examples of three types of vocabulary questions follow.

## Word Meanings

The simplest type of vocabulary question simply asks you the meaning of a word. Usually, the format is an incomplete statement to which you add one of several choices to complete the meaning. The following is a sample question of this type.

EXAMPLE **A** To whet one's appetite is to ——

a wean it
b salve it
c sharpen it
d appease it
e dampen it

Answer:[1]
**A** ⓐ ⓑ ● ⓓ ⓔ

Some questions of this type ask for a choice between *phrases* explaining the word's meaning or use; others offer *single words* and ask you to choose a synonym of the key word.

**EXERCISE 1.** Read the beginning of each sentence below and the choices that follow it. Choose the answer which best completes the sentence.[2]

**1** A person who is talkative is ——

a fervent
b reticent
c jocular
d loquacious

**2** To be nimble is to be ——

a gracious
b agile
c numb
d earthy

[1] Answer: ⓒ *sharpen it*. When you have marked your answer sheet for ⓒ, this is the way it will look. You will black in the circle containing the letter of the correct answer. Answers are shown this way for all sample test items throughout this chapter.

[2] Answers for this and all the following exercises will be found on page 705.

3 Material you can see through is called ——

a opaque
b potential
c imaginary
d transparent

4 Something that is powerful must be ——

a lavish
b lenient
c potent
d malicious

5 To condense something is to ——

a abridge it
b accelerate it
c abolish it
d acclaim it

## Synonyms and Antonyms

In a test on synonyms or antonyms you are asked to select, from four or five choices, the word *most similar* in meaning (synonym) to the word given *or* the word *most nearly opposite* in meaning (antonym). *Pay attention!* These are sometimes mixed together. Careful reading will help you here. There are very few true synonyms or antonyms in English; the "correct" answer, therefore, is the one most nearly the same or most nearly the opposite in meaning—it need only be better than the other choices.

Following are three sample questions in which you are to find the word *most similar* in meaning (synonym) to the underlined word.

EXAMPLE

**A** <u>disclose</u>

a react
b darken
c resound
d visualize
e reveal

**B** <u>impediment</u>

a agreement
b obstacle

c idiot
d outline
e utterance

**C** enervate
a encourage
b enlarge
c bemoan
d weaken
e cut

Answers:

**A** ⓐ ⓑ ⓒ ⓓ ●
**B** ⓐ ● ⓒ ⓓ ⓔ
**C** ⓐ ⓑ ⓒ ● ⓔ

You will note that in the last question, a common misconception of the word's meaning is included among the choices. Many people are confused as to whether *enervate* means to take "nerve" away or to give it; hence *encourage* is given as an incorrect choice.

**EXERCISE 2.** For each of the following questions, choose the word *most nearly opposite* in meaning (antonym) to the underlined word.

**1** abstract
a extract
b general
c concrete
d ideal
e difficult

**2** chronic
a occasional
b habitual
c public
d unimportant
e healthy

**3** detriment
a complement
b loss
c damage
d attribute
e benefit

**4** abate
- a fall
- b shrink
- c subside
- d increase
- e release

**5** transient
- a swift
- b permanent
- c polite
- d sure
- e passenger

## Verbal Analogies

Analogies are designed to measure your understanding of the relationships existing among words. Here is a sample set of directions and one question.

EXAMPLE In the items below, the first and second words are related in a certain way. The third word is related in the same way to one of the four words which follow it. You are to choose the word related to the third word in the same way that the second word is related to the first.

**A** *Inch* is to *foot* as *ounce* is to ——
- a weight
- b meter
- c yard
- d pound

Answer:
A ⓐ ⓑ ⓒ ●

In this sample question, the relationship tested is that of a unit of measurement to a larger unit in the same scale. An inch is a division of a foot. Hence, the correct answer is *pound* since an ounce is a division of a pound. *Weight* is an attractive wrong choice, since an ounce is a unit of weight, but the relationship is not parallel to that between *inch* and *foot*. If the first part of the analogy had been *inch* and *length,* then *weight* would have been the best answer.

Analogies may also be presented as shown in the following example.

EXAMPLE Below is a list of five pairs of related words. Choose the pair of words whose relationship is most like that of the first pair.

**A** INCH: FOOT::

a quart: measure
b weight: peck
c ounce: pound
d mile: length
e meter: yard

Answer:
**A** ⓐ ⓑ ● ⓓ ⓔ

The same relationship is being measured here as was measured in the first example. *Ounce* is related to *pound* as *inch* is related to *foot*. But here you are to find the whole pair. In the first example, the first part of the second pair was given to you. If you are not familiar with analogies, it may help to turn them into sentences such as the one in the first example.

Suppose the first pair of words were *glance* and *gaze*. They are both "ways of looking at something." But a *glance* is a quick look, usually superficial or casual, while *gaze* has the idea of a long, careful, or thoughtful look. Which of these combinations, then, has the same relationship between the words?

EXAMPLE **A** GLANCE: GAZE::

a blink: scowl
b glimpse: stare
c observe: note
d skim: peek
e peruse: study

Answer:
**A** ⓐ ● ⓒ ⓓ ⓔ

Option ⓑ would be the most similar pair to complete the analogy, since *glimpse* also implies a quick once-over, and *stare* gives the notion of a long and concentrated look. Another way to check your understanding of the analogy is to compare the first and third parts, and then check to see if the second and fourth parts have the same relationship. In the original example, this check would take the form: "*inch* is to *ounce* as *foot* is to ——?"

**EXERCISE 3.** In the items below, the first and second words are related in a certain way. The third word is related in the same way to one of the five words which follow. Choose the word related to the third word in the same way as the second word is related to the first.

1 Clear is to cloudy as definite is to ——

a sunny
b vague
c bright
d positive
e short

2 Reckless is to cautious as rash is to ——

a hasty
b impudent
c careless
d prudent
e smooth

3 Gaggle is to goose as pride is to ——

a lion
b vain
c king
d bear
e eagle

4 Calm is to storm as quell is to ——

a traffic
b crowd
c ink
d riot
e nerve

5 Encourage is to scold as chide is to ——

a punish
b praise
c query
d insult
e forbid

In the following items, choose the pair of words whose relationship is most similar to that of the first pair given.

**6** LIMP: WALK::
- a snore: sleep
- b walk: ride
- c whistle: sing
- d stutter: speak

**7** QUARRY: STONE::
- a rock: mineral
- b mine: ore
- c soil: field
- d oil: drill

**8** SALVE: WOUND::
- a eraser: pencil
- b drink: thirst
- c save: money
- d sword: scabbard

**9** LAVISH: STINGY::
- a quick: average
- b late: earlier
- c bright: brightest
- d profuse: grudging

**10** RELEVANT: PERTINENT::
- a wasteful: efficient
- b thoughtful: reasonable
- c implicit: explicit
- d quiet: slow

## READING ACHIEVEMENT

Your grasp of the meaning of what you read, and your understanding of concepts presented in written form, are abilities that are often measured in tests for school or vocational guidance. Reading abilities are usually measured in one of the two ways described below.

### Sentence Completion

This question format could be called "fill in the blanks." Sentences are presented with one or two blanks, each indicating that a word has been left out. You are to choose, from the possible answers given, the one which fits best in the sentence.

EXAMPLE

**A** We laughed at the clown —— he performed funny tricks.

a but
b until
c because
d unless
e although

Answer:
**A** ⓐ ⓑ ● ⓓ ⓔ

The sentence clearly calls for a conjunction, but the only one that makes any sense is *because*. Questions like this do not ask for the recall of information. Rather, they look for your ability to recognize the logic and coherence of the sentence—one aspect of comprehension.

## Reading Comprehension

The reading tests you are likely to be taking are not concerned with testing whether you understand, word by word, what you have read, but rather how well you can draw conclusions about what you read, and how well you can make judgments about it. The questions you will be asked about the passage you read should not require outside information, but should be based upon the information found within the paragraph itself. Here is a sample passage followed by three questions.

EXAMPLE

Two days after his sudden death on June 9, 1870, Charles Dickens was honored in a *New York Times* obituary covering more than five of the seven long columns on the front page. The length of this article accurately reflected Dickens' position among the American reading public of a century ago, when entire households waited anxiously from month to month to discover the fate of Little Nell, or Oliver Twist, or whichever Dickensian hero figured in the novel currently being serialized for United States audiences. In later years, the novelist's reputation diminished; critics dismissed him as a "popular" writer rather than a true craftsman. His remarkably vivid characterizations were considered caricatures, even though numerous outstanding writers such as Feodor Dostoevski, Joseph Conrad, and Henry James expressed their indebtedness to "the master." But during the 1940's, writers like Franz Kafka and Edmund Wilson brought readers to a fresh awareness of Dickens' unforgettable delineations of personalities whose very names—Scrooge, for instance—have assumed an independent meaning for people around the world. Readers today are also impressed by Dickens' vision, more than 100 years ago, of what the modern city was to become. For Dickens' London was a place of smoke and filth and a decaying social fabric, rather than the rich, bustling, upper-class London of virtually all his contemporaries.

**A** The main thrust of this article has to do with ——

a modern attitudes towards Dickens
b Dickens' descriptions of London
c changes in Dickens' literary reputation
d Dickens' treatment of fictional characters

**B** Dostoevski, Conrad, and James indicated that ——

a their writing was influenced by Dickens
b Dickens wrote for a lower-class public
c they had learned about London from Dickens
d Scrooge was a caricature

**C** Apparently other British authors of Dickens' day ——

a were upper-class Londoners
b ridiculed Dickens' London
c believed Dickens an expert on city life
d pictured London as an attractive place to live

Answers:

**A** ⓐ ⓑ ● ⓓ
**B** ● ⓑ ⓒ ⓓ
**C** ⓐ ⓑ ⓒ ●

These sample questions are fairly typical of the kinds of questions that may be asked in reading comprehension tests. Question 1, for example, asks for the main idea of the passage. Question 2 asks for a restatement of an idea clearly stated in the passage. And question 3 asks for an inference which the reader must draw from the passage. Other types of questions often used in this type of test may ask the meaning of a term or phrase as used in the paragraph, a recognition of the author's intent, or the identification of bias, exaggeration, value judgments, or the like.

**EXERCISE 4.** After reading the following passage, answer the questions given at its conclusion.

The computerized age in which we live, while enabling us to land people on the moon and accomplish vast feats of arithmetical figuring in seconds, has raised many new problems. One of these, according to D. Lee McMahon, a psychologist at the Bell Telephone Laboratories, is the need for communication between computers and between humans and computers. In order to facilitate such communication, Dr. McMahon developed, in 1966, a new "language" designed to eliminate computer confusion about the relation of words in a sentence. The language is called FASE, for Fundamentally Analyzable Simplified English, and although at first it appears indistinguishable from ordinary English prose, it is actually quite different, for FASE reduces English to a strict form in which syntax is absolutely clear and free of ambiguity. The resulting grammatical structures can be broken down easily by a computer, while ordinary English cannot. For example, consider how a computer would interpret the phrase "time flies." The computer would have to decide whether this meant "time speeds by" or "clock the speed of certain insects," and such a choice, unaccompanied by human guidance, is beyond the capacity of even the most advanced computers. But a computer programmed to "read" FASE would have no trouble with the phrase, for FASE is based on a strictly maintained sequence of subject, verb, and object, with other parts of speech falling regularly into line. FASE lacks the beauty of English, then, and its spontaneity, but can be very useful in indexing scientific documents, which would be punched on cards and stored in a computer until needed. Locating a particular subject would be a comparatively simple matter for the computer, since there would be no ambiguity of meaning. "Time flies," for instance, would be "FASE-indexed" under time, rather than speed or insects.

**1** FASE was developed by a ——

a psychologist
b computer programmer
c physician
d linguist

**2** A FASE-programmed computer could correctly interpret the phrase "time flies" because ——

a the phrase is an idiom
b computers work so speedily
c the phrase contains a verb
d the subject comes before the verb

**3** Sentences written in FASE are probably rather ——

a ambiguous
b idiomatic
c boring
d spontaneous

**4** The writer implies that a computer's ability to make decisions is ——

a unlimited
b limited to choices about grammar
c nonexistent, even in sophisticated machines
d controlled by the use of FASE

**5** In which of the following lines is a value judgment expressed?

a line 24
b line 26
c line 7
d line 16

## STANDARD WRITTEN ENGLISH

Tests on written English are designed to measure, at least indirectly, your knowledge of standard English – knowledge that you have gained in your language arts program in school. Ideally, of course, the best way to "test" your writing skill is to have you write. For many reasons, however, this is not always practical, so multiple-choice tests have been developed to measure your knowledge of correct spelling and usage, your skill in organizing material into a cohesive whole, and your sensitivity to nuances of tone, style, and choice of words. The paragraphs which follow give examples of some of the more commonly used methods of testing skills in standard written English.

### Spelling

Spelling may be tested in any number of ways. One of the most common formats consists of five words, one of which may be misspelled. You are to indicate the word spelled incorrectly or mark a choice indicating no errors. Another type of common spelling error derives from the misuse of homonyms – words which sound alike but differ in spelling, such as *to, too,* and *two*. In this sort of test question, four phrases with different homonyms will usually be given, and you will be asked to choose the phrase in which a homonym is used correctly or incorrectly. In the following sample, choose the phrase in which a homonym is incorrectly used:

EXAMPLE **A** a *too* hot
b grizzly *bear*
c *peace* of pie
d rough *seas*

Answer:
**A** ⓐ ⓑ ● ⓓ

**EXERCISE 5.** For each of the following questions, choose the one word which is misspelled. If no word is misspelled, mark the answer N for no error.

1 a seize
b percieve
c righteous
d salutary
N

2 a ruse
b laughter
c explannatory
d traveler
N

3 a peaceable
b edible
c salable
d changable
N

4 a picnicking
b prejudice
c foreigner
d desiccate
N

5 a mischievious
b grandeur
c gorgeous
d athletic
N

6 a *herd* of elephants
b *berth*place
c mountain *peak*
d apple *core*
N

7 a *whole* wheat
b *steel* pipe
c ice *floe*
d *idol* hands
N

8 a bumble *bee*
b *bowl* weevil
c string *bean*
d acting *troupe*
N

9 a bare *feet*
b boat *sale*
c *bail* of hay
d filet of *sole*
N

10 a pint of *beer*
b carving *board*
c *right* to work
d wild *hoarse*
N

## Error Recognition

Another way of testing writing skills indirectly is to ask you to detect or correct errors in written passages. Some type of error recognition questions ask you only to indicate that an error has been made; others ask you to specify the type of error it is. Here are samples of three types of questions.

EXAMPLES TYPE 1.

Mark the letter of the line containing an error in spelling, punctuation, capitalization, grammar, or usage. If there is no error, mark N for no error.

**A** a Actually, bats are fascinating
b animals. They are the only Mammals
c living today that are able to fly.
N

Answer:

**A** ⓐ ● ⓒ Ⓝ

TYPE 2.

Mark the letter of the underlined part that must be changed in order to make the sentence correct. (Be sure to note whether underlining includes the punctuation.) If there is no error, mark answer space e.

**B** During <u>the colonel period,</u> (a) many colonies had <u>their own flags,</u> (b) the <u>earliest of which</u> (c) was based on <u>the British flag.</u> (d) <u>No error.</u> (e)

Answer:

**B** ● ⓑ ⓒ ⓓ ⓔ

TYPE 3.

Some of the sentences below contain errors; others are correct as they stand. For each sentence, mark your answer sheet:

a – if the sentence contains an incorrect choice of words (error in diction)

b – if the sentence is wordy (verbose or redundant)

c – if the sentence contains an overworked expression (cliché) or a mixed metaphor

d – if the sentence contains an error in grammar or structure

e – if the sentence is correct as it stands

**1** Each day it was a daily occurrence to see the mail truck arrive.

2 The mass of detail is not penitent to the question at hand.

3 The young man was fit as a fiddle as he started work.

Answers:

1 ⓐ ● ⓒ ⓓ ⓔ
2 ● ⓑ ⓒ ⓓ ⓔ
3 ⓐ ⓑ ● ⓓ ⓔ

**EXERCISE 6.** Following the appropriate set of directions, record your answers to each of the following questions.

**TYPE I.** Mark the letter of the line containing an error in spelling, punctuation, capitalization, grammar, or usage. If there is no error, mark N for no error.

1 a Russias woman astronaut may have been
b the first woman to explore outer space,
c but she wasn't the first woman explorer.
N

2 a As long ago as 1805, woman were helping
b men find their dangerous way across
c the uncharted Rocky Mountains.
N

3 a Sacajawea whose name means "Bird Woman," was
b only 13 when she was captured by a tribe of
c enemies.
N

4 a She was living with them in North Dakota
b when Lewis and Clark asked her help
c in accomplishing this difficult feat.
N

5 a Charbonneau, her French-Sioux husband,
b was hired in the autumn of 1804
c as a guide for the exposition.
N

**TYPE II.** Mark the letter of the underlined part that must be changed in order to make the sentence correct. (Be sure to note whether the underlining includes the punctuation.) If there is no error, mark answer space e.

**6** Sacajawea's (a) geographical knowledge and her usefulness as (b) a guide was limited (c) to her native region of western Montana. (d) No error. (e)

**7** Nevertheless, (a) she traveled all the way from Fort Mandan, N.D. (b), to the Pacific Ocean (c) and back again with the exploring (d) party. No error. (e)

**8** The first-hand reports (a) of the expedition by Lewis, Clark, (b) Gass, and others, praised (c) her highly but, not her husband (d). No error. (e)

**9** Shortly before the expedition left to find (a) its way (b) to the coast, a healthy son (c) was born to Sacajawea on February 11, 1805. (d) No error. (e)

**10** Her son, who (a) was given the name Jean-Baptiste Charbonneau made (b) the entire trip with (c) his mother and father. (d) No error. (e)

**TYPE III.** Some of the sentences below contain errors; others are correct as they stand. For each sentence, mark your paper with one of the following letters as appropriate:

a – if the sentence contains an incorrect choice of words (error in diction)

b – if the sentence is wordy (verbose or redundant)
c – if the sentence contains an overworked expression (cliché) or a mixed metaphor
d – if the sentence contains an error in grammar or structure
e – if the sentence is correct as it stands

**11** Charbonneau was given five hundred dollars for his services as a guide, but Sacajawea received no pay.
**12** It was generally agreed by the leaders of the project, Charbonneau mistreated his wife and was unworthy of his pay.
**13** Their son returned back to St. Louis, Missouri, with William Clark, who brought him up and paid for his education.
**14** After all was said and done, Sacajawea faded from view and, to make a long story short, it is not known what fate befell her in her later years.
**15** Though it is a mistake to say that she guided the expedition, it is entirely possible that the roll played by Sacajawea made the difference between its success and its failure.

## Error Correction

Error correction questions indicate the inappropriate part of the sentence and ask you to choose a suitable correction from among the choices given you. Here are some samples.

EXAMPLES **A** Eating, drinking, and *to stay up* late at night were among her pleasures.

a correct as it stands
b she liked staying up
c staying up
d to remain up

**B** *On the snow-covered branch, two sparrows, they huddled close together.*

a correct as it stands
b On the snow-covered branch, two sparrows huddled close together.
c On the snow-covered branch, two sparrows, huddled close together.

d Closely, on the snow-covered branch, huddled the two sparrows together.

Answers:
A ⓐ ⓑ ● ⓓ
B ⓐ ● ⓒ ⓓ

## Sentence Revision

This type of question requires you to mentally restate a *correct* sentence, using a phrase that is given to you. Using the phrase will require change in other parts of the sentence as well. Then you must choose, from among the choices given you, a word or phrase that will appear somewhere in the restated sentence. (They may not necessarily follow directly after the given revision.) Study the sample given below.

EXAMPLE **A** Sentence: When night came and the temperature fell, my father lit the fire in the bedroom.

Revision: Begin with *"Each night . . ."*

a that the temperature
b upon the temperature's
c because the temperature
d when the temperature

Answer:
A ⓐ ⓑ ⓒ ●

There will often be several ways the new sentence could be completed. If none of the choices given is in your revised sentence, think of another way to rephrase the sentence, and check the choices again. But be sure you do not change the meaning of the original sentence when you revise it.

**EXERCISE 7.** Following the appropriate directions, answer each of the following questions.

**Error Correction.** Choose the letter which indicates the best correction for the underlined part of each sentence. If the sentence is correct as it stands, mark a.

**1** Traffic on the highway was blocked for an hour, this causing many drivers to have cold suppers.

a correct as it stands
b causing
c thus having necessitated
d which was responsible for

**2** I haven't but a few more pages to write for this report.

a correct as it stands
b have scarcely
c haven't any except
d have only

**3** Everyone due to the continued storm sat and sang around the fireplace.

a correct as it stands
b Sitting and singing around the fireplace were everyone, while the storm continued.
c The storm continued while everyone sits and sings around the fireplace.
d Everyone sat around the fireplace and sang while the storm continued.

**4** Harry, although tired, worked late, typed long into the quiet summer evening.

a correct as it stands
b lengthily typing
c and he typed late too
d typing long

**5** Suppose you tell us exactly where you hid and a thorough report of your precise reasons for doing it.

a correct as it stands
b and a report on why.
c and give us a report of your reasons.
d and precisely why you did it.

**Sentence Revision.** Mentally revise each of the following sentences according to the instruction given for each. Then choose the letter of the phrase most likely to occur in the sentence as revised.

**6** Sentence: Leaning on the arm of her granddaughter, the old woman slowly entered the room.

Revision: Begin with: *The old woman leaned*

a so that she could
b for her entrance
c as she
d to slowly enter

**7** Sentence: Aside from his dread of snakes, he was afraid of almost nothing.

Revision: Begin with: *He had a dread*

a but otherwise
b still
c outside of that fear
d and so

**8** Sentence: What have we been doing all week but preparing for the holidays?

Revision: Change to a declarative sentence.

a had done
b anything all week more than
c nothing all week but
d does

**9** Sentence: Bonnie told me she hadn't been there and didn't find out about what had happened until the next day.

Revision: Change the indirect quote to a direct quote.

a told me, "I'd never been there and didn't find out
b told me, "I wouldn't have gone and
c told me, "I wasn't there. I didn't find out
d told me, "I won't go. I'm not going to find out

**10** Sentence: She leapt to her feet and yelled, "I heard you say, 'What are they really worth?'"

Revision: Make the last direct quote an indirect quote.

a "I heard you say What are they really worth?"
b "I heard you ask what they're really worth."
c "I heard you ask What they're really worth."
d "I heard you say what they're really worth."

## Organizing Paragraphs

Another skill of written English that is often tested is organization. The most frequent exercise designed to measure organizational ability is the scrambled paragraph. This exercise takes a paragraph from any type of subject matter and presents the sentences to you in random order. Your job is to figure out the correct order, the order which will rearrange them so as to make a well-knit paragraph. This you do to some extent by studying the sequence of ideas presented; but primarily you have to concern yourself with the transitional words and phrases.

Here is the way the directions are likely to go:

DIRECTIONS Each group of sentences in this section is actually a paragraph presented in scrambled order. Each sentence in the group has a place in the paragraph; no sentence is to be left out. You are to read each group of sentences and decide the best order in which to put the sentences so as to form a well-organized paragraph.

Before trying to answer the questions which follow each group of sentences, jot down the correct order of the sentences in the margin of the test book. Then answer each of the questions by blackening the appropriate space on the answer sheet. Remember that you will receive credit only for answers marked on the answer sheet.

A sample paragraph follows:

EXAMPLE

**P** As you read, however, concentrate only on main ideas; don't try to remember everything.

**Q** If you develop an interest in what you read, you are more likely to remember the factual information in a passage.

**R** Finally, when you have completed the passage, pause to summarize the main ideas in your mind.

**S** You will have an even stronger motive for remembering those facts if you understand their importance to you.

**1** Which sentence did you put first?

a sentence **P**
b sentence **Q**
c sentence **R**
d sentence **S**

**2** Which sentence did you put after sentence **S**?

a sentence **P**
b sentence **Q**
c sentence **R**
d None of the above. Sentence **S** is last.

**3** Which sentence did you put after sentence **Q**?

a sentence **P**
b sentence **R**
c sentence **S**
d None of the above. Sentence **Q** is last.

Answers:
1 ⓐ ● ⓒ ⓓ
2 ● ⓑ ⓒ ⓓ
3 ⓐ ⓑ ● ⓓ

Note the use of words such as *finally, however, even stronger*. These words refer to previous statements. You may also find clues in sentences using pronouns or adjectives clearly referring to some noun in a previous sentence (*those* facts). Before you answer any of the questions, you should determine the correct order for all the sentences and write it down for your own reference. Most tests, however, will not ask you to give that order all at once. They will be set up so as to give you credit for each correct relationship you detect between the individual sentences. If you were merely asked for the order itself, you would lose all credit for a single mistake.

**EXERCISE 8.** Read the following sentences carefully and

write down their correct order before answering the questions related to them. Then choose your answer for each question that follows.

**P** Swim out and approach the victim from behind in order to avoid struggling.
**Q** Then go into the special procedure called a "carry," and swim back to shore with the victim.
**R** In order to save a drowning person, you must jump into the water, keeping your eye on the victim at all times.
**S** Bring the victim into a horizontal position by pulling back on the chin and resting the body on your hip, using your arms as a lever.
**T** Stick your elbow in the middle of the victim's back and cup the chin with your hand.

**1** Which sentence did you put first?
- a sentence **P**
- b sentence **Q**
- c sentence **R**
- d sentence **S**
- e sentence **T**

**2** Which sentence did you put after sentence **P**?
- a sentence **Q**
- b sentence **R**
- c sentence **S**
- d sentence **T**
- e None of the above. Sentence **P** is last.

**3** Which sentence did you put after sentence **Q**?
- a sentence **P**
- b sentence **R**
- c sentence **S**
- d sentence **T**
- e None of the above. Sentence **Q** is last.

**4** Which sentence did you put after sentence **R**?
- a sentence **P**
- b sentence **Q**
- c sentence **S**
- d sentence **T**
- e None of the above. Sentence **R** is last.

5 Which sentence did you put after sentence **T**?

a sentence **P**
b sentence **Q**
c sentence **R**
d sentence **S**
e None of the above. Sentence **T** is last.

## Essay Tests

Some examinations, such as the *English Composition Test,* may include an essay question. When writing an essay, keep in mind the principles of paragraph and composition organization taught in Chapters 21 and 22. You will be given only a limited amount of time to complete an essay question. Therefore, you must plan ahead, jot down an informal outline, and be careful not to omit any essential points in your essay.

### *Answers to Exercises*

| Ex. 1, p. 682: | Ex. 2, p. 684: | Ex. 3, p. 687: | |
|---|---|---|---|
| 1-d | 1-c | 1-b | 6-d |
| 2-b | 2-a | 2-d | 7-b |
| 3-d | 3-e | 3-a | 8-b |
| 4-c | 4-d | 4-d | 9-d |
| 5-a | 5-b | 5-b | 10-b |

| Ex. 4, p. 691: | Ex. 5, p. 693: | | Ex. 6, p. 696: | | |
|---|---|---|---|---|---|
| 1-a | 1-b | 6-b | 1-a | 6-c | 11-e |
| 2-d | 2-c | 7-d | 2-a | 7-e | 12-d |
| 3-c | 3-d | 8-b | 3-a | 8-d | 13-b |
| 4-c | 4-N | 9-c | 4-N | 9-e | 14-c |
| 5-b | 5-a | 10-d | 5-c | 10-b | 15-a |

| Ex. 7, p. 699: | | Ex. 8, p. 703: |
|---|---|---|
| 1-b | 6-c | 1-c |
| 2-d | 7-a | 2-d |
| 3-d | 8-c | 3-e |
| 4-d | 9-c | 4-a |
| 5-d | 10-b | 5-d |

# Speaking and Listening

## PART EIGHT

Chapter **38**

# Solving Problems Through Discussion and Debate

## Types of Discussion; Elements of Debating

It is natural for people to talk things over, either to exchange information or to dispute. The common kinds of discussion and debate are treated in this chapter.

## GROUP DISCUSSION

Societies of every kind – school clubs, civic organizations, labor unions, legislative assemblies – use discussion as a means of arriving at a solution to a particular problem or airing the opinions of members before making a decision. This method of problem solving gives each member a voice in deciding matters and ensures the right of everyone to be heard.

### 38a. Learn how discussion differs from conversation and debate.

Although conversation, discussion, and debate are similar, there are marked differences.

A *conversation* is unplanned and private. It ranges over many topics, casually touching on each. It may have no purpose at all other than fellowship, or it may aim to entertain, instruct, or persuade.

A *discussion* is planned and public. It is focused on one topic, which is examined in depth under the direction of a discussion leader. Its purpose is to consider a problem, evaluate proposed solutions, and arrive at the best solution.

A *debate* considers two sides of a problem. The supporters of each side attempt to defeat their opponents by arguments set forth in carefully reasoned and extended speeches. A debate usually follows a formal procedure and involves a decision by judges.

## Types of Group Discussion

### 38b. Learn the various types of group discussion.

Among the many types of group discussion, the most common are the *round table,* the *forum,* the *symposium,* and the *panel.*

A *round table* is an informal discussion in which the participants exchange views around a table—not necessarily round—under the direction of a discussion leader and most often without an audience. The number of participants usually does not exceed a dozen. Members of the group speak without rising and without being recognized by the chair.

The most common example of round-table discussion is the committee meeting. Many organizations conduct a large part of their business through committees. A committee considers business referred to it and reports its findings and recommendations to the entire organization.

In a round-table discussion everyone has a feeling of equality. This type of discussion is most likely to succeed when the participants are well informed and nearly equal in ability.

A *forum* is any type of speaking program that is followed by audience participation. For example, a lecture followed by questions from the audience is a forum.

A *symposium* involves several formal speeches on a single topic followed by audience participation. When the audience is large, audience participation is sometimes limited to questions; expressions of opinion from the floor are usually not allowed.

A *panel* is a discussion among a selected group of persons under a moderator in front of an audience which joins in later. The speakers represent different viewpoints. There are usually no set speeches, but sometimes speakers are asked to set forth their viewpoints in brief preliminary statements.

A panel is really an overheard conversation guided by a moderator. It may consist of four to eight members, who face the audience and remain seated while talking. The moderator keeps the discussion moving forward and, at some interesting point, invites the audience to join in. The panel conversation spills over to include the audience. At the conclusion of the discussion, the moderator summarizes what has been said and thanks the participants and the audience.

The purpose of a panel is to get important facts and opposing opinions into the open, stimulate audience thinking, and lay a basis for wide participation later.

### 38c. Select a topic that lends itself to profitable group discussion.

The success of a group discussion depends on the topic. Before selecting a topic, ask yourself:

1. Is it related to the needs, interests, and experience of the listeners and speakers?
2. Is it timely?
3. Is it controversial?
4. Is it many-sided?
5. Is it stated clearly?

What are good sources of topics for group discussion? Books, magazine articles, movies, and television programs can often stimulate discussion. Newspapers are another source. The discussion of current events, especially of controversial matters, can capture and hold an audience's attention. Topics that are trivial or timeworn, have no audience appeal, do not evoke strong differences of opinion, or can be answered by *yes* or *no* are not suitable.

A topic for discussion should be a question of policy rather than fact. "Have we a supply of energy?" is a question of fact and hence not discussible. The only appropriate reply is a direct, factual answer. "Should we control the use of energy?" is a question of policy which should stir discussion.

**EXERCISE 1.** List five topics suitable for group discussion. Test yours and those submitted by other members of the class against the criteria listed above. The topics may be related to school, community, state, national, or international affairs.

**EXERCISE 2.** Conduct a round-table discussion on a topic concerning all the participants. The discussion leader, appointed beforehand, will end the discussion after 20 minutes, summarize, and invite class discussion. Suggested topics:

1. City vs. country living
2. Improving the student organization
3. The school yearbook
4. Assembly programs
5. Building school spirit

**EXERCISE 3.** Conduct a forum. A student will lecture on a current, vital problem and propose a solution for it. At the end of the lecture the class will ask questions.

**EXERCISE 4.** Conduct a symposium on discipline. The speakers should represent the viewpoints of a young person, a parent, a law enforcement officer, an educator, and a community leader.

**EXERCISE 5.** Divide the class into groups. Each group will select a discussion leader and present a panel discussion before the class on any one of the following topics or a topic of its own. Each panel should meet beforehand to settle matters of procedure and scope.

1. Modern manners
2. Radio and television advertising
3. Youthful crime
4. The ideal school
5. Choosing a career
6. The honor system of conducting examinations
7. Professional vs. amateur sports
8. Vandalism
9. Prejudice—and how to overcome it
10. Student dress
11. The kind of world I'd like to live in
12. Extracurricular activities
13. Our foreign policy
14. Problems of the small farmer
15. Ways of preventing war
16. Selecting a college

**38d. Prepare for group discussion by thinking, talking, and reading about the topic.**

Many discussions fail because of insufficient preparation by the participants. When the topic is announced, think about it. Do your own thinking. If you simply swallow what you see, hear, and read without analyzing it, you are not acting intelligently. Make sure that there is sufficient evidence to substantiate the truth of every major point. Think things through and avoid making rash or erroneous judgments.

Talk to others about the topic. Discuss it with your friends and parents. Discuss it with someone who is an authority on the subject. Be ready to modify your previous opinion in the light of your new knowledge.

Consult reference books, recent publications, magazine articles, and editorials. Inform yourself as thoroughly as you can about the topic. Investigate the facts before arriving at a decision, for otherwise you may delude others as well as yourself.

## Problem-Solving Discussions

In problem-solving discussions, follow the steps of logical thinking. When you are confronted by a problem, your mind follows certain logical steps. For example, if your ball point pen fails to write, you ask yourself:

1. What is the trouble? [You define the problem.]
2. What *might be* the cause? [You mentally list various causes: a clogged point, defective mechanism, exhausted ink cartridge.]
3. What *is* the cause? [You consider each of the previously listed possibilities. The point is not clogged, the mechanism works smoothly, the cartridge is used up.]
4. What should be done about it? [Obviously you need a new cartridge or a new pen.]

This simple example illustrates the steps in problem solving. They are as follows:

I. Define the problem.
  A. Limit the problem.
  B. Phrase the problem.
II. Find the possible causes.
III. Propose and examine possible solutions. [What would be the effects of each? To what extent would each solve the problem?]
IV. Select the best solution.
V. Put the best solution into operation. [What obstacles will be encountered and how will they be overcome?]

When participants are familiar with these five steps, they follow them in their individual and group thinking, and an orderly discussion results. The discussion does not remain static and pointless. It marches forward.

**EXERCISE 6.** Listen to a television or radio discussion program and report on it orally to your class. Did the discussion follow the steps in problem solving listed above? If not, what order or sequence did it follow?

## Participating in Group Discussion

The success of a group discussion depends on the attitudes of the participants and the quality of their participation, the guidance of the discussion leader, and the response of the audience.

## 38e. Learn the responsibilities of a speaker in a group discussion.

As a speaker in a group discussion, you should have a cooperative attitude, recognizing that the common good of the group supersedes your own concerns.

Know your subject well. To have an adequate knowledge of the topic, prepare thoroughly by reflecting on it and by talking and reading about it.

Contribute willingly. Some of your ideas will come from previous reflection, and others will come on the spur of the moment, stimulated by what someone else has said. Don't hesitate to express tentative ideas for the other participants to consider, for these ideas may be just what are needed. Be careful, however, not to monopolize the discussion. Everyone should have a chance to be heard.

Listen intelligently. When you agree with another speaker, listen to increase your store of information. When you disagree, listen to accept a different viewpoint if it is supported by sufficient evidence or to refute it by sound reasons if it is fallacious.

Speak so that all can hear—not only the participants but the audience too, if there is one.

Recognize and admit the truth of what others say. There is no need, however, to pass judgment on every statement made by someone else.

Be courteous always. Sarcasm and ridicule are out of place. Self-control is a mark of maturity. Disagree reasonably—and with reasons.

## 38f. Learn the responsibilities of a leader of a discussion.

The skill and personality of a discussion leader are important. If you are chosen to lead a discussion, consider yourself complimented. Your teacher and classmates have recognized your leadership ability.

You should familiarize yourself with the subject and the special interests and backgrounds of the participants. If the discussion is to be held before an audience, arrange a preliminary meeting of the speakers to decide on procedure and the order in which the various aspects of the topic will be discussed.

Decide on the seating plan. "Set the stage" with an arc of chairs and tables on a slightly raised platform close to the audience. Do not seat members with similar viewpoints together; mix them up.

Introduce the speakers to the audience, telling something of each one's background or point of view.

Arouse the audience's interest in the topic by a brief introductory statement. Say just enough to spotlight the problem and then throw out the first question.

Address your questions to the group as a whole. Don't question individual members, as a rule. Let participation be as free and spontaneous as possible. Ask challenging questions – not the *yes* and *no* kind, but *why?* and *how?*

Dig out points of differences, not as in debate, but in a friendly, united pursuit of a solution. Work to find the common meeting ground.

Take time for occasional summaries. People like to know what progress is being made. In your final summary mention the loose ends, if any.

Keep your own viewpoint out of the discussion. Break in only to ask clarifying questions, bring the discussion back on the track, advance to the next point, or summarize. Be impartial.

Keep the discussion on the track. Encourage the give-and-take of opinion among the participants.

Invite audience participation at a point of high interest, usually about the halfway mark. Speakers from the floor may describe their own experiences, state their opinions, or ask questions. Do not answer questions; refer them to the panel.

Before closing, be sure to thank the speakers and the audience.

### 38g. Learn the responsibilities of a member of the audience.

By listening attentively, asking questions, and making clarifying statements, members of an audience can help make a group discussion stimulating.

As a member of the audience, you also have an obligation to prepare for the discussion by thinking, talking, and reading about the topic.

Listen with an alert mind. Ask yourself: What proof is offered in support of each important argument?

Join in when the discussion leader invites the audience to participate. Speak freely, briefly, sincerely. A discussion in which there is general participation is more stimulating and interesting than one in which only a few take part.

Focus on the main issues. Minor points of fact or opinion should be overlooked.

Speak audibly. While your remarks are addressed to the chair, speak so that all can hear.

## Nonverbal Communication

As you may have noticed in your conversations and discussions with others, people often gesture with their hands or use facial expressions to convey meaning. These body movements are examples of nonverbal communication.

Discussion skills should include effective nonverbal habits. For example, hand gestures should not distract listeners; they should support what you are trying to say. Hands can show size, shape, or direction. You can indicate the organization of your remarks by using fingers to count off the points you want to make. In fact, gestures are quite varied. Be sure that those you use convey specific meaning to your listeners. Needless hand waving can indicate nervousness.

**EXERCISE 7.** Divide the class into groups of six to eight members. Each group, under the direction of a leader, will select a question for discussion and phrase it properly. The discussions will be carried on simultaneously in separate areas of the room with the instructor moving from one to another. After a designated time, the class will reassemble, and the discussion leader of each group will report on the problems faced in its discussion, how they were handled, and where improvement is needed.

## Listening

As a member of the audience, you must be able to understand and evaluate the ideas of others in the discussion. You must *listen* to what is said, not just *hear* it.

### 38h. Learn to listen efficiently.

Studies show that the average listener recalls only a little more than half of what a speaker says. By understanding and applying the following points, you can close this communication gap between speaker and listener.

***Listen to acquire information and evaluate it.*** As you hear a speaker present ideas, you interpret them and pass judgment on them as sound or weak. Ask yourself: "Has the speaker presented enough evidence to justify these opinions? Is the evidence from reliable sources? Is the reasoning valid?"

***Listen with the right attitude.*** To listen efficiently, you must be unbiased and cooperative. People with fixed ideas find it difficult to listen to viewpoints different from their own. They develop a mental deafness to ideas that do not sit well with them. An intelligent listener, on the other hand, is fair-minded and receptive to all ideas that are supported by convincing evidence.

Do not strongly agree or disagree with a speaker early in a talk. Withhold final judgment until the topic is developed.

***Listen with attention.*** Concentration is hard work. We all have a tendency to listen for a few minutes, daydream for a while, and then turn our attention again to the speaker. To overcome this tendency, be aware of it and make an effort to concentrate continuously on the speaker's message.

***Listen for the main ideas.*** Usually only a few main points are presented in a discussion, although many minor points and some digressions creep in. Listen with the purpose of discovering the central ideas and fastening attention upon them.

***Listen for supporting information.*** A speaker should support assertions by offering evidence in the form of facts, statements of authorities, and logical reasoning.[1] The evidence must be sufficient to justify what has been said; otherwise the assertion fails for lack of proof. Whatever is asserted without proof can be denied without proof.

***Listen for faulty reasoning.*** In Chapter 24 you learned about faulty cause-and-effect arguments, irrelevant arguments, rationalizing, and wishful thinking.

As you listen to discussions, you may hear faulty reasoning of this sort, for this mistake is more common in oral than in written presentations.

***Listen for loaded words.***[2] The use of emotionally loaded words is natural in free discussion, particularly when the speakers are committed to a viewpoint. The active listener is aware of this danger and discounts arguments that are directed at emotions, not reason.

**EXERCISE 8.** Report on a radio or television discussion on a controversial question. Did the speakers present both sides of the question fairly? What evidence did they offer to support their opinions? What objections can you pose?

## Evaluating Group Discussion

By considering the merits and deficiencies of a group discussion after it is over, you can learn to improve future discussion programs. In your evaluation, consider the group as a whole, the individual participants, the discussion leader, and the outcome of the discussion.

[1] For a discussion of evidence, see pp. 421–22.
[2] For a discussion of loaded words, see pp. 308–09.

## 38i. Evaluate a group discussion by asking key questions about it.

The following questions will help you estimate the worth of a group discussion.

1. Was the discussion purposeful? Were the causes of the problem considered? Were various solutions proposed and analyzed? Did the discussion ramble or did it proceed in an orderly fashion? If the discussion was concerned with solving a problem, did it follow the steps of logical thinking?

2. Was the outcome worthwhile? A group discussion need not reach a solution or agreement. It may be successful if it brings areas of disagreement into the open.

3. Were the participants thoroughly familiar with the problem? Did they present facts, statements of competent and unbiased authorities, and statistics to support their opinions?

4. Was the discussion lively and general? Was there a give-and-take of opinion in an atmosphere of mutual respect? Did all participate? Did anyone monopolize the meeting, or did everyone speak briefly and to the point?

5. Were the audience's questions thought-provoking? Did the speakers answer them directly and fully?

6. Was the discussion courteous? Did each speaker exercise self-control by refraining from interrupting when another was speaking? Were statements and objections phrased courteously?

7. Was the discussion leader competent? Did the introductory remarks arouse interest? Did the discussion avoid pointless digressions? Was everyone encouraged to join in? Was there a summary?

**EXERCISE 9.** Prepare a rating sheet for use by class and teacher in rating group discussions.

## DEBATING

A debate is a contest in which arguments are used instead

of physical strength. It is a form of argument in which two sides publicly dispute a question in a systematic way.

Debating focuses attention on controversial questions, particularly those affecting the public interest. It stimulates thinking, develops ability in speaking, provides training in research, and encourages the habit of suspending judgment until all facts are at hand.

The team supporting the question or proposition is called the affirmative; the opposing team, the negative. Each team consists of two (or, rarely, three) speakers, who are called *first affirmative* (or *negative*), *second affirmative*, etc.

A debate is divided into two parts. During the first part (constructive speeches), both sides present their arguments for or against the proposition. After an intermission, both sides try to refute (with rebuttal speeches) the opposing arguments.

The order of speaking may be as follows:

1. CONSTRUCTIVE SPEECHES
   a. First affirmative
   b. First negative
   c. Second affirmative
   d. Second negative

2. REBUTTAL SPEECHES
   a. First negative
   b. First affirmative
   c. Second negative
   d. Second affirmative

Notice that the affirmative side opens and closes the debate and that the first rebuttal is made by the negative side.

## The Proposition

The characteristics of a proposition are discussed in Chapter 24, page 415. The following review should recall the main points in that discussion.

### 38j. A proposition is a topic stated in debatable form.

It may be phrased either as a question or as a resolution.

EXAMPLES Should football be prohibited as a high school sport?
Resolved: Football should be prohibited as a high school sport.

**(1) A proposition should contain only one central idea.**

NOT DEBATABLE Resolved: Fraternities and sororities should be banned in high schools, and every high school student should be required to participate in at least one extracurricular activity. [two ideas]

DEBATABLE Resolved: Fraternities and sororities should be banned in high schools.

DEBATABLE Resolved: Every high school student should be required to participate in at least one extracurricular activity.

**(2) A proposition should be debatable. It should have two sides.**

NOT DEBATABLE Resolved: The automobile has greatly affected the way we live. [This is so obviously true that it cannot be debated.]

NOT DEBATABLE Resolved: Space flights allow us to obtain valuable scientific information to aid human progress. [Since nearly all the arguments are in the affirmative, this is too one-sided to be debatable.]

**(3) A proposition should be stated fairly.**

UNFAIR Resolved: That the unjust and harmful cutbacks in school aid should be restored. [This assumes what has to be proved—that school aid cutbacks are unjust and harmful.]

FAIR Resolved: That the cutbacks in school aid should be restored.

**(4) A proposition should be timely.**

There are hundreds of vital questions relating to young people, schools, local conditions, and state, national, and international affairs which stimulate controversy.

**(5) A proposition should be stated affirmatively.**

CONFUSING Resolved: Capital punishment should not be abolished. [The affirmative side would have to argue,

"Yes, it should not be abolished," a confusing position.]

CLEAR Resolved: Capital punishment should be abolished.

**(6) A proposition should put the burden of proof on the affirmative.**

Anyone who makes an assertion should be ready and able to prove it. The affirmative side, which asserts the truth of a proposition, must present enough proof to establish its case beyond a reasonable doubt.

The affirmative side must show a need for a change; for example, that high school football should be prohibited or that a government lottery should be established. Existing conditions—called the *status quo*—are presumed to be satisfactory until the affirmative offers sufficient proof to show that a change is necessary.

NOT DEBATABLE Resolved: That our government should continue to support wildlife conservation. [This makes the affirmative defend the *status quo* and the negative advocate a change.]

DEBATABLE Resolved: That our government should stop supporting wildlife conservation.

The negative has only to prove that the affirmative case is false or unsound. It does not have to offer an alternative solution.

**(7) A proposition should contain no words of uncertain meaning.**

For example, "Resolved: That oil is more valuable than steel in modern civilization" is not debatable because "valuable" has no exact meaning. Does it mean essential? Costly? Efficient? Useful?

**EXERCISE 10.** Compose five propositions for class debate. Be sure that each of your propositions satisfies all the requirements listed above.

## The Issue

### 38k. An issue is a point of disagreement.

The points in a debate on which there are clashes of opinion are called *issues*.[1] A proposition rests on several issues. If they are proved, the proposition is proved. An issue is stated as a question which can be answered by *yes* or *no*.

PROPOSITION Resolved: That students should participate in the process of selecting high school principals.

ISSUE Is the present method of selecting principals faulty?

Issues often deal with the need for a change, the practicability of a proposed solution, and the desirability of adopting a different solution.

**EXERCISE 11.** List at least three issues for one of the propositions you submitted in Exercise 10.

## The Brief

### 38l. A brief is an outline for debate.

In Chapter 24, you learned the principles of argumentation. Those principles are as valid in debating as in writing. Debating is simply oral argumentation.

In a debate, arguments are not written in consecutive prose. They are prepared in the form of a detailed logical outline called a *brief*. A brief is an orderly arrangement of all the arguments needed to prove or disprove a proposition. All the statements in a brief are complete sentences.

The introduction summarizes the history of the question and defines terms. Sometimes, it sets forth issues and mentions any matters that are excluded from discussion by mutual agreement.

[1] An *issue* in debate corresponds to the minor proposition in other kinds of argument.

In the brief proper the issues are taken up one by one, and the evidence in support of each is given in the form of facts, figures, examples, authority, and logical reasoning.

The conclusion summarizes the main arguments and reasserts or denies the proposition.

The example that follows illustrates the form and content of a brief.

## *Model Brief*

*Resolved:* That the jury system in the United States should be significantly changed.[1]

### *Affirmative*

I. Jury trials in civil cases cause unfair delay and clog court calendars.
   A. Court calendars are crowded because only a few jury cases can be heard at a time while many others await trial. A national survey by the Institute of Judicial Administration showed that the average delay was 13.3 months.
   B. Delay is a great aid to wrongdoers.
      1. It erases the memories of witnesses.
      2. It may cause wronged parties to give up their cases.
   C. Delay inflicts hardship on the innocent, who have to wait before they can clear themselves.

II. Jury trials waste time and money.
   A. They take up the time of the courts, participants, and jurors.
   B. They increase the cost of court administration, including the payment of jurors' fees.
   C. In New York City alone, jury service each year is equivalent to taking 50,000 people away from their jobs for ten days—an enormous loss of time and money to the jurors' businesses.

III. Juries should be composed of fewer than twelve members.
   A. There is no sound reason for the number twelve.

[1] Based on *The Jury* by Lloyd E. Moore (Anderson Publishing Co., Cincinnati, 1973) and *Verdict: The Jury System* by Morris J. Bloomstein (Dodd, Mead & Company, 1972). Reprinted by permission of the publishers.

B. Many states have smaller juries, sometimes eight, often six, and the administration of justice has not suffered.
C. If juries were smaller, fewer jurors would have to be challenged, expenses would be cut, and verdicts could be reached more quickly.

IV. Unanimous verdicts should not be required.
A. Many states require only a majority or some number less than a unanimous vote.
B. In 1972, the Supreme Court ruled that a criminal jury need not be unanimous. (*Johnson* v. *Louisiana*)
C. By removing the need for a unanimous verdict, the time for deliberation would be reduced, and there would be fewer hung juries.

V. Juries should be eliminated in civil cases and verdicts rendered by a single judge.
A. The quality of justice would be improved if administered by a judge alone.
1. Judges are trained in law and bring experience and knowledge to each case.
2. Juries sometimes do not follow the law as explained by the judge but determine a case by their prejudices or common sense, and consequently they create a government by people, not by law.
B. Juries have been proved to be unnecessary, since thousands of nonjury cases are tried each year, and no one claims that such procedure is undemocratic.

### *Negative*

I. The jury system is a safeguard for citizens.
A. It is a protection against injustice and corruption and against prejudiced judges and overzealous prosecutors.
B. Experience over a period of 5000 years has shown that it is necessary for the evenhanded administration of justice.
C. Although imperfect, some of its shortcomings can be lessened without tampering with its basic structure.

II. Court congestion is not caused by jury trial alone but by:
A. Increasing population.
B. Failure of public authorities to create sufficient judgeships and to provide enough court facilities.

III. The jury system does not waste time, money, and human energy.
  A. Compared with what we spend on education, defense, and other aspects of government, the jury system costs little.
  B. In the Federal courts, jury expenditures constitute only 1/170 of 1% of total costs. (If you paid an income tax of $17,000, only one dollar of it would go to support the jury system.)
  C. A University of Chicago study found that 94% of those who served on juries wanted to serve again, 3% more were willing to do so, and only 3% were unwilling to serve again.

IV. The proposal to reduce the size of juries is fraught with danger.
  A. It would be the first step in doing away with juries entirely.
  B. It diminishes the protection given to those in the minority.
  C. It substantially reduces the likelihood of representation by people of diverse ethnicity.
  D. It would lower public confidence in jury verdicts.
  E. Innocent persons are more likely to be convicted if a jury is composed of fewer than twelve.

V. Unanimous verdicts should be required.
  A. There would still be a reasonable doubt about the guilt of a person convicted by less than a unanimous vote.
  B. Most juries are able to reach a unanimous verdict; hung juries occur very rarely.

VI. Justice might be weakened if administered by a judge alone.
  A. If a judge is biased, justice may be thwarted; but if one or two jurors are biased, the effect is diluted among twelve.
  B. On some questions, twelve minds are better than one, no matter how skilled that one is; for example, deciding whether or not a witness is telling the truth.
  C. Jury trials are of a higher quality than nonjury trials.
    1. Attorneys prepare their cases more carefully when they have to present them to a jury.
    2. Cross-examination is more effective.
    3. Attorneys take more trouble to have highly qualified experts present.

## The Rebuttal

### 38m. Plan the rebuttal while preparing the debate.

The rebuttal is the most interesting phase of a debate because it tests a debater's ability to analyze and answer an opponent's arguments. To refute effectively, a debater must be able to think quickly and speak extemporaneously.

Prepare for the rebuttal weeks before the debate, at the time you are gathering material and thinking about your case. As you learned in Chapter 24, you will be in a weak position if you ignore a major argument of the other side. Your success as a debater may rest on your ability to answer your opponents' arguments. As you prepare your brief, consider the arguments they will use, confer with your colleagues about them, and assemble arguments to refute them. Summarize each opposing argument and your answer to it on a separate card. Have your cards available for reference during the debate.

Refutation can start during the constructive speeches. Reply to your opponent's arguments when your turn comes to speak. Because of time limitations, however, most of your reply must wait until the rebuttal period. When refuting, state your opponent's arguments clearly and fairly, quoting your opponent's words if possible. Then present evidence to show that the argument is illogical, misleading, or unproved.

In rebuttal, limit yourself to the main arguments of the opposition. It is wasteful to spend time refuting minor points of fact or opinion. If you can demolish the opposition's main contentions, the minor arguments can be ignored.

## Participating in Debate

### 38n. Observe the conventions of debate.

Address the chair as "Mr. Chairman" or "Madam Chairman." Refer to the judges as "Honorable judges."

Instead of referring to participants by name, use the customary terms: "The first affirmative speaker," "My worthy opponents," "My colleagues," or "My teammates."

Ridicule, sarcasm, and personal attacks have no place in debating. A debate should be won or lost on the basis of reasoned argument and convincing delivery.

**38o. The judges' decision is based on the skill of the debaters, not on the truth or falsity of the proposition.**

The most common method of determining the winner of a debate is by decision of three appointed judges. The judges base their decision on the merits of the debate and not upon their own views of the question.

Another method is by decision of a critic judge who announces the winning team and gives the reasons for the decision.

A third method is by means of a shift-of-opinion poll. Before the debate ballots are distributed to listeners to record their opinions regarding the proposition. At the end of the debate another ballot is taken. Only ballots showing a change of opinion are counted. The decision is awarded to the team that caused the greater number of listeners to change their opinion.

**EXERCISE 12.** Divide the class into groups of four or six. Each group will decide on a proposition for debate, divide into affirmative and negative teams, prepare briefs, and on the appointed date present the debate in class under a chair, or leader, appointed by the teacher or elected by the class. If desired, another class may be invited to attend the debate. The following topics, which should be phrased as propositions, are only suggestions.

1. Coeducation
2. Homework
3. Jury system
4. Tipping
5. Freedom of the press
6. Abolition of football
7. Government support of TV
8. Electoral college
9. Compulsory voting
10. Eleven-month school year

11. Elective courses
12. Professional boxing
13. Nuclear energy
14. Role of the UN
15. U.S. foreign policy
16. Abolition of interscholastic athletics
17. Federal aid to schools
18. Honor system of examinations
19. Censorship of motion pictures
20. Protecting endangered species
21. Raising (Lowering) the driving age
22. Energy conservation
23. Labor unions
24. Ecology
25. Youthful crime
26. Compulsory military service
27. Lagging school spirit
28. Reorganization of Congress
29. A permanent site for the summer Olympics
30. Mass transit

Chapter 39

# Effective Speech

## Pronunciation and Enunciation

If you want to communicate your ideas and feelings to others so that they understand, feel, and act as you want them to, you must know how to speak effectively. Poor speech interferes with communication. It diverts attention from *what* is being said to *how* it is being said. "Mend your speech," said Shakespeare, "lest it mar your fortunes."

## PRONUNCIATION

The United States has several speech regions, each with its own standard of pronunciation. Fortunately, American regional differences are not great enough to hinder communication. The speech of one region is easily understandable in another.[1]

### 39a. Be particularly careful about stress or accent.

No pronunciation fault is quite so obvious as stressing the wrong syllable.

It occurs most often with words we encounter in books but rarely hear. For such words, a dictionary is usually a reliable guide to pronunciation. For the pronunciation of

[1] For further discussion of the varieties of English, see pages 74–76.

commonly used words, of course, careful speakers in your own area are your best guides.

There are a few general rules governing stress, but they have so many exceptions that you must be careful in applying them.

***Stress tends to be recessive in English; it recedes, or backs away from, the final syllable.***

When *automobile* came into English from the French, it was pronounced *automoBILE.* Later it became *autoMObile.* Today it is commonly *AUtomobile.*

*Chauffeur* and *menu,* once stressed on the last syllable, are now stressed on the first.

*Balcony* and *confiscate* were formerly stressed on the second syllable only. *Retail, detail,* and *address,* formerly accented on the second syllable only, may now receive a stress on the initial syllable.

***Words that contain the suffix* -able *do not usually put the accent on the syllable immediately preceding* -able.**

| | | |
|---|---|---|
| EXAMPLES | ádmirable | inéxplicable |
| | ápplicable | inéxtricable |
| | disréputable | inhóspitable |
| | fórmidable | irréfutable |
| | incómparable | préferable |

***In words ending in* -ity *and* -ety, *stress the third syllable from the end.***

| | | |
|---|---|---|
| EXAMPLES | aménity | satíety |
| | anonýmity | spontanéity |
| | inebríety | |

***The final syllable is stressed in many words taken from the French.*** In nearly every case these words have not been fully naturalized.

| | |
|---|---|
| EXAMPLES | bourgeoisíe |
| | entrepreneúr |
| | ragoút (rhyme this with "Drag who?") |

***Words ending in* –iacal *have a long* i *sound and are stressed on the* i.**

EXAMPLES hypochondríacal maníacal

***Stress is sometimes used to distinguish parts of speech.*** A word that has the same form when used as a noun, adjective, or verb is usually stressed on the first syllable when used as a noun or adjective and on the second syllable when used as a verb.

| NOUNS OR VERBS | ADJECTIVES OR VERBS |
|---|---|
| affix | absent |
| compress | frequent |
| contract | perfect |
| insult | present |
| rebel | subject |
| survey | |
| torment | |

***Compound nouns and adjectives usually receive primary stress on the first part of the compound; compound verbs are usually stressed on the second part.***

NOUNS bláckbirds, fírefighter, móonshine, síxpence, éarthquake

VERBS outdó, overcóme, counteráct, underráte

**EXERCISE 1.** The following words are often stressed on the wrong syllable. Check each in a dictionary and write it with an accent mark over the stressed syllable. Note that in some cases two pronunciations are permissible.

| | | |
|---|---|---|
| acumen | decorous | impious |
| admirable | desultory | impotent |
| adult | dirigible | incognito |
| alias | eczema | incomparable |
| awry | equitable | indefatigable |
| combatant | formidable | inexorable |
| condolence | gondola | infamous |
| contrary | grimace | integral |
| conversant | herculean | lamentable |
| curator | horizon | mischievous |
| debate | hospitable | municipal |

| | | |
|---|---|---|
| orchestra | recess | secretive |
| peremptory | respite | superfluous |
| prestige | robust | theater |

**EXERCISE 2.** Here are some foreign words frequently used in English. Look up their pronunciation in a dictionary.

*French* apropos, blasé, bon voyage, cuisine, de luxe, elite, en masse, en route, hors d'oeuvre, lingerie, née, petite, première, rapport, sabotage, trousseau

*Italian* adagio, concerto, fiasco, maestro, maraschino, cognoscenti, sotto voce

*Spanish* guitar, mesa, rodeo

*Latin* ad infinitum, ad nauseam, de facto, gratis, facsimile, status quo, data, via, vice versa

**EXERCISE 3.** Each of the following words can be used as a noun or verb. The accented syllable is shifted to denote the parts of speech. Read the list aloud, accenting the correct syllable in each case.

| | | |
|---|---|---|
| perfume (n.) | rebel (n.) | refuse (n.) |
| perfume (v.) | rebel (v.) | refuse (v.) |
| object (n.) | present (n.) | insult (n.) |
| object (v.) | present (v.) | insult (v.) |
| survey (n.) | torment (n.) | contract (n.) |
| survey (v.) | torment (v.) | contract (v.) |

### 39b. Avoid the omission or addition of syllables and the switching of sounds.

In nonstandard pronunciation, syllables are often omitted; for example, *s'pose* for *suppose, champeen* for *champion,* and *jool* for *jewel.*

Syllables are also added in nonstandard pronunciation, as in *umberella* for *umbrella; athalete* for *athlete.*

In certain cases, sounds may be switched or transposed; for example, *calvary* for *cavalry, irrevelant* for *irrelevant, prespiration* for *perspiration,* and *bronical* for *bronchial.*

**EXERCISE 4.** Careless speakers frequently omit a syllable or a sound in each of the following words. Practice saying this list aloud, taking care not to omit a syllable.

| | | |
|---|---|---|
| government | probably | cigarette |
| ideal | geography | finally |
| library | police | literature |
| company | poetry | particular |
| giant | geometry | ridiculous |

**EXERCISE 5.** Practice each of the following words aloud, being careful not to add a sound or syllable.

| | | |
|---|---|---|
| elm | extraordinary | laundry |
| film | idea | burglar |
| helm | chimney | translate |
| athlete | lightning | grievous |
| athletics | hindrance | mischievous |
| ticklish | banana oil | law |

**EXERCISE 6.** Practice each of the following words aloud, being careful not to transpose sounds.

| | | |
|---|---|---|
| perspiration | modern | western |
| southern | cavalry | irrelevant |
| hundred | larynx | prescription |
| prodigy | poinsettia | bronchial |

## 39c. Learn the rules for pronouncing *ng*.

The *ng* sound causes much confusion. You can eliminate any difficulty by learning three simple rules.

*1. All words ending in* **–ng** *and all words derived from them are pronounced with the final sound in* **sing.**

EXAMPLES bring, bringer, wing, winging

EXCEPTIONS Use the sound in *finger* in the following words: longer, longest, stronger, strongest, younger, youngest

*2. The combination* **nge** *at the end of a word is pronounced* **nj.**

EXAMPLES hinge, flange

*3. In all other words,* **ng** *is pronounced as in* **single.**

EXAMPLES hunger, anger, single
EXCEPTIONS gingham, Bingham

**EXERCISE 7.** Practice the following words and sentences aloud. In every case *ng* is pronounced as in *sing.*

| | | |
|---|---|---|
| tongue | among | harangue |
| ringlet | fangless | songbird |
| springier | thronging | prongless |
| slangy | clingy | twangy |

The slangy singer sang a song.
The bringer of good news came from Long Island.
He was coming in, not going out.
The youngish singer put the hanger in the closet.
The throng gathered around the bell ringer.
The young and lovely child had a ringlet on her forehead.

**EXERCISE 8.** Practice the following words and sentences aloud. In every case *ng* is pronounced as in *finger.*

| | | |
|---|---|---|
| anger | hunger | tangle |
| mingle | jingle | dangle |
| single | jangle | bingo |
| bangle | English | fungus |
| bungle | language | spangled |
| linger | younger | elongate |
| longer | stronger | angry |

When I was single, my pockets did jingle,
I wish I was single again.
Linger longer.
The English language is difficult to learn.
The angler hurt his finger.
If you are hungry for mangoes, do not linger.

## ENUNCIATION

Enunciation is the process of forming, uniting, and separating speech sounds. It has to do with distinctness of utterance.

When you enunciate correctly, your words are clearly shaped and easily understood, yet not overly precise. Here are some typical enunciation errors:

| | | |
|---|---|---|
| gimme | gunna | wanna |
| whyncha | dunno | wit' (for *with*) |
| wonnerful | didja | gover'ment |

## 39d. Enunciate clearly.

To enunciate clearly, you must move your lips, tongue, and jaw.

If your friends often have difficulty in understanding what you say or if telephone operators often ask you to repeat a number or message, your enunciation may be faulty.

The exercises that follow are useful in correcting the habit of mumbling. Practice them with exaggerated vigor, precision, and speed.

**EXERCISE 9.** Practice the following sound and word combinations.

| | |
|---|---|
| bah-bay-bee-baw-boh-boo | bool-ah, bool-ah |
| mah-may-mee-maw-moh-moo | raw beet, raw beet |
| mee-maw, mee-maw | meat ball, meat ball |

**EXERCISE 10.** Place the tip of the tongue on the gum ridge behind the upper teeth. Lightly and agilely practice:

t-t-t d-d-d t-t-t d-d-d

tah-tay-tee-taw-toh-too
dah-day-dee-daw-doh-doo
lah-lay-lee-law-loh-loo

**EXERCISE 11.** Old-fashioned tongue twisters are lots of fun—and good enunciation drills, too. Practice the following, at first slowly and then with increasing speed.

1. The big black bug bit the big black bear.
2. Fanny Finch fried five floundering fish for Francis' father.
3. Lemon liniment, lemon liniment.
4. Prunes and prisms, prunes and prisms.
5. The seething sea ceaseth and thus sufficeth us.
6. She sells seashells by the seashore.
7. The sixth sheik's sixth sheep's sick.
8. Truly rural, truly rural.

**EXERCISE 12.** Pronounce the following lists of words, giving special attention to the enunciation problem indicated for each list.

INITIAL SOUNDS

| | | |
|---|---|---|
| about | electric | exact |
| America | eleven | huge |
| because | eraser | remember |

MIDDLE SOUNDS

| | | |
|---|---|---|
| accidentally | February | library |
| all right | finally | mystery |
| already | geography | poem |
| automobile | giant | poetry |
| champion | government | really |
| company | history | recognize |
| cruel | interesting | shouldn't |
| diamond | jewel | wonderful |

FINAL SOUNDS

| | | |
|---|---|---|
| child | east side | meant |
| gold | west side | nest |
| hand | abrupt | past |
| kind | chest | post |
| second | last | left |

DIFFICULT CONSONANT COMBINATIONS

*cts:* conflicts, facts, respects, restricts, tracts

*dths:* widths, breadths, hundredths

*fts:* lefts, rafts, shifts, tufts

*lds:* builds, fields, folds

*pts:* accepts, precepts, concepts

*sks:* asks, desks, disks, risks
*sps:* clasps, lisps, rasps, wasps
*sts:* adjusts, frosts, digests, insists, lists, mists, rests, tests

**39e. Avoid substituting one sound for another.**

The substitution of one sound for another is a frequent fault: *ciddy* for *city, dis* for *this, tree* for *three.*

**EXERCISE 13.** Practice the following pairs of words, taking care to distinguish between them.

| t–d | | t–th | | d–th | |
|---|---|---|---|---|---|
| beating | beading | boat | both | bayed | bathe |
| bitter | bidder | tree | three | breed | breathe |
| matter | madder | true | through | dare | there |
| metal | medal | taught | thought | day | they |
| latter | ladder | tinker | thinker | doze | those |
| writing | riding | tin | thin | read | wreathe |

# Index and Tab Key Index

# Index

## A

## C

## D

## N

## Q

## T

## W

# Tab Key Index

# Key to *English Workshop* Drill

To supplement the lessons in *English Grammar and Composition, Complete Course,* there is additional practice in grammar, usage, punctuation, capitalization, composition, vocabulary, and spelling in *English Workshop, Review Course*. This chart correlates the textbook rules with the lessons in *English Workshop*.

| Text Rule | Workshop Lesson | Text Rule | Workshop Lesson | Text Rule | Workshop Lesson |
|---|---|---|---|---|---|
| 1a | 1 | 7a | 72,73 | 19c-h | 92 |
| 1b | 1 | 7b-c | 72 | | |
| 1c | 1 | 7d-e | 73 | 21b-c | 93 |
| 1d | 2 | 7f | 76 | 21d | 94 |
| 1e | 2 | 7g | 77 | 21g | 94 |
| 1f | 4 | | | 21h | 95 |
| 1g | 2 | 8a | 82,83 | 21i | 94–102 |
| | | 8b | 82 | | |
| 2b-d | 3 | 8c | 82,85 | 22b-c | 103 |
| 2e-f | 3 | 8d-e | 85 | 22d | 103 |
| 2g | 3 | | | 22e | 104 |
| 2h | 3 | 9a-b | 2 | | |
| 2i | 3 | | | 23 | 91–92 |
| 2j | 3 | 11a-b | 33 | | |
| | | 11c | 34 | 24e | 105 |
| 3a | 4 | | | 24f | 105 |
| 3b-d | 4 | 12a | 2,41 | 24g | 105 |
| 3e-f | 4 | 12b | 39 | | |
| 3g-h | 4 | 12c | 40 | 26a | 107 |
| 3i-j | 4 | 12d | 41 | 26b | 107 |
| 3k | 4 | | | 26c | 108 |
| | | 13a | 50 | 26d | 108 |
| 4a | 5 | 13b | 50 | 26e | 108 |
| 4b | 6 | | | 26f | 109 |
| 4c | 1,5 | 14a | 47 | 26g | 110 |
| 4d | 6 | 14b | 48 | | |
| 4e | 6 | | | 27a | 106 |
| 4f | 5 | 15a | 51 | 27b | 106 |
| 4g-h | 5 | 15b | 52 | | |
| | | 15c | 52 | 29c | 10,11,12 |
| 6a-c | 64 | 15d | 52 | 29d | 11 |
| 6d-f | 64 | | | | |
| 6g-i | 65 | 18a | 56 | 30a-e | 17 |
| 6j | 65 | 18b-c | 58 | 30f-g | 17 |
| 6k | 67 | 18d | 57 | 30h | 20 |
| 6l | 67 | 18e | 59,60,61 | 30i | 20 |
| 6t | 68 | 18g | 43 | 30j | 21 |

| Text Rule | Workshop Lesson | Text Rule | Workshop Lesson | Text Rule | Workshop Lesson |
|---|---|---|---|---|---|
| 30k | 8 | 31d | 17 | 32d | 107 |
| 30l | 17,18,19 | 31i-k | 27 | 32e | 107 |
| 30m | 17,18,19 | 31l-n | 28 | | |
| | | | | 33c | 107 |
| 31a-c | 26 | 32b | 107 | | |

# Correction Symbols

| | |
|---|---|
| **cap** | error in use of capital letters |
| **frag** | sentence fragment |
| **gr** | error in grammar |
| **k** | awkward sentence or passage |
| **ms** | error in manuscript form or neatness |
| **nc** | not clear |
| **p** | error in punctuation |
| **ref** | error in reference of pronoun |
| **rs** | run-on sentence |
| **sp** | error in spelling |
| **ss** | error in sentence structure |
| **t** | error in tense of verb |
| **w** | error in word choice |
| ¶ | You should have begun a new paragraph here. |
| ∧ | Something has been omitted and must be inserted. |

B 2
C 3
D 4
E 5
F 6
G 7
H 8
I 9
J 0